CHINESE FILMS IN FOCUS II

Edited by
Chris Berry

BFI   palgrave
macmillan

A BFI book published by Palgrave Macmillan

Second Edition published in 2008 by
PALGRAVE MACMILLAN
Houndmills, Basingstoke, Hampshire RG21 6XS and
175 Fifth Avenue, New York, N.Y. 10010
Companies and Representatives throughout the world

on behalf of the

BRITISH FILM INSTITUTE
21 Stephen Street, London W1T 1LN
www.bfi.org.uk

There's more to discover about film and television through the BFI.
Our world-renowned archive, cinemas, festivals, films, publications and learning resources are here to inspire you.

PALGRAVE MACMILLAN is the global academic imprint of the Palgrave Macmillan division of
St. Martin's Press, LLC and of Palgrave Macmillan Ltd. Macmillan® is a registered trademark in the United States,
United Kingdom and other countries.
Palgrave is a registered trademark in the European Union and other countries.

First Edition published 2003
Reprinted 2006
Second Edition © British Film Institute 2008
Introduction and editorial arrangement © Chris Berry 2008
Individual essays © the authors 2008

Cover design: couch
Cover image: 15 (Royston Tan, 2003), © 27 Productions/© Singapore Film Commission

Set by Cambrian Typesetters, Camberley, Surrey
Printed in China

This book is printed on paper suitable for recycling and made from fully managed and sustained forest sources. Logging, pulping and manufacturing processes are expected
to conform to the environmental regulations of the country of origin.

British Library Cataloguing-in-Publication Data
A catalogue record for this book is available from the British Library

ISBN 978-1-84457-237-3 (pb)
ISBN 978-1-84457-236-6 (hb)

Contents

Notes on Contributors

Annette J. Aw is Adjunct Associate Professor in the Department of Communication at the University of Maryland University College. She is also an independent research consultant in Washington, DC, where she conducts media-related studies for private businesses, trade associations and government agencies. Before working in the United States, she taught at Nanyang Technological University in Singapore between 1995 and 2001. Her research and teaching interests focus on public relations and intercultural communication in Asia and the United States.

Chris Berry is Professor of Film and Television Studies in the Department of Media and Communication at Goldsmiths, University of London. His research is focused on Chinese cinemas and other Chinese screen-based media. His publications include (with Mary Farquhar) *China on Screen: Cinema and Nation* (Columbia University Press and Hong Kong University Press, 2006); *Postsocialist Cinema in Post-Mao China: The Cultural Revolution after the Cultural Revolution* (Routledge, 2004); (edited with Feii Lu) *Island on the Edge: Taiwan New Cinema and After* (Hong Kong University Press, 2005); (editor) *Chinese Films in Focus: 25 New Takes* (BFI, 2003); (edited with Fran Martin and Audrey Yue) *Mobile Cultures: New Media and Queer Asia* (Duke University Press, 2003); and (translator and editor) Ni Zhen, *Memoirs from the Beijing Film Academy: The Origins of China's Fifth Generation Filmmakers* (Duke University Press, 2002).

Yomi Braester is Associate Professor of Comparative Literature and a member of the Program in Cinema Studies at the University of Washington in Seattle. He is the author of *Witness Against History: Literature, Film and Public Discourse in Twentieth-Century China* (Stanford University Press, 2003) and *Painting the City Red: Film and Drama as Agents of Chinese Urban Policy, from 1949 to the Beijing Olympics* (Duke University Press, forthcoming).

Felicia Chan is RCUK Fellow in Film, Media and Transnational Cultures, at the Research Institute for Cosmopolitan Cultures (RICC), University of Manchester. Her research interests lie in issues of cultural translation, intertextuality and modernity in film, literature and other cultural texts. She has published in *Critical Studies in Television*, *EnterText*, *Inter-Asia Cultural Studies*, *Refractory: Journal of Entertainment Media*, *Scope: An Online Journal of Film and Television Studies* and *English Studies in Asia*, edited by Araki, Lim, Minami and Yoshihara (Silverfish, 2007).

Esther M. K. Cheung is Associate Professor of Comparative Literature at the University of Hong Kong and a Research Associate of the Kwan Fong Cultural Research and Development Programme at Lingnan University. She is Director of the Center for the Study of Globalisation and Cultures at the University of Hong Kong. She has published on identity in Hong Kong films, pop song lyrics, and literary and historical writings. She is the co-editor of three collections, *Xiang-gang wen-xue@wen-hua yan-jiu* (*Hong Kong Literature as/and Cultural Studies*) (Oxford University Press, 2002), *Between Home and World: A Reader in Hong Kong Cinema* (Oxford University Press, 2004) and *Jijin qieyuan, jiyuan qiejin: Guan Jinpeng de guangying jiyi* (*In Critical Proximity: The Visual Memories of Stanley Kwan*) (Joint Publishing, 2007). Currently she is working on alternative and independent cinemas in Hong Kong and the PRC, paying specific attention to the production and circulation of Chinese-language films in the global context.

Robert Chi teaches in the Department of Asian Languages and Cultures at the University of California, Los Angeles (UCLA). His writings on Chinese-language cinemas have appeared in *Modern Chinese Literature and Culture, Tamkang Review, Zhongwai wenxue (Chung wai Literary Monthly), Dangdai dianying (Contemporary Cinema)* and elsewhere.

Rey Chow is Andrew W. Mellon Professor of the Humanities at Brown University, Providence, Rhode Island, and the author, most recently, of *The Age of the World Target* and *Sentimental Fabulations, Contemporary Chinese Films*. She is a member of the international advisory board of the Asian Film Archive (Singapore), and serves as well on the boards of numerous journals around the world, including *camera obscura* (USA), *Postcolonial Studies* (Australia), *Chung-wai Literary Monthly* (Taiwan) and *Journal of Chinese Cinemas* (UK).

Shuqin Cui is an Associate Professor of Asian Studies at Bowdoin College, Brunswick, Maine. She is the author of *Women through the Lens: Gender and Nation in a Century of Chinese Cinema* (University of Hawaii Press, 2003). Her research and teaching interests include cinema studies, modern Chinese literature, cultural and gender studies.

Mary Farquhar is Professor at Griffith University, Australia. She specialises in China studies and studied at Beijing University. Her publications include *Children's Literature in China: From Lu Xun to Mao Zedong* (M. E. Sharpe, 1999), which won the annual International Children's Literature Association Award for the most distinguished, scholarly book published in the field. Her most recent work is a book on Chinese cinemas with Chris Berry, *China on Screen: Cinema and Nation* (Columbia University Press and Hong Kong University Press, 2006).

Carolyn FitzGerald is Assistant Professor of Chinese Language and Literature at Auburn University, Alabama. Currently, she is working on a book manuscript entitled *Fragmenting Modernisms of the War of Resistance: Geographic and Cultural Border Crossings*, which examines formal experimentation in Chinese literature and art during World War II. Her recent article 'Imaginary Sites of Memory: Wang Zengqi and Post-Mao Reconstructions of the Native Land' was published in *Modern Chinese Literature and Culture*.

Ping Fu is Assistant Professor of Chinese and Asian Studies at Towson University. Her works on Chinese cinema, literature and theatre have appeared in *Encyclopedia of Modern Drama, Journal of Multilingual and Multicultural Development, Asian Theatre Journal, Dushu* and *Ming Pao Monthly*. Her recent article 'Reconfiguring *Jianghu* on Screen' was published in the anthology *The Jin Yong Phenomenon: Chinese Martial Arts Fiction and Modern Chinese Literary History*, edited by Ann Huss and Jianmei Liu (Cambria, 2007). She is completing a book on contemporary Chinese urban cinema.

Kristine Harris is Associate Professor of Chinese History and Director of the Asian Studies Program at the State University of New York, New Paltz. Her recent publications include 'The Metropolis in the Cinematic Imagination of Republican China and the City Symphony Film', in *Popular Culture and Social Change in Modern China* (Huadong, 2007).

Margaret Hillenbrand is Lecturer in Chinese Studies at the School of Oriental and African Studies, University of London. She is the author of *Literature and the Practice of Resistance: Japanese and Taiwanese Fiction, 1960–1990* (Brill, 2007), and has published articles in *Modern Chinese Literature and Culture, positions: east asia cultures critique, The Journal of Japanese Studies* and *Cinema Journal* (forthcoming).

Brian Hu is a PhD candidate in the Department of Film, Television and Digital Media at the University of California, Los Angeles. His research interests include post-war Chinese popular culture and the diaspora, and his writings on cinema have appeared in *Screen, Continuum* and *Post Script*.

Haiyan Lee is Assistant Professor of Asian Studies at Stanford University. She is the author of *Revolution of the Heart: A Genealogy of Love in China, 1900–1950* (Stanford University Press, 2007), and guest-editor of 'Taking It to Heart: Emotion, Modernity, Asia', a special issue of *positions: east asia cultures critique* (2008). Her scholarly articles have appeared in *Public Culture, positions, Journal of Asian Studies, Modern China, Twentieth-Century China, CLEAR* and elsewhere.

Vivian Lee is Assistant Professor in the Department of Chinese, Translation and Linguistics at the City University of Hong Kong. She has published articles on modern Chinese literature and Chinese cinemas in collections of essays and academic journals such as *Modern Chinese Literature and Culture*, *Asian Cinema*, *Journal of Chinese Cinemas* and *Scope*.

Helen Hok-sze Leung is an Assistant Professor in the Department of Women's Studies at Simon Fraser University, Canada. Her research interests include Chinese-language cinemas and media culture, queer and transgender cultural politics in Asia, and issues of nationalism and post-coloniality. Her work on queer cinema has appeared in numerous anthologies and journals. She is the author of *Undercurrents: Queer Culture and Postcolonial Hong Kong* (Vancouver and Hong Kong: University of British Columbia Press and Hong Kong University Press, 2008).

David Leiwei Li is Professor of English and Collins Professor of the Humanities at the University of Oregon. He is the author of *Imagining the Nation: Asian American Literature and Cultural Consent* (Stanford University Press, 1998) and editor of *Globalization and the Humanities* (Hong Kong University Press, 2004). He is working on a manuscript, *Globalization on Speed: Chinese Cinema and the Neoliberalization of Culture*.

Song Hwee Lim is Senior Lecturer in Film at the University of Exeter, UK. He is the author of *Celluloid Comrades: Representations of Male Homosexuality in Contemporary Chinese Cinemas* (University of Hawaii Press, 2006), co-editor of *Remapping World Cinema: Identity, Culture and Politics in Film* (Wallflower Press, 2006) and editor of the *Journal of Chinese Cinemas*.

Kam Louie is Dean of the Arts Faculty, Hong Kong University. Publications include *The Cambridge Companion to Modern Chinese Culture* (editor, Cambridge University Press, 2008), *Theorising Chinese Masculinity* (Cambridge University Press, 2002), *The Politics of Chinese Language and Culture* (with Hodge, Routledge, 1998), *The Literature of Chinese in the Twentieth Century* (with McDougall, Columbia University Press, 1997) and *Inheriting Tradition* (Oxford University Press, 1986).

Fran Martin is Lecturer in Cultural Studies at the University of Melbourne. Her publications include *Situating Sexualities: Queer Representation in Taiwanese Fiction, Film and Public Culture* (Hong Kong University Press, 2003) and *Backward Glances: Transnational Chinese Cultures and the Female Homoerotic Imaginary* (Duke University Press, forthcoming).

Jason McGrath is Assistant Professor of Modern Chinese Literature and Film at the University of Minnesota–Twin Cities. He is the author of *Postsocialist Modernity: Chinese Cinema, Literature, and Criticism in the Market Age* (Stanford University Press, 2008). His essays on Chinese cinema have appeared in *Modern Chinese Literature and Culture*, *The Urban Generation: Chinese Cinema and Society at the Turn of the Twenty-first Century* (edited by Zhen Zhang, Duke University Press, 2007) and *China's Literary and Cultural Scenes at the Turn of the 21st Century* (edited by Jie Lu, Routledge, 2008).

Corrado Neri (corradoneri@hotmail.com) received his PhD in Chinese Studies from the University Ca' Foscari, Venice, and Jean Moulin, Lyon 3. He has conducted extensive research on Chinese cinema in Beijing and Taipei and written various articles published in specialist journals. He is now teaching at the University of Venice and Lyon. He authored *Tsai Ming-liang* (Cafoscarina, 2004), a monograph on the Taiwanese director. His second book, *Ages inquiets: la jeunesse dans le cinéma chinois*, is forthcoming in 2008 from the IETT, Université de Lyon (Jean Moulin).

Jonathan Noble has taught contemporary Chinese Literature and Culture at the University of Notre Dame since 2003. His essays on contemporary Chinese film, theatre and society have been published by over a dozen presses, and since 1998 he has translated thirty Chinese plays and film screenplays. He is a member of the National Committee on US–China Relations' Public Intellectual Program and is currently serving in Notre Dame's Provost Office as Advisor for Asia Initiatives.

Bérénice Reynaud teaches Film Theory, History and Criticism in the School of Critical Studies and the School of Film/Video at the California Institute of the Arts and is Co-Curator of the Film/Video series at the Roy and Edna Disney/CalArts Theater

(REDCAT). She is the author of *Nouvelles Chines, nouveaux cinémas* (Editions *Cahiers du Cinéma*, 1999) and *Hou Hsiao Hsien's 'A City of Sadness'* (BFI, 2002). Her work has been published in periodicals such as *Sight & Sound, Screen, Film Comment, Afterimage, The Independent, CinemaScope, Senses of Cinema, Cahiers du Cinéma, Libération, Le Monde diplomatique* and *Ciném-Action*. She is currently working on a book on the Chinese martial arts film.

Julian Stringer is Associate Professor of Film Studies at the University of Nottingham, and co-ordinating editor of *Scope: An Online Journal of Film and Television Studies* (<www.scope.nottingham.ac.uk>). He is currently completing a monograph on *In the Mood for Love* for Hong Kong University Press and co-editing (with Gary Rawnsley and Ming-Yeh Rawnsley) a volume of critical essays on *Hero* for Routledge.

Tan See-Kam (PhD University of Melbourne, Australia) is Associate Professor in Communication at the University of Macau. He has publications in *Antithesis, Asian Cinema, Cinemaya, Intermedia, Jump Cut, Media Asia, Screen, Social Semiotic* and *The South East Asian Journal of Social Science*, book chapters in *Queer Asian Cinema: Shadows in the Shade* (Harrington Park Press, 2000), *Between Home and World: A Reader in Hong Kong Cinema* (Oxford University Press, 2004) and *The Cinema of Small Nations* (Edinburgh University Press, 2007). He is co-editor of *Hong Kong Film, Hollywood and the New Global Cinema: No Film is an Island* (Routledge, 2007), *Chinese Connections: Critical Perspectives on Film, Identity and Diaspora* (Temple University Press, forthcoming) and a special journal issue on gender in Asian cinema for *Asian Journal of Communication* (2001). He is currently writing a book on Tsui Hark's *Peking Opera Blues* (Hong Kong University Press).

Janice Tong received her PhD in Film Studies at the Department of Art History and Theory at the University of Sydney. Her thesis, 'Aporia of Time: The Cinema of Wong Kar-wai', is a full-length study of the films of Wong Kar-wai, and critically examines aspects of Deleuzian philosophy, with a particular focus on his cinema books. She has previously published on Pasolini in the philosophy journal *Contretemps*, no. 2.

Faye Hui Xiao is a PhD candidate in the Department of East Asian Languages and Cultures at the University of Illinois, Urbana-Champaign. Her special areas of interest are modern Chinese literature and culture, film studies and gender studies. Her publications have appeared in journals such as *Asian Cinema, China Media Research, Tianya* and collections such as *Globalization and Chineseness: Postcolonial Readings of Contemporary Culture* (edited by Song Geng, Hong Kong University Press, 2006) and *From Camera Lens to Critical Lens: A Collection of Best Essays on Film Adaptation* (edited by Rebecca Housel, Cambridge Scholars Press, 2007). Currently she is working on her dissertation, *Representing Divorce, Engendering Interiority: Narratives of Gender, Class and Family in Contemporary Chinese Literature and Culture*.

Gary G. Xu is Associate Professor of Comparative Literature and Cinema Studies at the University of Illinois, Urbana-Champaign. He is the author of *Sinascape: Contemporary Chinese Cinema* (Rowman and Littlefield, 2007) and numerous articles on Chinese literature and film.

Yiman Wang is an Assistant Professor of Film and Digital Media at the University of California, Santa Cruz. Her essays have appeared in *Quarterly Review of Film and Video, Film Quarterly, Camera Obscura, Journal of Film and Video, Literature/Film Quarterly, positions: east asia cultures critique, Cultural Identity, Gender, Everyday Life Practice and Hong Kong Cinema of the 1970s* (edited by Lo Kwai-cheung and Eva Man, Oxford University Press, 2005) and *Stardom and Celebrity: A Reader* (edited by Sean Redmond *et al.*, Sage, 2007). She is currently working on a book project on border-crossing film remakes.

Audrey Yue is Lecturer in Cultural Studies at the University of Melbourne. She is co-editor of *Mobile Cultures: New Media in Queer Asia* (Duke University Press, 2003) and *AsiaPacifiQueer: Rethinking Gender and Sexuality* (University of Illinois Press, 2008). Her essays on Hong Kong cinema appear in *Cultural Theory in Everyday Life; Youth Media in the Asia Pacific Region; Datutop; Feminist Media Studies; Asian Migrations – Sojourning, Displacement, Homecoming and Other Travels; Between Home and World: A Reader in Hong Kong Cinema; Actor: Leslie Cheung; The*

Horror Reader and *Inter-Asia Cultural Studies*. She is currently completing a book on Ann Hui's *Song of the Exile* (Hong Kong University Press, forthcoming).

Yingjin Zhang, Director of Chinese Studies Program and Professor of Comparative Literature, Cultural Studies and Film Studies at University of California–San Diego, is the author of *The City in Modern Chinese Literature and Film* (Stanford University Press, 1996), *Screening China* (Center for Chinese Studies, University of Michigan Press, 2002) and *Chinese National Cinema* (Routledge, 2004); co-author of *Encyclopedia of Chinese Film* (Routledge, 1998); editor of *China in a Polycentric World* (Stanford University Press, 1998) and *Cinema and Urban Culture in Shanghai, 1922–1943* (Stanford University Press, 1999); and co-editor of *From Underground to Independent* (Rowman & Littlefield, 2006).

John Zou received his PhD from University of California at Berkeley and is currently teaching at Arizona State University. His research interests include modern Chinese theatre and cinema. He has also published on Mei Lanfang, a major figure in Peking Opera.

Introduction: One Film at a Time – Again

Chris Berry

The original idea for the first edition of this anthology came during the Chinese Film Studies conference held at Hong Kong Baptist University in 2000. Listening to so many groundbreaking papers together with over one hundred other participants, I was impressed by the transformation of the field. Ten years before, the equivalent event could have been held around my kitchen table. When I edited the earlier BFI anthology, *Perspectives on Chinese Cinema* (1991), we had to translate material from Chinese to make up a full-length collection. By 2000, Chinese Cinema Studies in English had such a close relationship with its Chinese-language counterparts that they were beginning to constitute a transnational and translingual field that continues to be diverse, burgeoning, complex and wide-ranging. However, the keynote speaker of the 2000 conference, David Bordwell, leaned over and punctured my reveries by remarking that, great achievement though the event was, there was a dearth of papers on individual films. The first edition of this volume aimed to fill that gap. It has been sufficiently well received that the editors have commissioned a revised and much expanded second edition.

All the essays in *Chinese Films in Focus* have been specially commissioned for the anthology, and each one focuses on an individual film of the author's choice. With the first edition, there was no set list or canon of films to be written on. Rather, fresh angles and excellence of scholarship determined the selection of essays, in the hope that they would stimulate fresh engagement with individual films. To prepare for the second edition, the BFI carried out a survey of users. I was relieved that all respondents were happy with the quality of the existing essays. However, they reported that certain chapters were rarely read because the films could not be found, and they also asked for more essays on contemporary cinema. With these preferences in mind, we have removed four essays from the original volume, but added thirteen new essays, bringing the total up to thirty-four.

This introduction considers two questions. First, if the films have not been selected as a canon, what is their relationship to Chinese cinema and Chinese Cinema Studies in English? And second, what do they tell us about studying Chinese cinema one film at a time? In other words, why are single film analyses necessary and what do they contribute?

CHINESE CINEMA AND CHINESE CINEMA STUDIES

Chinese Films in Focus is neither an attempt to establish a canon of the best Chinese films nor is it a representative selection of all the Chinese films ever made. The collection is a resource to be dipped into rather than an effort to impose any particular order on Chinese cinema. It is designed for the reader who wants to sample the main debates in the field of Chinese Cinema Studies or for the teacher who seeks readings for a course on Chinese cinema – whether that course is organised historically, geographically or by academic debate. In order to leave it open for different readers to trace different paths through the collection, the essays are given in alphabetical order according to film title.

However, before discussing these features of the volume in more detail, it is necessary to define 'Chinese cinema'. My aim has been to create space for the widest range of films that readers might consider Chinese. Therefore, Chineseness is not defined according to territorial nation-state. Because non-Chinese languages are used in many diasporic Chinese films, even the recent broader concept of 'Chinese-language film' (*huayu dianying*) is not broad enough for my purposes. Indeed, the intersection of class and different languages in Singapore, including English, plays a major role in Song Hwee Lim's analysis of Royston Tan's 2003 exposé of teen life, *15*. The inclusion of *15* as the opening film in the volume foregrounds the catholic understanding of Chineseness applied here: its Chineseness exceeds both territorial and linguistic definitions.

Chinese Films in Focus may attempt to be inclusive in its range, but why is it not representative? This is primarily related to accessibility and secondly to reader demand. Chinese cinema dates back to the early part of the twentieth century. Whether the first screenings of films took place in Shanghai or in Hong Kong remains unclear, but certainly screenings took place in both cities in 1896.[1] The first Chinese film, *Dingjun Mountain*, was made in Beijing in 1905, although the cinema industry moved down to Shanghai soon after. *Dingjun Mountain* was an excerpt from an opera film, as were the first Hong Kong films, *Right a Wrong with Earthenware Dish* and *Stealing a Roasted Duck*, both made in 1909.[2] Yet none of these films has survived to the present day, making it impossible to consider them for a volume based on analysing individual films. During this early period, Taiwan was a Japanese colony, and the island did not generate its own film industry until it was handed over to the Republic of China at the end of World War II.[3]

The earliest surviving Chinese film is a 1922 comedy short, known variously in English as *Labourer's Love* and *Romance of a Fruit Peddler*. However, the great many 1920s martial arts action films and melodramas about the ethical dilemmas produced by modernity have not survived.[4] The 1930s is the earliest period from which substantial numbers of films are available today. It is represented in this volume by Kristine Harris's essay on the 1934 film *The Goddess*, featuring the great silent star Ruan Lingyu. After *The Goddess*, the next earliest film included here is *Spring in a Small Town*, made in 1948 by Fei Mu and analysed here by Carolyn FitzGerald as symptomatic of post-war trauma.

Yet, even as we enter the period after which substantial numbers of Chinese films survive, other problems of accessibility make representative selection impossible. In recent years, considerable numbers of 1930s and 1940s classics have become available, and the tendency to include English subtitles is growing. However, so far most of these subtitles are so poor that they are misleading. In Taiwan, the cinema took off in the 1950s and the output of both local *minnanhua*-language and Mandarin-language films was very substantial. But few of the films are available on DVD, and almost none have English

subtitles. As a result, the earliest Taiwan film discussed here is King Hu's 1971 film, *A Touch of Zen*, in Mary Farquhar's essay. In Hong Kong, output in both Cantonese and Mandarin also took off after revolution on the mainland closed its cinema off from the West in the 1950s. Although DVDs are coming out, few of the Cantonese-language films are subtitled in English. Therefore, the earliest Hong Kong film analysed in this volume is Li Han-hsiang's 1963 Mandarin-language film, *The Love Eterne*, discussed in Tan See-Kam and Annette Aw's essay.

Although representativeness is not possible, *Chinese Films in Focus* does attempt historical and geographical range. It aims to offer variety for the general reader, and to provide the teacher of a Chinese cinema course with appropriate resources, whether organised historically, geographically or by topics and debates in the field. As regards history, although the emphasis is on recent films in accord with the expressed wishes of readers of the first edition, films from every decade after the 1930s are included. Geographically, Hong Kong, Taiwan and mainland China all receive wide coverage, and one essay on the diasporic Chinese culture (Song Hwee Lim on *15* from Singapore) is also included.

In addition, the essays in the book could easily be mobilised for a course organised according to debates in the field. Most of the pieces in *Chinese Films in Focus* first summarise the existing debate around a well-known film – with references that readers can follow up – and then produce a new angle of their own. For example, at least three essays in the first edition already noted the domination of realism and realist aesthetics in much discussion of Chinese cinema, but then go on to challenge that status quo in different ways. Rey Chow's analysis of Zhang Yimou's film *Not One Less* notes the consensus that his recent works have been more realist than earlier productions. In contrast, she reads the film as a sly reflection on the strategy of making things appear transparent, obvious and real in the new 'mediatised' economy and culture of the People's Republic. Yiman Wang's essay on Zheng Junli's 1949 classic *Crows and Sparrows* argues that what is usually understood as realism in this particular film and in Chinese film in general needs to be reinterpreted as allegory. And Mary Farquhar's piece on *A Touch of Zen* counters the idea of action as purely formal play that suspends realist narrative. Instead, she traces a local Chinese operatic tradition informing Chinese cinematic traditions that is anything but realist yet also makes action a meaningful part of narrative development.

The currency of debates about realism in all its various forms is continued through some of the essays added for the second edition. Esther Cheung's analysis of Fruit Chan's *Durian Durian* emphasises that although Chan's work is characterised by a realist aesthetic, it is also highly interpretive. In my analysis of the particular on-the-spot realism favoured by Jia Zhangke in *Xiao Wu*, I focus on the rendering of time in a manner that, although still edited, gives the effect of watching nothing much happening – and so also communicating an interpretation of the small-town China featured in the film.

No doubt other essays could be grouped according to various topics. For example, sexuality is significant in Bérénice Reynaud's analysis of *Centre Stage*, Tan See-Kam and Annette Aw's work on *The Love Eterne*, John Zou's reading of *A Chinese Ghost Story*, Fran Martin's work on *Vive L'Amour* and my own essay on *Wedding Banquet*. Another group might be essays on globalisation and the response to it. This would include not only Jonathan Noble's essay on *Blind Shaft* but also Ping Fu's on *Ermo*, Rey Chow's on *Not One Less*, Yingjin Zhang's on *Big Shot's Funeral*, David Li's on *Yi Yi* and probably Gary Xu's on *Flowers of Shanghai*.

But by no means all the essays are particularly concerned with theme-related topics. For example, Janice Tong's essay focuses on the way time is constructed through the deployment of cinema in *Chungking Express*, whereas my essay pursues a similar question in regard to *Xiao Wu*. This echoes a general resurgence in interest in issues of time in Cinema Studies as a whole, with the rise of Deleuzian theory and awareness of time as a construct rather than a given.

Another direction in general Cinema Studies that is less focused on the film text is an interest in production and reception circumstances. Kristine Harris is concerned to understand issues stemming from the precise historical context of *The Goddess*, for example, and Brian Hu's analysis focuses on the industrial, economic and generic underpinnings of *Formula 17*. Jonathan Noble's essay on *Blind Shaft* includes questions stemming from the film's circulation on the festival and arthouse circuits in the West more than textual analysis of the film itself.

Finally, it must be noted that in some cases, the films were so new at the time of the anthology's production that there was no existing scholarly debate on them. Examples from the first edition have not been changed, and they include Edward Yang's *Yi Yi*, which David Li considers, and Ang Lee's *Crouching Tiger, Hidden Dragon*, discussed by Felicia Chan. In these cases, the essays map out some terms of debate for the film and produce one of the first sustained and serious interrogations of them. Li reads *Yi Yi* as an argument for the importance of reconfigured ethical engagement in response to the challenges of globalised modernity. Chan examines the variations in *Crouching Tiger, Hidden Dragon*'s reception in different Asian territories as well as the 'West', arguing that the different cultural knowledges audiences bring to the film not only shape their understanding of it but may hinder the film's translatability as much as help it.

In this second edition, an even greater number of new productions are included. *PTU*, *Riding Alone for Thousands of Miles*, *Kekexili: Mountain Patrol*, *Formula 17* and *Blind Shaft* are all too recent to have generated large debates yet. Cui Shuqin's analysis of Lu Chuan's 2004 hit *Kekexili: Mountain Patrol* follows David Li's interest in the ethical dimensions of cinema in his essay on *Yi Yi*. She considers the intersection of the film's ostensible ethical commitments to the environment and animal welfare and its equal commitment to commercial narrative film-making. The engagement with the consequences of globalisation on Chinese cinema pursued in Chan's essay on *Crouching Tiger, Hidden Dragon* also underlies Jonathan Noble's examination of Li Yang's 2003 festival success, *Blind Shaft*. As well as considering the film's focus on working conditions in China's burgeoning economy, Noble examines the currency of the 'underground' tag on the international festival circuit.

Kekexili: Mountain Patrol is an example of a new generation of commercial cinema to come out of the People's Republic. On Taiwan, *Formula 17* opened up a parallel new direction there in 2004. Brian Hu analyses this new mainstream cinema and its production circumstances in his essay here. Vivian Lee locates Johnnie To's *PTU* (2003), tracing the way it reinscribes the cinematic vision of Hong Kong post-1997 within the police action genre. And Faye Hui Xiao examines Zhang Yimou's exceptional low-budget arthouse film from 2005, *Riding Alone for Thousands of Miles*, which stars the Japanese veteran

Takakura Ken as a father seeking to redeem himself before his son. Xiao shows how this Japanese casting rewrites not only Zhang's well-established obsession with father–son narratives but also China's complex relationship with Japan, at a time of growing regional popular cultural circulation and connection.

SINGLE FILM ANALYSIS

Why study Chinese cinema one film at a time? The 'textual' emphasis in Film Studies, associated with single film analysis, came under attack in the 1990s. For example, in what he admits is a 'shameless polemic', Toby Miller argued that we should 'acknowledge the policy, distributional, promotional, and exhibitionary protocols of the screen at each site as much as their textual ones'. He continues: 'Enough talk of "economic reductionism" without also problematizing "textual reductionism". Enough valorization of close reading and armchair accounts of human interiority without establishing the political significance of texts and subjectivities within actual social movements and demographic cohorts.'[5] Calls for understanding the cinema as a social, economic and political institution as well as a set of texts are timely, and, as already indicated, taken up in various ways here. But approaches to the issue like Miller's can be problematic on at least three counts. First, they may exaggerate the degree to which Cinema Studies has neglected the institutional. Second, they risk empiricism. Implying a divide between the supposed subjectivity of textual interpretation and objectivity of investigations into the so-called 'real world', they ignore the fact that the 'data' of the latter is also selected and interpreted. Third, they risk falsely dividing Cinema Studies between the institutional and the textual. Important though all the areas Miller mentions are, seeing, responding to and making sense of individual films is at the centre of all of them. Policies are made in response to and in anticipation of films. Films are bought on the basis of distributor's perceptions of how they will be received by audiences.

Cinema Studies requires a range of approaches to the cinema that understands the singularity of the individual film and the importance of the cinema as an institution without trying to divide them or set them in opposition to each other. In Stephen Neale's classic study of genre – itself an example that challenges the claim that the institutional side of cinema has always been neglected – he points out that the singularity of the individual film-viewing experience is a primary and defining characteristic of the cinema and the film industry. Filmgoing differs from most other commodities. People go back to McDonald's because they want the product to be standardised and predictable. But film audiences expect a different experience every time. In their efforts to regulate and control the marketplace, film producers have developed genres and stars to balance the consumers' desire for originality with their desire to repeat previously pleasant experiences; the logic is that if you liked this musical or that Jackie Chan film, you'll like another one.[6] Understanding the process of genre formation and change requires attention to both the cinema as a socio-economic institution and to the range of individual film texts and how they both repeat and change existing generic norms in the play of predictability and originality that is built into the cinema as we know it.

Bearing this understanding of single film analysis in mind, I would argue that the essays in this volume focus on the individual film in a variety of different ways. Some of them place the text at the intersection of institutional and social patterns, helping to answer the concerns of writers like Miller, whereas others place them at the intersection of discursive patterns. But all of them have an important place within the study of the cinema. To simultaneously illustrate this argument and provide another pathway through the contents of the volume, the remainder of this introduction outlines some of the different types of single film work pursued in those essays not already discussed above. Although I will not use any essay to illustrate more than one tendency, most could be invoked more than once.

THE SINGLE FILM AND THE SOCIO-CULTURAL MOMENT

First, many of the essays account for the single film by placing it within the historical and social context of its initial production and circulation. This work resists the temptation to 'apply' theoretical formulas or large ahistorical generalisations about Chinese culture when reading Chinese films, erasing the singularity of the film in question. Instead, these essays emphasise the moment and location of their production to enable new insights. Felicia Chan's essay on the different responses to *Crouching Tiger, Hidden Dragon* is exemplary.

Yomi Braester notes that the dominant interpretations of *Farewell My Concubine* 'deplored' the film for its 'emphasis on national narratives … backed by catering to the taste for the exotic of an Orientalising overseas audience'. In contrast, Braester heeds director Chen Kaige's own claim that the film is a personal story. He argues that the emphasis on Beijing as a local city brings out the tension between grand narrative at the national level and personal experience represented by the local culture and cityscape.

The 1934 classic *The Goddess* also benefits from Kristine Harris's meticulous mapping of the circumstances surrounding the film's production and reception in Shanghai. Not only does she locate it among the anxieties around the figure of the fallen woman circulating in Shanghai at the time. But she also goes on to question the frequent critique of the film for being too hesitant in its damnation of the exploitation of women and the upholding of Confucian patriarchy. Using the strict censorship codes of the time, she undertakes a subtler search of the text for subversive 'visual cues' beneath its seeming narrative acquiescence with official optimism and traditional values.

Ping Fu's essay, like Harris's, places particular emphasis on visuality, but she investigates a much more recent film and places it in the particular moment of China's integration into the global economy. Zhou Xiaowen's 1994 *Ermo* is a 'vivid depiction of a rural woman in pursuit of the biggest TV in town'. The television set itself, the programmes on it and the way it and Ermo are visually represented all combine in Fu's analysis of the contemporary Chinese experience of globalisation at the intersection of the city and the countryside. Fu's awareness of China's tortuous pursuit of the modern as the context of the film's production leads her to note carefully that the film is fundamentally unsure yet about whether these transformations will be worth the price.

Audrey Yue's essay on *In the Mood for Love* locates the film precisely at the moment marked by Hong Kong's transition not only in but also after 1997. Furthermore, she mobilises the particular regional intersections marked by the histories of migration and cultural movement in the film to counter the common critical tendency to abstract Wong's Hong Kong as just another sign of urban cosmopolitanism. In so doing, she opens up new ways of thinking about the significance as well as the specificity of Hong Kong and Hong Kong cinema in the new post-1997

age, as well as prompting us to ponder the politics of our various passions for Chinese cinemas.

Carolyn FitzGerald notes how many other commentators and critics have claimed *Spring in a Small Town* as a 'timeless masterpiece'. Without disputing the quality of the film, her essay works to place it very precisely in its time and place. She argues for an understanding of the formal qualities of the film as working with the narrative to convey the effects of wartime trauma and its aftermath.

THE SINGLE FILM AND DIFFERENT VALUE SYSTEMS

A second major tendency in the essays contained here is to consider the individual film in terms of value systems. The discussion of value systems must feature strongly in any focus on a category of films defined by culture. Given the multiple and incompatible value systems from Confucianism to Marxism and environmentalism to the market economy that have been mobilised in Chinese cultures, this is even more true for Chinese Film Studies, and both David Leiwei Li and Cui Shuqin's essays on *Yi Yi* and *Kekexili: Mountain Patrol* pursue such conflicts of values arising from the Chinese experience of globalisation.

The legacy of the Maoist value system informs Helen Hok-sze Leung's focus in her essay on *Yellow Earth*. Whereas other authors emphasise this keystone film as emblematic of Chinese Fifth Generation film-makers' stylistic and political rejection of the Maoist legacy, her subtle reading takes us closer to the film. As she argues, *Yellow Earth* 'is at once a critique of Mao's dysfunctional political project and an embodiment of the desire such a project inspires but is unable to fulfil'. As well as offering a new take on *Yellow Earth* itself, she notes how the film-making process echoes the journey of the soldier in the film.

Robert Chi returns to the Maoist project and its cinema. He examines one of its most rousing and repeatedly filmed political epics, *The Red Detachment of Women*. Focusing on the 1960 version by Xie Jin, Chi looks beyond established debate on gender issues in the film and extends existing accounts of how these films work to mobilise their audience. He notes that the individual transformation of the main character not only provides a model for the audience, but that this transformation is crucially tied to the production of memory that is not just cognitively known but also felt and inscribed in the body. By highlighting the somatic grounds of ideological mobilisation, he reinvigorates our thinking about the core body of Chinese revolutionary films, which has been neglected recently.

Changing values about gender are also a key theme in the established debates on *Woman, Demon, Human*, with the film being acclaimed as one of China's few true feminist texts. Yet Haiyan Lee argues that beyond this film's apparent denaturalisation of gender is a deeper commitment to values based on *qing*, or human attachment. Focusing on the relationship between father and daughter, Lee analyses the narrative of the film as emancipating them and their relationship from conventional expectations and roles to re-establish it on the basis of *qing*.

Kam Louie's essay on *Hero* engages with this highly contentious film to demonstrate its engagement with Chinese values around masculinity. Drawing on his groundbreaking research in this area, Louie argues that the film portrays the emperor as a man able to combine the desirable characteristics of both martial and scholarly paradigms for Chinese masculinity. This makes him a man worth laying one's life down for. With this film, then, long-established gender codes reassert themselves.

Finally, in regard to this second tendency to focus on value systems, Margaret Hillenbrand's essay on Chen Kuofu's *The Personals* sees the film as an intervention in debates that transcend contemporary Taiwan, even though they have a particular significance there. Hillenbrand argues that *The Personals* is concerned with the impact on human relationships of the voyeuristic culture we all know so well from surveillance cameras to reality television. She argues that the narrative works demonstrate how easily the apparent power dynamics of the spy and the spied upon can be turned around within this dynamic.

THE SINGLE FILM AND INTERTEXTUAL ANALYSIS

Another mode of engagement with the single film that is centrally concerned with the cinema as at once institution and text is the attempt to place the film within networks of intertextual connections, such as genre conventions and other geneaologies, themselves inscribed in both industrial and critical practices. Yomi Braester's essay discussed above locates *Farewell My Concubine* within a lineage of films that represent Beijing, just as Mary Farquhar's essay places *A Touch of Zen* within the generic conventions of martial arts films.

However, not all the intertextual connections are necessarily with other films. Corrado Neri's essay on *A Time to Live, A Time to Die* looks to literature and specifically autobiography to account for some of the unique features of Hou Hsiao-hsien's autobiographical film-making. He notes that 'Autobiography (*zizhuan*) is far from the modern western tradition of … romanticism and psychology. It is more a matter of finding a place in society … It is also a way to pay respects to the memory of parents and family.' As well as tracing how these thematic concerns structure Hou's autobiographical films, Neri also suggests that they are a kind of cinematic *biji*, a literary genre that is much more impressionistic, poetic and distanced from state and politics than more conventional forms.

Jason McGrath's essay on the 1980s comic favourite *Black Cannon Incident* also mobilises intertextual connections relatively ignored in the West, in this case the spy genre. He points out that the production of spy films was a staple of 1950s and 1960s People's Republic cinema. Therefore, audiences for *Black Cannon Incident* would have viewed it in the light of their prior knowledge of the earlier films. By tracing the echoes of the key narrative elements, character types and iconography of the earlier genre, he enhances our comic enjoyment of *Black Cannon Incident* and our appreciation of its social critique, as well as solving the long mystery of why the main character is a Roman Catholic.

Tan See-Kam and Annette Aw work on *The Love Eterne*, the 1963 classic much loved by Ang Lee, the director of *Crouching Tiger, Hidden Dragon*. Lee's remarks on *The Love Eterne* work against the queer dimension of this cross-dressing opera in which two actresses perform as a male and female couple, one of whom cross-dresses as a man. In contrast, Tan and Aw work the intertext to maximise the queer dimensions of the film. Drawing on the literary tradition of scholar-and-beauty (*caizi jiaren*) romances, they highlight how both the film and its heritage depend on a carnivalesque play with gender and sexuality norms in mainstream Chinese culture.

Changing sexual norms are of course at the centre of Ang Lee's own popular gay farce, *Wedding Banquet*. But where other writers have focused heavily on this dimension of the film, I examine its generic intertext at the point where Hollywood and Chinese family melodrama meet. Although it is a hybrid text,

Wedding Banquet's ambivalence and ambiguity are mobilised by clear differences between the Chinese and Hollywood family melodrama. Tracing what those differences are helps us not only understand the two textual traditions but also the different values the film invokes.

THE SINGLE FILM AND FILM THEORY

Two further types of single film analysis are undertaken in the essays. These might be seen as the more purely interpretive types of single film analysis, but I want to argue that they continue to have a central role in Cinema Studies. First, there are those readings that look at a particular film as a site to investigate theoretical paradigms. Given that so much film theory has originated in the study of Hollywood or European films, Chinese films can be exciting to work with precisely because their origins may challenge existing paradigms.

For Janice Tong, time and the cinema, and Deleuze's ideas about the relationship between them, motivate her work on Wong Kar-wai's *Chungking Express*. As Tong notes, 'It is Wong's rendering of time in his cinematographic images that unhinges our perception of time when viewing *Chungking Express*. But how so?' Tong's meditations on time are enabled by Hong Kong's complex understanding of how its experience of time is refracted by the anticipation of its 'back to the future' 1997 return to China. It is this particular disruption of the linear time schemes of modern teleology that enables *Chungking Express*'s creativity with cinematic time, which Tong carefully demonstrates to explore 'the substance of Wong's cinematic time'.

Like Wong Kar-wai, Stanley Kwan works at the intersection of art film and popular genres. But the particular aspect of his films that interests Bérénice Reynaud in '*Centre Stage:* A Shadow in Reverse' is the tripartite relationship between his engagement with the genre of the woman's film, his now public homosexuality and feminist theory. Although generated by the particular circumstances of the Chinese history of gender and sexuality, Reynaud's investigation and theorisation of this crucial nexus has broader ramifications, as male homosexuality and femininity are linked in so many patriarchal cultures. In order to maintain an appropriately subtle and yet rigorous ambivalence about Kwan's use of female figures to talk about male homosexuality and at the same time

investigate precisely how this closeted textual operation functions, Reynaud focuses on denial, contradiction and reverse discourse as generative tropes.

John Zou's witty and incisive essay on the division of men into the 'lovable' and the 'edible' in *A Chinese Ghost Story* is part genre analysis, making it a candidate for the above discussion on intertextuality, and part extension of horror film theory. Zou draws on Carol Clover's ideas about the cross-gender identification of male audiences in many horror films, where they are asked to identify with the female protagonist who survives monstrous attack – the Final Girl, in Clover's terms. But, as he notes, in *A Chinese Ghost Story*, the survivor is a Final Boy. With this insight, he opens up both a new avenue in our understanding of the complex engagement of gender and subjectivity in horror film, and also questions whether this can ever be regarded as an eternal story about the production of selfhood. With this in mind, Zou pursues a surprising but convincing and original take on the film as a parable about Hong Kong's ambivalent relation to and anticipation of 1997 as both return to the (homogenous identity of the) motherland and arrival of another (heterogenous) colonial force. In this way, he also pushes the boundaries of conceptual models for understanding the colonial and post-colonial imagination.

THE SINGLE FILM AND CRITICAL INTERVENTION

Finally, there are a number of essays that, although they may also engage in some of the directions enumerated above, place a particular emphasis on a direct engagement with the text, emphasising the critical intervention of the interpreter in our understanding of the film. In Cinema Studies, we are frequently reminded that we are examining a piece of discourse, a text, and not a reflection of reality. Yet, as Rey Chow points out in her essay on *Not One Less*, 'the study of modern and contemporary China is so dominated by so-called realism that even the most imaginative writings and artworks, however avant-garde they might be, have tended to be read largely for factographic value'. All the essays in this volume are mindful of the dangers of such narrow foreclosure on other possibilities. But those collected in this section place particular emphasis on teasing out the textual specificity of the films as a way of countering attempts to read them as direct reflections of Chinese societies. As already noted in the earlier part of the introduction,

Chow's own essay on *Not One Less* and Yiman Wang's essay on *Crows and Sparrows* are key examples of this tendency.

For Fran Martin in '*Vive L'Amour*: Eloquent Emptiness', the stakes are somewhat different. She finds that most work in English on the film has attended to it as simply a reflection of alienation in modern Taiwan, but that it has neglected the specifically Taiwanese queer dimensions of the film. In her careful working through of elements such as the metaphor of the 'family' in the film and its particular resonance for queer subjects in Taiwan, she counters this. Furthermore, she takes issue with those critics who have attended to the queer dimension of the film but seen it as pessimistic. By focusing in close detail not only on the representational level but also on the cinematic level of lighting and framing, she produces a very different understanding of *Vive L'Amour*'s trajectory.

Also on Taiwanese cinema, Gang Gary Xu's essay on Hou Hsiao-hsien's *Flowers of Shanghai* may surprise readers, because it is about Taiwan as well as Taiwan film. Most writers have assumed that because it is set in colonial Shanghai over a century ago, *Flowers of Shanghai* has nothing to do with Taiwan. However, Xu teases out the significance of both the production process and of the film itself as continuing Hou's project of interrogating his homeland, its history and its contemporary condition. As he writes, 'Thematically, although "Taiwan" is no longer relevant to the story of the film, its absence becomes present in *Flowers of Shanghai* because of Hou's increasing awareness of MIT – Made in Taiwan.'

Finally, Julian Stringer's essay is on Ann Hui's *Boat People*, a 1982 film about the fate of the Vietnamese following the arrival of communism throughout the country. For a long time, writers on the film have assumed that it is an allegory reflecting fearful anticipation of Hong Kong's future return to mainland China, and that there is nothing more to say about it. Stringer notes, 'such arguments are perfectly valid and seemingly "correct." However, the simple repetition of this primary interpretation inevitably overshadows *Boat People*'s other variable and even contradictory meanings.' Attending to the film afresh and to its distribution context, Stringer emphasises the analysis of the role of photojournalism as an issue in the film. Placing *Boat People* within an internationally circulating cycle of such films, he argues that its less than heroic depiction of its non-Western main character is both what made it 'difficult' from the point of view of distributors and what makes it interesting.

I hope that readers will be as excited by the variety of the essays and freshness of their perspectives as I am. I would like to thank all the authors who have contributed to this anthology not only for their highly original and rigorous analyses but also for their patience and co-operation. Without their hard work, the volume could not exist. Thanks also to Wang Dun for helping to compile the Chinese character lists and to the Center for Chinese Studies at the University of California, Berkeley, for funding his diligent work. Last but certainly not least, Andrew Lockett, Rebecca Barden and Sarah Watt at the BFI have been incisive and constructive editors, and the institute's anonymous readers have given powerful and constructive feedback and guidance.

NOTES

1. Pang Laikwan, 'Walking into and out of the Spectacle: China's Earliest Film Scene', *Screen*, 47, no. 1 (2006): 66–80.

2. For more discussion of the operatic heritage in Chinese cinema and *Dingjun Mountain* in particular, see Chapter 3 of Chris Berry and Mary Farquhar, *China on Screen: Cinema and Nation* (New York and Hong Kong: Columbia and Hong Kong University Presses, 2006).

3. For a brief but useful discussion of this period, see Emilie Yueh-Yu Yeh and Darrell William Davis, *Taiwan Film Directors: A Treasure Island* (New York: Columbia University Press, 2005), 15–17.

4. For detailed discussion of these films, this period and early Chinese film culture in Shanghai, see Zhang Zhen, *An Amorous History of the Silver Screen: Shanghai Cinema 1896–1937* (Chicago: University of Chicago Press, 2005).

5. Toby Miller, 'Cinema Studies Doesn't Matter; or, I Know What You Did Last Semester', in *Keyframes: Popular Cinema and Cultural Studies*, ed. Matthew Tinkcom and Amy Villarejo (London: Routledge, 2001), 303, 308.

6. Stephen Neale, *Genre* (London: BFI, 1980), 48–55.

1   *15*: The Singapore Failure Story, 'Slanged Up'

Song Hwee Lim

Released in 2003, Royston Tan's debut feature film *15* can be situated in the context of a revival in Singaporean film-making that began in the early 1990s. Following the closure of the Shaw and Cathay studios in the late 1960s and early 1970s respectively, not a single film was made in Singapore until the abysmal *Medium Rare* (Arthur Smith) in 1991.[1] While there were attempts at making genre films aimed at the mass market in the subsequent years, resulting in films such as the comedy *Army Daze* (Ong Keng Sen, 1996), the thriller *God or Dog* (Hugo Ng, 1997), the disco-inspired *Forever Fever* (Glen Goei, 1998) and the teen movie *The Teenage Textbook Movie* (Philip Lim, 1998), all of which enjoyed varying degrees of box-office success, two noteworthy trends emerged outside of this genre-based milieu. The first is what Olivia Khoo calls 'local content films' that centre around the comedian Jack Neo,[2] such as *Money No Enough* (Tay Teck Lock, 1998), *Liang Po Po: The Movie* (Teng Bee Lian, 1999) and the Neo-directed hits, *I Not Stupid* (2002) and *Homerun* (2003). These films typically target a Mandarin-speaking audience who are already familiar with Neo's television work,[3] and are also well received in Malaysia, Hong Kong and Taiwan.[4] The second consists of more self-consciously stylised films, including Eric Khoo's *Mee Pok Man* (1995), *12 Storeys* (1997) and *Be with Me* (2005); *Eating Air* (1999) by Kelvin Tong and Jasmine Ng; and Tan's *15* and *4:30* (2005). These have begun to break into international film festival and arthouse cinema circuits in the West. Both groups of films are similarly invested in representing the underbelly of Singapore society that is at odds with the country's sparkling clean image, giving voice to different marginalised groups and to the officially censured Chinese dialects (in particular Hokkien) and Singlish (a local version of ungrammatical English mixed with other languages and dialects, including Malay). In their different ways,

these films engender a cinematic social realism that implicitly and at times explicitly performs a social critique function in a country whose government is not known for its tolerance of dissenting views.

It has been argued that the artistic sphere, to which the films of Eric Khoo and Jack Neo belong, has emerged as 'a "privileged" space for critical reflection on society', and that the all-pervasive presence of the People's Action Party government 'makes itself a relatively easy target for critique' that is 'almost too good to pass up'.[5] However, if it is accurate to say that, in Singapore, 'as in all authoritarian regimes, artists have a tendency to embed their work within quite explicit critiques of politics',[6] it must be emphasised that such a critical stance plays well not just locally but also globally. In this regard, there is a shared tendency for discourses on Singapore and the People's Republic of China (and their respective cinemas) to interrogate excessively (if not exclusively) issues surrounding official censure, alternative artistic practices and potential for resistance, sometimes leading to the specificities of films being conveniently overlooked, as Geremie Barmé has demonstrated in his dismissal of the early works of the PRC film-maker Zhang Yuan as 'bankable dissent', while leaving the 'oppressed' film-maker with no viable position other than that of a 'dissident'.[7] Within this dynamic, dissent or dissidence becomes what global audiences now expect of any film from countries with a presumed authoritarian regime, and simultaneously serves as the film-maker's almost compulsory passport to global recognition.

Appearing almost a decade after those of Khoo and Neo, Tan's film-making can be located in this tradition yet departs from it. On the one hand, Tan said in an interview about his debut film that 'It's time we washed some of our dirty linen in public',[8] thus locating *15* as a cinematic discourse of social critique. On the other hand, while his films to date, including his latest, *881* (2007), featuring song-and-dance street performances that proliferate in the 'ghostly' seventh month of the Chinese calendar, share the theme of social marginalisation, what distinguishes them is the *manner* in which this critical reflection on society is represented on screen. Aesthetically, Tan is not only unmistakably of the MTV generation for whom post-modern pastiche and parody, rather than social realism, reigns, but, like the American director Spike Jonze, Tan also 'cut his teeth on music videos',[9] winning awards for his music videos as early as his late teens.[10] What is paradoxical, as I want to suggest in this chapter and illustrate below, is that *15* does not totally eschew social realism but rather pushes it to an extreme documentary realism. Nevertheless, rather than present a linear narrative in which the bleak reality of the marginalised is played out for social critique, *15* fragments the narrative with a pastiche of musical interludes, arcade-game simulation and animation that playfully puts any sense of realism into relief. The result is a film that cannot be read merely as social-realist critique, but rather is full of contradiction and ambivalence in its effect and affect.

With the release of *15* in 2003, Tan immediately became the *enfant terrible* of Singapore film-making. Based on his eponymous 25-minute short film that won the Special Achievement Award at the Singapore International Film Festival (SIFF) in 2002, the 90-minute feature-length *15* premiered uncut at the 2003 SIFF where all 1,200 tickets were snapped up in just four days.[11] It subsequently stirred up a controversy when, for its general release, the Board of Film Censors granted the film an R(A) (Restricted [Artistic], for audiences aged twenty-one and above only) rating but demanded twenty-seven cuts.[12] As a result, Tan became, in his own words, 'the poster-boy of the anti-censorship movement'[13] and was named in 2004 by *Time Asia* magazine on its '20 Under 40' list of 'Asian heroes', in which he was categorised as an 'iconoclast'.[14] He also responded to the cutting of *15* by poking fun at the censorship system with a short film *Cut* (2004), which includes a musical item sung to the tune of Abba's *Thank You for the Music*: 'Thank you to the censors/The scenes you're chopping/Thanks for all the crime you're stopping'.[15] Predictably, the authorities, represented by the Minister for Information, Communication and the Arts, were not amused, nor did they 'appreciate such

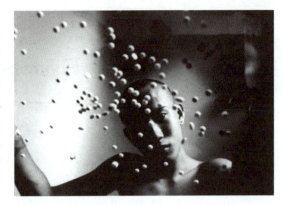

15

unbecoming attempts to undermine the standing of a public institution'.[16]

Based on the experiences of the real-life street kids who assume the lead roles, *15*'s narrative centres on the lives of five fifteen-year-old boys as they play truant, devise gangsta raps in preparation for a school singing competition, engage in gang fights, endure the pain of tattoo and body piercing, smuggle drugs from Malaysia into Singapore, search for buildings to jump off and commit suicide, watch porn on video and on the Internet, and role-play with a blow-up sex doll while worrying about their maths test, not having a celebration birthday cake and being thrown out by their parents. The film presents the flip side of a stereotypical Singapore in which economic growth is 'almost always the backdrop of both international and local constructions of the Singapore Story as synonymous with Success'.[17] As with Khoo and Neo, Tan's interest is not so much in the Singapore Success Story as in the Singapore Failure Story, with success and failure measured chiefly in academic and economic terms. The best education prospect for the teenagers in *15*, as one of them discloses his aspiration in the film, is the Institute of Technical Education, whose acronym ITE signifies colloquially as 'It's The End'.[18]

Drawing upon 'elements of the marginalised and the ready-to-be-discarded' like Khoo and Neo do can be seen as an 'intentional act of subversion' that deflates 'the triumphalism by pointing to the underbelly of the nation where failures are too well hidden under the new affluence'.[19] However, Tan's version of the Singapore Failure Story is aestheticised in ways that make the measure of its subversive force difficult to ascertain. Following the opening credits, the film begins with a low-angle shot of a high-rise housing estate in the background and a lower round tower in the middle of the foreground. Two of the characters, Melvin and Vynn, sit atop the roof of the entrance to the tower, and Melvin sings two lines of a song about Vynn committing suicide by jumping off a building and becoming flattened like a *roti prata* (a popular Singaporean Indian dough pancake dish).[20] The tune of the song is taken from the Singapore national anthem whose original lyrics are in Malay, Singapore's national language. It is safe to presume that the boys, like many Chinese Singaporeans, do not understand the meaning of the Malay lyrics in the anthem.[21] With Melvin's miscomprehension and mischievous adaptation of the national anthem, the film wastes no time in rupturing the myth of national unity and identity. While the housing estate, basking in the tropical sunlight, shows off its affluence, Melvin's lyrics hint at the dark tone of the protagonists' obsession with suicide. The opening sequence thus foregrounds this Singapore Story as one about failure: failure of its education system to inculcate respect for one's national anthem and to convey the meaning of the anthem's Malay lyrics to the Chinese pupils; failure of its schools to enforce attendance of students (as Melvin and Vynn are clearly playing truant); and failure to make life meaningful for some fifteen-year-olds to the extent that suicide is consistently on their minds.

So far, so social realist. As the ensuing conversation reveals, Vynn has a cunning plan of participating in a school singing competition so as to humiliate the school principal, who has publicly caned him and suspended him from school. His plan is to perform a Hokkien song and shout vulgarities on stage in the hope that the VIPs present will fire her. As Vynn and Melvin go through a list of possible songs, the film cuts to an MTV-style segment of gangsta rap in Hokkien. Similar segments are subsequently interspersed in the narrative as the boys progress in their 'rehearsals', the style of the songs ranging from gangsta rap to a sweet Japanese tune.[22]

The juxtaposition of two distinct styles – social realism on the one hand and post-modern pastiche and parody on the other – results in an ambivalence and contradiction in the director's voice, which is identifiable in at least three sources. The first is the director's voice-over before the opening credits in which he claims that making this film has unwittingly reminded him of a past self that he has forgotten, betraying a sense of nostalgia for his lost youth. (About ten years separate the director from his protagonists.) The second consists of social-realist and documentary-style narratives in which the camera, the director's voice by proxy, records episodes from the characters' lives or conversations that reveal their thoughts and emotions. The third is the director's diegetic and extra-diegetic treatment of the characters' experiences, including renditions of gangsta rap in Hokkien, gang fights transformed into PlayStation-style arcade games with words slammed over the screen declaring 'You Win', and contemplations about suicide turned into 'a breezily twisted animated suicide manual (a rapid *South Park* sequence of death by poison, shark, war or washing machine)'.[23] The latter two voices are interwoven, while the first haunts the entirety of the film, as we are encouraged not only to identify with the characters but also identify the director *in* the characters.[24] As a result, the film's jarring aesthetics becomes a question of ethics. Notwithstanding the director's proclaimed concern for street kids like his protagonists,[25] the postmodern pastiche and parody in the film re-orientate our attention away from the nature of the film's material, however controversial or potentially sensational, and towards Tan's treatment of it, and the ends it serves.

This aesthetic contradiction is most salient in relation to the issue of suicide, which is portrayed in at least three styles. The first is an extreme form of documentary realism, such as a 40-second sequence in which a character named Armani, squatting in the corner of a toilet, repeatedly slashes his arm with a penknife. The unflinching camera either adopts a high-angle shot that diminishes Armani's stature, hence emphasising his sense of helplessness, or else closes up on his arm while he self-mutilates. Second, a range of suicide methods is rendered, as mentioned above, as an animation accompanied by a cartoonish tune. Finally, in a montage, buildings and sites from across the island are offered for consideration as the ideal location for suicide, the soundtrack this time being a karaoke-style accompaniment to a Hokkien song while Armani and two other characters, Shaun and Erick, each holds up a placard with a Chinese character that collectively announces 'I want to die'. Can these different aesthetic treatments of the same grave subject be possibly reconciled? If not, what is the ethics behind the aesthetics, both in the individual segments and taken collectively?

In his article on 'traces of otherness in recent Singaporean cinema', Ho Tzu Nyen traces Tan's 'influence' to Wong Kar-wai and delivers a damning verdict on *15*, arguing that the swerving between documentary realism and Wong's aesthetics lies at the root of the film's contradiction:

> ... for the avowed 'compassion' or empathy of the director for his subjects, like the claim to 'realism', is perpetually betrayed by Tan's cinematic language, a language, which in its theatricality and mannerism, its perpetual recourse to the stock MTV techniques of 'jump-cuts, slow motion sequences, freeze frames, unusual camera angles and voiceovers' is inherited from Wong. [...] In this process, a kind of violence more ruthless than any gang fight is unleashed upon the subjects, whose everyday existence is flattened into a series of music video-like snippets, just as the complexity of social relations in which they are embedded is glossed over by the airless totality – or better yet, totalitarianism, of design.[26]

While I largely agree with Ho's critique of *15*, this does not explain Tan's aesthetic choices beyond his personal preference and stylistic affinity. I suggest that the contradictory aesthetics in *15* can be located in the conditions of production, indeed a certain condition of Singaporean film-making that is driven by a desire for decipherability beyond its borders. It is this desire that, despite its otherwise laudable intention to highlight the plight of juvenile delinquents in a social-realist mode, pushes the film to aestheticise itself in an instantly recognisable post-modern mode of pastiche and parody in its pursuit of decipherability.

A crucial figure behind Tan's film-making is Eric Khoo, who persuaded Tan to expand his short film into a feature,[27] which was then co-produced by Khoo's company, Zhao Wei Films.[28] Arguably the first auteur in the revival period of Singaporean film-making,[29] Khoo's *12 Storeys* was, in 1997, the first Singaporean feature to be officially invited to participate in the Cannes Film Festival.[30] For Gina Marchetti, Khoo's films exist

> on the borders between the high art world of the international art film and the low pop cultural environment of the B-grade exploitation film, the television soap opera,

and the cartoon. As such, the films contain enormous contradictions, narrative gaps, and inconsistencies of tone.[31]

By citing Marchetti's description of Khoo's films, which on the surface seems equally applicable to Tan's *15*, I am not suggesting an aesthetic affinity between the two film-makers, as any comparison of their films will readily shore up stark differences rather than similarities. Rather, I wish to highlight their shared condition of Singaporean film-making in terms of its need to situate itself 'in the global arena of the international art film and Chinese transnational cinema culture, while still appealing to a domestic market hungry for local images of the country's unique cultural mélange'.[32]

Shu-mei Shih has critiqued Ang Lee's films in terms of a 'decipherable localism' that presents local national culture 'with the anticipation of ready decipherability by the non-local audience'.[33] The *conditions* for decipherability, however, are dependent upon prior knowledge and the malleability of that knowledge, and clearly not all forms of knowledge are equally translatable. If both Khoo and Tan have an eye on the local audience and another fixed on the transnational and global audience, their films are almost invariably doomed to suffer from a schizophrenic contradiction precisely because those gazes are irreconcilable. Owing to its socio-political and linguistic specificities and the lack of global cultural capital, the local in Singapore in its present state remains too local to be decipherable to the non-local audience. One of the ways to overcome this communicative hurdle is to aestheticise the local so that it becomes recognisable in the global. In the case of *15*, the local is the social-realist content, while the global is the post-modern mode of pastiche and parody.

I shall call the film's dressing up in an immediately translatable aesthetic 'slanging up'. However, my use of this term differs from Olivia Khoo's. In her discussion of the two groups of Singaporean films, Khoo regards the 'local content films' of Jack Neo as too localised to be exportable, whereas films by Eric Khoo and Royston Tan deploy an

> aesthetic vernacular, or slang image, that can translate the local into a particular brand of foreignness that can be assimilated and understood by non-Singaporeans since it articulates a common experience of economic modernization employed to produce a cinematic modernity.[34]

I want to argue that the 'slang images' belonging to the second group of films, defined by Khoo as characterised by the impulses of authenticity production and self-consciousness,[35] are in fact as indecipherable as the first group of 'local content films'. Rather, there exists in *15* a different understanding of 'slang', rooted in a decidedly local inflection owing to Singapore's colonial legacy, that serves as a metaphor for Tan's dressing up of his film in a globally identifiable visual aesthetics. Tan's 'slanging up' of his films makes them globally accessible but at the same time invokes a local code that may be not so much indecipherable as invisible to global audiences, and this creates an ambivalence around the very act of slanging up.

Among the 'slang images' identified by Khoo that strive to self-consciously construct an authenticity in relation to social reality is the setting of scenes in a *kopitiam*, a local coffee shop.[36] In such a scene in *15*, an argument breaks out between two of the lead characters (Erick and Shaun) and a group of four male Chinese students dressed in pressed white school uniform. Speaking in fairly standardised English, the boys in school uniform assert that 'at least we speak better English' and call Erick and Shaun 'Chinese hooligans' before asking them: 'Need us to lend you dictionary or not, to find out the meaning of "hooligans"?'; 'And do you need me to spell the word out for you or not? H-O-O-L-I-G-A-N.' They also label Erick and Shaun using a Hokkien term '*chao* Ah Beng' (literally 'stinking Ah Beng'). Ah Beng is the generic name for any lower-class, Hokkien-speaking male in Singapore, as caricatured in popular television shows such as *Phua Chu Kang*.[37] The two groups subsequently call up their friends and conduct a gang fight in a pedestrian underpass.

Though the setting of this scene in a *kopitiam* qualifies it as a translatable 'slang image' in Khoo's terms, I would suggest it illustrates the film's indecipherability to an audience outside Singapore. This is because of the class issue embedded in the use of different languages by the two groups of boys and also because of the specifically local references. For example, audiences beyond Singapore (and possibly parts of Malaysia) would be unlikely to pick up on a reference made by the boys in school uniform about Erick and Shaun (despite the fact that they are not in their school uniform) as being from the 'normal' stream. In the Singaporean secondary school system, pupils in the normal stream take five years to complete rather

than the four years in the 'express' stream – a stigma of academic failure. In *15*, the different durations designated for the completion of this phase of education are manifested less in temporal and more in class terms. That is to say, students from the 'express' stream, to which the boys in uniform are likely to belong, perceive their superiority over those in the 'normal' stream not only because they are academically more successful but also because they 'at least speak better English'. That they insult Erick and Shaun as *Chinese* hooligans underlines a unique construction of Chineseness in Singapore wherein speaking the Chinese languages of Mandarin and Hokkien is perceived as inferior to speaking in English and also most plausibly associated with low lives such as hooligans. By emphasising the ethnicity of their opponents (which is the same as their own), the boys in school uniform place themselves at once above hooliganism and Chineseness. It is this amalgamation of ethnicity and language that turns an argument between the two groups of boys into a class conflict.

For Khoo, 'slang images' are aesthetic choices made by Singaporean film-makers to be at once local and foreign. Yet these images are constrained by the limits of the terrain of the larger filmic and linguistic systems to which they belong, and these limits include the government's attack on forms of colloquial speech such as Singlish.[38] Slang, then, in its common usage and for Khoo and the Singaporean government, is 'considered as below the level of standard educated speech',[39] and thus regarded as degeneration. However, I want to introduce here a different usage of 'slang' with precisely the opposite connotation: that is, 'slang' as elevation. This meaning of 'slang' is mobilised in *15* by Armani, who comes to the rescue of Erick and Shaun after members of the rival gang have beaten them up. When the rival gang leader (Erick and Shaun's chief tormentor in the *kopitiam* scene) is captured, Armani interrogates him using a mixture of Hokkien and Mandarin. Claiming that he has always despised '*angmoh gao*' (literally 'red hair monkeys') – '*angmoh*' being a Hokkien term for Caucasians – like the rival gang leader, Armani questions if his parents are Caucasians and challenges him: 'You're damned good at "slanging", aren't you?'; 'You want to "slang", don't you? Why don't you dare to "slang" now?'

'Slang' in this context refers to affecting an accent when speaking in English and, alongside the categorisation of 'angmoh gao', is employed to condemn such speakers as pretentious and desiring to imitate or to become Caucasians. Here 'slang' is not so much a debased form of a language but an elevating gesture that betrays the speakers' desire to promote themselves, via mimicry, to the rank of whiteness, a potent racial imaginary given Singapore's (post)colonial status.[40] Indeed, the word 'slang', together with its synonym 'accent' in the same context, is usually mobilised by the underclass and the Chinese-educated against the well-spoken English-educated, who are also caricatured in Hokkien as 'chia gangtang' ('eat potatoes'). While this rhetorical device is clearly imbued with racism, given the long-standing social privilege enjoyed by those educated under the British colonial system and endowed with economic and cultural capital that comes with a good command of the English language, it is also a self-defence weapon of the linguistically marginalised that exposes the user's own impotence with each utterance. Armani's hatred of 'slang'-as-elevation stems from a history of marginalisation and suppression of Hokkien and its speakers in Singapore. This has been described as 'a process of internal colonisation that is even more violent than the suppression [of Hokkien] in Taiwan under the KMT [Kuomintang, or the Nationalist Party]'.[41] The result of such internal colonisation, institutionalised through the education system, employment opportunities and social stigmatisation, is internal racism between two groups of Chinese Singaporeans that boils over in these scenes.

This local inflection of 'slang'-as-elevation can serve as a metaphor for Tan's 'slanging up' of his film's aesthetics for a global audience. Besides segments set in realistic locations such as the kopitiam, 15's local content is otherwise rendered globally decipherable through the use of pastiche and parody in its audio-visual form. The MTV-style visual vocabulary of the musical interludes, the popular rhythm of rap, and the computer game and animation aesthetics readily resonate with a younger generation across the world brought up on PlayStation and Japanese anime. Moreover, 15 cites from transnational Chinese cinemas both present and past, not only from Wong Kar-wai and Tsai Ming-liang (most evident in a campy musical interlude in which the characters are draped in boas) but also from early kung fu films (a conversation between Shaun and Erick on a rooftop turns into a fight scene complete with special-effects weapons colliding in mid-air). Tan's 'slanging-up' is therefore not simply one of colonial mimicry of Western aesthetics; it also accesses the cultural capital of auteurs of recent transnational Chinese cinemas who have achieved international fame as well as that of a more traditional genre that, thanks to the global success of Ang Lee's Crouching Tiger, Hidden Dragon (2000), has become increasingly decipherable to a global audience. The 'slanging up' of 15 is thus double-accented and double-voiced, speaking simultaneously to Western audiences and to those in the Chinese-speaking world.

It is in this sense that Tan's flamboyant and stylistically contradictory aesthetics can be appreciated as a different kind of 'slang image' – as a layering of cinematic and other visual styles that have already gained currency in the global consumption of culture and entertainment, at once engendering decipherability and enhancing one's status in the marketplace of world cinema. Like the films of Jack Neo and Eric Khoo, 15's success is predicated upon the Great Singapore Failure Story, only arguably more successful because 'slanged up'.

NOTES

1. Jan Uhde and Yvonne Ng Uhde, Latent Images: Film in Singapore (Singapore: Oxford University Press, 2000), 107.
2. Olivia Khoo, 'Slang Images: On the "Foreignness" of Contemporary Singaporean Films', Inter-Asia Cultural Studies, 7, no. 1 (2006): 81–98 (86–87).
3. Chua Beng Huat (with Yeo Wei Wei), 'Cinematic Critique from the Margins and the Mainstream', in Life is Not Complete without Shopping: Consumption Culture in Singapore (Singapore: Singapore University Press, 2003), 177–189 (186).
4. Megan Tay, the young actress in Homerun, won the Best New Performer award at Taiwan's Golden Horse Awards in 2003.
5. Chua and Yeo, 'Cinematic Critique', 177.
6. Ibid.
7. Geremie Barmé, In the Red: On Contemporary Chinese Culture (New York: Columbia University Press, 1999), 188–198. For a fuller critique of Barmé's position, see Song Hwee Lim, Celluloid Comrades: Representations of Male Homosexuality in Contemporary Chinese Cinemas (Honolulu: University of Hawaii Press, 2006), 190, note 7.

8. Nazir Keshwani, Review of *15*, *Cinemaya*, no. 59 (Summer 2003): 25–27 (26).

9. 'Royston Tan: New Voice that Wants to be Heard (But Singapore Wants to Censor)', *Voice Films* website, 16 July 2004. Available online at: <voicefilms.typepad.com/voicefilms/2004/07/royston_tan_new.html> (accessed 14 November 2005; the link was no longer active when I accessed it on 11 December 2007).

10. See Royston Tan's blog for a list of his filmography and awards. Available online at: <royston-tan.blogspot.com/2006_06_01_archive.html> (accessed 11 December 2007).

11. Clarissa Oon, 'Not Another Teen Movie', *The Straits Times*, 9 April 2003, L1, L4.

12. James Bell, 'Singing for the Censors', *Sight & Sound*, 15, no. 2 (February 2005): 6.

13. Ibid.

14. Anthony Spaeth, '20 under 40: The Bold and the Young', *Time Asia*, 4 October 2004. Available online at: <www.time.com/time/asia/2004/heroes/hopener.html> (accessed 11 December 2007).

15. Steve Rose, 'Bunny Peculiar', *Guardian*, 24 November 2004. Available online at: <film.guardian.co.uk/features/featurepages/0,,1358503,00.html> (accessed 11 December 2007).

16. 'Singapore Says Satire on Censorship Not Funny', *ABC News Online*, 26 March 2004. Available online at: <www.abc.net.au/news/newsitems/200403/s1074625.htm> (accessed 11 December 2007).

17. Chua and Yeo, 'Cinematic Critique', 180.

18. Ibid., 187.

19. Ibid., 180.

20. There are numerous errors in the English subtitles of the DVD released by Picture This Home Video. As the subtitles also tend to paraphrase what the characters say, throughout this article I will transcribe and translate the lines in a more verbatim manner to bring out either the actual lines spoken or make the connotative meanings clearer.

21. For example, the first line in Melvin's version is '*Mari kita rak*, Vynn Soh jumps off the building'. The first line in the national anthem is '*Mari kita rakyat Singapura*' (which translates as 'Come, fellow Singaporeans'). Melvin's breaking up of the word *rakyat* and his poor pronunciation of the Malay words are proof of his lack of understanding of the lyrics. Lyrics and translations of the Singapore national anthem can be found on the *Singapore Infomap* website of the Ministry of Information, Communications and the Arts. Available online at: <www.sg/explore/symbols_anthem.htm> (accessed 12 December 2007).

22. Musical interludes are a staple of Tan's film-making right from the start. In his 2001 short film, *Hock Hiap Leong*, set in the eponymous *kopitiam* (a distinctly local coffee shop), a first-person voice-over accompanying wide-angle close-ups of the protagonist is coupled with a sudden musical sequence with characters lip-synching to old songs by Grace Chang – a self-reflexive cross between Wong Kar-wai and Tsai Ming-liang. Indeed, the first song on the soundtrack on *Hock Hiap Leong* is Chang's 'I Don't Care Who You Are' ('Buguan ni shi shui'), the same song that closes Tsai's 1998 film, *The Hole*.

23. David Jays, Review of *15*, *Sight & Sound*, 15, no. 3 (March 2005): 50–51 (51).

24. As Ho Tzu Nyen notes, Tan's attempt to 'efface the distance between himself and his subjects' works 'in a strange twist of logic' so that his protagonists also 'speak for him (by helping him to reconnect with a forgotten part of himself)'. Ho Tzu Nyen, 'The Afterimage – Traces of Otherness in Recent Singaporean Cinema', *Inter-Asia Cultural Studies*, 8, no. 2 (2007): 310–326 (316).

25. Tan claimed he 'talked to more than 200 troubled teenagers over the period of a year, in order to "give a voice" to school dropouts and teen gangsters in his new film'. Oon, 'Not Another Teen Movie', L4.

26. Ho, 'Afterimage', 317.

27. Bell, 'Singing for the Censors', 6.

28. Zhao Wei Films also co-produced Tan's second feature, *4:30*, and produced Tan's latest film, *881*.

29. Uhde and Uhde consider Khoo's debut feature, *Mee Pok Man*, 'an *auteur* film', 'made not to please the audience but to express the personal vision of the author or filmmaker'. Uhde and Uhde, *Latent Images*, 112.

30. Biographical notes of Khoo are available on the website of Zhao Wei Films at: <www.zhaowei.com/index2.htm> (accessed 12 December 2007).

31. Gina Marchetti, 'Global Modernity, Postmodern Singapore, and the Cinema of Eric Khoo', in *Chinese-Language Film: Historiography, Poetics, Politics*, ed. Sheldom H. Lu and Emilie Yueh-yu Yeh (Honolulu: University of Hawaii Press, 2005), 329–361 (342).

32. Ibid., 330.

33. Shu-mei Shih, 'Globalisation and Minoritisation: Ang Lee and the Politics of Flexibility', *New Formations*, no. 40 (Spring 2000): 86–101 (100).

34. Khoo, 'Slang Images', 86.

35. Ibid., 87.

36. Ibid., 88–89.

37. See Chua, *Life is Not Complete*, 162.

38. Khoo, 'Slang Images', 82.

39. *OED* (*Oxford English Dictionary*) online, entry on 'slang'. Available online at: <dictionary.oed.com/cgi/entry/50226993?query_type=word&queryword=slang&first=1&max_to_show=10&sort_type=`alpha&search_id=1P3j-hUKicp-6407&result_place=1> (accessed 13 December 2007).

40. On colonial mimicry, see Homi K. Bhabha, 'Of Mimicry and Man: The Ambivalence of Colonial Discourse', *The Location of Culture* (London and New York: Routledge, 1994), 85–92.

41. Chua, *Life is Not Complete*, 172.

2 *Big Shot's Funeral*: Performing a Post-modern Cinema of Attractions

Yingjin Zhang

This essay interprets Feng Xiaogang's *Big Shot's Funeral* (2001) as an example of post-modern cinema of attractions – a bifocal perspective informed by discourses of post-modernity and early cinema. A blatant comedy lampooning a nationwide craze for money in the age of globalisation, Feng's film unabashedly deploys features increasingly associated with post-modern aesthetics (e.g. surface over depth, spatiality over temporality, simulacrum over authenticity, disjuncture over coherence) and at the same time flaunts attractions typical of early cinema (e.g. astonishment over absorption, exhibitionism over voyeurism, visuality over psychology, intertextuality over linearity). By referencing early cinema and late cinema together, I seek to demonstrate that Feng's subversion of the socialist legacy is both performative and carnivalesque. However, Feng's performative subversion is ultimately predicated on a deep-seated complicity with transnational capital on the one side and the post-socialist market economy on the other (evident in the Columbia Pictures–China Film Corp–Huayi Brothers & Taihe co-production). The titular funeral for Orientalism is nothing but a pretext to reap profits, and this pretext tends to hijack the film's subversiveness through its playful indulgence in a runaway performance of contradictions as attractions.

A POST-MODERN COMEDY FUNERAL

Recent English scholarship on *Big Shot's Funeral* focuses on its metacinematic construction, its symbiotic relationships with transnational capitalism and an emerging domestic partnership between cinema and real estate via advertisement, and its director's role as a culture broker intent on maximising profits while serving the masses with popular entertainment.[1] Chinese scholars, on the other hand, tend to interpret *Big Shot's Funeral* as a post-modern comedy. For Hu Ke, the film's post-modern features

include its loose structure, fragmented details, and lack of depth and purpose. True, the viewer admires Feng's wisdom, intelligence and humour, but it is difficult to pinpoint the director's exact position vis-à-vis an increasingly commercialised society.[2] What Hu characterises as post-modern irony is best exemplified in the film's apparent vilification of pervasive advertising in contemporary China. Yoyo (Ge You) is a Beijing freelance cameraman hired to document the remake of *The Last Emperor* by Don Tyler (Donald Sutherland), a renowned Hollywood big shot who entrusts Yoyo to stage a comedy funeral for him before he lapses into a coma under the pressure of his sagging creativity. Unaware of Tyler's improving health, Yoyo teams up with his friend Louis Wang (Ying Da), a resourceful local media entrepreneur, and the two launch an ambitious campaign to raise money nationwide by selling advertising space in the live funeral coverage to be globally televised. When Yoyo brings Lucy (Rosamund Kwan), Tyler's Chinese-American bilingual personal assistant, to inspect the funeral preparation, they are welcomed by seven slender young women lining up to greet them in chorus, 'IT'S NOT A BUST TO BE A WOMAN!' (*xia beizi zuo nüren tinghao*). The viewer may not comprehend this particular advertising slogan – which is printed in the ribbons the women wear – until the end credits start rolling and 'IT'S NOT A BUST TO BE A WOMAN!' turns out to be an advertisement for the Sun Run brand of breast enlargement cream. Here, the film's dozen or so corporate sponsors (including BMW and Sony) remind the viewer of a plethora of advertisements saturating all conceivable spaces inside the Forbidden City: balloons, banners, bill boards, floor coverings and stage props. In short, *Big Shot's Funeral* succeeds in staging a visual carnival where a façade of ordered disorder threatens to collapse at any moment.

Big Shot's Funeral

'Isn't it self-contradictory for a film critical of advertising to rake in money from advertising companies?' Hu Ke poses this question. For Hu and other critics, Feng Xiaogang's reliance on soft advertising reduces the effectiveness of the film's use of irony: 'This kind of advertising is endowed with post-modern characteristics – apparently self-negation but essentially self-glorification … [engendering] a coexistence of self-debasement and self-promotion, [ultimately] achieving the goal of self-promotion by means of self-debasement.'[3] Likewise interpreting the film as an 'imitation of the post-modern urban comedy', Yin Hong contends that *Big Shot's Funeral* eventually deconstructs its own deconstruction of the absurdity of the commercial society and throws itself into absurdity by making its cinematic deconstruction 'nothing but a play'.[4]

As a matter of fact, Feng Xiaogang himself regards 'playfulness' (*youxi*) as a major component of his directorial style critical of moral rectitude and constitutive of an 'opposite way of thinking' (*fanxiang siwei*).[5] Feng's key is 'opposite' – a tactical, often surprising move away from the norm or the normative – rather than 'oppositional' – a risky stance bordering on political dissent that implicated Feng in censorship problems a few years before.[6] Instead of moral rectitude claimed by an oppositional stance, Feng now prefers playful twists between the opposites, such as high and low, global and local, heroic and profane, and his preference for playfulness determines that his transgressive acts of border-crossing are characterised by compromise and complicity rather than commitment and confrontation. Interestingly, the resulting ambiguity and contradiction in his films work to reinforce playfulness as fundamental to Feng's signature style.

Moreover, Feng's penchant for playfulness is facilitated by marvellous technology, as evidenced in the sequence of Tyler's imagined reincarnation. When Yoyo visits Louis's company with Lucy, Louis insists on conducting a formal reception, complete with a photo op of him shaking hands with Lucy and an official conversation in a great hall translated back and forth between Chinese and English. All this is reminiscent of the documentary footage of the national leaders receiving distinguished foreign guests, now buried in the faded memory of the socialist era. As Louis boasts of the artists on his invitation list (e.g. Chen Kaige and Zhang Yimou), his animated video presentation astonishes even jaded Yoyo as Tyler shoots out from a firecracker, flying through the twinkling sky, and changes into a yellow-skin Chinese boy. In response to Lucy's protest and Yoyo's rationale for supporting the emergent African cinema, Louis changes computer codes and the second reincarnated Tyler now turns into a black boy. Post-modern technology and visual tricks are such that skin colours become changeable with a few clicks on the keyboards and racial-cultural differences seem to have lost their political and historical valence. Indeed, such post-modern tricks are carried to an extreme as the black boy suddenly changes to a punk-haired girl: 'It's a virus', Louis apologises, as if technology just engineered a prank on its own.

Lucy's protest against the technological manipulation of skin colours in Tyler's reincarnation is waged on the ground of her personal feeling for Tyler, but Louis is quick to defend that Chinese emotions are not to be toyed with, either. Ironically, it is in the name of the national (China) that Louis justifies his daring alteration of an image of the global (the US), using none other than Hollywood's prided visual tricks. The implied argument is that, cultural imperialism and clichéd Orientalism notwithstanding, it is now the Chinese turn to make big money, and the best way is to transform Tyler's funeral into a fierce competition whereby every inch of his funeral space is covered by advertisements.

Tyler's funeral preparation becomes a comedy through such a fanatic bid for advertising, which involves a high-profile public auction, extensive media coverage and direct interference from gangsters. This comedy funeral exposes striking contradictions in what Chen Xiaoming labels as 'postpolitics' in Chinese film, 'where everything is political and nothing is political at once and the same time. Politics is everywhere, and yet it subverts itself at any moment.'[7] Feng Xiaogang's post-modern tricks fit Chen's characterisation of postpolitics in post-socialist China: 'Under such an ecosystem, noble idealism and heroism are completely replaced by a real sense of comedy, manifested in a rhetoric of parody-travesty, irony and black humor.'[8] According to this post-modern logic, Feng's politics of criticising rampant advertising by using capitalism's logic inevitably subverts itself through its own complicity in generating money from soft advertising.

A further dimension of the post-modern comedy is embodied in the film's metacinematic structure. Elaborating on a film-within-a-film theme, Feng simultaneously subverts the authoritative position of the West as the unproblematic purveyor of truth across the globe and haplessly betrays his own dilemma in the transnational production of a block-buster. Feng's subversion is achieved through Tyler's abortive remake of *The Last Emperor* and his symbolic incapacitation through hospitalisation, both of which reveal that China is changing so fast that the outmoded Western epistemology is no longer functional in the age of globalisation. In light of this revelation, Lucy's rather contemptuous instructions to Yoyo at the pre-credit sequence of the job interview become profoundly ironic: 'You are just a pair of eyeballs … and the last thing we need is your creativity.' By the time Tyler wakes up from coma, he is utterly astonished to see Yoyo's creativity in pursuing the comedy funeral: 'This is theatre of the absurd.' Convinced by Yoyo's boundless imagination, Tyler admits to Lucy that Yoyo is a genius, an angel, a messenger from heaven who brings a perfect movie for him to make. Indeed, the conventional power structure seems to have been subverted as the local proves to have outsmarted the global in this post-modern play. However, the layered self-reflexivity in Feng's metacinema reaches an anticlimactic conclusion where the viewer comes to realise that Tyler, who has been shooting a comedy funeral inspired by Yoyo's ingenious performance, is the real authority who pulls strings behind the puppet show and who orders 'cut' only when he is fully satisfied by a Hollywood-type happy ending – agreed upon by both the global and the local – in which Lucy and Yoyo, now lovers admitting their true feelings, kiss each other off screen.

EARLY CINEMA OF ATTRACTIONS

Metacinema presupposes a degree of self-reflexivity – a trope integral to post-modern playfulness that thrives on irony, satire, parody, pastiche, even farce. Nevertheless, self-reflexivity is also a distinctive feature of early cinema, especially comedy, where an awareness of self-performance positions the actor in certain relations to the cinematic apparatus and the spectator. To contrast the IMR or institutional mode of representation exemplified by Hollywood classical cinema, Noël Burch describes early cinema as an alternative approach, a PMR or primitive mode of representation. 'The PMR consisted of a number of unfamiliar structures: a spatial approach combining frontality with non-centred composition and distant camera placement to create a "primitive externality"; a lack of narrative coherence, linearity, and closure; and an underdevelopment of character.'[9]

The remnants of the PMR characteristic of early cinema are present in the pre-title sequence of *Big Shot's Funeral*, in which Yoyo is rigidly placed in an uneasy frontal posture in a medium close-up and is seen rubbing his nose nervously in response to Lucy's disembodied voice coming from the front of the screen. Only until he is presented with a movie camera does Yoyo become confident, handling the equipment professionally and directing the camera straight at Lucy off screen. In a reverse shot, Lucy is revealed to have a pretty face, as the camera zooms in on the extreme close-ups of her charming eyes, sensuous lips and delicate hand. The foregrounding of the movie camera in this sequence makes the cinematic apparatus highly visible, and this self-reflexive visibility is punctuated throughout *Big Shot's Funeral* by means of the film's metacinematic structure as well as the playing of Yoyo's documentary footage.

While the point-of-view shots of Lucy suggest Yoyo's subconscious desire for intimacy, this pre-title sequence frustrates that desire by creating a primitive externality that keeps Lucy and Yoyo apart in separate shots. Their separateness is emphasised even when they subsequently appear together in the same frame, where Lucy and Yoyo are separated by a table in Yoyo's water-leaking apartment. However, the space between them looks farther apart due to the distant camera placement, and the frontality of the *mise en scène* suggests a stage ambience. 'Could you come here and hug me?' Lucy sobs, distressed over Tyler's unexpected lapse into coma. Astounded by this intimate request, Yoyo stops fumbling with a golf club (a pathetic phallic symbol pointing to his lack of gallantry), hesitantly takes two steps toward Lucy, but gives up his effort when she tells him to forget it. After Lucy departs in the rain, Yoyo rushes to where she had been sitting and hugs the chair (in a medium shot), murmuring to himself more than to absent Lucy, 'Don't be afraid. It's okay.' He rehearses the rush again (in a medium shot), and this time he picks up a porcelain bowl and rubs it gently with his fingers. 'Stop gazing at me like that,' he tells the inanimate object (in a point-of-view close-up), only to break it into two pieces, which frame his astonished look, with eyes and mouth open (in a reversed extreme close-up) to confront the viewer.

Yoyo's solo performance in this failed romantic sequence resembles the *pantomime*, the acting out of a story by expressive bodily and facial movements. Furthermore, the attraction of Yoyo's comic situation derives in part from his primarily *gestural gag*, which belongs to 'a form of visual humor' from the established tradition of early silent cinema 'in which amusement is generated by the play of alternative interpretations projected by the image or image series'.[10] The gag is thus regarded as 'an alternative model that begins to form with this early period' of cinema – alternative to the classical norms of seamless narrative and character development.[11] By tapping in on an alternative film tradition of the gag, *Big Shot's Funeral* not only justifies its disproportionate reliance on performances as visual spectacles but also achieves a new measure of self-reflexivity integral to its post-modern playfulness.

The merging of early cinema and post-modern comedy is occasioned by another pantomime of sorts in the middle of the film. Comedian Mr Biao (Fu Biao) is brought in to rehearse a one-man act of crying over Tyler's mannequin. To the amazement of Louis, Lucy and Yoyo, it only takes a few seconds for Biao to become fully emotional. With tears streaming down his face, he speaks in a trembling voice: 'We Chinese actors began taking calcium supplements [*jiti bugai*] long ago, but it's too late for you.' Early cinema and post-modernism merge perfectly here, as this simple skit of stand-up comedy delivers the expected expressivity of emotions only to serve as a trivial mimicry of an advertising message: take calcium supplements. The humour in question requires the viewer's knowledge of its intertextual reference to

the repeated appearances of famous Chinese actors in recent television commercials featuring calcium supplements, a deplorable practice mockingly termed as *jiti bugai* in the Chinese media.

Ge You's association with comic gestural gags makes him a perfect embodiment of the post-modern clown, who runs around town on a motorcycle, initially to amuse himself by deceiving people, but eventually to please others by being repeatedly deceived himself. In *Big Shot's Funeral*, Yoyo's insistence on the crucial difference between his comedy funeral and movie piracy nicely sums up his postmodern playfulness: funeral advertisers profit by 'stealing from themselves' (*chumai ziji*), whereas video pirates profit by 'stealing from others' (*chumai bieren*). Thus placing himself squarely in solidarity with bigshot advertisers, Yoyo musters enough courage to deliver a heroic act of revoking a piracy company's bid of over 1 million yuan and designating a prominent bill-board space for posting a 'public service message': 'fight video piracy'. This unexpected act of *fanxiang siwei* establishes Feng Xiaogang firmly on the side of transnational business and the Chinese state.

Yoyo's image as an unlikely yet likeable hero bears a striking resemblance to the *clown* in early cinema, an endearing figure who has made repeated appearances in film history. Having cast Ge You in all his films, Feng Xiaogang describes the actor as 'a guy whom everyone feels safe with, and wouldn't consider … a threat'.[12] As an embodiment of Feng's *fanxiang siwei*, of playfully 'perceiving things upside down',[13] Ge You's amiable comic character functions very much like the clown in silent cinema: an eccentric whose makeshift, often awkward performance connects the otherwise discontinuous, fragmentary, chaotic, contradictory, even traumatic elements of modern life. Miriam Hansen's characterisation of early cinema clowns like Charles Chaplin is enlightening at this juncture:

> While their antics have a long tradition, the clowns assume an acute alterity in relation to the ongoing process of modernisation; they inhabit the intermediary realm of *improvisation* and *chance* which … has come into existence only with the loss of 'foundation' or a stable order.[14]

As dramatised in *Big Shot's Funeral*, the rampant commercialisation has severely destabilised the moral foundation of post-socialist China, and an unlikely screen hero has emerged from a little man whose comic gags work to gloss over the missing self and the absent centre. Like Chaplin's laughter, Yoyo's performance 'welds together madness and happiness', appeals to the rich and the poor alike, and adds to the popularity of Feng Xiaogang's post-modern comedy that 'makes happy endings imaginable and at the same time puts them under erasure'.[15]

Another point of relevance between *Big Shot's Funeral* and Hansen's work on early cinema is her elaboration of Walter Benjamin's reflection on the sensory-aesthetic effects of advertising in modernity. Conceived as a form of *Wandelschrift*, advertising brings out

> two senses in which writing has become at once more moving and more mobile: a new mutability and plasticity of script (*Wandel* in the sense of change) … and the connotation of the verb *wandeln* (to walk, amble, wander), which suggests writing's migration into three-dimensional, public space.[16]

Advertising thus becomes a modern practice marked by the physicality, speed and directness of its presentation, a practice teeming with a powerful perceptual, tactile, even visceral appeal. 'For it is not the message of the advertisement that moves people …', Hansen asserts; rather, the 'profane illumination' from commercial lighting provides in advertising 'a medium of reflection, albeit an ephemeral one, exemplifying a type of reflexivity that inheres in the material'.[17]

In its tangible materiality, sensory immediacy, moving and mobile performativity, advertising displays much of what Tom Gunning theorises as an aesthetic of astonishment in early cinema of attractions. Early cinema is a cinema of discrete instants rather than developing situations; it specialises in delivering a series of visual shocks rather than a coherent narrative; it relishes in moments of revelation when the viewer's visual curiosity or desire for novelty is repeatedly satisfied. Instead of a spectator-in-the-text completely absorbed into the fictional world (as in classical cinema), early cinema entertains the viewer as a gawker who stands alongside its episodic presentation of attractions, whose attention is directed away from competing distractions on and off screen, and whose cinematic response goes beyond the purely intellectual or emotional to involve the kinetic, sensorial and visceral.[18] To a great extent,

attractions in early cinema, which 'work by interruption and constant change rather than steady development',[19] function less as means to some purposes than as ends in themselves, showcasing their physical immediacy and performative contingency in almost the exact way that modern advertising flaunts its material existence.

By bringing the sensory-aesthetic effects of advertising and early cinema together, *Big Shot's Funeral* pushes the logic of *exhibitionism* to the extreme: attention feeds on further attention (as in the auction scene), but when so much attention is multiplied, it verges on distraction (as in the funeral ground); at that point, certain distraction (e.g. the gangster's interference) becomes a new focus of attention (e.g. a faster musical tempo that makes a familiar solemn funeral tune sound lighthearted). What fascinates critics is that the logic of exhibitionism revealed in this post-modern cinema of attractions is precisely that of transnational capitalism, which has magically transformed contemporary China into an eyeball economy, where attention and attractions are measured increasingly in monetary terms and public space is frequently saturated with distracting advertisements.

Against this irresistible proliferation of attractions verging on distractions and distractions passing as attractions, Yoyo emerges as an unlikely hero whose gestural and verbal gags help reduce the viewer's anxiety in a rapidly changing society and who puts himself to all kinds of test, including an ultimate test of insanity. True, *Big Shot's Funeral* is saturated with verbal gags the moment Louis comes to Yoyo's aid in planning the funeral and the two start to compete in their masterful Beijing idiolect, but the most intriguing examples of verbal gags occur in several scenes in the psychiatric hospital, where Yoyo fakes madness to avoid advertisers' demand for a return of their investment. Louis, on the other hand, is insane for real. Characteristic of Feng Xiaogang's *fanxiang siwei*, the psychiatric hospital – literally a world turned upside down – is magically transformed into a place where people speak the truth. Former real-estate speculators and IT investors share their secrets of profiteering in a crowded hall, where conversations take place simultaneously and a dialogue often ends in a monologue. 'What is the definition of success?' a businessman asks the viewer in a frontal extreme close-up. 'Buy the most expensive things, not the highest quality,' he answers himself, and proudly adds his company's slogan: 'Not the best, just the most expensive' (*bujiu zuihao, danqiu zuigui*). Gestural and verbal gags notwithstanding, 'insane' truths like this become astonishing attractions in a post-modern comedy.

A GLOCAL EXHIBITION

The preceding discussion in light of the early cinema of attractions dovetails Mike Featherstone's argument that many post-modern features discovered in our contemporary time are actually traceable to earlier periods. At the turn of the twentieth century, the proliferation of signs and images in everyday urban life led to widespread information overload and commodity fetishism, and the subsequent development of scopic regimes of signification highlights the logic of simulation and the intensified working of desires through images.[20] For Featherstone, the 'post' in the term 'post-modernism' designates not just disjunctions but also continuities between historical periods. His discussion of post-modern characteristics in carnivals, festivals and county fairs – sites of pleasure, hybridisation and a controlled decontrol of emotions – finds echoes in my foregoing examination of *Big Shot's Funeral*.[21] Feng Xiaogang's post-modern cinema of attractions stages precisely such a carnivalesque site of ordered disorder, where the social hierarchy of elite versus popular is subverted, the power structure of global versus local is reversed and pent-up emotions are released safely in comic situations so as to prevent a narcissistic regression into schizophrenia or hysteria.

The carnivalesque nature of Feng's comedy determines its predominantly performative mode of presentation. While the figures of the clown and the pantomimist foreground the indispensability of comedians like Ge You and Fu Biao to a popular reception, I want to underscore *cinematic gesture* as a new dimension of performativity and exhibitionism in *Big Shot's Funeral*. For Lesley Stern, cinematic gesture is a ghostly performance through which filmic codes are deployed to generate desirable affects, to activate spectatorial performance (mimetic enactment) by putting into place bodily techniques (gestural modalities) and the techniques of communication technologies (cinema, television, etc.).[22] Instances of cinematic gesture can be found in Yoyo's handling of the movie camera in his interview, Louis's colour-recoding of Tyler's reincarnation in his

video presentation, the reverse black-and-white freeze-frame close-up of Yoyo's face when he shouts 'fight video piracy' at the auction, and Yoyo's meticulous assignment to every part of Tyler's mannequin a 'properly' displayed commercial product (from sports wears, leather shoes to a contact lens and a tea bag). Yoyo's verbal gags in articulating his rationale for product placement are intensified by cinematic gestural gags in locating all these commodities as phantasmagoric attractions. To further Tom Gunning's apt observation of early cinema – 'this experience of visual attraction plays a fundamental role in the phantasmagoria of commodities'[23] – I contend that cinematic gesture not only foregrounds the phantasmagoria of advertised commodities but also transforms comic performances into audio-visual commodities.

Just as '[t]he cinema of attractions develops out of a visual culture obsessed with creating and circulating a series of visual experiences to stimulate consumption',[24] so post-modern tricks in *Big Shot's Funeral* aim at a large-scale exhibition – yet another dimension of performance we must explore. The global ambition of this film is already visible in Columbia Pictures' casting of Hollywood star Donald Sutherland and Hong Kong diva Rosamund Kwan. Riding on the success of its enormously profitable distribution of *Crouching Tiger, Hidden Dragon* (Ang Lee, 2000), Sony Pictures dispatched a high-profile promotion team to the 2002 Berlin International Film Festival. Even though its international sales paled in comparison to Ang Lee's martial arts epic, *Big Shot's Funeral* set a domestic box-office record, raking in 38 million yuan during the traditional New Year release window from 21 December 2001 to 31 January 2002.[25] Successful marketing gimmicks included the director and stars' much-hyped media interviews, the simultaneous publication of a novel based on the film and nationwide anti-piracy measures in the first week of theatrical release.

The film's overwhelming success in the Chinese market raises the issue of *glocal* exhibition – 'glocal' as in the business motto of 'think globally, act locally'. Without Columbia Pictures' involvement, *Big Shot's Funeral* might not have accomplished an unprecedented success in 2002, and hypotheses like this compel one to reconsider the film's appropriation or manipulation of global signs. To wit: Tyler likens Yoyo to a messenger from heaven, but what message is delivered in this post-modern comedy? The reversed global–local power structure during Yoyo's staging of a comedy funeral is reversed again near the end, with rejuvenated Tyler firmly at the helm of directing. 'Cut!' he shouts. 'This is perfect.' As the camera pulls back from the *mise en scène* of Yoyo's insanity test in the hospital, the viewer suddenly realises that Yoyo, after all, is a puppet-like comedian in a larger scheme of post-modern attractions. A quintessential local, Yoyo succeeds in delivering what he is contracted to do in the first place – serving as a 'pair of eyeballs' to help his global employer see through the veils of a changing China. He breaches the contract only slightly by using his 'least needed' creativity to deliver a better than expected perform-ance, thereby helping to regain Tyler's lost creativity.

A peculiar note in this astonishing glocal exhibi-tion deserves further attention. Confronted by Yoyo's commitment to Tyler's comedy funeral and his refusal to entertain the possibility that Tyler is still alive, Lucy screams furiously, 'You are being fooled by us.' As a transnational cultural broker, Lucy occupies an ambiguous position, pledging her allegiance to the global while claiming her expertise on Chinese cul-ture. The logic of Hollywood's happy-ending formula convinces her to acquiesce to the final intimate scene of her romance with Yoyo. As Tyler waits patiently to shoot the lovers' off-screen kiss, Lucy is in effect transformed from a savvy businesswoman to an Ori-ental babe who decides to leave her Caucasian pater-nal figure (the global) and return home to the local. Ironically, this scene of romance is rehearsed before by Yoyo. The authenticity and spontaneity of intimate feelings are obviously not an issue any more, and this glocal exhibition is nothing but a staged exhibit, a façade of the global yielding to the local. The film thus ends happily as a comedy without a funeral (as 'funeral' was dropped from the Chinese title), a fan-tasy in which a local streetwise little man wins the affection of a cosmopolitan woman, who remains an exchangeable object of male desire circulating in the newly reconfigured global economy, in which China is definitely on the winning side.

NOTES

1. See Shuyu Kong, 'Big Shot from Beijing: Feng Xiaogang's *He Sui Pian* and Contemporary Chinese Commercial Film', *Asian Cinema*, 14, no. 1 (2003): 183–186; Jason McGrath, 'Metacinema for the Masses: Three Films by Feng Xiaogang', *Modern Chinese Literature and Culture*, 17, no. 2 (2005): 90–132; Shujen Wang, '*Big Shot's Funeral*: China, Sony, and the WTO', *Asian Cinema*, 14, no. 2 (2003): 145–154; Yomi Braester, 'Chinese Cinema in the Age of Advertisement: The Filmmaker as a Cultural Broker', *China Quarterly*, 183 (2005): 549–564.

2. Hu Ke, 'An Attempt at a Postmodern Comedy' ('Houxiandai xiju changshi'), *Contemporary Cinema (Dangdai dianying)*, no. 2 (2002): 7.

3. Ibid.

4. Yin Hong, 'Transnational Production, Commercial Film and Consumer Culture' ('Kuaguo zhizuo, shangye dianying yu xiaofei wenhua'), *Contemporary Cinema (Dangdai dianying)*, no. 2 (2002): 22–23.

5. Feng Xiaogang, 'I'm a Plebeian Director' ('Wo shi yige shimin daoyan'), *Film Art (Dianying yishu)*, no. 2 (2000): 48.

6. Before switching to commercial film, Feng Xiaogang's film *I'm Your Dad* (1996) and television serial *The Dark Side of the Moon* (1997) were banned, and his other film, *A Life under Pressure*, was abandoned in mid-production. See Michael Keane and Tao Dongfeng, 'Interview with Feng Xiaogang', *Positions*, 7, no. 1 (1998): 192–200.

7. Chen Xiaoming, 'The Mysterious Other: Postpolitics in Chinese Film', *Boundary 2*, 24, no. 3 (1997): 124.

8. Ibid., 140.

9. See Tom Gunning, 'Early American Film', in *The Oxford Guide to Film Studies*, ed. John Hill and Pamela Church Gibson (New York: Oxford University Press, 1998), 256.

10. Noël Carroll, 'Problematics of Film Comedy: Notes on the Sight Gag', in *Comedy/Cinema/Theory*, ed. Andrew Horton (Berkeley: University of California Press, 1991), 26.

11. Tom Gunning, 'Crazy Machine in the Garden of Forking Paths: Mischief Gags and the Origins of American Film Comedy', in *Classical Hollywood Comedy*, ed. Kristine Brunovska Karnick and Henry Jenkins (New York: Routledge, 1995), 89.

12. Quoted in Kong, 'Big Shot from Beijing', 181–182.

13. Feng, 'I'm a Plebeian Director', 46.

14. Miriam Bratu Hansen, 'America, Paris, the Alps: Kracauer (and Benjamin) on Cinema and Modernity', in *Cinema and the Invention of Modern Life*, ed. Leo Charney and Vanessa Schwartz (Berkeley: University of California Press, 1995), 372; original emphases.

15. Ibid., 373–374.

16. Miriam Bratu Hansen, 'Benjamin and Cinema', *Critical Inquiry*, no. 25 (1999): 333–334.

17. Ibid., 335–336.

18. See Tom Gunning, 'An Aesthetic of Astonishment: Early Film and the (In)Credulous Spectator', in *Viewing Positions: Ways of Seeing Film*, ed. Linda Williams (New Brunswick, NJ: Rutgers University Press, 1997), 114–133.

19. Tom Gunning, 'The Whole Town's Gawking: Early Cinema and the Visual Experience of Modernity', *Yale Journal of Criticism*, 7, no. 2 (1994): 193.

20. See Ben Singer, *Melodrama and Modernity: Early Sensational Cinema and Its Contexts* (New York: Columbia University Press, 2001), 59–99.

21. Mike Featherstone, 'Postmodernism and the Aestheticization of Everyday Life', in *Modernity and Identity*, ed. Scott Lash and Jonathan Friedman (Oxford: Blackwell, 1992), 265–290.

22. See Lesley Stern, 'Ghosting: The Performance and Migration of Cinematic Gesture, Focusing on Hou Hsiao-hsien's *Good Men Good Women*', in *Migrations of Gesture: Film, Art, Dance*, ed. Carrie Nolan and Sally Ness (Minneapolis: University of Minnesota Press, 2007).

23. Gunning, 'The Whole Town's Gawking', 196.

24. Ibid., 194.

25. See Yingjin Zhang, *Chinese National Cinema* (London: Routledge, 2004), 292.

3   *Black Cannon Incident*: Countering the Counter-espionage Fantasy

Jason McGrath

Black Cannon Incident (Huang Jianxin, 1985) is one of the defining works of the 'Fifth Generation' of Chinese film-makers – those who were among the first graduates of the Beijing Film Academy in the post-Mao era. Like other early Fifth Generation films, it reflects many of the dominant intellectual and aesthetic trends of the time, including a strong interest in formal experimentation, a renewed concern for individual subjectivity, an openness to artistic influences from abroad and an increased willingness to test the bounds of ideological control. The film is generally read as a direct comment on the contemporary reform era, exploring the question of whether reform-minded intellectuals would be adequately heeded by the socialist bureaucracy. Without contradicting such a reading, this essay seeks to complement it with a comparative study that looks back to the cinematic history of the Mao era. The Fifth Generation films of the 1980s, despite their stylistic differences from previous mainland Chinese cinema and their debts to international art cinema, served nonetheless as ideological interventions in a cinematic discourse distinctive to the People's Republic of China. In the case of *Black Cannon Incident*, I will argue that both narrative structure and visual rhetoric are used to unmask previous Mao-era spy-genre films as purely performative ideological operations rather than realist representations.

Black Cannon Incident begins with an engineer named Zhao Shuxin sending a mysterious telegram that reads simply: 'Lost Black Cannon. Look 301. Zhao.' A suspicious postal clerk reports the telegram to the police, who launch an investigation into the possibility that Zhao is a spy working for foreigners, engaged perhaps in industrial espionage. Managers and Party representatives from Zhao's own employer, a state-owned mining enterprise, take over the case. In the course of the investigation, Zhao is barred from his usual role as translator for a visiting German engineer, Hans Schmidt, who is helping with the installation of a large and expensive piece of equipment called the 'WD'. After much trouble and intrigue, it turns out Zhao's message was merely about a black cannon Chinese chess piece he had inadvertently left in a hotel room on a business trip. Moreover, in the end it is discovered that the incompetence of Zhao's replacement translator has led to an installation mistake in the WD causing over US$1 million in damage. The message is clear: the Party's lingering distrust of intellectuals seriously cripples the national project of modernisation in the reform era.

In a study of director Huang Jianxin's 1980s films, Paul G. Pickowicz reads *Black Cannon Incident* as a post-socialist critique of the Chinese Communist system, a dystopic 'red' comedy (i.e. a black comedy about Communism) expressing the continued disillusionment of the people with the government even during the reform era.[1] Chris Berry and Mary Ann Farquhar also analyse the film as a post-socialist political satire, but with a more detailed emphasis on artistic form rather than narrative political content. Berry and Farquhar show how the cinematography and set design of the film evoked the aesthetic and thematic concerns of modernist art, including alienation, expressionism/abstractionism and distanciation, which served to 'break the aesthetic stranglehold of socialist realism on the cinema'.[2] Similarly, Jerome Silbergeld relates some of the set designs of *Black Cannon Incident* to the modernist Chinese paintings and installation art that also began appearing in the mid-1980s.[3]

Indeed, the film's stylistic elements reflect a broader modernist or avant-garde aesthetic in much contemporaneous Chinese art and literature. In the case of cinema, the aesthetic experimentation of the 1980s is widely attributed to the very different sort of education the young post-Mao film-makers received in comparison to their elders educated before the Cultural Revolution (1966-1976). By the early 1980s, students at the Beijing Film Academy had access both to works of Western film theory in Chinese translation and to previously unavailable foreign art films.[4] Much has been made of the effect such a cosmopolitan education had on the style of the Fifth Generation. Nevertheless, while such genealogies may locate possible sources of various stylistic decisions, to explain how the Fifth Generation films of the 1980s functioned as interventions in an ideological field specific to post-Mao China it is necessary to place the films in the context of the cinematic history of the Mao era itself. Although Western viewers might be better attuned to the Fifth Generation's affinity with international art cinema, contemporary Chinese audiences would have been equally aware of their engagement with, and subversion of, the norms of Maoist realism established during the previous three decades. Beijing film scholar and cultural critic Dai Jinhua places *Black Cannon Incident* in this context by suggesting that 'the discursive forms and contexts' of the Mao-era spy genre are 'deconstructed through comic mimicry' in the film.[5] The remainder of this essay will explore the ideological implications of such a genre deconstruction by reading *Black Cannon Incident* against its antecedent patriotic spy films of the 1950s.

Unsurprisingly, in mainland China in the 1950s, the combination of the Korean War, the threat of attack or subversion from Taiwan and the menace of nuclear-armed America made for an obsession with national security and a strong fear of possible infiltration by spies who would enable the 'imperialist' forces to undermine the new socialist society from within. The typical counter-espionage film (*fante pian*) of the 1950s thus opens with a secret agent from Hong Kong or Taiwan, loyal to Chiang Kai-shek and the American imperialists, who enters China and establishes contacts with reactionary or foreign elements already inside the country. The spy ring then enacts a plan to steal Chinese security secrets or cultural relics, or perhaps to blow up a Chinese building or ship. Working with upstanding regular citizens and newly repentant collaborators, Chinese security forces gradually detect the plan and zero in on the spy ring, and the film ends with a dramatic confrontation and arrest of the spies, along with the unearthing of their secret weapons and other valuable objects.[6]

Despite the reality of its geopolitical context, the 1950s spy genre essentially constitutes an ideological fantasy – that is, an imaginary narrative in which public fears and desires are activated, manipulated and finally negated with a reassuring sense of closure. The imagined 'other' of the typical spy film was not so much a depiction of an actually existing antagonist but a condensation of the traits that needed to be negated by the hegemonic ideology of the Party. The spy's overdetermined position as 'other' is evident from the fact that sexual and even religious layers were often added to his or her political identity to provide elements of mystery, seduction and danger that extended well beyond the threat of military or political subversion. The Catholic Church, for example, was often depicted as the lair of dangerous spies inside China. In *Declawing the Devils* (Shen Fu, 1953), the leader of a spy ring is an Italian Catholic archbishop in China who supervises a spy sent from Hong Kong and manipulates mainland Catholic believers into aiding his subversive scheme to steal military secrets. In *Mysterious Travelling Companions* (Lin Nong and Zhu Wenshun, 1955), a foreign Catholic priest is the intended recipient of a secret shipment of arms being smuggled into China on horseback. Significantly, in both cases the rituals of religious belief are preserved even in the most private consultations among spies, with secret agents routinely making the sign of the cross, kissing the archbishop's ring and so on. Western religion is thus presented as not simply a cover, but rather an essential part of the alien and perverse ethical universe of the spies; their exotic Western superstitions are tied directly to their menace as 'other'. Excessive sexuality was another common means of characterising the subversive element in Mao-era spy films. For example, the priest in *Declawing the Devils* is finally discovered to have photographs of nude women among his hidden secrets; one of the main Chinese collaborationist smugglers in *Mysterious Travelling Companions* is depicted as a lecher who repeatedly tries to sexually molest an innocent young minority woman hired to accompany the horse train; and in *Secret Guards in Canton* (Lu Jue, 1957), the lead female spy is portrayed as a sexually insatiable middle-aged *femme fatale* whose temptations must be overcome by the double-agent Communist hero posing as a fellow spy.

Such portrayals of alien religious belief and transgressive sexual appetite are inseparable aspects of the overall ideological 'othering' of the spy as a threat to Chinese socialist normativity in the 1950s spy genre. Insofar as a villain resists the truth of Party doctrine, he/she must be defined as either profoundly misguided or inherently perverse. In the former case, as with the Chinese Catholic followers who later realise the error of their ways and cooperate with the authorities in *Declawing the Devils*, the collaborators learn the falsity of their position through correct education from concerned Party members. However, in the case of villains who are committed to foreign, imperialist values in a spirit of fully conscious (and therefore purely wicked) opposition to the Party's truth, a final confrontation must be enacted in which the guilty are arrested, their secrets exposed and the threat smashed. As the narrative builds to such a climax, details in characterisation clearly mark the ideological enemy as a subverter of Chinese normativity in general, while the Party line is synonymous with morality and national essence.

Black Cannon Incident skilfully cues the customary expectations of audiences well versed in the Mao-era spy drama by interspersing key signifying elements of the genre within the narrative. However, by emptying these ideological signifiers of their traditional signifieds, the film effectively 'traverses' the ideological fantasy – revealing its status precisely *as fantasy*, as lacking any real, material support – since, quite simply, it turns out that the foreigner Hans Schmidt is *not* a threat and neither is Zhao a spy or collaborator. The film's key opening scene clearly establishes its generic reference points. As Dai Jinhua has noted, this scene 'employs the stylised appearance of mainland counterespionage films from the "seventeen years" (1949–66): a rainy night, flashing lightning, a suspiciously behaving man sending a suspect cable at the post office'.[7] The scene is reminiscent, for example, of the rainy night scene in *Declawing the Devils* when an ominous-looking American agent in Hong Kong intercepts a letter between two Chinese engineers, or of the stormy scene in *Mysterious Travelling Companions* in which a minority peasant woman surreptitiously observes the horse train of the smugglers in the woods at night and then reports to the authorities, spurring an investigation. In *Black Cannon Incident*, a shot of the postal clerk reading the strange telegram and then looking inquisitively up at its sender cuts to a shot of Zhao lit in a style characteristic of villains in Maoist spy films, with the top half of his head covered by a dark shadow as lightning flashes and thunder rolls. The next shot is a close-up of the clerk's hand ringing up the police to launch the 'black cannon' case.

In the subsequent investigation, a background check reveals Zhao received his engineering education from China's top science and technology university and has had previous close contact with the German engineer/advisor Schmidt. It is duly noted that Zhao's 'family class background' is that of an 'office worker' (not a proletarian or peasant). He has no history of political involvement, but his parents were both Catholics and he was a believer himself, at least in childhood – a detail of obvious significance considering the generic precedents mentioned above. It is never explicitly asserted that Zhao is a secret agent engaged in deliberate subversion; rather, he may be more like the 1950s engineer Zhou Changmin who works at the defence factory that is the main setting for *Declawing the Devils*. In that film, Zhou is not a spy, but his status as a Westernised intellectual makes his position somewhat suspect, and his lack of vigilance does result in near disaster when a foreign agent posing as his nephew steals the design plans for a new anti-aircraft weapon. Educated in America and still maintaining contacts abroad, Zhou first appears dressed in Western suits, though later he has switched to the 'Mao suit' tunic preferred by Party cadres, thus implicitly indicating his growing identification with the masses. Like Zhou, *Black Cannon Incident*'s Zhao is a highly educated engineer with foreign contacts, not to mention a Catholic background, all of which are enough to reinforce the suspicions raised by the mysterious 'black cannon' telegram.

Other details periodically surface to play on the conventions established by the Mao-era spy drama. Many spy films of the 1950s, for instance, involve the smuggling of ammunition into China to arm counter-revolutionaries. *Declawing the Devils* and *Mysterious Travelling Companions* both include close-ups of stashes of pistols or bullets discovered when the spy ring is finally broken, while *Secret Guards in Canton* and *Ten O'Clock on the National Holiday* (Wu Tian, 1956) both revolve around the planned use of explosives by the spies. *Black Cannon Incident* also associates the foreigner with ammunition, but in a way that ironically subverts the narrative structure of the earlier films. The incompetent translator who replaces Zhao in working with Schmidt mistranslates the German *Kugel* as 'bullet' rather than its intended 'ball-bearing' when Schmidt requests the item during installation of the WD equipment. After a short while, the translator presents actual rifle bullets to the German engineer, who responds, dumbfounded, 'What am I supposed to do with these?' In effect, then, the foreign 'other' in the film is presented with the objects with which he would customarily be concerned in the generic Maoist spy drama, only to reject them as incomprehensible, underlining the apparent irrelevance of the former ideological fantasy to the present reform era.

Of course, the most essential element of the generic spy film referenced in *Black Cannon Incident* is the mysterious *object* of intrigue itself.[8] In the Mao-era spy drama, the fears and desires of all the characters, whether patriotic or subversive, centre upon some object of fascination, generally a technological tool such as communication equipment, firearms or explosives, or perhaps culturally significant archaeological treasures that apparently signify a Chinese essence in jeopardy of being stolen by foreigners. (Thus, it is far from irrelevant that the recipient of Zhao's mysterious cable about the black cannon happens to be the director of the 'Suzhou Antiques Office', or that Schmidt is said to have asked Zhao for help in procuring antiques during a previous visit.) Often in Mao-era spy films antique cultural objects are linked to objects of military use, as for example in *Secret Guards in Canton*, in which a spy ring based in an antiques shop hides a bomb intended to blow up a boat inside an ornate antique Chinese box. In *Ten O'Clock on the National Holiday*, the object is a bomb concealed in a child's clock. In every such case, the object of fear and desire sets much of the plot in motion, even though its real nature may only be revealed at the end of the film. In *Declawing the Devils*, as if the film-makers were afraid of leaving something out, besides the main plot element of stolen design plans for Chinese military equipment, the archbishop is ultimately found to be hiding guns, ammunition, communications equipment, dynamite, liquid explosives among Chinese antiques *and* the aforementioned dirty photographs of nude women.

In *Black Cannon Incident*, the mysterious object of intrigue is of course the 'black cannon' itself, which brings us to the ultimate subversion of ideological fantasy in the film: the revelation that 'the other does not exist' – the supposed agent motivating everyone's desires and identifications turns out to be a mere phantasm, a figment of the ideological imagination left over from the Mao era. The non-existence of the 'black cannon' *qua* object of fascination and fear is vividly illustrated in two crucial scenes that destroy any semblance of generic consistency between *Black Cannon Incident* and its Mao-era antecedents. The first is the scene in which Schmidt visits Zhao in his apartment, where his chess set is laid out with a small black canister replacing the lost black-cannon piece. Zhao's plant manager shows up unannounced and enquires about the canister. When Zhao explains that it is a substitute for a lost black cannon, his boss realises for the first time the true nature of the whole 'black cannon' case and soon departs. Schmidt, meanwhile, has noticed the intrigue surrounding the previous conversation (in Chinese) about the black-cannon substitute:

> Schmidt: What's this box?
> Zhao: It's just a box.
> Schmidt: What's inside?
> Zhao: Nothing.
> Schmidt: [suspiciously shakes box next to ear, opens it, sees nothing inside] Nothing? What was that about then? What was all that? [smiles in disbelief] I don't understand the Chinese.

In the span of a brief conversation ending with a shot of the mysterious object opened and displayed as containing nothing, the ideological fantasy of subversion from abroad is completely traversed; the object itself is revealed as insubstantial while the threatening foreign 'other' is depicted as not only ignorant of the entire intrigue, but honestly perplexed as to the discursive context of his Chinese counterparts. The message is reinforced when the authorities finally intercept the package sent back to Zhao in response to his original telegram. The parcel is unwrapped to reveal the absurdly literal nature of the mysterious 'black cannon' that had set the entire narrative in motion: it turns out to be merely a black chunk of wood with the character for 'cannon' written on it – a simple Chinese chess piece with no industrial or military implications whatsoever. In combination with the previous scene revealing the 'black cannon' substitute as an empty lack, this scene exposes the ideological fantasy of industrial or military subversion precisely *as fantasy*, suggesting that the Mao-era spy paranoia lacks the real-world referent of any actually existing threat but nevertheless continues to disfunctionally run its ideological course of its own accord. The 'black cannon' in *Black Cannon Incident* is a Hitchcockian McGuffin – an object imbued with great significance by the characters in the story, but which in fact is merely a pretext for setting the plot in motion – but it is a McGuffin exposed *as such* to both the audience and the characters.

The black-humour value of such a genre deconstruction is reinforced by the woefully inadequate responses of the characters to the revelation regarding the 'black cannon' case and the resulting expensive damage to a real piece of valuable equipment. Rather than criticising herself for her paranoid suspicions, the company's Party vice-secretary castigates Zhao for his irrationality in sending a telegram to recover something as cheap and inconsequential as a chess piece. For his part, Zhao pathetically vows that he will never play chess again, as if his hobby is to blame for the entire fiasco. This exchange humorously mimics the obligatory moment in 1950s spy films when the Chinese citizens who have mistakenly aided the foreign agents must tearfully admit their mistakes and express their remorse before the authorities. It is as if the characters in *Black Cannon Incident* are determined to cling to their faith in the power of the phantasmic McGuffin rather than acknowledge that what caused all the damage was the ideological fantasy itself.

Up to now, the parallels I have drawn between *Black Cannon Incident* and its 1950s antecedents have been mainly at the level of characterisation and plot, largely eliding the question of cinematic style. In fact, despite the generic visual cues parodied in the opening scene of the film as analysed earlier, *Black Cannon Incident* is profoundly different stylistically from counter-espionage films of the Mao era. In the 1950s spy films referenced here, the aesthetic of socialist realism, largely imported from the Soviet Union, was the formal standard in mainland Chinese filmmaking. Such an aesthetic, which actually owed much to the classical Hollywood style, aims at maximum narrative legibility and favours the story itself over any experimentation that might distract the audience or introduce ambiguity to the narrative. In contrast, as mentioned previously, *Black Cannon Incident* has been noted precisely for its modernist visual aesthetic, which is in fact the dialectical opposite of socialist realism in the context of 1980s China. Its stylistic oddities include the use of striking set designs, unusual formal compositions achieved with telephoto lenses, several scenes that seem superfluous to the narrative and a complicated temporal structure using multiple flashbacks.

These stylistic features have been analysed at greater length elsewhere,[9] but here I argue that the modernist visual style of the film can also be read, at least in part, as an element of the film's rhetorical undermining of the spy genre. We should first note that the point of *Black Cannon Incident* is not simply that the authorities mistakenly launched a counter-espionage investigation into the activities of a man who was in fact innocent – that is, some overzealous ideologues just went too far this time (particularly in the new era of opening to the West and so on). Rather, the true subversion of the film lies in its depiction of this investigation precisely *as a formal operation*; the film points not just to a gap between (past) ideology and (present) reality, but also to the very illusory nature of the ideological fantasy itself. That is, the counter-espionage effort is highlighted as a *performative* operation rather than a *descriptive* one: the dangerous spy is generated *by* the performance of the ideological ritual, instead of entering the social space as a presence from *out there* to be dealt with through ideological opposition.[10]

This essentially formal nature of the ideological ritual is illustrated in the film's most formalised, modernist scenes, which are precisely the ones most associated with the assertion of Party authority: the two scenes in a formal conference room where company officials and Party ideologues debate Zhao's fate in his absence. As a point of comparison, we can note the *mise en scène* of the meeting room in the defence plant of *Declawing the Devils*: in typical socialist realist style, a group of people are loosely gathered, as if spontaneously drawn to the spot, around a speaker/leader who stands slightly above them. The arrangement of figures suggests both the naturalness of the authority of the Party representative and the

Factory meeting room in *Declawing the Devils* (left); conference room in *Black Cannon Incident* (right)

solidarity of this authority with the masses themselves. In contrast, in *Black Cannon Incident*, Party ideologues and company managers meet not in a space formally defined by socialist realism – the presumed aesthetic and ideological support that would point to an objective reality they share and convey – but rather in a space of solipsistic modernist formalism reminiscent of cinematic fantasy-scapes from Lang's *Metropolis* to Kubrick's *2001: A Space Odyssey*. Their meeting room is completely white, arranged in perfect symmetry, and dominated by an absurdly gigantic stylised black clock that looms in the centre of the frame above the conference table. The stifling sense of formality conveyed by the set and composition is the exact opposite of the naturalness characteristic of socialist realist representations of group gatherings. In this way, the ideological underpinnings of authority are themselves denaturalised and revealed as consisting of a purely ritualistic performative operation rather than being a reflection of objective reality. In the first scene in the room, the establishing shot drags on for over two and a half minutes while those gathered chat aimlessly before finally getting around to Zhao's case. More remarkably, this long take is stretched further by the fact that the minute hand of the massive clock actually traces four minutes. Both scenes in the conference room last just over five minutes, with no obvious ellipses in the editing, but by reference to the clock the viewer realises each meeting actually has lasted well over an hour, thus emphasising the sense of the authorities' inertia and detachment from reality.

Perhaps the single most striking formal choice in *Black Cannon Incident* is the 360-degree pan shot

near the end of the film, when the principal characters at the company contemplate the disastrous mistake in the WD installation that their paranoia has caused. As the group sits in a loose circle in a bright, airy room, the camera pans across the characters from the centre of the room until its rotation has made a full circle – a daring shot that becomes a synecdoche for the entire film. By smoothly and methodically exposing all lateral off-screen space, the shot vividly illustrates the message to the company and Party bosses that there is no hidden and mysterious 'other' who can be blamed; there are only themselves. The full arc made by the camera echoes earlier images such as the circular face of the oscillating fan in the same room, the circle traced by the hands of the giant black clock in the company boardroom, the close-up of a spinning ball-bearing that ends the 'bullet' sequence and the circular forms of the empty 'black cannon' substitute as well as the harmless chess piece itself. Most particularly, the 360-degree pan shot epitomises a certain circular logic of the ideological spy fantasy in general. Director Huang Jianxin has said that inspiration for the film came from both *Catch-22* and computer scientist Douglas R. Hofstadter's idea of the 'Strange Loop' – any structure that, when its elements are traced in succession, paradoxically ends in the same place it began.[11] Hofstadter applies this concept to many phenomena, from M. C. Escher's drawings to conundrums of mathematical set theory such as Russell's paradox of 'the set of all sets that do not contain themselves'. The most simple visualisation of a Strange Loop is the Möbius strip, a favourite image of Lacan's which illustrates the fundamental interdependence of such binary oppositions as *self* and *other* while also exemplifying a system in which movement never ultimately gets anywhere but just continually turns in on itself. According to Huang, *Black Cannon Incident* depicts just such a movement: 'From the loss of the black cannon to its return, we have precisely the completion of a Strange Loop.'[12] The 360-degree pan and Strange Loop metaphor satirise the futility of the ideological spy fantasy's circular logic, which redundantly conjures and defeats its own threatening 'other' as a necessary element of its performance in the public sphere. Again, we have ideology as what Slavoj Žižek calls 'the pure performative, the tautology of pure self-reference'.[13]

The 360-degree pan shot ends with a view of a doorway; but does the film as a whole point to a way out? According to set theory, Russell's paradox can be resolved only by introducing a meta-proposition that can logically refigure a set containing its own contradiction. In the structure of *Black Cannon Incident*, an analogous meta-viewpoint is provided by none other than the visiting German engineer, whose function in the narrative is indicated by his simple conclusion, 'I don't understand the Chinese'. By reference to the scientific knowledge and earnest friendship of the foreigner, the spy fantasy of the authorities is revealed as paranoid and irrational, as incomprehensible to the 'objective' perspective of the Western visitor. In other words, in the process of debunking the Maoist ideological fantasy, *Black Cannon Incident* invokes its own foreign *other* to suit the ideology of the pro-reform 1980s intellectual. This 'other', now benign and rational rather than wicked and perverse, is depicted as an ally of the Chinese intellectual, the latter being invested in an ideology of liberalism and openness to the West and a teleology of technological and social progress that seeks to break out of the perceived circular futility of the inherited political culture.

In sum, in the context of the early reform era, the real subversion of *Black Cannon Incident* lay in its subversion *of* subversion. The point was not to oppose the Party with some dissident political plan, but rather to expose dissidence as being in some sense generated *by* the Party itself – or, more broadly, by the entrenched ideological fantasies of a public discourse that the young film-makers, with an ideological agenda of their own, wished to portray as inadequate to the task of modernisation.

NOTES

1. Paul G. Pickowicz, 'Huang Jianxin and the Notion of Postsocialism', in *New Chinese Cinemas: Forms, Identities, Politics*, ed. Nick Browne, Paul G. Pickowicz, Vivian Sobchack and Esther Yau (Cambridge: Cambridge University Press, 1994), 57–87.

2. Chris Berry and Mary Ann Farquhar, 'Post-socialist Strategies: An Analysis of *Yellow Earth* and *Black Cannon Incident*', in *Cinematic Landscapes: Observations on the Visual Arts and Cinema of China and Japan*, ed. Linda C. Ehrlich and David Desser (Austin: University of Texas Press, 1994), 110.

3. Jerome Silbergeld, *China into Film: Frames of Reference in Contemporary Chinese Cinema* (London: Reaktion, 1999), 245–249.

4. See Hu Ke, 'Contemporary Film Theory in China', *Dangdai dianying*, 2 (1995): 65–73. Trans. Ted Wang, Chris Berry and Chen Mei at: <www.latrobe.edu.au/screeningthepast/reruns/hkrr2b.html>

5. Dai Jinhua, *Wuzhong fengjing: Zhongguo dianying wenhua, 1978–1998* (Beijing: Peking University Press, 2000), 195.

6. This sketch of a model narrative is distilled from the plot structures of the 1950s counter-espionage films discussed later in this essay; its basic elements can also be found in many other films of the Mao era.

7. Dai, *Wuzhong fengjing*, 195.

8. For a suggestive reading of the 'black cannon' and technology itself as the twin Lacanian object-causes of desire in the film, see Kwai-cheung Lo, 'Feminizing Technology: The *Objet A* in *Black Cannon Incident*', in *Significant Others: Gender and Culture in Film and Literature East and West*, ed. William Burgwinkle, Glenn Man and Valerie Wayne (Honolulu: University of Hawaii Press, 1993), 88–95.

9. See Berry and Farquhar, 'Post-socialist Strategies', 100-110; Silbergeld, *China into Film*, 245–249.

10. On ideology as a pure performative rather than descriptive operation, see Slavoj Žižek, *The Sublime Object of Ideology* (London: Verso, 1989), 98–100.

11. Hofstadter's *Gödel, Escher, Bach: An Eternal Golden Braid* (New York: Vintage, 1979) had been translated into Chinese in 1984. See the director's comments in 'Cu ren shensi de *Heipao shijian*', *Dianying yishu*, 4 (1986): 10.

12. Ibid., 10.

13. See Slavoj Žižek, 'The Fetish of the Party', in *Lacan, Politics, Aesthetics*, ed. Willy Apollon and Richard Feldstein (Albany: State University of New York Press, 1996), 12.

4   *Blind Shaft*: Performing the 'Underground' on and beyond the Screen

Jonathan Noble

Blind Shaft, Li Yang's first feature film, opens with one of the most powerful and provocative scenes in new Chinese cinema.[1] A 2003 review of the film in *Time Asia* zeroed in on this hauntingly forceful scene:

> … a trio of men descends into the bowels of a fly-by-night Chinese coal mine. As darkness blots out the men's faces, the camera swings upward to linger on the shrinking rectangle of light above their heads. Then it, too, disappears. And for a claustrophobic moment we and the actors are left in stifling blackness.[2]

The image of the 'stifling blackness' of the 'bowels' of a coalmine serves an emblematic role in performing particular political processes that are instrumental in constructing an image of the production, circulation and reception of 'underground' film from mainland China. This essay explores the relationship between the visual and discursive representations of the underground in *Blind Shaft* and the film's social life, in terms of its circulation and consumption as a product of 'underground' currency. I argue that the underground in *Blind Shaft* is not simply a metaphor for social and economic conditions under global capitalism in China as well as around the world. More importantly, the film exemplifies the complex relationship between on-screen representation and the performances of underground cinema off the screen in a globalised, and politicised, context. But what is the underground cinema in China? Is it really a dangerous pursuit analogous to the dissent literature of the former Soviet bloc? Or is it closer to the underground culture of the avant-garde in the West?

Analyses of the ideological meanings of strikingly emblematic scenes have long assisted in constructing paradigmatic models for the linkages between social and visual processes in the contemporary visual culture of mainland China. A number of

these analyses have gained near canonical status in the study of Chinese cinema. For example, Esther Yau interprets Zhang Yimou's non-perspectival cinematography of the landscape in *Yellow Earth* (1984) as representing a Daoist aesthetic constitutive of a non-Western alternative filmic style.[3] Rey Chow reads the scene in *Ju Dou* (1990) in which Judou exhibits her naked body to her voyeuristic nephew as representative of Zhang Yimou's exhibitionism that 'returns the gaze of orientalist surveillance' and as a 'critique of the voyeurism of orientalism itself'.[4] Lydia Liu interprets a scene in the 1980s hit television series *Beijing Sojourner in New York* of the male protagonist tossing hundred-dollar bills at an American prostitute as representing a popularised and commercialised form of Chinese nationalism.[5] All of these images emblematise spectatorship processes inscribed in a complex web of visual politics involving transnational flows of cinematic production, circulation and consumption.

Blind Shaft's striking images of the pitch-black underbelly of the Shaanxi terrain are not facilely interpreted in accordance with the analytical paradigms discussed above. Instead, I argue that they are less about Orientalism, nationalism or even the West/non-West, but rather invoke a universal

Blind Shaft

predicament of self-destruction motivated by the global demand on energy and the global desire for wealth. Products of new Chinese cinema are often analysed as national allegories. But although *Blind Shaft*'s visual iconography appears as symbols on a local or national level, it more poignantly tells a story of a world that survives only through the venal exploitation of natural resources and human innocence. The sordid depths of the coalmine are the veritable abysses of humanity.

At the dawn of the twenty-first century, illegal and unauthorised coalmines dot the central earthen plateaux of northern Shaanxi province in China. Despite China's record-breaking economic performance, the number of workers who desperately toil in the depths of shoddily constructed mineshafts continues to mount. According to one report, deaths in the coalmines total at least 7,000 per year.[6] The vast majority of the makeshift mines lack the safety measures and equipment required to adhere to the government's construction standards. For many of these unauthorised operations, higher pay attracts miners who are willing to face the poor conditions and life-threatening risks. Illicit mines are often allowed to remain open on account of pay-offs to local officials.

Li Yang adopts this poignant and troubling socio-economic issue in *Blind Shaft*. While the illegal operation of coalmines reflects China's economic reforms and political state of affairs, Li Yang weaves together a captivating plot that integrates suspense and intrigue, elements of black comedy, social critique and existential crisis. The film tells a story about a duo of scam artists, Tang Zhaoyang and Song Jinming, who defraud illegal mines into paying compensation to them for the death of 'blood-relatives' in mining 'accidents'. After falsifying their relationship with the unsuspecting victims to the mine owners, the scam artists murder the victims while engineering a mine collapse to appear as the cause of death. The duo's last target is a desperate but optimistic teenage boy, Yuan Fengming, whose youth, innocence and honesty spark doubts in Song's commitment to carrying out the murder. The film concludes with the crooks killing each other in the depths of a mine seam, while the boy escapes the collapse of the mine and reluctantly collects compensation for the death of his 'uncle'.

The emblematic force of the 'abyss' stems from the way it functions as a composite of the narrative, figural, literal and social meanings of 'underground' in *Blind Shaft*. The abyss, however, is not solely a linchpin of different layers of meaning on a vertical axis but also functions as a type of liminal space that motivates the film's different stories. These stories include: Tang Zhaoyang and Song Jinming's murderous scamming of mines and unwitting victims; the gradual unfolding of their mistrust for each other that eventually undermines their scam; Yuan Fengming's quest to earn money to help out his family and the manipulated loss of his innocence; Xiao Hong's selling of her services that transforms Fengming into a 'man' and legitimises him as the next victim.

In terms of the narrative of the film, the audience views the miners working in the abysmal depths of the coalmines in four interconnected sequences. The depths of the coalmines represent an 'underground' space hidden from view that is both potentially dangerous as well as unknown. Each sequence is shot with low-key lighting, as the only light emanates from the miners' helmets. The faces of the miners can barely be distinguished, and the humans in the mines are transformed into silhouettes and shadows. In the first sequence, the miner, surnamed Yuan, is hit over the head and killed with a pickaxe by Tang Zhaoyang. Tang and Song then cause the mine to collapse, so that they can demand compensation for the death of Tang's 'brother'. In this first sequence, the mineshaft functions as not just the site for Tang and Song's scam but also as the enabler – it is precisely the illicit and hidden nature of the mine that allows their scam to succeed.

The second sequence in the mineshaft occurs after Yuan Fengming has been recruited by Tang and Song as their next victim. This sequence focuses on Fengming's experience, the danger of the mine emphasised through his expression of mild fear. The exploitation of the miners' labour is also highlighted by montage editing that parallels the mined coal with the miners' labour, i.e. coal is equated with the exploitation of labour under dangerous working conditions. The sordidness of the mineshaft is also highlighted in the subsequent sequence in which the miners take a bath to clean the black coal dust from their weary bodies.

In the third mineshaft sequence, Tang and Song disagree on when to kill Fengming. Tang wants to kill him immediately, while Song insists upon waiting two more days. This disagreement represents the erosion of the duo's mutual trust and foreshadows the narrative action in the final mineshaft sequence. Tang kills a miner and asks Fengming if he 'wants to go home', which is a coded signal for Song to kill Fengming. However, motivated by mistrust, Tang first hits Song over the head with a shovel and prepares to kill Fengming himself, but Song recovers enough to smash him over the head. Fengming runs out of the mine before a dynamite blast causes the mine to collapse on Song and Tang.

In terms of the film's narrative, this last sequence represents failed trust and a betrayal of the duo's partnership in crime, but it also enables Fengming to collect compensation for the false death of his fake uncle. In the end, Fengming is the beneficiary of multiple layers of deception, from his identity to the events that occurred in the mine, as well as the illegal operation of the mine, which pays out to avoid being shut down by the authorities. One of the major questions raised by the film's narrative is whether or not the mineshafts, and the greed, desperation and corruption that they represent, have permanently blemished if not destroyed Fengming's childlike innocence and innate goodness. Fengming's knowledge is also restricted in comparison to the audience, who has reason to believe that his father was Song and Tang's previous victim. Would having this knowledge justify Fengming's collection of the compensation, despite its dubious origin? In terms of the film's diegesis, the mining abyss represents a liminal space in which the fates of the characters can suddenly change, and the liminality of the space motivates the suspense of the film.

Figuratively, the depths of the coalmines are also ritualised spaces, in which lives are sacrificed for the sake of the pursuit of money and social status. They represent a place of lawlessness in which, complicit with corruption, morality and humanity are sacrificed in the pursuit of avarice. The figurative space of the mines extends beyond their depths and motivates the actions of the characters above ground. For example, the reparation received after the wrongful death of Yuan enables Song and Tang to purchase the services of prostitutes, thereby sustaining illegal sexual workers. Their scam also necessitates the acquisition of fake identity cards and supports such illegal activities. From one perspective, the mineshaft represents the extreme commodification of human lives. A key contradiction within the film is Song's struggle to reconcile the commodification of human life with his growing recognition of Fengming's innocence, kindness and generosity. Song, importantly, shares with Fengming a motivation for earning money: they both wire money home to pay for the schooling of family members: Song for his son, and Fengming for his sister. Figuratively, the mineshaft therefore represents a final battleground between innocence and guilt, humanity and commodification, and life and death.

Parts of the film were literally filmed 'underground' 700 metres below the surface in bona fide illegally operated mineshafts in rural China. Li Yang and several of the actors and crew spent fifty hours filming underground. The dangers involved with the filming process are emphasised by the fact that one of the mineshafts where the crew had been filming collapsed only days after the shoot.[7]

The film can also be interpreted as an 'underground' cinematic product within a social context: the film cinematically reveals certain previously undisclosed facts about the dangers faced by miners and the complicity that exists between illegal mines and government officials in perpetuating their operations and life-threatening work conditions. Li Yang did not apply, and hence could not receive, permission from the State Administration of Radio, Film and Television to film *Blind Shaft*. On the basis of the film's 'illegal' (i.e. unauthorised) production, *Blind Shaft* is often considered to be an 'underground' cinematic production.

The emblematic performances of the mineshaft sequences link together the diegetic – the cinematic images on the screen – with the non-diegetic – the lives of miners in China's mammoth mining industry, and the non-diegetic with the socio-political reception and circulation of the film in a transnational context. I refer to the convergence of the diegetic, non-diegetic and socio-political nexus within these sequences as the film's 'undergroundedness' – constituted by the narrative, figurative, literal and social aspects of the 'underground' in *Blind Shaft*. One of the most common questions journalists asked Li Yang about *Blind Shaft* and his second feature film *Blind Mountain* (2007) was whether he felt his film would be able to help the underprivileged and disenfranchised individuals portrayed in his films.[8] Li Yang often replied that he hoped his films would increase awareness about aspects of social strife in

China, such as the exploitation of miners and bride trafficking represented in *Blind Shaft* and *Blind Mountain* respectively. From one perspective, it would seem that Li Yang gained critical success through a type of privileged visual broadcasting of the less fortunate; however, his boldness of vision and action have clearly directed greater global media attention to issues of social injustice in China today.

The 'undergroundedness' of *Blind Shaft* is constructed not solely by the production of images on the screen but also by how these images were politicised and marketed as the film circulated within the international media and international film circuit. *Blind Shaft*, one of the 'dark horse' sensations of 'Chinese' cinema in 2003, won nearly twenty awards at international film festivals, including the Silver Bear for Artistic Contribution in Directing and Writing at the Berlin International Film Festival and Best Narrative Feature at Martin Scorsese and Robert De Niro's Tribeca Film Festival.[9] The film was successfully sold to prestigious distributors in major film markets, including Kino International in the US market. *Blind Shaft* was also selected by *The New York Times* critic Manohla Dargis as one of the top ten films of 2004.[10]

The emergence of the 'Sixth Generation Directors' in the global film market was closely connected to the political currency attributed to their films' 'underground' production in China. The early films directed by Zhang Yuan (before 1998), Wang Xiaoshuai (before 2005) and Jia Zhangke (before *The World* in 2004), for example, were often referred to as 'underground' films by festivals and the media because of their taboo subjects, production outside China's official studio system and censorship bureaucracy, and their illegal submission to (or screening at) international film festivals outside China. The production and global circulation of Li Yang's *Blind Shaft* is similar to the experiences of the 'underground' films made by these directors, as well as by others, including Lou Ye, Cui Zi'en, Wang Chao, Zhu Wen, Li Yu, Liu Fendou and Han Jie.[11]

The underground phenomenon in new Chinese cinema from mainland China is a result of global and local politics. However, underground cultural production is not unique to China. How do China's 'underground' films, for example, compare to the student radio channel B92 in Serbia that, according to Matthew Collin,

chose the international call-signs of techno and rock 'n' roll to overturn the suffocating censorship of Milosevic's media ... [their] quest for the truth ... was a lifeline to reality from the universe of distortion which they were condemned to inhabit, a totem held up against the encroaching darkness.[12]

Or, are they like rock music that was rigidly circumscribed by a bureaucratic state apparatus during the Brezhnev era from the 1960s.[13] Are China's 'underground films' closer to zines in the US, which according to Stephen Duncombe are 'variegated voices of a subterranean world staking out its identity through the cracks of capitalism and in the shadows of the mass media ... speaking to and for an underground culture'.[14] Such comparisons suggest the importance of historicising China's 'underground' cinema. This can in part be accomplished by avoiding the pitfall of assuming that underground film in China is a product of an absolute dichotomy between legal and illegal film production, official sanction versus official censure, and market availability versus proscribed access. A discussion of the hybridity of *Blind Shaft* provides a model for a more accurate understanding of the operations of the underground film industry within a local and global context.

Blind Shaft received substantial global attention, including reports in mainstream media, such as Reuters, *The Washington Post*, *The New York Times*, the BBC, *LA Weekly*, Australian Broadcasting Corporation and *Time Asia*, in addition to regionally based media, such as the *Taipei Times* and the *South China Morning Post*, and less mainstream media including *The Nation*, *The Village Voice* and the *Guardian*. A number of these articles directly use the term 'underground' (e.g. 'Going Underground' and 'Film from the Underground' in the *Guardian* and *Taipei Times* respectively[15]) in their titles, whereas others emphasise descent and darkness ('Descending into the Pit of Humanity' and 'Filming the Dark Side of Capitalism' in *The New York Times* and 'Dark Night of the Soul' in *Time Asia*[16]). In addition to a relatively facile employment of the term 'underground', the majority of these articles mention that the film was banned in China, and, as result, implying that the film is 'exiled' from China, along with director Li Yang himself. A quote from the *Guardian* sums this up nicely: '*Blind Shaft* officially does not exist within China. The film is banned and its director is regarded as an outcast.'[17]

The print advertisements released by Kino International featured a banner printed in bold capitals that reads: 'BANNED IN CHINA!'.

However, 'banned' is an obfuscating term that is primarily used for its currency as a marketing buzz-word rather than for its descriptive accuracy. Li Yang did not apply for official permits to make the film, and thus, according to the Film Bureau's regulations, *Blind Shaft* was made illegally in China. By using the term 'banned', the media is misleading readers into thinking that the film was officially censured – 'ban' equals 'to prohibit, especially by official decree'.[18] This term also creates a false picture of the 'censorship' apparatus in China as well as simplifying the complex relationship between the country's artists and government. The maker of a 'banned' film in China is suddenly promoted to the status of political dissident, victim of an oppressive Communist regime and martyr for free speech. In Li Yang's case, for example, the Chinese government allegedly forced the International Film Festival of India to withdraw *Blind Shaft* from competition.[19]

In fact, *Blind Shaft* could never have been produced without receiving support from certain authorities within the Chinese government. For example, the scouting of sites received devoted assistance from certain unnamed cadres in the provincial government.[20] Also, much of the post-production work was completed in Beijing with the knowledge of film officials. Since *Blind Shaft*, film officials have in the main encouraged Li Yang to co-operate and work within the system.[21] It is likewise important to keep in mind that many of the directors (such as Zhang Yimou and Tian Zhuangzhuang) who currently hold official positions within the China Film Directors Association (*Zhongguo dianying daoyan xiehui*) had their own films 'banned' at one time or another. China's film establishment apparently pursues a course of engagement rather than containment – encouraging formerly 'underground' directors such as Wang Xiaoshuai, Jia Zhangke and Wang Chao to follow the trajectory of 'Fifth Generation' predecessors Zhang Yimou, Wu Ziniu, Chen Kaige and Tian Zhuangzhuang by making films that both receive government approval and target the domestic box office.

Contrary to what one may be led to believe by Western media reports, *Blind Shaft* has not been 'exiled' from China. News coverage in Chinese about *Blind Shaft* has been and continues to be available in China. For example, news of the Best Narrative Feature award at Tribeca was reproduced by Xinhua News Agency, China's official news organisation, after having been printed in the *Beijing Evening Post* (*Beijing Wanbao*), in factual if not slightly laudatory terms.[22] In addition, *Blind Shaft* was screened for students at Peking University, and currently a cut version of the film is being distributed throughout China on DVD and has been widely available in video stores in Beijing.[23]

Complicities with the official establishment are necessarily overlooked as part of the official/anti-official bipolarisation that results from glamorisation of 'undergroundedness' in the Western media and the international film festival circuit. Such hybridity is often conveniently overlooked in the international film circuit for purposes of publicity and political ideology and spectacle. *Blind Shaft* was clearly promoted at various film festivals as a film subversive of the Chinese government. When Nora Ephron presented Li Yang with the award for Best Narrative Feature at the Tribeca Film Festival, he told the audience: 'I hope this won't get the film festival in trouble with the Chinese government.'[24] The statement was heartily received with cheers and enthusiastic clapping. Though Li Yang undoubtedly did face certain risks in the production of *Blind Shaft*, personal risks that he faced for breaking the law in China were lessened because of his status as a German citizen. Li Yang's citizenship was downplayed on the international film circuit, as was his transnational identity and the film's transnational production. According to Chinese law, *Blind Shaft* is a Chinese production (as more than half of the lead actors are Chinese), despite the fact that the financing came primarily from 'German' sources and the post-production work was done in Australia, Thailand, Hong Kong and Germany. The portrait of Li Yang often presented in the film festivals was of a dissenting 'Chinese' auteur who scrounged up the money and risked his life to film the 'truth' that had been hidden from the 'international community' by the Chinese government.

Such cultural hybridity complicates the 'undergroundedness' of Chinese 'underground' film, and, in particular, the spatial bipolarisation between underground and above-ground films. An 'underground' film is clearly much more complex than simply a film that contains anti-Party or anti-official content. The case of *Blind Shaft* exemplifies the pitfalls of equating 'underground' with 'anti-official' in cultural production in contemporary China, as it simplistically reduces the circulation of cultural products to terms that are in many ways already intertwined.

Whereas scholars have often articulated how Zhang Yimou's films seduce Western audiences with their sensuous and exotic visual imagery and mythic allegory, 'underground' films seduce the Western media, festival circuit and audiences with their politics of presenting a harsh, 'real' China in a cinéma-vérité style that conceals a film's fictional construction.[25] In this way, 'underground' films become a category of convenience governed by an implicit contract held between film festivals and the media and producers of the 'underground films'. The rubric does much to obscure the film and mystify the audience, and little to clarify how the film is actually produced, circulated and interpreted by different audiences within the international film circuit. In his discussion of the circulation and interpretation of Iranian films in the international film circuit, Bill Nichols notes: 'The international film festival, and the new directors and new visions offered by it, affords an ideal opportunity to enjoy the pleasure of film's imaginary signifiers.'[26] Like Iranian films, 'underground' Chinese films have benefited enormously from the international film festival circuit, especially in terms of its promotion of a 'real' China as captured and projected through cinéma-vérité techniques.

The flipside of the fascination with the 'underground' is the almost total disregard by the media, film festivals and scholarship of both 'state-sponsored' films (also called 'main melody films') and China's commercial blockbusters. For example, Wu Ziniu, the director of a number of films that failed to receive certification for release, such as *Dove Tree*, turned to making 'official' productions, such as *National Anthem*, in 1998, and has only recently been attracting greater attention.[27] Western media attention on China's top-grossing films, such as Feng Xiaogang's *Cell Phone*, number one at China's box office in 2003, and Ning Hao's 2006 sleeper *Crazy Stone*, is greatly overshadowed by media attention on 'underground' directors, such as Lou Ye's 2006 *Summer Palace*, the illegal screening of which at the 2006 Cannes Film Festival resulted in a prohibition

that forbids Lou Ye from making another feature film in China for five years.

As China's commercial films become officialised and official films are commercialised, underground films and their makers have already submitted to a global market. On the one hand, the surge of DV films, especially documentaries, and the use of Internet technology to disseminate them, may indicate a type of democratisation of film-making and viewing in China. At the same time, amid the onslaught of commercialisation and surfeit of commodity-signs, the fate of 'underground' film-making in China may be similar to that of the zines. According to Duncombe, the underground culture of the zines did not seem to be changing the above-ground world; rather, 'alternative culture was being celebrated in the mainstream media and used to create new styles and profits for the commercial culture industry … The underground is discovered and cannibalised almost before it exists.'[28] Paul Pickowicz asks:

> Will Li remain underground for a few more pictures? Will he be recruited by the state sector? … Only time will tell, but the main point is that a simple binary interpretive approach that pits heroic political dissidents against a ruthless police state does not work very well in the complicated Chinese case.[29]

Given the pressures of the government and the market, Li Yang's future filmic output will most likely increase in its commercial and official appeal. *Blind Shaft*, therefore, will remain as a tropic intervention with a particular historical moment in the history of new Chinese cinema and its sacramental representation of the underground will remain as visually iconic of the intersection between the cinematic representations and the social life of Chinese 'underground' film.

NOTES

1. *Blind Shaft* (2002) was based on Liu Qingbang's novel *Sacred Wood* (*Shengmu*). Li Yang wrote the screen adaptation, produced and directed the film, as well as co-edited it. Li Yang discusses the process of adapting the novel in *Today*, 76, no. 1 (2007): 32.
2. Susan Jakes, 'The Dark Night of the Soul', *Time Asia*, 162, no. 17 (3 November 2003): <www.time.com/time/magazine/article/0,9171,526556,00.html> (downloaded 27 June 2007).

3. Esther C. M. Yau, 'Is China the End of Hermeneutics?'; or, Political and Cultural Usage of Non-Han Women in Mainland Chinese Films', in *Multiple Voices in Feminist Film Criticism*, ed. D. Carson, L. Dittmar and J. R. Welsch (Minneapolis: University of Minnesota Press, 1994), 280–292.

4. Rey Chow, *Primitive Passions: Visuality, Sexuality, Ethnography, and Contemporary Chinese Cinema* (New York: Columbia University Press, 1995), 170–171.

5. Lydia Liu, 'Beijing Sojourners in New York: Postsocialism and the Question of Ideology in Global Media Culture', *Positions*, 7, no. 3 (1999): 763–798.

6. According to *The New York Times*, China's 'government also seems inclined to tolerate a high death rate to keep coal, which still supplies about 75 per cent of China's energy needs, abundant and inexpensive'. See Joseph Kahn, 'Filming the Dark Side of Capitalism in China', *The New York Times*, 7 May 2003.

7. Bill Smith, 'An Interview with Director Li Yang', *South China Morning Post*, 8 January 2003.

8. Based on interviews with Li Yang at the 2007 Cannes Film Festival. I served as Li Yang's interpreter.

9. *Blind Shaft* received the following awards: Silver Bear for Artistic Contribution in Directing and Writing, 53rd Berlin International Film Festival; Best Film, Best Director, Best Actor (Wang Baoqiang), Audience Award, Critics Prize, Deauville Asian Film Festival; Best Cinematography Award, Buenos Aires Film Festival; Best Narrative Feature, 2nd Tribeca International Film Festival; Silver Firebird Award, Hong Kong International Film Festival; Outstanding Film Award, 57th Edinburgh International Film Festival; Best Film, Seville International Film Festival; Film and Literature Prize, 2003 Film by the Sea (Holland) Film Festival; Jury Award, Bergen (Norway) International Film Festival; nominations for Best Film, Best Screenplay and Best New Actor, Taiwan's Golden Horse Film Festival; selected for competition at the Seattle Film Festival, Pusan Film Festival, Chicago Film Festival, Moscow Film Festival, The Karlovy Vary International Film Festival (Prague), Three Rivers Film Festival (Pittsburgh), as well as at film festivals in Sydney, Melbourne, Bangkok and Portland.

10. Manohla Dargis, 'The Best Films of the Year', *The New York Times*, 26 December 2004.

11. For a comprehensive list of underground films made in China, see the appendix in Paul G. Pickowicz, 'Social and Political Dynamics of Underground Filmmaking in China', in *From Underground to Independent: Alternative Film Culture in Contemporary China*, ed. Paul Pickowicz and Yingjin Zhang (Lanham, MD: Rowman & Littlefield, 2006), 215–244.

12. Matthew Collin, *Guerrilla Radio: Rock 'n' Roll Radio and Serbia's Underground Resistance* (New York: Thunder's Mouth Press, 2001), 4–8.

13. Thomas Cushman, *Notes from Underground: Rock Music Counterculture in Russia* (Binghampton: State University of New York Press, 1995).

14. Stephen Duncombe, *Notes from Underground: Zines and the Politics of Alternative Culture* (London: Verso, 1997), 2.

15. See Xan Brooks, 'Going Underground', *Guardian Unlimited*, 3 November 2003; and Yu Sen-lun, 'Film from the Underground', *Taipei Times*, 9 December 2003.

16. See Elvis Mitchell, 'Descending into the Pit of Humanity', *The New York Times*, 4 February 2004. See also Kahn, 'Filming the Dark Side of Capitalism', and Jakes, 'Dark Night of the Soul'.

17. Brooks, 'Going Underground'.

18. *The American Heritage® Dictionary of the English Language*, 4th edn. (Boston: Houghton Mifflin, 2000).

19. Jakes, 'Dark Night of the Soul'.

20. Bill Smith, in 'Interview with Director Li Yang', notes that the filming took place on the border between Hebei and Shaanxi provinces, but 'Li is unwilling to be more precise about the location, to protect those who helped him gain access'. Li Yang mentioned in conversation that provincial and local government officials facilitated the scouting of filming sites and were provided with certain remuneration for their assistance. Li Yang also mentions having received the assistance of a journalist for the official publication *Coal Industry in China* [*Zhongguo meitan gongye*]. See Michael Berry, *Speaking in Images: Interviews with Contemporary Chinese Filmmakers* (New York: Columbia University Press, 2005), 218.

21. Li Yang's second feature film, *Blind Mountain*, about the kidnapping of brides, was shot after having received approval from the Film Bureau. This shows the effectiveness of the government's courting of 'underground' film-makers. As of May 2007, however, China's Film Bureau has not yet approved the film for exhibition.

22. Wu Yong, 'Mang jing huo Tribeca dianyingjie zui jia gushipian jiang' ('Blind Shaft Wins Prize for Best

Feature Film at the Tribeca Film Festival'), Xinhuanet (14 May 2003): <news.xinhuanet.com/newsmedia/2003-05/14/content_868552.htm> (downloaded 27 June 2007). (Originally printed in *Beijing Wanbao*.)

23. The video compact disc (VCD) was distributed at the end of November 2003. In February 2004, a DVD version (uncut) was released in Hong Kong. It was quickly bootlegged and became available throughout China as a 'pirated' copy. Also, of course, the authorised version of the DVD could be easily ordered online by mainlanders. The Hong Kong release of the DVD has English subtitles.

24. I stood on stage with Li Yang to interpret his acceptance speech at the 2003 Tribeca Film Festival.

25. On the other hand, Yingjin Zhang discusses how the independent film-makers' claims to represent truth in China challenge 'the hegemony of official film-making and media representation'. Yingjin Zhang, 'My Camera Doesn't Lie? Truth, Subjectivity, and Audience in Chinese Independent Film and Video', in Pickowicz and Zhang, *From Underground to Independent*, 23–45.

26. Bill Nichols, 'Discovering Form, Inferring Meaning: New Cinemas and the Film Festival Circuit', *Film Quarterly*, 47, no. 3 (1994): 17.

27. Wu Ziniu's career helps to demonstrate the complex dynamics between social critique and state compliance in China's film industry. See Yingjin Zhang, *Screening China: Critical Interventions, Cinematic Reconfigurations, and the Transnational Imaginary in Contemporary Chinese Cinema* (Ann Arbor: University of Michigan Press, 2002), 176–90; and Paul Clark, *Reinventing China: A Generation and Its Films* (Hong Kong: The Chinese University Press, 2005), 90–105.

28. Duncombe, *Notes from Underground*, 5.

29. Paul G. Pickowicz, 'Social and Political Dynamics of Underground Filmmaking in China', in Pickowicz and Zhang, *From Underground to Independent*, 10.

5 *Boat People*: Second Thoughts on Text and Context

Julian Stringer

Following a television drama (*The Boy From Vietnam*, 1978) and prequel feature film (*The Story of Woo Viet*, 1981), *Boat People* is the third instalment of Ann Hui's 'Vietnamese Trilogy.' Shot on location on Hainan Island, the film sparked an international controversy over its politically incendiary subject matter. The movie opens with Akutagawa (George Lam), a Japanese photojournalist, covering the liberation of Da Nang, Vietnam, in 1975. Three years later he returns to the country as a guest of the government's Cultural Bureau.

As well as spending time with communist officials, Akutagawa strikes up a friendship with Cam Nuong (Season Ma), a teenage street urchin, and her two young brothers. One of them, Ah Nhac, is later killed by a land mine. After witnessing the youngsters scavenge from the bodies of execution victims at the nearby 'chicken farm,' Akutagawa tries to help them. The journalist had been impressed by the organisation of a new economic zone (NEZ) he had been invited to visit. However, he is told by To Minh (Andy Lau), an ex-translator for the American army who now plans to escape from Vietnam by boat, that the zone he toured, number 16, is a show model designed to impress visitors: the other zones are much more inhumane. After witnessing further examples of social injustice, Akutagawa resolves to help Cam and her brother escape. Akutagawa is killed in the attempt, but the two young Vietnamese succeed in reaching the boat and put out to sea. A final freeze-frame depicts the two of them looking out across the ocean, an uncertain future ahead.

A commercial and critical event in Hong Kong, *Boat People* was the subject of intense political debate and the precursor of other similarly-themed allegorical narratives. It remains a powerful, if suppressed, document of its time.

Entry on *Boat People* in *Encyclopedia of Chinese Film*.[1]

Barbara Klinger has outlined the limitations of the 'single-discourse' approach often taken in Film Studies to the text–context relation. All too frequently a neat correspondence is posited between these two terms, resulting in the production of critical work that imposes 'a unity between a film and its historical moment at the expense of considering the intricate untidiness of this relationship'. In Klinger's view, scholars seeking to account for the diverse meanings particular films may be ascribed in specific historical circumstances should work to provide a sense

> not of *the* ideology the text had in a historical context, but its *many* ideologies. By placing a film within multifarious intertextual and historical frames – the elements that define its situation in a complex discursive and social milieu – the film's variable, even contradictory, ideological meanings come into focus.[2]

As the above entry from *Encyclopedia of Chinese Film* implies but never quite spells out, *Boat People* (Ann Hui, 1982) – in common with many films produced in Hong Kong throughout the 1980s and 1990s – has often been assessed in terms of an overarching single discourse, namely, the '1997 factor'. A key text of the post-1979 'New Wave', *Boat People* is ostensibly concerned with the contemporary Vietnamese refugee 'problem'. However, the movie has been widely interpreted as an allegory concerning the then-British colony's possible future fate under Chinese sovereign rule. For example, Derek Elley suggested in 1984 that Hui's film demonstrates how the 'shadow of 1997 is already making itself shown in Hongkong cinema as the colony reasserts its ties with the Mainland'; and Tony Rayns wrote in the same year that while 'Western critics have tended to see the film as a lurid exposé of Communist brutalities and hypocrisies, Hong Kong audiences, less naively, took it as a troubled commentary on the tensions within *China*'s Communist Party – and, consequently, on their own prospective future after 1997'.[3]

Subsequent academic scholarship has consolidated this dominant viewpoint. In a particularly influential formulation, Li Cheuk-to claims that the 'importance of the film lies in the remarkable way in which today's Vietnam is used as a metaphor for tomorrow's Hong Kong. ... When the film was released in Hong Kong, the local audience had no trouble in equating the Vietnamese Communist characters with their Chinese counterparts. Postliberation Vietnam was tantamount to post-1997 Hong Kong.' (Li further claims, however, that 'in *Boat People* there is a sense of hope as signified in the [final] freeze-frame shot of the young girl hugging her brother, both staring into the distance at dawn.') Stephen Teo, too, regards Hui's film as 'the most allegorical treatment up to that time of the China syndrome haunting Hong Kong people in the early 80s', while Patricia Brett Erens and Leung Ping-kwan both reproduce the view that the film was received 'as an intended allegory of the future condition in Hong Kong after 1997'. In a recent Hong Kong filmography published in the USA, John Charles reiterates that Hui's film must be 'an obvious metaphor for the trepidations over Communist rule that many HK citizens were starting to experience around this time'.[4]

It is important to point out that such arguments are perfectly valid and seemingly 'correct'. However, the simple repetition of this primary interpretation inevitably overshadows *Boat People's* other variable and even contradictory meanings. To be sure, work does exist which has adopted a different take on the film or framed analysis from an alternative perspective. This work includes recent articles by both Erens and Elaine Yee-lin Ho on the place the movie occupies in the context of Hui's overall artistic career, and in particular her identity as a 'woman director'; and Law Kar's discussion of the importance of the social-realist aesthetic *Boat People* and other New Wave titles injected into Hong Kong's cinema in the early 1980s.[5] Yet such pieces only underline the need to be more aware of the variety of elements that define the film's situation in a complex discursive and social milieu.

One of the historical frames largely unexamined by the existing critical literature is the crucial role played by international film festivals in the transnational circulation and reception of *Boat People*. By adopting a perspective that considers the significance of overseas distribution practices, it becomes possible to raise issues largely overlooked in previous accounts of the film's importance. My argument in this essay, then, is that in order to grasp more clearly the intricate untidiness of the text–context relation, it is necessary to consider *Boat People* in terms of the art world of the international festival circuit. The 'second thoughts' I want to explore are these. First, that *Boat People* proved a difficult movie for this art world to position. Second, that this contextual situation mirrors with uncanny appropriateness the film's thematic focus on travelling political 'problems' (i.e. refugees).

As a way of illustrating the latter of these two points, it is helpful to bear in mind that Klinger discusses the key role played at moments of historical reception by areas 'closely affiliated with a film's appearance ("intertextual zones")': these include other media and arts, review journalism and fan cultures, but also exhibition circumstances such as art-museum and film-festival screenings and revivals.[6] Similarly, in their introduction to the excellent *Traffic in Culture: Refiguring Art and Anthropology*, George E. Marcus and Fred R. Myers differentiate more specifically between key spaces of the contemporary art world's various 'intertextual zones'. For Marcus and Myers, there exists on the one hand a 'zone of speculation', wherein the international art market – its dealers, gallery owners and art writers – recognises and registers interest in avant-garde or emergent forms, in new work or newsworthy material. On the other hand, there is the 'zone of legitimation', wherein artworks play their privileged role in the formation of canons and take up their privileged place in the memory work of cultural narratives. For Marcus and Myers, 'the crucial point of intersection' is the 'interzone': this is where artworks move, or do not move, from speculation to recognition; it is the in-between space that determines whether or not artworks 'break through'. The interzone is where 'particular contemporary artists and works of art move from the location of speculation and recognition, registered by a small world of dealers, gallery owners, curators, collectors (private and corporate), and art writers (journalists, critics, scholars), into the legitimated art world which is the world of art history'.[7] In short, the interzone is where artworks sink or swim.

In 1983, as it sailed into the festival interzone, *Boat People* might have been expected to make quite a splash. After all, contemporary reports make clear that when first released in Hong Kong in 1982 Hui's movie constituted a social 'event'. Mel Tobias writes that it was

> by far the most popular, much written-up and talked about contemporary Hong Kong film since King Hu's heralded *A Touch of Zen* in Cannes ... *Boat People* had a good 'hype' even before the final sequence was envisioned by respected femme director [*sic*] Ann Hui. ... *Boat People* was both a financial (grossed HK$15 million) and a critical success.[8]

Unfortunately, though, such words now sound rather ironic, because it has been relatively difficult to actually get to see *Boat People* outside Hong Kong since its original theatrical release. The simple reason for this regrettable situation is that despite its initial status as a highly controversial and contested 'must-see' attraction, Hui's movie experienced a reversal of fortune once it entered international waters. The globalised festival circuit presented Ann Hui with the same question it habitually poses other film-makers seeking overseas distribution and exhibition rights for their work: will this movie stay afloat? However, unlike *A Touch of Zen*, *Boat People* was not exactly 'heralded' at Cannes when screened there in 1983. Sure, it had its throng of vocal supporters. Yet, as Harlan Kennedy documents, this Official Selection was protested by the Vietnamese government, and attacked on grounds of political naivety and opportunism as well as aesthetic superficiality and crude melodrama (the virulence of these attacks was enough to force the film out of competition). Patricia Brett Erens further reports that 'critics at the New York International Film Festival [1983] objected to the rather one-sided representation of the Vietnam government and the film's lack of historical perspective. Others found the work politically simplistic and sentimental.'[9]

As a result of negative reactions such as these, *Boat People* did not secure widespread international distribution and became for all intents and purposes a canonical unseen film. This inability to 'break through' internationally created the curious situation that exists today, whereby a body of English-language critical writing exists on a movie much talked-about but apparently seldom viewed. I have not undertaken a full study of how many prints or copies of *Boat People* exist in libraries or archives in the Western

world. However, I do know that New Yorker Films in the USA distribute a subtitled 16mm copy (this is the version I have had access to) and, according to John Charles, a Star Entertainment (Hong Kong) unsubtitled laser disc is available for import, as is a China Star (Hong Kong) unsubtitled DVD. The point to make here, though, is that whereas subtitled versions of other Ann Hui feature films are readily available through such exhibition 'windows' as VCD and DVD, *Boat People* – her event movie – is much harder to track down.

By a curious twist of fate, then, the narrative drama of *Boat People* accurately parallels the chilly reception the film itself received on the globalised festival and distribution circuits circa 1983. The film's international exhibition fate mimics its thematic dynamics. To repeat, the story concerns a small group of characters caught up in a web of political turmoil and ultimately cast out onto the open seas (literally or metaphorically). On its initial overseas festival screening at Cannes in 1983 (in September 2001 *Variety* is still referring to Ann Hui as a director of so-called 'festival films'), the movie generated political controversy but subsequently failed to achieve widespread international distribution. The film remained stuck in a 'no-man's land', waiting to arrive.

By positing the international festival circuit as a key part of the contemporary art world broadly conceived, a new text–context relation has now come into view. *Boat People* revolves diegetically around displaced persons seeking a place of safety, a new legal 'home'. The film's own reception history testifies to the occupation of a similar in-between liminal status. The movie made waves within the international film world's zone of speculation, but failed to move into the zone of legitimation. It became stuck in the interzone, cast adrift in the limbo it regrettably remains in to this very day. Moreover, one result of this unavailability is that critical writing has had a virtually free hand in embalming *the* ideology this text had in a particular historical context over the *many* meanings it may have in diverse contexts. In short, in the absence of regular screenings and opportunities for reassessment, it has proved hard for international film culture to 'remember' much about *Boat People* outside the '1997 factor'.

So, why exactly was this movie difficult for this art world to position? The critics cited above raise a number of observations concerning the perceived limitations of *Boat People* as a text – namely, that it is naive, opportunistic, deficient in matters of historical perspective and melodramatic or sentimental (all readings largely swept aside by the force of the 1997 discourse). Yet two further contextual considerations are also worth suggesting.

To begin with, Hui's movie had a troublesome relationship to a then-current international genre. *Boat People* is a rare Asian entry in what Claudia Springer has identified as a cycle of 1980s 'third-world investigation films'.[10] Produced most frequently by the US movie industry, such films combine 'two established genres: the action-adventure genre set in the Third World and the reporter-film genre' (167). The result of this 'generic hybrid is a narrative pattern that combines adventure with investigation, all revolving around an outsider who interprets an unfamiliar location' (168). Across the various examples cited by Springer – including *The Year of Living Dangerously* (Peter Weir, 1982), *Last Plane Out* (David Nelson, 1983), *Under Fire* (Roger Spottiswoode, 1983), *The Killing Fields* (Roland Joffe, 1984) and *Salvador* (Oliver Stone, 1985) – the spectator is 'typically' positioned 'in the role of cultural outsider by virtue of techniques that encourage identification with the reporter protagonist … but more importantly, they are concerned with constructing white Western male subjectivity' (168).

Boat People shares many of the dominant generic features of this cycle, including the following key elements: a preoccupation with 'a journalist who investigates a situation, typically increasing his or her knowledge as the narrative progresses' (167); a specific narrative movement, whereby an initially uncommitted journalist-protagonist gradually invents a new self through aligning himself with an individual and a cause (174); the equation of vision with understanding ('the more he sees, the better he is able to achieve what the film presents as the correct interpretation' [178]); and the utilisation of 'a seamless representational style of realism' (187) – albeit tempered with melodrama in *Boat People*'s case. All of this is achieved through the central dramatic focus on Akutagawa's awakening to the truth concerning the Communist regime's brutal activities in Vietnam.

Just as importantly, however, *Boat People* deviates from this generic 'model' in a number of important ways. Clearly, its central character is Japanese, not a white Westerner, and while the plot creates a vivid sense of Akutagawa's 'helplessness in the face of unpredictable violence' (171), it nevertheless denies him the kind of optical point-of-view shots granted central characters throughout other entries in the cycle. Indeed, Akutagawa's position as adventurer-hero is consistently undercut. This particular photo-journalist may well investigate and report, but he is relatively ineffectual when it comes to action and derring-do. (Compare this with the hunky physicality of the Nick Nolte character in *Under Fire* or lithe James Woods in *Salvador*.) At the most extreme, it is difficult to imagine the Third World investigation films' white Western male subjects – Sydney Schanberg (Sam Waterston) in *The Killing Fields*, say – immolated in flames, as Akutagawa is at the end of *Boat People*. That would just be too much of a 'downer'.

The 'problem' of Akutagawa has been argued before by Tony Rayns in terms of casting.[11] However, in the context of this specific film cycle, the character as written is already a problematic figure of audience identification. Symptomatically, in *Boat People* the hero-function of the 'typical' reporter film becomes split between a range of subsidiary characters, all of whom are revealed as unable fully to take control of their own destinies. In refusing to offer a simplistic foregrounding of any one central character, Hui's film devotes narrative interest to Cam and her family, To Minh (the ex-translator for the American army who is killed trying to escape on a refugee boat) and his best friend An Tranh (who is killed by a land mine), Comrade Vu (the party official who accompanies Akutagawa) and Commander Nyugen (the melancholy military officer who cannot get over his earlier life experiences in France), as well as the restaurant owner, played by Cora Miao, who ultimately resolves to help Akutagawa help others.

Devoting screen time to a variety of secondary characters works to deny the subjectivity and narrative stability of the reporter-protagonist. Moreover, Akutagawa's status as hero and adventurer is further undermined by the absence of what Springer terms a 'recuperative switch' (180), wherein stock narrative tropes are introduced at opportune moments to bolster the foreign reporter's normative masculinity (for example, matey banter and rivalry between journalists, derring-do and a heterosexual romance). As Springer further elaborates, to 'heighten the aura of

Boat People: George Lam as Akutagawa

seductive danger, the films consistently introduce a character who individually embodies the culture as a whole and evokes the reporter's simultaneous attraction and confusion. The object of the reporter's fascination is usually a woman' (171).

Like the photojournalist Billy Kwan (Linda Hunt), in *The Year of Living Dangerously* – along with *Boat People*, by far the most distinguished entry in the cycle – Akutagawa tries his best to help save a woman and a child. However, Hui's film presents no story line comparable to the relationship between *The Year of Living Dangerously*'s hero (played by Mel Gibson) and love interest (Sigourney Weaver). Such refusal of easy romantic pleasure is only exacerbated by *Boat People*'s non-exploitative presentation of Cam Nuong. (Springer claims that 'the camera participates in the narrative investigation by scrutinizing both [the woman's body] and the setting' [173].)

In the particular context of the other films in the Third World investigation cycle, the result of all this undermining of Akutagawa is that as a central protagonist he comes across as a severely compromised figure – a loner, ineffectual, a walking funeral pyre.

Boat People ends up resembling what *The Year of Living Dangerously* might have been like had the Gibson and Weaver characters been written out and Billy Kwan taken centre stage.

A second reason why Hui's film was difficult to position, or may have generated discomfort internationally in 1983, is because of its internal critique of cross-cultural looking relations. One of the most intriguing aspects of *Boat People*'s plot is its ability to indicate or anticipate the very reading positions through which the art world of the international festival circuit would comprehend it. This occurs through a narrative foregrounding of the processes through which cultural institutions frame or interpret new work or newsworthy material.

As my point of embarkation for analysis of this particular argument, I want to start at the end of the journey, with that final freeze-frame shot of the two young refugees looking out across the sea. The reproduction of this still as accompaniment to Li Cheuk-to's article in the groundbreaking 1994 anthology *New Chinese Cinemas: Forms, Identities, Politics* makes clear that this is an iconic moment in contemporary

Hong Kong cinema. It is also a powerfully haunting image, one that in the seven years since I first viewed *Boat People* I have been unable to banish from my own mind's eye. In terms of sheer dramatic power it is comparable to (and more than a little reminiscent of) the stunning freeze-frame that ends *Les Quatre cents coups/ The Four Hundred Blows* (François Truffaut, 1959) – another classic social-problem drama and 'controversial' Cannes festival title, concerning an orphan child who ends up gazing out across an endless ocean, an uncertain future ahead.

Boat People's freeze-frame image – presented as the final climactic shot of the entire film – captures and suspends a moment in time. It 'arrests' one fleeting second and offers it up for the viewer's contemplation, if not interrogation. What does this moment mean? What does it represent? However, the shot also has the simultaneous effect of suggesting the very limitations of photography as a medium. Consider the fact that just as folk wisdom is doubtless correct to claim that 'every picture tells a story', it is also true that a picture cannot tell every story. Certainly, this particular still image does not exist in isolation: it carries much cultural and historical baggage – namely, the context provided by the rest of *Boat People's* narrative – which viewers who have watched the entire film will already be aware of.[12] Given this, one of the ways in which this freeze-frame works is as evidence of the static image's inadequacy fully to account for the tragic life and situation of two young Vietnamese refugees (much as the '1997 factor' is unable fully to account for the text–context relation).

Another way of putting this is to say that after being presented with one hundred minutes of dramatic and compelling narrative information, viewers of *Boat People* are now confronted with the 'story' as it will appear in the global media – that is, as a single discourse depicting anonymous 'boat people' as a newsworthy 'social problem'. Ironically, then, at the very moment Akutagawa – the 'world famous' Japanese photojournalist who sacrifices himself in order to save Cam and her young brother – is killed, the film takes upon itself the task of fulfilling the professional and personal goal that drove his actions throughout each prior narrative development. Akutagawa had sought to capture, with a single click of his Nikon camera, the one symbolic image that would sum up the significance of what he saw around him in Vietnam. (His images are destined, in the words of a Party

cadre from the Cultural Bureau, for 'foreign magazines'.) It turns out in the end that Akutagawa himself never gets to take that picture, but the film does still provide it. The final freeze-frame supplies the solitary captivating image Akutagawa had all along hoped would enable the story to travel. The paradoxical nature of this situation is clear. The photograph eventually revealed in the final scene denies the background story of the individual boat people's lives, at the same time as it finally makes their predicament known to the outside world.

By such means, *Boat People* reveals itself to be centrally concerned with the processes through which international journalism frames and presents topical or newsworthy social dramas for overseas consumption. Indeed, this issue is raised explicitly in the very first scene. The re-creation of the liberation of Da Nang in 1975 is achieved through what John Gillett describes as 'a superbly shot victory parade', characteristic of Hui's direction as a whole in that 'the staging is confident and expert with a highly mobile camera'.[13] Camera mobility is the antithesis of the photographic freeze-frame. One represents motion, the other stasis. Here and elsewhere in her work, the means by which Hui's graceful tracking and craning movements are used so as to foreground social and political themes has perhaps been under-appreciated.

Through the lens of Hui's ever-mobile camera, we see Akutagawa taking snapshots of tanks as they roll down the street and crowds of onlookers cheering military muscle as it parades in front of their eyes. What *Boat People* therefore presents, and explores, in this powerful opening scene is an official public spectacle. Moreover, due to Akutagawa's presence as a photojournalist documenting this event for the foreign media, a connection is forged between text and context. The spectacular political display depicted through the staging of this victory parade corresponds to the moment *Boat People* announces itself to be an artwork self-conscious of – and ultimately self-questioning about – its own event status.

On both textual and contextual levels, then, we might say that the story is now able to develop in ways that expose the single discourse, or 'big picture', as insufficient. On the one hand, Akutagawa comes to realise that the NEZ he had been so impressed by is in reality a showpiece constructed for the benefit of foreign onlookers enlisted in the staging of the government's political spectacle. On the other hand, *Boat*

People's own self-critique of its exploration of issues of cross-cultural looking relations provides some indication of why the film may have been an uncomfortable viewing experience for some outside observers.

As a further indication of the interweaving of textual and contextual levels, it is useful to consider what happens at the end of the movie's first scene. Akutagawa walks away from the street where the victory parade is taking place in order to go in search of the one key iconic image he is looking for. His attention is before long drawn to the sight of a small child hobbling pitifully on crutches down a side street. The photojournalist pursues him, perhaps thinking that the boy's maimed physical condition might provide a 'human interest' angle, or could be made to function as a symbol that sums up the 'state of the nation'. Either way, Akutagawa follows the boy. The next scene then cuts to 1978, three years later, when Akutagawa returns to Vietnam and will eventually meet up with Cam and her family. These individuals come to represent the 'reality' Akutagawa searches for behind all the falsehoods he is confronted with by the *apparatchiks* of the state-propaganda machine.

An important theme has been introduced at this point. As we have already seen, Akutagawa, with his desire to snap that one iconic image, may provide the film's requisite narrative drive, but he is far from being the only point of narrative interest. While the young child on crutches depicted early on turns out to be 'unimportant' to the unravelling of the rest of the plot, various other characters will soon be introduced as 'more important'. The development of all of these characters, in turn, allows the film to take a multi-dimensional approach to the subject of the 'boat people'. Tellingly, these separate individuals all represent lives whose existence is not captured in the single discourse of the final freeze-frame image. And because these people are not actually photographed by Akutagawa as he pursues the 'real' story lying beneath the surface of the staged public spectacle, *Boat People* complicates Akutagawa's 'heroic' status by implicitly questioning some of his own motives and actions. Once again, audiences have been invited to identify with a character they may end up having a problematic investment in.

In conclusion, it is worth picking up on the film's awareness of itself as a self-aware political spectacle and public event so as to consider more closely international distribution practices. The narrative of *Boat People* foregrounds the workings of cultural institutions whose job it is to provide discursive frames around 'difficult' media material. Specifically, aside from the phenomenon of international photojournalism, there are the activities of the Vietnam government's Cultural Bureau, which regulates the potentially incendiary symbols created by the foreign photojournalist's Nikon camera. As one party official puts it, the Cultural Bureau's role is to ensure that Akutagawa's photographs cannot be 'misused' once circulated internationally.

Both the structuring centrality of the role cultural institutions play in the framing of 'difficult' visual representations, and the suggestion that the meaning of such representations are contested, and open to 'misuse', suggests an appropriate analogy to the importance of international film festivals. Akutagawa seeks to publish his images of Vietnam overseas; festivals activate multifarious intertextual and historical frames as they project local subject matter for international consumption. However, in this particular case, Cannes, New York and other similar events were in 1983 unwilling to keep afloat a troublesome movie highly self-aware of its own existence as a public political spectacle. This drama was played out against the backdrop of the emergence of a cycle of (mostly) Western films that took a more distanced view on the investigation of the Third World and offered a variety of more standard recuperative pleasures.

To say all of this is not to try to impose a neat sense of closure on the matter at hand. I have sought in this essay to offer a number of claims about why Hui's film was a relative failure at its original sites of overseas exhibition. These claims draw upon issues both internal and external to the 'text' of *Boat People* itself. Yet other ways of reading the film, and other ways of accounting for the significance of its moments(s) of international reception, are no doubt available. In order to further explore the inherent untidiness of the text–context relation, a variety of – variable, even contradictory – critical perspectives need to be advanced. Renewed attention to the interest and importance of *Boat People* should undermine the force of the single discourse, or the 1997 factor, and will hopefully shed new light on the historical relevance of what remains an impressive cinematic achievement.[14]

NOTES

1. Julian Stringer, '*Boat People*', in *Encyclopedia of Chinese Film*, ed. Yingjin Zhang and Zhiwei Xiao (London: Routledge, 1998), 99.

2. Barbara Klinger, 'Film History Terminable and Interminable: Recovering the Past in Reception Studies', *Screen*, 38, no. 1 (1997): 110.

3. Derek Elley, 'Hongkong', in *International Film Guide 1984*, ed. Peter Cowie (London: The Tantivy Press, 1984), 154; Tony Rayns, 'Chinese Changes', *Sight & Sound*, 54, no. 1 (1984/1985): 27.

4. Li Cheuk-to, 'The Return of the Father: Hong Kong New Wave and its Chinese Context in the 1980s', in *New Chinese Cinemas: Forms, Identities, Politics*, ed. Nick Browne, Paul G. Pickowicz, Vivian Sobchack and Esther Yau (Cambridge: Cambridge University Press, 1994), 166, 167, 168. Li's article includes a frame-grab of the movie's final frozen image together with the caption, 'Today's Vietnam as a metaphor for tomorrow's Hong Kong', 168; Stephen Teo, *Hong Kong Cinema: The Extra Dimensions* (London: BFI, 1997), 150–151; Patricia Brett Erens, 'The Film Work of Ann Hui', in *The Cinema of Hong Kong: History, Arts, Identity*, ed. Poshek Fu and David Desser (Cambridge: Cambridge University Press, 2000), 176–195; Leung Ping-kwan, 'Urban Cinema and the Cultural Identity of Hong Kong', in Fu and Desser, *The Cinema of Hong Kong*, 242; John Charles, *The Hong Kong Filmography 1977–1997* (North Carolina: McFarland and Company, 2000), 100.

5. Erens, 'Film Work of Ann Hui'; Elaine Yee-lin Ho, 'Women on the Edges of Hong Kong Modernity: The Films of Ann Hui', in *At Full Speed: Hong Kong Cinema in a Borderless World*, ed. Esther C. M. Yau (Minneapolis: University of Minnesota Press, 2001), 177–206; Law Kar, 'An Overview of Hong Kong's New Wave Cinema', in Fu and Desser, *The Cinema of Hong Kong*, 31–52.

6. Klinger, 'Film History', 113.

7. George E. Marcus and Fred R. Myers, eds, 'The Traffic in Art and Culture: An Introduction', in *The Traffic in Culture: Refiguring Art and Anthropology* (Berkeley: University of California Press, 1995), 31.

8. Mel Tobias, 'Two Views of *T'ou-Pen Nu-Hai* (*Boat People*)', in Cowie, *International Film Guide 1984*, 156.

9. Harlan Kennedy, '*Boat People*', *Film Comment*, 19, no. 5 (1983), 41–43, 47; Erens, 'Film Work of Ann Hui', 184.

10. Claudia Springer, 'Comprehension and Crisis: Reporter Films and the Third World', in *Unspeakable Images: Ethnicity and the American Cinema*, ed. Lester D. Friedman (Urbana: University of Chicago Press, 1991), 168. Hereafter cited in text.

11. 'The major weakness is the central casting: Lam is hopelessly unconvincing as both a Japanese and a professional photographer.' Tony Rayns, '*Boat People*', in *Time Out Film Guide*, tenth edition, ed. John Pym (London: Penguin, 2002), 128.

12. The opposite effect is achieved at the very start of *A Fishy Story* (Anthony Chan, 1991). Here, still photographs of the 1960s anti-colonial riots in Hong Kong – accompanied with great poignancy (especially when we see images of police firing tear gas into the crowd) by the The Platters' classic ballad 'Smoke Gets in Your Eyes' – are juxtaposed with still images of the film's heroine on a shopping spree. These two levels – the political and personal – will be kept in tandem throughout the film, albeit in uneasy combination.

13. John Gillett, 'Two Views of *T'ou-Pen Nu-Hai* (*Boat People*)', in Cowie, *International Film Guide 1984*, 156.

14. A DVD version of *Boat People* with English subtitles was finally released by Edko Films (Hong Kong) in 2008.

6   *Centre Stage*: A Shadow in Reverse

Bérénice Reynaud

Maggie Cheung, star of Stanley Kwan's *Centre Stage*, won a Silver Bear at the 1991 Berlin Film Festival, the first Chinese actress to receive such an award. A few months later, the director's 146-minute cut was reduced to less than two hours for commercial release in Hong Kong.[1] This partial invisibility is poignant, for *Centre Stage* revolves around the search for the missing image of legendary star, Ruan Lingyu, most of whose films have disappeared.[2] It is also a metaphor for another form of hindered vision: the image is *there*, but *not seen*. The second unseen image is that of the Chinese queer subject.[3]

Stanley Kwan 'came out' through his documentary, *Yang + Yin: Gender in Chinese Cinema* (1996). Since then, he has directed performances, another documentary (*A Personal Memoir of Hong Kong*, 1997) and feature films (*Hold You Tight*, 1998; *Island Tales*, 1999; *Lan Yu*, 2001) with gay themes and/or characters. In the context of the frequent denial of *real* homosexual practices in Chinese culture, Kwan's courageous assertion of his sexuality was of paramount importance. It has allowed a number of queer analyses of the work he has completed since 1996, but so far this has not extended to his earlier films.[4]

Until the late 1990s, there were virtually no sympathetic or realistic representations of homosexuals in Hong Kong cinema. Like the left-wing Shanghai film-makers who got round Japanese censorship by inserting coded allusions, gay directors like Kwan resorted to metaphors and *double entendre* to suggest an alternative reading. The most effective strategy in *Centre Stage* is inspired by Foucault's 'reverse discourse' that duplicates and subverts 'the same vocabulary, the same categories by which [homosexuality is] disqualified' and rendered invisible.[5] The denials that structure the film are therefore also *double entendre* asserting *simultaneously* one thing and its opposite 'I know very well, but ...' Three such denials can be identified:

- Ruan Lingyu is not alive (*but* Maggie Cheung is).
- Ruan Lingyu did not live in Hong Kong (*but* she spoke Cantonese).
- Ruan Lingyu is not a man (*but* she is an object of desire and/or identification for male homosexuals).

Such identification maps out a space allowing for queer analysis. As a female spectator with a vested interest in the representation of women, I conduct this analysis *within* the framework of contemporary gender and feminist film theory. First, I examine how the figure of Ruan/Cheung is constructed through the cinematic equivalent of Freud's *fort–da* mechanism. Then I follow how, in the Republican era, 'the immoral woman' and 'the homosexual' were subjected to similar rebukes, ejecting them from what was socially acceptable in Chinese culture. Finally, I decipher the interplay of identification and objectification that connects male subjectivity to the figure of the 'suffering woman' through the double process of denial and displacement described by Tania Modleski: 'the male finds it necessary to repress certain "feminine" aspects of himself, and to project these ... onto the woman, who does the suffering for both of them'.[6]

RUAN LINGYU IS NOT ALIVE

An 'experimental biopic', *Centre Stage* recounts aspects of the life and legend of Ruan Lingyu. One of the most famous Shanghai silent cinema stars, she made her first film at the age of sixteen, and committed suicide at twenty-five on 8 March 1935 – International Women's Day – after being attacked by the media about her relationships with the bankrupt family scion, Zhang Damin, and the wealthy tea merchant, Tang Jishan.

Centre Stage's fragmented texture intertwines fictional reconstructions of Ruan's life with black-and-white video interviews with survivors from the Golden Age of the Shanghai studios and Ruan's biographer, as well as the cast and crew of the contemporary film; excerpts of footage from still-extant films; reconstructions of scenes from lost films; production stills; and photographs. This *mise en abyme* allows several Ruan Lingyus to coexist, diffracting her image to the point of vertigo. Here she appears as Maggie Cheung, there in her role as *The Goddess* (Wu Yonggang, 1934), here again in Cheung's re-creation of the same sequence of *The Goddess*, and finally in black-and-white pictures taken on her deathbed. To 'capture' the elusive 'essence' of the star, Kwan stages several 'mirror scenes' such as the moment when Ruan stands alone at night, gazing at her diffracted reflection. She holds the bowl of *congee* that we have seen her pour two bottles of sleeping pills into. Under the shimmering seduction of appearances, Kwan weaves a dialectic between the visible and the *invisible*. He playfully uses cinema to indulge in a grown-up game of what Freud called '*fort–da*' ('gone–there'), after the exclamations of a little boy throwing and recovering a cotton reel to re-enact and master his mother's departure.[7] Now you see Ruan Lingyu, now you don't – or maybe a little bit of her, a reflection, a copy, or a trace: *mise en scène* creates a symbolic control over the appearance and disappearance of the object of desire.

'Cinema, like the *fort–da* game, constitutes itself as a continually renewed search for a lost plenitude', writes Mary Ann Doane, analysing *Gilda* (Charles Vidor, 1946)[8] – a film with barely disguised homosexual overtones.[9] The questions are: Whose loss? Whose plenitude? And at whose expense? Both *Gilda* and *Centre Stage* stage the punishment of their heroines by wounded and flawed males (Gilda's two husbands, Ruan's two lovers). In *Centre Stage* this also generates a friendly rivalry between the director and his star based on the tacit question, who will *benefit* most from identification with Ruan Lingyu?

Cheung first appears as herself, while off screen Kwan asks if she hopes to be remembered in fifty years. She replies, 'If people do, it'll be different from Ruan, because she is remembered when she was at the pinnacle of her success. She's become a legend.' In his desire to use Cheung as a 'medium' to access the dead star, Kwan seeks overlaps between her and Ruan and to involve her in the (re)construction of her character. Yet Cheung refuses to be seen as an icon. In

turn, her resistance fuels the film's unspoken suggestion: isn't a *man* better equipped to incarnate Ruan Lingyu?

Centre Stage's first narrative sequence takes place in an all-male bathhouse. The camera glides sensuously over the bodies of half-naked men getting massaged, smoking and talking. In *Yang + Yin*, Kwan identifies this moment as a 'marker' of his homosexuality, adding: 'the person who first took me to a bathhouse was my father'. However, Kwan also acknowledges *two* patterns of queer identification. One is defined by the search for intimacy with an older man, the other by his love for gender-bending performances in Cantonese opera (starring women playing male roles), where his *mother* took him. The bathhouse sequence unfolds between allusions to these two 'founding moments'.

First, *before* she appears on the screen, the *fictional* Ruan is already constructed as a *figure of speech to be passed between a chorus of men*. The narrative part of the film is book-ended by two such choruses. The brotherly banter of the beginning corresponds to the film-makers' bonding around Ruan's deathbed. The imaginary brotherhood of Shanghai film-makers is tightly knit first by passing Ruan on from film to film then through the death of 'their' common star.

Second, Kwan introduces a disruptive element: an unnamed young man sashays into the discussion of Ruan's acting abilities. Assuming the comical role of 'the sissy', he offers himself as the melodramatic lead for *Wayside Flowers* (Sun Yu, 1930), in case 'Ruan is not up to scratch'. Rebutted, he replies 'I'll go compare sizes with the others'. On the one hand, he suggests that he could be a *better female impersonator* than Ruan. On the other, he reasserts his manhood through both his desire to look at other men's penises and the existence of his own member. This brief exchange gives an edge to Kwan and Cheung's later conversation, when they good-naturedly compete to impersonate Ruan. An acknowledged director of melodrama (*wenyi pian*), Kwan mimics her saddest poses, while, as a modern young woman, Cheung reproduces her happy smile in *The Peach Girl* (Bu Wancang, 1931).

Some men, gay and straight, think the construction of femininity is too serious a business to be left to women. This attitude may be best exemplified by the tradition of female impersonators (*huadans*) in Peking opera following a 1772 law barring women from the stage. The cognoscenti believed that the exquisite essence of femininity conveyed by the *huadans* was superior to anything a 'real woman' could do. *Centre Stage* poses the question of female impersonation (by men *and* women) in a way that denotes a queer sensibility in 'the awareness of the social constructedness of sex roles',[10] the suspicion that 'gender is a kind of persistent impersonation that passes as the real',[11] or the discovery, as Kwan aptly coins it in *Yang + Yin*, that 'gender need not be a boundary, but can also be a game'. Also queer is the implicit assumption that too-much-femininity may be a mask over masculinity, as in the case of Joan Riviere's patient.[12]

Examples of femininity-as-masquerade abound in the film. When future star Chen Yanyan tells Cheung/Ruan she has heard that in Peiping 'it takes you an hour to do one eyebrow', Cheung splendidly replies, 'in Harbin, it took me two hours'. The gesture of carefully painting an eyebrow over a face reduced to a blank canvas invokes the make-up sessions of the *huadan*. In their stylised femininity, did not the actresses of Shanghai's Golden Age try to compete with the *huadans* who had displaced their forebears? Filmic realism demanded 'an authentic object called "woman" – to be *seen*, and then "known" and "had"'.[13] But where did these bodies copy their version of the feminine from?

Ruan is also shown to face the double bind of fashion and male authority. As she and Tang Jishan are being sued for 'adultery' by her previous lover Zhang Damin, Tang ponders how he should dress to go to court. 'I'll wear a dark suit and a green tie to match that new dress of yours … . I want all Shanghai to know that we are high class adulterers', he says. Ruan replies, 'I live with you, knowing you're married. I admit being a loose woman. What we wear wouldn't make a difference.' Tang slaps her twice.

Later, when a friend invites her to a party that night, Ruan replies, 'Then I must look my best …' and extends her hand to Tang in a conciliatory gesture. However, the tension between them resurfaces at the party when Ruan, dazzling in a superb *cheongsam*, uses the very codes of feminine masquerade he's imposed upon her to upstage him. This is a strategy of 'self-parody' Doane identifies as 'double mimesis'.[14] A bit tipsy, Ruan kisses all the men, speaks too much and dances without restraint. As she utters a mock feminist statement about Women's

Day, Tang protests: 'You women have arisen, whereas we men have fallen.'

Later, Tang falls on the polished floor. Angrily refusing a helping hand, he screams, 'She's my mistress!', while Ruan continues to dance alone. Cheung's exuberant yet dreamlike dancing is spectacular, seeming to express Ruan's silent *jouissance* – a *jouissance* beyond the phallus, 'proper to her and of which herself may know nothing, except that she experiences it'.[15] However, what Cheung imitates is not the body language of the dead star, but that of Stanley Kwan, who had felt the need to demonstrate the appropriate movements,[16] yielding to the pleasure of 'dancing like Ruan Lingyu'. Kwan's performance, covered over by the glamour of his star, was nevertheless a way to experience 'the suicidal ecstasy of being a woman' which Leo Bersani identifies as a component of male gay *jouissance*.[17] By intercutting the party sequence with shots of the wake, Kwan further intimates that the whole 'act' gave its performer such intense pleasure that only death could follow, again closely linking it to male masochism.

While he stages the performance of femininity as a *contest* between women and gay men, Kwan also views it as an essential component of the *impasse sexuelle* between women and straight men. Whether contained and fabricated by the codes of acting or gender roles, or produced to excess as a covert form of retaliation and resistance, femininity is perceived by straight men as a challenge.

Against the grain of his noted sensual filmmaking, Kwan depicts Ruan's affairs as devoid of intimate sensuality; their physicality is reduced to male hysteria from Zhang Damin, abuse from Tang Jishan and emotional withdrawal from Cai Chusheng. Over-evaluated and fetishised, Ruan *can't* be 'possessed' by boorish men who don't 'deserve' her. That husbands and lovers tend to abuse, mistreat and demean 'woman' is a widespread queer belief – as seen in the cult of Judy Garland.[18] Femininity is too serious a business to be left to heterosexuals.

RUAN LINGYU DID NOT LIVE IN HONG KONG
By asking a famous Hong Kong star to embody Ruan Lingyu, Kwan 'reclaims' her by stressing her Cantonese origins. Like the modern Cheung in her conversations with Kwan, her fellow actors and the crew, Ruan speaks Cantonese at home. She uses

Shanghainese for mundane exchanges and to talk with director Bu Wancang, while trying to master Mandarin when speaking to actresses Chen Yanyan and Li Lili. Kwan's oeuvre is thoroughly informed by a sense of fractured Chinese identity, leading to the intimate dialectic between Hong Kong and Shanghai in the 'nostalgic trilogy' formed by *Centre Stage*, *Rouge* (1988) and *Red Rose White Rose* (1994).

Rouge starts with a close-up of Anita Mui (as the courtesan Fleur) carefully making up her face, and segues into a scene in which she sings Cantonese opera in male drag, under the fascinated gaze of a young brothel patron. After committing suicide – on the same date, yet one year earlier, than Ruan[19] – Fleur returns as a ghost fifty-three years later in 1987 Hong Kong.

Red Rose White Rose is an adaptation by noted queer writer and artist Edward Lam, who later wrote *Yang + Yin*'s voice-over, of a novella by Eileen Chang – a cult figure among Chinese intellectuals, especially but not exclusively, in queer circles. Set in 1930s Shanghai, the story explores the relationships of a selfish Chinese businessman, Zhenbao, with two women, his mistress, the passionate adulteress Jiaorui, and his wife, the masochist Yanli.

Nostalgia in these films has been thoroughly analysed,[20] but I will focus on its queer connotations, following Russo's interpretation of the longings expressed by cross-dressing *Queen Christina* (Rouben Mamoulian, 1933) as 'a nostalgia for something [gay people] had never seen on screen'.[21] Similarly, Kwan's investigation of Chinese cinema history in *Yang + Yin* articulated a longing for a symbolic *space* within pan-Chinese culture that would allow queer desire to unfold. However, this longing proves painfully contradictory, as homosexuality had been 'marked' as *un*-Chinese.

In spite of a classical Chinese homosexual tradition, colonial Hong Kong and Republican Shanghai perceived homosexuality as a 'recent importation from the decadent West …. going against traditional Chinese moral concepts'.[22] Moreover, 'prostitution and sodomy represented the two forms of non-procreative sex which needed to be eliminated for the sake of the family and the nation'.[23]

When Ruan Lingyu started acting in 1926, film actresses were equated with loose women and prostitutes. This changed in the 1930s, with increased professionalism in the industry and well-orchestrated publicity campaigns turning movie stars into media darlings. Escaping her working-class background, Ruan attained a glamorous lifestyle – once the privilege of imperial courtesans, who had been downgraded to prostitutes as movie stars now entertained the new urban elites.[24]

In a telling moment, Ruan is at home, rehearsing the role of the prostitute in *The Goddess*, smoking and striking semi-lascivious poses to inhabit her character. As Tang arrives, she blows smoke in his face and imitates the streetwalker's gait. Tang asks if this is her true self. Unruffled, she whispers, 'If Miss Liang upstairs and I were whores, tell me, who would you pick?' The situation might be fictional, yet the anxiety was not, for Tang is depicted as a womaniser.

It is in *New Women* (Cai Chusheng, 1934), where she is cast as Wei Ming, an intellectual who resorts to prostitution to buy medicine for her daughter, that the thin wall between 'acting' and 'being' collapses. The object of a slanderous media campaign much like Ruan herself, Wei Ming commits suicide, but on her hospital bed she has a last surge of energy and vows to live. The scene completed, Ruan/Cheung cries uncontrollably under the sheets. Cai Chusheng/Tony Leung stands uncomfortably by the bed. Kwan steps in: 'You forgot to lift the sheet to look at Maggie.' Who forgot? The fictional Cai? The Hong Kong actor? While a beautiful woman crying for the camera is an object of specular consumption, an excess of sobbing is potentially obscene, for it threatens the boundaries of the acting profession. So, an actress playing a prostitute may think she's become one. Maybe it is better not to look. Now you see her, when she's a star, now you don't, when she's a tart.

In the 1930s, 'movie actresses … were still placed … on this prostitute–courtesan continuum [that] gave them ambiguous status'[25] and put Ruan in the constant risk of 'falling'. Kwan shows her obsessed by the fear that people may not perceive her as a 'good woman'. His 'nostalgic trilogy' creates an association between sexual subjects traditionally thought of as 'bad': the courtesan in *Rouge*, the foreign-born adulteress in *Red Rose White Rose* and the actress in *Centre Stage*. Gliding along this chain, Kwan hides a fourth term, providing a hint with the bathhouse 'sissy'. As much the object of social reprobation as the prostitute, as 'influenced by foreign mores' as the overseas woman, as vulnerable to gossip as the movie star, is the homosexual in Chinese society.

Centre Stage: Maggie Cheung as Ruan Lingyu

Public discourse in the Republican era equally condemned the prostitute, the socially mobile woman and the 'sodomite'. While often coupled with left-wing politics, the upsurge of nationalism caused by the war also gave way to xenophobic tendencies. It was believed that in treaty ports contacts with foreigners put prostitutes at greater risk of disease,[26] while young men were exposed to seduction by Western perverts.

Already *out of place* in 1930s Shanghai, the queer subject is neither here nor there, but has instead the tragic freedom to glide between worlds like a ghost. So Kwan can jump between 1934 and 1987, collapsing Hong Kong into Shanghai in *Rouge*[27] or creating a scintillating game of equivalences between 1930s Shanghai and 1990s Hong Kong in *Centre Stage*. For, if 'stories about Hong Kong always turned into stories about somewhere else',[28] the 'negative hallucination (not seeing what is there)' facilitates the queer

strategy of now you show it, now you don't. The moralising discourse of the 1930s 'was meant to exclude and delegitimise anyone who might become … influential through the medium of film – [a goal achieved] via the trope of "woman"'.[29] It attacked film actresses to take aim at an ineluctable modernity. By reversing the trope, a gay director may also reverse the exclusion. You thought you saw the victimisation of a woman – while I showed you the trials of a gay man.

RUAN LINGYU IS NOT A MAN

And yet Maggie Cheung triumphantly and effortlessly wins the contest with Kwan. As he fights as a director does with his star, he also gives her literally 'room to breathe', for example when the camera captures her breathing on the fictional Ruan's deathbed, and then sitting up laughing. However, this perpetual oscillation between different sides of the representation was hard on Cheung: 'To play Ruan Lingyu, Stanley and I agreed on one thing ... she had to wear a mask at all time .... So I find my acting a little fake, hieratic .... Stanley wanted this alienation effect, he wanted representation to be visible as a process.'[30]

However, the effectiveness of Cheung's presence in the film goes beyond mere equivalence to Ruan. Like the *xiuyang* (mystique) of the Shanghai actresses of the 1930s, her charisma retains its opacity. So far, literature on the fascination of gay men for female movie stars has been limited to the West: Garbo, Dietrich or Garland. There is no such scholarship on the cult of Ruan. About one hundred thousand mourners attended her funeral,[31] and some *young men* committed suicide.[32] However, 'the majority of these mourners were women, especially female students'.[33] So, what does this say about the young men who 'adored Ruan'? At this stage, nothing. The queer subject was not only invisible, but he was also silent.

If the cult of certain movie stars has become a code of recognition for gay men in the West, has Ruan Lingyu's played a similar role in contemporary Hong Kong? *Yang + Yin* lists some of the denials encountered by Kwan when tracking down possible signs of queerness in Chinese cinema: 'I've never taken Brigitte Lin as anything but female' (film archivist Law Kar); 'You cannot project modern attitudes onto the friendship between two Peking opera actors' (Chen Kaige, director of *Farewell My Concubine*); 'We Chinese see this kind of relationship differently from Westerners' (veteran director Xie Jin); 'No Chinese reader thinks of homosexuals when he reads *Romance of the Three Kingdoms*' (martial-arts film director Chang Che). At the core of these denials is a suspicion of Western-induced modernity, which ejects the queer subject outside 'Chinese culture'. On the other hand, woman *is* marginalised as a subject, but as a figure of speech, she is *at the centre* of the discourse on the effects of modernity. So the female movie star, as the site of multiple contradictions, provides the Chinese queer subject with a possible anchor for identification.

Centre Stage explores many avenues through which this identification is possible. The issue of mask is central for gay men, who view 'performance [as] an everyday issue, whether in terms of passing as straight [or], signaling gayness in coming out ...'.[34] Although Ruan's female masquerade is mostly performed for the benefit of men, Kwan throws clues that subvert this reading. When Ruan and Chen Yanyan discuss make-up, they achieve a subtle bonding, 'which demonstrates the masquerade's potential to draw women closer together and to function as non-verbal homoerotic expression'.[35] In several instances, Ruan is seen dancing with other young actresses, with whom she seems freer and more at ease than with men. At the final party, however, she theatrically overplays her heterosexuality by loudly announcing she 'won't kiss the girls'.

Another clue occurs when Ruan interviews another actress about the pain of childbirth – something she *knows* she will never experience herself – and explains her decision to adopt a little girl, Xiaoyu. Thus, the family composed of Ruan, her mother, Xiaoyu and first lover Zhang Damin resembles a gay household. Zhang plays the role of a kept lover and Ruan, who keeps writing expenses in her ledger, is the responsible breadwinner. This role reversal continues throughout, with Ruan taking more 'masculine' responsibilities: she 'directs' her partner Li Lili in a crucial scene in *Little Toys* (Sun Yu, 1933), convinces Bu Wancang to let her play a more socially conscious role, and asks director Cai Chusheng to elope with her. While humouring Tang Jishan by pretending to be his kept mistress, she was actually financially independent.[36]

The mechanism of identification with a female actress/character by a male subject is complex, especially for films that foreground female suffering. The subjective position of the gay man complicates matters further, for his 'denial of the feminine' differs from that of the male heterosexual subject. His ambivalence toward femininity is best exemplified by the 'bifurcated position' of the bathhouse 'sissy' (identification, competition *and* phallocentrism). Moreover, queer subjects are often faced with a situation unknown to heterosexuals: the impossibility of identifying with a mirror image on the screen, where they are only constructed as *absent*. To draw a parallel with other misrepresented minorities, how is the Chinese queer subject 'sutured into a place that includes [him] only as a term of negation? *What* does [he] identify with when his own mirror image is structurally absent or present only as an Other?' This could be the explanation for James Baldwin's 'adolescent identification with Bette Davis',[37] since images of black gay men were unavailable on screen.

Reading Lacan, Kaja Silverman stresses that it is through fantasy that the subject learns both how to desire and to build an identity. The two are 'complexly imbricated' through 'the insertion of the subject into a particular syntax or tableau', so the subject can only exist if under the gaze of the Other, as well while 'assuming a position within the *mise en scène* of desire'.[38] A subject whose desiring identity keeps being denied and/or rendered invisible has no other recourse than to project himself into a specular fantasy. While there are many avenues to queerness, including those far removed from feminine identification, recent scholarship has focused on the feminisation that overplayed male theatricality entails: 'masquerading as a man' feminises the 'macho' wearer's relation to the costume.[39] These analyses strengthen Silverman's thesis that 'woman seem[s] to function at times not only as the focus of gay identification, but as the pivot of gay desire'.[40]

What is more problematic – and interesting – is the *internalisation* by the queer subject of this feminine *mise en scène*. Of the variety of ways this phenomenon has been analysed, the one that concerns us here is narcissistic object-choice of 'what [the subject] once was' and/or 'someone who was once part of himself',[41] a process made more complex by the congruence between object of desire and object of identification. Identification and desire rest on the loss of both the little boy that the subject once was – and his mother loved – and the first object he ever lost – his mother.

Ruan Lingyu, the lost object par excellence of Chinese cinema, becomes a stand-in for all these losses. By mourning her, Kwan identifies with the mainstream Chinese culture that outlaws his queerness; with the community of film-makers, husbands and lovers that used her 'glamour value' to strengthen their male bonds; and with all the Chinese gay men and women that secretly identify with her. By mourning her, he also mourns himself – what he never was, what he has lost without even ever possessing it.

The *pleasure* caused by *Centre Stage* stems from Kwan's ability to simultaneously play on several registers – while anchoring himself in the *wenyi pian* 'melodrama' tradition. *Centre Stage* may be the story of a female impersonator who thought s/he was Ruan Lingyu, who, in turn, thought she was Maggie Cheung. Or it may be the story of a modern Hong Kong actress who is asked to play a star of the past,

as the latter discovers that she was only 'playing' at being Ruan Lingyu. 'Truth' lies in this interplay of surfaces and *trompe l'oeil*, this collage of eras, cities, genres and media, this hall of mirrors in which identity is many times diffracted and only exists as seduction.

NOTES

1. This essay is based on the director's cut.
2. Kwan mentions ten films, five of them 'lost'. Since 1991, four other films starring Ruan have been recovered.
3. Chinese lesbian representation is beyond the scope of this essay. Here, I refer to the 'Chinese queer subject' in the masculine only.
4. Existing texts on *Centre Stage* include: Natalia Chan Shui Hung, 'Memory, Gender, History: Female Sensitivity and Queer Spectatorship of Stanley Kwan's Films' ('Jiyi, xingbie, lishi: lun Guan Jin-peng dianying di nuxingchujue yu kuyiguanzhao') in *City on the Edge of Time: Gender, Special Effect, and the 1997 Politics of Hong Kong Cinema* (*Shengshi di bianyuan: Xianggang dianying di xingbie, teji, yu jiuqi zhengzhi*) (Hong Kong: Oxford University Press, 2002), 43–72; Shuqin Cui, 'Stanley Kwan's *Center Stage*: The (Im)possible Engagement between Feminism and Postmodernism', *Cinema Journal*, 39, no. 4 (2000): 60–80; various essays in *Stanley Kwan: la via orientale al melodrama*, ed. Giovanni Spagnoletti, Alessandro Bori and Olaf Möller (Pesaro: Fondazione Pesaro Nuovo Cinema/Il Castoro, 2000); and Julian Stringer, '*Centre Stage*: Reconstructing the Bio-Pic', *Cinemaction*, no. 42 (1997): 28–39. Queer analyses of Kwan's work include Helen Hok-sze Leung, 'A Time to Dance: Stanley Kwan's Queer Fable of 1997 Past' (paper presented at the After the End – Hong Kong Culture After 1997 conference, UCLA, 26 May 2001); Yau Ching, 'Bisexuality and Duality in *Hold You Tight*', *Cinedossier: The 35th Golden Horse Award-Winning Films* (Taipei: National Film Archive, 1999), 116–122. Since the original writing of this text, Mette Hjort has written a monograph on *Centre Stage* (Hong Kong: Hong Kong University Press, 2006).
5. Michel Foucault, *The History of Sexuality*, vol. 1 (New York: Vintage Books, 1980), 101.
6. Tania Modleski, *The Women Who Knew Too Much* (London: Methuen, 1988), 13.
7 Sigmund Freud, *Beyond the Pleasure Principle* (New York: Norton, 1961), 8–9.

8. Mary Ann Doane, '*Gilda:* Epistemology as Strip-Tease', *Femmes Fatales* (London: Routledge, 1991), 102.

9. Vito Russo, *The Celluloid Closet* (New York: Harper & Row, 1987), 78–79.

10. Richard Dyer, *Heavenly Bodies* (New York: St Martin's Press, 1986), 178.

11. Judith Butler, *Gender Trouble* (London: Routledge, 1999), xxviii.

12. Joan Riviere, 'Womanliness as Masquerade', *The Inner World and Joan Riviere* (London: Karnac Books, 1991), 90–101.

13. Michael G. Chang, 'The Good, the Bad and the Beautiful: Movie Actresses and Public Discourse in Shanghai, 1920s–1930s', in *Cinema and Urban Culture in Shanghai 1922–1943*, ed. Yingjin Zhang (Stanford, CA: Stanford University Press, 1999), 129.

14. Mary Ann Doane, *The Desire to Desire* (Bloomington: Indiana University Press, 1987), 181.

15. Jacques Lacan, 'God and the Jouissance of the Woman', in *Feminine Sexuality*, ed. Juliet Mitchell and Jacqueline Rose (London: Norton, 1982), 145.

16. Interview with Kwan, April 1997.

17. Leo Bersani, 'Is the Rectum a Grave?', *October*, no. 43 (1987): 212.

18. Dyer, *Heavenly Bodies*, 141–194.

19. Ackbar Abbas, *Hong Kong, Culture and the Politics of Disappearance* (Minneapolis: University of Minnesota Press, 1997), 45.

20. Ibid., 39–47; Leo Ou-fan Lee, *Shanghai Modern* (Cambridge, MA: Harvard University Press, 1999), 335–338; Kristine Harris, 'The *New Woman* Incident', in *Transnational Chinese Cinemas*, ed. Sheldon Hsiao-peng Lu (Honolulu: University of Hawaii Press, 1997), 198; Rey Chow, 'A Souvenir of Love', in *At Full Speed*, ed. Esther C. M. Yau (Minneapolis: University of Minnesota Press, 2001), 209–229.

21. Russo, *Celluloid Closet*, 66.

22. Bret Hinsch, *Passions of the Cut Sleeve* (Berkeley: University of California Press, 1990), 165.

23. Frank Dikötter, *Sex, Culture and Modernity in China* (Hong Kong: Hong Kong University Press, 1995), 137.

24. Chang, 'The Good, the Bad and the Beautiful', 150.

25. Ibid., 157.

26. Dikötter, *Sex, Culture and Modernity*, 127–130.

27. Lee, *Shanghai Modern*, 335.

28. Abbas, *Hong Kong*, 25.

29. Chang, 'The Good, the Bad and the Beautiful', 140.

30. *Libération*, 4 December 1999, interview with J. M. Lalanne.

31. Harris, ' The *New Woman* Incident', 291.

32. Shu Kei, '*La Légende de Ruan Lingyu*', in *Le Cinéma chinois*, ed. Marie Claire Quiquemelle and Jean-Loup Passek (Paris: Centre Georges Pompidou, 1984), 149–154.

33. Chang, 'The Good, the Bad and the Beautiful', 297, note 88.

34. Richard Dyer, 'Believing in Fairies: The Author and the Homosexual', in *Inside Out*, ed. Diana Fuss (London: Routledge, 1991), 188.

35. Chris Straayer, 'The Hypothetical Lesbian Heroine in Narrative Feature Film', in *Multiple Voices in Feminist Film Criticism*, ed. Diane Carson, Linda Dittmar and Janice R. Welsch (Minneapolis: University of Minnesota Press, 1994), 351.

36. Chang, 'The Good, the Bad and the Beautiful', 297, note 93.

37. Isaac Julien and Kobena Mercer, 'De Margin and De Center', *Screen* 29, no. 4 (1988): 9.

38. Kaja Silverman, *Male Subjectivity at the Margins* (New York: Routledge, 1992), 6–7.

39. See, in particular, Jamie Gough, 'Theories of Sexual Identities and the Masculinization of the Gay Man', in *Coming on Strong: Gay Politics and Culture*, ed. Simon Shepherd and Mick Wallis (London: Unwin, 1989), 121.

40. Silverman, *Male Subjectivity at the Margins*, 355.

41. Sigmund Freud, 'On Narcissism: An Introduction', *General Psychological Theory* (New York: Collier, 1963), 71.

7 *A Chinese Ghost Story*: Ghostly Counsel and Innocent Man

John Zou

Whenever ghosts appear on a screen, we realise, intuitively and without hesitation, that they are going to do something. For all the illuminated or closed depths they suggest beyond this world of ours, ghosts cannot be described as contemplative beings. In that sense, ghost stories are always strangely human stories. Ghosts may act strangely, but we know what the strangeness is about. They are action figures of a special kind. However, the consequences of this reciprocity are not happy, for ghostly rationality tends to drive humans out of their wits. Ghosts may take different approaches but they all send one message: your life is in strange hands.

Maybe this is why we have flocked to the movies in modern times, savouring the maddening moments of our life embraced by the Other. We are not only scared stiff by ghostly liminality, but also immensely attracted to their predatory appetite that shocks us into living, into demanding our own being. It is not enough to reiterate Benjamin's idea that as messengers of death, ghosts impart counsels of great authority to the living.[1] In ghost stories, we, the frightened listeners, the barely breathing audience, are often more ghostly than human. Is it not we who have developed this insatiable appetite for human life that seems, alas, denied to us? Is it not true that it is ultimately 'we' who desperately want 'us'? The exceptional joy of scary movies is mischievously autoerotic. It registers the foreignness of our own touch on our half-numb bodies.

GHOSTS ARE US

This essay studies how the Hong Kong film *A Chinese Ghost Story* (1987) rhetorically positions and constitutes its audience in anticipation of the colonial city's traumatic repatriation in 1997. I employ the basic Lacanian notion of symbolic castration to discuss the anxious ghostly acquisition of 'live humanity', gendered male in the film and an element

perceived as fantastically complementary to the abject lack that energises an audience in need of masculine conquest. Beyond existing interpretations that emphasise the film's narrative and visual hybridity and innovation,[2] I highlight the configuration of masculine and feminine identities at the centre of the visual imaginary concerning 'post'-colonial Hong Kong.

In *Men, Women, and Chain Saws*, Carol Clover argues that the cinematic constitution of the male gaze and subsequent male embodiment for the audience in the horror film may be facilitated by identification with a female victim-hero.[3] Moving beyond this thesis of cross-sexual identification, however, I argue that in *A Chinese Ghost Story* the cinematic subject's assumption of female embodiment and obsession with the acquisition of manhood manifest male homoerotic moments in the 'post'-colonial making of an allegedly 'straight' male gaze. Furthermore, the invitation of male conquest by the 'feminised' audience becomes a particularly compelling trope of political negotiation when it is reframed as an amorous process of seduction and castration. In the disorientating historical context of the Hong Kong handover, I argue that seduction and castration register an ambiguous instrument of political engagement counterbalancing the tremendous weight of British and mainland Chinese powers of domination and conquest.

Since its 1987 release, *A Chinese Ghost Story* has become a cult classic of Hong Kong cinema. Its memorable music, outrageous randomness and fleeting eroticism precipitated two sequels and numerous imitations. Indeed, it is often said to represent the pinnacle of Hong Kong horror. Partly because of its impact, the retrospective section at the 13th Hong Kong International Film Festival in 1989 was dedicated to the ghost film. Although the film seems to haphazardly combine romance, martial arts and period drama, its programmatic imprudence, excessive self-mockery and dizziness resulting from hasty production all contribute to a uniquely potent configuration of sexuality, history and contemporary Hong Kong politics. A remake of an earlier picture, the film's prominent literary origin is a familiar episode in *Strange Stories from a Chinese Studio*, an eighteenth-century compilation of ghost stories and a favourite sourcebook for ghostly reverie in Hong Kong cinema. The story relates a young man's solitary encounter with a female ghost in a desolate place.[4] At the most accessible level, the film takes the form of a quest narrative. A young tax collector, Ning Caichen (Leslie Cheung), sojourns in a haunted temple and thus subjects himself to the mercy of a beautiful female ghost, Nie Xiaoqian (Joey Wang), and a cohort of zombies. These zombies are human victims wasted by her bloodsucking master, the hermaphroditic Tree Monster by the name of Lao Lao or, literally, 'Grandma'. Yet because of Caichen's innocent respect for her body and his feeble but sincere effort to keep her out of harm's way, Xiaoqian falls in love with him, and entrusts herself to him for delivery from Lao Lao and a prospective marriage to a more terrifying figure – the Black Monster. Also resident at the temple is a powerful Taoist hermit, Yan, who prefers the company of ghosts to human troubles. Finally, with the Taoist's help, Caichen succeeds in defeating Lao Lao and the Black Monster and sends Xiaoqian away for reincarnation and a new life.

According to Carol Clover:

> Students of folklore or early literature recognize in horror the hallmarks of oral narrative: the free exchange of themes and motifs, the archetypal characters and situations, the accumulation of sequels, remakes, imitations. This is a field in which there is in some sense no original, no real or right text, but only variants; a world in which, therefore, the meaning of the individual example lies outside itself.[5]

To greatly simplify the folklorist Vladimir Propp's basic terms, the narrative of the film may be said to consist of four classes of characters: the hero, Caichen, who sets out on a journey to acquire his desired prize; the prize, Xiaoqian, whose acquisition testifies to the hero's success and full self-realisation; the donor, Yan, with whose help the hero accomplishes his mission and fulfils his identity as hero; and

the villainous guardian, Lao Lao/Black Monster, who initially blocks the hero's acquisition of the prize and then yields to the additional power he receives from the donor.[6] However, such a structural interpretation is only true to a limited extent. Those who are familiar with *A Chinese Ghost Story* may be aware that, in the end, it is revealed that the female ghost's interest in the travelling man far precedes and exceeds his interest in her. Caichen's initial attraction to Xiaoqian's music playing and personal charm is in fact a scenario she has orchestrated as a fatal scheme. In that first meeting between them, his love for her is not awakened by her 'spontaneous' presence but indeed conditioned by her premeditated and seductive design. His need for her is programmed to fulfil her objective of turning him into a sacrifice to Lao Lao. Therefore, we have also to acknowledge that the quest narrative works in both directions. It is not just a mundane and male-centred romance where 'boy sees girl, and boy gets girl'. At a less obvious, but certainly more primordial level, we may read an extraordinary ghostly quest in which 'girl sees boy, and girl gets boy'. Caichen's pursuit of Xiaoqian is always situated within a larger context in which he plays only a passive and compliant role. In Clover's terms, one may say that by identifying with the subject of both narratives, the audience is at once Caichen and Xiaoqian, male and female, conqueror and conquered.

The fact that Caichen, the boyish man, constitutes the ultimate object of desire is further demonstrated at the end of the movie, when his romance with Xiaoqian concludes with her departure. Whereas her loving gaze that has so far directed and framed the audience's attention on him is now formally withdrawn, Caichen nevertheless still occupies the centre of the screen. The last shot of the movie follows him and Yan riding off towards an open pasture under a rainbow. Besides the emotional catharsis and sublimation mediated through the disappearance of the female and ghostly figure, the importance of this seemingly impersonal and objective look of the camera moves the audience to take the position left open by Xiaoqian. Indeed, when Xiaoqian's desire for Caichen ceases to stage him as the object of desire, the film exposes the tenacious persistence of its audience's own fascination with such a male figure. Of course, like Xiaoqian's, this parting look by the audience at Caichen is filled with a sense of longing and discontent. But whereas Xiaoqian's unrequited love opens up a space of desire in which he is situated, the movie's structural longing for him seems to indicate the necessity for narrative continuation. Predictably, in the box-office driven Hong Kong cinema, both the cinematic character Caichen and its actor Leslie Cheung would soon be reincarnated for further commercial and narrative exploitation. In that partially sublimated but also somewhat ominous parting shot of Caichen, one could almost be sure that he was to be accosted by other ghosts down the road. *A Chinese Ghost Story* was followed by two successful sequels, and Leslie Cheung was soon cast in another equally, if not more famous, Hong Kong ghost movie, *Rouge* (1988), in which he is remembered and pursued by the spectre of his youthful lover fifty years after her death.[7]

What becomes clear in this reiteration of the desiring characters of Xiaoqian, the impersonal camera and the female lead in *Rouge* is that the immediately evident quest narrative of male agency is situated within a framing narrative, in which the male protagonist serves as a rather passive object of desire with predetermined functions. Behind the

masks of Xiaoqian and the figure of Caichen are pre-designated functions operative in a larger context that Clover compares to the folkloric in her discussion of slashers or low-genre horror movies in the West. Citing Andrew Britten's remark that '[The] highly ritualistic and formulaic character is the most striking feature of contemporary entertainment film', she argues that the modern Western horror genre consists of a 'set of fixed tale types that generate an endless shadow of what are in effect variants: sequels, remakes, rip-offs'.[8] The limitation of her reading, from the perspective of *A Chinese Ghost Story*, is twofold. First, when interpreting the female identification by the male audience as an essentially masochistic process that contributes to the constitution of male subjectivity, she largely lays aside the issue that whereas the male audience may cross the boundary of sex to assume cinematic womanhood, the same 'straight' male cohort may also cross the boundary of sexuality to assume a homosexual position in their quest for masculine self-realisation. Citing Kaja Silverman, Clover agrees that 'it is always the victim – the figure who occupies the passive position – who

A Chinese Ghost Story: Caichen and Xiaoqian

is really the focus of attention, and whose subjugation the subject (whether male or female) experiences as a pleasurable repetition of his/her own story', and that 'the fascination of the sadistic point of view is merely that it provides the best vantage point from which to watch the masochistic story unfold'.[9] What is important in the present context is that when the cinematic gaze is focused upon Leslie Cheung, a gay man playing the heterosexual lead, the masochist identification with his threatened body by a 'straight' audience is inevitably correlated with a male homosexual projection of desire, for which the Final Boy constitutes the object of passion rather the designation of the self.

Second, the folkloric reading, though mindful of larger structures of social discourse and process, is somewhat underdeveloped to account for catalytic and revolutionary moments of historical trauma. The Hong Kong horror genre in the last two decades of the twentieth century, for all its borrowings from Western vampire themes and classical Chinese ghost stories, specifically addresses subject formation under the shadow of agonising and riveting anticipation of radical socio-political change – Hong Kong's 'post'-colonial repatriation. Here, the source of anxiety is not so much the reconfiguration of pre-existing structures as the advent of the absolutely new. In the following pages, I provide an analysis that may lead to some tangible means to critically engage this political and psychological subject and assess its formative impact upon colonial Hong Kong's imagination of its own terminal moment. Clover's Final Girl, the sole survivor among numerous dead female and male bodies, serves as a pivotal link that allows the cinematic gaze to assume male subjectivity through exhilarating pains gendered as female. In contrast, I argue that in the Final Boy – rather than the Final Girl – embodied in the charismatic Leslie Cheung, Hong Kong sets up a lucky, innocent but helplessly gullible, imperialist figure, to be eternally staged, tantalised and seduced by a feminised Hong Kong undergoing repeated colonising ravishment. The presumed straight male gaze of the cinematic subject undergoes a similar process of masochistic self-articulation, not through identification with a female final survivor, but by projecting a feminised passion by which the want for men is satisfied through a seemingly passive but indeed predatory entrapment.

MALE DIFFERENCE: THE EDIBLE AND THE LOVABLE

The modernist message of ghostly narratives may ultimately concern the Lacanian law regarding being versus having.[10] According to Lacan, the acquisition of language – fundamental to the achievement of human subjectivity – presupposes a fundamental loss of unmediated connection to material reality, which the linguistic subject tries forever to recuperate. He names the acquisition of language the symbolic stage of the subject's development and likens that fundamental loss to castration. Because of this loss, the subject may only 'have', but not 'be', what it is distanced from: the dimension of materiality to which the pre-linguistic infant had spontaneous access. In her adaptation of this Lacanian insight in the seminal *Powers of Horror*, Kristeva states that

> [t]he abject of the self would be the culminating form of that experience of the subject to which it is real that all its objects are based merely on the inaugural *loss* that laid the foundations of its own being. There is nothing like the abjection of self to show that all abjection is in fact recognition of the *want* on which any being, meaning, language, or desire is founded.[11]

For Kristeva, horror or its vehicle, the abject, is fundamentally an experience that brings the subject back into proximity with what the subject has to expel from itself in order to establish itself. Abjection is designated as an ambiguous process precisely because the desirable is here intrinsically related to the repellent.

In modern horror cinema, maybe since *Nosferatu* (Murnau, 1922), ghostly figures mark ambiguity for cinemagoers precisely because they are both attractive and disgusting, and because they are attracted to and disgusted by their own objects of desire. Like linguistic subjects, they are forever in pursuit of live human bodies, as the latter may provide some form of material complement. The haunted Lanruo temple, the allegorical Hong Kong, is a breeding ground for just such forlorn ghosts neurotically waiting for male blood and lively being. There is an unambiguous preference among the ghostly population in the film for male blood and, together with it, male essence. Female victims do exist, but they are not sucked dry, as if their blood does not yield the same relished taste. Furthermore, in comparison to the wasted men, who are consistently turned into zombies and left in desolate places such as the temple, the female ghosts – the undead women – are at least selectively treated with favour by Lao Lao. They become members of his/her murderous retinue and reside in illusory but swanky houses, such as the one where Caichen's erotic rendezvous with Xiaoqian takes place. In the business of blood sucking, therefore, gender difference conforms unconventionally to the difference between object and subject. Whereas the coveted object is male essence, without which man becomes a zombie and loses his sexual identity, the desiring agency is perversely highlighted as female: Lao Lao is half-female, as indicated by the almost equal distribution of his/her voice between male and female registers; and his/her entourage seems to consist only of female ghosts. Since the victimisation of men is prominently gendered as a female enterprise, the zombies' attempt on Caichen's life, by following the 'female' routine of blood sucking, serves only a female agenda.

This ghostly economy of consumption in human fodder, gruesome as it is, has counsel for the audience. An ideologically conformist project, the movie trains us to desire and mystify a certain version of manhood, and warns against its unhappy loss. Even in the ghostly world, the unethical loss of manhood is punished more severely than its mere absence. A good ghost, such as Xiaoqian, is redeemable. A bad ghost, such as Xiaoqian's 'sister', exercises supernatural powers, such as flying. But zombies, once men, either languish in that eternal want for manhood, or are haplessly crushed without compensation, as indicated in Caichen's (non)encounter with them at the temple. Furthermore, within the category of desirable men, there is a crucial distinction between Caichen and earlier visitors to the temple. Those visitors were turned into zombies for one main reason: their inability to resist Xiaoqian's ethereal charms. Caichen, however, is represented as exceptional when he manifests a certain unresponsiveness to her sexual form. Xiaoqian only withdraws her attempt on Caichen's life, allowing herself to note his other admirable qualities, when she recognises this strangeness in Caichen, which the movie – and then she – apparently interprets as 'heterosexual innocence'. In an interpretive leap, Caichen's deficiency in heterosexual responsiveness is understood as his surplus in heterosexual charm. When he fails to express interest in her

heterosexual advances – indeed for that reason – the Chinese Final Boy does not look too different from the Western Final Girl in her sexual inactivity. Unsurprisingly, Leslie Cheung's gay escapades were already common knowledge by this time, thanks to the tireless Hong Kong paparazzi.

'Heterosexual innocence' is not only a factor in Caichen's disinterested moral self-possession, but also an important self-defence protecting him from being devoured by his ghostly neighbours. Translatable into his male physical integrity, this moment of heterosexual default also lays the ground for the transformation of Caichen's vulnerable male body into an entirely different figure of desirability. His innocence converts her evil obsession with his physical body into a romantic and therefore positive fascination with his emotional, intellectual and spiritual being. Xiaoqian stops seeing him as a food item and begins desiring his attention, company and ultimately his help in delivering her from indenture to Lao Lao and the prospect of marriage to Black Monster. Caichen's heterosexual innocence thus miraculously turns him from wretched victim into a benefactor with considerable leverage over Xiaoqian.

If manhood is made the focus of attention and the ultimate figure of desire in *A Chinese Ghost Story*, innocent manhood is even more so, because it inspires a higher denomination of desire. A man is but meat, and thus a matter of mere digestive and nutritional consideration for a ghost. An innocent man, however, can be a ghost's lover, benefactor and superior. Caichen goes from being an object of palatal attachment to one of sentimental attachment. As an innocent man, he renders the ghost an exceptional service. A ghost remains a ghost while consuming licentious and ordinarily heterosexual men, but she acquires a chance to be reincarnated as a human when she is consumed by the love for an innocent and exceptionally 'heterosexual' man. A man's lack of heterosexual response is therefore the definitive apparatus that distinguishes a lovable man from an edible man. As a movie, *A Chinese Ghost Story* celebrates Caichen's triumphant metamorphosis from food to conqueror of evil, though at the behest and always to the benefit of his ghostly lover. The ghostly counsel to the innocent male conqueror therefore reads: 'Desire not my body, but my soul.'

There is one further point to be made about the figure of male heterosexual innocence. Given its false

materiality, attraction to the ghost's form is by definition vain. In not fixating upon this form and in seeing
through that medium into the depth of the ghost's
'body', Caichen, the innocent and therefore dubiously
heterosexual man, not only discovers Xiaoqian's
'heart', the locus of her real worth as a caring and vulnerable woman. He also discovers us, the audience for
whom Xiaoqian's ghostly appearance functions as our
mask, our concealment. The astonishing fantasy of *A
Chinese Ghost Story* is not one in which man redeems
ghost, or ghost seizes man, but one about Caichen in
love with us. Functioning as some external and separate form of power and figured as the Lacanian pound
of mortgaged flesh, he miraculously comes into lively
connection with us and willingly attaches himself to
us, to our invisible and therefore ghostly bodies in dire
need of a physical complement.

However, the desiring agency of the ghostly
women also takes on a distinctly masculine gender
within the Lacanian scenario, where the having of
phallus – as inscribed in the pursuit of Caichen – is
conventionally represented as male, whereas the being
of such phallus – Caichen himself – is female. To the
extent that Caichen is a figure to be had by Xiaoqian
and the audience, he is fundamentally correlated with
that inaugural loss (or rejection) that makes possible
the cinematic subject. In this sense, Caichen incar-
nates a typically vulnerable woman embodied as man.
The ghostly women, on the other hand, reveal a forbidding male countenance. Particularly in the figure
of Lao Lao, we witness a phallic mother capable of
penetrating or castrating men.[12]

HEART OF GHOSTLINESS

Critics and fans of Hong Kong cinema agree that *A
Chinese Ghost Story* is one heck of a ghost story. However, to describe it as a statement about colonialism
may raise some eyebrows. Where is the international
relevance? Who are the colonised? What constitutes
the economic incentive? To answer such queries, one
has only to turn to the film's conspicuous conquest
themes. An audience familiar with Conrad's Africa
may appreciate the irresistible attraction of the dark,
oppressive world of the spectral beings, its intrinsic
madness, and the necessity for a drastic final departure on the part of the sane 'humans'.[13] There is also
romance: the film is about a languid female member
of the ghostly tribes falling in love with a vibrant
male intruder and betraying her own kind. Behind

her lie unspeakable intrigues, savageness and cruelty.
With him stands triumphant 'human' technology:
Sanskrit sutras, martial arts and a weapon called 'love'
that is capable of melting Turandot's heart. Stepping
into the heart of darkness, the intruder brings with
him not just satisfaction but also therapy. He gives
her happiness, but he also gives her a cure. On the
other hand, there is the constant possibility of the
intruder's own victimisation. He who enters the dark
world by accident is under the constant threat of
being consumed by darkness. Caichen could be food
for Lao Lao at any point before he/she is finally
defeated. To redeem Xiaoqian, Caichen makes a
heroic exertion for which he can never be adequately
rewarded. In the end, the narrative of colonial self-
making is also central to the film. Whereas Xiaoqian's
world remains in general ghostly and Caichen's friv-
olous, there is a magic mutual recognition that elevates them both. Caichen comes out of the ordeal not
just a seasoned warrior against the forces of darkness,
but also more of a man: sublimated, wiser and better
prepared to meet with troubles in his future. Conquest here is represented as a formative experience, a
Bildungsroman.

But what does it mean for such a story of
(con)quest to be placed within a reversed framing
narrative? Whereas the ghostly audience of Hong
Kong cinema implied in *A Chinese Ghost Story* comes
forth as a coveted object of desire in Caichen's eyes,
Caichen's quest for Xiaoqian obviously becomes
meaningful only within Xiaoqian's primordial quest
for him. Why does the positioning of Xiaoqian, our
surrogate cinematic subject or audience, have to
assume the narrative forms of a (con)quest of herself?

To answer these questions, we have to revisit the
fundamental ambiguity and transgression of the
ghostly beings, most sensationally articulated in the
monstrous person of Lao Lao. Between Xiaoqian and
Lao Lao there is a ghostly community torn between
agendas to save and destroy men. Like the colonising
figure, Caichen, who is also both masculine and feminine, the ghostly world is never one and the same,
but always divided between rejection and invitation,
and between murderous hatred of and sentimental
longing for the intruder. If we take Xiaoqian and Lao
Lao as two aspects of the self-same colonised subject,
they complement each other in such a way that the
conventional colonial object of desire becomes immediately recognisable.

As Homi Bhabha states, the designation of objects or values of English origin in the dark colonial world becomes necessary in colonial travels and conquests, because there they produce signs of difference within that world that help consolidate the discriminatory relationship between Europe and its colonies.[14] In *A Chinese Ghost Story*, Caichen's discovery of some form of humanity in the heart of Xiaoqian fulfils that purpose. In Xiaoqian, Caichen locates a responsive human image among the dark cohorts. This image reminds him not only that his own 'humanity' is linked to the dark world around him, inspiring his anger and energy for conquest and cleansing, but also of the fundamental inconsistency of the ghostly world, giving him leverage and making his intervention practical.

Conversely, what stands out within the framing narrative of Xiaoqian's interest in Caichen is that unique desire for, and the attendant techniques to manipulate and victimise, the intruding conqueror. To Xiaoqian, love for Caichen always involves betrayal, violation and condemnation of the self. Even though her self-hatred may precede the intruder's advent, the latter certainly supplies a means for its sustenance and materialisation. Caichen's presence gives Xiaoqian opportunity to repeat confessions of past wrongdoings and to express yearning for future improvement. Xiaoqian, like Lao Lao, is a dualist figure. Whereas Lao Lao is both man and woman, Xiaoqian is both human and ghost, or a human value among the ghosts. Therefore, her *raison d'être* in the film is self-incrimination. She is totally subjected to the overwhelming power of Caichen's human interpellation. As explained in Judith Butler's recent discussion, the Althusserian allegory of the policeman's 'hey, you there' postulates that subjects achieve their identity by forming a conscience which systematically incriminates and demands compliance with the law.[15] Between Xiaoqian and Caichen, the scenario of interpellation may be a form of conquest that forever demands Xiaoqian's reform on account of her past crimes against masculinity, humanity and colonial consistency.

Yet, *A Chinese Ghost Story* is ultimately interesting because it does not stop at such a mode of colonial self-incrimination. The female, ghostly conscience that presupposes a debt to the masculine human runs side by side with mockery of masculinity. If nothing else, masculinity is the butt of the joke throughout the film. The romantic hero Caichen is almost pissed upon by Swordsman Yan. The archetypal warrior Yan is prone to emotional breakdowns, when he bewails his confusion about worldly affairs. He is even pierced in the buttock by a clumsy Caichen, his dignity compromised in his duel with Lao Lao. Lao Lao's swimming tongue, shaped like an oversized penis, is maybe visually the most striking and ridiculous metaphor of masculinity. Though its horrifying function is to force open the lustful heterosexual man's mouth, in the end Yan chops it off: the film's passion for masculinity is checked by a fundamental disbelief in its inherent powers.

More importantly, although Xiaoqian's agency as subject is delineated as female, wanting and often self-punishing, to a certain extent this is a camouflage, because the masculinity idealistically embodied in the intruder is not only undermined but also ultimately her victim, her toy, and a source of her pleasure and karmic gain. In the movie, at the same time as we the audience are engaged in conquering ourselves by imagining ourselves receptive of a robust and innocent masculinity, we realise that such a masculinity is as artificial as that simulated foreign touch. Leslie Cheung, the Final Boy, is not a triumphant figure in the end, but constantly subjected to the cinema's voluptuous, threatening and disabling gaze. Benjamin's great dictum about death that ghosts impart counsels of great authority to the living may therefore also require a different reading. Through the masks of death, the colonised subject does come forth, but only to tantalise and castrate the living presence of the colonising forces. Maybe such ghostly counsel for the innocent man is the ultimate and ambiguous message of the film, as Hong Kong cinema of the late 1980s foresaw another strange conqueror at the gate.

NOTES

1. Walter Benjamin, 'The Story Teller', in *Illuminations: Essays and Reflections*, ed. and intro. Hannah Arendt, trans. Harry Zohn (New York: Schocken Books, 1968), 93–94.

2. Stephen Teo, *Hong Kong Cinema: The Extra Dimensions* (London: BFI, 1997), Chapter 14, 219–229; Lisa Odham Stokes and Michael Hoover, *City on Fire: Hong Kong Cinema* (London and New York: Verso, 1999), 101–103; and David Bordwell, *Planet Hong Kong: Popular Cinema and the Art of Entertainment* (Cambridge, MA: Harvard University Press, 2000), 165–168.

3. Carol Clover, *Men, Women, and Chain Saws: Gender in the Modern Horror Film* (Princeton, NJ: Princeton University Press, 1992), 16–17.

4. Pu Songling, *Strange Stories from a Chinese Studio* (*Liaozhai zhiyi*), trans. Herbert A. Giles (London: T. W. Laurie, 1913). On this Chinese classic, see Judith Zeitlin, *Historian of the Strange: Pu Songling and the Classic Chinese Tale* (Stanford, CA: Stanford University Press, 1993). The film is roughly based on a story entitled 'Nie xiaoqian'. Another movie with the same Chinese title and known in English as *The Enchanting Shadow* was made in 1960 by the famed Hong Kong director Li Hanxiang.

5. Clover, *Men, Women, and Chain Saws*, 10–11.

6. Vladimir Propp, *Morphology of the Folk Tale*, trans. L. Scott (Austin: University of Texas Press, 1968). For a relatively recent discussion, see Fredric Jameson, *The Political Unconscious* (Ithaca, NY: Cornell University Press, 1981), esp. Chapter 2, 151–184.

7. For a discussion of the ghostly business of memory, see Rey Chow, 'A Souvenir of Love', in *At Full Speed: Hong Kong Cinema in a Borderless World*, ed. Esther C. M. Yau (Minnesota: Minnesota University Press, 2001), 209–229.

8. Clover, *Men, Women, and Chain Saws*, 9–10.

9. Ibid., 62.

10. For a discussion of Lacan's binary divide between meaning and life, see Kaja Silverman, *Male Subjectivity at the Margins* (New York: Routledge, 1992), 35–48.

11. Julia Kristeva, *Powers of Horror: An Essay on Abjection*, trans. Leon R. Roudiez (New York: Columbia University Press, 1982), 5.

12. For a discussion of the castrating mother as a regulating factor in horror movies, see Barbara Creed, *The Monstrous Feminine: Film, Feminism, Psychoanalysis* (London and New York: Routledge, 1993), 88–104.

13. Joseph Conrad, *Heart of Darkness* (Harmondsworth: Penguin, 1983).

14. Homi Bhabha, 'Signs Taken for Wonders: Questions of Ambivalence and Authority under a Tree outside Delhi, May 1817', in *Location of Culture* (London: Routledge, 1994), 102–121.

15. Judith Butler, ' "Conscience Doth Make Subjects of Us All": Althusser's Theory of Subjection', in *The Psychic Power of Life* (Stanford, CA: Stanford University Press, 1996), 106–131.

8 *Chungking Express*: Time and its Displacements

Janice Tong

The world as we see it is passing.

Paul of Tarsus

Four shots of an indeterminate steel-blue pre-dawn or twilight sky follow each other. Framed by the jutting contours of dirty housing commission flats and factory-like buildings, they offer a view of the 'world' between the gaps of an urban concrete jungle. White clouds pass, their motion is sped up. A voice-over begins in Mandarin: 'We rub shoulders every day … although we may not know one another now, it may be possible to be friends some day. My name is He Qiwu. I'm a cop, my number is PC 223.' Jostled and incoherent images of an overcrowded street provide glimpses of this plain-clothes detective in a *mise en scène* that is indistinguishable. A series of quick cuts interrupt this already over-loaded vision – handcuffs, a mannequin with a blonde wig, an Indian with a paper bag over his head who suddenly and doggedly runs off. The cop makes chase – around him the streetscape flashes by in a multitude of colours and frozen movement, recalling the multi-perspectival blur of Futurist paintings. The action freezes into stop-motion as He Qiwu bumps into a woman in dark glasses, beige raincoat and a blonde wig. An abrupt cut to a close-up of an old-fashioned electronic 'flip-card' clock interrupts the frame. It reads 'Friday, 28 April, 8:59pm', which, at that moment, changes over to '9:00pm'. Then the frame cuts back to a succession of mid- to long shots of the blonde woman turning to look at the figure disappearing towards camera and out of frame. Over this image, we hear He Qiwu's voice-over: 'At our closest point, we were just 0.1 centimetres apart … 55 hours later, I fall in love with this woman.' This is the second part of the opening sequence to *Chungking Express* (Wong Kar-wai, 1994).[1]

The experience of time in cinema, particularly in post-World War II cinema, opens up a fundamental and irreversible change in our basic perception and conception of time and temporal relations. The technology of cinema directly calls for a manipulation of time and in doing so the visual fabric of time is altered definitively. The multitudinous presentation of time – time can be accelerated, compressed, stretched, spliced and even evacuated – means that time itself can be (re)produced in cinema. Directors such as Jean-Luc Godard, Alain Resnais and more recently Krzystof Kieslowski, David Lynch, Raoul Ruiz, Tsai Ming-liang and Wong Kar-wai belong to a handful of directors whose films contribute to a new cinematic rendering of time by complicating the materiality, or the visuality, of time. What I mean by this is that these directors do not necessarily follow the convention of a narrative-driven structure. Instead, their films unfold in a kind of temporal exegesis. Their films toy with and challenge our experience of time as a linear succession of moments, as well as the rudimentary notion that time's trajectory is that of a past, present and future. Take Quentin Tarantino, for example. His *Pulp Fiction* (1994) throws this linear notion of time into disarray. At the end of the film, we are returned to the opening sequence to give this episode (and the film) closure. (Hitherto, the opening sequence has only functioned as a kind of adjunct to the story.) Not only is Tarantino able to neatly and inventively tie up loose ends, but he is also able to resurrect the heroes of the story, Jules and Vincent, from their respective exits – Jules's untimely retirement and Vincent's memorable but somewhat unheroic death. However, although the temporal structure of this film does indeed loop in on itself and is for the most part fragmented, with the story interlocking in a multi-perspectival and splintered way, I would argue that Tarantino's films are still unable to alter or challenge our perception of time. This is both because Tarantino's fragmentation and looping of time still obey a coherent narrative structure that is episodic, and, more importantly, because his films generally do not attempt to complicate or extend the boundaries of the *visuality* of time. It is this second idea, to do with stretching our perception of cinematic time that I believe Wong's films give access to and that fuels this essay.

This is not to say that Wong, Resnais or Ruiz are attempting to make non-diegetic films. In fact, what makes *Chungking Express* so compelling and delightful to watch is precisely its two unrequited love stories. What I am suggesting, however, is that in these films there is a lot more at stake than the storyline. Films like *Ashes of Time* (Wong Kar-wai, 1994), *Last Year at Marienbad* (Alain Resnais, 1961), *Mulholland Drive* (David Lynch, 2001) and *Time Regained* (Raoul Ruiz, 1999) bring to the fore certain kinds of images which are difficult to grasp through an analysis of narrative alone. In fact, this specific concern with images and their representational power are what constitute the film's aesthetic being, an ontology that is specifically of the temporal kind.

Chungking Express presents its viewers with such images. They are what I would like to call images of time. It is Wong's rendering of time in his cinematographic images that unhinges our perception of time when viewing *Chungking Express*. But how so? This essay sets out to describe what I mean by the visual fabric of time which constitutes Wong's images of time. It asks how Wong's film defies conventional readings of time by displacing temporal relations so as to open up possibilities for non-linear, disseminative and discontinuous reading.

Tony Rayns rightly calls Wong Kar-wai the 'poet of time',[2] in whose films we see a vital engagement of time in its many guises – speed, recollection, memory, waiting. The cinematographic images in *Chungking Express* bear witness to this not only through the overlapping narrative's focus on deadlines and expiry dates, which are shown in close-ups of recurring images of clocks and dates stamped on tins of food. Also, his image repertoire and its incongruities suggest that Wong's manipulation of time is experienced more obliquely. For me, his films raise the question of what it means for time to be cinematic, while at the same time remaining open to how cinema, in turn, affects this temporal event. In other words, what sort of time is cinematic? And, furthermore, how can the 'substance' of cinematic

time be experienced, especially the substance of Wong's cinematic time?

In order to engage with these questions we need first to approach Wong's films from a historico-cultural viewpoint so as to contextualise and give a fuller understanding to their *image* of Hong Kong and its citizens.

HONG KONG: CULTURAL DIASPORA AND THE HORIZON OF LOSS

Hong Kong in the mid-1990s was experiencing the state of its own disappearance. A shroud of uncertainty has bathed the city-state since the 1984 Sino-British Joint Declaration returning Hong Kong to China. But even before this, the history of Hong Kong has always reflected a city in flux: from its origin as a territory of the Qing Dynasty, Hong Kong was then annexed to the British for a period of ninety-nine years after the Opium War, during which time it also experienced a period of Japanese occupation. In its status as a British colonial-state it thrived as an entrepôt, an unparalleled 'nexus' through which the cultural and economic traffic of the East and West passed and still passes.

It is therefore not surprising to find Hong Kong as a city with an identity that is for the most part culturally fragmented. With its return to mainland China in 1997, instability and indeterminacy advances on its citizens. It is as though Hong Kong itself, along with its identity, is vanishing before the very eyes of its people. There is a rapid sense of time passing and, in this process, a calling forth towards an indeterminate future.

This experience of flux is reflected in Wong's destabilising cinematographic self-image of Hong Kong. The city epitomises Paul Virilio's description of geography as no longer the measuring of space alone, but now as determined by a 'chrono-space'; what he calls geography 'by speed'. Virilio sees this 'space of speed' as an image of the 'city of the beyond', which he calls 'the City of Dead Time'.[3] This is exemplified in the experience of having 'dawn and dusk in a single window' of an airplane: appearance and disappearance. This is how Wong presents the image of Hong Kong and its citizens to us. The images of Faye at the Midnight Express food stall are typically 'slit-framed', giving us only a partial view of her actions (or inaction). Christopher Doyle's hand-held camera and William Chang's fast-paced editing combine to disorient the viewer. Take the opening sequence described at the beginning of this essay as an example. Only glimpses of the sky are visible and, even so, they are 'denatured' with the clouds moving at an abnormal speed. The following action sequence through the streets is a jumbled incoherent mess of colours, which makes the surrounding architecture and its location indistinguishable. The camera then freeze-frames on a woman we do not and cannot recognise, because she is in disguise. All this is combined with a haunting fairground-like music, its repetitive bass riff oscillating not more than three to four semi-tones apart, adding to our growing sense of displacement. These are not familiar images of Hong Kong. They are not even familiar cinematic images of Hong Kong. How, then, are we able to read these images of Hong Kong and to make sense of what escapes us visually?

These 'visual slippages' reveal that Wong's camera is not given over to a direct representation of the anachronistic spaces of Hong Kong. In fact, his images extend Ackbar Abbas's view of the new Hong Kong cinema as one that is sensitive to 'spatial issues', eloquently summed up in his phrase 'image[s] of history as palimpsest'.[4] Instead of trying to capture spaces, geography, architecture or location, Wong is 'trying to capture time'.[5] Wong's rendering of cinematic time can be experienced in the ambiguous nature of his images, and not only does time displace the characters and locations, but also it is *time itself* that is ultimately displaced in *Chungking Express*.

In Ewa Mazierska and Laura Rascaroli's essay 'Trapped in the Present: Time in the Films of Wong Kar-wai',[6] and in a recent interview with Hou Hsiao-hsien, both the critics and director have commented on Wong's ability to 'capture contemporary life'[7] or 'catch the spirit of the time'.[8] *Chungking Express* bears this out, as it has often been described as a post-modern slice of contemporary Hong Kong exemplified by 'a new wave editing style, on-location realism and narrative dissonance'.[9] But these readings have only located this experience of contemporary life as that of living in the *present*. Mazierska and Rascaroli refer to Hong Kong as a 'throw-away society': its citizens consume fast foods, rent 'small apartments furnished with simple, mass produced furniture', doing so through 'choice rather than necessity', because for them 'the past and memory matter very little'.[10] For Mazierska and Rascaroli, Wong has no

'appetite for dead styles and fashions' and the 'contemporary culture he depicts … does not appear to be founded on past achievements, but on the strength of the present'.[11] This view echoes Abbas's description of Hong Kong people as having 'little memory and no sentiment for the past', their 'general attitude to everything sometimes indistinguishable from the spirit of enterprise', that is, to 'cancel out and pass on'.[12]

A focus on the narrative level alone indicates that the four main characters in *Chungking Express* do seem to belong to this kind of disposable and transient society: the two cops, He Qiwu and Cop 663, both live alone, renting small and inexpensively furnished apartments, and frequent the Midnight Express take-away food stall where a third character, Faye, works. But the images reveal a different story; in fact, their experience of Hong Kong is *not* of the present.

The first story in the film involves Cop 223 (He Qiwu) and a drug-trafficker (an unrecognisable Brigitte Lin in a blonde wig, dark glasses and trench-coat). Time is of paramount importance to both these characters. We can literally see the minutes ticking away for them. 223's presence was first 'documented' by a flip-card clock in the opening sequence, propelling him ceaselessly into the future. The significance of time for him is that of time running out. As Wong says, he has to make 'every minute of his life count for something'.[13] So, from the deadline of 1 May he sets for his ex-girlfriend, May, to return (represented by the expiry date stamped on tins of pineapples, her favourite fruit), to his pager password ('to love you for 10,000 years'), to counting the hours until he or someone else falls in love, he is trying to capture a bit of time. But these attempts are failures, and time slips from his grasp. Despite all the technology that enables immediacy, his phone calls never reach their destinations and become but a series of further detours and delays. Presence inevitably escapes him. Tellingly, his character appears in 'smudge-motion' more than any other character in the film, as if to suggest that change is always effacing his sense of himself.[14]

For the other two principal characters, 663 and Faye, the present is not a rapid succession of ceaseless moments, as suggested by the name of the take-away stall they frequent, Midnight Express. Instead, they are out-of-sync with the present: Faye listens compulsively to 'California Dreamin' and 663 to his lover's favourite tune, Dinah Washington's 'What a

Difference a Day Makes'. Both songs are from a different era and a different culture. In 663's case, we are doubly trapped in the past. The song belongs in his flashback of his time with his air-hostess former girlfriend. This flashback, in turn, plunges us into Wong's own memory of Hong Kong when he was a boy, his nostalgia for the toy planes he played with then (no longer fashionable and difficult to find when Wong decided to have them in the film), and his fondness for this song (used in a PanAm advertisement several years ago).[15] The only song in the film current at the time of its filming is 'Dreams' by The Cranberries. But even as you hear the opening strain your familiarity is immediately displaced, because it is a Cantopop version remade and sung by Faye Wong.

Chungking Express offers us an experience of Hong Kong in Abbas's sense of '*déjà disparu*', the feeling that 'what is new and unique about the situation is always already gone, and we are left holding a handful of clichés, or a cluster of memories of what has never been'.[16] It is as though even this desire to preserve is problematic: Abbas writes that in the very 'act of looking … the more you try to make the world hold still in a reflective gaze, the more it moves under you'.[17] Let us return to the opening sequence where Takeshi's character is running through a background that is totally blurred. His movements seem to be staggered or disjointed, yet he is visible and in focus. In contrast, his surroundings are a mere blur of colours and movement. This sequence is shot in Wong's signature 'smudge-motion' or 'step-printing' technique,[18] for Wong feels that Hong Kong is too fast-paced, but that with this technique he can 'concentrate on [things which] don't move while everything around them moves fast'. For him, this process is a way of 'trapping time', to 'change' and 'play with time', to do to time what you can't do to it in real life.[19] What happens to the visuality of time in these images? And what is our experience of Wong's cinematic rendering of time?

The scene is shot at double-speed, forty-eight frames per second, and played back at twenty-four frames per second through the projector. At the lab, frames one to twelve are allowed to run consecutively, then frame twelve gets repeated for the next twelve frames to achieve a 'pause' in the motion; frames thirteen to twenty-four are discarded, and frames twenty-five to thirty-six get to run consecutively, and so forth. By letting the same frame run through the projector this process distinguishes itself from the device of the 'jump-cut' – another editing process used to show temporal discontinuity.[20] Something gets lost in this process – we lose sight of our surroundings. Space becomes ambiguous, things and objects around the foreground and background merge and blend with each other. Hong Kong has been stripped of its appearance, the signs that are so easily recognisable have been replaced by an underbelly of non-signs. I would like to recall Virilio's metaphor here: appearance, disappearance. Sylvere Lotringer describes this as the tension between '[t]he urbanist … whose art made the city appear' and 'the acceleration of speed … now making it disappear'.[21] The urbanist is now the *cineaste* whose camera is able to not only speed things up, but also able to slow things down to make visible what is previously invisible to the human eye.

Takeshi's character caught in Wong Kar-wai's signature smudge-motion style. This technique offers up a new visuality to our experience of cinematic time

TIME, MULTIPLE FRAGMENTATION, DISPLACEMENT

Wong's manipulation of time enables us to see incongruous and divergent states of time in the same image. Simultaneously represented, these states of time appear to be in the process of dissemination; the images dilate and stretch, and seem to slip and pull away from each other. It is this displaced sense of time that is experienced in the opening sequence and throughout *Chungking Express*. Perhaps the most significant scene supporting this view in the second story is when 663's past and future collide at Midnight Express: Faye (future air-hostess and 663's future love interest) and his ex-girlfriend (dressed in an air-hostess uniform) stand side by side, sizing each other up. It is an image that conjures up a visual representation of a present that is split, both past and future appearing in the one image. This image prefigures my reading of Wong's cinematic images, and specifically their visual activity in the displacement of time. Gilles Deleuze describes these images as time-images, when '[w]hat is specific to the image … is to make perceptible, to make visible, relationships of time which cannot be seen in the represented object and do not allow themselves to be reduced to the present'.[22] What is significant in Deleuze's concept of the time-image to Wong's project is that when 'a little time in the pure state … rises up to the surface of the screen' it privileges the 'seer'. In other words, Wong's cinema is a 'cinema of the seer'[23] which privileges seeing rather than acting, making images rather than following plot-lines, making visible time and temporal relations rather than spaces or movements.

A few image sequences can illustrate this. 663's ex-girlfriend leaves behind a letter for him at Midnight Express (having gone there on the wrong night), only to have 663 delay their 'end' by leaving it

behind the counter indefinitely. Wong makes visible these temporal dislocations in a beautiful image sequence. A two-shot of 663 and Faye shows 663 frame left, leaning against the side of the counter and staring into the distance. Faye is frame right; motionless, she watches him drink his coffee. The two are almost entirely still in this whole sequence, and deep in their own thoughts. She is watching him and he is looking but doesn't see, for 663 has plunged into the past, into his memory. The foreground is a blur of shadows, indistinct figures whose movements are speeded up, an effect that punctuates the stark neon-lit backdrop of 'inaction'. This scene faithfully renders what Deleuze would call a 'pure optical situation',[24] where time can be seen as being freed from movement. In this scene, we can see how Wong makes visible this other temporality that exists for his characters. He renders visually the interiority of Faye and 663 – contemplative, waiting, weighed down by memory. The different components of the image come together to make time and temporal relations visible: the lack of a soundtrack; Faye's stillness; her quiet gaze at 663; and his banal everyday gestures, steeped in the past here. People speed past around them, in sync with each other and the world they live in. But Faye and 663 are isolated, absorbed in their own timeframe, and for them time *drags*. The materiality of time is fractured visually, opening itself up to different temporal intensities in the one shot.

Jean-Marc Lalanne's analysis of Wong's images closely describes this rendering of cinematic time:

> The images break loose from any context of enunciation to drift through the narrative; space splits into pieces; the film's direction is no longer governed by a spatial scenography based on continuity, but becomes an abstract device of pure optic and sonic sensations; as in the sublime verse from *Hamlet*, 'the time is out of joint', it breaks up into atoms of disparate and overlapping lengths of time.[25]

This fracturing of time is not only present in special-effects shots, but is found throughout Wong's film: in everyday gestures infinitely mutated with every repetition. This is especially the case with 663, who is not only out-of-sync with the present, but whose identity is also displaced. When his ex-girlfriend asks for him at Midnight Express, the owner of the stall

Cop 663 and Faye: caught in their own timeframe

mistakenly refers to him as 633 (as he does through-out the film), but she does not seem to register this error. Later on in the film, one of the kitchenhands corrects his mistake, only to have him shrug his error off. To compound this displacement further, writing on the film perpetuates this slippage of identity. Nei-ther Ackbar Abbas in his essay 'The Erotics of Dis-appointment' nor David Bordwell in his chapter on *Chunking Express* in *Planet Hong Kong* picks up on the cop's displaced identity. In *Hong Kong: Culture and the Politics of Disappearance*, Abbas slips from one badge number to the other. Perhaps these 'slippages' only testify to the inevitability of change and, in the end, it doesn't really matter whether his real number is 663 or 633. Even as he purposefully and incessantly resists change by sticking to the same foods (we see huge stacks of Del Monte tomato sardines in his cup-board) or the same places to eat, or by even failing to notice the alterations Faye makes to his apartment (we see him reprimanding his dishcloth for changing when it should be steadfastly holding onto its sense of self). He seems to be unaware that his everyday gestures and habits are already made up of 'a daunt-ing number of minutely varied repetitions of locales and routines'.[26]

Chungking Express shows Hong Kong to be a compressed space that forces its people to make phys-ical contact with one another without making any connections, even effecting disconnections from their selves. Just as the city and its citizens embrace time in the express speed of communication via mobile phones, emails and faxes, so too these technologies elicit distance and displacement between people. Therefore, it is not surprising to find the swift and efficient drug-trafficker contracting a group of drug-smugglers and concealing the heroin in the opening fast-paced sequence only to lose her charges at the airport, a place of transit with multiple destinations and time zones. When her own 'expiry date' is stamped on a tin of sardines she should be forced into action. Yet, paradoxically, she spends her last night in apparent inaction. The series of images of her and 223 sitting together at the bar show a motionless couple. Time passes. They are still motionless, except for their different poses and the collection of empty glasses in front of them. It is hard to say how much time has actually passed. More images of 223 and the blonde woman follow, this time in a hotel bedroom where she is sprawled out asleep on the bed, still in

her disguise. He is consuming plates of chef's salads and chips while watching Chinese opera on TV. Tele-vision is the only allusion to the present moment, encapsulated by the notion of televisual presence as the most immediate form of time, a perpetual pres-ence, direct, continuous and uninterrupted, leaving one with no time to think or to dwell on the past. Why these images of listlessness, of stillness, instead of the images of action usually associated with these characters?

Martin Scorsese's editor, Tom Rolf, talks about investing a little bit of time into the image when edit-ing *Taxi Driver* (Martin Scorsese, 1976). In a partic-ular shot, Robert de Niro's character, Travis Bickle, puts an effervescent tablet into his glass of water. We see his hands putting the tablet in the glass in a zoom-in, which cuts to a zoom-in of a motionless de Niro staring fixedly at the fizzing water and then a final cut back to the glass – the camera zooms in slowly, until the bubbles fill the entire frame. The whole sequence took about twenty seconds, which is very long in terms of screen time for the little action that is taking place. Rolf explained Scorsese's insis-tence in 'hanging on to the shot' when he was about to edit it out: 'By hanging onto an image for an inor-dinately long time, the audience questions why they are looking at this image for such a long time … and they reinvest their interest into the image, and begin to look at it with a new perspective.'[27]

This investment of time is what leads to the sev-ering of the action/reaction response that many mainstream films offer their audiences. Traditional narrative cinema has conditioned audiences to respond in a certain manner to its conventions: for example, matching eye-lines, shot/reverse shots; or a close-up of a face used to induce an emotional response; or a special-effects sequence slowed down to heighten its effects which may not otherwise be visible to the naked eye. For Deleuze, the 'break in the sensory-motor link'[28] frees time from its subor-dination to movement. In traditional narrative cinema, time is subordinated to movement that allows the story to unfold in a logical, linear manner. Deleuze's 'time-images' are established by breaking with this convention. In Wong's films, especially in *Ashes of Time*, we are often shown a series of images that no longer follow a cohesive narrative structure. In turn, the narrative is further displaced by these images, which are aberrant and ambiguous. In fact,

Time stands still for Cop 663 at the California bar

'we no longer know what is imaginary or real, physical or mental in the situation, not because they are confused, but because we do not have to know and there is no longer even a place from which to ask'.[29] In *Chungking Express*, Wong's rendering of a time freed from movement can be found everywhere, such as in the slow-motion images of Faye daydreaming, as if her daydreaming has altered even the camera's perception of time. Or it can also be found in the image of 663 and Faye sitting together at his apartment (their image is further displaced because it is their mirror reflection that we see), as if they are only able to be together when they are absent from each other, absent even in their presence. And again, it appears in the smudge-motion images of 663 while he was waiting for Faye at the California bar. His voice-over tells us that he is wondering whether she will remember their date in her California that evening. The fragmentation of time in this scene is experienced in 663's stillness by a juke-box contrasting the rush of bar-goers, and the slippage of place as well as time zones, between an imaginary California (from the song, which nonetheless conjures up images of Faye) and the real California, a destination where she will physically arrive. The temporal relations in these image sequences come together to testify to a new experience of cinematic time.

For the most part, *Chungking Express*'s images of mutability depict conditions of lostness in the characters – loss of identity, failure of communication, impossibility of reconciliation and the inability to hold on to time. These are conditions that, in turn, infuse Wong's images of Hong Kong with a sense of nostalgia, a kind of sentimental yearning for a history that has disappeared too quickly. In Wong's world it is not memory or the past that do not matter to his characters. In fact,

the very opposite seems to be true. Rather, it is as though for Wong, the people of Hong Kong do not know how to *think* the history of Hong Kong; the relationship between the people of Hong Kong and the place is displaced temporally. BBC Hong Kong correspondent Damian Grammaticas recently described Hong Kong as a 'rootless refugee city' that even six years after its return to the mainland is still 'struggling to find its own identity'.[30]

The last section offers a close reading of the opening sequence to *Chungking Express* as described at the beginning of the essay. In my analysis, I hope to further and more concretely describe how Wong's rendering of his cinematographic images illustrate a split or displacement in time itself, and how, as a viewer, the substance of his cinematic time can be experienced.

THIS IS NOT OF THE PRESENT

Time is out of joint.

Gilles Deleuze[31]

Chungking Express opens *in media res*, as if to suggest that time is always already split and could only open up to its 'variable present'[32] in every instance. The 'present' for Deleuze is a disjunction – it joins the present that is 'still to be' with a present 'that has already passed'. In other words, the present is 'variable', it is a paradox that speaks of a fold in time. While the present calls forth a ceaseless opening towards an indeterminate future, it simultaneously disappears into a concrete but infinitely variable pastness. Made possible only through a loosening of the sensory-motor schema, the challenge now lies in the '*interstice* between images',[33] where temporal relations open up to all possibilities not based on determinate logic.

Wong's film begins with Cop 223's voice-over: 'We rub shoulders every day … we may not know each other, but we could be friends some day.' As the voice-over is the first thing we hear, the viewer is immediately compromised temporally. The device of the voice-over suggests a displacement in time, a casting back in time from a narrative point of view that normally places the viewer in a privileged position of knowing in advance the outcome of the narrative. But instead of shedding insight for the viewer, this voice-over conveys its message in Mandarin where the local dialect is Cantonese. Immediately, the audience is disadvantaged and a distance between audience and narrative effectively opens up. This displacement is further compounded by the subsequent voice-over – when 223 bumps into a woman in a blonde wig – that tells us: 'At our closest point, we were just 0.1cm apart … 55 hours later, I fall in love with this woman.' The use of the present tense here – 'I fall in love' – confuses the flashback convention of a voice-over, which would normally employ the past tense: '… 55 hours later, I fell in love …' This temporal incongruity found in the voice-over returns us to the present unfolding of events and to the temporally parallel stories that follow this space of encounter. It is only as the first story draws to a close that we will find a further and more destabilising fracture within his voice-over: that there was no possibility of 223's voice-over being a flashback, since he could not have known that this woman was the one he would fall in love with at the time they were 'closest' to one another. Thus, the fold doubles in on itself, the voice-over becomes a non-diegetic insert of time, and radically puts into question what the audience is seeing or experiencing.

Wong's image-narrative in *Chungking Express* presents Hong Kong as a city with an absent centre. In its place, we find a mobile state of rupture where images, space, time, characters and narratives fold in upon each other, weaving a skein of images that threaten to slip from our gaze. These are images of a little 'pure time' which rises to the surface of the screen: time that has taken flight from spatial relations, abstracted from the real world. Wong's visual fabric of time has more to do with affect, memory, displacement. It is about seeing, as well as not seeing: appearance, disappearance.

NOTES

1. All translations and descriptions of scenes from *Chungking Express* used in this essay are my own.
2. Tony Rayns, 'Poet of Time', *Sight & Sound*, 5, no. 9 (1995): 12–14.
3. Paul Virilio and Sylvere Lotringer, *Pure War*, trans. Mark Polizotti (New York: Semiotext(e), 1983), 6.
4. Abbas's new cinema is one that captures these kinds of spaces. Ackbar Abbas, *Hong Kong: Culture and the Politics of Disappearance* (Minneapolis: University of Minnesota Press, 1997), 27.
5. Wong says that he became aware of this when filming around the Wanchai area for *Fallen Angels* (1995).

Jimmy Ngai, 'A Dialogue with Wong Kar-wai: Cutting between Time and Two Cities', in *Wong Kar-wai*, ed. Danièle Rivière (Paris: Dis Voir, 1998), 85.
6. Ewa Mazierska and Laura Rascaroli, 'Trapped in the Present: Time in the Films of Wong Kar-wai', *Film Criticism*, 25, no. 2 (2000–2001): 2–18.
7. Lee Ellickson, 'Preparing to Live in the Present: An Interview with Hou Hsiao-hsien', *Cineaste*, 27, no. 4 (2002): 13–19.
8. Mazierska and Rascaroli, 'Trapped in the Present', 3.
9. Stephen Teo, *Hong Kong Cinema: The Extra Dimensions* (London: BFI, 1997), 196.
10. The notion of the 'throw-away society' is Alvin Toffler's. See Mazierska and Rascaroli, 'Trapped in the Present', 4–5.
11. Here the writers use Jameson's ideas on post-modern societies. Mazierska and Rascaroli, 'Trapped in the Present', 16.
12. Abbas, *Hong Kong*, 26.
13. Rayns, 'Poet of Time', 14.
14. The same goes for Brigitte Lin's character, who is permanently in disguise. She says, 'Whenever I put on a raincoat, I put on sunglasses as well. You never know when it will rain and when it will be sunny.' She is in disguise so as to avoid the effects of change, be it a change in the weather or a change in her emotions. Is it possible that the only disguise she has on is, in fact, a disguise that hides her from herself?
15. These references are Wong's comments on the making of *Chungking Express*. Rayns, 'Poet of Time', 14.
16. Abbas, *Hong Kong*, 25.
17. Ibid., 26.
18. The two terminologies refer to the same device: 'step-printing' describes the actual lab process, whereas 'smudge-motion' describes what you can see.
19. John Ashbrook, 'Available Light', in *The Crime Time Filmbook*, ed. John Ashbrook (Harpendon: No Exit Press, 1997), 165.
20. All technical terminology here is the result of conversations with documentary film-maker Rick Farquharson, whose documentary on Christopher Doyle, *Orientations: Chris Doyle – Stirred Not Shaken*, was part of the Sydney Film Festival programme in 2000.
21. Virilio and Lotringer, *Pure War*, 6.
22. Gilles Deleuze, *Cinema 2: The Time-Image*, trans. Hugh Tomlinson and Robert Galeta (Minneapolis: University of Minnesota Press, 1997), xii.
23. Ibid., 2.

24. For further reading, see Chapter 1 'Beyond the Movement-Image' and the last section in Chapter 2 'Recapitulation of Images and Signs', ibid., 2–24 and 34–43.

25. Jean-Marc Lalanne, 'Images from the Inside', trans. Stephen Wright, in Danièle Rivière, *Wong Kar-wai*, 25.

26. From David Bordwell's description of *Chungking Express*'s plot-line in *Planet Hong Kong: Popular Cinema and the Art of Entertainment* (Cambridge, MA: Harvard University Press, 2000), 283.

27. Taken from a documentary on the shooting methods in *Taxi Driver*. *Taxi Driver* DVD special feature, Collector's Edition, Columbia TriStar Home Video Australia (1999).

28. Deleuze, *Cinema 2*, 173.

29. Ibid., 7.

30. Damian Grammaticas, 'Hong Kong Searches for New Identity', *BBC News: Asia-Pacific*, 4 February 2003: <news.bbc.co.uk/2/hi/asia-pacific/2721029.stm> (7 February 2003).

31. Deleuze, *Cinema 2*, xi.

32. For a Deleuzian description of the present as open-ended, see 'Peaks of Present and Sheets of Past: Fourth Commentary on Bergson', in ibid., 98–125.

33. Ibid., 179.

9 *Crouching Tiger, Hidden Dragon*: Cultural Migrancy and Translatability

Felicia Chan

Migration and cultural translation are symbiotic concepts. In the course of a migration, two or more cultures are inevitably brought up against each other requiring a process of translation of one culture to another. When a film like *Crouching Tiger, Hidden Dragon* (Ang Lee, 2000) makes the headlines around the world as a *unique* triumph for Chinese film, many issues are raised. What happens when a cultural text travels from one place to another? The wide disparity in responses to the film provokes larger questions of how we read what we see. How are cultural images and narratives translated by, or into, a different culture? What conditions our reading? Do Chinese audiences necessarily have a greater insight into the film compared with a Western one?

CULTURE MIGRATING

'Migration' usually refers to the movement of people from one locality to another, and physical migration usually involves the resettlement of an individual or community into a different geographical location. Whether the movement is of migrants in search of economic opportunities or the movement of imperial armies and missionaries across continents, each migrating community brings its own cultures to interact with those of the new location giving rise to a diasporic community. In the current technological environment, physical movement is no longer necessary to effect cultural change as ideas, cultures and ideologies are now brought in closer contact on a wider scale than ever before. The rate and reach of its impact on individuals and cultures is of an extent that one needs to speak of it as a state of cultural *migrancy* rather than an act of cultural migration.

In the face of *Crouching Tiger*'s success, Sony Pictures Classics executive Michael Barker was prompted to declare that the film had ushered in a 'new globalism in motion pictures'[1] and a majority of the Western press appears to echo this view. Lauren

Hunter of *CNN.com* outlines in her article the international flavour of the 2001 Academy Awards and lists a whole string of 'foreign' contenders for the golden statue: for example, Judi Dench (Britain), Juliette Binoche (France), Russell Crowe (New Zealand and Australia) and Javier Bardem (Spain).[2] And yet, the entry of such 'foreign' talent into Hollywood's biggest industry award ceremony is not unique to 2001. Many Anglo-Europeans have made Oscar headlines over the years, including Laurence Olivier (Britain), Sophia Loren (Italy) and Peter Weir (Australia), though not specifically for their *foreignness*. Ang Lee and *Crouching Tiger* are the first East Asian entrants to attract such media attention since Akira Kurosawa was nominated for *Ran* in 1986. *Crouching Tiger* was nominated for an unprecedented ten awards and won four, including Best Cinematography and Best Foreign Language Film, encouraging the perception that East Asian cinema has finally 'arrived'. In other words, the Chinese-language film is seen to have completed the global circuit for the Oscars, in the sense that *Crouching Tiger* now makes the Oscars even more 'global' than they had already been. Ironically, the film's success at this *American* sponsored event is what would open doors for it to the rest of the world, including East Asia itself.

When attempting to account for the film's phenomenal success, most credit its action sequences. Paul Dergarabedian, president of a box-office tracking service, Exhibitor Relations, says: 'The reason *Crouching Tiger* may transcend its foreign-language status is that it's an action film. There's a lot of visual information. That translates well in foreign markets.'[3] Similarly, Paul Tatara, also for *CNN.com*, gushes, 'The first fight, which springs to sudden, exquisite life … surely will elicit rounds of applause from audiences the world over – action, after all, has become cinema's universal language.'[4] And yet many mainstream Hong Kong films, such as those by Jackie Chan, John

Woo or Tsui Hark for example, boast a far higher and more spectacular action quotient, as well as a considerably higher body count. In fact one Hong Kong viewer even complained that 'there's simply not enough action … *Crouching Tiger* is so slow, it's a bit like listening to grandma telling stories'.[5]

Perhaps the cultural phenomenon may be better explained as an economic phenomenon. Rather than any profound textual mystery, record earnings at the US box office are what actually catapulted the film into an international acclaim. The film earned about US$128 million at the US box office – in comparison, the threshold for 'foreign hit status' is a mere US$1 million[6] – and this in turn fuelled its international success (about US$208 million). However, the appeal of the film to mainstream US audiences was not a historical accident, but the result of a particularly shrewd marketing campaign, rendered even more exceptional given that American audiences are notorious for shunning subtitled films. If Tom Bernard, Co-President of Sony Pictures Classics, could suggest that 'Ang Lee has hit the button for every demographic',[7] it is only because his marketing team had cleverly tailored its publicity campaign at specific segments of the mass market.[8] Basically, the producers divided the US audience into five target groups – 'the arthouse crowd, the young, the females, action lovers, and the popcorn mainstream'[9] – and tailored the publicity of the film to each group by anticipating their respective needs. For example, one group was composed of the fans of *The Matrix* (1997). *Crouching Tiger* was sold on the strength that action choreographer Yuen Wo-ping was also responsible for the action in *The Matrix*. Ironically, the quasi-martial arts display in *The Matrix* is itself a modified cultural import from the Hong Kong martial arts and action genres. Such blurring of boundaries between primary and secondary texts is not new. Kurosawa's adaptations of the Western for his samurai films were later remade as Westerns by Hollywood, the most famous of which is *The Magnificent Seven* (1960) from *Seven Samurai* (1954). What is different and interesting about *Crouching Tiger* is that it was not *only* marketed as a *Matrix*-type film, but also as an art film, a woman's film, as well as a combination of all these, which complicates its positioning. According to David Saunders, 'Just 700 of 37,000 U.S. screens are available for foreign films',[10] but *Crouching Tiger* opened not only in arthouse venues

but in mainstream multiplexes as well. This too was planned. In seeking to subvert the arbitrary association of foreign-language films with the arthouse, the producers deliberately withheld the film from competition at the Cannes Film Festival, in an effort to break from what they called 'the art-house ghetto'.[11] The fact that the move did not fail made distributors sit up and take notice. Daniel Battsek, Managing Director for Buena Vista International, says that the film 'acts as a vanguard for all foreign language films'.[12] Thus it would seem that the migratory success of this ostensibly Chinese text is made possible only when the *conditions* allowing for its (apparently) successful translation and favourable reception are adequately attended to.

However, the cultural migrancy of *Crouching Tiger* lies not only in the capture of Western markets but also in the re-capture of Asian ones. The lukewarm reception of the film in China and other parts of East Asia has been well publicised.[13] And once again numerous theories abounded, the most common of which is that Lee has simply pandered to Western tastes. Chinese film-maker Xie Fei bluntly suggests that 'Lee is clever. He knows what they like.'[14] Li Xun, director of the Graduate Programme of China Film Arts Research Centre, likewise surmises that 'What is appealing to American audiences is the exoticism: the totally fresh aesthetic of Chinese martial arts and the imaginary artistic conception. But that turned out to be mundane to Chinese viewers.'[15] While Hong Kong viewers appear to expect a greater dose of action, mainland Chinese viewers appear to expect a degree of realism. Zhong Gang, a bank employee, is quoted as saying: 'The action scenes weren't as good as the old kung fu movies …. People flew around way too much. If you put me on wires, I could fly around too …. There was no real martial-arts skill.'[16] Xie Fei expresses a similar view: 'Some in China say that the movie's *gongfu* [*kung fu*] is not very exciting because it's quite artificial. They can feel the wires and cables used.'[17] And yet, are aesthetic considerations the only reason for the film's lacklustre performance in China and Hong Kong?

While the West may be looking to reformulate its distribution strategies, China continues to be plagued by more mundane problems of excessive bureaucracy and video piracy. Attempting to distribute a film in the mainland is an arduous process. Films are not allowed to be independently distributed in China without official sanction. A private distribution company must form a joint venture with a state-run firm in order to have any access to the China market. In the case of *Crouching Tiger*, the rights to its distribution were shared by a private production firm, Asian Union Film and Entertainment, and China Film Co-Production, a state-run company. Of the US$1 million it cost to distribute the film in China, Asian Union invested 80 per cent and China Film 20 per cent. Problems arose when China Film, on realising that the film was about to be a hit, tried to oust Asian Union from the partnership. In the tussle, the film was withheld from exhibition for 'three crucial months'.[18] By the time permission was given to release the film, there was 'no time to remarket the movie'.[19] Furthermore, during that time, the streets became 'flooded with pirated DVD and video compact disc copies of the movie, selling for about [US]$2.50 each, or less'.[20] Ironically, it was precisely in the bid to combat piracy that the film was 'scheduled for almost simultaneous openings across the region'.[21]

In addition, the film's Oscar triumph saw a revived interest in many parts of East Asia, which basked in a collective cultural pride. This is evident in cinematographer Peter Pau's Oscar acceptance speech: 'It's a great honour to me, to the people of Hong Kong and to Chinese people all over the world.' Donna Tung, a spectator, called Lee a 'credit to all Chinese people'.[22] In Hong Kong, the film did not even make the top five box-office earners of that year, and yet 'as Oscar night neared, video discs of the movie were selling for nearly double the price of other local movies at around HK$95 (US$12)'.[23] In Taiwan, Lee was honoured with a personal visit from the Taiwanese President, Chen Shui-bian, who congratulated him on being the first Taiwanese national to win an Academy Award.[24] The Taiwanese premier, Chang Chung-hsiung, also offered public congratulations: 'We recognize the hard work and contribution that Ang Lee has made to our movie industry and his achievements on the international stage also honour us.'[25] Interestingly, the film's Taiwanese financier had backed out in the early stages of pre-production,[26] and the film's only links to Taiwan are the director's own ethnic origin as well as those of his Taiwanese actors, Chang Chen and Cheng Pei Pei. Nevertheless, Scarlet Cheng, writing for the *Far Eastern*

Economic Review, calls it a 'cultural homecoming'[27] for Ang Lee, while a Taiwanese office worker is reported to have exclaimed: 'I am so proud of Ang Lee … . He never forgot his roots in Taiwan, and he also traced his roots back to China.'[28] Never mind that Lee himself has said that the China he envisioned was a fantasy China of his boyhood dreams.[29]

Although in no way a Chinese culture specialist, my own personal observation from living in Chinese-dominated Singapore is that the attitudes towards the film's Western success seem to reveal a characteristic, though paradoxical, mix of cultural chauvinism and deference towards Western culture. Despite a great resistance to being dictated to by the West, a foreign success is at the same time almost always seen as something to be emulated, praised and welcomed. This cultural schizophrenia, at least with regard to *Crouching Tiger*, stems in part from a history of being inundated by high production value Hollywood films, which set a commercial standard, and a sense of self-effacement characterising Chinese culture. Chinese film scholars like Zhang Nuanxin and Li Tuo, for example, seem inordinately concerned with 'why the development of our film *lags behind* the rest of the world'.[30] Their essay calls for Chinese film-makers to learn from foreign films in order to 'hasten the development of our own cinematic language',[31] laying the blame for its aesthetic 'backwardness' on China's contemporary history and political struggles, specifically the 'stagnation and retrogression created by the Gang of Four'.[32] Even in Singapore, film-makers, artists and theatre practitioners often aim to make a name for themselves in international festivals before they are confident that the local public will accept them. So, while Chinese audiences may initially express reservations about *Crouching Tiger*, a Western success may not only convince them to the contrary, but also assure them that it was a winning product to begin with.

I should emphasise that for the sake of argument and convenience, I am making some unqualified assumptions about the unity of Chinese culture, which as history has shown is far from unified. However, the general situation is interesting and worthy of pursuit insofar as this process of what I can only call a 'double migration' – from East to West and back to East again – has an impact on local industries and films. The Hong Kong film industry for instance is already looking to emulate *Crouching Tiger*'s success. Joe Cheung of the Hong Kong Film Directors' Guild says, 'This movie is a benchmark and it shows that we must all be professional, that we must put together the best to create something of such high standards.'[33] Hong Kong cinema, which used to outsell Hollywood blockbusters in domestic markets, saw a reverse trend in the 1990s, caused in part by changing audience demographics, rampant piracy and the political uncertainty leading up to the British handover of the colony to Chinese rule in 1997. Thomas Chung, an influential Hong Kong producer, is described by *Asiaweek* as being on a 'mission – to revitalize Hong Kong's ailing film industry'.[34] Most of his efforts are directed at changing the signature slap-dash style of production in Hong Kong films in favour of stronger scripts and high value productions designed to appeal to foreign audiences as well as local audiences weaned on foreign imports. This includes writing most of the dialogue in English, as with *Gen-Y Cops* (2000) and *The Touch* (2002), produced by and starring Michelle Yeoh. The kinetic energy of a regular Hong Kong film resulting from the spontaneity of churning out a film in forty days or less, and the rapid-fire witticisms tossed out in Cantonese, look set to be sacrificed in favour of Hollywood-style big-budget action flair.

In addition, the ersatz copies have surfaced. One example, *Flying Dragon, Leaping Tiger* (2001), starring Sammo Hung, is unabashed in its resemblance, complete with a brooding middle-aged hero, lengthy desert scenes, a feisty young heroine and the theme of lost love. Interestingly, Miramax is said to have acquired the film for distribution in the US,[35] and it was reported that the ending of the film was changed after a US screen-test audience was found to have disliked the original ending. However, given the complex conditions for *Crouching Tiger*'s success, does it necessarily mean that *any* Chinese-language film could replicate its appeal? Have the traditional barriers to entry really been eradicated? It remains to be seen if Miramax's other acquisitions such as Stephen Chow's slapstick *Shaolin Soccer* (2001, released as *Kung Fu Soccer* in the US), a top-earner in Hong Kong, will translate well and take in any substantial box-office revenue in Western markets.

CULTURE TRANSLATING

To translate something generally means to express it in another language, and yet embedded in the act of translation is the notion of the untranslatable. Those on the receiving end of the foreign language or product need to translate it into a language they can understand; those on the producing end need to translate it into a language they think the other can understand. The fissure between the two is where the untranslatable lies – an *aporia*, if you will. *Crouching Tiger*'s migration to the West, and back to the East, necessitates a translation, not simply of language, but of *cultures* as well. By 'cultures' I mean more than the ethnological sense of culture; I mean also the culture of the medium itself – the culture of film developed over its history, and the culture of reading that has developed out of that history.

The main difficulty of translation in *Crouching Tiger* is the Chinese notion of *jianghu*. The closest equivalent in English to the term is 'world of knightly chivalry', which is mostly unsatisfactory since it conjures up images of Sir Galahad and maidens in need of rescue, which confines us still within the English context. *Jianghu* encompasses an abstract community within the Chinese literary tradition that is ruled not by state legislation but by moral principle and decorum. It exists simultaneously outside as well as within society. Its members are not above state laws, but are accorded the moral authority to reject the implementation of those laws should they serve corrupt ends. *Crouching Tiger* is sustained by the tension between the various characters and their varying abilities to adhere to *jianghu* principles. The inability of Li and Shu Lien to act upon their love, for example, stems from their *jianghu* code of honour. They are bound by a respect for Li's sworn brother and Shu Lien's betrothed, Meng Sizhao. That Meng was killed in battle does not free them from this obligation and in fact binds them further into honouring his memory. Li's responsibility to avenge the death of his master is another barrier between them. A viewer unfamiliar with the cultural resonances of this decision may ask why Li is unable to court Shu Lien and avenge his master at the same time. The answer is that that would mean privileging his personal desires over his social and filial responsibilities. Indeed, Li's initial attempt to retire from his *jianghu* obligations and give up on the search for Jade Fox only resulted in a situation that forced him to stay on and accomplish his mission.

The intrusion of Jade Fox and her disciple Jen into Li's life provides a different perspective on the notion of *jianghu*. Jade Fox sees the *jianghu* world as a world of freedom in which she can roam freely. At the end of the film, she tries to persuade Jen to remain with her: 'But why go home now? We've gone this far, we won't stop now …. At last we'll be our own masters. We'll be happy.' For Jade Fox, the life of a wandering pugilist represents an entirely different world from the life within the governor's household. She sees the *jianghu* world as an escape from society, though her excessive concern with the martial combat ('Kill or be killed. Exciting, isn't it?') over the moral aptitude necessary to operate within that world forces her to remain in hiding behind the walls of the governor's mansion.

Her protégé, Jen, is the most complex character in the film. The narrative momentum of the film is sustained mainly by her failure to comprehend *jianghu* etiquette and values. When chided for stealing the Green Destiny sword, she says it was just 'for fun'. Note that the brawl she causes in the tavern stems from her insolence and arrogance, causing her

opponents to later complain about her lack of manners. It is Jen's waywardness that also leads Jade Fox to attempt to poison her, for Jen has committed the ultimate offence in *jianghu* terms: she has betrayed her own master. Li's desire to train her is in part an attempt to impart the moral discipline required to wield her talent responsibly.

No knowledge of the *jianghu* context is necessary to access or enjoy the narrative of the film. On a basic level, the film supplies sufficiently recognisable signs for the story to be understood. However, some of the gaps in the narrative can only be filled by a knowledge of the cultural context within which the film operates. When that knowledge is absent, and the narrative gaps are filled by signs from a different cultural system, the context for the narrative could be altered to the extent that meaning in the narrative is also altered.

One example is to read the film as a feminist film, as Matthew Levie has done:

> It is a sign of tremendous skill on Lee's part that he manages to insert into his epic such a profound

Crouching Tiger, Hidden Dragon: Jen

commentary on the situation of the modern woman. Imagine Jade Fox as the strong professional woman who is perceived as too 'aggressive' and even 'bitchy', while her equally aggressive male colleagues are spared this criticism; Shu Lien as the woman who works twice as hard as her male colleagues to reach the same stature, sacrificing her personal happiness for professional success; and Jen as a beautiful, capable teenager trying to set her priorities: career or family?[36]

Although the similarities may exist on the level of a Lévi-Straussian 'deep structure', the three categories of women Levie depicts represent problems women face within *Western* cultural discourse. This is not to say that Chinese women don't necessarily face the same problems of patriarchal domination, but that the discourse employed by Chinese films tends to approach gender roles differently. I refer to Esther Yau's article about the difference in representation of gender politics in Chinese and Western texts. Although the text she analyses is Chen Kaige's *Yellow Earth* (1984), the point she makes is relevant to my argument: 'Inasmuch as the sense of social identity defines the person within Chinese society, individuals in Chinese films are often cast as non-autonomous entities within determining familial, social and national frameworks.'[37] The familial and social, perhaps not so much the national, framework of *Crouching Tiger* is the framework of the *jianghu* world. Each character has a social role to play within this world, and the gender relations depicted in the film are but part of this larger framework. There is no direct evidence of male oppression in the film other than the one we are primed to expect from the period setting of ancient China. Li Mubai and Lo (Jen's lover) struggle as much with the restrictions of *jianghu* society as the women. Gender relations are not presented in dialectical opposition in the film, and if we assume that they are, then we run the risk of turning it into a different film.

A different kind of misreading involves the imposition of other cultural texts onto the film. One extreme case is Elvis Mitchell's review in *The New York Times*, which describes *Crouching Tiger* as a 'picture [with] a knockabout, screwball comedy bounce' and that it is 'just the film for an audience transfixed by the weekly girl-power cool and soap-opera bloodshed of "Buffy, the Vampire Slayer"'.[38] How far has the fissure widened between producer and receiver

that a film deemed too slow and tedious by a Hong Kong viewer can be perceived as one having a 'screwball comedy bounce'? The comparison with *Buffy*, though incongruous, is more understandable, although their similarity is acknowledged as based on the lowest common denominator between the two texts – the martial arts. This leads to questions of genre and how awareness of generic conventions may influence a reading of a film. Are genres dependent upon a particular culture? Can a genre sufficiently translate from one culture to another? In addition, do genres themselves create a culture of reading?

According to Stephen Neale:

> Genres ... help render films, and the elements within them, intelligible and therefore explicable. They offer a way of working out the significance of what is happening on the screen: why particular events and actions are taking place, why the characters are dressed the way they are, why they look, speak and behave the way they do, and so on.[39]

In other words, genres depend on a spectator's familiarity with its conventions, built upon knowledge gained from other films of the same genre. This inherently circular process can sometimes complicate rather than clarify readings of a film. For instance, while we can say Kurosawa's samurai films resemble Westerns, we cannot say that *The Magnificent Seven* resembles a samurai film. Different genres depend on different sign systems: a Western, it seems, can be recognised without the cowboy costumes and frontier setting, but a samurai film cannot be identified as such without the actual representation of a samurai figure or Japanese period setting. Like the samurai film, the Chinese martial arts film is identified mainly though its *mise en scène*, a criterion which *Crouching Tiger* fulfils, and which in turn influences audience expectations.

So Mitchell's identification of *Crouching Tiger* as possessing 'a knockabout, screwball comedy bounce' appears to be influenced by his expectations of a martial arts film. Before *Crouching Tiger*, American audiences used to experience these films as low-budget, low-quality 'chopsocky flicks', usually with poor to laughable English subtitles. While martial arts films are mainstream fare for Eastern audiences, for US audiences Hong Kong martial arts films tend to be available mainly from cult video stores and

Chinatown theatres. For this reason, *Crouching Tiger*'s mainstream release is seen to have crossed a major hurdle. Does the cultural context under which one had experienced a genre then affect one's response to a new film seemingly of that genre?

So far, I have been arguing that the lack of cultural knowledge and familiarity can impede the understanding of a cultural text. Ironically, that same knowledge and familiarity may conversely alienate viewers from the film as well. For instance, one of the reasons for which the film is said to be unpopular among Chinese viewers is that the characters are not portrayed according to type. Larry Teo reports that critics on the mainland 'assailed [the film] as a shallow story about anti-heroes – a debasement to the traditional martial arts genre'.[40] And indeed, Li Mubai fails as a traditional *wuxia* (knight errant) hero. Although he succeeds in killing his master's mortal enemy, he is killed by her *by accident*, and dies with regret on his last breath. Jen, whom he had set out to save, is not given a chance to redeem herself, arrives too late with the antidote and leaps to an uncertain death. There is no showdown in *Crouching Tiger*, no dialectical clash of good and evil, and thus no catharsis its resolution is expected to provide.

Instead what Lee has chosen to emphasise is the film's emotional quality, underscoring the personal price each character has to pay as members of the *jianghu* world. The heroism in *Crouching Tiger* is thus not the heroism of action but of *effort*. Early in the film, when Jen expresses a longing for the *wuxia* lifestyle, her fantasies are countered very quickly by the level-headed Shu Lien:

Jen: I've read all about people like you. Roaming wild, beating up anyone who gets in your way!

Shu Lien: Writers wouldn't sell many books if they told how it really is.

Jen: But you're just like the characters in the stories.

Shu Lien: Sure. No place to bathe for days, sleeping in flea-infested beds .... They tell you all about that in those books?

Central to the aesthetic of *Crouching Tiger* then is a degree of self-reflexivity about the conventions of the genre that does not yet resort to parody. This is achieved in part by merging two different cinematic sensibilities – the older Taiwanese melodrama and swordplay films and the more recent Hong Kong martial arts films.

Martial arts films are generally divided into two categories: the *wuxia* (or sword-fighting) films and the *kung fu* (or fist-fighting) films. According to Stephen Teo, swordplay narratives were traditionally set 'in medieval dynasties and other mythical fantasies which, in turn, became stylistic conventions of the genre', such as 'the effortless facility of swordfighting heroes and heroines to leap, somersault and generally levitate in defiance of gravity'.[41] *Kung fu* films on the other hand 'emphasised the body and training rather than fantasy or the supernatural'[42] as in the films of Bruce Lee and Jackie Chan. *Wuxia* films, mostly made in Taiwan, gave way to Hong Kong *kung fu* films by the early 1970s[43] and have currently adapted to television in the form of lengthy serials. The other difference between Taiwanese and Hong Kong films is that the former favoured domestic and rural themes (melodrama was popular) while the latter favoured a more kinetic cinema leaning towards action, comedy and mass entertainment.[44] In some ways, Ang Lee brings a Taiwanese sensibility into what is now commonly perceived as a Hong Kong genre. Indeed, there are several homages to earlier *wuxia* films, such as the tavern scene and the bamboo grove scene. Interestingly, the casting of Cheng Pei Pei as Jade Fox seems to be a nod towards a film genre long past. As the 'queen' of the *wuxia* films in the 1960s, Cheng symbolically makes way for a new generation of actor the way Jade Fox must make way for her disciple.

The translation of *Crouching Tiger* at the level of its cultural milieu thus requires knowledge not only of the conventions of genre but also of the history of the genre. This cultural milieu, however, extends equally to the circumstances under which it is received. Singapore audiences, for example, were extremely conscious of the fact that the four lead actors spoke with four different accents: Zhang Ziyi with a Beijing accent, Chang Chen with a Taiwanese accent, Chow Yun-fat a Cantonese one, and Michelle Yeoh with a Malaysian-English lilt to her Mandarin which she had memorised phonetically. Though Yeoh's acting was sufficiently nuanced, her awkward Mandarin drew laughter during the three occasions I watched the film at theatres in Singapore, mainly because Malaysia is the closest neighbour and the accent was so familiar to us, yet oddly unfamiliar in the context that it came across on screen.

Thus what I have tried to explore in this essay are the various conditions under which a cultural text may operate, which hopefully reveal that the processes of cultural migration and translation are never simply bilateral in nature. In fact, Rey Chow argues that 'cultural translation needs to be rethought as the co-temporal exchange and contention between different social groups deploying different sign systems that may not be synthesizable to one particular model of language or representation'.[45] She calls for a reassessment of the 'transactional reading' when discussing the process of cultural translation, suggesting that the emphasis might fall less on the 'reading' than on the 'transactional' aspect of the process. She says:

> the translation between cultures is never West translating East or East translating West in terms of verbal languages alone but rather a process that encompasses an entire range of activities, including the change from tradition to modernity, from literature to visuality, from elite scholastic culture to mass culture, from the native to the foreign and back, and so forth.[46]

This transactional aspect is what I have tried to explore with my analysis of *Crouching Tiger*, in order to illustrate that while culture may be infinitely translatable, it is not easily translated. And when particular readings of culture can also be shaped by particular cultures of reading, its problems can be exponentially compounded.

NOTES

1. Richard Natale, 'The Film Business's New Globalism Makes Its Mark', *LA Times*, 26 March 2001, *calendarlive on latimes.com*: <www.calendarlive.com/top/1,1419,L-LATimes-Search-X!ArticleDetail-26825,00.html> (12 May 2002).

2. Lauren Hunter, 'More than Ever, Oscars Go Global', *CNN.com*, 22 March 2001: <www.cnn.com/2001/SHOWBIZ/Movies/03/22/international.oscar/index.html> (11 April 2002).

3. Quoted in Dan Biers, 'Chasing the Tiger's Tail', *Far Eastern Economic Review*, 164, no. 3 (25 January 2001): 67.

4. Paul Tatara, ' "Crouching Tiger, Hidden Dragon": A Gripping Poetic Tale', *CNN.com*, 11 December 2000: <www.cnn.com/2000/SHOWBIZ/Movies/12/11/review.crouching.tiger/index.html> (7 July 2001).

5. Quoted in Steve Rose, 'The Film Is So Slow – It's Like Grandma Telling Stories', *Guardian*, 13 February 2001, *Guardian Unlimited*: <www.film/guardian.cu.uk/features/featurepages/0,4120,437326,00.html> (29 July 2001).

6. Robert Koehler, 'How Auds Learned to Love Subtitles', *Variety* (14 January 2002): <www.findarticles.com/cf_Ø/m1312/8_385/82262324/print.html> (23 May 2003).

7. Quoted in Biers, 'Chasing the Tiger's Tail', 66.

8. See John Lippman, 'Buzz Gets "Crouching Tiger" a Leg Up"', *Asian Wall Street Journal*, 12–14 January 2001, 1 and M1; and Charles Pappas, 'Improbable Eastern Hit Proves It Can Fly in the U.S.', *Advertising Age* (Chicago), 26 March 2001, S2.

9. Pappas, 'Improbable Eastern Hit', S2.

10. David Saunders, ' "Crouching Tiger", Hidden Profits', *Chicago Sun-Times*, 8 April 2001, Sunday Late Sports Final Edition, F41.

11. Lippman, 'Buzz Gets', M1.

12. Quoted in Vanessa Thorpe, 'A Tiger Burning Bright', *Observer*, 14 January 2001, 6.

13. See, for example, David Rennie, 'Chinese Unimpressed by "Crouching Tiger" ', *Chicago Sun-Times*, 13 January 2001, Sunday Late Sports Final Edition, 30.

14. Quoted in Jessica Tan, 'Gongfu Not Good Enough?', *The Straits Times* (Singapore), 12 February 2001, L10.

15. Quoted in Dai Limin, ' "Crouching Tiger" Scoops 10 Academy Award Nominations', *China Daily*, 15 February 2001, 1.

16. Quoted in Henry Chu, ' "Crouching Tiger" Can't Hide from Bad Reviews in China', *Los Angeles Times*, 29 January 2001, A1, 1.

17. Quoted in Tan, 'Gongfu Not Good Enough?', L10.

18. Chu, ' "Crouching Tiger" ', A1, 1.

19. Ibid.

20. Ibid.

21. Scarlet Cheng, 'Ready to Pounce', *Far Eastern Economic Review*, 163, no. 27 (6 July 2000): 85.

22. Quoted in 'Asia Roars as "Crouching Tiger" Pounces on 4 Oscars', *Mercury News*, 26 March 2001: <www.mercurycenter.com/justgo/special/tiger/feature-oscarroar.htm> (23 October 2001).

23. Ibid.

24. 'President Chen Meets with Ang Lee and Lee's Father', 24 April 2001, *The Office of the President of the Republic of China website*, news release:

<www.president.gov.tw/php-bin/docset/
showenews.php4?_section=5&_rid=586> (7 July 2001).

25. Quoted in Larry Teo, 'A Triumphant Roar for Taiwan
    Filmmaker Lee', *The Straits Times*, 26 January 2001,
    A1.

26. See 'Interview with Ang Lee and James Schamus',
    Guardian Unlimited, 7 November 2000:
    <www.film.guardian.co.uk/interview/interview-
    pages/0,6737,394676,00. html> (29 July 2001).

27. Cheng, 'Ready to Pounce', 84.

28. Quoted in 'Many Asians See "Crouching Tiger" as an
    Example of China's Power' (2001), *Mercury News*:
    <www.mercurycenter.com/justgo/special/tiger/
    feature-power.htm> (23 October 2001).

29. Ang Lee, 'Foreword', *Crouching Tiger, Hidden Dragon:
    A Portrait of the Ang Lee Film* (New York: Newmarket
    Press, 2000), 7.

30. Zhang Nuanxin and Li Tuo, 'The Modernization of
    Film Language', trans. Hou Jianping, in *Chinese Film
    Theory: A Guide to the New Era*, ed. George S. Semsel,
    Xia Hong and Hou Jianping (New York: Praeger,
    1990), 10, my emphasis.

31. Ibid., 18.

32. Ibid., 19.

33. Quoted in ' "Crouching Tiger" Oscars Bring Hope to
    HK Filmmakers', *Mercury News*, 26 March 2001:
    <www.mercurycenter.com/justgo/special/tiger/
    feature-hkfilm.htm> (23 October 2001).

34. Jeremy Hansen and Alexandra A. Seno, 'A Touch of
    Realism', *Asiaweek*, 20 July 2001, 1.

35. 'Copying Tiger, Ripping Off Dragon', *The Straits
    Times* (Singapore), 5 July 2001, L3.

36. Matthew Levie, '*Crouching Tiger, Hidden Dragon*: The
    Art Film Inside the Chop-Socky Flick', *Bright Lights
    Film Journal*, 33, July 2001: <www.brightlightsfilm.com/
    33/crouchingtiger.html> (23 October 2001).

37. Esther C. M. Yau, '*Yellow Earth*: Western Analysis and
    a Non-Western Text', in *Perspectives on Chinese
    Cinema*, ed. Chris Berry (London: BFI, 1991), 69.

38. Elvis Mitchell, ' "Crouching Tiger, Hidden Dragon":
    Fans, Be Prepared for Heart and Feminism', *New York
    Times* on the web, 9 October 2000:
    <www.nytimes.com/2000/10/09/arts/09TIGE.html>
    (27 July 2001).

39. Steven Neale, 'Questions of Genre', *Film Genre Reader
    II*, ed. Barry Keith Grant (Austin: University of Texas
    Press, 1995), 160.

40. L. Teo, 'A Triumphant Roar', A1.

41. Stephen Teo, *Hong Kong Cinema: The Extra
    Dimensions* (London: BFI, 1997), 98.

42. Ibid.

43. Ibid., 102.

44. See Chiao Hsiung-ping, 'The Distinct Taiwanese
    and Hong Kong Cinemas', *Perspectives on Chinese
    Cinema*, ed. Chris Berry (London: BFI, 1991),
    155–165.

45. Rey Chow, *Primitive Passions: Visuality, Sexuality,
    Ethnography, and Contemporary Chinese Cinema* (New
    York: Columbia University Press, 1995), 197.

46. Ibid., 192.

10   *Crows and Sparrows*: Allegory on a Historical Threshold

Yiman Wang

Crows and Sparrows (Zheng Junli, 1949) was produced by the Shanghai-based and left-leaning Kunlun (Peak) Film Company. Production started in April 1949 but did not finish until after the Chinese Communist Party (CCP) overcame the Nationalist Party (Kuomintang: KMT) government in October. The film has been canonised in mainland China's official film history as a masterpiece that realistically reflects the disintegration of the KMT government in the storm of the Communist revolution.

> Armed with exuberant revolutionary zeal, sharp social observation, and masterful skills, the filmmakers created biting political satire. By depicting the gradual transformation of a group of ordinary cityfolk ... from pessimism and fantasy to heightened consciousness in their struggle against the oppressive and reactionary KMT government represented by Mr. Hou, the film delivers a realistic and vivid reflection of the social landscape in the KMT-controlled area on the brink of Liberation, a landscape vacillating between chaotic darkness on one hand and brightness on the other.[1]

The screenwriter, Chen Baichen, agrees with this judgment, recalling that all the film-makers were motivated by the desire to act 'as witness to the disintegration of the Chiang Kai-shek dynasty, and an urge to record the last page of its wicked history so as to welcome Liberation'.[2] This agreement has two important implications: first, the film-makers were convinced of the possibility and necessity of a *realistic* cinematic representation of social circumstances; and second, realism was established as a primary criterion for judging good films.

Contrary to the official evaluation that emphasises the film's sympathy with the CCP, Leo Ou-fan Lee seeks to wrest the film from the CCP co-optation by re-evaluating it as a paragon of what he calls 'social realism'. According to Lee, where socialist

realism compels ideological conformity to the CCP's radical political agenda and the subjugation of art to politics, social or critical realism represents 'a social stance of discontent' and leads to 'a committed art burdened with ethical and emotional weight but not necessarily with doctrinaire propaganda'.[3] *Crows and Sparrows* demonstrates precisely that:

> ... in China artistic creativity prospered on the eve of the revolution ... [Committed art] is 'revolutionary' only in the sense that through its exposé ethos it lays bare the darkness before the revolution, rather than glorifies propagandistically the revolutionary victory itself ... [Leftist film-makers'] independence of spirit and their critical conscience were given full release precisely because in the last years of the Kuomintang (Guomindang) rule they had to confront the chaos and darkness of a disintegrating society.[4]

Lee's analysis achieves two things for my purpose. First, he demystifies the canonised 'socialist realism' by proposing 'social realism' as a positive counterterm. Second, he usefully emphasises the on-the-eve mentality inscribed in the film diegesis as well as the *ambiguous* political conditions of its production. Nevertheless, his thought-provoking rethinking of realism is limited to a concern with the indexical tie between the film and its *immediate* context.

This begs an important question: if the value of the film exists solely in its indexical tie with its time, whether in a straightforward or an ambiguous manner, why does it remain significant now? To address this question, I re-focus on the other side of realism, that is elements that exceed indexicality, thus making it possible to relocate the work in a different context. These elements remain in the textual substratum as moments of 'excess', defined as 'the random and inexplicable, that which remains ungovernable within a textual regime presided over by narrative'.[5] Excess in fiction films is built into the very attempt to represent an external world. Such extra-textuality, according to Nichols, can be generalised as 'history', which 'always stands outside the text'; 'Always referred to but never captured, history, as excess, rebukes those laws set to contain it; it contests, qualifies, resists, and refuses them.'[6] My refocus on excess sheds a new light on realism and enables us to read *Crows and Sparrows* with a different frame of reference.

In this essay, I question the orthodox realist discourse by showing how realism is inevitably imbricated with excess. On this basis, I propose an alternative approach to *Crows and Sparrows* as an *allegory*. This allegorical quality, as analysed below, is inscribed in the film's temporal and spatial configurations. However, I will conclude counter to the usual understanding of allegory as utopian by arguing that in this case excess reverses into a dystopic ideology.

My reading of the film as an allegory is premised on Jameson's re-conception of this device as 'an unstable and provisory solution to an aesthetic dilemma which is itself the manifestation of a social and historical contradiction'.[7] The aesthetic dilemma in question is precisely the dilemma of representation. That is, whereas available strategies of representation are necessarily circumscribed by certain conditions, they are nonetheless indispensable for one's speculation on the realm beyond representation. If Nichols considers history as the origin of excess, Jameson similarly sees history as an ultimate term that exceeds representation, but nevertheless is accessible *only through* representation: 'History is *not* a text, not a narrative, master or otherwise, but … as an absent cause, it is inaccessible to us except in textual form, and … our approach to it and to the Real itself necessarily passes through its prior textualization, its narrativization in the political unconscious.'[8] When history exceeds the extant conceptual categories, it results in a crisis of representation, which in turn demands new representational parameters. This is precisely how Jameson's 'allegory' becomes necessary. Jameson's conceptualisation of history and allegory casts a new light on the signifying system of *Crows and Sparrows*.

Produced at the crucial historical moment of 1949, when KMT control was giving way to the would-be CCP government, *Crows and Sparrows* straddles a historical threshold moment, the complexity and instability of which constituted a repre-sentational problem. This problem, following Nichols and Jameson, leads to moments of excess, which can be located in director Zheng Junli's 1979 reflections on the film.

Entitled 'Recording an Outline of the Transitional Moment between the Old Times and the New Era', Zheng's essay displays pronounced reservation, even scepticism, despite surface agreement with the orthodox position on the film. His claim that the film succeeds in recording (*jilu*) its time is bracketed by qualifications such as 'to a certain degree' and 'one aspect' or 'a sidelight'. As a result, realism in the film becomes conditional and partial at the best.[9] Written in 1979 shortly after the end of the Cultural Revolution, Zheng's self-deprecating recount echoes schoolteacher Mr Hua's self-criticism at the end of the film, when he urges all the characters – himself included – *and* the film audience to transform themselves into new people in the new society.

The major 'defects' of the film, according to Zheng, lie in its framework, which was not modified according to the changed situation after the CCP conquered Shanghai. The concentration on the struggle for a two-storey lane house forecloses the possibility of a more penetrating exposé of the KMT in a wider social context. Also, due to KMT censorship and the screenwriter's limitations, the film focuses on the 'sparrows', or narrow-minded urban residents who lease rooms from a domineering KMT official, Mr Hou the 'crow'. Thus, it overlooks the more organised workers and peasants who were named as the masters of the new China. Consequently, the film fails to represent the awakening of the real people – the creators of the new era and the gravediggers of the old dictatorship.[10] Zheng further pinpoints three faulty characterisations. First, the transformation of Mr Hua and the old newspaper editor Mr Kong from weak conciliators to unyielding resistors seems too abrupt and unconvincing. Second, the film fails to highlight Mr Kong's enthusiasm for the People's Liberation Army (PLA), which should be a spontaneous response given his son's CCP affiliation. Third, the film fails to portray Ah Mei, maid of Mr Hou's mistress, as a pivotal figure. As a sheer oppressee, Zheng reasons, Ah Mei should have the strongest sense of justice and the deepest class sympathy, and her good personality should be instrumental for the other characters' transformation.[11]

Zheng's self-criticism is circumscribed by the CCP ideology that dictates who should be the hero, how a hero should behave and why. Ironically, however, his recount carries the CCP terminology overboard, thus undermining the orthodox discourse by converting what the People's Republic official critics have praised as realistic details into subversive moments of excess. These moments undermine the real-to-reel correspondence assumed by the ideology of realism and joins Jameson's 'allegorical spirit'.

To view the film as an allegory entails an emphasis on the temporal-spatial 'edge', which is arguably connected with utopian futures. Allegory thrives at the threshold moment insofar as it provides a provisory solution to the problem of representation by way of a visual projection, that is proffering a figure as proxy for the pre-formed and not-yet-representable realm. The film stemmed precisely from a historical threshold moment, registering a series of images that presumably point toward a desirable future. The film's investment in the future is manifested in three interweaving timelines, all spanning the transition from KMT to CCP control. They are diegetic time, production time and historical time. Diegetic time covers the last two weeks before lunar New Year's Day on 18 January 1949. Production time started in April 1949, was soon suspended by KMT censorship, resumed in May, nearly finished by the end of 1949 and released in early 1950. Historical time includes the CCP conquering north-east China, beating the KMT along the Huai River in the winter of 1948, taking over Shanghai in May 1949 and finally establishing the People's Republic on 1 October 1949. Although diegetic time slightly precedes production time, radical future change is already clearly prefigured in the film. Largely couched in the present tense, indicating contemporariness, diegetic time nevertheless takes on a pronounced forward-looking, or allegorical, dimension. Within the framework of this progressive timeline, diegetic time is strictly chronological. Flashbacks are laboriously eliminated and current happenings consciously extended toward the future – the future delivered by the CCP. The intersection of the film's progress with the pace of CCP victories not only sutured the film into the socio-historical fabric, but was also calculated to visually prefigure the future from this side of the threshold moment.

The investment in the present and the future determines that events that took place fours years ago right after China's victory in the anti-Japanese war (1937–1945) are consigned to mere verbal references, instead of being fleshed out in flashbacks. These events are referred to by Boss Xiao, the American merchandise peddler nicknamed 'Little Broadcast' for his rumour-spreading habit,[12] and Mr Kong, the original house owner. They cover how Hou, the former collaborator with Japan during the anti-Japanese war, was suddenly transformed into an undercover agent, obtaining a high KMT position, subsequently framing Kong's son as a Communist soldier, having him jailed, and usurping Kong's lane house. In the absence of visual flashbacks, these brief verbal allusions in the past tense fill in the background without distracting the audience, so that the present events, fully visualised in the film, can be emphasised and endowed with forward momentum. To modify Winston's comments on pre-war Griersonian documentaries, 'the "problem moment" structure [the problem of housing and class struggle in my context] has an implicit narrative trajectory ... there was a [problematic past]; there is a current problem; there will be a [hopeful] future'.[13] Such a linear and irreversible plot-line implies inevitability, or the 'weight of the temporal axis. The parallel between plot development and temporal progress allows the latter to be perceived and experienced as concrete materiality.'[14] In this light, the chronological narrative in Crows and Sparrows implies a specific future-oriented perspective.

In accordance with the weight of the temporal axis, the confrontation between the 'crows' and the 'sparrows' can be viewed as a struggle to control *time* for their individual interests. The film starts with a newspaper advertisement about an urgent house sale. The hasty sale advertised by the 'crow' Hou causes an instant housing problem for the 'sparrow' tenants. The ensuing story describes their unsuccessful struggle to find other housing before the last day of the year, the deadline set down by Hou. Failure forces them to rebel against Hou's timeframe, replacing it with their own simple one: 'We will unite together. None of us will budge. Let's see what he can do.' The ability to determine their own timeframe (which really means frustrating that of Hou) marks the emergence of a certain subaltern agency. Passive as it seems to be, it outlasts Hou, whose timeframe turns out to be determined not by himself but by the larger historical force of the CCP tug-of-war with the

KMT. This larger force is conveyed through the headlines Little Broadcast disseminates, which serve as a timepiece tolling the knell for Hou and the KMT government.

The tenants' tactic of procrastination implies their vague, sometimes blind, optimism about what the future can bring. For Little Broadcast, the headline news reporting CCP's victory means that peace is coming, that Mr Hua the schoolteacher and Mr Kong's son will be released from prison, and that his business in American goods will prosper. Similarly, Mr Hua tries to ameliorate Mr Kong's pessimism by proclaiming that 'Your account will be settled one day. The forces of evil will be eradicated one day, but the time is not ripe yet ...' Hua's inaction and ostrich-like reliance on the future are largely ineffectual. Nevertheless, he provides a verbal harbinger for future fulfilment. When the calendar in the last sequence turns to the last day of the old lunar year in close-up, the original deadline set up by Hou has become the sparrows' day of celebration. The threshold date finds a perfect visual illustration in the 'happy ending' sequence.

After the fall of Nanking, the base of the KMT government, Hou the crow hurries to leave Shanghai, then a financial centre approximately 400 kilometres to the south of Nanking, reluctantly leaving the house to the sparrow tenants, who represent a wide range of urban classes oppressed by KMT to different degrees. The unexpected resolution of the housing problem, resulting from Hou's hasty escape leads to the final sequence, with all tenants gathering for a joyful lunar New Year. A medium shot toward the end includes all the major characters, significantly positioned on the threshold of the front gate and arranged as in a theatrical tableau, with Mr Kong and Mr Hua – the two intellectuals among the sparrows – delivering clinching remarks for the entire film. After Kong, the original owner, rejoices about regaining his house and looks forward to a promising New Year, Hua, whose consciousness was raised by recent imprisonment, voices his self-criticism and determination to renew himself: 'A new society is coming! We should get rid of our old weaknesses. We must live a new life as new people!'[15] This anticipation of a utopian society merges with the traditional New Year couplet (duilian) that Kong pastes on the gate: 'The firecracker sends off the past; a peach wood mascot brings in the new (baozhu yisheng chujiu, taofu wanhu gengxin).'

This couplet is framed in a close-up at the end, when the tenants-turned-masters go back 'home', closing the gate behind them. A few neighbours run past the gate, setting off firecrackers amid loud festival music. The music track continues long after the image track has turned black. If the gate suggests these characters' on-the-eve and anticipatory mentality,[16] the prolonged music suggests continuation into a utopian future that literally exceeds and lies beyond visual representation. During actual screenings in early 1950, the music track would have accompanied audiences of the New Chinese exiting the theatre after the show, probably around lunar New Year, inspiring them with great expectations for a new year and a new society. By telling an ultimately triumphant story set in the recent past, the film strives toward an undefined yet apparently utopian future.

The encounter between the crows and the sparrows operates not only along the temporal axis, but also on the spatial level. The allegorical dimension of the film accordingly shifts from utopian projection to the spatial reconfiguration of the lane house. Director Zheng recalls that the five-person scriptwriting group (including Zhao Dan who plays Little Broadcast) had to resort to allegory or metaphor (yingyu) in order to dodge KMT censorship. As a result, they deployed

> Hou as a figure for the reactionary KMT, and centred the main story on the house. The house is like the nation (jiangshan), which had belonged to the people, but was usurped by collaborators and KMT lackeys .... their doomsday is approaching ... and the house is returned to its original owner. [17]

Interestingly, Zheng dismisses this allegory as too obscure to be understood by the audience.

Nevertheless, I argue that spatial allegory structures the central conflict by allowing it to develop in a site orchestrated by elaborate camerawork.

First, the two-storey house epitomises and literalises the social hierarchy of the crows and the sparrows. Hou and his mistress lord it over the tenants and live upstairs, where Kong used to live as the original owner. The tenants divide up the rooms below according to their social positions and professions. As part of 'garret literati' (tingzijian wenren) in 1930s and 1940s Shanghai, the schoolteacher Mr Hua and his family live in the garret room to the right of the stairway landing, an intermediate position between upstairs and downstairs.[18] The peddler Little Broadcast and his relatively better-off family live in the front living room, next to the kitchen. In contrast, the original owner Kong, an old and poor newspaper editor, is crammed into the windowless back room. Besides these 'family rooms', there are two 'communal spaces' – the kitchen downstairs and the clothes-drying terrace on the roof. The sparrows gather here to discuss their tactics against the crow. Also, Little Broadcast and Hua's children play games in these places and sing a satirical song that compares Hou to an ugly and oppressive 'monkey'.[19]

This spatial configuration not only epitomises the social hierarchy, but also inscribes its self-deconstruction. The opening sequence, for example, powerfully illustrates porosity between contrasting worlds. The camera first shows Hou's mistress lighting a cigarette in her room upstairs, then tilts down past the floor to reveal the noisy and messy room of Little Broadcast downstairs. This cross-section shot underlines the co-implicating relationship between the oppressor class and the oppressed class by visualising their simultaneous distance *and* proximity. Such proximity produces porosity that allows the sparrows to monitor the crows, thus facilitating their subversion of social hierarchy. The resultant leaking of information is shown often when the sparrows, especially Little Broadcast and his wife, eavesdrop on the stairs. The porous boundaries in the house both

The camera tilts down vertically from the warlord's mistress (her legs seen in upper part of the frame), across the floor (the black plank running horizontally through the frame), to 'Little Broadcast's' wife (lower part of the frame) taking off her hoarded American goods

intensify the conflict and render it susceptible to subaltern corrosion.

As a major site of adjacency and porosity, the stairs constitute an important stage for conflict and struggle as well as connection. Director Zheng emphasises shots at the stairs and the door area in that they help to alleviate the theatrical look resulting from the large quantity of shooting within rooms.[20] The stairs not only diversify the shots, but also imply vertical mobility, thus converting encounters between crows and sparrows into a metaphor for class conflict and re-negotiation of social hierarchy, threatening to collapse boundaries and reverse the hierarchy. This is born out in changes in Hou's physical relationship with other characters and the audience.

Hou, referred to as the 'master' from the very beginning, remains mysteriously invisible to the audience for the first third of the film. The audience hears his voice and coughing sound as '*acous-mêtre*', a disembodied voice that commands ubiquity, panopticism, omniscience and omnipresence.[21] The authoritative voice is located in a body after a set of deferring shots that whet the audience's desire to see Hou. His final materialisation is couched in satiric terms. The camera first tracks up to a close-up of Little Broadcast announcing with a heavy Zhejiang accent: 'Now we've found a solution [to my housing problem].' A graphic match cuts to a picture of the uniformed Chiang Kai-shek (a Zhejiang native) in Little Broadcast's posture, accompanied by a stern off-screen voice. The camera tracks right, stopping briefly at another picture of an ugly uniformed man, then resumes tracking right until it falls upon the back of a man, subsequently revealed to be Hou – the ugly man in the picture. This scene begins with Little Broadcast parodying the dictator Chiang and ends by satirising Hou as a self-important monkey who ludicrously mimics Chiang, his master. The move to locate the domineering voice in Hou's body, or de-acousmatisation, serves to undermine his power, as Chion argues.[22]

Further demystification takes place in an important stairs sequence, where Hou is forced to literally lower himself to face the united tenants at the bottom of the stairs. Zheng recalls that this scene was shot with a wide-angle camera to elongate the stairs and increase the distance between the two parties, thereby to enhance the tension.[23] Two other

A wide-angle over-shoulder shot of Mr Hou (the warlord and crow) from the perspective of 'Little Broadcast', his wife and other tenants (sparrows) behind them outside the frame

types of camerawork contribute to building the tension. First, the clash is deferred by focusing on the tenants listening attentively to off-screen steps walking down the stairs, approaching them. Second, the encounter is registered visually by alternating high-angle and low-angle shots that take the positions of Hou and the tenants in turn. This confrontation on the stairs is a transitional point when the crows and the sparrows switch positions. Their confrontation on the stairs begins with Hou's aggressive threat. Then, with Mr Kong visibly animated by Little Broadcast's words, the children starting to chant their satirical song, and the other tenants forcing their way up the stairs, Hou is compelled to retreat and the old social hierarchy is visually subverted.

This trajectory illustrates Zheng's allegorical conception of the house as a nation usurped by dictators but eventually returned to its original owners, who promise to construct a new future. Insofar as the house is poised on the threshold between the old and the new, bearing marks of both, it evokes Benjamin's 'dialectical image'. Benjamin describes the dialectical image as 'that in which the Then and the Now come into a constellation like a flash of lightning .... the image is dialectics at a standstill.'[24] The collapsing of the past and the present serves to liberate the utopian potential buried in the 'prehistory' (*Urgeschichte*) of the object into an 'afterlife' (*Nachleben*).[25] Such liberation depends precisely on an 'allegorical gaze', because allegory is a form of premonition that 'sees the object as it will appear in its "afterlife"'.[26]

In these terms, the house is wrested from its previous context and reconstructed as a home by, of and for the former sparrows. The moment when the maid Ah Mei replaces Hou's picture with one of Mr Kong and his son suggests momentary superimposition of the past, the present and the future in a montage that quickly turns out to be a dissolve, one image giving way to the other. The whole house *and* the wall thus become a palimpsest, inscribed with multiple temporalities and competing meanings, from Kong's home to Hou's loot, and then to the home of Kong *and* the other sparrows.

Having established the forward-looking and promising side of allegory, I now proceed to discuss how this vision is fractured by excessive moments when viewed with historical hindsight. In other words, I show how history is both figured in the film and exceeds its parameters, turning the utopia of the film upside down, thereby complicating the notion of allegory. To recall Zheng's 1979 reflection on the film, the film fails to focus on the broader social landscape and the more politically conscious classes, and instead limits itself to the self-interested petty bourgeoisie. By reconsidering these apparent faults in terms of excess, we can see how allegory entails constant transformation and inversion when placed in a new context.

In order to show how inversion takes place in the film, I refer to Benjamin's comments on the Soviet experiment with socialism in the late 1920s. Regarding the elimination of private space in late 1920s

A close-up shot of a photograph of Mr Kong (the original owner of the lane house) and his son being hung on the wall, replacing the usurper warlord's picture, illustrating Walter Benjamin's notion of the 'dialectical image'

Moscow, Benjamin observes, 'apartments that earlier accommodated single families in their five to eight rooms now often lodge eight'.[27] While he sees the socialist vision as a potential redemption of what he contemptuously calls 'the petty-bourgeois interior' and its de-politicisation, he implicitly voices a concern, even anxiety, about over-emphasis on the 'correct political tendency' to the exclusion of 'free intellect'.[28] This concern was to become prevalent among Chinese intellectuals as socialism unrolled in the post-1949 China. The film's release was to be followed by similar sweep of collectivisation, which was to provoke ambivalence and even alienation among Chinese people, especially intellectuals, as it did in Benjamin.

Ironically, the film itself contains instances that begin with utopic potential only to turn into their own opposites. With the completion of collectivisation by 1952, a private house owner like Mr Kong would have had his house appropriated – again – for public use this time. Peddlers, especially those trading in foreign merchandise like Little Broadcast, would have been phased out due to economic and political reorientations and re-channelled into socialist collective units, instead of being allowed to expand their private business. Mr Hua's voluntary self-criticism in the happy ending would become the staple in the state-sponsored ideological interpellation that constantly prodded the entire intellectual sector toward self-reflection and realignment with the masses. The encouraging vision of becoming masters of a nation offered at the end of the film was soon to flip into something unexpected, even dystopic, to the sparrows. If hope and utopia lie in the provisory and dreamlike quality of the vision, they become disillusioning when realised in the form of an ossifying and imposing ideology. The utopia postulated in the film can be described as Raymond Williams's 'structure of feeling'. Contrary to an ideology more concerned with maintaining the status quo, 'structure of feeling' is 'at the very edge of semantic availability', and therefore characterised by 'pre-formation' or 'intensity of experience'.[29] The choice to focus the film on the so-called self-interested petty bourgeoisie instead of more politically conscious classes tends towards the production of excess that subverts the original vision. The petty bourgeois conviction in private ownership will ultimately clash with the socialist ideology, although it

may be temporarily harnessed as a rebellious voice against the KMT government and a demand for social change.[30] Reconsidered with the benefit of historical hindsight, the film becomes a complex allegory, its figures being reversible, and its apparently straightforward narrative closure giving rise to indeterminable excess. In this sense, 'realistic' details take on multiple shifting significations as allegorical nexuses.

NOTES

1. Cheng Jihua, Li Shaobai and Xing Zuwen, eds, *The History of Chinese Film (Zhongguo dianying fazhanshi)* (Beijing: Zhongguo dianying chubanshe, 1963), vol. 2, 248.
2. Chen Baichen, 'Thoughts on the Re-release of *Crows and Sparrows*' ('Cong "Wuya yu Maque" chongying shuoqi'), *People's Daily (Renmin ribao)*, 11 January 1958. Quoted in Cheng *et al.*, *The History of Chinese Film*, 244.
3. Leo Ou-fan Lee, 'The Tradition of Modern Chinese Cinema: Some Preliminary Explorations and Hypotheses', in *Perspectives on Chinese Cinema*, ed. Chris Berry (London: BFI, 1993), 7–8.
4. Ibid., 11.
5. Bill Nichols, *Representing Reality: Issues and Concepts in Documentary* (Bloomington: Indiana University Press, 1991), 141.
6. Ibid., 142.
7. Fredric Jameson, *Fables of Aggression: Wydham Lewis, the Modernist Fascist* (Berkeley: University of California Press, 1979), 94.
8. Fredric Jameson, *The Political Unconscious: Narrative as a Socially Symbolic Act* (Ithaca, NY: Cornell University Press, 1981), 35.
9. Zheng Junli, 'Recording an Outline of the Transitional Moment between the Old Times and the New Era' ('Jiluxia xinjiu jiaoti shidai de yige ceying'), in *Voiceover (Huawai yin)* (Beijing: China Film Press, 1979), 19–38.
10. Ibid., 21.
11. Ibid., 27–8.
12. 'Xiao' functions as a pun referring to 'Xiao', his last name, and 'xiao', meaning small or little.
13. Brian Winston, *Claiming the Real: The Documentary Film Revisited* (London: BFI, 1995), 107.
14. Li Suyuan, 'Narrative Modes in Early Chinese Cinema' ('Zhongguo zaoqi dianying de xushu moshi'), in *Melting National Characteristics into Film – Chinese*

Film-Television and National Culture (Minfeng hua jing – Zhongguo yingshi yu minzu wenhua), ed. Zhou Xuan (Beijing: Beijing Normal University Press, 1999), 238.

15. Interestingly and unfortunately, the reformation of intellectuals through the practice of repeated self-criticism and confession was to become a means of persecution during the Cultural Revolution (1966–1976). Ironically, among the persecuted intellectuals were well-known film workers, including Zhao Dan who plays Little Broadcast.

16. It is significant that the front gate appears in the film only in this sequence. Throughout the film, characters enter and exit through the run-down back door. The implication is that only the legitimate master of the house can use the front door, which is associated with the future and progress.

17. Zheng, 'Recording an Outline', 20.

18. Intellectuals in 1930s and 1940s Shanghai were conventionally known as 'garret literati' because their meagre income could only afford the rent of a garret room in a lane house, a cheap accommodation due to its narrow space and noisy environment.

19. Hou's name and the Chinese character for 'monkey' are homophones.

20. Zheng, 'Recording an Outline', 35.

21. Michael Chion, *The Voice in Cinema*, trans. Claudia Gorbman (New York: Columbia University Press, 1999), 24.

22. Ibid.

23. Zheng, 'Recording an Outline', 38.

24. Quoted in Gary Smith, ed., *Benjamin: Philosophy, Aesthetics, History* (Chicago: University of Chicago Press, 1989), 49.

25. Graeme Gilloch, *Myth and Metropolis: Walter Benjamin and the City* (Cambridge: Polity Press, 1996), 111.

26. Ibid., 137.

27. Walter Benjamin, *One-Way Street and Other Writings*, trans. Edmund Jephcott and Kingsley Shorter (London: Verso, 1985), 187. Quoted in Gilloch, *Myth and Metropolis*, 50.

28. Quoted in Gilloch, *Myth and Metropolis*, 53.

29. Raymond Williams, *Marxism and Literature* (Oxford: Oxford University Press, 1985), 134.

30. A similar reversal is mapped out in Jameson's comparative study of *The Godfather I* and *The Godfather II*:

> It is as though the unconscious ideological and Utopian impulses at work in *Godfather I* could in the sequel be observed to work themselves towards the light and towards thematic or reflexive foregrounding in their own right. The first film held the two dimensions of ideology and Utopia together within a single generic structure, whose conventions remained intact. With the second film, however, this structure falls as it were into history itself, which submits it to a patient deconstruction that will in the end leave its ideological content undisguised and its displacements visible to the naked eye. ('Reification and Utopia in Mass Culture', in *Signature of the Visible* [New York: Routledge, 1990], 33.)

11 *Durian Durian*: Defamiliarisation of the 'Real'

Esther M. K. Cheung

THE TRIPARTITE ART OF MAKING

Scholarship on Fruit Chan's films often focuses on issues of realism and the theme of marginality. Some critics have explored these concerns in the context of independent film-making in Hong Kong. *Durian Durian* (2000*)* is particularly often hailed as a fine example of independent film production in the tradition of social realism in Hong Kong.[1] What has not been addressed is the way in which Chan's realism in the film is less a faithful reflection of contemporary reality than an attempt to use 'quasi-realism' to make sense of the phantasmagoric mutations in the global world today. 'Quasi-realism' refers to Chan's adoption of the realistic film style in his fiction films to enhance the impressions and effects of the 'real'. This assertion does not suggest that *Durian Durian* is not 'realistic', nor does it argue that it cannot be described in the tradition of social realism. Undoubtedly, the film exhibits many traits in the tradition of realism: the aesthetics of the long take, the employment of amateur actors and the use of hand-held camera. These 'techniques' are used to tell an intersecting story of social concern: the life experiences of two marginalised characters – an illegal immigrant and a prostitute – in Hong Kong. All these demonstrate what Kristin Thompson and the neo-formalists call 'realistic motivations'.[2] It was produced with a low budget outside the industrial film institution. While the realistic 'aura' adhering to this film is easily recognisable, this paper argues that these 'realistic' traits are better understood in specific historical and cultural context as the film-maker's attempt to *make sense* of the urban mutations in post-handover Hong Kong and post-socialist China. As film art is a conscious process of sense-making, which is particularly true in independent films, our analysis will have to rely on the understanding of the dynamics of art-making and the context of independent film-making. The connection between the two, seldom analysed previously, will illuminate Chan's film practice as what

I would call the 'tripartite art of making', shedding light on how alternative film art can be practised in our contemporary world.

By 'making sense', I refer to an existential and cultural stance borne by independent film-makers who mediate their agency through film art. Rather than acting as auteur in a Romantic sense, they create a cultural space for themselves by negotiating with the constraints imposed upon them. The choice of a realistic style is a matter of actualising this independent endeavour. It is important to point out that reality and realism as a mode of representation are not to be confused with each other. As critics have observed, realism, which is fundamentally associated with social transformation, may emerge in various forms such as naturalism, social or socialist realism and 'healthy realism'.[3] Realism is thus better understood as a style that needs to be studied in specific historical and cultural contexts than a representational mode that articulates a natural relationship between art and world. After his first three films, *Made in Hong Kong* (1997), *The Longest Summer* (1998) and *Little Cheung* (1999), often called the 'Handover Trilogy', Chan was intrigued by the changing cultural space in Hong Kong and ended up making *Durian Durian* 'for fun', as he himself put it. When making *Little Cheung*, Chan was already interested in further exploring the story of the illegal immigrant girl Fan. At the same time, he saw the many prostitutes from the PRC frequenting Wan Chai and Mongkok and decided to make a film about them. In an interview, Chan talked about how the genesis of the film did not start with a concrete idea:

> I didn't write a script for *Durian Durian* – not a word. I just went to Wan Chai to do research. ... I thought I had something, but I still hadn't figured out the structure. ... I thought their lives were fascinating but that was not enough, I needed an angle to go deeper.[4]

Finding an angle in Chan's sense is an attempt of 'making sense'. It therefore does not imply a reflective and natural connection between film and the world; it also involves two other kinds of 'making' – 'making strange' and 'making-do'. If artistic creation can be aptly considered as a kind of interpretation, *Durian Durian* demonstrates a process of 'making strange', providing viewers with an angle of grappling with the changing reality that exceeds their ability to comprehend. Or, we can call it 'defamiliarisation', following the neo-formalists.[5] One can even say that defamiliarising the 'real' is the film-maker's crudest way of facing the 'real'. According to Chan's own recollection, this angle was solidified when he travelled to the PRC with Qin Hailu, the actress who plays the prostitute:

> So I went with her back to her hometown to have a look. … suddenly it all became clear – I knew how to make this film. It was at that moment that the whole structure came to me. … Over the course of interviews with many prostitutes, I discovered that a lot of them actually came from this type of background [from special arts school]. So we put these elements together and suddenly the story was born.[6]

This new artistic angle of articulating reality was acquired when Chan shifted his attention from Hong Kong to the PRC, unlike his earlier films, which focus more on Hong Kong's situation before and during the 1997 handover. In this essay, it is argued that this new angle is a technique of making strange a 'familiar' situation, namely the presence of two groups of illegal border-crossers in Hong Kong. It is accomplished, as we shall see later, not only by depicting the inner lives of the characters but also by the use of the uncanny narrative structure and the quasi-realistic *mise en scène*. It is thus more interesting to read *Durian Durian* as an art of defamiliarisation that mixes documentary realism with dramatic elements to shape a critical cultural discourse on self and other. Intriguingly, this new angle also brings forth the defamiliarisation of a realist docudrama. It illustrates that artwork will be disappointing if it is only subordinated to the strict principle of realism, no matter whether the imperatives come from market constraints or political dicta.[7] Independent art also has its own ideal notions such as authenticity and objectivity, which do not necessarily help one render a powerful artwork. The value of *Durian Durian* lies in its openness and seriality in both content and form. It did not start with a preset idea; Chan utilised leftover ideas from *Little Cheung*, the previous film, simultaneously exploring the dynamics of the contingent environment around him.

If 'making strange' is a means of making sense, Chan's film art is also a practice of 'making-do' because of his status between industrial and arthouse cinemas. After the 'Handover Trilogy', *Durian Durian* marks his other attempt to shift from the mainstream to the independent. Chan started his career in the industry in the 1980s as an assistant director before he made his explosive independent debut, *Made in Hong Kong*.[8] While it is generally true that Chan adopted an independent film-making mode, his in-between status allows him to gain financial assistance from film producers in the mainstream. In his legendary making of *Made in Hong Kong*, he stockpiled 80,000 feet of film stock off-cuts, secured the support of superstar Andy Lau, relied on a limited fund of US$80,000 and a crew of only five people to produce his film. Following his enhanced international fame after the 'Handover Trilogy', *Durian Durian* was produced by Nicetop Independent Limited and Golden Network Limited, and supported by funding from France. As Golden Network distributes not only art films but also those with mainstream appeal, he is not completely separated from the industry. I agree with Tony Rayns, who remarks that Chan shows 'an insider's attempt to unlearn some bad industry habits, a professional's bid to beat commercial rivals at their own game'.[9] To some extent, we can name this mode of film-making 'an art of making-do'. It is similar to de Certeau's idea that one can make-do by constructing one's own space within and against the other's space, speaking one's own meanings with other people's language.[10] While *Durian Durian* did not make impressive box-office records, its artistic value was affirmed by a few film awards in Hong Kong, which had mainly been paying attention to commercial productions until the emergence of *Made in Hong Kong* in 1997.[11] While it is true that *Durian Durian* is less adhered to commercial genres than his earlier films and is more like an arthouse production, the film can nonetheless be aptly described as an alternative at the edge of the mainstream.

THE 'REALISTIC' SUBJECT MATTER

In his films, Chan often expresses a consistent interest in the lives and experiences of the lower-class people. The gangsters and lost youth in *Made in Hong Kong*, the disbanded Chinese soldiers of the British Army in *The Longest Summer*, the illegal immigrants in *Little Cheung* and *Durian Durian*, the prostitutes in *Durian Durian* and *Hollywood Hong Kong* (2001) form an array of socially and culturally marginalised characters. This persistent concern has earned him the title of a 'grassroots film-maker', placing him in the tradition of social realism.

In her book on *Durian Durian*, Wendy Gan observes that the film shows some shifts in the images of the two kinds of illegal border-crossers from China to Hong Kong, all of which also reveal a changing cultural relationship between the two places. Since the 1980s, Hong Kong's vibrant economic developments and China's opening up during the Reform Era have coincidentally generated continuous cross-border human traffic. The massive influx of illegal immigrants to Hong Kong in the late 1970s and the onset of handover in 1997 seemed to be key factors that have contributed to an unequal Self–Other relation in the society at large or on screen, no matter whether the 'Other' is legal or illegal. Public discourses began to differentiate the earlier immigrants who fled China during social and political upheavals in the 1950s and 1960s from these more recent immigrants who are economically driven.[12] In film culture, from images of the invasive masculine 'Other' in Johnny Mak's *Long Arm of the Law* (1984) or ludicrous feminised 'Other' in Alfred Cheung's *Her Fatal Ways* series (1990–1994), the centrality of these marginalised images is exploited for sensual pleasure. However, in *Little Cheung, Durian Durian* and other films, this image of the 'Other' has become more sympathetic, as Fan and her family show us. In different ways, more and more mainland women who came to Hong Kong with a legitimate permit often breached their terms by extending their stay and working as prostitutes. Their presence in Hong Kong, abstracted and solidified into Yan's role, not only drew public attention but also created a new category of sex-workers on the Hong Kong screen.[13] While previous images are more or less localised, as portrayed in Lawrence Ah Mon's *The Queen of Temple Street* (1990), mainland prostitutes have acquired greater and more sympathetic exposure in films like *Durian Durian*, Yu Lik-wai's *Love Will Tear Us Apart* (1999) and Derek Yee's *One Nite in Mongkok* (2004).

As illegal immigrant and sex-worker from mainland China, Fan and Yan signify two major strands of ethnoscape drifting across the border between Hong Kong and the PRC. They stand out prominently as prototypical figures of marginality in Hong Kong society. As new kinds of unequal relationships are formed between these illegal border-crossers and Hong Kong people, the inclusion of these characters naturally leads one to anticipate a realistic story of social victimhood, although such a story is not automatically realistic. In terms of subject matter and its inherent ideology, it is interesting to note that the film manifests double-coded meaning. On the first level, the story depicts rather objectively and realistically the two lower-class people's experiences in Hong Kong and China, drawing our attention to the inner worlds of the neglected people and the interiors of the abject city spaces in Hong Kong. The low-cost cafés, dirty and wet back alleys, and the congested brothel houses in Hong Kong help to re-situate the lower-class people's lives in the film's *mise en scène*. The film does not propagandise any socialist ideology of class struggle, although the class issue is prominently foregrounded, with constant references to what is often repressed in the grand narrative of the Hong Kong economic miracle, as is also the case in Chan's earlier films.[14] In fact, both characters, but in particular Yan, are closer to what Aihwa Ong calls the '*homo-economicus*' who are not only economically driven but also indifferent to social and economic inequality.[15] On the second level, this realistic and socialist connection, which is class-specific, is constantly mixed with a subtle thrust toward what is more universally shared. As Chan himself explains, the film is about the sense of dislocation and homelessness that people feel; it emphasises 'the power of space and the attachment one feels to the place they call home, one in the north, one in the south'.[16] As the Chinese title of the film, *Liulian piaopiao*, literally means 'the floating durian', migratory experiences suggest a sense of heaviness, very much like the drifting durian, which is weighty, spiky and unacceptable to many people's taste. Differentiated from political refugees and émigrés, these kind of urban exiles and their nostalgia are caught up with the waves of globalisation in what Chris Berry calls the 'post-socialist' world.[17] In the case of 'post-socialist' China, ever since the country opened up in the 1980s, there has been a gradual decline in the socialist ideology and revolutionary ideal in the context of people's everyday life, even though the official grand narrative of socialism is yet to be renounced. It is within this context that the second level of meaning can be deciphered.

In the following, I argue that these double-coded meanings of the specific and the general form a double bind, which is made possible by the techniques of defamiliarisation. It is also due to the latter coding that a story seemingly grounded in social realism has acquired the lyrical and personalised traits of a border-crosser's travelogue.

QUASI-REALISM IN *DURIAN DURIAN*

THE QUASI-REALIST *MISE EN SCÈNE*

Durian Durian demonstrates a mixed use of documentary realism and dramatic elements to create the thematic double bind. Although there are clear realistic motivations that cue viewers to associate the film with notions of authenticity, technical crudeness is not Chan's trademark. Chan once remarked on his preference for not teaching the non-professionals how to act because their natural and unskilled rendition would convey an illusion of authenticity, everydayness and ordinariness.[18] That is why the use of non-professional actors is emphatically presented toward the end before the credits roll on. It is quite true that Fan and most of the actors are amateurs but Qin Hailu, the actress playing Yan, is not strictly untrained. Yan's ordinariness, enhanced by her unfamiliarity to Hong Kong viewers, is mixed with her professional finesse as a mainland opera artist. Her impressive acting skills, which won her the Best New Artist in the 20th Hong Kong Film Awards in 2000, were acquired from her Chinese opera background. Her acting and artist background helped Chan to achieve the 'angle' of articulating the experience of urban exile, which brings him somewhat closer to other contemporary urban film-makers in the PRC. Jia Zhangke, Wang Xiaoshuai, Zhang Yuan and others have all turned self-reflexively to the image of artist/intellectual to explore the impact of the unprecedented waves of modernisations and globalisations on the cultural realm.[19] Although Chan, unlike his mainland counterparts, seldom seeks to emphasise authorship to assert the significance of

Durian Durian

artistic independence in his other films, Yan's 'professional' performance of Peking opera in an open space at the end of the film conveys nostalgic sentiments. As a metanarrative device that defamiliarises the 'realistic' depiction, the nostalgic performance clings onto a traditional art form as a way to resist the global currents of change that threaten to wipe out one's cultural roots. It is a lonesome, persistent performance, which acquires a Sisyphean absurdist, if not heroic, outlook in the midst of inevitable changes.

Undoubtedly, the ordinary façade of the film is also maintained by on-location shooting, occasionally accompanied by the use of hand-held camera, especially in the first half of the film. The use of the hidden camera as an observational device documents the contingent sense of the mundane and the trivial spaces and happenings as 'evidences' and 'records'. The scenes in the back-street cafés where pimps and sex-workers gather display strong documentary realism. In addition, long shots also enhance the distance and the sense of objectivity of cinéma vérité, capturing actions in process. In many instances in *Durian Durian*, however, long shots and long takes create quasi-realistic effects. For example, the scene where Fan's family tries hard to open the durian is closer to a contrived studio production than a random on-location record of action-in-process in a medium-range shot. The scene is clearly not scripted, because the characters improvise amiably as they go along, but its paradigmatic relation with other scenes about people's love–hate relationships with the durian adds a symbolic dimension to the episode. Shot in one long take of more than four minutes (timecode 42:45–46:54) with a stationary camera, it captures not only the action-in-process in a horizontal manner but also stresses how the movement of narrativity depends on the vertical, metaphorical relation of paradigmatic events. The use of symbols does not necessarily make things less 'real' but symbols clearly defamiliarise the 'real' through their artificiality. It is the recurrence of this artifice that allows the theme of homelessness to be coherently developed.

THE GHOSTLY SOUND/VOICE

The feeling of time–space dislocation that border-crossers experience in an age of globalisation can be further explored in the audio dimension. As Yan's moneymaking career in Hong Kong is hectic, she relaxes by performing a series of stretching exercises in a back alley in Mongkok, Hong Kong. The scene is composed of several edited shots taken from a great distance with an objective camera angle lasting for two minutes (timecode 29:36–31:30). She starts off with routine exercises but ends up practising operatic acrobatics. On the soundtrack, the non-diegetic music of Peking opera is heard in a ghostly manner as if spirits from another space and time have been invoked. It is not only a moment of relaxation through recollection but also of time–space dislocation. Elizabeth Wilson argues that the city 'naturally evokes a sense of the past and of change', arguing that 'the changing fabric of cities congeals that process of the passage of time in a way that is both concrete and somehow eerie and ghostly'.[20] I would add that the feeling of homesickness in the city is intensified because of the dislocation of affect and place. Ghosts as symbols of the past appear in the city because of this continuing process of change, more so in the case of border-crossers.

This interesting amalgam of the phantasmagoric *mise en scène* and the ghostly sound is further paradigmatically linked to two other scenes where the voice-over is heard: the surrealist superimposition of images of the Hong Kong Victoria Harbour and Mudanjiang in North-eastern China when the film opens and her reading of Fan's letter when she returns home. In both cases, one character's voice runs into the other's in the same way that one changing space (Hong Kong) opens up into another (North-east/Shenzhen). It is close to what Michel Chion calls the '*acousmêtre*'.[21] It is an off-screen voice that does not correspond to the visual representation. In some films, they are literally ghostly, because they are the voices of the dead that narrate the events. While Fan and Yan's voices are not exactly like that, they are

also dislocated from the bodies to which they correspond. Together with the opening shots of Hong Kong and Mudanjiang, this kind of image–voice dislocation ironically suggests a somewhat optimistic Bakhtinian dialogical relationship between two selves, implying that the self cannot be constructed without an interaction with the other. The Self–Other relation is more like gift-giving than unequal exploitation. These scenes, however, are also extremely open to interpretation because of the multiple meanings of the visual signifiers. Whether this ideal can be actualised in the context of 'one country, two systems' – Deng Xiaoping's political model for post-handover Hong Kong – is questionable; its dialogic interaction also suggests the consequences of the homogenising force of globalisation. While the erasure of differences in a global context might imply the realisation of a cosmopolitan ideal, it might also foreshadow a dystopia where the sense of homelessness is universally shared. It cannot be denied that Yan and Fan can be described as border-crossers who feel homeless, regardless of their class differences and motivations; their sense of attachment to place is constantly threatened by incessant urban mutations that no one can arrest.

THE UNCANNY NARRATIVE AND HYBRID GENRE

Besides symbolism and the ghostly soundscape, the parallel but intersecting narratives and mixed genre also create defamiliarisation effects. The double narrative embodies an uncanny structure, which refers to repetitive events that recur with a difference; what is familiar returns as the unfamiliar, just as the double semantic of the German uncanny, *unheimlich*, suggests.[22] This doubleness helps to depict the characters' paradoxical estrangement to places they call 'home'.

The film can be neatly divided into two halves. The first part focuses on both characters' lives in Hong Kong, while the second concentrates on Yan's journey back home. The first narrative is structured in such a realistic way that events are basically incidental, with a few coincidences that create some dramatic moments: for example, the attack of the pimp and the police's search for illegal immigrants. But these incidents are not important enough to alter the characters' fate. There is no significant difference between what the narratologists call 'kernel' and 'satellite' events, as they are mostly mundane and trivial, recorded in a documentary style.[23] A certain rhythm of the real events is created by the objective recording of the characters' everyday life. Fan and Yan's activities are delivered in a fast-paced alternating manner, creating details for verisimilitude. Many of them are similar to actions-in-process in cinema vérité. The second part shifts to Yan's experience back in China, where her background is revealed, although events are more or less incidentally structured. The pace of events is slower than the first, without its elaborate alternation with Fan's story. Her divorce and her friends' departure from the North-east are not climactic events of any sort that entice a final denouement. The film ends *in media res*, looking into an uncertain future just as Yan loses herself in the vast, agoraphobic space of snowy Mudanjiang, which is experiencing drastic mutations.

Despite all these, in both parts, the objective effect of documentary realism is mixed freely with the use of subjective shots such as shot/reverse shots and close-ups. Together with the voice-over, the characters' inner subjective feelings allow the documentary mode to coexist with the genre of the travelogue. If the film documents changing reality, it also captures reality through psychological reflections. Undoubtedly, Fan and Yan's voices deviate from the National Geographic-like documentaries in which the narrator is often a male, disembodied voice, imparting information and knowledge. Their voices help to add a personal and lyrical dimension to the objective narrative, providing viewers with access to their inner lives. Hearing their narration is like reading a traveller's log that provides information, epiphany and expression. It is thus documentary, exploratory and expressive. The film does not rely entirely on voice-over; it utilises edited subjective shots and close-ups to stress the impact of the impersonal global forces on the personal. The sense of objectivity enhanced by documentary realism is not undermined but augmented by 'evidences' through the means of subjectivisation. While it does not propagandise any socialist ideology, it opens up a subtle critique of the encroachment of the global upon the local through the use of the hybrid genre.

The film expresses the characters' feeling of homesickness not only in exile but also at home. The unprecedented processes of globalisation have swept through southern cities like Shenzhen and the more remote parts of China. Yan returns to discover this huge wave uprooting her sense of attachment, which she can never restore after a short span of separation. It is through the uncanny narrative structure that this double sense of homelessness is articulated. Similar to the sense of time–space dislocation that is conveyed when Yan practises in the Hong Kong back alley, her dislocated feeling is expressed when she returns home, even in everyday matters like the choice of cosmetics and use of gloves. She also finds her homeland shifting ground as friends and relatives are following waves of urbanisation and globalisation to seek opportunities elsewhere. Home has indeed become uncannily unfamiliar. The parallel spatial configuration in the double narrative further perpetuates this sense of uncanniness. Both Yan and Fan's spacious homes in China contrast with their congested sojourns in Hong Kong, whether it is the back alley or the crammed interior. Agoraphobia and claustrophobia seem to be diametrically opposite but they are in fact two sides of the same coin. Both reflect feelings of homelessness that result from a sense of time–space dislocation. One can even venture to say that Yan's agoraphobia is an uncanny recurrence of her earlier claustrophobia. The double spatial configuration functions like the double semantic of the *unheimlich* to convey the sense of homelessness but with a difference.

CONCLUDING REFLECTIONS

All cultural representations are uncanny; without the techniques of defamiliarisation, they are stuck in the subordination to doctrine, dictum and propaganda. Chan's quasi-realism, just like the double-coded theme of the film, makes *Durian Durian* a 'pleasurable' text to read, in Roland Barthes's sense. It helps to express his 'independent', personal vision of the mutable reality in both post-handover Hong Kong and post-socialist China, although we are well aware that limited autonomy is everyone's ontological condition. His art of making-do is practised in the space between the mainstream and the alternative; it is important to add that the process of negotiation also exists between the global and the local.

Chan's incentive to articulate Hong Kong and China's changing cultural space is intimately tied with Hong Kong's relation with China after the handover, globalisation and his aesthetics of quasi-realism. It also arose out of the changing film scene in Hong Kong when industrial film-making declined in the mid-1990s. This coincidence created an opportunity for alternative or non-industrial film-makers to expand the cinematic public sphere in Hong Kong. Some have sought Hong Kong government's funding; others like Chan have acquired sponsorship here and elsewhere.[24] Global cinematic connections have provided Chan with opportunities to produce and exhibit his films. Similar to Jia Zhangke and other contemporary Chinese urban film-makers, he is better received overseas than locally. Identified now as Hong Kong 'arthouse' produced and circulated in the space between the global and the local, Chan's films, together with those of Wong Kar-wai and Stanley Kwan, bifurcate the international viewing reception of Asian films. In addition to Hong Kong action cinema, their films disturb the tendency of mono-culturalisation or homogenisation in global cinematic culture, providing diversification not only in generic innovation but also in modes of production and distribution.[25] However, we can also argue that Chan's 'tripartite art of making' has no choice but to benefit from the processes of economic and cultural globalisation. The subtle critique of globalisation through quasi-realism in *Durian Durian* has provided viewers with a better understanding of the plight of border-crossers, but the sense of helplessness inherent in the characters' actions and choices seems to suggest that the absorption into, or collaboration with, the global is simply inevitable. In so-called 'independent' film, the notion of agency may be a better reference than the idea of 'auteur' to indicate that the film-maker is bound up in local and global relations, audience expectations and industrial/state desires in the process of negotiating with one's own incentive *to make sense*, *make strange* and *make-do*.

Acknowledgment

The work described in this paper was fully supported by a grant from the Research Grants Council of the Hong Kong Special Administrative Region, China (Project No. HKU 7416/05H).

NOTES

1. See Natalia Sui Hung Chan, 'The Cruel Tragedy of Youth: On Fruit Chan's *Made in Hong Kong*', in *Cinedossier* (Taipei: Taipei Golden Horse Film Festival, 1998), 77–81; Esther M. K. Cheung, 'The City that Haunts: The Uncanny in Fruit Chan's *Made in Hong Kong*', in *Between Home and World: A Reader in Hong Kong Cinema*, ed. Esther M. K. Cheung and Chu Yiu-wai (Hong Kong: Oxford University Press, 2004), 352–368; Chu Yingchi, 'Hong Kong Cinema after 1997', in *Hong Kong Cinema: Coloniser, Motherland and Self* (London and New York: RoutledgeCurzon, 2003), 119–133; Wendy Gan, *Fruit Chan's Durian Durian* (Hong Kong: Hong Kong University Press, 2005).

2. Kristin Thompson, *Breaking the Glass Armor: Neoformalist Film Analysis* (Princeton, NJ: Princeton University Press, 1988).

3. See Laikwan Pang, *Building a New China in Cinema: The Chinese Left-Wing Cinema 1932–1937* (Lanham, MD: Rowman & Littlefield, 2002); Yingjin Zhang, *Chinese National Cinema* (New York: Routledge, 2004); and Chris Berry and Mary Farquhar, *China on Screen* (Hong Kong: Hong Kong University Press, 2006).

4. Michael Berry, 'Fruit Chan: Hong Kong Independent', in *Speaking in Images* (New York: Columbia University Press, 2005), 474.

5. See Thompson, *Breaking the Glass Armor*, 11–21.

6. Ibid., 475.

7. See Jean-François Lyotard, 'Answering the Question: What is Postmodernism?', in *Modernism/ Postmodernism*, ed. Peter Brooker (London: Longman, 1992), 144–145.

8. Berry, 'Fruit Chan', 461–464.

9. Tony Rayns, 'Made in Hong Kong', *Sight & Sound*, 8 (1999): 48. Available online at: <www.bfi.org.uk/ sightandsound/review/173/> (accessed 27 February 2007).

10. Michel de Certeau, *The Practice of Everyday Life* (Berkeley: University of California Press, 1984), 30.

11. It took the Best Screenplay prize and Qin Hailu won as Best New Artist at the 20th Hong Kong Film Awards.

12. Gan, *Fruit Chan's Durian Durian*, 62.

13. Ibid., 48.

14. See Cheung, 'The City that Haunts'.

15. Aihwa Ong, 'On the Edge of Empires: Flexible Citizenship among Chinese in Diaspora', *Positions*, 1, no. 3 (1993): 745–778.

16. Berry, 'Fruit Chan', 477.

17. Chris Berry, 'Facing Reality: Chinese Documentary, Chinese Postsocialism', in *The First Guangzhou Triennial: Reinterpretation: A Decade of Experimental Chinese Art (1990–2000)*, ed. Wu Hung, Wang Huangsheng and Feng Boyi (Guangzhou: Guangdong Museum of Art, 2002), 121.

18. Berry, 'Fruit Chan', 473.

19. See Xiaoping Lin, 'New Chinese Cinema of the "Sixth Generation": A Distant Cry of Forsaken Children', *Third Text*, 16, no. 3 (2002): 261–284; and Shuqin Cui, 'Working from the Margins: Urban Cinema and Independent Directors in Contemporary China', *Post Script*, 20, nos. 2–3 (2001): 77–93.

20. Elizabeth Wilson, 'Looking Backward, Nostalgia and the City', in *Imagining Cities: Scripts, Signs, Memory*, ed. Sallie Westwood and John Williams (London: Routledge, 1997), 127.

21. Michel Chion, *The Voice in Cinema*, ed. and trans. Claudia Gorbman (New York: Columbia University Press, 1999).

22. Sigmund Freud, 'The Uncanny', trans. James Strachey et al., in *The Standard Edition of the Complete Psychological Works of Sigmund Freud*, vol. XVII (London: Hogarth Press, 1964), 224–225. The use of the uncanny here deviates from the original Freudian psychosexual context.

23. See Steven Cohan and Linda M. Shires, *Telling Stories: A Theoretical Analysis of Narrative Fiction* (New York: Routledge, 1988), 54.

24. Bryan Chang's *After the Crescent* (1997) and Vincent Chui's *Leaving in Sorrow* (2001) are two representative productions of government sponsorship.

25. See Audrey Yue, '*In the Mood for Love*: Intersections of Hong Kong Modernity', in *Chinese Films in Focus*, ed. Chris Berry (London: BFI, 2003), 128–136.

12   *Ermo*: (Tele)Visualising Urban/Rural Transformation

Ping Fu

Focusing on Zhou Xiaowen's 1994 film *Ermo*, this essay asks how contemporary Chinese film-makers use visual motifs to delineate the new urban space that has been socially reconfigured by transnational capital and globalised cultural practices. The corresponding urban–rural dichotomy dynamics reflect new political assertions, ideological underpinnings, historical conditions, social transformations, and cultural practices and negotiation. In the late 1980s and early 1990s, a striking number of films about rural migration, and the plight of rural women migrants in particular, appeared on the screenscape, counter-intuitively focused more on economic reform than gender issues *per se*. For example, one of the earliest films about rural women seeking business opportunities in the city, Peng Xiaolian's 1987 *Women's Story*, attracted the attention of international film critics for its portrayal of women's changing role in the labour force. And Zhang Liang's 1990 film, *Girls from the Special Economic Zone*, tells the story of a group of rural women becoming employees of a joint-venture electronic factory in Shenzhen, the Special Economic Zone near Hong Kong in the 1970s.

Film-makers started to question economic reform, re-embracing humanitarian themes concentrating on women's identities and their social repositioning in the course of unanticipated side effects from this socio-economic revolution. Based on the novel by Xu Baoqi, *Ermo* keenly depicts the dislocation of gender, society and culture faced with the lure of new work roles and economic prosperity. Rural women like the leading figure, Ermo, embody all the contradictory effects of this 'dislocation' in relation to transnational capital and heterogeneous cultural practices.

Most of existing writing on *Ermo* examines how the film's content demonstrates issues concerning the power of capital, economic development, technological phantasmagoria, consumer culture and the role of women's bodies in the formation of power.[1] My project is to treat the 'technologised visuality'[2] of both the film itself and its televisual theme as a discourse in which the filmic spectacle demands further critique by pointing to its own ideological connotations and social implications. By elaborating on how these elements interact with the story, I analyse the urban–rural dichotomy as it is condensed into the vivid depiction of a rural woman in pursuit of the biggest TV in town.

My close reading aims to supplement exiting critiques by unpacking visual clues to scrutinise the representational value of the commodity-on-display and its cinematic iconography. I discuss how experiencing the power of a spectacle is transmitted by the film, and how post-socialist consumerism and the new urban phantasmagoria are turning the commodity form into an ideology in its own right. If, as Michel Foucault puts it, 'urban space has its own dangers',[3] how does 'danger' intersect with emergent hybrid political and economic cultures and change human behaviour? How do people in post-socialist China, including the film-maker, comprehend and respond to modernity in this period of political and economic transition?

Cultural representations of rural and urban identities are taking on increasing significance in China today under conditions of state retreat and marketisation. These conditions are creating a space shared by the desirable and profitable grandeur of transnational capital, and the unexpected and debatable splendour of the global culture – the two most prominent inputs from Western culture. Transnational capital provides Chinese people with mobility and autonomy while global culture moves society toward post-industrial ideological practice. In this filmic instance, the parallel economic and cultural inputs reflect the political economics and cultural politics at play in contemporary Chinese modernisation. And in this mirrored hybridity, we see an emerging dichotomy of China and the world, the rural and the urban, the individual and the collective, the traditional and the modern, and woman and man.

THE SOCIAL BACKGROUND AND SYNOPSIS

Launched in the late 1970s, reform of the old socialist state-owned economy has penetrated every fibre of people's lives with irresistible force. The leading-edge sectors of this economic transformation are foreign investment and domestic private enterprise. The influx of imported goods and foreign culture, and the experiences and expectations that travel with them, have followed three decades of relative isolation.[4] The combination of these two sectors with the continued existence of the old state-run sector signals the emergence of a hybrid state and society. Less politically and ideologically harsh policies have provided farmers, in particular, with more chances to take advantage of the market economy, leading many to seek out business opportunities and new roles in the urban landscape. In major cities, the presence of multinational corporations signifies speedy modernisation of the economy while also posing a challenge to domestic enterprises. Hence the contest and compromise of the domestic and the foreign, the traditional and the modern, and the rural and the urban, forming a landscape of hybridity. These heterogeneous cultures, politics and regional practices and traditions have found common ground to invent the Chinese urban scenario of the 1990s. But the global reach of capitalism, which has transformed China's old integrated economic system and hybridised its culture, has come at the price of human and cultural dislocation.

'*Ermo*' in the Chinese north-western dialect literally means 'the second daughter' of the family. '*Mo*' in classic Chinese refers to a plain woman. Nevertheless, the female protagonist Ermo is a good-looking and hard-working peasant woman, whose journey to modernity is one of spatial transition and mental transformation. As a mother and the wife of a physically, sexually and politically impotent man, Ermo is the breadwinner and decision-maker in her family. Her aspirations include buying a huge colour television set for her son, whose spare time is spent watching the television of a sharp-tongued neighbour with a daughter his age. The neighbour's husband Xiazi

(literally meaning 'blind') is the *nouveau riche* owner–driver of the only truck in the village. He encourages Ermo to take her roadside business selling twisted noodles and hand-woven baskets to the city. There she sets her sights on a 29-inch colour television that attracts daily crowds and that not even the mayor can afford. Her new obsession with the large television fuels her ambition to enter the city marketplace and increase her earning power. She commutes with Xiazi, and, through his connections, becomes a noodle-making expert in a city restaurant. Her new job requires her to relocate to an urban women's hostel. When a co-worker suffers an accident demanding a transfusion, she discovers that cash is paid for blood. Selling her blood regularly, her health declines.

Sharing rides with Xiazi promotes their relationship. He praises her ability to support her family and produce a son. Denigrating his own wife as a narrow-minded couch potato, he suggests they each divorce their spouses to be together. This intensifies their clandestine love, until she discovers that Xiazi secretly boosted her wages through an arrangement with the restaurant manager. Outraged at being treated like a whore, she quits her job and returns home to resume making and selling twisted noodles in the local market.

Finally, Ermo makes enough money to buy the highly sought-after 29-inch television set and bring it home. It has to be manoeuvred in through the window and placed on the bed – the only place large enough to hold the monstrosity. As soon as the television set is settled in, Ermo collapses from exhaustion. As the coloured light display of the television and the promise of viewing the outside world attracts the villagers to squeeze into the room, Ermo leans on the set, helplessly turning herself into part of the show.

SEARCHING FOR MODERN CIVILISATION

Ermo does not have the typical Chinese glamour that Zhang Yimou and Chen Kaige intentionally and effectively created to attract the gaze of the international film market. It is not a tale of 'a helpless victim or self-sacrificing saint who has suffered the usual varieties of sexist exploitation'.[5] Nor does the story reveal feudal Chinese oppressiveness in the form of an unreasonable and domineering male figure, which was Zhang Yimou's trademark 'secret

Ermo: to market with twisted noodles

weapon' in international film festivals. Rather, *Ermo*, anchored in contemporary rural China, depicts a strong-willed peasant woman on a mission to buy a 29-inch television. According to director Zhou Xiaowen, the film is about 'a peasant's pursuit of a new lifestyle and her wish for upward mobility'.[6] In other words it is, as most Chinese critics say, about 'modern civilisation'.

Evidently, 'modern civilisation' here is largely and loosely associated with material abundance, foreign commodities and modern technology. As a symbol of Western influence, the city and the television set embody the new urban phantasmagoria equated with 'modern civilisation'. The term indirectly but forcefully manifests a challenge to the past, a denial of tradition, and a belief in social advancement and historical progress. It is the lure of modern civilisation that initiates Ermo's desperate pursuit of the symbolic television, which is a perfect cipher for the meaning and effect of change in rural China. Nevertheless, the meanings of her mission are multiple. They include a fight for dignity, an

emotional competition with her neighbour, an overwhelming desire to possess the best, the capacity to consume within the new national economic environment, a woman's effort in a domestic power struggle and an unconscious departure from patriarchal tradition.

However, the misfortune that Ermo experiences in pursuit of her dream undermines all the above positives. Modern civilisation and all it signifies becomes a new hegemony that monitors, justifies and shapes the thoughts and deeds of each individual. What most represses rural women like Ermo is no longer traditional ethics but modern civilisation itself in the form of the commodity. Showing how Ermo is captured by the power of the commodity and in the end turns herself into a commodity to realise her dream further illustrates the dialectic and contradiction of the promise of modern civilisation.

Ermo begins with her hawker's cry as she sells her twisted noodles by the roadside. The tightly framed shot of Ermo squatting behind her noodle basket becomes the film's visual leitmotif and associates her with the arena of commerce, suggesting a woman farmer's separation from the land and changing identity. Her stubborn bargaining demonstrates that she is an inflexible but profit-minded rural business-woman. This new image of a rural woman suggests this will not be a tale about the countryside but about the city where a woman farmer's social status and identity are dislocated, as indicated by the basket-selling episode in the film.

After Xiazi has found a shop where Ermo can sell the hundreds of surplus baskets she wove all summer, she is shown sitting on top of the load of baskets in his truck and heading to the busy urban marketplace. A freeze-framed close-up of her fearful face cuts to a moving long shot, which captures the fully loaded truck rumbling through the village gate and into the distance, where it becomes a dot hovering across the mountains. Ermo can hardly be made out anymore as a human being on top of the pile of baskets. This cine-matic effect dislocates Ermo to associate her with the baskets, registering the subjugation of human con-sciousness to the form of the commodity, in which human alienation and its reification find their expres-sion.

The filmic presentation of Ermo's fetishistic desire for a 29-inch colour television set further illus-trates how human desire for material civilisation has been alienated by irresistible global commercialisa-tion. No sooner does Ermo wander into a city depart-ment store than she finds a horde of people mesmerised by the television set and watching a Chinese-dubbed tape of a Western soft-core sex film. The scene baffles her; she cannot understand why the foreign actors are speaking Chinese. Her first encounter with the 'Other' – the foreign commodity as well as the foreigners on television – in such a hybridised condition 'infuses the fetish's initial role as the material sign of a cross-cultural agreement' and an in-between experience.[7]

As a spectacle, the object – the TV set – becomes image and belief, secured by an erotic aura manifested through the Western soft-core sex film. Such a dis-play emphatically registers both the television show and the set itself as commodities to the consuming world by directing consumers' libidinal drives towards the whole package. Susan Buck-Morss's interpreta-tion of Walter Benjamin's *Arcades Project* gives an even more precise account of the quietly persistent process of commodity fetishism:

For Benjamin … the key to the new urban phantasma-goria was not so much the commodity-in-the-market as the commodity-on-display, where exchange value no less than use value lost practical meaning, and purely representational value came to the fore. Everything desir-able, from sex to social status, could be transformed into commodities as fetishes-on-display that held the crowd enthralled even when possession was beyond their reach. Indeed, an unattainably high price tag only enhanced a commodity's symbolic value. Moreover, when newness became a fetish, history itself became a manifestation of the commodity form.[8]

Indeed, what attracts Ermo's gaze are the represen-tational value of the television set, its giant size, its unaffordable price and the incomprehensible conver-sation on it. Its status 'beyond reach' transforms the television into a spectacle, in the sense elaborated by Debord. Debord's core thesis is that the spectacle constitutes a social relationship mediated by images:

The spectacle is both the outcome and the goal of the dominant mode of production …. It is the very heart of society's real unreality …. [It] epitomizes the prevailing model of social life. It is the omnipresent celebration of a choice already made in the sphere of production, and the consummate result of that choice. In form as in content the spectacle serves as total justification for the conditions and aims of the existing system [transmitted visually].[9]

In Ermo's case, the affect of visuality that upholds the power of the spectacle is not just individual; rather, it is group-based. Collective viewing in the department store leads to collective enthusiasm for the TV show and comments about the unaffordability of the set, reflecting a shared vision of the modern, the foreign and the Other, as well as shared and visualised imag-ination of the near future. The Chinese dubbing of the US soap opera *Dynasty* minimises verbal signifi-cation and further emphasises the visual. In the end, it is the visual – both the show and the set – that counts and haunts.

The spectacle is what drags Ermo into the imag-inary space where she can fantasise the power of pos-session, and also propel herself towards empowerment. 'The real consumer, in this case, thus becomes a con-sumer of illusion.'[10] This illusion enriches and enlarges her original goal, which was simply to buy a television for her son so he would not have to run next door to endure the neighbour's insults while he watched their television.

The iconography develops further by emphasising her compulsive viewing of the television, demonstrating the perfect logic of capitalist commercialism whereby 'watching' leads to 'wanting'. Ermo is captured by this cunning logic in the name of pursuing modern civilisation. Through the other visual leitmotif of counting money, which draws attention to her role as bread-winner, decision-maker and book-keeper, Ermo anticipates being able to count body hair in the clearness of the television image: 'the TV set is so big, its colour is so beautiful, and its picture is so clear that you can see every strand of the foreigners' blond body hairs.' This demonstrates her naive perception of the foreign/Other through the window of the 'global village',[11] which also perfectly echoes Anne Friedberg's analysis of a 'mobilised virtual gaze':

> Cinema and television – mechanical and electronic extensions of photography's capacity to transform our access to history and memory – have produced increasingly detemporalised subjectivities …. The cinema developed as an apparatus that combined the 'mobile' with the 'virtual'. Hence, cinematic spectatorship changed, in unprecedented ways, concepts of the *present* and the *real*.[12]

The department store television set and the television show have profound effects on Ermo. They open up her 'optical unconscious',[13] letting her experience what they present and represent as *real*. The set attracts her 'virtual gaze' and the show mobilises her desire to possess the set, which holds the promise of foreign eroticism. This opening of her 'optical unconscious' makes her more desperate than ever to pursue the set as icon of modern civilisation. She takes more aggressive steps to reach her goal, such as leaving home for a city job and selling her blood. The latter underlines the fact that she is turning her body into a commodity valued only for its exchange value – its worth as another commodity. Her reaction to 'the external culture'[14] turns civilisation into fetishism.

Broadly speaking, fetishism involves the attribution of autonomous power to a manmade artefact. It is therefore dependent on the ability to disavow knowledge and suspend disbelief. However, the fetish is always haunted by the fragility of the mechanisms that sustain it. Both Freud and Marx use fetishism to explain a refusal or phobic inability to understand a symbolic system of value, one within the psychoanalytic and the other within the social sphere.[15] For Freud, the body that is the source of fetishism is the mother's body, uncanny and archaic. For Marx, the source of fetishism is in the erasure of value of the worker's labour. Both are repressed as the unspeakable and the unrepresentable in commodity culture.

However, the unspeakable and unrepresentable are openly, cheerfully and sarcastically exhibited by the film-makers through the image of Ermo selling blood and repeating, 'I have plenty of blood. Women lose their blood anyway.' To mistakenly and innocently identify medically drawn blood with menstrual blood signifies Ermo's need to become 'civilised', i.e., educated, about human physiology. Instead of showing a block or phobic inability of the psyche, her innocence about her own body manifests itself as a natural impulse driving her search for modern civilisation. However, at the end of the film, she appears to be a fragile, totally worn-out and lifeless object compared to the gigantic television set with all its vibrant and colourful movement, implying the internal and external dislocation that is the price of achieving modern civilisation.

(RE)ENVISIONING THE GLOBAL–LOCAL AND THE URBAN–RURAL

The market economy has speeded up urbanisation as urban migration has become an avenue to make money. Throughout the 1980s, rural migrants including women like Ermo overturned the social immobility imposed on them by the old collective system.[16] The proliferation of markets made commerce a significant alternative for rural women. Saskia Sassen remarks that migration is a representation of globality in terms of economics, politics and culture. It transcends locality, Otherness and marginality, transforming all three into the core of power.[17]

The filmic imagery of Ermo's country-to-city trips not only showcases her geographical travelling but also the way in which her identity and power travels, elevating her gender and social status, and releasing her from rural exclusion from the urban, the modern and the global. Ermo's power is never visualised on the screen through her role as a farmer but only in her role as an agricultural migrant entering the urban sphere. On the one hand, her naiveté, diligence and endurance in her efforts to make a better life for herself and her family challenge patriarchal dominance and empower her. On the other hand, the same imagery diminishes the significance of farming in contemporary China and signifies its constant movement towards further modernisation and globalisation.

The visual juxtaposition of her husband's physical and political impotence simultaneously signifies the diminution of his male power and his once respected rural leadership. He is almost always confined to the edge of the frame, consuming medication as a dietary staple, reminding everyone that he is no longer the village chief. He pushes for a larger house instead of the television, insisting that 'A TV set is an egg but a house is a hen'. Ermo's powerful status, as someone mobile and autonomous, is symbolised by her frequent business trips to the city, her taking over the role of male labour in her household and her new buying power. Her geographical border-crossing and gender-crossing in terms of labour seem to help her win female subjectivity and agency. Sassen contributes a keen insight into such power formations:

> We learn something about power through its absence and by moving through or negotiating the borders and terrains that connect powerlessness to power: Power is not a silence at the bottom; its absence is present and has consequences.[18]

Superficially, Ermo is empowered. When she fills the vacancy at the 'International Grand Restaurant' as an expert noodle-maker, she designates a new element in a new urban regime, facilitating its operations. Her noodle-making expertise changes her urban status from temporary to permanent, and also empowers her as master of her own family. The film-makers communicate this to the audience in a distinctive way during one of Ermo's rare home visits.

Following a close-up of two naked male backs, the audience sees Ermo sitting in front of the two half-naked males – her son and her husband – giving them new shirts purchased from a city store. This symbolic act not only signifies that she is a caring wife and mother but also that she is in financial control. The visible nakedness and their passive seated position suggest their vulnerability compared to her

fully clad mobility, as she stands over them and even dresses her husband. From this position, Ermo's husband looks remarkably similar to his son in height and stature, further marking out his loss of power.

Ermo returns to powerlessness when she breaks up with Xiazi, quits her restaurant job and resumes her position selling twisted noodles in the local market. Her husband's renewed bossiness signifies the power shift associated with these changes. Power is suddenly lost because of her withdrawal from the city. Furthermore, this loss is exacerbated by her husband's suspicion of her infidelity. Her infidelity compensates for the diminution of his patriarchal power because of his physical mutilation and loss of political power when he ceased to be the village chief, because it propels him to reaffirm his role as husband and father.

Ermo's body is inscribed by sexual politics demonstrated in the circulation and transformation of power, which director Zhou Xiaowen communicates through recurring boundary crossings.[19] These male–female and urban–rural transpositions can be regarded as a modern allegory of location where power, morality and economics construct and deconstruct the power of individuality, subjectivity and autonomy.

In conclusion, by almost any measure, China's opening to the world economy has been a spectacular success. Film-makers participate in this transformation when they focus on the geographical and cultural spheres that make up the rural–urban context. In John Revne Short's analysis:

> Cities are embedded in a world economy; they are nodes in a global network of production, consumption and exchange of commodities, goods, and services. The cities of the world make solid in time and space the nature of changing economic transactions. They are the physical embodiment of social and economic change.[20]

His remark echoes Raymond Williams's canonical thesis on the relation of *The Country and the City*,[21] denoting the city as an achieved centre of learning, communication and light (an embodiment of modernisation). However, because the city is situated in globalised politics, economics and cultural conditions, the moment is only 'solid' as a snapshot in time, forever moving forward and then backward in our memory-banks. Furthermore, travelling between the city and the country does not necessarily entail a struggle between advancement and backwardness. As Aihwa Ong suggests, understanding it requires the new concept of 'flexible citizenship'.[22] She suggests there is an internal logic in capitalist consumption and that the movement between different spheres is such that, in order to improve one's political and economic situation, some fluidity is necessary.

The city as a 'physical embodiment of social and economic change' in the Chinese context sustains a complex hybridisation, which enhances the contact between the global and the local, the foreign and the indigenous, and the centre and the marginal. This loosens the ties between the rural and the urban, and produces a new 'cultural logic', in which transportability and transformation become possible. In the final frame, the world-weather forecast is ending the China Central Television (CCTV) broadcast on the large 29-inch screen. This underscores the reality and existence of a larger world and climate. This modernisation that has invented the Chinese contemporary urban scenario – viewed by Foucault as a 'danger', by Jameson as 'commodity production', by Benjamin as an 'aura-killer' and by Debord as a 'spectacle' or as fetishism – does in fact bring Chinese people, and especially farmers, substantial wealth alongside the ineluctable confusion that accompanies the rupture and dislocation of their culture and traditions.

Ermo's overwhelming pursuit of the symbolic icon of the 29-inch television set forces her to take on all the baggage associated with the above-mentioned discursive practices, irreversibly intertwining the beautiful and the ugly. In the end, any judgments about either the intent or outcome of China's ongoing modernisation and modernism must be suspended, for they cannot be read as more than an unfinished script.

Furthermore, the visuality of Ermo's rural–city–rural journey enacts ceaseless but clueless debates on the dichotomy between mobility and stability, the domestic and the foreign, and the national and the global throughout the century-long process of Chinese modernisation. This specific cinematic visual cipher, to echo Rey Chow's thesis on visuality,[23] 'enables us to notice [our] position of spectator and observer', reminding us of the reciprocity of viewing and receiving, and warning us to ponder what projects our gaze upon the spectacle and what shapes our vision of the social panorama, particularly in the age of globalisation.

NOTES

1. David Leiwei Li, 'What Will Become of Us If We Don't Stop?: Ermo's China and the End of Globalization', *Comparative Literature*, 53, no. 4 (2001): 442–461; Beth Notar, 'Blood Money: Woman's Desire and Consumption in *Ermo*', *Asian Cinema*, 12, no. 2 (2001): 132–153; Stephen J. Gould and Nancy Y. C. Wong, 'The Intertextual Construction of Emerging Consumer Culture in China as Observed in the Movie *Ermo*: A Postmodern, Sinicization Reading', *Journal of Global Marketing*, 14, nos. 1 and 2 (2000): 151–167; Judith Farquhar, 'Technology of Everyday Life: The Economy of Impotence in Reform China', *Cultural Anthropology*, 14, no. 2 (1999): 155–179; Anne T. Ciecko and Sheldon H. Lu, 'Televisuality, Capital and the Global Village', *Jump Cut*, 42 (December 1998): 77-83; Tani E. Barlow, 'Green Blade in the Act of Being Grazed: Late Capital, Flexible Bodies, Critical Intelligibility', *Difference: A Journal of Feminist Cultural Studies*, 10, no. 3 (1998): 119–158; Tony Rayns, 'The Ups and Downs of Zhou Xiaowen', *Sight & Sound*, 5, no. 7 (1995): 22–24.

2. Rey Chow, *Primitive Passions: Visuality, Sexuality, Ethnography, and Contemporary Chinese Cinema* (New York: Columbia University Press, 1995), 16.

3. Michel Foucault, 'Space, Knowledge, and Power', in *The Foucault Reader*, ed. Paul Rabinow (New York: Pantheon Books, 1984), 243.

4. Margaret Peterson, *China's New Business Elite: The Political Consequences of Economic Reform* (Berkeley: University of California Press, 1997).

5. Tony Rayns, 'The Position of Women in New Chinese Cinema', *East–West Film Journal*, 1, no. 2 (1987): 32–44.

6. Chai Xiaofeng, *Zhou Xiaowen is Also Crazy* (*Zhou Xiaowen ye fengkuang*) (Changsha: Hunan wenyi chubanshe, 1996), 313. For more detailed discussion, see Dai Jinhua, '*Ermo*: Modern Allegorical Space' ('*Ermo*: xiandai yuyan kongjian'); Wang Dehou, '*Ermo*: A Crystallization of Sturdiness and Blindness' ('*Ermo*: zhuozhuang yu mangmu de jiejing'); and Wang Yichuan, 'A Realistic Representation of Power Exchange and Repetition' ('Rushi biaoyan quanli jiaohuan yu chongfu'), in *Film Art* (*Dianying Yishu*), no. 5 (1994): 39–43, 36–38 and 44–47.

7. See Patricia Spyer, ed., *Border Fetishism: Material Objects in Unstable Spaces* (New York: Routledge, 1998) for details.

8. Susan Buck-Morss, *The Dialectics of Seeing: Walter Benjamin and the Arcades Project* (Cambridge, MA: MIT Press, 1991), 81–82.

9. Guy Debord, *The Society of the Spectacle*, trans. Donald Nicholson-Smith (New York: Zone Books, 1994), 13.

10. Ibid., 32.

11. In Marshall McLuhan and Bruce Power's book, *The Global Village* (New York: Oxford University Press, 1989), McLuhan invents this term to refer to globalised telecommunication. According to McLuhan, all Western scientific models of communication are linear, sequential and logical as a reflection of efficient causality. McLuhan thinks speed-of-light technologies could be used to postulate possible futures (globalisation). The 'global village' (or 'international arena') is controlled by those with the most advanced technology. To a great extent, an advanced telecommunication determines the legitimacy of speech, information flow and, in short, global control in this 'global village'.

12. Anne Friedberg, *Window Shopping: Cinema and the Postmodern* (Berkeley: University of California Press, 1993), 2–3.

13. The term originates from Walter Benjamin's thesis of mimesis with reference to the camera, which he suggests is capable of generating 'the aura' of works of art in the age of mechanical reproduction. For a detailed analysis of the notion, see Michael Taussig's *Mimesis and Alterity* (New York and London: Routledge, 1993), 44–69.

14. Georg Simmel states that 'the deepest problems of modern life derive from the claim of the individual to preserve the autonomy and individuality of his existence in the face of overwhelming social forces, of historical heritage, of external culture, and of the technique of life'. See his 'The Metropolis and Mental Life', in *Classic Essays on the Culture of Cities*, ed. Richard Sennett (New Jersey: Prentice Hall, 1969), 47.

15. See Sigmund Freud, 'Fetishism', *Standard Edition of the Complete Psychological Works*, vol. 21 (London: Hogarth Press, 1961) and Karl Marx, *Capital*, vol. 1 (Moscow: Foreign Languages Publishing House, 1961) for details.

16. Ashwani Saith, ed., *The Re-emergence of the Chinese Peasantry* (London: Croom Helm, 1987), and Kate Zhou, *How the Farmers Changed China* (Boulder, CO: West View Press, 1996).

17. Saskia Sassen, *Globalization and Its Discontents* (New York: The New Press, 1998), 81–111.

18. Ibid., 86.

19. Rong Weijing, 'Zhou Xiaowen, a Director Knocked Dead by Films' ('Zhou Xiawen bei dianying kesi de daoyan'), *Film Art* (*Dianying yishu*), no. 3 (1994): 45–49.

20. John Short, *New Worlds New Geographies* (New York: Syracuse, 1998).

21. Raymond Williams, *The Country and the City* (New York: Oxford University Press, 1973).

22. Aihwa Ong, *Flexible Citizenship: The Cultural Logics of Transnationality* (Durham, NC, and London: Duke University Press, 1999).

23. Rey Chow, *Primitive Passions: Visuality, Sexuality, Ethnography, and Contemporary Chinese Cinema* (New York: Columbia University Press, 1995), 6.

13   *Farewell My Concubine*: National Myth and City Memories

Yomi Braester

The dazzling images and sweeping narrative of Chen Kaige's *Farewell My Concubine* (1993) might blind the viewer to the more intimate associations of the film's locations and themes. The director insists, however, that the film is 'not an epic ... It's a personal story about a few individuals.'[1] By paying homage to Chen's native Beijing and to Beijing opera, *Farewell* engages in personal memories, contrapuntal and even conflicting with collective memory. I argue here that the film shows how memories are fetishised and re-articulated through intimate objects, bodily scars and perhaps most importantly urban spaces, all of which resist the myths of the Chinese nation-state.

My essay challenges the existing critical response, which has mostly accused the film of presenting a patronising national allegory. Together with Zhang Yimou's *Raise the Red Lantern* (1991), *Farewell* marked a turning point in so-called 'Fifth Generation' movies. Critics had hailed earlier films by the new directors, which presented alternative models of nationhood. A shift away from the focus on rural themes – notably in Chen's own *Yellow Earth* (1984) and *King of the Children* (1987) – to epic plots coincided with a novel reliance on foreign investment. In this context, *Farewell* was deplored as backsliding to an emphasis on nationalist narratives and to the dominant culture represented by Beijing opera, and as catering to an Orientalising overseas audience's taste for the exotic.[2] Hong Kong critic Yar See, punning on the film's title – literally 'hegemon king bids farewell to his concubine' – alluded to the domineering position of PRC culture and called the movie 'hegemonic cinema' (*bawang dianying*).[3]

Yet such criticism does not fully take into account the politics of memory in Chinese cinema. Since the establishment of the People's Republic, the government has used specific public spaces to forge a collective national identity. Even these places, however, have often been re-appropriated for contending

meanings, and urban locations have largely resisted national myths. *Farewell* uses political changes as a backdrop for the story of a locale whose inhabitants strive to retain an identity free from the state's ideological manipulations. As such, Chen's film foreshadows the 'Sixth Generation' film-makers' use of urban settings as spaces of personal memory.

The tension between these different uses of memory is exemplified by the two sequences that open *Farewell*. In the first, presented before the credits, two Beijing opera actors walk onto the floor of a dark sports hall. The attendant recognises them: 'Oh, it's you two! ... It's been over twenty years since you performed together, hasn't it?' One actor answers, 'twenty-one', and the other rebukes him, 'twenty-two!' The scene introduces some of the film's major themes – the failure of recognition, the fickleness of memory, the use of recollection as a stake in personal grievances and the staging of these issues in theatrical spectacles. The scene also links personal memories to larger historical narratives, foreshadowing the film's epic span of fifty-three years, marked by key political events. The next sequence, immediately following the credits, transports the viewer to another place and time. A transition to sepia-tinted photography cues spectators that the scene takes place in the more distant past, and an intertitle identifies the place and time as 'Beijing, 1924: The Warlord Era'. A woman makes her way through food and porcelain stalls, itinerant vendors of toys and musical instruments, and advertisers of foreign tobacco. The crowded alleys may be recognised as Tianqiao district, which lies to the west of the Temple of Heaven in Beijing's southern, lower-class quarters. This carnivalesque space presents the underbelly of respectable performance.

The two opening sequences – the last and first, respectively, in the story of the two opera actors – frame the epic and foreground the film's main symbols. The two scenes are, however, also very different in tone and may stand for two diverging ways of reading the film. The first sequence places the operatic spectacle and the gender roles played by the two actors in the context of larger political changes. The second shows the street savvy of the child apprentices and the power struggles among local groups in the dusty alleys of old Beijing. Critical discussion of *Farewell* has largely targeted the more heavily ideological issues, and in particular the construction of national history and the performance of queer desire, at times mentioned in the same breath.[4] Yet the actors' hesitant and contradictory answers in the pre-credits sequence cast doubt on the validity of translating personal experience to the national level. In response to the attendant's statement that their troubles are all due to the Gang of Four, leaders of the Cultural Revolution, the actors concede in a hollow voice and without conviction. One should notice the director's choice to frame the film as a story about personal memories of old Beijing. The detailed representation of the Tianqiao stalls, vendors and performers indicates the importance of the film's location in Chen Kaige's native city. Through references to urban landmarks and earlier cinematic representations of Beijing, *Farewell* offsets the national narrative with a focus on the intimate spaces of the city and their past. The references to Beijing locales present a parallel plot-line that mitigates the melodrama and the national historical narrative.

Farewell's myth-making has overshadowed Chen's use of cinema as a facilitator of personal memory. *Farewell* commemorates old Beijing, makes urban spaces into places of post-traumatic recall and works through the director's unresolved memories of growing up in the capital during the Cultural Revolution. *Farewell* offers not only a grand national epic but also intimate urban vignettes, amounting to a statement about the interaction between personal and collective memory and on the importance of film for reclaiming otherwise lost experience.

BEIJING'S ARCHITECTURAL SYMBOLISM

Farewell does not offer grand vistas of Beijing, nor does it show many recognisable landmarks. Indeed, the film is shot mostly on sets, or in enclosed courtyards and

Farewell My Concubine: Leslie Cheung as Cheng Dieyi

opera houses – courtyards were rebuilt on the Beijing Film Studio lot – and is sprinkled with occasional glimpses of an old alley or an ancient wall. Yet it is precisely by turning inward, to the more intimate architectural spaces typical of Beijing, that *Farewell* captures the experience of the lived-in city. Rather than reproduce camera-ready images of touristy sites, Chen's film re-creates the practices that have defined local identity. At the heart of the film, visually and thematically, is the *siheyuan*, a rectangular courtyard surrounded by one-storey tile-roofed houses, typical of Beijing's residential architecture since the thirteenth century. The opera school where the two opera actors meet is made of three courtyards strung together; when the actors move out, they settle in private courtyards. Images of the courtyards are complemented by typical Beijing sounds, from the telltale accent to street peddlers' cries and pigeon whistles.[5]

Even though the film also presents extravagant operatic and political spectacles, Chen gives as much attention to aspects of everyday life in Beijing's alleys. *Farewell* follows earlier filmic depictions of Beijing's southern quarters, notably *My Memories of Old Beijing* (1982), which shows unabashed nostalgia for the city's layout and customs before its transformation since 1949. Like the cameraman for *My Memories*, the cinematographer for *Farewell*, Gu Changwei, was careful to block out views of the rapidly modernising metropolis. The resulting eye-level photography of the enclosed alleys and courtyards adds to an intimate and sometimes claustrophobic atmosphere.

The visual and auditory clues not only help locate the plot but also motivate the storyline. A case in point is the architectural symbolism that stresses the theme of the overlap between operatic spectacle and political struggles. The film tells the story of two Beijing opera apprentices, Douzi and Shitou, who grow up to become famous actors under the names Cheng Dieyi (played by Leslie Cheung) and Duan Xiaolou (Zhang Fengyi). The friendship between the two is marred by Dieyi's undeclared attraction to Xiaolou and jealousy of his wife, Juxian (Gong Li). The two protagonists' schooling extends to using their acting skills off stage, whether to confront gangsters in a brothel or procure the favours of politically connected patrons. The intimate theatrical spaces protect the two protagonists, even as the opera

hall hosts political rallies and riots. On one occasion, a rehearsal in the school courtyard turns into a cruel display, when Shitou forces a pipe into Douzi's mouth as ostensive punishment. Despite the brutality, the episode further strengthens the bond between the two actors. Later the two grown-up actors return to the same courtyard to enact another punishment upon each other, in a scene that stresses the ties between the actors and their teacher, to the point of excluding Juxian, an outsider to the courtyard.

The symbolism of the courtyards as private spaces, seemingly impenetrable to outside regulation, is made clear when the plot turns to the Cultural Revolution. After the establishment of the PRC in 1949, Dieyi's adopted son, Xiaosi'r, refuses to take part in the operatic tradition. He gives up his training, resists his adoptive father's discipline and denounces him before leaving for good. A pivotal scene takes place in Dieyi's residential courtyard, where the established opera singer uses against Xiaosi'r the same punishments that had been inflicted upon him. The younger man, however, rebels; instead of letting Dieyi flog him, Xiaosi'r leaves for the 'new society' and joins the revolutionary masses. Xiaosi'r's betrayal of his adoptive father is coded also in spatial terms by his departure from the courtyard, in a shot/reverse shot sequence that places Dieyi in the middle of the *siheyuan* and Xiaosi'r behind the 'ghost wall' that blocks the line of vision from the street. The courtyard and the street stand for two separate viewpoints.

When the conflicts are no longer contained within the private courtyards and erupt in public spaces, the protagonists face their undoing. The spectacles of the Cultural Revolution spill into the streets. Dieyi and Xiaolou are dragged into a 'struggle session'. Unlike previous personal and political conflicts, the scene takes place in an open space, large enough to contain a big crowd. The actors are made to wear opera costumes and make-up that mocks their profession. The protagonists' stage skills do not help them this time. In fact, they are drawn into making mutually incriminating accusations. Without the protective traditional architecture around them, they are reduced to complicity in the cruel spectacle staged by the state. The difference between the small Beijing courtyards and the large, barren public square foregrounds the distinction between personal and collective narratives.

FACING PERSONAL MEMORY

By Chen Kaige's own testimony, the film allows the director to return to Beijing's intimate spaces and come to terms with his experience of growing up in the city. In particular, the director associates the city's spaces with his parents' home and with his betrayal of his father. In a recent autobiographical account, Chen expresses his desire to return to live in a *siheyuan* like the one in which he grew up and laments the recent gentrification of old courtyards, which have become status symbols for new entrepreneurs. Chen also tells about his interest from childhood in the capital's history. He associates Beijing opera with his memories and wonders 'whether Beijing opera has impacted Beijing people or Beijing people influenced Beijing opera'. Chen also identifies specific Beijing locations used in the film, in particular a fortress in Xiangshan, in the capital's north-west suburbs. 'When shooting *Farewell* I felt an unknown force taking hold of me,' he recalls. 'I believe that I put into the film all my understanding of Beijing and all that old Beijing left in me. After the shoot, I dreamed that Leslie Cheung as Cheng Dieyi was bidding me farewell; I wept in my dream.'[6]

Farewell may thus be seen as Chen's farewell to the city of his childhood. I do not suggest reading the film as an autobiography in disguise. Yet Chen admits that he used film-making to reflect upon his relationship with his father, Chen Huaikai, a celebrated film-maker in his own right. The son grew up among the Beijing film establishment until he was sent down to the countryside together with many youths of his generation during the Cultural Revolution. Upon his return to Beijing and graduation from the Film Academy in 1982, Chen Kaige directed four films reflecting his experience as a sent-down youth and as a People's Liberation Army soldier, and then turned to *Farewell*, in which he pays tribute to his birthplace.

Chen's experience in the period from 1966 to 1978 is of major importance to his subsequent career and stands at the centre of his autobiography.[7] Chen tells how as a Red Guard he denounced his father, who had been associated with the KMT Nationalist pre-1949 regime, and how he has lived with the ensuing guilt ever since. *Farewell*, which starts with a reference to the Gang of Four and depicts a son's betrayal of his adoptive parents only to be exposed as their successor, is Chen's closest brush with his guilt-ridden past. It is apt that the movie should pay homage to film-makers of his father's generation, both in showing the torture to which stage professionals were subjected during the Cultural Revolution and in alluding to the locales they had frequented and portrayed in their films.

Many have commented on the formative importance of the Cultural Revolution for Chen and his peers. Critic Dai Jinhua notes that the Cultural Revolution may be viewed as a collective patricide – the fathers, formerly regarded as 'valiant hero[es] of revolutionary historical myth', were denounced and victimised by their children.[8] Sheldon Lu draws attention to the obsessive interest in child–parent relations in Fifth Generation films. This concern informs *Farewell*'s focus on the rapport between the two opera actors and their master on the one hand and their adopted disciple, Xiaosi'r, on the other.[9] The director would continue to try to come to terms with his past in *The Emperor and the Assassin* (1998).[10] Chen is explicit about the relation between film-making and his family history in his comments on the later film. Chen plays the court historian Lü Buwei, who according to the fictional script is the Emperor's unacknowledged father. Explains the director:

> One reason I wanted to play this part is that I wanted to pay respect to my father ... [During the Cultural Revolution] I was asked by the revolutionaries to denounce my father. I did that, and it did huge harm to my father and my family. He was deeply hurt by what I did to him ... What I learned from my father was the word 'forgiveness' ... I was sent to the countryside, and my father came to the train station to see me off ... Then I realised how much he loved me, despite the terrible things that I had done to him. This is [similar to] the situation between the prime minister and the emperor.[11]

The mature Chen Kaige takes over the role of the forgiving and self-sacrificing parent to re-enact his father's actions during the Cultural Revolution. Acting the role becomes Chen's belated atonement, repaying his father by forcing himself into a position of identifying with the father's pain.

Chen draws attention to the scene in *Emperor* in which the son is confronted with the choice to either implicitly acknowledge his illegitimate provenance and imperil his legitimacy as Emperor or kill his father. Comments Chen: 'That's when I understood my father better and better ... I had tears in my eyes ... I can't forgive myself ... I did it because I was selfish.' The younger Chen's conflicting emotions are transferred to the Emperor, who cannot bring himself to kill his father but is nevertheless relieved by the latter's subsequent suicide and then denounces him as a traitor.

While the director has not made similar remarks to explicitly link *Farewell* to his personal memories, the plot alludes to the problem of facing the past. Both *Emperor* and *Farewell* contrast two men who deal with their memories in diverging ways. In the later film, the Emperor is motivated by his pledge never to forget his plan to unify the empire; he faces an assassin brought to inaction by the memories of his own past conduct. The final showdown between the two protagonists takes place on a bridge that literally floats up from the king's memory. In *Farewell*, Dieyi struggles to keep memories alive, while Xiaolou pays little attention to them. Their memories finally resurface during the Cultural Revolution, where their past is held against them and claims the life of Xiaolou's wife. In light of the director's comments on *Emperor*, one may better understand his interest not so much in Xiaosi'r (roughly his own age) as in that of Dieyi and Xiaolou (of his parents' generation). Inasmuch as the two protagonists' fate reflects Chen's view of the Cultural Revolution, it shows that the dynamics of mob persecution not only caused the victims to betray one another and themselves[12] but also that the period's most devastating effect was the betrayal of memory itself, by remoulding recall of the past into a tool of torture.

BEIJING AS THE SPACE OF TRAUMA

In *Farewell*, Chen sets out to rescue memory from state ideology, such as the one that taints the recollections of the Mao-like emperor in *Emperor*. Many ways in which the film addresses memory lie outside the scope of this essay, yet one should notice that the plot foregrounds the existence of unresolved mental traumas by constant reference to unhealed scars. Douzi's road to success starts when his mother chops off a sixth finger on his right hand, and Shitou dresses the wound. Later, Shitou's forehead is bruised; Dieyi tenderly applies make-up to the scar before each performance throughout their career. Their relationship is sealed in the film's last scene with another wound, as Dieyi slits his throat. The scene takes up

the episode at the sports hall, presented in the film's beginning. Surprisingly, it is Xiaolou, usually resistant to nostalgia, who brings up the past and starts to recite an aria that re-establishes the bond between the two actors. Next, they play a routine from *Farewell My Concubine*, an opera piece that has earned them fame. At this moment, when the two return to the experiences that defined their relationship, Dieyi avails himself of Xiaolou's sword – also an object that evokes multiple memories – and commits suicide. Dieyi has consistently tried to remind Xiaolou of their common past, at times addressing Xiaolou by his childhood name. The film's last shot, in which Xiaolou relinquishes his dramatic persona as Hegemon King and calls Dieyi by his childhood name, denotes the return of memory, in the form of a freshly opened wound.

The reunion scene brackets the film and is key to understanding not only the role of reminiscence but also the specific kind of memory at stake and the importance of place. The significance of the scene can be glimpsed from comparing the filmed version to the description in the 1985 novel of the same name by Li Bihua (aka Lillian Lee). Chen and Li collaborated on the script, and following the film's success Li published a revised edition of the novel in 1993. Yet Li's novel retains scenes excised or modified in Chen's film. Two specific changes in the concluding scene stand out: the novel locates the actors' reunion in Hong Kong and Dieyi only feigns suicide. Dieyi derives satisfaction from Xiaolou's renewed recognition, then gets up, parts with his former stage partner and leaves for his home in the People's Republic.[13]

By placing the scene in Hong Kong, Li touches on questions never mentioned in the film. Hong Kong residents often regarded the British colony as a sanctuary of a Chinese culture, such as Beijing opera, vandalised in Maoist China. Xiaolou, now a resident of Hong Kong, worries about its freedom after the impending 1997 handover. The film, on the other hand, is set in Beijing from beginning to end. Anchoring the narrative in the capital of the People's Republic pre-empts a contending narrative based on Hong Kong identity. Moreover, the novel fashions the concluding scene as a relocation if not dislocation of memory, whereas the film emphasises the return to the original point of departure – Dieyi becomes Douzi again, in the city where the two actors grew up.

The semblance of return is of course illusory. Re-opening the wounds of memory on the floor of the empty hall stresses the failure of constructing a collective memory outside the landscape of old Beijing. The modern, barren sports hall draws attention to the urban restructuring projects that destroyed much of the old capital and left Beijing short of good opera stages at the end of the Cultural Revolution. The failure to reconstitute the spaces of memory is echoed also in Dieyi's self-immolation. His suicide, whether real or feigned, is the last of many dislocations of the operatic spectacle. Dieyi, who has consistently fetishised scars, re-opens his old wounds, literally and irrevocably. Posthumously triggering Xiaolou's recognition, in an empty Beijing arena, is Dieyi's paradoxical and misplaced attempt to bring his memories back to life.

THE CINEMATIC MEMORY OF BEIJING

The thematic reference to belated recognition, reified memories and displaced recall goes hand in hand with the use of cinematic allusions that pay tribute to the old capital, its vanishing spaces and earlier films that have captured Beijing's image.

In the context of post-Cultural Revolution cinema, the casting alludes to Beijing's place in earlier fiction and films. Side by side with Gong Li and Leslie Cheung, most likely chosen for their international star power and appeal to Hong Kong investors, the cast includes some of the capital's better-known actors. Ge You, as Master Yuan, had often been typecast as a young Beijing hooligan, from *The Troubleshooters* (1988) to *Conned Once* (1992) and *After Separation* (1992). Of special note is Zhang Fengyi as Xiaolou. Although Zhang had attained some fame in Hong Kong by the time of shooting *Farewell*, he had risen to fame in films about the capital, from his debut in *My Memories of Old Beijing* and his successful lead role in *Camel Xiangzi* (1982) to *No Regrets about Youth* (1992). In his performances in *My Memories* and *Camel Xiangzi*, Zhang Fengyi took an active role in rehabilitating an image of Beijing that had been erased during the Cultural Revolution. *Camel Xiangzi* invokes also the memory of Lao She, the author whose novel provides the film's plot and whose works document 1930s Beijing. *No Regrets* (and *The Troubleshooters*) were among the earliest scripts inspired

by Wang Shuo's vision of a new consumerist society in post-Mao Beijing. *Farewell* joins these pieces and can be considered among the earlier Chinese urban films after the Cultural Revolution. *Farewell* lacks the rough edge of Wang Shuo's plots and the documentary-like realism of later 'Sixth Generation' urban cinema. Yet in significant ways, *Farewell* demonstrates an important link between the grand productions of Fifth Generation film-makers and the understated pieces usually associated with urban cinema.

Farewell not only pays homage to recent Beijing cinema but also alludes to earlier, largely forgotten films. Many have noted the precedent set by Xie Jin's *Stage Sisters* (1965). Set in the Republican period, the film depicts the life of two opera singers who are separated by their political views. Even though *Farewell* is indebted to *Stage Sisters*, Chen disregards the local opera variation in Xie Jin's film, which draws much of its vitality from representing the southern-style Shaoxing opera, with its unique costume, singing and staging. Yet *Stage Sisters* is itself an homage to an earlier film, namely Zheng Xiaoqiu's *Opera Heroes* (1949). Despite its historical importance, *Opera Heroes* has largely been neglected by critics. The assistant director was Xie Jin, in his debut, and his *Stage Sisters* reworks themes present already in *Opera Heroes*. The earlier film describes the careers of two actors dedicated to the Communist cause. Yuan Wenguang drops out of high school to become an opera singer, under the stage name Yuan Shaolou, and teams up with female singer Liu Yanyun. Yuan is imprisoned by the Japanese, and Liu saves him at the price of her chastity. Liu drifts in and out of Yuan's life, but the latter becomes involved in political protest. Many of the political and social messages are conveyed by modifying existing opera plots. *Opera Heroes* paves the way for *Stage Sisters* and *Farewell* in foregrounding the political use of the stage.

Reading Chen's film may be informed not only by the similarities with Xie Jin's films but also by the dissimilarities. While the earlier pieces stress the positive propagandistic value of theatre, *Farewell* foregrounds the abuse of the stage for political means. As such, *Farewell* is clearly a product of post-Maoist ideology. Chen's film also differs in that it challenges Xie Jin's national epics by placing the plot in Beijing and depicting Beijing opera. The focus on Beijing opera, rather than invoking 'national essence', can also be seen as the director's tribute to his city and to his father – Chen junior mentions that his advisor on the history of Beijing opera was Chen Huaikai.[14] Counter to the logic that made some critics identify Beijing opera with the nation-state, it was the opera of the area around Shanghai that had become a symbol for revolutionary nationalism in earlier films. In fact, in the 1930s and 1940s – the period in which *Opera Heroes*, *Stage Sisters* and much of *Farewell* take place – the capital was moved away from Beijing, which was renamed Beiping. It was not until 1949 that Beijing became identified with the modern Chinese nation-state, and Chen's emphasis on Beijing should not be confused with reference to political hegemony.

Farewell acknowledges portrayals of Beiping also by re-using earlier cinematic form. *Opera Heroes* features teahouse shows typical of the capital and a sequence of Beijing opera training remarkably similar to the ones in *Farewell*. Like Zhang Shichuan's *Fate in Tears and Laughter* (1932), *Farewell* starts with establishing shots of Beijing at Qianmen and Tianqiao District. However, Chen's consistent focus on Beijing diverges from the earlier films – unlike *Farewell*, *Fate in Tears and Laughter* and *Opera Heroes* shuttle between Beiping and the south. In terms of the cultural rivalry between the Beijing and Shanghai styles, *Farewell* is a rare proponent of Beijing, and as such it promotes a local and decentralised identity no less than its southern equivalents. In the context of earlier cinematic treatments of Chinese opera, the film's relocation of the ending from Hong Kong to Beijing should not be mistaken for siding with nationalist hegemonic discourse.

In retrospect, *Farewell* signals the beginning of a shift of emphasis in non-government-sponsored Chinese cinema away from a national grand narrative to the history of specific cities. It is easy to understand why the film's attempt to use Beijing symbolism to counter nationalist myth has been misread. Chen himself admits to the difficulty of parting with the myths of the People's Republic, which was established only three years before his birth: 'You have no way to disbelieve a rhetoric as old as you, of which you have become part, until you muster the bravery to deny yourself first.'[15] *Farewell My Concubine* turns to Beijing's local history to displace national myth. To reshape personal and collective memory in post-Maoist China, Chen Kaige reframes the political theatre within a filmic screen of personal memories.

NOTES

1. Jianying Zha, *China Pop: How Soap Operas, Tabloids, and Bestsellers Are Transforming a Culture* (New York: The New Press, 1995), 98.

2. See, for example, Jenny Kwok Wah Lau, '"Farewell My Concubine": History, Melodrama, and Ideology in Contemporary Pan-Chinese Cinema', *Film Quarterly*, 49, no. 1 (1995): 16–27; Liao Binghui, 'Time and Space and Gender Disorder: On *Farewell My Concubine*' ('Shikong yu xingbie de cuoluan: lun *Bawang bieji*'), *Zhongwai wenxue*, 22, no. 1 (1993): 6–18; Lin Wenji, 'Drama, History, Life: National Identity in *Farewell My Concubine* and *The Puppetmaster*' ('Xi, lishi, rensheng: *Bawang bieji* yu *Ximeng rensheng* zhong de guozu rentong'), *Zhongwai wenxue*, 23, no. 1 (1994): 1139–1156.

3. Yar See, 'The Hegemon's Film' ('Bawang dianying'), *Sing Tao Evening News*, 11 December 1993, quoted in Lau, '"Farewell My Concubine"'.

4. See, for example, Benzi Zhang, 'Figures of Violence and Tropes of Homophobia: Reading *Farewell My Concubine* between East and West', *Journal of Popular Culture*, 33, no. 2 (1999): 101–109.

5. For a description of Chen's childhood in Beijing's old quarters, see Ni Zhen, *Memoirs from the Beijing Film Academy: The Genesis of China's Fifth Generation Filmmakers*, trans. Chris Berry (Durham, NC: Duke University Press, 2002), 13.

6. Chen Kaige, 'Sometimes Growing up Takes Only an Instant' ('Zhangda youshi zhishi yishunjian de shi'), in '*The Fifth Generation' in the '90s* (*90 niandai de 'diwudai'*) (Beijing: Beijing guangbo xueyuan chubanshe, 2000), 251–260 (253).

7. All references are to the Hong Kong edition, entitled *The Dragon-Blood Tree* (*Longxieshu*) (Hong Kong: Cosmos, 1992). The book has also appeared under the title *Young Kaige* (*Shaonian Kaige*).

8. Dai Jinhua, 'Severed Bridge: The Art of the Sons' Generation', trans. Lisa Rofel and Hu Ying, in *Cinema and Desire: Feminist Marxism and Cultural Politics in the Work of Dai Jinhua*, ed. Jing Wang and Tani E. Barlow (London: Verso, 2002), 16.

9. Sheldon Hsiao-peng Lu, 'National Cinema, Cultural Critique, Transnational Capital: The Films of Zhang Yimou', in *Transnational Chinese Cinemas: Identity, Nationhood, Gender*, ed. Sheldon Hsiao-peng Lu (Honolulu: University of Hawaii Press, 1997), 105–136.

10. 'Director's Commentary', included in the DVD edition of *The Emperor and the Assassin* (Culver City, CA: Sony Pictures Classics, 2000).

11. Minor changes made to comport with standard English grammar and style.

12. In his autobiography as well as in the Director's Commentary to *The Emperor and the Assassin*, Chen describes in detail the dynamics of betrayal and self-betrayal, and attributes them to the fear of becoming an outcast and the need to remain part of the collective. See, for example, Chen, *Dragon-Blood Tree*, 69.

13. Li Bihua, *Farewell My Concubine – New Edition* (*Bawang bieji – xin banben*) (Hong Kong: Tiandi tushu, 1993), 352.

14. Chen, *Dragon-Blood Tree*, caption for photo on unnumbered page.

15. Ibid., 3.

14 *Flowers of Shanghai*: Visualising Ellipses and (Colonial) Absence

Gary G. Xu

Flowers of Shanghai (1998) is Hou Hsiao-hsien's fourteenth film. Based on the eponymous 1892 novel by Han Bangqing (1856–1894), it presents sensuous visual details of the inner space of the most elegant brothels in Shanghai's foreign concessions during the late nineteenth century. While fascinated again by Hou Hsiao-hsien's stylistic innovations, including the daring use of low-key lighting, low-contrast colour, the long take, and the fade-in and the fade-out, audiences and critics also raised questions about the drastic differences between *Flowers of Shanghai* and Hou's previous films, which were exclusively about Taiwan's culture and history: Why not Taiwan? Why colonial Shanghai one century ago? Why the adoption of Shanghai-dialect for most of the dialogue? To some, it seemed Hou Hsiao-hsien had gone too far in pursuit of individual style and artistic idiosyncrasy,[1] so much so that he had departed completely from his concern for his native land at conspicuous historical junctures.

Hou Hsiao-hsien answered some of these questions during an interview in Cannes. When asked why he chose to make a film on 'China' instead of 'Taiwan', he explained:

> On the one hand, the choice was random. I happened to come to like the novel *Flowers of Shanghai*, which I stumbled upon when preparing materials for another film. On the other hand, I felt that I was artistically mature enough to jump out of Taiwan and make something new.[2]

The pursuit of innovation in both theme and style seems to be the motivation behind Hou's daring attempt. However, on closer examination of the film and its production process, I find that he has neither 'jumped out of Taiwan' nor departed completely from his previous stylistic and thematic patterns.

Stylistically, Hou's camera is still slow moving, and his trademark long takes still dominate the entire film. Although fades are rare in Hou's previous films, in *Flowers of Shanghai* they are used in such a way as to enhance long-take continuity; the scene does not change after the fade-out and fade-in, which seems to function as if the camera were pausing to take a deep breath. Thematically, although 'Taiwan' is no longer relevant to the story of the film, its absence becomes present in *Flowers of Shanghai* because of Hou's increasing awareness of MIT – Made in Taiwan.

In fact, the entire film was shot in Taiwan for logistical and political reasons. Hou originally planned to shoot street scenes in Shanghai after finishing the interiors in a Taiwanese studio. His request to shoot was rejected by the mainland Chinese authorities, because the film's subject of 'prostitutes' indicated 'decadence'.[3] Therefore, Hou had to sacrifice all the outdoor scenes and build the indoor set from scratch. From the perspective of the local Taiwanese film industry, this forced choice nevertheless has had trailblazing significance. For the first time, as this film's screenwriter Zhu Tianwen exclaims, Taiwan was able to build and maintain a set for late imperial-period Chinese scenes. Antique furniture was carefully designed and hand-crafted by Vietnamese carpenters; clothes were hand-sewn in Beijing; jewellery, decoration, make-up and other props were purchased in Nanjing, Suzhou and Shanghai. All these were shipped back to and assembled in Hou's studio in Yangmei, thus establishing a new way of producing Chinese history films. 'Building files, maintaining reserves, and building up productivity'[4] are major contributions this film has made to Taiwan's independent film industry, which simultaneously resists and co-operates with the increasing trend towards globalisation and syndication in film production.

The complete indoor enclosure of *Flowers of Shanghai* seems a drastic departure from Hou's famous panoramic representations of Taiwan's natural scenery and calm observations of characters from a distance, and it was forced upon him. However, the enclosure also better conveys Han Bangqing's original understanding of space under the colonial situation. On one hand, Han emphasises the importance of enclosure for the interactions between patrons and high-level prostitutes, who are exclusively Chinese. On the other hand, this stands in contrast to a complete absence of colonial authority in a colonial territory, so much so that the absence itself becomes questionable. The more enclosed the space of the brothels, the more fearfully unknown and vast the colonial territory. Without displaying colonial presence, Han's enclosed pleasure quarters thus paradoxically reveal the colonial presence in a more emphatic way, which may be termed a 'non-present presence'. Similarly, without referring to 'Taiwan', Hou's representation of Shanghai's brothels points to Taiwan's 'non-present presence' by touching upon the peculiar invisibility of Taiwan in a postcolonial setting. The 'MIT' assembly of sets from materials made outside Taiwan, for example, symbolises the difficulty and irony of establishing a 'Taiwanese' identity, which also had to be built from scratch using the 'imported materials' of the histories and identities of various ethnic groups including mainland immigrants after 1945 and 'local' Taiwanese, who were also immigrants in earlier times. For the different ethnic groups to coexist peacefully under political and military pressure from mainland China, 'Taiwan' as a geographical and political entity must be upheld but also downplayed to the extent that it seemingly fades into the shadows of superpowers. In what follows, I will detail how Hou Hsiao-hsien masterfully visualises the 'non-present presence' originally rendered by Han Bangqing's narrative manoeuvres, and how Taiwan's invisibility becomes part of Hou's reflections upon film-making and his previous films.

The film begins with a drinking scene in a brothel. Facing the audience are Pearl (Carina Lau) and her primary patron Hong Shanqing (Luo Zaier), a merchant. To their left are Jasmine (Vicky Wei) and her patron Wang Liansheng (Tony Leung), a foreign-affairs official from Guangdong. To their right are some other patrons. During the carousal, Wang Liansheng remains silent. No sooner than he takes leave does the crowd turn to gossip about him: Wang is said to be trapped in a triangular relationship with Crimson (Hada Michiko) and Jasmine. Since it is hard to catch all the names and events in this first glimpse of brothel life, the gossip may interest the audience less than its presentation – the entire scene is shot in an eight-minute long take. The slow action and the unusually long duration allow the audience to observe not only the mannerisms of the characters, but also the way the camera moves and *observes* the characters. Although the camera cannot appear in the scenes it shoots, in this long take it becomes like a character. It is alert – when hearing someone speak, it immediately turns in the direction of the sound; it remains at the same level as the characters' eyes, evidenced in the picture's lack of depth. The camera, in other words, forcibly asserts its 'non-present presence' through cinematographic manoeuvres from the very outset.

This prefatory scene is representative of the entire film, which is shot exclusively in long takes. The total number of forty shots is the lowest of all Hou Hsiao-hsien's films. But this does not necessarily signify a drastic change. As Shen Xiaoyin points out, lengthening each take and decreasing the total number of shots has been a consistent tendency of Hou's films. In *The Boys from Fenggui* (1983), for example, there are three hundred and eight shots, averaging twenty seconds per shot; while in *The Puppetmaster* (1993), there are only one hundred shots, averaging eighty-five seconds each.[5] Limiting the number of shots also guides Hou Hsiao-hsien's focus, which is on three groups of characters picked from among hundreds of characters in the original novel. The go-between Hong Shanqing, Pearl and her understudy courtesan Jade belong to the first group based in the brothel in Gongyang Enclave. There is almost no intimacy between Hong and Pearl, who only talk about happenings in the pleasure quarters. This demonstrates that Hong uses the brothel not for pleasure but for business, skilfully squeezing ten thousand *taels* of silver from Jade's inexperienced lover Zhu Shuren as compensation for her fabricated marriage with someone else when Zhu himself is forced by his family into an arranged marriage.

The second group, associated with the brothel in Shangren Enclave, consists of Emerald, her patron Luo Zifu and her madam Dame Huang. Sold into the brothel at the age of seven, Emerald understands the value of her body better than anybody. She gains

Flowers of Shanghai

control of Dame Huang by swallowing raw opium in a suicidal gesture. However, her renowned intractability attracts patrons such as Luo Zifu, who believes that Emerald is an exemplar of virtue in a place where virtue is not supposed to exist. Relying on Luo, Emerald buys herself out from the brothel and exits from the film in a spectacular scene where she carefully counts every piece of jewellery and returns them one by one to Dame Huang.

The third group, consisting of Wang Liansheng, Crimson and Jasmine, is at the centre of the film's plot. Crimson, who lives in Huifang Enclave, is bitter about Wang's courtship with Jasmine. As Wang is her only customer, this points to financial disaster for her. Hong Shanqing arranges for Wang to offer compensation to Crimson, only to have his proposal flatly turned down. Crimson claims that she wants Wang's exclusive affection, not money. After they resume their relationship, however, Wang catches Crimson in bed with an opera singer. Infuriated by her transgression of the implicit 'ethical' rule of the pleasure quarters that a courtesan should be loyal to her exclusive customer much as a wife is faithful to her husband, Wang trashes Crimson's

room and immediately marries Jasmine. However, during the farewell banquet marking Wang's return to Guangdong, it is revealed that Wang has kicked Jasmine out because she has had an affair with his nephew. The final scene witnesses Wang's return to Crimson; they face each other silently, letting the surroundings fade into complete darkness.

These three groups often mingle, and the storyline is difficult to follow, especially for general audiences unfamiliar with the original novel. But for Hou Hsiao-hsien, clarity of story seems to be of less concern than the *aura* of the brothels. His focus is not on character interaction but on the unique surroundings enabling interaction. To emphasise the 'elegance' of the most expensive brothels, the prostitutes' rooms are filled with furniture, decorations and other details unrelated to plot. An antique oil lamp, sitting on a round Ming-style redwood dining table, often occupies the centre of the frame, and the lighting is deliberately subdued, as if the lamp is the only source of light. The yellowish light enhances the soft and elegant profiles of the prostitutes, adding a feeling of cosy intimacy. Other details include engraved beds, doors, windows, screens, exotic clocks, silver tobacco pipes, opium utensils, and so forth, which combine to create a beguiling atmosphere. The details, however, are by no means extravagant. In fact, they exhibit both the usefulness and the uselessness of the every-day furnishing, so much so that they create an aura that is thoroughly familial and indicates the brothel's mimicry of family relationships.

The familial aura made possible by the labori-ously created *mise en scène* is Hou Hsiao-hsien's true focus. As a special costume consultant, Hou Hsiao-hsien hired the mainland novelist Ah Cheng, known for the tranquil, concise and 'natural' writing in his famous 'three king' novellas: *King of the Children*, *King of Trees* and *King of Chess*.[6] Ah Cheng told the costume designers: 'What you have so far found are all useful things; let's start to look for useless ones.'[7] These 'useless' items could be anachronistic, since they would not have any particular use. A Chanel lip-stick, for example, was placed on a plate full of opium-smoking utensils. Bombarded by the excess of visual detail, the audience would not notice the anachronistic lipstick. According to Zhu Tianwen, 'useful things are stage props, while useless things are traces of real life', but the anachronism and unsuit-ability of the added items raise questions regarding not only the claimed naturalness of the *mise en scène* but also the very notion of naturalness in representa-tion.[8] Ah Cheng's own fiction often juxtaposes highly polished language with closeness to life, so it seems Hou may have been striving to extend his own trademark style of pushing naturalism to the point where it becomes artificial and vice versa.

The familial aura in the film is both natural and artificial. It is natural, because of the family-like set-tings and because brothels from the era of polygamy and arranged marriage provided rare chances for one-to-one bonding between romantically attracted men and women. Naturalness in acting is also consistent with Hou's performance ideals. For example, Tony Leung was repeatedly reminded by Hou to act 'as little as possible' and to 'give up all your weapons as a great actor'.[9] Therefore, Leung had to remain silent and emotionless, especially in his dinner scene with Hada Michiko in her room. Both say nothing, yet the silence suggests the quiet intimacy of a married couple.

It is ironic, of course, that domestic bliss between husband and wife can only be found in a brothel, which threatens family structures. This irony also indicates the artificiality of the seemingly natural family atmosphere and performances. The more care-fully the prostitutes and their patrons create and maintain the mock family, the more incompatible the aura and setting – as incompatible as the verisimilar *mise en scène* and the Chanel lipstick. Likewise, the more restrained the actors' performances, the more artificial they actually are.

The technique of creating a familial aura in the most improbable place that Hou visualises is bor-rowed from Han Bangqing. Unlike most authors of traditional Chinese fiction, Han was clearly conscious of technique. In particular, he proudly points out in his preface that he makes two narrative inventions: 'knitting' (*chuancha*) and 'hiding and eluding' (*cang-shan*). By 'knitting', he refers to overlapping plot threads by ellipsis and recollection: 'Before one wave subsides another comes chasing its tail … When reading the novel, you feel there are many more words hidden underneath the text – even if they are not explicitly written into the narrative, you can sense them hermeneutically.' 'Hiding and eluding' refers to similar techniques:

> Something suddenly flies out of nowhere, giving no hint to readers and making them more curious about what will come next. However, the passage that follows turns away to other events. The first event is not picked up again until after some unrelated events, and the whole story does not become clear until the very end. Only then can readers grasp the relevance of every little detail.[10]

Han Bangqing deploys these principles, best termed 'strategies of ellipsis', to create numerous discrepan-cies between what has been announced by chapter titles and pretexts and what is actually hidden or omitted. Han's consistent use of these strategies calls attention to an intriguing dialogical imagination between the silent and the obvious. One of the most conspicuous discrepancies in the novel, for example, is the exclusively Chinese presence in the foreign concession. Hidden clues, however, often point up this obvious discrepancy between historical reality and fictional representation. In one case, the guests are startled by a dark shadow on the roof of the house across the street:

> It turned out to be a foreign policeman, standing straight up on the top of the building opposite. He was all

wrapped up in a black uniform, with a big steel knife in his hand. Illuminated by the electric light, the knife flashed brilliantly.[11]

The stunned guests are quickly distracted by an ensuing incident in which policemen arrest several gamblers. (Gambling was illegal in the concessions, while whoring in a brothel registered with the concession authorities was legal.) Flirting with the courtesans, they appear undisturbed by the incident. But the towering image of a foreign policeman in dark uniform lingers on as an unknown and heterogeneous force, threatening to end the banquets at any time. This episode also highlights the 'extraterritoriality' enjoyed by foreigners in Chinese treaty ports – although physically on Chinese land, Western citizens possessed the privilege of immunity from Chinese laws. In other words, they were untouchable – 'invisible' or 'non-present' – while Chinese citizens were subjected to the laws of the concessions.

In Hou's film, the towering image of the colonial presence does not appear. Hou has kept the scene, but all we see is a stir of excitement among the crowd in a courtesan's room. People whisper about gamblers next door being caught and one having plunged to his death. They rush to the window, but the focus of the camera stays with Wang Liansheng, who seems preoccupied and ignores the disturbance. Although the foreign policeman is not shown, this is the only reference in the film to the existence of a world beyond the brothel, further intensifying the sense of a self-sufficient enclosure threatened by non-present presence. This subtle example of off-screen space is reminiscent of Hou's use of off-screen radio sound and other similar devices to hint at the existence of a larger world in such films as City of Sadness.[12]

Han Bangqing's strategies of ellipsis also harbour an essential visuality. The visual image, as correctly understood by Rey Chow,

is characterized by two seemingly opposite features: obviousness and silence. While the obviousness of the image expresses an unambiguous presence, the silence of the image suggests, instead, nonpresence – that is, all those areas of 'otherness' that are an inherent part of any single 'presence'.[13]

Han Bangqing's novel is fraught with moments of 'nonpresence', such as the absence of romantic passion and erotic desire in a place where they are supposed to be present, the deliberate disruptions and ellipses in the plot, and the lack of colonial presence in colonial territories. These 'nonpresences' nevertheless point up their surprising 'nonpresentality' in places where presences are expected, thus emphasising the contrast between silence and obviousness. Such a contrast is precisely what makes things 'visible'. Furthermore, in order to 'make sense' of the novel, readers must engage in incessant backtracking to locate and fill in the ellipses whenever a seemingly displaced clue pops up. New for Han Bangqing's time, this reading technique uncannily anticipated the arrival of the motion picture and its accompanying viewing habit of suturing, which relies on the viewer's incessant retroaction to fill in previously created ellipses whenever new hints are given. As Jean-Pierre Oudart notes in his seminal essay on suture, after their initial jubilant response to filmic images, the audience tends to be reminded that any single filmic image is but one link in the chain of signification that is not 'being there' but 'being there for' – for indicating the necessary filling up the 'absent field' in the viewer's imaginary. Suturing, at once 'retroactive at the level of the signified' and 'anticipatory at the level of the signifier', is precisely the way of coping with the dialectics between the present and the absent in the cinema.[14]

It is the contrast between silence and obviousness, or absence and presence, which Hou Hsiao-hsien visualises through filmic technique. Hou's Flowers of Shanghai is in this sense a 'meta-film', a film about how visuality is visualised and how film is apprehended. The long take is one visual means of conducting the dialogue between silence and obviousness, for it draws the audience to observe the observation of the camera. Other means include the use of the fade. Conventionally used to transition from one scene to the next, in Flowers of Shanghai fades do not mark changes of scene. While the characters and the settings remain the same, the angle of the camera changes slightly, as if the animated camera has just taken a closed-eye yawn and shifted its attention. In the scene immediately following the prologue, for example, there is a fade after Hong Shanqing and another friend take leave of Wang Liansheng and Crimson. The audience would assume this marks a cut to another scene in another place. However, after the fade-in, this assumption is proven wrong, for the only change is that Wang Liansheng has moved from the left to the right of the screen. Crimson suddenly begins to cry, and Wang goes over to comfort her. This fade in mid-scene raises many questions: What has happened between the fades? What triggered Crimson's crying? How long is the real interval? Could it have been one minute, one night, or even several nights, during which Wang Liansheng first left and now has returned? In other words, the gap between the fade-out and the fade-in, albeit very brief, implies infinite elliptical possibilities in its very mode of silence, and points to the gap between filmic representation and reality exemplified in temporal differences.

During an interview, Hou discusses his new understanding of camera movement:

From *The Boys from Fengkuei* to *Flowers of Shanghai*, my understanding of space has changed. I used to think that the camera had to be set at a distance to show emotionless and objective observation. But in *Flowers of Shanghai*, I realized that objective observation had to depend on subjective manoeuvres in presenting characters. I could be cool or emotional toward the characters when shooting. My feelings are not important in terms of objectivity, because there is another pair of eyes simultaneously watching the characters. No matter how close the camera is, there is same effect of a double gaze. The camera is like a person standing beside me watching the group of characters.[15]

Hou's words imply that the camera becomes a character in the film by participating in the banquet. The role of the camera thus helps us to achieve a doubled viewing experience. On one hand, our eyes follow the camera, so that what we see is exactly what is shot by the camera. On the other hand, the animated camera reminds us of its limitations in the field of vision, pushing us to reflect on how filmic scenes are presented by an optical device.

The subtlety of Hou's reflections on film-making makes them easy to overlook. Without taking this self-reflexivity into consideration, one might suspect Hou of eroticising the image of Asian women. The lack of movement seemingly makes the camera the equivalent of the male gaze, which caresses the passive, hyper-feminised and exotic female characters, performed not only by Chinese but also by Japanese beauties. Nicholas Kaldis, for example, easily equates this male gaze with a tendency towards Orientalism in *Flowers of Shanghai*. He does try to defend Hou Hsiao-hsien, emphasising that the excessive sensuous detail tends to 'overstuff' the audience, so much so that surface Orientalism is subverted.[16] Maybe this is another 'meta-filmic' feature, in the sense that Hou deliberately creates Orientalist imagery to reflect on the film's own Orientalism. However, without recognising the silent beyond the obvious or the absent hidden beneath the present, Kaldis's explanation seems at best far-fetched and at worst reduplicative of the Orientalist logic that emphasises the glossy results of the Orientalist imaginary instead of the process and the agent of cultural production behind it.

By reflecting upon visuality itself, Hou's visual dialogue between the silent and the obvious conveys well Han Bangqing's understanding of space in a colonial situation. In the context of the late nineteenth century, how to redefine space became a major concern for Chinese intellectuals after Western colonisers forcibly demystified the notion of the 'Central Kingdom'. The most representative and widespread redefinition of space was Liang Qichao's polemics that imagined a new Chinese citizen integrated into the world system of modernisation against the old China as an isolated, closed and dilapidated house.[17] As a well-informed Shanghai intellectual, Han Bangqing must have been aware of Liang's rhetoric, but he chose to retreat back into the old house full of opium smoke and etiolated desires. However, his retreat reveals a much more acute sensibility about the colonial implications behind the drive to redefine space than Liang's utopian vision. His depiction of the lethargy and gluttony of the banqueting crowd in a completely closed and self-sufficient space would have been a mere celebration of decadence without the reference to the 'absent-presence', symbolised by the towering image of the coloniser whose gaze from *outside* keeps the colonised under constant surveillance. Space, therefore, is understood by Han as a closed and homogenous entity, but its closedness and homogeneity are enabled by colonialism, an outside and heterogeneous force made invisible by its disguise as a call for modernisation and global participation.

Closeness in this understanding of space is manifested in Hou's exclusive focus on the sealed and isolated inner space of the brothel. Defining cinematographic space has always been at the centre of

Hou's experiments. In his previous films, Hou has often juxtaposed a space that is wide open and infinitely extending with an inner space of enclosure and self-sufficiency. In *A Time to Live and a Time to Die* (1985), for instance, the isolated life of a family of three generations does not prevent Grandma from going out in search of the bridge leading to Meixian, the home town she and her family left behind in the retreat from the mainland. Combined with the infinite possibilities posed by identical bridges and rivers is the frequent intrusion of outside space into the family's enclosure. The dialectics between these two spaces, as Li Zhenya points out, reflect Hou's conscientious construction of history through redefining a space in which the relics of historical events are preserved and constantly excavated.[18] However, as in many other Hou Hsiao-hsien films, the apparent message in *A Time to Live and a Time to Die* is too direct and obvious to disclose the truth of history. Grandma's search for home clearly signifies the tragic nature of the migrants' forced choice of Taiwan as their home; caterpillar tracks from tanks on the ground speak volumes about the Nationalist military occupation of Taiwan. In other words, the interaction between the outside space and the inner space is clearly associated with historical traces, to the extent that personal histories are subordinated to the grand history of the nation-state, which is retrievable based on traces of the former.

Much as the construction of grand history has been questioned by the likes of Foucault, the visual representation of history and space in Hou's previous films is reflected upon, if not completely overturned, by Hou himself. The absence of an outside space in *Flowers of Shanghai* enables Hou to distance himself from overtly immediate concerns about Taiwan's local history. This deliberate distancing is discernible in the dialogue Hou's stylistic innovation performs with his previous films, a dialogue that helps make the ellipses and absences in *Flowers of Shanghai* full of implications.

NOTES

1. For example, 'With *Flowers of Shanghai*, Hou seems to have reached an aesthetic dead end, a breakthrough, or both.' Peter Keough, 'Cinema of Sadness: Recapturing

Lost Illusions in the Films of Hou Hsiao-hsien', *The Boston Phoenix*, 2–9 March 2000.

2. Zhu Tianwen, ed., *The Ultimate Dream: The Complete Record of* Flowers of Shanghai *(Jishang zhi meng: Haishanghua dianying quan jilu)* (Taipei: Yuanliu, 1998), 16.

3. Ibid., 9.

4. Ibid.

5. Shen Xiaoyin, 'Meant to be Watched Several Times: Film Aesthetics and Hou Hsiao-hsien' ('Benlai jiu yingai duo kan liangbian: dianying meixue yu Hou Xiaoxian'), in *Performance that Loves Life: Researching the Cinema of Hou Hsiao-hsien (Xilian rensheng: Hou Hsiao-hsien dianying yanjiu)*, ed. Lin Wenqi, Shen Xiaoyin and Li Zhenya (Taipei: Maitian, 2000), 76.

6. For an analysis of the film version of *King of the Children*, see Rey Chow, *Primitive Passions: Visuality, Sexuality, Ethnography, and Contemporary Chinese Cinema* (New York: Columbia University Press, 1995), 108–141.

7. Zhu, *The Ultimate Dream*, 126.

8. Ibid.

9. Ibid., 99.

10. Han Bangqing, *Flowers of Shanghai (Haishanghua liezhuan)* (Taipei: Sanmin, 1998), 1.

11. Ibid., 274.

12. I am indebted to Chris Berry for this observation.

13. Chow, *Primitive Passions*, 117.

14. Jean-Pierre Oudart, 'Cinema and Suture', *Screen*, 18, no. 4 (1977–1978): 35–57. In the same issue, see also Stephen Heath's article 'Notes on Suture' (48–76), which clarifies some of the confusions in Oudart's as well as Dayan's conceptualisation of suture based on Lacanian psychoanalysis.

15. Chow, *Primitive Passions*, 344.

16. Nicholas Kaldis, 'Desire-denying Oriental Exoticism: On Hou Hsiao-hsien's *Flowers of Shanghai*', *Jintian (Today)*, no. 52 (2001): 266–272.

17. See Xiaobing Tang, *Global Space and the Nationalist Discourse of Modernity: The Historical Thinking of Liang Qichao* (Stanford, CA: Stanford University Press, 1996).

18. Li Zhenya, 'Historical Space and Spatial History' ('Lishi kongjian/kongjian lishi'), in Lin *et al.*, *Performance that Loves Life*, 113–139.

15   *Formula 17*: Mainstream in the Margins

Brian Hu

On 30 November 2004, a posting on the message boards of Yahoo! Taiwan's movie website asked readers a question that has long perplexed directors, critics and policymakers: 'Why can't Taiwanese cinema rise?'[1] Given how stubbornly little interest local audiences had shown to Taiwanese cinema in the past ten years, it was amazing how vocal – and often heated – were the respondents who came out to trash or defend local cinema in the mere five days after the initial posting. As expected, the main response was that Taiwanese films are boring. 'The scripts don't attract audiences', wrote one Yahoo! user. 'Please, we need some content', added another. And there's the perennial 'our directors only make films to win awards at international festivals'. In other words, it seemed like the usual gripes against the usual auteurs.

However, every few posts, one encountered the titles of a few local films that 'aren't too bad', as one poster put it. *Double Vision* (Chen Kuo-fu, 2002) and *Blue Gate Crossing* (Yee Chin-yen, 2002) came up regularly, as did *Formula 17*, which was a surprise hit among teenage and college-aged audiences, grossing NT$6 million, making it Taiwan's highest grossing fiction film in 2004. Like *Blue Gate Crossing*, *Formula 17* is a romantic comedy with homosexual themes made by young film-makers who know little about attracting audiences, only that it needs to happen.[2] With classic movie houses vanishing (captured most famously in Tsai Ming-liang's *Goodbye, Dragon Inn* [2003]), and megaplexes popping up in the island's many trendy malls, more than ever, going to the movies is a youth-driven social activity – something to do on dates and with friends. Hollywood spectacles are still popular of course, but suddenly so are films that reflect middle-class, teenage, urban lifestyles with humour and style; it's not surprising then that the Chinese title for *Formula 17* means '17-Year-Old's World'. While such films still receive limited releases compared to American pictures, they now play in more than one theatre for more than a week, the usual sentence for local productions. I would argue that these films are not anomalies, but a signal of the resuscitation of mainstream film in Taiwan.

Since the decline of the Taiwan New Cinema movement in the early 1990s, the discourse on Taiwanese national cinema (*guopian*) locally has centred on the issue of cultural and industrial survival under the threat of Hollywood, an approach representative of what Toby Miller *et al.* describe as the global effects model.[3] The apprehension over the demise of local cinema (embodied most emphatically in the anti-New Cinema manifesto *Death of the New Cinema*[4]) and the unprecedented approval of Taiwanese art cinema in overseas film festivals have led scholars of Taiwanese film to fixate disproportionately on the works of 'quality' directors like Hou Hsiao-hsien, Edward Yang and Tsai Ming-liang, celebrating their aesthetic and cultural accomplishments (however deserved) while neglecting the efforts by film-makers and policymakers to reconfigure local cinema as a social and economic practice in light of Taiwanese cinema's shifting place in the global and regional imaginaries. In this essay, I want to draw attention to this running 'parallel cinema', and then suggest that Chen Yin-jung's 2004 film *Formula 17* represents new aesthetic, thematic and marketing possibilities in mainstream Taiwanese cinema arising in a transitional commercial environment that could accurately be described as 'post-sadness'.[5] In so doing, I hope to show how the previously marginalised mainstream – *Formula 17* in particular – is now playing a central part in Taiwanese cinema's self-definition as *guopian* at home and as national 'brand' in festivals and markets abroad.

That *Formula 17* was so successful was shocking given that the entire film has no women characters. Better yet, the film is constructed in such a way that the audience can safely assume that every character in the romantic comedy is a gay man. In Hollywood, this idea would have been stricken before the script phase; in Taiwan, post-Hou film-makers have a hazy conception of what mainstream audiences want, so anything goes, even a conceit as seemingly radical as a gay utopia. The story is standard fare with a twist. A bashful country bumpkin named Tien (played by Tony Yang) treks north to Taipei to rendezvous with a chat-room acquaintance. The meeting is a disaster, but Tien soon finds a new love interest in an infamous playboy named Bai. What follows is essentially boy wants boy, boy gets boy, boy loses boy, boy regains boy; the turning points grind like clockwork, complete with flamboyant sidekicks who nurse heartache with flowers and romantic prose.

Yet those audiences who complained that Taiwanese films do not have original scripts did not seem to mind. (They also tolerate Hollywood films, but that is a different story.) Apparently, young audiences were won over by the freewheeling style. More than one comment on the discussion forum noticed the film's 'interesting camerawork', probably referring to Chen's use of flashbacks, dream sequences, ellipses, song montages, intercutting and direct gazes at the camera. Unhampered by demands from distributors and studios (who have long since abandoned local film production), these younger mainstream film-makers have inherited Hou, Yang and Tsai's spirit of independent experimentation, but not the endless takes and long shots. In short, Chen has perfected the incorporation of music video techniques in creating an idiosyncratic, popular film style. Music video, a medium many fledgling local directors rely on to finance their own works, has considerable cultural penetration thanks to cable networks MTV and Channel [V], TV screens in buses and subway stations, and pop music CD/DVD bundles. It was Chen Yin-jung who synthesised the music video style into a vernacular young people understand. At a Taiwanese film festival in 2005, *Formula 17* was heralded as one of the representative works of the 'seventh graders' generation, which refers to the seventh decade of Taiwanese born after the beginning of the Republic of China in 1911: that is, Taiwanese born between 1981 and 1990.[6] In popular local discourse, the 'seventh graders' are known as a privileged generation born during the economic boom and therefore did not undergo the economic, cultural and political turbulence of their parents and

grandparents' generations. The incorporation of music video styles is one way the seventh-grade film-makers are reaching out to their peers. Another is the integrated use of middle-class technology. In *Formula 17*, as well as *Taipei 21* (Alex Yang, 2003), *Love of May* (Hsu Hsiao-ming, 2004) and even Hou Hsiao-hsien's *Three Times* (2005), cellular phones, instant messaging and e-mail are not just props, but are media through which communication, misunderstandings and reconciliations in the narrative are made possible.[7]

However, style and content alone do not draw audiences into theatres, especially in a market where locals are so prejudiced against their own films. *Formula 17*'s miracle was that it found the right image to attract the desired audience. The film was produced by Three Dots Entertainment, whose founders began in film marketing and distribution and are now the symbolic leaders of the new wave of teen-oriented popular films.[8] They designed a movie poster that shows the leading man Tony Yang in nothing except boxers and a blazer unbuttoned to reveal his bare, sculpted chest. On the poster, both Tien and Bai are casually smiling, deflecting the stereotype of Taiwanese cinema characters as being terminally despondent. In the poster, as well as the trailer, the homosexual relationship is more than suggested (the trailer even reveals their big kiss) but it is not made to feel 'heavy' as it is in the films of Tsai Ming-liang, so as to retain the atmosphere of a romantic comedy while squeezing squeals out of giddy teenage girls. Featured prominently in the commercial is the film's theme song 'I Think Your Happiness is Because of Me' by local pop-rock act Rock Bang, whose debut CD *Proof of Life* was released only a month before *Formula 17*. The symbiosis between the two industries was spearheaded by the song's music video, directed by Chen Yin-jung herself and featuring clips from the film. While the use of theme songs is hardly new in Chinese cinemas, the use of the music video here shows that the film is directly targeting a certain audience and is promising an adherence to a particular music video vocabulary, namely quick edits, unusual camera setups and of course popular song.[9]

In terms of marketability, the film's greatest assets are the actors. Though *Formula 17* was Tony Yang's first film, he was already known as an actor in serial television dramas including *First Love* (2003), *Love Train* (2003) and *Crystal Boys* (2003), the last of which is based on the groundbreaking gay novel by

Formula 17

Taiwanese writer Pai Hsien-yung. The film's other major actor, Duncan Chow, was even more well known, having appeared in the series *Lover of Herb* (2004) and *Legend of Speed* (2004) among others. Both Yang and Chow are well built and undeniably good lucking, while they project amiable personalities. The audiences for these TV programmes are young, energetic consumers, and by recruiting Yang and Chow, *Formula 17* exploited a built-in audience. In many ways, *Formula 17* is a flashier, livelier retelling of a standard soap opera story, condensed to 90 minutes and featuring the gay twist. From this point of view, the film is less a cliché than something of a transmedia genre experiment, where one medium's successful formula is moulded into what would ideally become the formula for a re-emerging mainstream cinema.

What sets *Formula 17* apart from earlier popular films is that critics and highbrow viewers actively took notice. Nobody hailed the film a masterpiece by any means, but festival programmers found its freshness and popularity hard to ignore. *Formula 17* debuted at the Taipei Film Festival in March 2004, played at the Pusan Film Festival in September and screened at the Golden Horse Film Festival in November, where Tony Yang won an award for Best Newcomer. The film's success led the programmers of the 2004 Tailly High – New Talents, Young Cinema Film Festival to dedicate an entire showcase to the emerging acting talents of Taiwanese cinema, with both Yang and Chow highlighted as faces to watch. Tailly High took place at Spot – Taipei House (*Guangdian – Taibei zhijia*), which, since its opening in 2002, has become a hub for cinephilia in Taipei. In fact, the rise in popularity and critical acceptance of a

film like *Formula 17* is made possible by Spot, which is run by the Taiwan Film and Culture Society and managed by Hou Hsiao-hsien, who has in recent years been among the most vocal supporters of a mainstream cinema in Taiwan.[10] Spot's mission is to provide a venue for non-Hollywood productions ranging from local features and documentaries, to arthouse programming like a Robert Bresson retrospective in late 2006. The restored Western-style architecture of Spot contributes to an atmosphere conducive to 'serious' filmgoing; in the same building are a coffee shop and bookstore that has Taiwan's best collection of film books and local films for sale. Spot attracts college-aged film lovers who trust that films playing at Spot are pre-screened for quality. And whereas smaller films playing at mainstream theatres close after a week if business cannot compare with Hollywood competitors, Spot schedules its programmes in advance so audiences can rely on a fixed calendar. *Formula 17* was so popular among the Spot crowd that even after its initial three-week run, the film was rolled back out for a Valentine's Day programme, as well as for the Tailly High festival.

Now that *Formula 17* has proposed a possible formula for a mainstream Taiwanese cinema – incorporating music video and soap opera formulas, joining forces with the music industry, recruiting good-looking acting talent and appealing to both the mall-culture crowd and the cinephiles – is there hope for a progressive new film movement in Taiwan? Nobody expects the teen genre to supplant the festival boys – Hou, Yang, Tsai – as some of the most exciting voices in world cinema. However, as I mentioned earlier, the fact that mainstream Taiwanese cinema is still unmapped territory means that film-makers, distributors and marketers have the freedom to produce socially relevant products that project a multiplicity of voices, especially crucial in a time of political and social uncertainty. Things do look promising in terms of gender and sexuality. While the masters of the Taiwan new wave (Hou, Yang, Wu Nien-jen), the 'second wave' (Tsai, Ang Lee) and the new generation (Lin, Chang Tso-chi) are mostly men, *Formula 17* is directed by a 24-year-old woman and is explicitly about sexual orientation.

However, is *Formula 17* as radical as the premise suggests? The film's joyous skipping over of 'gay issues' allows it to avoid the dramatic and moral confrontations that led a film like *Wedding Banquet* (Ang

Lee, 1993) to be interpreted by some as patriarchal and nationalistic.[11] Meanwhile, it functions by presenting standard gay archetypes: the flamboyant homosexual, the cross-dresser, the well-dressed playboy, etc. Also, like *The Wedding Banquet*, none of the leading gay characters are played by homosexual actors, so therefore part of the audience's pleasure in seeing the film isn't to see homosexual representation, but to see straight teenage guys kissing each other.[12] In addition, as the film plays on clichés of the romantic comedy genre, audiences, particularly straight female ones, can easily identify with the Tien character by switching his gender without a huge stretch of the imagination. There are plenty of cues for standard generic emotional identification: kissing one's reflection in a mirror, sulking after a breakup, drawing messages in the sand on a beach, mushy phone conversations, reciting 'I love you' in a dozen languages, gossiping about each other's romantic escapades. In essence, the film's gay male utopia can be read as a straight female utopia; in this way, *Formula 17* is like pre-digested, pre-'poached' slashings of mainstream heterosexual screen romances, a commodified version of the fan fiction romanticised as anti-corporate by Henry Jenkins in his classic text on fan cultures.[13]

However, I would argue that the very fact that every character in the film is potentially a gay man is a daring, if not radical, move. When an old man Tien and Bai meet on the street turns out to be gay, it is not only a comical moment but also a fresh and liberating one. In addition, the very evident effort the film-makers paid to removing all female characters and making the city a squeaky-clean gay male utopia draws attention to its constructedness, and consequently the fact that this blatant non-reality is incongruous with Taiwan's actual culture of intolerance. That such a utopia includes instantly recognisable Taipei locations such as Warner Village, Hsimenting and especially Chiang Kai-shek Memorial Hall (the ultimate symbol of conservatism in Taiwan) also suggests a playful queering of Taipei.[14] Finally, the big revelation at the end of the film is that Bai's fear of commitment stems from childhood trauma: a fortune-teller predicts that all of Bai's future lovers will be cursed, a standard trope in Chinese melodrama and soap operas, but in this case could also refer to the fact that Bai is a homosexual. (The fortune teller in contemporary Taiwanese society is a symbol of old, patriarchal and repressive beliefs;[15] to further press

the point, directly behind the seated fortune-teller are drawings of a man and a woman, perhaps suggesting that he stands for heterosexuality.) The resolution of this problem (and thus the film) rests on Bai's breaking free from his reliance on traditional superstition and embracing his own desires. 'What's fate got to do with it? If you're afraid of getting hurt, just admit it!' screams Alan, one of the film's three flamboyantly gay characters. So when Bai decides to run after his lost love, we can read the melodramatic resolution as a radical (homosexual) act breaking the character from outmoded (heterosexual) tradition.

In the years following *Formula 17*'s release, the film has been evoked by policymakers as a symbol of Taiwanese cinema's populist reawakening. More specifically, the film is at the centre of the industry's co-ordinated strategy to revamp the image of theatrical Taiwanese cinema locally, turning *guopian* (national cinema) away from art cinema and toward teen-oriented, star-driven genre films. The aforementioned Tailly High Film Festival, which highlighted *Formula 17*'s leading men, is actually a project of Taiwan's Government Information Office (GIO), which in recent years has shifted its emphasis from harvesting festival wins to promoting young talents.[16] The GIO is also responsible for the pan-Chinese Golden Horse Awards, which consistently awards its 'best newcomer of the year' award to Taiwanese actors and film-makers, including Tony Yang for *Formula 17*.

Meanwhile, other film-makers, producers and distributors have taken advantage of *Formula 17*'s unexpected success in marketing their own films. Naturally, Three Dots Entertainment splashed 'From the creators of *Formula 17*' on advertising for their subsequent films *Catch* (Chen Yin-jung, 2006) and *The Heirloom* (Leste Chen, 2005), and naturally, films like *The Shoe Fairy* (Robin Lee, 2005) that feature *Formula 17* stars explicitly note their *Formula 17* connection in publicity materials. What is surprising is that aside from the name-dropping, the trailers for these films also draw attention to the fact that they are part of a new brand of Taiwanese film-making; this is a self-conscious attempt to draw the tonal and demographic boundaries of an emerging local film movement. *The Shoe Fairy*, which was financed by the much-discussed 'Focus: First Cuts' series aiming to promote new talent in Chinese-language cinema, has a trailer that boasts a quote from local film critic Wen

Tien-hsiang: '[The film] possesses the humor and creativity missing in Taiwanese cinema for a long time'. Humorous and creative 'post-sadness' director Tsai Ming-liang clearly is not included in this new formulation, which, as the trailer for *The Heirloom* suggests, is the terrain of maverick 'seventh graders' like director Leste Chen. *Formula 17* was also among several films that revitalised a long tradition of using theme songs in trailers, a well-established practice in other film industries. We see (and hear) subsequent examples of trailers that deploy pop songs to brand their films within the island's various pop culture constituencies and to target the cherished teenage demographic. A short list includes the trailers for *Love of May*, *La Mélodie d'Hélène* (Yin Chi, 2004), *Do Over* (Cheng Yu-chieh, 2006), *Chocolate Rap* (Chi Y. Lee, 2006) and *Gogo G-Boys* (Yu Jong-jong, 2006). Finally, the success of *Formula 17* has made mainstream films with LGBT (lesbian, gay, bisexual and transgender/transsexual) themes commercially viable, as evidenced by a handful of recent theatrical features that take sexual orientation as a theme, such as *Splendid Float* (Zero Chou, 2004), *Eternal Summer* (Leste Chen, 2006), *Spider Lilies* (Zero Chou, 2007) and *Gogo G-Boys* ('*Formula 17* meets *Miss Congeniality*' proclaims the trailer).

While the authenticity of the gay themes in *Formula 17* and its successors has been debated within Taiwan – they are 'gay films for straight audiences', one local film-maker told me – the films are finding acceptance abroad in LGBT film circles. The programme notes for Frameline 29 (also known as the San Francisco International LGBT Film Festival) states that *Formula 17* is 'an insistent testament to gay friendship, as the always optimistic pals help each other past heartaches and back to happiness as fully realized queers'.[17] Meanwhile, the notes for the Miami Gay & Lesbian Film Festival declare that 'For anyone who remembers the tumultuous feelings of that time when you were "new," *Formula 17* brings them back to life.'[18] The gay Thai website Dragoncastle.net includes *Formula 17* in its list of thirteen 'best gay movies' and celebrates the film for providing 'enough bare flesh to give the film a realistic view of gay life and get your juices moving'.[19] In all three descriptions, the film is depicted as resonant with the realities of gay life and film spectatorship. In this case, the film's status as 'Other' in foreign film festivals and arthouses absolves it from the scrutiny and suspicion it faces locally, where the film is more likely to be judged by how well it 'speaks for' the community it has chosen to depict. Whereas critics typically describe the 'burden of representation' as symptomatic of the Western consumer's Orientalist 'othering' of foreign texts, for a populist film – particularly one that makes money – in an industry where local production is both self (as a local cultural product) and Other (as marginal to the dominant Hollywood), the burden of representation and cultural authenticity is ironically stronger at home. Abroad, the film's 'realism' is more readily accepted, because it bears no such burdens, as it is one of many international LGBT films circulating in the film festival circuit, unlike in Taiwan where it is for many at the time the sole representative of 'gay' local film-making. The film's banning in culturally conservative Singapore is also played up in the international discourse as a badge of honour (or authenticity). The Miami festival programme even adds that the film 'is progressive in some ways that American youth movies are still working towards', a sentiment rarely heard at home.

Formula 17's dent in the international art film world may be small, but given how miniscule Taiwanese mainstream cinema still is in terms of visibility and market share, its impact on cosmopolitan festivalgoers and distributors will have a significant effect on the international definition of 'post-sadness' Taiwanese cinema. At the 2006 American Film Market (the largest gathering of international film buyers and sellers in the United States), the GIO rented a booth to tout the latest in Taiwanese film-making. As I approached the desk of flyers and pamphlets celebrating predominantly teen-oriented features (conspicuously missing was the new Tsai Ming-liang film, which was handled at the market by its European sales agent), I listened in on a conversation between the Taiwanese representative (a 'seventh grade' film distributor) and an international buyer. The representative was trying to promote Leste Chen's gay-themed teen drama *Eternal Summer* as the latest 'big thing' in Taiwanese cinema; the buyer's response was simply, 'Is it anything like *Formula 17*?', which poses the question where does this new wave of Taiwanese mainstream films stand in the international 'interzones'[20] of cultural commodities? Will local cinema need to find a new niche to replace the old one of art films? Will domestic anxieties of Taiwanese representation be obviated or exacerbated by their international acceptance and profitability?

For anybody familiar with the recent history of Chinese-language cinemas, these questions are hardly new, and their persistence is indicative of the limits of policymakers' and film-makers' abilities to self-define *guopian* in a local mainstream vernacular given enduring international categories such as 'Taiwanese', 'Chinese' and 'LBGT film'. From a production standpoint, *Formula 17* represents the liberating effects of a largely unregulated, inchoate mainstream market; film-makers are free to experiment with style, themes and marketing to target their desired local audience. But the success of *Formula 17* closes certain doors as others are opened. In the wake of *Formula 17* came a wave of homogeneously homosexual youth films armed with the full backing of Taiwan's GIO, which, through international film markets and regional awards ceremonies, has conducted a co-ordinated re-branding of Taiwanese national cinema on a number of transnational stages. Following Alan Williams, who argues that 'national cinemas' are not the corpus of nations' films, but rather 'sites of conflict among different interest groups',[21] we can read the GIO's re-branding of Taiwanese national cinema as an institutionalised minimisation of intranational difference in the name of the local industry's survival within the international flow of film commodities. In regards to the role of the nation-state in the disjunctive global economy, Arjun Appadurai writes that:

> [N]ational and international mediascapes are exploited by nation-states to pacify … the potential fissiparousness of all ideas of difference. Typically, contemporary nation-states do this by exercising taxonomical control over difference; by creating various kinds of international spectacle to domesticate difference; and by seducing small groups with the fantasy of self-display on some sort of global or cosmopolitan stage.[22]

'Gay' cinema as exemplified by *Formula 17* and its successors is precisely that 'international spectacle' (as 'authentic' Asian queer) on a cosmopolitan stage (the film festival and film market), while the GIO's purchasing of the 'Taiwanese cinema' booth at film markets around the world is an active way in which the government exercises 'taxonomical control'. The liberating potential of an open market may be energising for local film-makers in search of the precious mainstream, but the control of distribution, publicity

and the 'Taiwan brand' remains subject to the usual political and cultural forces at home and abroad. In this way, there is continuity between the new mainstream and the 'alternative' Taiwan New Cinema movement, which Kuan-hsing Chen argues was 'swallowed up' by a government wishing to define a nativist history for national and transnational markets.[23] With new self-definition comes the reorganisation of old boundaries, and the rise of the marginalised mainstream will continue the confrontations between Taiwanese cinema and the international film festival circuit, the Asian regional market and the true Taiwanese mainstream: Hollywood.

This chapter is expanded from '*Formula 17*: Testing a Formula for Mainstream Cinema in Taiwan', *Senses of Cinema*, 34 (January–March 2005): <www.sensesofcinema.com/contents/05/34/formula_17.html>

NOTES

1. All references here are to 'Why can't Taiwanese films rise?' ('Wei shenme taiwan de dianying qi bu lai … sha yuanyin a …'), 30 November 2004: <tw.mb.yahoo.com/movie/board.php?action=l&sod=2&tid=ac0a40bbra5xfwaaba9qbcv0a4a3a8sta3adl&sid=152955249> (2 December 2004). Over a dozen of the original postings have since been removed and the message thread has moved to a new URL: <tw.mb.yahoo.com/movie/board.php?bname=152955249&tid=2660&action=m&keyword=%B0_%A8%D3&type=title> (17 February 2007).
2. Ada Tseng, 'Boys Just Wanna Have Fun: An Interview with DJ Chen', *Asia Pacific Arts*, 23 June 2005: <www.asiaarts.ucla.edu/article.asp?parentid=25969> (17 February 2007).
3. Toby Miller *et al.*, *Global Hollywood 2* (London: BFI Publishing, 2005), 35–40.
4. Mi Tsuo and Liang Hsin-hua, eds, *Death of the New Cinema: From 'Everything for Tomorrow' to 'A City of Sadness'* (*Xindianying zhi shi: cong 'yiqie wei mingtian' dao 'beiqing chengshi'*) (Taipei: Tangshan Press, 1991).
5. Meiling Wu, 'Postsadness Taiwan New Cinema: Eat, Drink, Everyman, Everywoman', in *Chinese-Language Film: Historiography, Poetics, Politics*, ed. Sheldon H. Lu and Emilie Yueh-yu Yeh (Honolulu: University of Hawaii Press, 2005), 76–95.
6. 'Festival introduction', Tailly High Film Festival website, 2004: <www.twfilm.org/taillyhigh_web/intro.htm> (29 April 2007).

7. The use of technology also makes possible product placement, as was the case with *Love of May* and BenQ, a maker of cellular phones.

8. Caroline Gluck, 'Can Youth Save Taiwan Film?', *International Herald Tribune* (26 November 2004): <www.iht.com/articles/2004/11/26/taifilm_ed3_.php> (17 February 2007).

9. This marketing technique was also employed for *Love of May*, which fully exploited the popularity of pop-rock sensation Mayday, although to lesser success.

10. For Hou's thoughts on Taiwanese popular cinema, see his comments made at a seminar at Spot in 2002. Hou Hsiao-hsien, 'In Search of New Genres and Directions for Asian Cinema', trans. Lin Wenchi, *Rouge*, 1 (2003): <www.rouge.com.au/1/hou.html> (17 February 2007).

11. Cynthia W. Liu, 'To Love, Honor, and Dismay: Subverting the Feminine in Ang Lee's Trilogy of Resuscitated Patriarchs', *Hitting Critical Mass: A Journal of Asian American Cultural Criticism*, 3, no. 1 (Winter 1995), 1–60.

12. The making-of featurette on the Taiwanese version of the DVD includes a humorous section on the preparation of the love scene, showing that the film is not necessarily promoting acceptance of gay themes, but is offering the thrill of seeing heterosexual TV idols flirt hesitatingly with deviant sexuality, which is hardly a radical reading.

13. Henry Jenkins, *Textual Poachers: Television Fans & Participatory Culture* (New York: Routledge, 1992).

14. The film's queering of public spaces runs parallel to Taipei's government-funded gay and lesbian pride parades in these very spaces, suggesting that *Formula 17* is not in any strict sense 'revolutionary', but rather is in a dialogical relationship with other above-ground attempts by the LGBT community to work in accord with the government, which commonly evokes gay and lesbian issues for political purposes. Scott Simon, 'From Hidden Kingdom to Rainbow Community: The Making of Gay and Lesbian Identity in Taiwan', in *The Minor Arts of Daily Life: Popular Culture in Taiwan*, ed. David K. Jordan, Andrew D. Morris and Marc L. Moskowitz (Honolulu: University of Hawaii Press, 2004), 67–88.

15. For a discussion of the sexual politics of fortune-telling in Taiwanese soap operas, see Lin Szu-Ping, 'The Woman with Broken Palm Lines: Subject, Agency, Fortune-Telling, and Women in Taiwanese Television Drama', in *Multiple Modernities: Cinemas and Popular Media in Transcultural East Asia*, ed. Jenny Kwok Wah Lau (Philadelphia: Temple University Press, 2003), 222–237.

16. Yu Sen-lun, 'Tomorrow's Stars of the Screen Today', *Taipei Times*, 27 August 2004: <www.taipeitimes.com/News/feat/archives/2004/08/27/2003200481> (17 February 2007).

17. Shannon Kelley, '*Formula 17*', Frameline 29: San Francisco International LGBT Film Festival, 2005: <www.frameline.org/festival/29th/programs/formula_17.html> (17 February 2007).

18. 'Formula 17 (Shi qi sui de tian kong)', *Miami Gay & Lesbian Film Festival*, 2005: <www.mglff.com/2005/films/sl_33.htm> (17 February 2007).

19. 'Best gay movie reviews', *Dragoncastle's Gay Asia*: <dragoncastle.net/reviews.shtml> (17 February 2007).

20. Julian Stringer borrows George E. Marcus and Fred R. Myers's 'intertextual zones' to describe spaces of artistic contact, speculation and legitimation, in particular the international film festival. Julian Stringer, '*Boat People*: Second Thoughts on Text and Context', in *Chinese Films in Focus: 25 New Takes*, ed. Chris Berry (London: BFI, 2003), 15–22.

21. Alan Williams, 'Introduction', in *Film and Nationalism*, ed. Alan Williams (New Brunswick, NJ: Rutgers University Press, 2002), 5.

22. Arjun Appadurai, 'Disjuncture and Difference in the Global Cultural Economy', *Public Culture*, 2, no. 2 (Spring 1990): 13.

23. Kuan-hsing Chen, 'Taiwan New Cinema, or a Global Nativism?', in *Theorising National Cinemas*, ed. Valentina Vitali and Paul Willeman (London: BFI, 2006), 138.

16   *The Goddess*: Fallen Woman of Shanghai

Kristine Harris

The goddess ... struggles in the whirlpool of life ...
In tonight's streets, she is a cheap goddess ... When she
takes her child into her arms, she is a pure, holy mother.
In both these lives, she has shown great moral character.

Accompanying this elliptical epigraph, a cryptic emblem of a female figure huddled over an unclothed child foreshadows the precarious cycle of humiliation and devotion propelling *The Goddess*. The title itself conveys this sense of duplicity: literally it means 'divine woman', but colloquially 'goddess' was a mordant euphemism for streetwalking prostitutes. This haunting prelude portends the uneasy tensions embedded in this silent film. The background image, rendered in a Western-style relief sculpture of a nude woman and child, looms behind two Chinese characters conveying the mocking title. Juxtaposing imported aesthetics and local idiom, physical sacrifice and immortal divinity, vilified prostitution and glorified motherhood, *The Goddess* invokes the idolatrous, if ambivalent, obsession with female icons that so occupied the urban imagination of 1930s China.

This particular goddess is an unnamed young woman raising a child alone in the city, and surviving only by streetwalking. One night, she is cornered by the police, but saved from arrest by a small-time crook offering protection in exchange for submission. He blackmails her into a mock marriage, then siphons off her meagre earnings for his gambling habit. The goddess moves away and searches for other work, but continually fails to escape. She secretly saves up for her son's schooling, but wary parents discover her true occupation and have the child dismissed, despite the headmaster's impassioned speech condemning their intolerance. The hoodlum, meanwhile, wagers away all her remaining cash. The goddess confronts her adversary, inadvertently killing him. Sentenced to twelve years in prison, she receives a visit from the sympathetic educator, who assures her he will raise her son attentively. Hoping to free her child from ill repute, the woman beseeches the headmaster to tell the boy his mother has died.

When *The Goddess* premiered at Shanghai's Lyric Theatre on 7 December 1934, it played to full houses and instantly won attention from critics.[1] Newspapers and movie magazines lauded Wu Yonggang's directorial debut for his sophisticated use of expressive film language, hailing the 27-year-old filmmaker as the new wonder boy of Chinese cinema.[2] They also showered praise on the mature, nuanced performance by actress Ruan Lingyu, then at the pinnacle of her career.[3] This popular release from Lianhua film studios was one of its last silent productions, and politically more reticent than its previous releases.

Depicting marginal outcasts of the urban underclass, *The Goddess* stimulated public debate over the capacity of individual action and cinematic representation to effect social change. Some journalists were concerned about the film's fatalistic ending, but even these critics considered *The Goddess* 'one of the three best films of 1934', and praised its courage in taking on such sensitive subjects as unemployment, intolerance and prostitution.[4]

Half a century later *The Goddess* came into global circulation, through retrospectives of Chinese cinema across Europe, Asia and North America.[5] International festivals foregrounded Ruan Lingyu alongside renowned stars like Marlene Dietrich and Barbara Stanwyck with the affectionate moniker 'Garbo of the Orient'.[6] Chinese and foreign critics alike reclaimed *The Goddess* as a masterpiece of 'the first golden age of Chinese cinema'.[7] These viewers considered Wu's use of the silent medium world-class, recognising resonances in genre and technique between *The Goddess* and European or American films. They also discerned a certain restraint and apparent Confucian conservatism.

This essay examines *The Goddess* closely in the context of writings by Wu Yonggang and his contemporaries. What we discover is that the director was indeed intimately engaged with global developments in cinema, including the 'fallen woman' film and maternal melodrama, but that he was also compelled to craft his film to conform with the changing outlines of China's cultural politics during 1934. Seen in this light, the strikingly restrained visual language in Wu's film dramatised not only the sacrifices of his nameless protagonist, but also, implicitly, the film-maker's own sense of limits demanding self-regulation.

FALLEN WOMAN OF SHANGHAI

Focusing on a prostitute, *The Goddess* resonates with narratives about the 'fallen woman' who violates conventional codes of sexual morality incurring tragic consequences. Early Chinese film-makers, enamoured with this genre, drew upon local and foreign precedents to produce titles like *New Camille* (Asia-Xinmin, 1913; Li Pingqian, 1927), based on the nineteenth-century novel *La Dame aux Camélias*, and *A Lady of Shanghai* (Zhang Shichuan, 1925). For the 1920s and 1930s New Youth culture emerging in Chinese cities, this complex 'fallen woman' figure embodied the predicament of individuals flouting restrictive boundaries of social convention.

Wu Yonggang's early education in cinema was filled with 'fallen woman' films from the United States and Europe. In a memoir written shortly before his death in 1982, the director recalled his teenage years watching third-run features at Shanghai's Carter Theatre during the mid-1920s.[8] American silents like *Way Down East* made an especially deep impression on Wu. Released in China as *Laihun*, or 'Mock Marriage', D. W. Griffith's classic featured Lillian Gish as a young woman duped into a false marriage and then maligned for bearing a child out of wedlock.[9] Shot through with the tensions of intolerance, such films provided powerful inspiration for the young Wu Yonggang.

Just steps away from the pathos of these tarnished screen heroines were the 'miserable sights', Wu remembers, of desperate women milling about the Shanghai streets at dusk. Unlicensed prostitutes, proliferating there during the late 1920s and early 1930s, were more vulnerable to danger and uncertainties than the city's legally registered courtesans in tax-paying

brothels, and were scorned as criminals polluting public health and morality.[10] Wu pitied these streetwalkers 'forced to sell their own flesh to live': 'Every time I watched this scene, my heart was filled with indignation. I sympathised with these misfortunate women and detested this dark society. I was dissatisfied; I was despondent; I wanted to cry out!'[11]

Wu Yonggang eventually realised he could channel this indignation into a film of his own. He abandoned a frustrating job in set design at the Shaw Brothers' Tianyi Film Company, and completed art-school training in Western painting. Inspired by new films of social conscience released by studios like Lianhua in 1933, Wu began to envision *The Goddess* as a film with universal, allegorical weight: 'I thought that speaking out about so many women's misfortune and oppression through the concrete images of cinema might serve as a repudiation and denunciation of this dark society in general.'[12]

MATERNAL VIRTUE

To develop the pathos of this 'fallen woman' figure, Wu lavished attention on her daytime life as a virtuous mother. Wu's camera respectfully observes her nursing the baby after staggering upstairs at dawn. He tracks her tireless missions to locate a new boarding house, a factory job, a school for her son. Even the final expository intertitle underscores her self-effacing devotion: 'The lonely, quiet prison cell is the only rest she has had in this life. In her hopes and dreams, she imagines with great yearning a bright and glorious future for her child.'

The woman who sacrifices everything for her child's future was, of course, a mainstay of Hollywood maternal melodramas like *Stella Dallas* (Henry King, 1925; King Vidor, 1937), *Madame X* (Lionel Barrymore, 1929), *The Sin of Madelon Claudet* (Edgar Selwyn, 1931) and *Blonde Venus* (Josef von Sternberg, 1932).[13] Yet the goddess's maternal virtue also conjured up local ideals, including the renowned mother of Mencius, who worked night and day to provide for her son's Confucian education, and the contemporary 'good wife, wise mother' model, which encouraged women to contribute to the nation by raising children.[14]

Seen in the same Confucian framework, the headmaster typifies paternal benevolence and righteousness as he extols the need for education: 'It's true the child's mother is a streetwalker, but this is due to broader social problems. ... Education is our respon-sibility and we must rescue this child from adversity.' Embedded in a series of long, didactic intertitles (in a film where dialogue is otherwise minimal), the headmaster's indictment of intolerance is conspicu-ous; he even addresses the camera straight on, direct-ing his speech at the trustees *and* the film audience. Indeed, Wu Yonggang subsequently explained that he had 'borrowed' the 'conscientious' voice of the educator to register his own cry for social justice.[15] If the headmaster offers a possible source of legitimate male authority, then the imprisoned goddess's final request that he tell her son 'his mother is dead' would appear to represent a parallel surrender of maternal influence.

When viewed alongside American melodramas and social conditions in Shanghai during the mid-1930s, *The Goddess* certainly seems to project a con-servative morality. William Rothman points out, for instance, that this female character's only fulfilment comes vicariously, through her son and his education. Comparing *The Goddess* to *Blonde Venus*, Rothman sees in the Chinese film a virtual absence of the eroti-cism, romance, feminism or self-fulfilment so common in American 'fallen woman' films.[16] Along similar lines, Rey Chow searches for hints of sexual-ity in the film, concluding that 'even though she is a mother, the prostitute's access to her own feminine sexuality is continually obstructed, policed, and pun-ished by society's patriarchal codes of female chastity'.[17]

Yingjin Zhang likewise interprets the film's emphasis on motherhood as an evasion and conceal-ment of female sexuality, ultimately 'marking the film as conservative'. Supporting his conclusion that *The Goddess* is primarily a male fantasy, Zhang offers some compelling examples: the goddess's virtue does appear to depend on the fulfilment of an 'expected role in cultural reproduction'; the headmaster, as a potential surrogate father, seems to 'secure patrilineal continuity on a symbolic level'; and the camera's focus on locked gates and prison bars does indeed lock the goddess away.[18]

Some of Wu's contemporaries likewise took issue with the conservatism in *The Goddess*, though from a different angle. Critics influential in China's 1930s left-wing underground admitted *The Goddess* sur-passed other releases that year, but questioned whether the film's ending was sufficiently revolution-ary. Wang Chenwu contended that if prostitution is a 'broader social problem' rather than an isolated moral failing, as Wu's headmaster asserts, then *The Goddess* should offer a 'total indictment of social forces' and clear-cut resolution, emulating recent Soviet fiction.[19] A Ying concurred; he felt the plot focused excessively on the goddess's personal misfortune and her ill-fated conflict with the gambler, when in reality only a wholesale dismantling of the entire social system could resolve this woman's adversity.[20] Notably, neither critic took issue with patriarchal morality in *The Goddess*; instead, both worried that the film's protest against social injustice was politically inconclusive.

A NEW LIFE

Was *The Goddess* simply a maternal melodrama that accommodated and reinforced the social or political status quo, as these reactions might suggest? In response to his contemporary critics, Wu Yonggang promptly responded in print: 'When I first set out to write about the goddesses, I wished to show more of their real lives, but circumstances would not permit me to do so.'[21] The obliqueness of Wu's reference to 'circumstances' and 'permission' implies that the spe-cific obstacles were sensitive, even unspeakable.

The Goddess would have been a likely target for censors. During the film's production in October and November 1934, China's KMT Nationalist Party was already intensifying its ideological efforts to regulate literature and cinema, concurrent with military cam-paigns targeting Chinese Communist Party bases in the hinterland. Under the government's broad cen-sorship law, reinforced by increased police powers, any imported or domestic film that might 'harm good customs or public order' was ineligible for a licence.[22] This included any works advocating class conflict or socialism. By some counts, the script inspection com-mittee rejected over eighty submissions from Novem-ber 1934 to March 1935.[23] Surprisingly, however, extant public records provide no evidence of formal directives requiring alterations to *The Goddess*.[24]

More conceivably, Wu self-censored to navigate the diffuse and pervasive anxieties about ideology, politics and the market confronting China's film-makers in 1934, when official censorship was rein-forced by broader conservative restrictions and state surveillance. The government's New Life Movement, designed to bolster popular loyalty to the Nationalist cause, had been unveiled in February 1934, just months before *The Goddess* went into production.[25] Film-makers were encouraged to champion this cultural mobilisation effort, promoting Confucian revivalist morality along with sacrifice, discipline and endurance in everyday life. Just months later, Lianhua's weekly newsletter prominently reported that New Life organisational committee members, as well as high-ranking government ministers like Chen Gongbo, had paid several visits to the set half-way through the shooting of *The Goddess*; they were lavishly banqueted by studio head Luo Mingyou.[26]

The Goddess's idealisation of domesticity and virtuous motherhood dovetailed conveniently with the New Life Movement's prescribed roles for women. One line in *The Goddess* may even be interpreted as an allusion to the movement. After the goddess enrols her son in school, an expository title at this juncture declares emphatically, 'The start of a new life gives her new happiness.' Wu's self-conscious appropriation of New Life rhetoric would appear to fulfil national mandates and public expectations.

Additionally, Chinese studios like Lianhua were competing in a market dominated by imports. By 1934, the new talking pictures playing in Shanghai were generally light-hearted musicals, comedies, mysteries and adventures from the United States and Britain. American films, especially, seemed to be taking fewer risks, owing to new Production Code limitations and concomitant self-regulation.[27] Cumulatively these factors made the miserable 'social and economic conditions of fallen women' – Wu's stated concern – virtually unrepresentable on Shanghai screens.

Thus the street scenes of the 1920s and early 1930s that had first inspired Wu Yonggang's despondent indignation gradually evolved into a new, arguably more complex, narrative. Wu explains how he came up with the idea of a double life for the film: 'The story's emphasis shifted to maternal love, with the life of the streetwalkers as a background, until it became about the struggle of a streetwalker living two lives for her child.'[28]

A DOUBLE LIFE
Moving beyond the straightforward 'fallen woman' narrative, and also transcending a 'New Life' conservative maternal melodrama, Wu Yonggang silently dramatised the implications of the protagonist's double life through suggestive visual language. The film shifts between a few recurring spaces, and between the two 'regions' of public and private.[29] Nearly all – exteriors and interiors alike – are deliberately confined: the street corner set, her single-room dwelling, a pawn-shop threshold, the tight alleyway, a montage of factory smokestacks. The artificiality and alternation of these spaces underscores the highly circumscribed patterns of daily life for this goddess, as she attempts to maintain a separation between her two roles as mother and streetwalker.

Wu's careful use of lighting also helps establish a 'double life' for the goddess. Offsetting daytime exterior shots are frequent night scenes, when the sun sinks below the horizon, gas lamps illuminate otherwise dark streets and incandescent bulbs cast shadows across interiors. Oscillating between natural and artificial lighting, the film conveys a sense of the passage of time, a sense of inexorable routine reinforced by frequent close-ups on the clocks that regulate this goddess's brutal schedule.

The 'double life' in *The Goddess* is as skilfully crafted as the best American silent melodrama or Weimar street tragedy. Wu Yonggang augments the film's oppressive claustrophobia through a rhythmic repetition of spaces and shots.[30] He also heightens its stark melodramatic contrasts by making the characters virtually anonymous, with almost mythological power. In fact, by transforming these figures into transcendent types, Wu arguably succeeds in extending the significance of *The Goddess* far beyond the individual to the universal.[31]

The film's restrained visual style effectively expressed the otherwise unnameable limits Wu had referred to as 'circumstances'. He conveyed his bleak vision less through intertitles than through spare sets, stark lighting and jarring montages. Granted, this economy was partly borne from necessity – as a first-time director, Wu was given a spartan budget and a schedule that involved shooting at night. But the evocative *mise en scène* demonstrates Wu's decade of artistic training and experience designing sets for studios like White Lily and Tianyi, where he had managed with even fewer resources.

In fact, shortly after *The Goddess*'s nation-wide release, Wu Yonggang published an article about the 'power of suggestion' [*anshi*] that sets and lighting design could instil in a film.[32] Wu's advice would be useful to any film-maker trying to move beyond the narrow limitations of written scripts deemed acceptable. Seen in this light, the story of a marginalised woman striving for her ideals while maintaining a secret life might also be understood as an allegory of the 'double life' a film-maker might construct by necessity, to negotiate the constraints of 'circumstances'.

Silent actress Ruan Lingyu seemed to incarnate such duplicity. On the one hand, Ruan was a mother herself, and had attained public acclaim by playing tragic, suffering women in films such as *Peach Blossom Weeps Tears of Blood* (Bu Wancang, 1931), *Little Toys* (Sun Yu, 1933), *Life* (Fei Mu, 1934) and *Return* (Zhu Shilin, 1934). This element of Ruan's star persona translated into *The Goddess* well, generating sympathy for this solitary woman striving to maintain maternal virtue. On the other hand, the image of actresses was highly commodified, and at this peak period of her career, pictures of Ruan adorned advertisements for perfume, soap and other consumer products. These images played into the popular notion that female movie stars, like prostitutes, were merchandise for public display and consumption – making Ruan seem even more plausible in the role of the goddess.

Wu Yonggang attributed much of the film's success to Ruan's skill in character development, which often went far beyond what he could possibly have envisioned. Noting her talent for complex scenes, Wu commented on Ruan's masterful gestures and facial expressions, which could convey conflicting emotions simultaneously (hysteria, fear, sorrow, anger, resignation), enhancing key moments such as the incarceration scene. The director even intimated that the actress's self-effacing performances were inseparable from her own painful life and past experiences – a reference to Ruan's wretched childhood as a servant girl and her troubled relationships while making this film, which culminated in suicide only months later in March 1935 at age 24.[33]

SHATTERING THE GAZE

If the goddess at first manages to survive by maintaining a double life, any attempt to keep the two spheres separate is constantly frustrated. She becomes a target of surveillance, and the camera's voyeuristic gaze intimates her vulnerability to physical violation and abduction. The opening scene of the film, for instance, wends its way from the

rooftops of Shanghai through a window to enter the goddess's home.

This pursuing, consuming gaze gets replicated in successive scenes. In the dark streets, potential clients casually survey the goddess's figure. Vigilant police and the gambling scoundrel stalk her in back alleys. Echoing the film's opening shots, the headmaster's initial housecall methodically scans her room for signs of vice; soon afterwards, the gambler similarly searches crevices in her room for cash.

One might interpret this visual surveillance as a 'male fantasy' of 'penetration' into a 'female world of prostitution', reaffirming male authority and 'control of the city', as Yingjin Zhang argues.[34] Or one might determine, as William Rothman does, that it demonstrates the camera's 'capacity for violence, for villainy', indicating that even the film-maker himself is 'implicated in the hypocrisy [he] attacks'.[35] Zhang and Rothman make absolutely crucial points. Yet in the light of our understanding about Wu's circumstances, it is possible to conclude that his camera does not simply participate in the controlling male gaze; rather, by foregrounding the camera's potential for visual domination and physical violation, Wu also presents coercion and force as part of the goddess's problem.

The gambler's imposing perspective and physical frame visibly dominate his scenes with the goddess. When this gambling thug takes her child hostage, the stunned goddess shrinks to a diminutive powerlessness in a disorienting shot framed by his legs. Then, lunging his hand directly at the camera – at

Held hostage

the goddess, and the spectator – the grinning gambler slowly tightens it to a steely grip, warning, 'The monkey king struggles but he can't jump out of the palm of the Buddha's hand.' This line asserts the omnipotence of an enormous Buddha prevailing over misguided sinners, and it is full of bitter irony. For if the hoodlum once offered a moment of salvation for the fallen woman absconding from police raids, his underworld blackmail schemes soon approximate eternal damnation.

Wu's camera condemns this male domination in other ways too – replaying scenes structurally to magnify their impact, or positioning the camera as antagonist. By presenting analogously the police pursuit, the headmaster's investigation and the scoundrel's encroaching search, Wu's reiterations cumulatively insinuate a critique of such harassment.

When the goddess's anger finally erupts in the film's penultimate murder scene, Wu offers a brief moment of settlement for this fallen woman struggling to escape the grip of her oppressors. Bloody and beaten, the goddess musters up a bottle and smashes it on the unsuspecting gambler, instantly eliminating the antagonist. This murder scene fulfils an earlier moment of symbolic patricide in the film. When asked about the head of household's occupation, the goddess replies after some thought, 'His father is dead.' She cautiously conceals the truth for her son's sake; the film never reveals his phantom paternity.[36] Even the child's surrogate father (headmaster and film-maker stand-in) finds himself powerless to lead in the face of intolerance, and can only secede in righteous resignation.

Shattering the gaze

Yet if *The Goddess* is permeated with anxiety about the absence of legitimate authority, paternity is only one aspect of the crisis dramatised here; Wu Yonggang also implicates class relations as part of the problem. Gossiping parents and neighbours scorn the disreputable woman and her son; school trustees expel the child to satisfy the parents' 'call for accountability'. As these men and women track the goddess's behaviour, the film conveys their 'looks' as menacing surveillance shots through extreme high angles or apertures: a next-door woman spies on the goddess and gambler through a keyhole; other women look down on her child in the street from overhead. The class scrutiny becomes even more troubling when shots that appear to convey a point of view actually have no direct source – such as an isolated bird's-eye view of the goddess soliciting on the pavement below.

The goddess's violent blow of vindication against the scoundrel becomes a blow against the totality of this surveillance. As she smashes the bottle against the camera lens, Wu Yonggang's brief shot shatters the film spectator's gaze upon the action, single-handedly positioning its audience as complicit in the power structure. But if this 'symbolic attack', as Rothman rightly calls it, succeeds in stunning the viewer into a consciousness of the lethal consequences of intolerance, then what happens to that awareness during the anticlimax of the film? Wu's concluding sequence dramatises the court's judgment of this goddess; newspapers report her twelve-year prison sentence; she is incarcerated. These disciplining scenes could well have satisfied the public (and state

Surveillance

censors) that the lethal threat of streetwalkers was properly contained and neutralised, as Yingjin Zhang suggests.

Yet again, Wu's film insinuates a compelling alternative interpretation. In the courthouse, the camera eye looks down upon the goddess through high-angle shots (from the judges' perspective), and up at the bench far above (low-angle shots from the goddess's position). The angles suggest an indictment not simply of this fallen woman, but also of a repressive justice system subordinating powerless individuals before the law. This double meaning was, of course, not fully speakable under the censorship code, but at least one contemporary reviewer noticed it, commenting obliquely that 'only through thoroughly skilled techniques [like these] can the fullest content be expressed'.[37]

ENDINGS

Wu Yonggang allows us to understand *The Goddess* in two ways. On the one hand, his narrative appears to fulfil Confucian convention and patriarchal moral codes: it affirms the maternal aspirations of this sympathetic female protagonist and enacts a final punishment for the fallen woman. But on the other hand, key visual cues in the film (especially sets, lighting and camera angles) imply that social convention is not always reliable or just.

Wu implicates the goddess, but he also incriminates the anxieties and hypocrisies of neighbours, parents, children, the justice system and even her last resort, the educational system. The fallen woman is left to negotiate the brutalities of the underworld alone, with all routes to reform closed off. Seen in this light, the school gates, walls and prison bars represent not simply protection and reassurance, but also bulwarks between the ruling powers and the defenceless. Wu deconstructs these barriers as artificial, even permeable, yet the confinement remains.

The child embodies her aspirations for the future, but by the end of this film, any hope for the goddess, even through her offspring, is bleak. Having implored the headmaster to tell her son that his mother has died, she now sits alone in a bare jail cell. The woman hallucinates a dim vision of the future – a vignette of her boy appearing against the blank prison wall – but then even this picture fades to 'the end'.[38] As his image vanishes, so does the goddess's joyful expression. The film's earlier faith in her redemption

through her son's education – as 'the start of a New Life' and 'a new happiness' – now seems to have paled, even disappeared.

If, as Wu Yonggang's technique and his writings imply, *The Goddess* dramatises the individual's struggle within 'circumstances' that limit free expression, might a resolution of that 'double life' be found in his subsequent cinematic retelling of the story? Only four years after he made *The Goddess*, Wu created a new version of the film, entitled *Rouge Tears* (1938). Rather than concluding his new scenario with a grim scene of imprisonment, Wu now showed the freed goddess twelve years hence, eager to see her grown child graduated from music conservatory and engaged to be married. The mother approaches the headmaster's home, and observes through a window her son performing 'Ode to a Devoted Mother'.[39]

The remake may have offered a somewhat more rousing glimpse of future freedom for the goddess – and a potential source of hope for a public now surrounded by the Anti-Japanese War – especially since it incorporated the new technology of sound, along with an established entertainer from drama and comedy, Butterfly Woo, in the lead role.[40] The revised conclusion, where the fallen woman gains reassurance of her child's survival and success, was certainly consonant with American maternal melodramas like *The Sin of Madelon Claudet*, and particularly *Stella Dallas*, remade by King Vidor just a year earlier, in 1937.[41]

Yet Wu's 1938 conclusion turned out to be no less disquieting than the original. Content to know the boy has been raised well, and adhering to her own erasure and anonymity, the woman ultimately resists the opportunity to meet her grown son. Instead, she slowly walks away from the headmaster's house in the falling snow.[42] Like *The Goddess*, Wu's remake offers neither a conventional 'happy ending', nor a fully reformist one: mother and child remain separated, and the social stigma of the goddess persists.

ACKNOWLEDGMENTS

I am grateful to Margherita Zanasi and the University of Texas, Austin, China Seminar, for valuable feedback on an earlier draft, presented 22 March 2002.

NOTES

1. *Lianhua huabao*, 4, no. 23 (9 December 1934): 1;
   Lianhua huabao, 4, no. 24 (16 December 1934): 1.

2. Mu Miao, '*The Goddess*: Review 2' ('*Shennü* ping er'),
   Chenbao (December 1934), reprinted in *The Chinese
   Left-Wing Film Movement* (Zhongguo zuoyi dianying
   yundong), ed. Chen Bo (Beijing: Zhongguo dianying
   chubanshe, 1993), 553.

3. *Lianhua huabao*, 4, no. 24 (16 December 1934): 2.

4. Chen Wu (pseud. Wang Chenwu), '*The Goddess*:
   Review 1' ('*Shennü* ping yi'), *Chenbao* (December
   1934), reprinted in *Chinese Left-Wing Film*, 551–552;
   Wei Yu (pseud. A Ying), 'Painful Words Transcribed –
   On *The Goddess* and *Plunder of Peach and Plum*'
   ('Kuyan chao – guanyu *Shennü* yu *Taoli Jie*'), *Wenyi
   dianying*, 1 (1934), reprinted in *Chinese Left-Wing
   Film*, 554–555.

5. For instance, Turin, Italy (1982); China Film Archive,
   Beijing (1983); National Museum of Modern Art,
   Tokyo (1986); Hong Kong Arts Centre (1988);
   Pordenone, Italy (1995); Guggenheim Museum, New
   York (1998).

6. Programme notes, *Three Goddesses of the Silver Screen
   from the Thirties* (Hong Kong Arts Centre, 1988).

7. For example, Marie-Claire Quiquemelle and Jean-
   Loup Passek, eds, *Le Cinema chinois* (Paris: Centre
   Georges Pompidou, 1985); Miriam Hansen, 'Fallen
   Women, Rising Stars, New Horizons: Shanghai Silent
   Film as Vernacular Modernism', *Film Quarterly*, 54,
   no. 1 (2000): 10–22.

8. Wu Yonggang, *My Explorations and Pursuits* (*Wode
   tansuo he zhuiqiu*) (Beijing: Zhongguo dianying
   chubanshe, 1986), 176–177.

9. Ibid., 176. *Way Down East* (1920) first appeared in
   China in 1921. On Griffith's film, see Robert Lang,
   American Film Melodrama: Griffith, Vidor, Minnelli
   (Princeton, NJ: Princeton University Press, 1989),
   65–78; Lucy Fischer, *Cinematernity: Film, Motherhood,
   Genre* (Princeton, NJ: Princeton University Press,
   1996), 56–72.

10. See Gail Hershatter, *Dangerous Pleasures: Prostitution
    and Modernity in Twentieth-Century Shanghai*
    (Berkeley: University of California Press, 1997),
    286–287; Yingjin Zhang, 'Prostitution and Urban
    Imagination: Negotiating the Public and the Private
    in Chinese Films of the 1930s', in *Cinema and Urban
    Culture in Shanghai, 1922–1943*, ed. Yingjin Zhang
    (Stanford, CA: Stanford University Press, 1999),
    160–180.

11. Wu, *My Explorations*, 130.

12. Ibid., 131.

13. See Christian Viviani, 'Who is Without Sin?: The
    Maternal Melodrama in American Film, 1930–39',
    and E. Ann Kaplan, 'Mothering, Feminism and
    Representation: The Maternal in Melodrama and the
    Woman's Film 1910–40', in *Home Is Where the Heart
    Is: Studies in Melodrama and the Woman's Film*, ed.
    Christine Gledhill (London: BFI, 1987), 83–99;
    113–117.

14. See Sally Taylor Lieberman, *The Mother and Narrative
    Politics in Modern China* (Charlottesville: University
    Press of Virginia, 1998), 27–35.

15. Wu Yonggang, 'After Completing *The Goddess*'
    ('*Shennü* wancheng zhihou'), *Lianhua huabao*, 5, no. 1
    (1 January 1935); reprinted in *My Explorations*, 134.

16. William Rothman, '*The Goddess*: Reflections on
    Melodrama East and West', in *Melodrama and Asian
    Cinema*, ed. Wimal Dissanayake (New York:
    Cambridge University Press, 1993), 59–72;
    see esp. 66.

17. Rey Chow, *Primitive Passions: Visuality, Sexuality,
    Ethnography, and Contemporary Chinese Cinema* (New
    York: Columbia University Press, 1995), 24.

18. Zhang, 'Prostitution and Urban Imagination',
    169–171.

19. Chen, '*The Goddess*: Review 1', 552.

20. Wei, 'Painful Words Transcribed', 554–555.

21. Wu, 'After Completing *The Goddess*', in
    My Explorations, 134.

22. See 'Film Inspection Law' ('Dianying jiancha fa')
    (3 November 1930), in *Chinese Left-Wing Film*, 1089.
    Also see Zhiwei Xiao, 'Film Censorship in China,
    1927–1937' (PhD dissertation, University of
    California: San Diego, 1994).

23. Cheng Jihua, Li Shaobai and Xing Zuwen, eds,
    History of the Development of Chinese Cinema
    (*Zhongguo dianying fazhanshi*), vol. 1 (Beijing:
    Zhongguo dianying chubanshe, 1963, 1980), 304.

24. I thank Zhiwei Xiao for confirming the censorship
    record.

25. See Lloyd E. Eastman, *The Abortive Revolution: China
    under Nationalist Rule, 1927–1937* (Cambridge, MA:
    Harvard University Press, 1974).

26. *Lianhua huabao*, 4, no. 15 (14 October 1934): 1;
    Lianhua huabao, 4, no. 16 (21 October 1934): 1.

27. Accompanying self-regulation, institutional
    enforcement of the 1930 US Production Code
    intensified in spring 1934. Lea Jacobs, *The Wages of*

Sin: Censorship and the Fallen Woman Film, 1928–1942
(Madison: University of Wisconsin Press, 1991), 153.

28. Wu, *My Explorations*, 134.

29. On 'regions of the camera', see Rothman, '*The Goddess*:
Reflections on Melodrama', 71.

30. On such techniques in Weimar melodrama, see
Patrice Petro, *Joyless Streets: Women and Melodramatic
Representation in Weimar Germany* (Princeton, NJ:
Princeton University Press, 1989), 176.

31. For a stimulating reading of Wu's minimalist film
language and the 'archetypal' effect of the nameless
characters, see Chow, *Primitive Passions*, 24–25.

32. Wu, 'Speaking of Film Sets' ('Lun dianying bujing'),
Lianhua huabao, 5, no. 5 (1 March 1935): 3; reprinted
in *My Explorations*, 171–174.

33. Wu, *My Explorations*, 132–133. Ruan made several
dozen popular melodramas during her eight years on
screen. On her suicide, see the film *The Actress/Centre
Stage (Ruan Lingyu)* (Stanley Kwan, 1992); also,
Kristine Harris, '*The New Woman* Incident: Cinema,
Scandal, and Spectacle in 1935 Shanghai', in
*Transnational Chinese Cinemas: Identity, Nationhood,
Gender*, ed. Sheldon Hsiao-peng Lu (Honolulu:
University of Hawaii Press, 1997), 277–302.

34. Zhang, 'Prostitution and Urban Imagination', 168.

35. Rothman, '*The Goddess*: Reflections on Melodrama',
71–72.

36. This marginalisation of the father echoes China's
literary trends in the 1920s and 1930s, when male
intellectuals rehearsed their own sense of 'general

emasculation and powerlessness in the modern world',
according to Lieberman, *The Mother*, 81.

37. Mu, '*The Goddess*: Review 2', 553.

38. For a thoughtful analysis of this scene's analogies to
the cinematic experience, see Rothman, '*The Goddess*:
Reflections on Melodrama', 71–73.

39. Zhang Junxiang and Cheng Jihua, eds, *Dictionary of
Chinese Cinema (Zhongguo dianying dacidian)*
(Shanghai cishu chubanshe, 1995), 1162.

40. Several Chinese film historians have commented
that the remake was a more commercial venture;
Wang Yunman finds it inferior to Wu's original
silent version. Neither Wu nor Woo (Hu Die)
mention *Rouge Tears* in their memoirs. Zhu Jian,
*Movie Queen Butterfly Woo (Dianying huanghou Hu
Die)* (Lanzhou daxue chubanshe, 1996), 252; Wang
Yunman, '*The Goddess*: Simple yet Profound' ('Supu
yunhan de *Shennü*'), in *My Explorations*, 192; Hu Die
and Liu Huiqin, *Memoirs of Butterfly Woo* (Hu Die
huiyilu) (Beijing: Wenhua yishu chubanshe, 1988).

41. In fact, the ending of *Rouge Tears* is nearly identical to
Stella Dallas. On the debate over ambiguous closure in
Stella Dallas, see E. Ann Kaplan, 'The Case of the
Missing Mother: Maternal Issues in Vidor's *Stella
Dallas*' (1983), and Linda Williams, '"Something Else
Besides a Mother": *Stella Dallas* and the Maternal
Melodrama' (1984), reprinted in *Feminism and Film*,
ed. E. Ann Kaplan (Oxford: Oxford University Press,
2000), 466–478; 479–504.

42. Zhang and Cheng, *Dictionary of Chinese Cinema*, 1162.

17 *Hero*: The Return of a Traditional Masculine Ideal in China

Kam Louie

The movie *Hero* has won many prizes and has been popular with audiences both in China and the West. Yet it has been attacked by many critics, who see it as glorifying a tyrant. Critics claim that the film contradicts traditional understandings of heroism by its lionising of the First Emperor of Qin. This essay argues that, in fact, the film reinforces traditional thinking because it engages with the ancient and well-established *wen-wu* masculine ideals at a mythological level.

Qin Shihuang (lit. First Emperor of Qin), has been depicted as a cruel and merciless tyrant ever since his conquest of the then six major kingdoms to form the Qin Dynasty (221–206 BC), creating what is now known as China. He has been particularly vilified by intellectuals because he is said to have burnt books and buried scholars alive to suppress dissent. This negative view of the First Emperor lasted until 1973–1974, when a national campaign to 'rehabilitate' him was waged as part of the Criticise Lin Biao Criticise Confucius Movement. Qin Shihuang's harsh measures and suppression of scholars were reinterpreted at that time as a struggle between his progressive Legalist policies and the reactionary ideas of the Confucianists. This movement was a desperate attempt by the radicals to reinforce their hold on power, and its failure to make any substantial changes signalled the end of the Cultural Revolution. Following the death of Mao Zedong in 1976, and the subsequent arrest of his 'Gang of Four', the Cultural Revolution was declared officially over.[1] The 'rehabilitation' of Qin Shihuang also collapsed as suddenly as it had begun, and it was not until 2002, and the release of Zhang Yimou's movie *Hero*, that the First Emperor's position once again became an issue for debate.

While short-lived, the politically motivated campaign during the Cultural Revolution to change the image of the First Emperor from villain to hero still touches a raw nerve in many people. Thus, despite the fact that *Hero* has won many domestic and international awards and has broken box-office records both in China and abroad, it sparked outrage and denunciation by well-known figures such as the authors Jin Yong and Liu Xiaobo and the film director Chen Kaige.[2] Released at a time when China's image was improving in the wake of continuous economic growth, entry into the WTO, winning the Olympic bid and the return of Hong Kong and Macau, *Hero* and the ensuing debate became part of the discourse on nationalism, and the movie was denounced as a vehicle for strengthening dictatorial rule because of its positive portrayal of the First Emperor. Film critics such as Evans Chan claim that by representing Qin Shihuang as a true hero, rather than the traditional interpretation of him as tyrant, Zhang Yimou is selling out to the authoritarian elements in the current regime.[3]

This paper attempts to show that rather than departing from tradition, the film adopts a truly conventional understanding of what constitutes a hero. This may explain why, despite its purported political incorrectness, the film was a phenomenally successful Chinese blockbuster, and audiences continue to enjoy it as 'a feast for the senses'.[4] This does not mean that arguments about the political use of the film are not valid. Indeed, the use of the past to comment on the present is also part of the return to tradition. Rather than examining this general question of history, I will concentrate on the issue that bothers critics most: why do audiences flock to see the movie despite its portrayal of Qin Shihuang as a hero? To do this, I will focus on the notion of 'hero' and its connections to the *wen-wu* paradigm that I have developed in my previous work.[5] As I will discuss, most commentators on the movie have tried to look for the 'real hero' among the many heroes in the movie, but so far, none has used the *wen-wu* dyad in their analysis. I believe, however, that considering how *wen–wu* masculinity works is absolutely essential if we are to understand why the film has won so many prizes and is so popular with audiences. *Wen–wu* also provides the key to my claim that the film harks back to tradition rather than departing from it.

I should briefly rehearse the characteristics of the *wen–wu* dyad before using it in my analysis. Literally, *wen–wu* translates as literary–martial, and refers to the dichotomy between the mental and the physical. It has been an ideal throughout Chinese history, from the first mythical sage kings until the present day. Thus, in the imperial courts, the officials were always seated or standing in two rows, one on either side of the emperor: one was the *wen* officials and the other the *wu*. The emperor is meant to have both attributes. The ways in which this dyad operates in Chinese ideology bring out many interesting formations relating to power and gender. *Wen* has always been perceived as more elite than *wu*, and women have not been able to attain true *wen–wu*. The Chinese language itself is steeped in traditional idioms to describe perfect men as having both *wen* and *wu*. Supreme leaders and real heroes are men who excel in both *wen* and *wu*, and this principle has been upheld in Chinese tradition for millennia.

By way of contrast, two other films made by high-profile directors – Zhou Xiaowen's *The Emperor's Shadow* (1996) and Chen Kaige's *The Emperor and the Assassin* (1998) – take a more conventional path. The premise of a ruthless and psychopathic Qin Shihuang is never challenged in these movies, even though they may attempt to offer psychological explanations for his sick mind. *Hero* adopts a completely different premise. The structure of the movie is such that different 'truths' are interrogated, and in the process of teasing out the real truth we are led to appreciate why ordinary heroes would elect one man as *the* hero. The movie has a very simple plot: an unknown magistrate, Nameless (played by Jet Li), is given an audience with Qin Shihuang because he has defeated and killed three of the most wanted assassins who have been trying to kill Qin Shihuang to stop his move towards absolute power – the lone swordsman Sky (Donnie Yen) and two lovers, Broken Sword (Tony Leung) and Flying Snow (Maggie Cheung). The dialogue between Qin Shihuang and Nameless is ostensibly a means of explaining how the three assassins were killed, but it

is also an interrogation of the nature of heroism and its relationship to enlightenment and power.

As Nameless recounts how he eliminated the other assassins, he is allowed to move within ten paces of Qin Shihuang, thereby enabling him to use his 'killer strike from ten paces' to slay the monarch. Thus, in computer-game fashion, the end of each of Nameless's mini-tales of how he vanquished one enemy moves him closer to his target. However, his first version of events is contradicted by an alternative narrative presented by Qin Shihuang, who alleges that Nameless and the assassins are in fact co-plotters against him. Nameless invents another story, and Qin Shihuang finally deduces that, in fact, none of the assassins is dead, and all Nameless's stories are part of a strategy to enable him to get close enough to administer the fatal blow. By the time this version is delivered by Qin Shihuang, however, Nameless is near enough to deliver the deadly blow. But seemingly inexplicably, he changes his mind and sacrifices himself (and the other assassins) because, like Broken Sword, he sees that the greatness of Qin Shihuang's wisdom is worth dying for.

Similarly, in the episode in which Broken Sword and Flying Snow storm the palace, Broken Sword could have killed Qin Shihuang, but again abandoned the assassination attempt, causing a rift between himself and Flying Snow. Like Qin Shihuang and the audience, Flying Snow cannot understand why he does not proceed with their mission, and is dismayed to find out that Broken Sword admires Qin Shihuang's vision of unifying China. In the context of the *wen–wu* paradigm, that is hardly surprising. After all, she is a woman. And women are supposed to be concerned only with matters such as love and family – the little things – not with big picture issues such as nationalism and power. This big picture emerges in one of the stories Nameless relates to Qin Shihuang, in which he describes Broken Sword tried to dissuade him from the assassination attempt by presenting as a parting word of advice the Chinese characters '*tianxia*' ('all under heaven'), drawn in the desert sand. Qin Shihuang, despite his notoriety as a tyrant, is acknowledged as having been the first person to unite the then warring states into what has become known as Qin (thus Chin-a), which at the time was the known world, or 'all under heaven'. And it is this unification that is meant to bring peace to the world, as Qin Shihuang indicates in the film.

The logic, then, seems to point to Qin Shihuang as the superhero who was able to bring stability and peace to the chaotic world by, when necessary, ruthless suppression. This elevates him to a position above the other heroes, and is what irks the critics. Most are horrified that Zhang Yimou could go against the traditional aversion to the First Emperor by painting him as a wise statesman. As one exasperated scholar proclaimed, the film does not even mention the 'stinking notorious deed of burying scholars'.[6] Many of these critics allege that the film condones authoritarianism and Chinese nationalism. Even those who praise the film, like Mary Farquhar, are uneasy about its 'dark' side, pointing out that:

> The awesome military power of Qin is not only painted in dynastic black; it also begins and ends each flashback just as it begins and ends the film. In terms of the martial arts genre … its heroic knights are overawed by the dark grandeur of the military machine.[7]

Critics claim that by portraying Qin Shihuang as at worst a politician who builds a military machine to pacify all under heaven, Zhang Yimou has become an apologist for the First Emperor (and by extension all the unpalatable politicians in Beijing), overlooking his horrible deeds, and condoning despotism and fascist rule. Some American Sinologists extrapolate even further by, for example, rhetorically asking 'Is the movie advocating the retaking of Taiwan or the deculturation of the Tibetans? Is one bit of hokey dialogue pronounced by Qin Shihuang from his throne intended to reveal China's latent desire for superpower status well beyond its present borders?'[8] Among many Chinese intellectuals, the reaction is equally strong. Some of them lived through the Cultural Revolution, the only time in history when Qin Shihuang was eulogised nationally in a political campaign. In the minds of many, Mao Zedong was responsible for that campaign and its elevation of Qin Shihuang.

It is generally believed that towards the end of the Cultural Revolution, in a last desperate attempt to stay in power, the 'Gang of Four' tried to revive Qin Shihuang as unifier of the nation and make him into a hero. The assumption is that Mao Zedong was power-hungry and wanted to emulate Qin Shihuang. But the situation is more complex than this, and Mao's personal reflections tell a different story. One of his most famous poems, 'Snow' (*Xue*) (1936),[9] is often cited to show that he was ambitious and full of self-importance. Describing the beautiful landscape in snow-covered China, he comments that countless heroes have paid homage to this land, including Genghis Khan, the first emperors of the Tang and Song Dynasties, and, of course, Qin Shihuang. 'Paying homage', of course, means conquering the land and establishing dynasties, as these emperors did. Mao ends the poem by saying that while all of these heroes are past and gone, 'for the truly great, look only to the present day'. With hindsight, we now know that he meant none but himself could truly be a great hero.

What quality does he possess that is lacking in all these other conquerors and founders of dynasties? In his poem, Mao Zedong dismisses them by saying that they only knew how to shoot eagles and did not possess poetic souls. He specifically describes Qin Shihuang as lacking in *wen* qualities (*wencai*). If Mao was scornful of Qin Shihuang for not possessing any literary graces, then *Hero* definitely presents a different figure to the one understood by Mao. For in *Hero*, Qin Shihuang, more than anyone else, was able to decipher and embrace literary graces. Nameless hesitated in his mission to kill Qin Shihuang because Broken Sword had alerted him to the importance of *tianxia*. Thus, in the movie, the ordinary heroes – the male assassins – all come to realise that Qin Shihuang is the man to unite the world, and, for the sake of *tianxia*, lay down their lives and pay homage. They are, therefore, like all the historical figures that Mao enumerates in his poem. They are heroic, love the land and pay homage to it.

However, this seems to be the extent of their comprehension, even though in practice they seem to recognise the link between *wen* and *wu*. Thus, Broken Sword and Flying Snow fine-tune their fighting skills by practising calligraphy. In other words, they sharpen their *wu* skills by improving their *wen* expertise. That is the craft they pursue, and it is the character 'sword' (*jian*), written by Broken Sword, that ultimately inspires Qin Shihuang. This insight into the essence of the writing, the *wen* spirit, however, only comes to Qin Shihuang right at the end of the film. It is for this insight that Nameless pays homage to him and makes the ultimate sacrifice. Even Broken Sword, who crafted the script on the scroll, and who is aware that the principles of calligraphy and swordsmanship are the same, only comes to realise the significance of *tianxia* from perfecting these skills. It is an understanding that is beyond a mere woman, but less than Qin Shihuang's understanding of the mythic significance of *wen* and *wu*.

The implication is that the ability to conceive the big picture instead of the personal one of seeking revenge, so common in little people and ordinary movies and novels, qualifies one to be an ordinary hero. The big picture involves kingdom, empire or *tianxia*. Only those who have gone beyond what mere mortals and women want can comprehend *tianxia* (for example, as women, both Flying Snow and Moon can only talk of love and personal loyalties). This is the level reached by Broken Sword and Sky. And, presumably, the level reached by most critics, judging by the number of comments and articles about the political uses of the movie and the attacks that Zhang Yimou has had to endure for his presumed selling out to a dictatorial regime. However, the final enlightenment that Qin Shihuang embraces is not about *tianxia*, but the spiritual mutuality of *wen* and *wu* that occupies a yet higher level.

In fact, this spiritual link between *wen* and *wu* is intimated throughout the movie. The very first combat scene between the two real-life martial arts experts Jet Li and Donnie Yen is a magnificent spectacle. As well as the weapons of sword and spear, the icons of *wen*, lute and chess, are highlighted. The symbols are blended together perfectly, each emphasising the other. Most importantly, the contest is conducted in the mind. Playing chess by conducting the game in one's mind without the pieces is a well-rehearsed trope to stress the importance of control of the mind, and therefore *wen* accomplishments. It symbolises the players' skills not just in terms of technique but also in terms of spiritual accomplishments. Here, the fight itself is conducted in the mind, with each anticipating the other's moves. The spiritual is therefore illustrated as a duel, a determination to kill the other. *Wu* is thus not just physical force but a cultivated achievement on a higher plane.

Not only does this scene emphasise both *wen* and *wu*. More importantly, it emphasises the principle that the ultimate goal of *wen* and *wu* is self-control. Controlling one's physical being is hard enough, but to be able, in the stress of combat, to control the mind is supreme mastery indeed. This fantastic match sets the tone for later combat episodes. For example, in

another beautifully photographed sequence between Nameless and Broken Sword, the sword fight is also portrayed as mental combat, above the lake and over the dead body of Flying Snow. And when the fight becomes physical, they engage in a struggle, pinball-machine-like, with a drop of water. Again, not only is the computer-game element very much in evidence; the mental over the physical is highlighted. Other combat scenes demonstrate even more directly that *wen* and *wu* cannot be separated. Thus, in both scenes in which Nameless shows off his 'killer strike from ten paces', the display of his swordsmanship is conducted in the library, where his sword movement first unties the bamboo scrolls and later literally turns the writing brush into an exploding puff of fine hair. And when the Qin army rains arrows onto the Zhao State, it is the calligraphy academy that stands firm and refuses to run away. Here, the old calligraphy teacher admonishes that it is the spirit of the written word that is unbending against military might. Even if the Zhao State is demolished by Qin, he insists, its spirit will live on. Indeed, the idea that the mind and the spirit dominate over military power and physical might is manifested in the game of mental tug-of-war between Nameless and Qin Shihuang, which persists for the entire length of the movie. And the prize is life or death.

In my book *Theorising Chinese Masculinity*, I argue that the *wen–wu* paradigm is generally used as a way for *wen* men to dominate *wu* men throughout Chinese history, despite the fact that both attributes are meant to be equally important. This is similar to *yin-yang* philosophy, in which *yang* is always placed above *yin*. While *yin-yang* can be used to categorise and divide everything in the universe into two classes – men *yang*, women *yin*; ruler *yang*, subject *yin* and so on – *wen-wu* refers exclusively to men. *Wen* men are superior, *wu* men less so. This hypothesis is certainly present in *Hero*, where the mental is in every way superior to the physical. Moreover, while the women yell and cry and stamp their feet, they cannot even begin to understand the mental games that are being played. Thus Flying Snow, for example, only understands love and vengeance. When Broken Sword refuses to kill Qin Shihuang, her response is to sulk, rather than try to comprehend the principles involved. The Zhang Ziyi character, Moon, does not even have any opinions. On the rare occasions when she does say something, it is usually an outburst such as 'whatever my master does is for a good reason', expressing her blind devotion to the master by trying to stab herself, oblivious to what he is trying to achieve. Again, as always, the 'heroes' who understand the big picture have to be men.

There is, however, a level that is above gender and politics. It has to do with 'myth-making'. As Richard Alleva insightfully indicates, *Hero* is unlikely to become a blockbuster in the USA because 'Americans like their violence gaudy and the characters domesticated (how many good fathers and husbands Schwarzenegger and Stallone have played!). But *Hero*'s violence is transcendent, and its characters will never remind you of anyone you have ever met.'[10] And Alleva concludes, 'the action is mythic from first to last, never novelistic, never worldly'. This is the crux of the matter. However, the myth that is created here is not universal. It is solidly grounded in Chinese culture, and Chinese audiences have met Qin Shihuang before in one form or another. That is why the movie has been such a success in China, compared to, say, *Crouching Tiger, Hidden Dragon* (2000). Most non-China experts would be puzzled by the heated debate in China (and among Sinologists in the West) about the relationship between heroism and authoritarianism, imperialism and so on.

In fact, the myth-making that is at work here, while not universal, is grounded in Chinese notions of manhood. The culturally rooted principle that Zhang Yimou is appealing to here relates to the *wen-wu* spirit of the hero. Many are not happy that of all the heroes in the film, Qin Shihuang is the only 'superhero'. Some find his pronouncements – such as war is peace, because you need bloodshed to unify the states so that peace can be established – too Orwellian for comfort. Other film critics such as Shelly Kraicer are aware that this is 'a cinema spectacle allied to a philosophical program'.[11] That programme, according to these critics, is the nothingness so lauded in Daoism. Kraicer remarks that 'The film's most insistent visual motif is the empty circle; a zone of complete emptiness that a hero creates around him or herself.' Jia-xuan Zhang, another critic who alludes to the symbolic significance of incompleteness and emptiness in the film, concludes by suggesting that Qin Shihuang's power seems so insignificant in the way it is portrayed in the movie that it is as if the movie has no real hero, and that in fact for over two millennia, the search for a true sage leader in China has not produced one.[12]

All that may be true, but the dominant motif in the film is, in fact, the mythic creation of the unity of the sword and the brush. This may seem obvious, yet its significance is not diminished by its conspicuity. The final comments from Qin Shihuang before Nameless decides to abort the assassination mission are to the effect that the spirit of the sword is in the spirit of the word. *Wen* and *wu* are the supreme principle that the sage has to grasp. While we may or may not want to agree with this principle, the film plays it out in every scene. The brush writing out the word 'sword', the displays of swordsmanship in the library, the gymnastics of the mind when fighting, the impossibility of the women grasping the big picture, and so on, all point to the same thing: an exposition of *wen-wu* at work. This is a principle that predates Empire. It is something the audience will instinctively respond to.

This may explain why the movie received such a hostile response from critics but was so popular with audiences. Chen Mo points to this dilemma when he claims that *Hero* is a good-looking film but that it does not stand up to analysis. He argues that a successful commercial movie should not go against the ideologies accepted by the masses, and correctly points out that in the popular imagination Qin Shihuang is hated as a ruthless tyrant who burned books and buried scholars. Yet, Zhang Yimou has painted exactly the opposite picture, depicting Qin Shihuang as the true hero while the other 'heroes' in the movie seem to inexplicably sacrifice themselves, achieving only ordinary hero status, and leaving superhero stature to a historically hated figure. Chen Mo claims that the movie is contrary to popular ideology, despite the fact that it achieved record sales at the box office in China and abroad. Surely its success at the box office negates Chen's own argument.[13]

Interestingly, the reason Chen Mo gives for the 'failure' of the movie is that it attempts to involve the conventional Robin Hood-type hero with big ideas, to transform him into a figure who thinks about *tianxia* instead of fighting injustice. Neither Chen Mo nor any of the other critics attack Zhang Yimou for resoundingly repeating *wen-wu* ideology, in which the true hero has to have both *wen* and *wu*, with *wen* always having primacy over *wu*. More importantly, there is no mention of the mythic element of this ideology in the movie. Chen Mo claims that the movie is unsuccessful because Zhang Yimou

Hero

has inverted the conventional notions of a wandering swordsman (*xia*) and the hero (*yingxiong*). The *wuxia* genre is traditionally about people of low cultures (that is, swordsmen who possess *wu* only). But true heroes belong to the more cultured class (the *wen* people), and Chen Mo claims that by confusing the two and making fighters into cultured sages, the movie is a failure.[14]

Chen Mo and others may be right in saying that the film has mismatched heroes with ordinary assassins or even tyrants. Indeed, Zhang Yimou himself has insisted that he wanted to change the martial arts convention when he made the film:

> If you look at the history of Chinese martial-arts literature, the plot always hinges on revenge: 'You killed my master, now you must die'. It's the same for American Westerns. For years, this has been the only theme in Chinese martial-arts films, whether it's Bruce Lee or Jackie Chan. I want to take the genre in a new direction. In my story the goal is the negation of violence. The characters are motivated by their desire to end the war. For real martial-arts masters, true heroes, the heart is far more important than the sword.[15]

He does not specify what the 'heart' means. Nonetheless, as we have seen, the most consistent message in the movie is that the true hero is one who understands, as well as practises, *wen-wu*. In traditional Chinese thought, the 'heart' refers to the mind. In fact, the Chinese character '*xin*' represents both the 'heart' and 'mind'. Thus, a state of enlightenment is one in which a person becomes aware of the mythic truth of *wen* and *wu* and the relationship between them – namely, that the brain dominates the body. In fact, mind over matter is taken to such extraordinary lengths that a fight can be conducted over a lake by mental engagement alone. We might dismiss this as fascist, reactionary or mumbo-jumbo nonsense, but it is an ideology that the Chinese masses accept and love. So to claim that the film is a failure because the masses do not like it is blatantly untrue.

It is therefore necessary to look elsewhere to discover why some scholars hate the film so much. Partly, this has to do with the perceived betrayal by Zhang Yimou of the scholar class. Thus, the Nanjing University professor Wang Binbin claims that Zhang Yimou 'is not *wen-ized* (*wenhua*)':[16] that is, he is not cultured, or has not undergone the process of having *wen* instilled in him. This is echoed by other critics such as Dou Jiangming, who explains the difference between Chen Kaige's and Zhang Yimou's renditions of the assassination attempts on Qin Shihuang by claiming that Chen Kaige is a '*wen* person' whereas Zhang Yimou is not.[17] Perhaps, too, it is the recognition that tyrants and those who talk about saving the country and worry about the 'big picture' also consider themselves heroes. That, moreover, horror of horrors, they have pretensions to being scholars! As I have shown elsewhere, *wen-wu* is about power. To pretend, as scholars always have, that one can wield power without a knowledge of how the sword kills and how to manipulate people is self-deception. And Chinese scholars have been very good at deceiving themselves.

Whatever we may conclude about why the movie was a success, the fact remains that it has reached a blockbuster status that few Chinese movies have been able to achieve. The audiences may or may not like its politics, but the film definitely harks back to the *wen-wu* ideal. And while it is a common enough one, the movie mythologises it to such an extent that it overrides all logical considerations. The philosophising about the unity between the brush and the sword may seem unnecessarily pretentious, or, in Nylan's words, a bit of 'hokey dialogue'.[18] High pretensions or clichéd nonsense, it is what the populace like. It finds resonance in their cultural make-up. Thus, the film is without a doubt preaching a traditional ideology, but one that stretches even further back than Qin Shihuang's conquering and unification of 'all under heaven' to establish an empire. The primeval desire to be a 'real man' involves the acquisition and understanding of a spiritual union of *wen* and *wu*, and it is this basic tradition that the movie has returned to. It is a tradition that is above politics, one that everyone understands, especially when it comes to talking about heroes and what a man should strive to achieve.

NOTES

1. See Kam Louie, *Critiques of Confucius in Contemporary China* (Hong Kong: Chinese University Press, 1980).

2. The Chinese critics' denunciations can be seen in 'Zhang Yimou zhi *Yingxiong* zai shou piping: shijiao xianfeng, sixiang zhuru' ('Zhang Yimou's *Hero* is again criticised: far-sighted vision, midget thinking'): <ent.sina.com.cn/m/c/2003-08-13/1503185188.html> (15 December 2006).

3. Evans Chan's essay 'Zhang Yimou's *Hero* – The Temptations of Fascism' appeared in *Film International*, no. 8 (2004). This webpage has since been deleted from the Internet.

4. Chen Mo, *Ten Directors in Chinese Cinema* (*Zhongguo dianying shi daoyan*) (Beijing: Renmin chubanshe, 2005), 20.

5. Kam Louie, *Theorising Chinese Masculinity* (Cambridge: Cambridge University Press, 2002).

6. Dou Jiangming, 'Xiang "Yingxiong" jugong; ranhou shuqi zhongzhi' ('I Salute "Hero"; then I Give it My Middle Finger'), cited in 'Zhang Yimou zhi "Yingxiong" zai shou piping.

7. Mary Farquhar, '"The Realm of Marvels": Landscape in Chinese Swordplay Martial Arts Movies', unpublished paper.

8. Michael Nylan, 'Hero', *American Historical Review*, 110, no. 3 (June 2005): 770.

9. This poem and an English translation can be found on: <www.asiawind.com/forums/read.php?f=2&i=5479&t=5479> (14 March 2007).

10. Richard Alleva, 'Mythmaking', *Commonweal*, 131, no. 16 (2004): 23.

11. Shelly Kraicer, 'Absence of Spectacle: Zhang Yimou's *Hero*': <www.chinesecinemas.org/hero.html> (29 January 2007).

12. Jia-xuan Zhang, '*Hero*', *Film Quarterly*, 28, no. 4 (Summer 2005): 47–52.

13. For a discussion of *Hero* as blockbuster, see Chris Berry and Mary Farquhar, *Cinema and Nation: China on Screen* (New York: Columbia University Press, 2006), 205–213.

14. Chen, *Ten Directors in Chinese Cinema*, 20–21.

15. Stephen Short and Susan Jakes, 'Making of a Hero': <www.time.com/time/asia/features/hero/story.html> (18 January 2007).

16. Wang Binbin, cited in cited in 'Zhang Yimou zhi "Yingxiong" zai shou piping'.

17. Dou, 'Xiang "Yingxiong" jugong'.

18. Nylan, 'Hero'.

18 *In the Mood for Love*: Intersections of Hong Kong Modernity

Audrey Yue

INTERSECTION AND MODES OF PRODUCTION

Hong Kong, 1962. Two neighbours meet and seek solace in each other as they discover their respective spouses are having an affair. They play-act what they will say to their spouses when they confront them with what they know. As they begin to spend more time together, they soon find that they too are falling in love and drifting into an affair. To allay neighbours' gossip, one moves to work as a reporter in Singapore. Four years later, in Cambodia covering General de Gaulle's visit, he finds himself unburdening the secret of this affair.

The above synopsis of Wong Kar-wai's *In the Mood for Love* (*IMFL*) reveals three sites of intersection. First, there is the theme – the mood of love is rendered through the intersection of the sanctity of marriage and the restraint of the affair. Second, there is the space – the narrative of the story is structured through Hong Kong's intersection with its region, including Cambodia, Singapore and Thailand (where the film was shot). Third, there is the time – history is replaced by a Jamesonian display of post-modern historicism, where the past surfaces as an intersection through the aesthetics of style.

The device of the intersection is a Wong Kar-wai hallmark. He has used two parallel stories since his directorial debut in 1988: triad big brother Ah Wah and his younger buddy-lackey, Fly, in *As Tears Go By*; teddy boy Yuddy and the cop-sailor in *Days of Being Wild*; cop 663 and 223's relationships with their respective lovers in *Chungking Express*; the hit man and his assistant in *Fallen Angels*; Evil East and Poison West in *Ashes of Time*; and Yiu-fai and Bao-wing in *Happy Together*. Ackbar Abbas formulates this as 'metonymic substitution', a device of doubling where characters are interchangeable in a narrative cycle of repetition.[1]

IMFL features a similar parallel-story structure,

with reporter Chow Mo-wan (Tony Leung Chiu-wai) and housewife Su Li-zhen, usually referred to as 'Mrs Chan' (Maggie Cheung Man-yuk). Instead of Wong's usual protagonists' voice-over monologues interweaving the narrative, the film follows his period martial arts epic, *Ashes of Time*, by opening and ending with titles quoting from popular fiction:

> It is a restless moment.
> She has kept her head lowered,
> To give him a chance to come closer.
> But he could not, for lack of courage.
> She turns and walks away.

> That era has passed.
> He remembers those vanished years.

> Nothing that belonged to it exists any more.
> As though looking through a dusty window pane,
> The past is something he could see, but not touch.
> And everything he sees is blurred and indistinct.

This adapted narration from Liu Yichang's novella *Duidao* reveals the three sites of intersection: a theme evoking a mood about two lovers and their failed encounter, a story that spatialises here and there, and a temporality that freezes memory in a perpetual present.[2] Wong explains the significance of intersection in a book accompanying *IMFL*:

> The first work by Liu Yichang I read was *Duidao*. The title is a Chinese translation of *tête-bêche*, which describes stamps that are printed top to bottom facing each other. *Duidao* centres round the intersection of two parallel stories – of an old man and a young girl. One is about memories, the other anticipation. To me, *tête-bêche* is more than a term for stamps or intersection of stories. It can be the intersection of light and colour, silence and tears. *Tête-bêche* can also be the intersection of time: for

instance, youthful eyes on an aging face, borrowed words on revisited dreams.[3]

This essay takes Wong's evocation of *tête-bêche* as a point of departure for an exploration of intersection in the film. Two practices of *tête-bêche* as intersection are evident in *IMFL*. First, *tête-bêche* is the intersection of *Duidao* and *IMFL*. The film intersects with the novella through the cinema, the space of Hong Kong and China, and popular media from Hong Kong, Taiwan and South-east Asia.[4] Second, *tête-bêche* resonates with the temporality of Hong Kong before and after 1997, when the British colony returned to its socialist motherland, China. I have written elsewhere about how Hong Kong cinema expresses this temporality of pre-post-1997 as a culture that simultaneously forecasts and recollects.[5] I extend that idea here, to suggest that intersection functions as a point in Hong Kong's period of transition – both pre-1997 to Chinese rule and post-1997

In the Mood for Love: Tony Leung and Maggie Cheung

in the following fifty years of the unique 'one country, two systems' administration. This can be seen in *IMFL*'s conception and release. The film originated when Wong visited Beijing for a month in 1996, and he gave it the working title *Summer in Beijing*. He writes: 'Between *Summer in Beijing* and *In the Mood for Love*, eras changed, locales changed, and the music changed. We moved from contemporary jazz to nostalgic waltz.'[6] *IMFL* is Wong's first post-1997 film, shot on location in Thailand while filming *2046*, a science-fiction film set fifty years after Hong Kong's 1997 return, highlighting its status as a product of temporal (before and after 1997) and spatial (China, Hong Kong and South-east Asia) intersections. In *IMFL*, '2046' is the number of the hotel room occupied by Chow.

These two practices of *tête-bêche* produce intersection as a point in transition characterised by convergence and divergence. In the next section below, I use convergence to explore the cinema. I critically review the politics of recent theorisation of Hong Kong cinema to interrogate how the mood of the popular is produced in the global reception of *IMFL*. In the section after that, I use divergence to examine the space between Hong Kong and China by exposing how the film uses Asian popular media to construct Hong Kong's relationship to the region. I argue that convergence and divergence question the presumed intersections of Hong Kong modernity. *IMFL* captures this modernity as that which is accented by its specific history of emergence. My conclusion addresses the politics of its present by evaluating the film's temporality through its aesthetics of style.

A THEME OF CONVERGENCE: IN THE MOOD FOR THE HONG KONG POPULAR

Convergence is a practice synonymous with media globalisation. In the past five years or so, the globalisation of Hong Kong cinema has witnessed the popularity in the West of the industry's martial arts action genre, which has resulted in Hollywood-produced blockbuster 'remakes', celebrity advertising and the emergence of a new breed of pan-Asian superstars in Hollywood. Against such a backdrop, the Wong Kar-wai film has also gained popularity, through the patronage of the likes of Quentin Tarantino and the arthouse and independent festival circuits. Using convergence as the first moment of intersection, I suggest here that the Wong Kar-wai genre functions as a site that crosses the high–low divide stereotyping Hong Kong action cinema in the West. I argue that as a site of convergence, the genre reveals the practices of current Hong Kong cinema theorisation and consumption to expose the politics surrounding Hong Kong cinema's transnational success. This success is the result of Hong Kong's transition that has witnessed the migration of people, cinema and industry throughout the world.

IMFL was released internationally in 2000 and 2001, around the same time as Ang Lee's award-winning *Crouching Tiger, Hidden Dragon*. Equally as critically acclaimed, the film's numerous awards included Best Actor (Leung) and Grand Prix technique (Christopher Doyle, Mark Li Ping-bin and William Chang) at Cannes 2000 and Best Actor, Best Actress (Cheung), Best Costume Design (Chang), Best Art Direction (Chang) and Best Editing (Chang) at the 20th Hong Kong Film Association Awards. These accolades attest to Wong Kar-wai's popularity. After the licensing of *Fallen Angels* to thirty-four countries in 1994, his UCLA interview with Tarantino in 1995 and the US release of *Chungking Express* in 1996, Wong's meteoric rise was unprecedented, culminating with the Best Director award for *Happy Together* at Cannes 1997, on the eve of Hong Kong's return to Chinese rule. *IMFL* crossed the high–low divide in 2000 when it was listed in various global annual top-ten film polls.[7]

As arthouse, Wong's films repeat the comfort of a familiar formula. But as 'Hong Kong arthouse', they disrupt the larger generic economy. The prefix 'Hong Kong' is a signifier of difference, as a post-modern and post-colonial space that attenuates the gap between cult and mass, and hip and unhip. As a practice of convergence between action and art, the Wong Kar-wai genre exposes the politics of the Hong Kong popular. It modulates the cult of martial arts films and the mass appeal of the new Hollywood action by suggesting that there is a difference between what is 'hip' and 'unhip' in the global consumption of Hong Kong cinema. By problematising the Hollywood-produced action blockbusters of Jackie Chan and John Woo as mass and almost B-list unhip, the genre's hipness produces the Hong Kong popular as a mood that structures a mode, reflecting the intersections of the post-modern collapse of categories, the global celebration of difference and the

neo-colonial new modern. The film's theme – its mood – governs this structure.

Most popular reviews of *IMFL* speak of it as 'a veritable mood piece'.[8] It communicates claustrophobic desire. Bound by the legal union that a marriage demands and the transgression of an illicit affection, Mr Chow and Mrs Chan try to curb their emotions. Claustrophobia is literalised through tight shot composition. Alleyways are angled from the turns of corners while interior shots of the apartments and the rooms are encased by windows, corridors, stairways and hallways, with characters framed through mid-shots, small tilts and slight pans. Yearning is structured through the finesse of Chang's editing and cinematography – a brush of fabrics, a turn of looks, a change in the film speed and tempo.

Theorisations of Wong's films have attributed the claustrophobic effect of his trademark fish-eye wide-angle lenscape to his unique understanding of the city.[9] These theorisations consign the city to a subject and a subjectivity by pointing to a prevailing Hong Kong structure of feeling concerning intensity, proximity and modernity. Some of these celebrate Wong's style often at the expense of undermining the specificity of Hong Kong, where the Hong Kong popular emerges only as a mood that is hip in current theorisations about the cinema and as a mode that structures a genre of film, maintaining the universality of film-as-art formula.[10] It is ironic that the modernity of Hong Kong that is used to characterise Wong's style is now the same site used to wipe out the specificity of the Hong Kong locality. For example, writing about the post-modern hipness of *IMFL*, Teo suggests that the privileging of 'abstraction rather than plot' allows the audience to engage in 'a ritual of transfigured time … and … each member of the audience, depending on their ages, could in theory go as far back in time as they wish to the moment that holds the most formative nostalgic significance for them'.[11] Abstractions such as this deny the politics demanded by the transfiguration of Hong Kong modernity's 'emergence of qualitatively new desires, social relations, and modes of association within the … community … *and* between that group and its … oppressors'.[12]

Such a politics consists of a desire to enact new modes of expression consequent on exposing the internal fissures of the transition. Elsewhere, I have argued that the politics of transition has produced a cinema post-1984 (the year of the Sino-British Joint Declaration that announced British Hong Kong's 1997 return to Chinese rule) that expresses Hong Kong's post-colonial identity as modern, mobile, transnational and hybrid. Both Hong Kong action and arthouse films have emerged in such a milieu as instances of their own socio-cultural circumstances: the former, a high-octane genre that resonates with Hong Kong's panic culture and saw the emergence of the first modern, romantic-thriller, gangster hero (e.g. Chow Yun-fat in John Woo's 1986 *A Better Tomorrow*); the latter, the maturity of a style and an indigenous subject matter that achieved international acclaim and recognition.

I extend this here, to suggest that in *IMFL*, the mood of claustrophobia can be read as an effect of the inscription of phobic spaces by a transnational film-maker such as Wong, reflecting his experience of 'liminality and multifocality'.[13] This is evident in both the film-maker's intent and his filmic strategies. Of *IMFL*, Wong noted that he was influenced by his own experience as an immigrant child growing up in the 1960s in Hong Kong among the diasporic Shanghainese community where rumours, lies and gossip were rife and people tried to pretend that all was well. Gossip and pretence are anchored in the film through Mrs Suen's disapproval of Mrs Chan's late nights out alone, the protagonists' make-believe marriages and play-acting of their partners' infidelity. These events mediate social order (duty, propriety, monogamy) and disorder (love affairs, extra-marital relationships, adultery) and encode, in the process, the subjectivity of claustrophobia. As noted earlier, the film's formal strategies attest to this desire.

More significantly, this desire is the desire for a forbidden love that has to remain a secret. Hence, the film is an ode to the acting of acting where everyday practices such as eating and walking are denaturalised to convey the oscillation between feeling secure and trapped. Not surprisingly, the use of Shigeru Umebayashi's 'Yumeji's Theme' as the main love theme for the encounters between Mr Chow and Mrs Chan captures the breathlessness of this desire. In these sequences, the camera pans are longer and wider, and the movement stylised and slowed. Rather than displacing intimacy to outside public spaces as Abbas and Siegel have suggested about Wong's earlier films, these sequences punctuate the film through the labour of its haunting rhythm, and function as a non-diegetic

(interstitial) space for the consummation of love.[14] Clearly, this non-diegetic space returns to the liminality of Hong Kong-in-transition, as a third 'border' space caught between the East and the West. Here, the politics of transnationality exposed by the popularity of the Wong Kar-wai genre helps return the film to its cultural location. The following section further suggests, maybe ironically, that *IMFL* returns to Hong Kong via the mobility of transnational routes engendered by Asian popular media, only to produce a space of regionality.

A PROJECT OF DIVERGENCE: REGIONALITY AND MODERNITY

Jeffrey Ressner's *Time International* report on the 'controversy' created by *IMFL* – together with Ang Lee's *Crouching Tiger, Hidden Dragon*, Jiang Wen's *Devils on the Doorstep*, Shinji Aoyama's *Eureka* and Edward Yang's *Yi Yi* – at Cannes exposes regionality as a benchmark for measuring standards of acceptability.[15] Its headline, 'Asia Scores: The Region's Movies Come of Age at the Cannes Festival, with Four Big Awards', foregrounds the discourse of regionality as part of the politics of transnationality. The article once again marks 'Asia' as the other evaluated against the normative orthodoxy of international film acclaim. 'Coming of age' is an event that intersects the disjunctive projects of Western and Asian modernities as claims to both representation (of the films) and self-representation (from the films). This section shows how regionality is produced in *IMFL* through the emergence of Hong Kong modernity.

Regionality highlights divergence through the reterritorialisation of place as an effect of the cultural-economic contradictions of globalisation. The changing geopolitical configurations of Asia and Europe have witnessed culturalist, statist and economic projects of self-representation that construct new regional imaginations to patch the fissures of identity and difference.[16] Against such a backdrop, regionality produces the image as a practice of the transnational imagination, as a way of negotiating between different sites, individuals and agencies.[17]

IMFL belongs to such an imagination where, as the previous section has shown, the 'hipness' of the Wong Kar-wai genre has produced an image of style. I argue that this image is characterised by a pan-Asian pastiche of Eastern and Western influences.

These influences question the authenticity of cultures and the different histories of the West in Asia. In *IMFL*, this pastiche is evident not only in the nostalgic 1960s *mise en scène* (e.g. modern apartments, modular furniture, pattern-design and floral wallpapers) but also in the use of Asian popular media. This use locates and problematises Hong Kong as an intersection for regional flows. As a strategy of divergence, intersection shows how the hegemony of Hong Kong cinema mobilises the process of reterritorialisation to produce its cultural location as a centre for Asian popular culture.

The eclectic references to Asian popular media in the film highlight Hong Kong as a modern space of regional cultural mix. For example, the use of Liu's *Duidao* archives an indigenous literary tradition in Hong Kong. A Shanghainese immigrant like Wong, Liu is one of Hong Kong's leading fiction writers. He is also the founder and chief editor of the journal *Hong Kong Literary Monthly* (*Xianggangwenxue*). The protagonists' penchant for reading martial arts pulp serials and Mr Chow's desire to write one himself show the popularity of the genre, one that Wong has also referred to in his use of Jin Yong's *Eagle Shooting Heroes* in *Ashes of Time*. Wong's quotations inscribe not only local literature and vernacular pulp fiction, but also Japanese film, art and music. 'Yumeji's Theme' is borrowed from Suzuki Seijun's 1991 film, *Yumeji*, a bio-fantasy about the turbulent life of Japanese artist Takehisa Yumeji (1884–1934), played by popular singer Kenji Sawada, who embodied the romanticism of Japan's Taisho era (1912–1926) with his hybrid woodblock and art nouveau style, and was renowned for his sketches of nude women. Other influences include the use of Cantonese, Beijing and Zhejiang operas. Notably, the recorded excerpts of *silangtanmu* and *sangyuan jizi* pay tribute to Tan Xin Pei, a legendary figure in the Beijing opera who was also involved in *Ding jun shan* (1905), China's first indigenous film.

Clearly, Wong's pastiche samples images and sound bites from the present and the past, producing Hong Kong as a modern space constructed by its location as an intersection for regional Asian influences. In particular, I argue that the strategy of divergence reterritorialises the space between Hong Kong and China by engendering the image through the female voice and the female star as constitutive sites for the emergence of Hong Kong modernity.

First, the space between Hong Kong and China is rendered through Shanghai in the film. The story partially uses Shanghainese and is set in an immigrant Shanghainese community where everybody knows each other. The advent of Chinese communism in 1949 saw the fall of Shanghai with the emigration of its people and capital and the consequent emergence of modern Hong Kong. Since the 1997 return and China's vigorous economy, Shanghai has returned to its former status as the more 'senior' city in the Chinese cultural imaginary. Writing on heritage renewal projects in Shanghai and Hong Kong, Abbas suggests different histories of colonialism: Shanghai exhibits 'a cosmopolitanism of extraterritoriality' while Hong Kong displays 'a cosmopolitanism of dependency'.[18] Although both forms of cosmopolitanism show how colonial presence is used to 'construct a Chinese version of modern cosmopolitan culture',[19] I suggest here that the regionality of Shanghai rendered in the film complicates the chronology and shows the incommensurability of Chinese cultural history: the film functions as an axis of divergence revealing a Hong Kong modernity also shaped by the social imagination of Shanghai.

Hong Kong exists in the film as a space of displacement. Shot on location in Thailand because Wong could not find enough old buildings in Hong Kong, Hong Kong exists as an effect of two forces, migration and modernity. Both are evident in the narrative. Migration appears as Mrs Chan works for a shipping company selling tickets, Mr Chow leaves to work as a reporter in Singapore and Mrs Suen joins her family in America. Modernity appears, for example, in the use of radio broadcasts, Japanese electric rice-cookers, the telephone, and dining on steak and mustard sauce.

The setting of the film in 1962 is significant because the 1960s marked the beginning of Hong Kong's post-colonial modernity. Historian Frank Welsh dates Hong Kong's 'official' period of 'autodecolonisation' to 11 April 1963, when Hong Kong's House of Commons reviewed post-war Hong Kong. Welsh observes that it was in the 1960s that Hong Kong 'acquired what have become its typical modern attitudes: that single-minded dedication to money-making which powered the engine of expansion'.[20] The film inscribes this history through the narrative by using the displacement of Shanghainese and South-east Asian migration, and the politics of transition. Transition here is evident from the use of the archival footage of Charles de Gaulle's visit to Cambodia in 1966, on the eve of the Vietnam War and the start of China's Cultural Revolution, as a historical and metaphorical staging for Hong Kong, as a transit destination for Chinese migrants and Indo-Chinese and Vietnamese refugees, as well as for Hong Kong's 1997 return to Chinese rule.

The radio broadcast of popular 1930s and 1940s Shanghainese singer Zhou Xuan's '*Huayang de nianhua*' consolidates the film's narrative as a transitional history between Hong Kong and China. Indeed, the film even pays homage to the singer through its Chinese title, *Huayang nianhua*. The practices of radio listening (and listening to imported music) and making song requests in the film highlights radio in the 1960s as a form of popular domestic technology. It also locates the popular memory of Zhou as Shanghai's 'golden voice' of the 1930s and 1940s. Her repertoire included more than one hundred songs. More significantly, she sang in the national language of Mandarin Chinese (*putonghua*). Jonathan Stock suggests that her use of the national language, along with radio broadcasts, and gramophone replays in nightclubs, restaurants and bars, 'mark [her] music as "popular"' through 'its intimate relationship with the mass media'.[21] Andreas Steen states that she is placed at 'the heart of a cult of romantic nostalgia which has accompanied the growth of modern Shanghai since the early 1990s'.[22] The film's broadcast not only inscribes this history; its aurality functions as a technical device that disembodies Mr Chan's love through the cult of Zhou, relaying a romance with an image made present by technology as a female voice.

Another female voice in the film is that of Rebecca Pan, who plays the landlady, Mrs Suen. Like Zhou Xuan, Pan is also a Shanghainese who recorded songs in Mandarin and English in Hong Kong, but in the 1970s. *IMFL*'s official website acclaims her as a Chinese popular music legend throughout East Asia. This legendary status is anchored in the film through her rendition of 'Bengawan Solo', the national song of Indonesia. Margaret Kartomi notes the post-colonial significance of this song not only in Indonesia but also in East and South-east Asia through its reflections on anti-colonial resistance and political independence. Tracing multiple renditions in Tagalog in the Philippines and in Cantonese or Mandarin in Singapore,

Hong Kong, Taiwan and China, she notes that it has been performed 'in virtually every popular style, from *kroncong* to swing, jazz to bossanova, rock-and-roll, national song to march band, and brass band to symphony orchestra', becoming 'a regional symbol' that represents 'the hegemony and power struggles within Indonesia and the East/Southeast Asia as a whole, with its economic dynamism and self-assertiveness'.[23]

This song anchors the arrival of Mr Chow in Singapore. An interior shot of his office pans across the *Singapore Daily* sign, echoing an earlier pan in Hong Kong of Mr Chow at his *Sing Man Yit Pao Daily* newspaper office. The references to print media further add to the film's narrative of modernity through its role as a technology for the formation of the modern nation-state. More significantly, this narrative of modernity also reveals a self-reflexive re-turn to the cinema of Wong Kar-wai and the politics of its emergence where *tête-bêche*, as the intersection of Mrs Suen (Pan) and Mr Chow (Leung), functions as a form of binding between *IMFL* and *Days of Being Wild*. Styled with the same vaselined hair, attired in the same mod suit and tie, the intersection of Leung and Pan re-places the song through the intertextuality of *Days of Being Wild*. Hence, the use of Nat King Cole's 'Aquellos Ojos Verdes', 'Quizas Quizas Quizas' and 'Te Quiero Dijiste' in *IMFL* makes sense when rendered through the surface of the Philippines as an image without memory, a cultural plastic of sound bites that makes familiar the foreignness of style. Like the band musicians in Hong Kong's nightclubs that croon familiar, romantic and exotic Latin ballads, here post-modern historicism produces a presence of the image as style.

CONCLUSION: AD(DRESS)ING ASIAN POP

The modishness of Cheung's *cheongsam* dresses in the film also foregrounds this post-modern historicist practice of making the image present as style. Her costumes epitomise the temporality of the film as a form of presentness marked by the new, where the progress of time is ritualised in the changing of her wardrobe. This temporality connotes a dailiness accentuated through the ephemerality of fashion. The style of the dress is not only newly fashionable again in the global consumption of Chinoiserie. The actualisation of style is also heightened through the aestheticisation produced by slow pans, low speeds and close-ups. This exteriority reflects the image of the Wong Kar-wai genre as a cinema of style, speaking to the politics of global fashion tourism. However, its literalness not only translates the logic of cross-cultural exchange; the style of dress also locates a politics about the history of modern Hong Kong cinema. This is also the style of dress adorning Cheung in *Centre Stage*, a film archiving the life of the legendary pan-Chinese movie star Ruan Lingyu and the attendant emergence of film in Hong Kong.[24] Cheung's performance won her the Best Actress Silver Bear award at the 1991 Berlin International Film Festival, considered as the first international acclaim for new Hong Kong cinema, but also marking the modernity of that cinema as one that questions the form of its relationship to the present and itself, signalling a self-consciousness about its presence in a world structured by the fissures of transition. Popularly described as the most recognisable female Asian face in the world, Cheung's image has not only appeared in films by Wong Kar-wai, Tsui Hark and Jackie Chan, but it also has currency as the face of the namesake style magazine, the hair of Lux shampoo advertisements and 'the latex fit' of French vampires[25] (*Irma Vep*) and martial arts cult aficionados (*Augustin, roi du kung-fu*). Her iconicity converges to address the Oriental, neo-Oriental and self-Oriental commodification of contemporary pan-Asian popular culture. It problematises the Hong Kong cinema interface as a form of marginal imperialism in the Asian region,[26] a genre of fusion pan-Asian kitsch in the global imagination[27] and a structure of mood in the nostalgic present. This is a cosmopolitan image that tells the modern story of the intoxication of love, but also a passion that returns to the politics of cinema, its look and its tale.

NOTES

1. Ackbar Abbas, *Hong Kong: Culture and the Politics of Disappearance* (Minneapolis: University of Minnesota Press, 1997), 48–62.

2. Liu Yichang, 'Intersections (*Duidao*)', trans. Nancy Li, *Renditions*, nos. 29–30 (1988): 92.

3. Wong Kar-wai, *Tête-bêche: A Wong Kar Wai Project* (Hong Kong: Block 2 Pictures, 2000), no pagination.

4. Set in 1970s Hong Kong, *Duidao* tells the parallel stories of Chunyu Bai, an old reporter from Shanghai who fled to Hong Kong in the 1940s to escape the

Japanese Occupation, and Ah Xing, a young single woman who lives with her parents. Bai is nostalgic, fuelled by his memories of Shanghai, his youthful liaisons with dancehall girls and his failed marriage. Ah Xing is forward-looking. Always day-dreaming about herself as a famous singer or a movie star, she longs to find love and marry a handsome husband, someone 'a bit like Ke Junxiong, a bit like Deng Guangrong, a bit like Bruce Lee, and a bit like Alain Delon' (Liu, 'Intersections', 92). Triggered by songs, old photographs, and magazine covers and posters of movie stars, the two characters' temporalities are retrospective and projective. In the story, they only meet once sitting next to each other in a crowded cinema. Everyday practices like walking, commuting, listening to music, watching television and going to the movies highlight their close encounters. These practices construct Hong Kong, already a Chinese migrant enclave and a metropolis dizzy with escalating property prices and swirling in the popular media mix of Taiwanese Mandarin pop songs, Filipino renditions of American Top Ten hits, Hollywood cinema and French film icons. The oft-repeated phrase, 'a bit like Ke Junxiong, a bit like Deng Guangrong, a bit like Bruce Lee, and a bit like Alain Delon', epitomises the cultural mix. As this essay will show, these practices are also significant to *IMFL*, because they function as the film's historical and cultural mode of production.

5. Audrey Yue, 'Preposterous Horror: On *Rouge, A Chinese Ghost Story* and Nostalgia', in *The Horror Reader*, ed. Ken Gelder (New York: Routledge, 2000), 365–399; 'Transition Culture in Clara Law's *Autumn Moon*: Refiguring the Migrant and the Foreigner', *Intersections*: <www.sshe.murdoch.edu.au/intersections> no. 4 (2000) (20 September 2000); and 'What's so queer about *Happy Together*? aka Queer (N)Asian: Interface, Mobility, Belonging', *Inter-Asia Cultural Studies Journal*, 1, no. 2 (2000): 251–263.

6. Wong Kar-wai, 'From *Summer in Beijing* to *In the Mood for Love*', in *Tony Leung: In the Mood for Love* (Taiwan: Block 2 Music Co. & Universal Music Ltd, 2000), no pagination.

7. For example, David Ansen, 'Ansen's Top 15: Our Critic Picks his Best and Brightest from the Pack', *Newsweek*, 14 January 2000, 58; Richard Corliss, 'Cinema (Arts and Media/The Best and Worst of 2001)', *Time International*, 24 December 2001, 78; and Anthony D'Alessandro, 'Top Grossing Pics of 2001', *Variety*, 7–13 January 2002, 38.

8. Stephen Teo, 'Wong Kar-wai's *In the Mood for Love*: Like a Ritual in Transfigured Time', *Senses of Cinema*: <www.sensesofcinema.com/contents/01/13/mood.html> (10 April 2001).

9. See for example: Kent Jones, '*In the Mood for Love* (Review)', *Film Comment*, 37, no. 1 (2001): 22. Teo refers to *IMFL* reflecting 'an ideal dreamtime of Hong Kong' (ibid.). Abbas suggests that the city functions as 'leitmotif of a space that enforces physical proximity but forbids intimacy', and has become a protagonist that is only perceptible in 'fragments, metonymies, displacements', in 'Dialectic of Deception', *Public Culture*, 11, no. 2 (1999): 362–363. Marc Siegel extends this to show that it produces 'new kinds of intimacy' that exist 'outside in the public sexual world', in 'The Intimate Spaces of Wong Kar-wai', in *At Full Speed: Hong Kong Cinema in a Borderless World*, ed. Esther C. M. Yau (Minneapolis: University of Minnesota Press, 2001), 290, 285.

10. See Jones, '*In the Mood for Love* (Review)'. See also Jean-Marc Lalanne, 'Images from the Inside', trans. Stephen Wright, in Jean-Marc Lalanne, David Martinez, Ackbar Abbas, Jimmy Ngai, *Wong Kar-wai* (Paris: Editions Dis Voir, 1997), 9–28; Ewa Mazierska and Laura Rascaroli, 'Trapped in the Present: Time in the Films of Wong Kar-wai', *Film Criticism*, 25, no. 2 (2000): 2–20.

11. Teo, 'Wong Kar-wai's *In the Mood for Love*'.

12. Paul Gilroy, *The Black Atlantic: Modernity and Double Consciousness* (London: Verso, 1993), 37; emphasis in original. Gilroy's counter-modernity relates to Hong Kong modernity as forms of alternative modernity. On alternative modernities, see also Dilip P. Goankar, 'On Alternative Modernities', *Public Culture*, 11, no. 1 (1999): 1–18.

13. Hamid Naficy, 'Phobic Spaces and Liminal Panics: Independent Transnational Film Genre', in *Global/Local: Cultural Production and the Transnational Imaginary*, ed. Rob Wilson and Wimal Dissanayake (Durham, NC: Duke University Press, 1996), 130.

14. Abbas, 'Dialectic of Deception'; Siegel, 'The Intimate Spaces'.

15. Jeffrey Ressner, 'Asia Scores: The Region's Movies Come of Age at the Cannes Festival, with Four Big Awards – and, in Ang Lee's Martial-arts Fantasy, One Peerless Triumph', *Time International*, 115, no. 22 (2000): 54.

16. On 'Asia' as a discourse of regionality, see: Rob Wilson and Wimal Dissanayake, ed., *Asia/Pacific as Space of Cultural Production* (Durham, NC: Duke University Press, 1995); Chen Kuan-hsing, ed., *Trajectories: Inter-Asia Cultural Studies* (London: Routledge, 1998); Aihwa Ong and Donald Nonini, eds, *Ungrounded Empires: The Cultural Politics of Modern Chinese Transnationalism* (London: Routledge, 1997); Tu Wei-ming, ed., *Confucian Traditions in East Asian Modernity* (Cambridge, MA: Harvard University Press, 1996); Arif Dirlik, ed., *What is a Rim?* (Boulder, CO: Westview Press, 1993); Ron Martin, ed., *Money and the Space Economy* (Chichester: John Wiley & Sons, 1999); Kris Olds *et al.*, eds, *Globalisation and the Asia Pacific: Contested Territories* (London: Routledge, 1999); Myong-gon Chu, *The New Asia in Global Perspective* (New York: St Martin's Press, 2000); and Leo Ching, 'Globalizing the Regional, Regionalizing the Global: Mass Culture and Asianism in the Age of Late Capital', *Public Culture*, 12, no. 1 (2000): 233–257.

17. Appadurai's disjunctive scapes point to the production of the image as a practice of transnational imagination, in 'Disjuncture and Difference in the Global Cultural Economy', *Public Culture*, 2, no. 2 (1990): 1–24. An example of this image in Asia is evident in Leo Ching's writings on mass Asianism.

18. Ackbar Abbas, 'Cosmopolitan De-scriptions: Shanghai and Hong Kong', *Public Culture*, 12, no. 3 (2000): 778.

19. Ibid., 775.

20. Frank Welsh, *A History of Hong Kong* (London: HarperCollins, 1994), 458, 461.

21. Jonathan Stock, 'Zhou Xuan: Early Twentieth-century Chinese Popular Music', *Asian Music*, 26, no. 2 (1995): 123.

22. Andreas Steen, 'Tradition, Politics and Meaning in 20th Century China's Popular Music. Zhou Xuan: "When will the Gentleman Come Back Again?"' *Chime*, 14–15 (1999–2000): 150.

23. Margaret Kartomi, 'The Pan-East/Southeast Asian and National Indonesian Song Bengawan Solo and its Javanese Composer', *Yearbook for Traditional Music* (1998), 97–98.

24. On *Centre Stage*, see Brett Farmer, 'Mémoire en Abîme: Remembering (through) *Centre Stage*' (review essay), *Intersections: Gender, History and Culture in the Asian Context*, 4 (September 2000): <wwwshe.murdoch.edu.au/intersections/issue4/centre_review.html> (10 October 2000); and Shuqin Cui, 'Stanley Kwan's *Center Stage*: The (Im)possible Engagement between Feminism and Postmodernism',

Cinema Journal, 39, no. 4 (Summer 2000): 61–76; as well as Bérénice Reynaud's essay in this volume.

25. Olivia Khoo, ' "Anagrammatical Translations": Latex Performance and Asian femininity unbounded in Olivier Assayas's *Irma Vep*', *Continuum*, 13, no. 3 (November 1999): 383–395.

26. Ding-tzann Lii, 'A Colonized Empire: Reflections on the Expansion of Hong Kong Films in Asian Countries', in Chen, *Trajectories*, 122–141.

27. On the nature of commodity consumption in Wong Kar-wai's other films, see Gina Marchetti, 'Buying American, Consuming Hong Kong: Cultural Commerce, Fantasies of Identity, and the Cinema', in *The Cinema of Hong Kong: History, Arts, Identity*, ed. Poshek Fu and David Desser (Cambridge: Cambridge University Press, 2000), 289–313.

19 *Kekexili: Mountain Patrol*: Moral Dilemma and a Man with a Camera

Shuqin Cui

In contrast to China's current film industry, dominated by Hollywood imports and domestic commercial releases, Lu Chuan's *Kekexili: Mountain Patrol* (2004) places the audience in an explicit confrontation with environmental catastrophe and moral investigation. A newcomer to the film industry, the young director refuses to identify himself with either the mainstream or independent film-making. Instead, his films seek possibilities between aesthetic quality and commercial appeal. In his directorial debut, *The Missing Gun* (2002), for instance, the theme of searching for the missing gun and by extension a man's lost identity engages the audience with psychological anxiety and visual thrills. *Kekexili* continues the theme of searching, but here the outcome of a search for environmental resolution and moral justice remains doubtful. Inspired by the story of a Tibetan patrol team whose members sacrifice their lives to fight poaching, Lu makes it his mission to screen the moving drama and its heroes.[1] In doing so, the film establishes a primary viewpoint through an embedded Beijing journalist and the lens of his camera. This engaged viewpoint leads our vision to antelopes slaughtered for their pelts and a virgin land under global-commercial exploitation. Due to this very perspective, watchful but ambivalent, however, the film falls into moral dilemma and narrative uncertainty.

In this essay, I consider how in *Kekexili* a journalist with a camera perceives the Tibetan wilderness and an environmental catastrophe unfolding there. I argue first that the land and the animals are viewed as gendered others. Framed as virginal terrain with treacherous conditions, Kekexili excites the imagination as it tests human capacities. Tibetan antelopes, their slaughtered bodies foregrounded in the film, signify poaching violence and commercial exploitation. Second, the Beijing journalist finds it difficult to make moral choices, as the perspective he embodies blurs the line between villains and heroes. In the

peasants who become poachers and the volunteers who patrol the wilderness, we find 'Tibetan' as a hybrid rather than an essential ethnic identity. Finally, the director's desire to bring a true story to the screen gives *Kekexili* a documentary quality and the camera view a semblance of justice. The film narrative, however, does not examine deeply the conflicts within the social-cultural world of Kekexili; it primarily advances through a succession of dramatic events and disastrous outcomes. The tragic heroes die for their noble cause, but their mission remains unexplored and the film closes with justice unfulfilled. In addition, the filming process reveals how the director negotiates between moral commitment and commercial pressures, between his personal pursuit and official ideology.

IMAGE OF THE LANDSCAPE, BODY OF THE ANTELOPE

Kekexili, located about 4,700 metres above sea level, is the last natural reserve for Tibetan antelopes. Worshipped by the locals as 'the beautiful mountain and the beautiful girl', the topography embodies a mixture of masculine power and feminine beauty. The feminine beauty lies in its virginal nature, where 'one's footprints could be the first left by humankind'.[2] The sublime view of the snow-covered mountain peaks, expansive deserts and silent water entices the camera and our vision. The masculine force emerges from the destructive conditions under which unpredictable snowstorms and inevitable accidents can take one's life silently in seconds. The beautiful and treacherous landscape encompasses far more than the setting of the film. Being the primary framework of the film narrative and discursive measure of human conflict, Kekexili, the space of otherness, both invites and challenges cinematic representation. For the director, the voyage through the wilderness allows him to engage personally with

Kekexili: Mountain Patrol

a culture and pursue cinematic possibilities unimaginable in his previous film-making experience. The landscape presents a visual as well as a virtual site against which notions of good and evil, man and nature, life and death may be reconsidered. To the audience, the landscape invites as well as rejects the extension of wishful imagination. We are led to face the brutal reality of antelope poaching yet are kept helplessly at a distance. The untouched land, which preserves the environment and nurtures its wildlife, is exposed to commercial exploitation and cinematic exploration.

The virgin land and the antelope are the desired images that the camera tries to capture. In addition to human characters, the film foregrounds the antelope as a highly feminised body image and the central configuration of the narrative. A pre-credit sequence, for instance, starts with a voice-over narration and images of antelopes in the open landscape. The voice-over informs us that Kekexili is the last natural reserve for the animals. The peaceful image then dissolves first into a close-up of a dismembered body, then a wide-angle shot of a mass of corpses. A man with a camera

in the film is photographing the scene, and the voice-over continues, 'Hundreds and thousands of antelopes have been slaughtered for the needs of European and American markets since 1985. The population has declined from over a million to less than 20,000.'[3] In different *mise en scènes*, where hundreds of antelope carcasses and pelts dominate the screen, the film accelerates a bleak contrast between human brutality and animal vulnerability that goes beyond any imagination of environmentalism.

While depicting the antelope as a feminised victim, the film links briefly to the human female figure. Excluded from men's life-and-death dramas and located in domestic or commercial places, women are identified with nature and primary needs, ready to nurture men with body or beauty. For example, the woman speaking in Sichuan dialect is a migrant working in the local sex industry. The film defines her screen identity as one patroller's girlfriend; her function is to offer sexual and financial consolation to her lover, who is distraught after his expedition in the wilderness. The Tibetan girl, with her exotic beauty and minority status, seems to exist only to add visual and sexual attraction. In Kekexili, this 'no man's land', there is no room for women's narratives. It is not surprising that in a film industry where the female image is too often a matter of breast size and body figure, a serious film such as *Kekexili* is no exception.[4]

The animal body image, penetrated by bullets and shorn of its pelt, personifies a feminised victimisation through which the film seeks possible explanations to environmental crises. Feminisation of the antelope comes to signify the subordinated Tibetan *Other*, subject to ethnic and political regulations. Today's poaching violence and commercial exploitation could well remind us of the British expedition to Tibet in the early twentieth century and the communists' militant intrusion in the 1950s. Hunted and slaughtered for the pelt to make *shahtoosh* shawls, the antelopes today are subject to collective profiteers – the poachers, the fur business and the fashion industry. Situated against the capitalist corporate machine operating behind the scene, the endangered wildlife and landscape bespeak the need for media exposure, legal regulation and, above all else, cinematic investigation.

As introduced in the pre-credit sequence, the figure of a journalist becomes our eyes and ears. He is identified with Beijing, the centre of political and cultural authority, and thus the law that legitimates his position to speak and document. The film begins, then, with a negotiation between the centre and the margin, Beijing and Tibet, on the question of the antelope patrol. Tibetan burial traditions and the patrollers' community do not welcome strangers. Identification of the journalist from Beijing breaks this convention, however. After the credits, for instance, the film introduces its journalist protagonist to the Tibetan locale. At first, a shot/reverse shot keeps the head of the patrol, Ritai, and the journalist, Gayu, briefly in opposing positions. After Gayu presents himself as a journalist from Beijing who has come especially to gather and report news about Kekexili, he then wins immediate acceptance. Through the journalist's position, the film places confidence in the moral mission to document the patrol and protect wildlife. Such a commitment should meet no resistance. In addition, the film identifies the journalist as half-Tibetan and half-Chinese. The double status allows him to be viewed as either one of us (Tibetan) or one of them (Han Chinese). This us–them duality, while allowing his voice-over to narrate story and his photo-images to reveal the brutal reality, indicates a power relation between urban and rural, centre and margins, official and minority. Questions arise as to whether the Beijing journalist can explain the patrol's suicidal obsession to protect the antelopes or whether the central government can bring order to its frontier.

MINORITY IDENTITY AND PROBLEMS IN REPRESENTATION

The world seen through the camera lens rejects moral measures, as the very notion of minority identity is forged with ambiguity. The peasants-turned-poachers and the volunteer patrol members, composed of poor Han Chinese and local Tibetans, are ultimate minorities on the social-economic periphery. The hybrid identity first subordinates conventionally measured oppositions between Han Chinese and Tibetans, then blurs the lines between heroes and villains. Confused and uncertain, the film's journalist and his camera often alternate between the conflicting sides. On the one hand, the journalist attempts to prevent misconduct he thinks violent or against the law. On the other, the journalistic perspective often limits his moral exploration. The role of the journalist as agent of moral judgment and his position as viewpoint of the film narrative renders the film paradoxical.

For instance, the photojournalist often turns his camera towards the 'villains' and engages their stories. The 'villains', except for the armed poaching organisers, share a minority position with ethnic Tibetans, as both are located at the social-economic periphery. The question of what happens when the embodiment of minority identity includes both the poverty-driven peasants and Tibetans of low socio-economic status challenges the film in its narrative and representation. In a conversation between the journalist and the head of the peasants-turned-poachers, Ma Zhanlin, we are informed that poverty rather than evil impulses drives them to hunt antelopes. Ma Zhanlin tells the journalist that he was once a shepherd but could not make a living after the grasslands turned into desert and the herds died of starvation. He is the most skilful one among the group and makes 5 yuan (US$0.65) for flaying one animal. The insertion of the minority voice in different categories invites the audience to reject a simple moral judgment and think deeply about the causes of poverty and the social-economic factors that motivate illegal hunting.[5]

The film, however, has no room to investigate the social-economic consequences further. Instead, it is trapped in moral ambiguity. The journalist and his camera eagerly seek justice, only to discover that violence and unlawful deeds exist among the patrollers as well as the poachers. Poachers sell pelts for profit, but so do the patrollers to sustain their operations. In terms of violence, there is no confusion when the sympathetic camera seizes the moment as a gunman coldly executes one patroller. In contrast, the camera lens appears to lose focus when patrollers beat their prisoners. Despite the violence, heroes and villains can be equally merciful to each other. In a chase sequence, for instance, as the patrollers pursue the escaped prisoners, both suffer from oxygen deprivation. When one patroller falls and almost dies of pulmonary congestion, his young opponent offers emergency assistance.

While the lines between heroes and villains are blurred, and poachers and patrol members are situated similarly at the social-economic margin, the film leaves the journalist and his camera as the agent of justice and in the position of a speaking subject. In the final chase sequence, for instance, Gayu challenges Ritai with the comment that selling pelts is an unlawful act. Ritai confronts the accusation by responding, 'I understand that selling pelts is against the law, but what concerns me most is Kekexili and my friends. Haven't you seen those performing prostration? Their hands and faces are dirty but there's beauty in their hearts.' This is the critical moment when the Han journalist and the Tibetan volunteer finally confront each other's different values. The issues that the confrontation poses cannot be explained only as ethnic difference. They are also power relations between speaking subject and the spoken object as well as tensions between official ideologies and ethnic moral codes, and between urban civilisation and minority customs.

In his discussion of ethnic minority writing, Joseph Pivato indicates that representation of ethnic minority assumes a political position. Questions of who is speaking and from what perspective generate power relations. When a person from outside the minority group assumes to speak about the experience of and for the people of the marginalised group, it is not just a political problem but an aesthetic one as well.[6] Assuming the position of the speaking subject yet uncertain how to speak for the Other, the journalist loses confidence in the camera's ability to adequately represent the cultural collision. 'I'm a journalist, how can I draft a reliable report?' Gayu wonders. 'Thanks to you journalists, Kekexili can survive,' Ritai answers, satirically. From the conversation and the confrontation, one sees that the film intends to impose media power over the environmental catastrophe and minority Other. The intention is challenged, however, as the Other speaks back and refuses to be represented. Their differences go deeper, as Gayu asks whether the prisoners and patrollers left behind will walk out of the desert. Ritai repeats, in responding to or ignoring his question, 'wish it won't snow, wish it won't snow', as a snowstorm might take anyone's life, hero or villain. The audience too is left thinking about the conflicts between the Tibetan concerned about life and death and the Han journalist concerned about reporting news according to his moral code. As an outsider and therefore an unreliable narrator, however, the journalist is unable to fully comprehend the local patrollers' suicidal obsession with their 'mission impossible'.

The film touches on important issues but leaves them to the audience to ponder. First, would Kekexili and its wildlife be appropriately protected if the government really considered its western plateau? Kekexili is under official conservation according to China's environmental law. But little has attracted government attention before the murder of the local volunteers gains international media publicity. As volunteers outside the official system, the local patrols have been short of funds, personnel and firearms for years. Second, would the peasants engage in the antelope pelt business if they were not subject to economic impoverishment and social or institutional neglect? Finally, the film points to leaders of the poaching organisations and the increasing demands of global capitalism as the real threats to the Tibetan antelopes, but cannot elaborate. The film can hardly address these questions. The narrative and the expedition end in death. At the close of the film, the journalist can only watch as the poacher kills Ritai on site; his camera is completely helpless. The visual moment seriously challenges the question of whether the man with the camera, hence the media, can uphold moral principles and the conservation of wildlife.

DEATH AND THE DOCUDRAMA EFFECT

With its constrained viewpoint, the film seeks moral sense in the point of death. In addition to the slaughtered antelopes, the film begins and ends with human sacrifices. In the opening of the film, for instance, the *mise en scène* of one poacher flaying an antelope and another executing the captured patroller are framed in the same screen. This spontaneous, horrific contrast shows how wildlife and human life are equally vulnerable to deadly violence. At the end of the film, a long shot frames Ritai surrounded by armed poachers. The unarmed individual asks his opponents to surrender, assuming that justice will triumph over evil. The film refuses a melodramatic collision between the innocent and the abusers, however. In a shot that mimics the shooting of antelopes, a poacher opens fire on Ritai, and the head poacher pumps additional bullets into the body. Finally, the film creates a tragic stillness as the narrative and its hero come to a disastrous end.

The film situates its protagonist somewhere between tragic hero and social victim. The tragic hero with moral strength and innocent intentions is in the end unable to triumph over evil; instead, he sacrifices his life for the noble cause. The desire to protect wildlife and infuse order in the wilderness stems not from heroism, however, but from the realm of Tibetan culture. Yet the question of these cultural origins remains unexplored due to the restraints of the perspective. The patrolling team, organised voluntarily by Tibetans themselves and working outside official administration, had operated for years before the making of *Kekexili*. Two of its leading figures lost their lives in conflicts with poachers. In respect to their dedication, the film director rejects melodramatic excitement. Instead the 'heroes' are doomed to die and their moral mission ends in disaster. In doing so, the environmental significance of the struggle between poaching and patrolling is transformed into the aesthetics of tragedy as representation. Moral strength and personal sacrifice need no explanation when an individual faces armed force backed by global imperatives. Only inevitable death will penetrate one's nerves to make tragedy excessive and unbearable. Columbia Pictures, the film's production company, requested that the director give the film an uplifting conclusion, with heroes fighting villains and justice triumphing over evil. Lu Chuan refused to do

so, insisting that he could not sacrifice what he was looking for: a life-and-death tragedy.[7]

Beyond human conflicts, the film further evokes the idea of life-and-death struggle in the forces of nature. The snowstorm and the treacherous conditions in Kekexili challenge everyone. Nature reinforces tragedy with overpowering, fatal destruction. In a panoramic shot, for instance, the group of captured peasant-prisoners is ordered to stand in line. Then a two-shot in close-up frames the patrol's leader, Ritai, and the head peasant, Ma Zhanlin, face to face. Ritai decides to release the prisoners, as he does not have enough supplies to feed them. Ma Zhanlin refuses to accept the offer, because walking 300 kilometres through the wilderness in the storm means certain death. Ritai insists, 'It's your fate if you fail to make it.' The film shows the released peasants walking in freezing conditions against the driving snow. After each dissolve, one man falls and the others strip off pieces of his clothing and move on. Villains are dwarfed before nature, as are heroes. The film situates its heroes in the same circumstances as the villains, as the sequence cuts to the three patrollers left behind due to a gas shortage, fighting their way out of the storm-whipped wilderness. In addition, the production process itself faced a life-and-death challenge. Alex Graf from Columbia Pictures died in a car accident on site and almost half of the crew resigned or ran away from their positions due to the treacherous shooting conditions.[8]

The death code, while used as a visual device to dramatise the tragic mode of the film, also imbues tragedy with certain documentary qualities. *Kekexili* is a feature film based on true stories. Lu Chuan's script takes actual events and figures as original resources. With real-location shooting and locals playing themselves (except for the two leads), the film invites the audience to accept it as a re-creation of actual events. Moreover, the film is punctuated with dates, and each day is marked with a specific location. But as each day unfolds, events remain unknown and unpredictable. A moment of happy reunion among members of the patrol station might occur, or a fatal encounter with poachers might ignite. The actual spatial-temporal framework ensures a documentary quality and the unexpectedness of events a dramatic effect.[9] Steven N. Lipkin, in his study on film and television docudrama, observes that 'The overall thrust of docudrama is neither exposition nor logical argumentation, but persuasion. ... Docudrama strives to persuade us to believe that what occurred happened much as we see it on the screen.'[10] In considering how docudrama presents persuasive arguments, one finds that an important strategy is to intensify the tragedy but not the emotional excess.

In *Kekexili*, the most unexpected death occurs when quicksand buries one patroller, Liu Dong. Liu's jeep breaks down at a critical moment as the trapped patrolling team waits for him to send supplies. As he attempts to unload the car and find the mechanical problem, he steps accidentally into quicksand. Only seconds of struggle elapse before the sand swallows him completely. What is left behind is the loss of life and deadly silence. This silent death and its dramatic effect provide the most forceful death image in the film. Inescapable and irresistible, the tragedy and the tragic hero draw the audience into terror and a feeling of helplessness. According to the director's shooting notes, this death scene was added deliberately. Lu Chuan explains, 'Quicksand is quite uncommon in Kekexili, but I decided to include the scene to enhance the sense of tragedy.'[11] Indeed, the specifically designed *mise en scène* and re-created death sequence add to the sense of tragedy, as the film poses the question of boundaries between fact and fiction. I suggest that the director pursues both documentary quality and dramatic effect in his rhetorical approach to social reality: the documentary mode legitimises antelope poaching as an environmental crisis and the dramatic effect reinforces its urgency. One should not assume that docudrama means reproduction or reconstruction of actual events and figures, however, as any real events, when framed on screen, are subject to narrative organisation and visual articulation. A general audience may not easily recognise the boundaries between documented facts and melodramatic intentions (insertion of the quicksand sequence, for instance), but the distortion of the 'real' exemplifies how controversial and slippery the notion of docudrama can be.

Kekexili engages the audience with the visual splendour of the Tibetan wilderness and directs attention to the efforts to fight the encroachment of antelope poachers. Exposure to the unfamiliar landscape and the threatened wildlife reveals not only an environmental catastrophe but also the life-and-death drama centred on the struggle over the fate of the antelopes. The film and the spectator fall into a moral dilemma when apprehending Tibetan culture through the camera lens of the Beijing journalist. *Kekexili* uses death as a visual device and narrative force to heighten the drama and make the heroes fatally tragic. Determined to form Kekexili – the space and the film – into a cinematic monument, Lu Chuan only succeeds in showing that art and justice yield to different hierarchies.

The film director has to reconcile the tensions between ideological concerns and commercial expectations. The film concludes its tragic drama on an irreverent note. 'Gayu, the journalist, returned to Beijing. His reports astonished the world. A year later, the Chinese government declared Kekexili a national natural reserve and established the Forest Public Security Bureau. The population of Tibetan antelopes is back to 30,000 and still growing.' The stark contrast between the previous death scene and the reassuring epilogue is not coherent. But it is unsurprising that the film needs to yield to official views, audience expectations and commercial concerns. One might find relief in the notion of government protection, but the lives sacrificed in the effort to stop poaching make us wonder how effective a security bureau will be. How can Kekexili retain its pristine nature and the antelope avoid exploitation in the face of increasing commercial pressures and the growing dominance of the Han on the Tibetan plateau?

NOTES

1. The inspiration originates from a newspaper report about the 'Wild Yak Brigade', a volunteer group organised to patrol Kekexili against poaching. Two members, Suonan dajie and Zhaba duojie, lost their lives in gunfights with the poachers. See Su Qiqi, 'Kekexili: *zhenshi, shiheng yu tuoxie*' ('*Kekexili*: Truth, Imbalance and Compromise'): <www.fanhall.com> (accessed 20 January 2007).

2. A geologist, lost in the Kekexili wilderness during his field exploration, made the statement, and a patrol member in the film repeats the lines to the Beijing journalist.

3. The voice-over is in Chinese. This is my translation based on English subtitles.

4. An illustrative example occurs in Zhang Yimou's recent feature, *The Curse of the Golden Flower* (2006). In addition to the spectacular setting and colour scheme, the film means to lure the audience with female body images, especially overexposed breasts. To

do so, Zhang requested special costume designs inspired by corsets and bras from eighteenth-century Europe as well as Tang China: <enjoy.eastday.com/eastday/enjoy1/e/20070215/u1a2631591.html>.

5. The cast list indicates that the patrolling members are composed of Tibetans and Han Chinese. But almost all the poachers share the family name 'Ma', a popular surname among the Hui minority centred in the Qinghai region. The minority issues raised by the film invite us to think about minority identity as transcending cultural and ethnic differences.

6. See Joseph Pivato, 'Representation of Ethnicity as Problem: Essence or Construction', *Journal of Canadian Studies*, 31, no. 3 (1996): 48–58.

7. For information on how Lu Chuan struggled to get the film made, see Zhang Ying, 'Kekexili: *cong xinwen dao dianying*' ('*Kekexili*: From News to Film'), *Nanfang zhoumo* (*Southern Weekend*) (28 October 2004): <www.southcn.com/nfsq/ywhc/ss>.

8. See Lu Chuan's explanations in James Bell, 'Living on Thin Air', *Sight & Sound*, 16, no. 10 (2006): 26.

9. For the idea of docudrama, see Tony Rayns's review of *Kekexili*, *Sight & Sound*, 16, no. 10 (2006): 70–71.

10. Steven N. Lipkin, *Real Emotional Logic: Film and Television Docudrama as Persuasive Practice* (Carbondale and Edwardsville: Southern Illinois University Press, 2002), ix. I see the film as a consolidation of documentary quality and dramatic effect. The film engages the audience by portraying an environmental crisis that endangers the antelopes and by representing in documentary mode the patrolling as well as the poaching of the animals. The actual people and real incidents, however, serve as the documentary reference. The confused perception of the moral dilemma between poaching and patrolling as well as the blurred lines between hero and villain reinforce the reality-based subject with dramatic effect. In so doing, the director negotiates a balance between fiction and reality, documentation and representation.

11. *Sight & Sound*, 16, no. 10 (2006): 25.

20   *The Love Eterne*: Almost a (Heterosexual) Love Story

Tan See-Kam and Annette Aw

In *Farewell My Concubine* (Chen Kaige, 1993), Leslie Cheung and Zhang Fengyi play two opera stars best known for their rendition of the concubine and the Emperor in the eponymous Beijing opera. On the opera stage, they epitomise an ideal heterosexual couple. Off stage, the two stage-brothers, that is the Cheng Dieyi and Duan Xiaolou characters, are as close as men can be; the former wishes for greater intimacy, but the latter is avowedly heterosexual. Cheng's intense but unrequited love for Duan – along with his cross-sex acts in *Farewell My Concubine* – opens a window to the queer sexual potential of Chinese film and film-opera culture for international film audiences of the early 1990s. For audiences well acquainted with this culture, the history is far longer. Between 1948 and 1964, at least eight film versions of the Liang Shanbo and Zhu Yingtai legend circulated in the diasporic Chinese film circuits of East and South-east Asia. They were all opera films, made in various Chinese languages. The story is typically about Zhu's quest for a formal education, and her subsequent love affair with her classmate, Liang. It starts as a comedy based on mistaken identities and cross-dressing masquerades, before turning into a fully fledged tragedy about love that transgresses class boundaries, so shoring up a critique of Confucian patriarchy and oppression. The star-crossed lovers finally find eternal bliss as immortal butterflies. Shaw Brothers' production, whose English title is *The Love Eterne* (Li Han-hsiang, 1963), was the best known.

The Love Eterne is a *Huangmei diao pian*, or *Huangmei* opera film.[1] *Huangmei* opera films are Mandarin productions that overlay traditional Chinese narratives, be they oral, folk, literary or theatrical, with the technology of film-making. They primarily draw on *Huangmei* opera from the Anhui Province of China, which itself has a history of creatively blending different Chinese folk arts, such as tea-picking music and peasant folk dance, and

regional theatrical repertoires and traditions, such as Anhui and Shanghai opera.[2] They feature gentle and melodic orchestral music and natural singing. Though defunct now, they were all the rage from the late 1950s until the late 1960s. They were high-budget productions with star-studded casts, extravagant sets and lavish costumes.

The Love Eterne was no exception. Shot on Shawscope, this colour widescreen production recounted the familiar legend in seven chronological acts.[3] It boasted a record thirty-four songs, variously inspired by three librettos from the Republican China period: *The Willow Shade Account* (Sichuan opera), *Liang Zhu* (Shanghai opera) and *Butterflies on a Skirt Hem* (Cantonese opera).[4] Its ingenious camera movements and shot framings had the effect of turning the *mise en scène* into an imaginative dance of images that moved with the pace and rhythm of the singing. Occasional dialogue was interspersed among the songs, while stylised acting added to the film's appeal.

Upheld as a 'screen miracle' of its time,[5] *The Love Eterne* was a box-office sensation and a multi-award-winning film.[6] It affirmed Li Han-hsiang's status as the foremost director of *Huangmei diao pian* and catapulted actress Ivy Ling Po, who played the male protagonist Liang, to stardom. The film's success in turn helped Shaw Brothers secure its growing reputation and prestige as the major studio for Mandarin film-making.

Writings on the film are largely restricted to anecdotes in film-related literature (newspapers, magazines and books), reminiscences of film directors and stars in their autobiographies or biographies, and website postings of archival material by fans and commercial enterprises. The lack of any sustained study on the film can be attributed to the fact that scholarly interest in Hong Kong cinema is a recent phenomenon, resulting in research that has tended to focus on its cinematic practices and phenomena of the last two decades. In the last few years, however, there appears to be a more concerted effort to study Hong Kong cinema, prior to the 1970s, which our present study joins.

Our essay is also partly triggered by an interview which Chinese/transnational film-maker Ang Lee granted Rick Lyman of *The New York Times* in 2001. Lee's interview is noteworthy on two counts. First, it draws timely attention to the relatively neglected *The Love Eterne*. Second, it attests to the film's enduring impression on people who saw it as a child. For Lee, *The Love Eterne* 'reminds me always of my innocence … [I]n every movie I make, I always try to duplicate [and recapture] that feeling of purity and innocence that I got when I saw this movie' at the age of nine.[7]

Lee's take on 'audiences at the time' with regards to *The Love Eterne* is insightful at times, but leaves something to be desired. As Lee suggests, it is plausible that some people were oblivious to the 'kinky' and 'very sexy' facets of the film manifested in the love story and the casting. But his assumption of a universe of prudish viewers is at issue. Lee claims that the film's 'pure' and 'sexless' love story conveys 'no sense of lust for the audience', and that the performance has the innocence of 'an all-boys choir' because it has two actresses (Ivy Ling Po and Betty Loh Ti) in the lead roles. These claims reach ridiculous heights when he asserts that the sight of 'a real man expressing romantic feelings for a woman on the screen … would have been too strong for the audiences then', and adds, 'China was a very repressed society'.[8] This explanation smacks of (self)-Orientalism. Its first part is also erroneous. The romantic couples in Li Han-hsiang's earlier *Huang-mei* opera films *Tiau charn* (1958) and *The Kingdom and the Beauty* (1959) were all performed by actors whose on- and off-screen genders corresponded.

Lee's insistence that two actresses playing a chaste heterosexual couple could not generate sexualised identification for the viewers also belies a latent homophobia. His insistence accords with Judith Butler's 'heterosexual matrix', which constructs heteronormativity and the heterosexist logic that identification and desires must be mutually exclusive: 'if one identifies as a given gender, one must desire a different gender'.[9] The cross-dressing themes in *The Love Eterne* challenge Lee's viewpoint. The corresponding narrative and performance mechanisms through which these themes find articulation can

generate fantasies of gender crossings and passings, fantasies which drive the queer gaze where 'multiple, contradictory, shifting, oscillating, inconsistent and fluid' identifications and desires are found.[10] In other words, Lee's take on the audience in regards to the love story and cross-sex acts amounts to a denial of the queer gaze.

Of course, the queer gaze as an academic model for conceptualising the spectatorial process finds more critical and cultural leverage now than during the era of *The Love Eterne*. However, while we are reluctant to force the model of queer spectatorship retroactively, we are also hesitant to block out the possibility of queer identification by film audiences of some forty years ago, for several reasons. First, reports exist that men perceived Ling as a woman while women perceived her as a man after watching her performance as Liang Shanbo.[11] Second, cross-sex acting where an actress appeared in a male role, or a female role included cross-dressing as male, was common in *Huangmei* and other opera films. This shows that viewers at the time accepted cross-sex acting in films. Furthermore becoming a *fanchuan*er[12] – an actor who specialises in cross-gender acting – was a career option at the time.

Ling's case demonstrates that this career choice was a rewarding one. The extent to which cross-sex identification was socially acceptable can be further glimpsed in the way Ling's public embraced her as 'Liang Xiong', or Elder Brother Liang – the pet name Zhu uses to address Liang in the film. This public declaration of adoration, reverence and worship for the actress has endured to the present-day, especially in Taiwan where the 'screen miracle' first appeared in 1963. In 2002, there was a Taiwan-wide commemoration of the fortieth anniversary of the phenomenon that was *The Love Eterne*. It included a stage production of *The Love Eterne*, featuring surviving members of the Shaw Brothers cast, Ling included, in their original roles. The poster for the stage production includes a still of Ling as Liang Xiong. Beneath it is Ling's signature. On the top left-hand corner is an extract from a duet in *The Love Eterne* consisting of Liang's pledge to Zhu: 'In life or death, I want to be with you.'

Ling capitalised on the allure of her gender malleability. It allowed her to build up an impressive repertoire of both female and male leads. Shaw Brothers also milked that allure for all it was worth. This manifested most blatantly in its production of

Love Eterne: Ivy Ling Po (standing) plays a young man, while Betty Loh Ti's character, a young girl, is presently in male drag

The Perfumed Arrow (Kao Li, 1965), not just because Ling was cast in the role of the occasionally cross-dressing female lead, but more because Shaw Brothers' execution of this *Huangmei* opera film rested on the decision to give viewers '*equal* excitement and enjoyment'.[13] As a result, Ling's character underwent frequent cross-gender make-overs, and variously found her/himself the amorous focus of three other 'straight-playing' characters: two men and one woman. This production clearly recognised the marketability of cross-gender fun predicated on multiple spectatorial positions, and Ling's diverse repertoire enhanced rather than negated her polymorphous appeal.

With respect to *The Love Eterne*, the narrative traditions of the *caizi-jiaren* or scholar–beauty romance and the performance conventions of traditional Chinese opera, from which the film derives its style, form and content, can give further insights into the film's shifting spectatorial positions. A leitmotif of popular folklores, vernacular period novels, traditional opera and opera films, *caizi-jiaren* romances typically tell a highly romanticised love story between a scholar (*caizi*) and a beauty (*jiaren*), who, without hesitation, would make a pledge of eternal love, most typically along the lines of 'we may not be born in the same

year, month and day, but we wish to die on the same year, month and day'. Their stories characteristically unfurl in a Confucian setting in traditional China, and have a strong populist orientation that has the characteristics of the Bakhtinian carnivalesque: ridicule of officialdom, inversion of hierarchy, violations of decorum and proportion, and celebration of bodily excess.[14] In *The Love Eterne*, the carnivalesque defies Confucian authority and articulates an intricate interplay of youthful rebellion, young love, same-sex conspiracy and cross-sex masquerades, producing subtexts that append a queer dimension to the film's heterosexual love story. This dimension dovetails well with, and lends itself to, contemporary queer scholarship.

In *caizi-jiaren* romances, the lovers are usually matched in terms of intelligence, moral fibre and appearance. They both seek love and romance, and above all, marriage to a partner of their choice. However, while pursuing affairs of the heart, they are mindful of their status as Confucian subjects, and act in accordance with the compulsory morality of legalised Confucianism.[15] Legalised Confucianism stringently upholds patriarchal familism, and endorses gender segregation, arranged marriage and female chastity. In *caizi-jiaren* narratives, these Confucian practices engender conflicts along as well as across class, gender, generational and other social lines, generating conflict-driven resolutions based on the playful breaching and restoring of Confucian norms. As such, the queer possibilities generated by themes of Confucian contestation and containment are generic. The resultant tension forges a plurality of Confucian subjectivities. In *The Love Eterne*, these include a conservative patriarch (Zhu's father), a loving mother figure (Zhu's mother), a liberal scholar with a conservative streak (Liang), a rebellious but chaste daughter who is also a brilliant scholar (Zhu), and a silent observer of Confucian familism and its attendant conflicts (Zhu's maid). These subjects are in turn multi-dimensional. For example, Zhu is variously an anti-Confucian rebel, a dutiful daughter, a cheeky male physician, a clever male student, a martyr of love, her own ambitious younger sister and the Goddess of Mercy incarnate. These personae allow her to wield carnivalesque power at will, but within the constraints of Confucian strictures.

More often than not, it is the *jiaren* who is the most rebellious. She has good reasons to be so since she has more to gain than lose from struggling against a world where masculinist Confucianism holds sway. Here, Zhu is an archetype. She embodies the quintessential *jiaren*: she is young, beautiful, intelligent and resourceful. Above all, she has ambition. If the beauty's motto in *caizi-jiaren* romances is 'Though in body I am a woman, in ambition I surpass men',[16] then the cross-dressed 'male' Zhu's self-referential description of 'his' imaginary sister to Liang in a song alludes to this 'ambition':

> My younger sister has high aspirations.
> She strives to be equal or superior to men.
> She has no need for rouge, only ink and brush.
> She does not like jewellery, only literature.

Zhu's quest for equal opportunity, self-fulfilment and self-determination spurs her journey into the male world. It rests on her overwhelming desire to compete with men, morally and intellectually. These themes are common in *caizi-jiaren* romances, and visible in the scene where Zhu has a debate with Liang over the Confucian dogma that 'Women are the source of all troubles.' Bursting into song, Liang argues in support of this dogma, citing the historical figures of Daji and Baosi, whom he says caused the respective downfalls of Kings Zhou and You.[17] In retort, Zhu sings: 'My dear elder brother, you are not critical of the books you read ... Those tyrannical emperors ruined themselves/[But Confucian historiography] puts the blame on women.' Finally, 'he' offers a list of counter-examples: Nüwa, Luo Zhu, and Mengmu.[18] All are 'intelligent and virtuous women' from ancient times, but forgotten by Confucian historians. This list taps a different epistemological genealogy, producing alternative models of subjectivity, variously noted for female resourcefulness, resolution, enterprise and courage. Awed by Zhu's scholastic brilliance, Liang promises to learn to be critical of the books he reads. In this way, Zhu proves herself intellectually superior to Liang.

A condition for Zhu's entry in the man's world, paradoxically, is that she cross-dresses as a male. Sartorial disguise grants Zhu privileges otherwise exclusively enjoyed by men – autonomy, mobility and education. To achieve these by recourse to sartorial disguise highlights female marginalisation within the Confucian society at large. This marginalisation is not equivalent to hopelessness. Instead it points out an aspect of social injustice that needs addressing, including gender discrimination. At the same time, it also points to the possibility of alternatives. Borrowing Butler's words, the significance of the 'man' Zhu occasionally performs can be understood as 'a crucial part not only of subject *formation*, but of the ongoing contestation and reformulation of the subject as well. The performative ... is one of the influential rituals by which subjects are formed and reformulated ... [It] can work in ... counter-hegemonic ways.'[19] In other words, Zhu's efficacious performance of what it might mean to be a man, or what it takes to be one, also grants her the carnivalesque power a woman-man can wield.

Conventionally, the *jiaren*'s final goal is no more than marriage, which is a narrative constraint on her development into a revolutionary heroine who breaks all restrictions. However, Zhu's insistence that marriage be based on love and mutual consent does demonstrate an active struggle for self-determination. 'I will marry the man of your choice,' she sings to her father curtly, 'only if the sun rises from the West!' Her eventual decision to choose death over a marriage not of her choice manifests similar defiance of Confucian patriarchal power and confirms her virtue, in that she remains true to herself and faithful to Liang to the end. In these ways, Zhu counters the hegemonic

Confucian dogma that *nüzi wu cai shi de*, 'a virtuous woman is one without literary abilities or literacy'.

In addition to feminist potential, *Huangmei* opera films such as *The Love Eterne* have narrative mechanisms for enabling multiple points of identification. Two interrelated performance techniques commonly employed by opera/opera film actors to effect cross-sex transformations are pertinent to our present task. One is what we would call female maling.[20] The other is called *kaiguang*.[21] These techniques are also central to the performance of subject-constitution (in the Butlerian sense) in opera and opera films.

In *The Love Eterne*, the transformation of Zhu into an occasional cross-dresser and actress Ling into Liang is achieved through female maling, while *kaiguang* sustains their cross-sex acts. The *kaiguang* technique separates the host body (that of the actor/actress) and the role body (that of the character) by dismantling the former to allow the latter to 'shine' through. The female maling technique is chiefly concerned with wrapping the role body over the host body so that the two become enshrouded in an aura of maleness and masculinity.

Female maling involves body, gender and erotic maling. Body maling gives the host body a physical make-over, using codified make-up and costumes, and the mimicry of movements, gestures and mannerisms typically associated with the *xiaosheng* (young man) prototype in opera and opera films, including his distinctive speaking and singing style. In short, it is most concerned with appearance. Zhu the scholar is thus different from Zhu the daughter in looks: the former has the appearance of a *xiaosheng*, while the latter that of a *dan* (young woman). As male, 'he' wears a hat and sports eyebrows shaped like a pair of willow leaves. As female, she has arched eyebrows and neatly combed hair, adorned with bejewelled hairpieces. The two also have different foot movements. For instance, Zhu the scholar walks with exuberant masculinity like a *xiaosheng*, rather than shuffling gracefully. The latter is the footwork for a *dan*, which Zhu the daughter adopts.

Gender maling overlaps with body maling, but mainly concerns the many ways malers assume the behaviour and emotions associated with being male, or those of the *xiaosheng* type. For example, when sorrowful, Zhu the scholar would shed a quiet tear, whereas Zhu the daughter would bawl her eyes out. In sum, both body and gender maling endow the host/role body with male and masculine character-istics. Together they produce erotic maling as an after-effect. Charged with a sexual energy, erotic maling arouses the spectators' erotic desires because it holds out the promise of (cross-)sexual pleasure. The tripartite process of body, gender and erotic maling thus helps bring to presence the performance or *biaoyan* – *biao* (express) and *yan* (act out) – of a sexed, gendered and sexualised entity that is connected to yet distinct from the host body's.

This *biaoyan* therefore turns on a performance that helps bring about the (cross-)gender transformation of the performer. Rather than becoming a biological man *per se*, s/he carries the aura of one. It is this aura that enables her/him to pass as a 'man'. In short, s/he is a 'make-believe' man. A 'make-believe' man embodies camp: as androgynous figures, they concurrently encapsulate the beauty of the feminine and femininity in masculine men, and the masculine and masculinity in feminine women.[22] In a sense, 'he' is *feinan feinü* (non-man, non-woman). Yet 'he' is not a transvestite, even though 'he' is a cross-sex cross-dresser of sorts. Nor is 'he' a female transsexual, for there exist scenarios in *caizi-jiaren* romances in which 'he' is endowed with procreative capability. Here *The Mermaid* (Kao Li, 1965) is an example: scholar Chang Cheng (also played by actress Ling in a male role) impregnates a beauty who is a carp incarnated in human form (played by actress Lee Ching). Finally, 'he' may be androgynous, but is not an androgyne. The gender identity of a female maler is therefore – as Butler might put it – 'performatively constituted by the very 'expressions' that are said to be results' of the performance.[23] That is to say, gender is a performance: it is what the character *biaoyan*s at particular times. Hence the maler may stand for any of those entities (man, woman, transsexual, transvestite, androgyne, non-man and non-woman), or various composites of them, at any given time, but is ultimately irreducible to any one of them. The challenge for the performer then is to call forth the appropriate entity or composition, as and when required by the plot.

If female maling simultaneously wraps the host and role bodies with the male aura, then the performative art of *kaiguang* would tie that aura more firmly to the role body than the host body. As mentioned, *kaiguang* subjects the latter to an 'opening process'. It cuts it up into separate units of articulation, and replaces it, part by part – the eyes, hands, fingers and feet – with those of the role body.

It necessitates 'emptying' the performer's body of 'its personal or individual essence (soul)' so as to allow for the *qi* (presence, life, energy) of the performed body to emerge, or to 'shine' through.[24] The process of simultaneously dissecting the host body, hollowing it out and reassembling it into another harmonious whole is the crucial technique by which the role body becomes both narrator and subject. Meanwhile the *qi* that maintains and dissolves both distance and proximity between the two bodies bring to the fore the personae as required by the plot. Not only that, it also throws a *kaiguang*-feel on the spatial-temporality of the fictive world, much as the female *maling* aura affects the actions, events and objects, in addition to the performer (body, self and identity). The fictive world, now belonging more to the role body or bodies than the host body or bodies, in turn connects with the many gazes of the viewers, enticing them to enter into the performance space. The audience in turn makes the entry, not as passive observers, but as interested parties who would read that space, connecting layers of meaning the performed bodies throw up and out, in relation to the situations and contexts of the performance. This form of participation inevitably demands the suspension of disbelief.

The presence of female malers in *The Love Eterne*, be it actress Ling in a male role or actress Loh in a female role who periodically cross-dresses as a male, does not necessarily cancel out viewers' prior knowledge of their host body. Nor would they be overwhelmed by the spectacle of their role body to the point of becoming stunned by it: the sight of the carnivalesque is all too familiar in opera/opera films. Nonetheless, the resultant discordance between prior knowledge and the spectacle opens up a space for negotiation. In this space is room for anyone who wants, or dares, to indulge in polymorphous desires and identification to do just that, with respect to the films' narrative and performance of cross-sex masquerades. In so doing, such viewers would imbue the film's themes of compulsory heterosexuality with a polymorphous appeal. This is not to repudiate the fact that *The Love Eterne* features a narrative progression favouring a heterosexual closure, but to point out that the films' gender-bending activities can generate subject-positions other than heteronormative ones. Nuances of performance become especially pertinent for viewers seeking alternative, even oppositional,

modes of identification. The narrative interstices simultaneously opened up and covered over by cross-gender *biaoyan*s allow for this. They also permit all sorts of readings, including against-the-grain ones. The love story's overtly heterosexual slant therefore cannot foreclose on alternative or oppositional readings. At face value, the love story may well accede to compulsory heterosexuality, but its narrativisation and performance can produce (unintended) subtexts. In *The Love Eterne*, carnivalesque comedy is in the air most when actresses Ling and Loh are concurrently male on screen. The double entendres that Zhu the cross-dressed scholar uses to convey 'his' desire for Liang have the effect of confusing Liang. Bursting into an angry song, Liang (played by a woman) scolds Zhu, 'I am not a female!' *The Love Eterne* is therefore at most almost a heterosexual love story.

NOTES

1. For a detailed study of this subgenre of Chinese-language musical films, see Tan See-Kam, 'Huangmei Opera Films, Shaw Brothers and Ling Bo: Chaste Love-Stories, Genderless Cross-Dressers and Sexless Gender-Plays?', *Jumpcut: A Review of Contemporary Media*, no. 49 (Spring 2007): <www.ejumpcut.org>.

2. See Wang-ngai Siu, *Chinese Opera: Images and Stories* (Vancouver: University of British Columbia Press, 1997), 22–23.

3. According to the film's production notes, the legend originated in folklores around the time of the Eastern Jin Dynasty (317–420). It first appeared in print during the Song Dynasty (960–1279), while theatrical adaptations appeared only during the Yuan Dynasty (1271–1368). By the time of the Republic (founded in 1911), there were some twenty to thirty opera librettos based on the legend in circulation. *Nanguo*, no. 59 (1963): <66.216.18.55/%7Elingboh/web/drama/Eterne/Eterne01.htm> (25 December 2002). *Nanguo* was Shaw Brothers' in-house film journal. It carried information on Shaw Brothers productions in Mandarin and English. Its English title is *Southern Screen*.

4. Ibid.

5. *Nanguo*, no. 65 (1963): <66.216.18.55/%7Elingboh/web/drama/Eterne/Eterne07.htm> (25 December 2002).

6. See *Nanguo*, no. 63 (1963): <66.216.18.55/%7Elingboh/web/drama/Eterne/Eterne06.htm> (25 December 2002); *Nanguo*, no. 68 (1963): <66.216.18.55/%7Elingboh/web/info/shaw

shaw01.htm> (25 December 2002); and *Nanguo*, no. 72 (1964): <66.216.18.55/%7Elingboh/web/drama/Eterne/Eterne10.htm> (25 December 2002).

7. Rick Lyman, 'Watching Movies with Ang Lee: Crouching Memory, Hidden Heart', *New York Times*, 9 March 2001: <nytimes.qpass.com> (6 January 2002). In this feature article, Lyman gives the film's English title as *Love Eternal*. This title differs from that in the film's opening credit: *The Love Eterne*. The film's Chinese title is *Liang shanbo yu zhu yingtai*, not *Qi cai hu bu gui*, as reported by Lyman. *Qi cai hu bu gui* (known in English as *Eternal Love*) is the Chinese title of a Cantonese opera film, directed in 1966 by Li Tie and starring Josephine Xiao Fangfang and Chen Baozhu. The story for that film is not based on the Liang–Zhu legend.

8. Ibid.

9. Judith Butler, *Bodies that Matter: On the Discursive Limits of 'Sex'* (London: Routledge, 1993), 239.

10. Caroline Evans and Lorraine Gamman, 'The Gaze Revisited, or Reviewing Queer Viewing', in *A Queer Romance: Lesbians, Gay Men and Popular Culture*, ed. Paul Burston and Colin Richardson (London: Routledge, 1995), 46.

11. See, for example, '1963 belongs to Ling Boh!' (25 October 1963; source of original publication and author unknown): <66.216.18.55/%7Elingboh/web/lingpo/lingpo631025_2.htm> (25 December 2002).

12. See Tan See-Kam, 'The Cross-gender Performances of Yam Kim-Fei, or the Queer Factor in Postwar Hong Kong Cantonese Opera/Opera Films', in *Queer Asian Cinema: Shadows in the Shade*, ed. Andrew Grossman (New York: Harrington Park Press, 2000), 201–212.

13. *Nanguo*, no. 92 (1965): <66.216.18.55/%7Elingboh/web/drama/perfumed/perfumed01.htm> (25 December 2002).

14. Mikhail Bakhtin, *Rabelais and His World*, trans. Hélène Iswolsky (Cambridge, MA: MIT Press, 1973).

15. John C. H. Wu, 'The Individual in Political and Legal Traditions', in *The Chinese Mind: Essentials of Chinese Philosophy and Culture*, ed. Charles A. Moore (Honolulu: University of Hawaii Press, 1968), 340–364. See also Tani Barlow, 'Theorizing Woman: Funü, Guojia, Jiating (Chinese Woman, Chinese State, Chinese Family)', in *Body, Subject and Power in China*, ed. Angela Zito and Tani Barlow (Chicago: University of Chicago Press, 1994), 253–289.

16. Keith McMahon, 'The Classic "Beauty–Scholar" Romance and the Superiority of the Talented Woman', in Zito and Barlow, *Body, Subject and Power*, 227–252.

17. See Lu Yanguang, *100 Celebrated Chinese Women* (Singapore: Asiapac Publication, 2001), 21 and 25.

18. Ibid., 1, 11 and 55.

19. Judith Butler, *Excitable Speech: A Politics of the Performative* (New York: Routledge, 1997), 160.

20. Richard Ekins, 'The Career Path of the Male Femaler', in *Blending Genders: Social Aspects of Cross-dressing and Sex-changing*, ed. Richard Ekins and Dave King (London: Routledge, 1996), 39–47.

21. Jo Riley, *Chinese Theater and the Actor in Performance* (Cambridge: Cambridge University Press, 1997), 117.

22. Susan Sontag, 'Notes on Camp,' in *A Susan Sontag Reader* (London: Penguin, 1983), 108.

23. Judith Butler, *Gender Trouble: Feminism and the Subversion of Identity* (London: Routledge, 1990) 25.

24. Riley, *Chinese Theater*, 115.

21   *Not One Less*: The Fable of a Migration

Rey Chow

In one of his more recent films, *Happy Time* (1999), Zhang Yimou has inserted a remarkable scene that may be cited as a summation of his consistently dialectical treatment of visuality. At the home of the fat lady who just received a marriage proposal from her suitor, Lao Zhao, we encounter the blind girl, left in her care by her previous husband, who has moved to Shenzhen. In order to impress her suitor, the fat lady, who normally treats this stepdaughter rather cruelly, serves the latter some ice cream. But this gesture of kindness lasts only as long as the brief duration of the suitor's visit. Once he has left, the fat lady snatches the cup of ice cream from the blind girl and, scolding her as someone not worthy of such a luxury item, puts it back in the refrigerator.

Although it is possible to derive a moral lesson from this scene (for instance, by seeing it as yet another illustration of the lamentable condition of human hypocrisy), what is much more interesting is the suggestive reading it offers of the semiotics and politics of seeing – indeed, of sight itself as a kind of material sign around which specific values are implicitly enacted and negotiated. The fat lady's opportunistic manner of handling the ice cream indicates that sight, as what renders the world accessible, is not a natural but an artificial phenomenon, one that is, moreover, eminently subject to manipulation. The fat lady consciously performs to Lao Zhao's sight by making an appearance of her own generosity; yet once that sight is no longer around, there is no need for this performance to continue. Sight, in other words, is not a medium of transparency or a means of understanding, as we commonly think; rather, it is a surveillance mechanism installed on (other) human bodies, which means that one must behave appropriately when someone else is watching, but that otherwise there is no intrinsic reason to do so. What Lao Zhao 'sees' is actually the opposite of what he thinks he has obviously seen or understood. The fat lady's

behaviour is disturbing because, contrary to what most people believe, she has not internalised or naturalised the function of sight in such a way as to make it her own conscience, her *automatised self-surveillance*. Sight remains for her something of an arbitrary and external function, a device to be exploited for her own benefit. As the film goes on to show, with the events that unfold around the blind girl, sight can also be a disability, an elaborate network of mendacity devised to fool others that ends up, ironically, trapping oneself more and more deeply. Having sight is not necessarily the opposite of being blind but may under some circumstances become an extension of blindness, a kind of handicap that distorts or obstructs reality as much as the physical inability to see.

This distinctive grasp of the materiality of a medium that has traditionally been associated with clarity, wisdom and transcendental vision continues to mark Zhang Yimou's films of the mid- to late 1990s and early 2000s, despite the rather misleading critical consensus that his recent films depart sharply from the early ones – *Red Sorghum* (1987), *Ju Dou* (1990) and *Raise the Red Lantern* (1991) – that made him internationally famous.[1] It is now often suggested that Zhang has more or less abandoned the Orientalist styles of the early classics, which portray a mythified timeless China in order to pander to the tastes of foreign devils, for a realist cinematic style that depicts simple people's lives in contemporary Chinese society. The well-known cultural critic Zhang Yiwu, for instance, has argued that this stylistic change, observed in films such as *The Story of Qiu Ju* (1993), *Keep Cool* (1997) and *The Road Home* (1999-2000), as well as *Not One Less* (1999–2000) and *Happy Time*, may be traceable to the changing trends in the mainland Chinese film industry, which has been compelled by the pressures of globalisation to produce a more inward-looking approach, centred on China's internal problems and aimed at a predominantly Chinese audience.[2] Having allegedly made such a change, Zhang Yimou has, it seems, finally been accepted and endorsed even by the Chinese authorities, once his most hostile critics, who not only consented to having him serve as the director of the unprecedented, internationally collaborative performance of Puccini's opera *Turandot* in Beijing in September 1998 (with Zubin Mehta as the conductor), but also appointed Zhang to film the official documentary showcasing Beijing in China's competition for hosting the 2008 Olympics. While this saga of how a native son who was first accused of selling out to the West is subsequently fully co-opted by his critics for purposes that are, strictly speaking, no less Orientalist, no less opportunistic and no less commodification driven, has to be dealt with in detail elsewhere, my point in bringing it up is simply to emphasise how the story of alternating rebuke and embrace that has followed Zhang's career, too, may itself be taken as an example of the power struggle over seeing and visuality in post-colonial post-modernity, a power struggle of which Zhang's work to date has provided some of the most provocative demonstrations.[3]

My aim, then, is to argue, in part through a reading of *Not One Less*, that the warm reception of Zhang's more realist films is perhaps as problematic as the hostile reactions to his early ones.

While the early films are consistently accused of Orientalist tendencies involving ungrounded fantasies, the realist ones are generally considered as a return to more authentic subject matter and a faithful documentary style. But as one critic, Shi Wen-hong, points out in relation to *Not One Less*, the subject matter of present-day poverty, too, can be exotic in the eyes of some (Western) audiences.[4] The valorisation of realism as an ethnographically more authentic/faithful representation of a culture remains, strictly speaking, part and parcel of an ideological legacy, in particular that accompanying the treatment of non-Western peoples. (One need only think of *National Geographic* to see my point.[5]) Indeed, the study of modern and contemporary China is so dominated by so-called realism that even the most imaginative writings and artworks, however avant-garde they might be, have tended to be read largely for factographic value, for making contributions to the production of empirical knowledge about China. This

critical proclivity towards realism in the institution of area studies is inseparable from the strategic targeting of non-Western political regimes during the Cold War, and the representational politics surrounding China remain tightly in its grip. If the preference for realist depictions belongs to a thoroughly politicised history of reading and viewing China (one in which the aesthetic qualities of works tend to be sidestepped or dismissed in order to legitimate the dogged attempts at information retrieval), then the critical, indeed laudatory, revaluation of a director such as Zhang in the form of 'Ah, he is finally becoming more realist!' must itself be subjected to rethinking.

As I will argue in the following reading of *Not One Less*, what is intriguing about Zhang's work is the possibility it offers for a critique of the historical import of the mediatised image, a critique that may have little to do with Zhang's personal intention *per se* but that nevertheless takes shape through the semiotic movement discernible in his handling of visuality. If Zhang has chosen more realist-looking locales, characters and happenings in comparison with the mythical stories of his early films,[6] his recent work nevertheless continues to deliver shrewd reflections on the politics of visuality and cultural identity, and their imbrications with the massively uneven effects of globalisation.

Such shrewd reflections have to do with Zhang's grasp of visuality as a second-order labour – labour not in the physical sense but in the form of cinematic and mediatised signification. Hence, strictly speaking, the early films displaying China's decrepitude were not only about poor peasants struggling against the injustice of life in the countryside but also about a process in which such struggles are transformed, through the film apparatus, into signs for a certain encounter, signs that convey the cross-cultural imaginary, 'Chineseness', to those watching it from the outside. Making these signs, building entertaining stories around them and rendering them visually appealing are for Zhang never a matter of realist reflectionism but always a matter of the specificities of film-making, of experimenting with colour, sound, time control and narrative. His critics, by contrast, have repeatedly ignored the materiality of this film-making process and insisted on the reality that is somehow always lying beyond it. For the latter, that reality is, of course, always China and its people, a

Not One Less

reality that 1) must, it is implied, direct and dictate how films should be made; 2) will always escape such framing; yet 3) must nonetheless continue to be used as a criterion for judging a film's merits.

In light of the hegemony of realist reflectionism in the field of China studies and of the obdurate moralism of his critics, it is interesting to consider the tactical adaptations Zhang makes in his evolving work.[7] As a way perhaps to distract and elude his critics' sight, he has been, over the past several years, making films that indeed seem more documentary-like in their contents and settings. Often, these films are about poor rural folk or *xiao shimin* (ordinary citizens) in big cities, whose lives are unglamorous but filled with hardships. Like *Red Sorghum*, *Ju Dou* and *Raise the Red Lantern*, these films are marked by Zhang's characteristic fascination with human endurance: the female characters in *Qiu Ju*, *The Road Home* and *Happy Time*, like those in the early films, stubbornly persist in their pursuit of a specific goal. But whereas Jiu'er, Judou, Songlian and Yan'er (the servant girl in *Raise the Red Lantern*) pay for their strength of character with their own lives or their sanity, the more contemporary female characters tend

to be successful in getting what they want. Similarly, in *Not One Less*, we witness a young girl's struggle against systemic indifference that ends happily. Whereas the earlier films seem to be exhibits of a bygone cultural system, sealed off with an exotic allure, a film such as *Not One Less* seems to offer hope. Is this indeed so?

The story of *Not One Less* is briefly as follows. At the primary school of an impoverished northern Chinese village (Shuiquan Village), a group of pupils are learning under difficult conditions. Their teacher, Mr Gao, has to go home to tend to his sick mother, and a thirteen-year-old girl from a neighbouring village, Wei Minzhi, is hired as his substitute for one month. Before leaving, Mr Gao advises Wei that quite a number of the pupils have been dropping out and instructs her to make sure that the remaining twenty-eight stay until he returns – 'not one less'. For her substitute teaching, Wei is promised 50 *yuan*. As she starts teaching, the pupils are not exactly co-operative, and Wei is confronted with various obstacles, including the relative lack of chalk, which she must use sparingly. One day, a boy named Zhang Huike fails to show up: his mother is ill and in debt, and can no longer afford his school fees, so the boy has been sent off to the city to look for work. Wei is determined to bring this pupil back. After a series of failed efforts at locating him, she succeeds in getting the attention of the manager of the city's television station, who arranges for her to make an appeal on a programme called 'Today in China'. Zhang Huike, who is washing dishes at a restaurant and sees Wei on TV, is moved to tears by Wei's appeal and turns himself in. Teacher and pupil return to the village with a crowd of reporters as well as a large supply of classroom materials and gift donations to the village from audiences who have watched the programme.

If stubbornness, persistence and endurance are human qualities that recur in Zhang's films, in *Not One Less* they take on the additional significance of being constituents of a humanism *vis-à-vis* an impersonal and inefficient official system, which is impotent in remedying the disastrous conditions of the village school. But how does this humanism express itself? Ironically, it does so through the very spirit of *productionism* that is, arguably, left over from official socialist propaganda, a productionism most clearly evident in the form of quantifiable accumulation (we recall the slogans of the Great Leap Forward period, for instance, during which the campaign for national well-being was promoted in terms of measurable units – so many tons of steel, so many tons of iron, so many tons of agricultural produce, etc.). As critics have reminded us, Wei Minzhi has come to Shuiquan Village to work for 50 *yuan*. Money, however, is only part of the issue. As the film progresses, we are made increasingly aware of the ideological as well as economic problem of how *resources* (of which money is an important though not the exclusive component) are (supposed) to be garnered and produced.

The clearest example of such productionism is the elementary method of counting and permuting adopted by Wei and her pupils to collect her bus fare for the city. Moving a brick (in a nearby factory), they discover, will earn them 15 cents, so to make 15 *yuan*, they should move one hundred bricks. Although this method of making money is based on a basic exchange principle – X units of labour = Y units of cash – its anachronism is apparent precisely in the mechanical correspondence established between two different kinds of values involved – concrete muscular/manual labour, on the one hand, and the abstract, general equivalent of money, on the

other. Sustained by the belief that if they contribute their labour they will indeed get the proper remuneration, the girl teacher and her pupils put themselves to work. At Zhang's hands, this simple event, what appears at first to be a mere narrative detail, turns out to be the manifestation of an entire economic rationale. As is demonstrated by the numerical calculations Wei and her pupils perform on the blackboard, this rationale is based not only on manual labour but also on the mathematics of simple addition, multiplication and division. At the heart of this rationale is an attributed continuum, or balance, between the two sides of the equation – a continuum whereby effort logically and proportionally translates into reward.

The tension and, ultimately, incompatibility between this earnest, one-on-one method of accounting, on the one hand, and the increasingly technologised, corporatised and abstract (that is, Enron-esque) method of value generation, on the other, is staged in a series of frustrations encountered by Wei, who is confronted each time with the futility of her own calculations. First, having earned 15 *yuan* for moving one hundred bricks, she and her pupils discover that the bus fare is actually 20.50 *yuan* each way. She attempts to solve this problem with her physical body, first by trying to get on the bus illegally and then, reluctantly, by walking. She is finally able to get a ride with a truck driver. On arriving in the city with 9 *yuan* (having already spent 6 *yuan* on two cans of Coca-Cola for her pupils), she has to agree to pay 2.50 *yuan* to the girl who was last with Zhang Huike before this girl will take her to the train station to look for him. The two girls end up paging him with a loudspeaker announcement around the station – to no avail. Wei spends the remainder of her money, 6.50 *yuan*, on ink, paper and a brush in order to write out her notices one by one, only to be told by a passer-by that such notices are useless and then to have them blown all over by the wind and swept away by the morning street-cleaners. By this time Wei has, at the passer-by's suggestion, made her way to the television station. After a long and stubborn wait, she finally succeeds in getting the attention of the manager.

Unlike her counterparts in Zhang's early films, women who have become immobilised in their rural positions or household status, Wei is the heroine of a migration, the migration from the countryside to the city. Even the countryside, however, is not the pure, original, primitive locale it is often imagined to be: the bus fare and the price of a can of Coke are but two examples of how a remote poor village, too, is part of the global capitalist circuit premised on commodified exchanges. If there is a residual primitivism here, it is, I'd contend, the ideology of accounting that Wei embodies, an ideology that has her believe that the expenditure of physical efforts will somehow be balanced off by due compensation and that, if she would try just a little harder, an equivalence can somehow be found between the two. To this extent, the film's title, *Yige dou bu neng shao* – literally, 'not even one can be allowed to be missing' – foregrounds this ideology of accounting in an unexpected manner: the ostensible goal of bringing back the missing child becomes simultaneously the epistemological frame over which a residual and familiar kind of passion unfurls – one that is organised around actual, countable bodies, in an economy in which resources are still imagined as successive, iterative units that can be physically stockpiled, expended or retrieved at will.[8] Wei's migration to the city is thus really a migration to a drastically different mode of value production, a mode in which, instead of the exertions of the physical body, it is the mediatised image that arbitrates, that not only achieves her goal for her but also has the ability to make resources proliferate beyond her wildest imagination.

Despite her strenuous physical efforts (moving bricks, walking, writing out notices longhand, sleeping on the street, starving, waiting for hours), it is when Wei transforms herself into an image on metropolitan television that she finally and effortlessly accomplishes her mission. As Wang Yichuan comments, there are two stories in Zhang's film: one is about 'human struggle'; the other has to do with the importance of money and television, and the emergence of the mediatised sign:

> Money has been playing a fundamental role throughout the entire film: it is closely linked to Wei Minzhi's job as a substitute teacher, her attempt to save chalk, the collective moving of bricks, her ride to the city, and her search [for the missing pupil] through television; what's more, money controls it all … . My sense is that the narrative structure of the entire film contains two stories: underneath the story about a girl as a substitute teacher lurks another story – the story about the magic of television or money … .

When the bumpkin-ish and flustered Wei Minzhi is brought before the TV screen by the program anchor as the interviewee making her appeal to the public, her bumpkin-ness and simplicity are no longer just bumpkin-ness and simplicity but instead turned into a powerful and conquering sign.[9]

The return to Shuiquan Village must therefore be understood as a post-migration event, when the system of value-making has been fundamentally altered, when the fatigued, confused and powerless figure of the girl herself has been transformed into an image signifying 'the rural population'. Recall how Wei's appeal is dramatised on television: she is featured on the programme 'Today in China', aimed explicitly at educating the metropolitan audiences about China's rural areas. As the anchor introduces the objectives of the programme, in the background appears a bucolic, bright-green lawn with pretty bluish hills in the distance and a clean white tricycle with flowers in front. This fantastical landscape, in stark contrast to the landscape of Shuiquan Village we have already seen, conjures the national imaginary by drawing attention to the plight of the countryside as an urgent social problem. Anonymous and unrelated TV consumers are thus interpellated as 'the Chinese people' and, although they have never met the villagers in the flesh – how materially deprived they are, how hard they must work to keep surviving, and so forth – the effect of Wei-the-image is such that it forges 'meaningful links' among this network of strangers at the speed of virtuality.

Once the rural population has been disseminated as a televised image, charitable donations pour in, and the return of Wei and Zhang to the village is accompanied by a plenitude of supplies, including especially colour chalk of various kinds, which allow the students to practise writing a character each on the blackboard. As well, this return is accompanied by eager reporters with cameras, intent on 'documenting' the village and its inhabitants with a relentless, henceforth infinitely reproducible gaze. In a public sphere made up of electronically transmitted signals, virtuality transforms exponentially into cash, in ways that would never have been achievable by the earnest logic of calculating resources on which Wei and her students had sought to rely. The closing credits offer a glimpse of the positive outcomes of this migration towards the image: Zhang Huike's family debt is paid off; Wei is able to return to her own village; the girl pupil who is a fast runner has gone on to join the county's track meet, and the village is now renamed Shuiquan Village of Hope. Finally, we read this important message: 'One million children drop out of school because of poverty in China every year. With financial assistance from various sources, about fifteen percent of them are able to return to school.'[10]

If what Zhang has provided with his early films is an imaginary ethnographic treatment of China – as a decrepit primitive culture – what he accomplishes in *Not One Less* is, to my mind, a similar kind of ethnographic experiment, albeit *within* Chinese society itself. What is often criticised as the Orientalist gaze in Zhang's early films, a gaze that produces China as exotic, erotic, corrupt, patriarchally repressive and so forth for the pleasurable consumption of Western audiences, is here given a thought-provoking twist to become none other than the national gaze. Whereas the object of the Orientalist gaze in the early films is arguably an ahistorical 'China', in *Not One Less* that object is more specifically China's 'rural population' living in wretched conditions, especially children deprived of education. In the latter case, the similarly fetishising and exploitative tendency of the media is underwritten not by the discourse of Orientalism (read: depraved Western imperialist practice) but instead by the oft-repeated and clichéd discourse of national self-strengthening and concern for future generations ('Save the children!').[11] These two seemingly opposed discourses are affined paradoxically through the magic of the image, which not only supersedes older notions of the exchange value of labour but eradicates the validity of manual labour and production altogether. The image asserts itself now as the indomitable way of creating resources, displacing an obsolete method such as moving one brick = fifteen cents to the abject peripheries of contemporary Chinese society.

This migration towards the dominance of the image, which Zhang explores through an apparently more realist contemporary story is, therefore, in tandem with the experimental attitude expressed towards visuality in his early films. The humanistic impulses that guide the narrative, leading it towards the telos of collective good, are at the same time punctured by a firm refusal on Zhang's part to idealise or eulogise the image, including especially that of Wei making her sentimental plea. Instead, the latter

is consciously presented as a media event in the new information economy. The image *works*, as it were, by deflating the currency of (human) work. Seen in this light, *Not One Less* rejoins the explorations of the non-urban others in the Chinese films of the 1980s (*Yellow Earth* [Chen Kaige, 1984], *On the Hunting Ground* [Tian Zhuangzhuang, 1985], *Sacrificed Youth* [Zhang Nuanxin, 1985], *Horse Thief* [Tian Zhuangzhuang, 1986], *A Good Woman* [Huang Jianzhong, 1986], *King of the Children* [Chen Kaige, 1987], just to mention a handful), albeit with a different emphasis. In the 1980s, when cultural introspection took shape in the aftermath of the Cultural Revolution, film offered the Fifth Generation directors and their contemporaries the exciting possibility of experimenting with technological reproducibility and artful defamiliarisation. As China becomes globalised at the turn of the twenty-first century, the anthropological impulses of the 1980s films have given way to a sociological one. From an investment in, or a fascination with, China's otherness, filmmaking at the hands of Zhang has shifted to a seasoned and cautionary approach to visuality as social regimentation, discipline and surveillance, but above all as *benevolence-driven coercion*.

In dramatising this trans-valuation of the labour performed over quantifiable, slowly cumulative time (bricks, hours, days, dollars, written notices) into an instantaneous spectacle, *Not One Less* stages a schism between two irreconcilable kinds of philosophical trajectories. There is, on the one hand, the trajectory opened in accordance with a pro-Enlightenment telos of a better and brighter future, towards which human will power and media capability inadvertently join forces. On the other hand, as is demonstrated by the usurpatory nature of the mediatised image and its tendency to cannibalise human labour, we are confronted with an aggressive radicalisation of the terms of communication, communal relations and, increasingly in the case of the People's Republic of China, communism's own political agenda. The image's limitless potential, in this regard, cannot be seen naively as an ally to human will power or simply as its latest instrument. Rather, its smooth and speedy superficiality announces a new collective reality to which human will power is likely to find itself increasingly subordinated, and to which human beings, especially those struggling against any kind of social inequity, will need to resort just to be recognised. As the ending of the film shows, it is to the image that people will give their concern and compassion, and it is the image, rather than the actual suffering human body, that now generates capital and, with it, social influence and political power. Instead of propelling us towards the telos of an improved future, then, this other philosophical trajectory lays bare the expanse and intensity of a new kind of oppression.

This dialectical narrative method, which is as astute in its cynicism (in the etymological sense of scepticism) towards the mediatised image as it is skilled in conveying a warm, sentimental story, remains Zhang's unique contribution. His work is about the relationship between labour and the image, about the transit from an economy in which humans can still make the world with their physical bodies to one in which the image has taken over that function, leaving those bodies in an exotic but also superfluous condition (a condition in which being 'real' simply means being stuck, that is, unable to trans-valuate into cash).

As in *Happy Time*, the ability to see, the availability of sight and the possibility of becoming a spectacle that are made such palpable events in contemporary Chinese life are turned by Zhang into the ingredients of a fable with a certain moral. But the notion of fable is rooted in the process of fabulation, and the moral at stake in Zhang's work is often elsewhere from the place at which his critics try to see it. However artificial, being and becoming imaged is, his recent work says, something no one can afford not to desire; yet the ever-expanding capacities for seeing and, with them, the infinite transmigrations of cultures – national, ethnic, rural – into commodified electronic images are part and parcel of an emergent regime of value-making that is as utterly ruthless as it is utterly creative. With the harsh *and* flexible materiality of this regime, critics of contemporary Chinese cinema have yet, seriously, to come to terms.

ACKNOWLEDGMENTS

Thanks to Chris Berry, Yomi Braester and Yvonne Leung for their assistance with this essay.

NOTES

1. See, for instance, the discussions of Zhang's evolving work in the special issue devoted to *Not One Less* entitled *Yige Dou Buneng Shao yingpian gean fenxi*, in *Aesthetics of Chinese Film: 1999* (*Zhongguo dianying*

meixue: 1999) (Beijing: Beijing guangbo xueyuan, 2000), and various discussions of the film in *Film Art* (*Dianying yishu*), nos. 1, 3 and 5 (2000).

2. See Zhang Yiwu, 'Once Again Imagining China: The Challenge of Globalization and the New "Inward-Looking Tendency" ' ('Zaidu xiangxiang Zhongguo: quanqiuhua de tiaozhan yu xin de "neixianghua"'), *Film Art* (*Dianying yishu*), no. 1 (2001): 16–21.

3. For a discussion of the implications of Orientalism raised by Zhang's early work, see Rey Chow, *Primitive Passions: Visuality, Sexuality, Ethnography, and Contemporary Chinese Cinema* (New York: Columbia University Press, 1995), Part 2, Chapter 4, and Part 3. For related discussions, including Zhang's responses to some of his critics, see the interviews with Zhang regarding the making of *Not One Less* in the following: *Aesthetics of Chinese Film: 1999* (*Zhongguo dianying meixue: 1999*), 29–35; *The Fifth Generation of Chinese Filmmakers in the 1990s* (*Jiushi niandai de diwudai*), ed. Yang Yuanying, Pan Hua and Zhang Zhuan (Beijing: Beijing guangbo xueyuan chubanshe, 2000), 121–127. For general interest, see also *Zhang Yimou: Interviews*, ed. Frances Gateward (Jackson: University of Mississippi Press, 2001).

4. See Shi Wenhong, 'The Sadness of *Not One Less*' ('Yige Dou Buneng Shao de aichou'), *Film Critics Quarterly* (*Yingpingren jikan*), nos. 6, 7 (2000).

5. For a sustained critique of the magazine's politics of representing non-Western cultures, see Catherine A. Lutz and Jane L. Collins, *Reading National Geographic* (Chicago: University of Chicago Press, 1993).

6. The cast of *Not One Less*, for instance, was made up of amateur actors, many of whom were actual villagers from the film's location. However, as Xiaoling Zhang points out, 'the whole suggestion of reality is entirely artificial: the school was chosen from a few dozen schools in that area, the eighteen pupils were selected from among thousands of pupils, and the girl playing Wei Minzhi was picked from twenty thousand girls, in an auditioning process which lasted more than half a month'. See Zhang, 'A Film Director's Criticism of Reform China: A Close Reading of Zhang Yimou's *Not One Less*', *China Information*, XV, no. 2 (2001): 138.

7. As one critic, Zeng Guang, writes:

Under the current political system, he [Zhang Yimou] feels that the biggest difference between himself and directors from foreign countries, Hong Kong, and Taiwan lies in the fact that 'when I receive a film script, the first thing I think about is not whether there will be an investor for the film, but how I can make the kind of film I want with the approval of the authorities.

This passage is cited as the epigraph in Sheldon H. Lu, 'Understanding Chinese Film Culture at the End of the Twentieth Century: The Case of *Not One Less* by Zhang Yimou', *Journal of Modern Literature in Chinese*, 4, no. 2 (2001): 123–142.

8. Note that although the film was adopted from Shi Xiangsheng's story 'A Sun in the Sky' ('Tian shang you ge taiyang'), *Feitian*, no. 6 (1997), Zhang changed the title to one that highlights the act of counting (bodies).

9. Wang Yichuan, 'Civilization and Civilized Barbarity' ('Wenming yu wenming de yeman'), *Aesthetics of Chinese Film: 1999* (*Zhongguo dianying meixue, 1999*), 67–75; the cited passages are on pages 71 and 73; loose translation from the Chinese is mine. This is the only reading I have come across that identifies money and the media as the decisive issues of the film.

10. Hu Ke writes that Zhang's narrative method is like an 'ad for charity'. See his 'Documentary Record and Fictional Construct' ('Jishi yu xugou'), *Aesthetics of Chinese Film: 1999* (*Zhongguo dianying meixue: 1999*), 41–49; the point about 'ad for charity' is on page 42. This view is shared by other critics: see, for instance, Wang Ailing, 'Obedient Children' ('Tinghua de haizi'), in *A Look Back at Hong Kong Cinema of 1999* (*1999 Xianggang dianying huigu*), ed. Wang Ailing (Hong Kong: Xianggang dianying pinglun xuehui, 2000), 301–302; Valerie Wong, '*Not One Less*', *Cinemaya*, no. 45 (1999): 20–21. This type of reading is not incorrect, but the main problem I have with it is that these critics tend to read Zhang's film as a completed realist *message* rather than as a process and a structure in which a dialectical understanding (of the changes brought to Chinese society by the new media) is being actively produced. For an opposite type of reading that sees Zhang's film not as propaganda but as a laudable piece of social criticism, see Zhang, 'A Film Director's Criticism of Reform China'.

11. For the latter point, as well as an informative discussion of Zhang's film in relation to recent conditions of film production and reception in mainland China, see Lu, 'Understanding Chinese Film Culture at the End of the Twentieth Century'.

22   *The Personals*: Backward Glances, Knowing Looks and the Voyeur Film

Margaret Hillenbrand

INTRODUCTION: RE-WATCHING *THE PERSONALS*

The opening shot of Chen Kuo-fu's *The Personals* (1998) shows a red-hued sun setting over a lake, its command of the urban vista in the distance making it look, to all intents and purposes, like a mammoth eye spying on the city. The next shot reinforces the impression by superimposing on this sun the image of a retina, filmed in extreme close-up during examination, and then washed in different colours as the sequence segues into montage. The backdrop for this montage is an ophthalmologist's clinic, and in almost the first words of the script, the eye doctor – Du Jiazhen, the protagonist of the film – tells her patient that tears serve two functions: 'One is to moisten the membrane of the eye; the other is a response to our emotions.' In other words, the eye is both a mechanism for seeing and a window on the soul, a duality that Du will explore in the rest of the film as she gives up her job as an expert in the science of seeing in order to probe what lies behind the eyes. Without the protection of her white gown, however, Du's status quickly shifts and she becomes fair game for other eyes – a transition made explicit in the next sequence, which shows the camera peering into the hospital lavatory, panning left and right in search of its quarry, before finally trailing Du into her own bathroom and lingering intently on her half-clad figure. This brief prologue to the movie ends as Du wipes the steamed-up mirror to reveal her face to viewer and camera, as if in a gesture of surrender to the latter's gaze.

These opening minutes of *The Personals* use the eye – as a shape, as a symbol, as a physiological function – to create a preface to the linked preoccupations of the film: voyeurism, eavesdropping, surveillance and self-exposure.[1] This preface works syntagmatically, through the studied juxtaposition of shots and scenes in which the ocular motif is deployed in its successive separate guises. The result is a manifesto of sorts, an invitation to read the film that follows as a study of life in a panoptic, even panauditory world. And the remainder of the movie does not disappoint. Recounting Du's search for love through the personal columns, it presents the rituals of courtship and desire – and, by extension, human interaction across the board – as a regimen of mutual surveillance. Du's advertisement attracts a horde of suitors, whom she interviews one by one in a coffee shop, probing their eligibility, and their secrets, just as they consume her greedily with their eyes – while the camera hovers keenly over the entire proceedings. These highly coloured encounters, which range from the tragic-comic through the suggestive to the burlesque, are spliced in between more monochrome, melancholic segments that show Du either sharing heartfelt confessions with her former university professor, or home alone weeping into her ex-lover's answering machine. These bridging passages, which reveal that Du's quest for love is really a form of therapy for her broken heart, are filmed with equal attention to the encroachment of external eyes and ears on moments of intimacy. The denouement, in which Du discovers that her ex-lover's wife has overheard every desolate word of her phone messages, drives the point home with finality. Indeed, the movie's ultimate point is the interchangeability of the spy and the spied-upon, and the implication of us all in the gradual sullying of private life.

Despite the clarity of its intent, however, the status of *The Personals* as a study of invaded space has so far escaped real scrutiny. Nick Kaldis's recent paper, the only substantial analysis of the film so far, makes no mention of voyeur-as-theme, preferring instead to read the film as a vaguely reactionary lament to an imagined heterosexual monogamy of yore, when men were solid types and women did not need to advertise themselves in newspapers.[2]

Ru-shou Robert Chen, meanwhile, focuses on the unusually skilful marketing of the film, which won it decent box-office returns among an audience mostly jaded by Taiwanese cinema.[3] Shelly Kraicer gets closest to voyeurism, raising the subject tantalisingly in a review of 1999, but the brevity of the review form prevents him from doing justice to the full complexity of the subject.[4]

The present essay spotlights Chen Kuo-fu's filmic exposition of what Foucault termed the 'techniques of surveillance'. It argues that *The Personals* sets out to present itself as a 'voyeur-reflexive' film, a movie that – according to Norman Denzin – uses notions of scopophilia to ponder the role played by cinema in a society under watch.[5] Chen works from the premise that voyeurism is interactive: a changing dialectic, willingly entered into, between those who watch and those who receive the gaze. Our lives are nothing without an audience, *The Personals* suggests; and, just as Chen's protagonists compulsively court attention, so does the director himself repeat the theme metatextually through the cinematic comparisons he solicits with virtually every voyeur film in the canon. Yet this need to be known – and known, moreover, in our most intimate moments – is ultimately an invitation to prurience and the social management of desire. This focus on surveillance and privacy under siege begs exploration from different cultural perspectives. In some senses, the film seems to hint at the old truism that China has no sense of personal space; but at the same time, it also homes in on the emerging surveillance society in post-martial law Taiwan, where tabloid journalism and personal data collection on a grand scale are squeezing the dignity of the individual on all sides. Yet *The Personals* also reveals the extent to which cinema anywhere is complicit in subtle regimes of social control, providing a space for infinite others to watch, compare and pass judgment. Indeed, the film proves itself most incisive of all when it suggests the ways in which cinema has made watchers of us all, transforming itself from a medium that told its audiences how to live into one that incites these audiences to exercise such control over one another.

LINES OF SIGHT: VOYEURISM IN *THE PERSONALS*

Throughout the film, this notion of voyeurism as interactive is explored across three linked axes: Du

Jiazhen and her suitors, Du Jiazhen alone and the workings of the camera across all these interactions – through which, of course, the audience becomes fully implicated in the process. At first sight, it is probably Du's assignations in the coffee shop that provide the most conducive forum for this dialectic between voyeurism and self-exposure. Chen Kuo-fu presents these encounters as a kind of candid camera slideshow, in which a troupe of undesirables shuffle into shot one after the other, and reveal their unvarnished sexual selves with barely a by-your-leave. The foot-fetishist who struggles to tear his eyes from under the table; the sweaty married man in search of no-strings sex; the would-be pornographer who wants a cinematic muse; the betelnut-chewing machinist so desperate for a wife that he proposes before the introductions are out of the way; the personable musician with a 'thing' for nurses' uniforms that he cannot stop mentioning: with few exceptions, Du's suitors are both 'perverse' – at least in their deviation from prevailing socio-sexual norms – and cheerfully uninhibited about it. Indeed, the readiness with which they confide in her suggests that the rendezvous, for them, is as much about the pleasure of getting emotionally naked in front of a stranger as it is a quest for the fulfilment of their desires. Each date is orchestrated around the climactic moment of revelation, the point at which these psychological flashers – for that is what they are – expose themselves to Du's scandalised eyes.

Yet to see the heroine as the unwilling recipient of these intimacies would be to misread Chen's take on the voyeuristic impulse. The coffee-shop sequences work because they are predicated on symbiosis, on the relationship of shared pleasure that obtains between the watcher and the watched. Du Jiazhen, with her doe eyes and heightened powers of empathy, is the perfect receptacle for the risqué confidence: combining innocence with understanding, her screen presence pries secrets from their hiding places more effectively than any interrogation. More to the point, perhaps, the movie dwells deliberately on her sexual curiosity, on the compulsion/repulsion she feels towards her suitors and their erotic lives. Again and again, the film displays her torn between outrage at some indecent proposal – and a prurient desire to know more that keeps her rooted to her seat. For Du, the dates become a whistle-stop sentimental education, a means of learning more about the sexual world without giving any of herself away; indeed, she even changes her name in an attempt to safeguard her privacy. Du herself knows that her motives are suspect – and have little to do with finding a husband – but the curiosity has become obsessive. Small wonder that she winces in embarrassment when a blind suitor turns the tables on her by announcing that he was once her patient and that he knows her real name.

In other words, then, the coffee-shop scenes that give *The Personals* its basic structural grammar are about reciprocity: a gentle frisson crackles between watcher and watched, and both are, at base, aware that they are performing a service for the other. Yet the ultimate beneficiary of this performance is, of course, the viewer; and in this sense, it is we who are the true voyeurs. Certainly, Chen Kuo-fu's cinematography proves adept at inveigling the audience into this compromising position, both in relation to the suitors, and to Du herself. Most obviously, perhaps, it is the former who are laid out for our delectation. Each candidate for Du's affections is introduced through a framing shot, tagged with a label in the lower right-hand corner that lists the man's name, age and occupation. These labels create an irresistible impression of taxonomical analysis – a sort of butterfly-collecting, in which recherché specimens are pinned under glass so that they can be better inspected. Chen's use of several non-professional actors, whose anonymity heightens the curio factor, is surely deliberate here. Just as important are the carefully eclectic ways in which Chen shoots these scenes. Thus we have shot/reverse shot (betelnut boy), straight-on medium long shot, shifting from one to the other (foot fetishist), cutting from face to face without shot/reverse shot (the philanthropist who woos Du with a falsetto song), high camera angle (the personal defence devices salesman who attempts to flog Du his wares), and so on. Up to a point, this variety is simply expedient, a strategy for keeping the interview format fresh across numerous repetitions. But at a deeper level, the cinematography of the coffee-shop encounters is at once exhibitionist and voyeuristic, showcasing the director's inventiveness at the same time as it blatantly turns the dates into a spectacle. When viewed as discrete, self-contained cinematic moments, the individual encounters look innocent enough; but as a collective, they become oddly redolent of the nature documentary:

expertly informative, but based on a fundamental disparity between man and beast. Indeed, as the camera manoeuvres itself around the coffee shop in search of different vantage points from which to film the dates, it turns increasingly anthropological, recording the mating rituals enacted before it in ways that begin to seem clinical, even dehumanising. Just like the labels, Chen's cinematography becomes a mode of inspecting oddball specimens – 'look how weird *this* one is!' – that encourages the viewer to pass judgment on what he or she sees.

By contrast, the camera's treatment of Du Jiazhen seems infinitely kinder. She acts as the mediator between us and the 'wildlife' that is her suitors – the presenter of the show, as it were – and thus although she is in the field with them, she remains one of us, more watcher than watched. Yet at the same time, and in keeping with her camera-friendly role, she is continually offered up, in the words of Shelly Kraicer, for 'our viewing pleasure'. In a way, this is nothing more than simple crowd-pleasing. Du Jiazhen, played by Rene Liu, has a photogenic face, and Chen Kuo-fu conspires to turn her into a visual treat, through high-key lighting, soft focus, lingering close-up and all the manifold devices of point of view. But just as the peccadilloes and physical quirks of the suitors (betelnut-stained lips, compulsive blinking, sweaty palms, desperate eyes) encourage a kind of punitive voyeurism, so does Du's appeal, and the delicate expressiveness of Liu's acting, promote the opposite: voyeurism as empathy and approval. We become the visual consumers of every reaction registered on her face, from compassion to guilt to the shivers of distaste; but the 'normality' of her desires is meant to make this process one of identification. Du, too, is a self-exposing spectacle, but one that we are told to relish, both aesthetically and morally.

These coffee-shop scenes, then, explore the dialectic between voyeurism and exposure on many levels: the suitors denude themselves in front of Du, she watches transfixed while all the time providing a performance of her own, and we, via the camera, play the fly on the wall that gets to savour the entire show. The sequences with Du alone, however, push this exploration along rather different lines. These solitary scenes are shot, by and large, in her apartment, a setting as chilly and inhospitable as the coffee shop is warm-hued and candlelit. Here, Du disgorges her misery to her lover's answering machine, in many ways as oblivious to the recklessness of her confidences as the suitors on whom she turns such a clear-eyed gaze. Just like them, she craves an audience, and the process of self-exposure becomes, correspondingly, an end in itself; the fact that the phone is repeatedly ignored, a mirror of her own rejection of the suitors, troubles her far less than we might expect. Indeed, throughout these scenes, Du moves unblinkingly into the role vacated by her would-be lovers; and in this sense, Kaldis's observation that the 'comedic scenes clash awkwardly against the privacy and intimacy of the scenes revealing Du's emotional suffering'[6] misses the deep structural similarities that transect the film. The mood may be more sombre (chirpy extra-diegetic music recedes, the colours bleach and jokiness vanishes), but the dialectic between self-exposure and surveillance remains the same.

If anything, in fact, the theme of surveillance is drummed out more forcefully when Du is filmed alone. At the surface level, Du's 'voyeur' is her ex-lover's wife – this time an eavesdropper rather than peeping Tom, a permutation on the theme that gives the technologies of spying a broader sensory remit. That Du's nemesis should become privy to her most intimate secrets seems a revengeful twist: Du has used her suitors as therapy, without much intention of pursuing marriage, and now she in her turn becomes the prey of another wounded soul in search of similarly vicarious consolation. Yet at the same time, and in much the same way as the suitors before her, Du seems to derive a certain pleasure from her own unmasking. When her ex-lover's wife finally answers the phone and begins to speak, Du is so stunned that she hangs up; but when the wife calls back moments later, she picks up the phone in state of high nervous excitement. Curiosity about her rival mingles with a deeper gratification that she has had some kind of audience for her torment, without which her existence has begun to seem forlorn and meaningless. The illicit thrills of voyeurism begin to pall as the peeping Tom begins to hunger for some limelight herself, and the positions of watcher and watched – the successive seizing and abnegation of control – are prone to slippage. The result is a social world in which privacy is neither available nor, for that matter, particularly desired.

This point becomes all too clear when we consider the ways in which the film's cinematography inculpates us, the audience, in this process of attrition. Nowhere in *The Personals* is this more obvious than in Du's apartment, where the camera abandons all pretence of neutrality and openly declares itself to be a device for surveillance. For a start, and in keeping with her identity switch, Du is made every bit the specimen in these scenes: no longer the darling of the camera, she is bathed in cold, fluorescent light, and her face left drained and pallid. This faint air of laboratory conditions is reinforced by the telling way in which her apartment is made to resemble a hospital ward. The colour white predominates, from the walls to her dressing gown, but is nowhere more striking than the bed itself – always filmed from above – with its reading lamp poised overhead like surgical lighting, and the anguished body of Du beneath, prone on an expanse of white sheets. This connection between the snooping camera and the hospitalised patient reaches its apotheosis in the scene where Du tells her lover's answering machine that she has recently undergone an abortion – principally, she indicates, because her lover had vanished and she felt she had no other choice. The intense whiteness of the room, Du's terrified sobs and the overbearing presence of the camera above the bed works to re-create the scene of Du's operation before our eyes. The result is perhaps the most grimly voyeuristic moment in the entire film.

Coming a very close second in this contest, however, is the sequence right at the end of the film when Du finally discovers the truth about her lover's disappearance. Here, the camera becomes more predatory than ever, stalking Du in the privacy of her bedroom, and then feasting its eyes quite shamelessly on her shock and misery. As if to signal its voyeuristic intent, the sequence begins with a momentary flashback to the eye washed in blue and orange that loomed large in the film's opening montage; only this time, the eye is dilated as if in a state of arousal. Next, we glimpse Du, captured through the window of her apartment by the camera that lurks like a peeper in the dark outside. Du is on the telephone, oblivious to the high irony of her situation, telling her lover's answering machine about her self-disgust at playing the voyeur on the dates: 'They tell me their private stuff, their secrets, without the slightest reservation – it doesn't feel like conversation, it feels like snooping. They're in the light, and I'm in the dark.' All the while, the camera pans slowly across the window, the bead curtains hung over the window quivering as in response to its presence, until Du is gradually pushed out of shot. She appears a split second later, this time in a long mirror that is angled towards the camera and frames her exactly as the window did earlier, only now the dimensions are fashioned like a keyhole, complete with blurred edges to the image. Again, the camera zooms in purposefully, as the lover's wife informs Du that her husband has been killed in a plane crash. The sequence ends with the camera moving into close-up to capture every conflicted expression on Du's face, as the wife tells her rival that the husband was on his way back to Taiwan after ending their marriage so that he could be with Du and their child. Just like Du before her, the lover's wife is candid about her conduct: she is a cruel 'eavesdropper' who deliberately waited by the phone so that she could discover the details of her husband's affair. For both women, watching and listening has brought cheap thrills, but also a lingering revulsion at themselves that can only expiate itself through some gesture of confession or exposure. Only the camera, it would seem, is immune from this remorse.

The Personals

THE PERSONALS: AN 'ESSAY' ON THE GAZE

But if the camera does, indeed, implicate the audience in its doings, then what does Chen Kuo-fu's film have to tell us about ourselves and, moreover, the lives we lead in a society under constant watch? Chen's dialectic of surveillance and self-exposure, the mutual implication of watcher and watched, implies more than anything else the impossibility of privacy – and more pertinently, perhaps, the failure to mourn its absence. In some ways, therefore, it is tempting to read the film as a meditation on the lack of a secluded sphere for selfhood in the traditional Chinese worldview, which has tended to value the virtues of the public sphere (*gong*) over the more dubious pleasures of private life (*si*). Popular pundits have been quick to draw attention to the pejorative connotations associated with the modern coinage *yinsi* (privacy), and its related terms such as *sixin* (selfish motives), *sitong* (illicit intercourse or adultery) and *zisi* (selfishness).[7] The perception that the Chinese-speaking world has no culturally attested notion of privacy remains a well-circulated one, despite the best attempts of recent scholars to expose it as myth.[8] Viewed in this context, *The Personals* becomes an updated take on old tale, in which the whispering *hutong* (alleyways) of the past are replaced by mobile phones, answering machines, security cameras and the whole paraphernalia of a wired-in

society. The setting may be contemporary Taiwan rather than traditional China, but the same lack of a protected interior space, safe from prying eyes and ears, still apparently prevails.

In fact, contemporary Taiwan may provide a still more pertinent cultural context for *The Personals*. The freedoms enjoyed on the island since the lifting of martial law have been accompanied by stealthy but steady inroads into civil liberties via such insidious routes as smartcard ID projects, national fingerprint databases, illegal wiretapping and sundry other mechanisms deemed essential for the 'total information society' – a process that has been abetted by a lack of robust resistance at the grassroots level.[9] In more recent years, governmental surveillance has found itself an unlikely bedfellow in the media, whose decisive turn towards tabloidisation began around the time that *The Personals* was released. Here, as elsewhere, the reign of the tabloid has been predicated on the spread of technologies – satellite news gathering, live on-the-spot recording, multiple cable channels – that fuse immediacy, sensationalism and blanket coverage. This unholy alliance has colonised the entire media apparatus, from new-style gutter newspapers and gossip magazines to TV news bulletins and chat/call-in shows, and these different sectors of the industry routinely conspire to turn the doings of politicians and celebrities into full-blown causes célèbres. Inevitably, this 'news' is all about sex, and as such, it is rooted in the violation of individual privacy.

It is surely unarguable that *The Personals* can be viewed as a kind of cautionary tale for a society on the cusp of these changes. And most striking is the complicity of the general public in the new culture of surveillance, either through their failure to resist the incursions of a nosy bureaucracy, or via their unseemly appetite for gossip. Indeed, in this latter connection, Chen Kuo-fu's theme can be seen as life under watch far more generically; and all he needs for his exposition is a city, its inhabitants and the whole host of technologies we use to keep tabs on one another. The reality he describes is both unutterably banal, because it happens everywhere, and yet all the more disturbing because we are so indifferent to its ubiquity. To underscore this sense of the everywhere, Chen – who was a noted film critic and film festival programmer before moving behind the camera – discreetly namedrops his way through the canon of cinematic voyeurism as he ponders his theme. Thus Du Jiazhen's status as an emotional invalid who watches others as recuperative therapy recalls Hitchcock's *Rear Window* (1954), and the wheelchair-bound Jeff's attempts to while away the hours by spying on his neighbours. Both are eye specialists of different kinds: Jeff a photographer, Du an ophthalmologist; and both find their own skewed reflections in the people whom they watch. Further in the background is Michael Powell's *Peeping Tom* (1960), and the insidious ways in which it lures the audience into the pleasure that Mark takes in his kill. Rather closer to home is *sex, lies, and videotape* (Steven Soderbergh, 1989), in which Graham's filming of erotic interviews is closely mirrored by the revelations of Du's suitors, who are 'catalogued' by the labels discussed earlier just as Graham marks his videos with a name, time and place. Or there are the resemblances to *Sea of Love* (Harold Becker, 1989) and *Single White Female* (Barbet Schroeder, 1992), with their fusion of the personal ad/mad stalker/urban loneliness theme.

What all these movies have in common is their status as voyeur-reflexive films – and it is membership of this genre to which Chen Kuo-fu would seem to aspire in *The Personals*. Cinema of this kind traverses the spectrum, but its exemplars share certain traits. The apparatus of voyeurism – cameras, binoculars, tape recorders, telephones, eyes – is fetishised, visually ever-present and freighted with symbolic meaning; the ethnographic impulse is also on prominent display as the voyeur attempts to encompass as much human life as possible within his powerful ocular purview (hence the lists, labels and interviews); the endless mutuality of voyeurism is implied, as we watch the watcher watch the watched; and, most crucial of all,

the voraciously voyeuristic nature of cinema as a medium – a fact ordinarily finessed to save our feelings – is dragged out into the open, often through the use of the camera as an instrument of menace. *The Personals* ticks all of these boxes. Indeed, its enthusiastic reflexivity may be why some observers have found the film too studied and mannered, a 'Godardian film-essay' in Kraicer's words. Mannered or not, Chen Kuo-fu's essay on voyeurism cannot but invite a kind of in-joke gaze itself, asking as it does to be 'watched' not just as a film about voyeurs, but – and more subtly – as a voyeur-reflexive film that engages with the conventions of the genre, and expects an appraising eye. Just like his filmic subjects, Chen wants an audience with his peers.

CONCLUSION: THE EYES HAVE IT

In a sense, this heightened self-awareness on the part of the film-maker is only appropriate given the key managerial role that cinema plays in the running of a surveillance society. After all, the cinematic medium has legitimised, even naturalised, the desire to snoop, peer and pry into other people's lives, and it has done so in the most entertaining and populist of ways. Many of its best-loved and most time-honoured genres (the spy thriller, the detective film, the political exposé, the courtroom drama) are predicated on the uncovering of illicit secrets – which is, needless to say, just another term for invaded privacy – and the result is that the cinematic voyeur has swapped places with his victim on the scale of virtue. The predictable corollary to this is the emergence of an all-too-eager confessional impulse that prefers to 'out' its own skeletons rather than wait in suspense for them to be unceremoniously dug up. We see this process taken a stage further with Du Jiazhen's suitors, who have internalised the value system of the surveillance society so well that they take positive pleasure in revealing all. Their readiness to divulge represents the voyeur logic operating at full tilt, with confession functioning as a means of gaining social acceptance, even identity: I confess therefore I am.

Rather than liberation, however, *The Personals* shows that all confession brings is the judgment of others – just as voyeurism, the flip side of the coin, is nothing other than a means of social control. The suitors, their secrets packaged up as bite-sized morsels for Du's consumption, meet only with pity, anger, indifference or disdain from their confessor.

And this process of moral evaluation is magnified a thousand-fold as these same secrets are consumed, and considered, by audiences with all their legion biases. Of course, Chen Kuo-fu skews the scales, encouraging our voyeurism to be punitive or empathetic – as discussed above – through prejudicial casting and cinematography. But at root, his point could not be more egalitarian: the surveillance society, and its signature behaviours of voyeurism and self-exposure, make us all vulnerable – not to the ministrations of some omnipotent Big Brother, but to the petty, subjective judgments of other people. Indeed, *The Personals* is less concerned with the cinematic society as one 'that would know itself through the reflections that Hollywood produced'[10] – or, for that matter, with what Laura Mulvey famously saw as the inequitable sexual politics of voyeurism in the filmic mode[11] – than with the ways in which cinema extends and democratises the power of the gaze. Chen's interests lie not in conspiracy or gender theory, but in the countless mundane ways in which we deny each other the right to be our unselfconscious selves.

This point is made quite poignantly in the coda to the film. Here, we see a final montage, in which selected suitors – the machinist, the actor, the musician, the autistic boy whose mother accompanied him on his date with Du, the cross-dressing lesbian reluctant to confirm her gender – live their real lives, and are filmed with a sudden delicacy and innocence that restores them to a fuller subjectivity. No longer are they tagged specimens, creatures of the camera, whose 'difference' is the sum total of what we watch and who they are. Instead, the film-maker – paradoxically enough – is showing us the integrity that their lives might perhaps possess away from the brutal glare of the gaze. Now, moreover, it is Du's turn to be labelled for our observation: her real name, her occupation and her age appearing in the corner of the screen in what seems at first sight to be a gesture of retribution. But if this is the case, then all it really proves is that the previous sequence was simply a flight of utopian fancy, a momentary respite from the law of the look. Du's incorporation into the taxonomy of voyeurism – which sees her trapped under glass and tagged for posterity just like all the others – is the final and abiding image of the film; and it suggests not so much that she is getting her comeuppance, but that surveillance is the fate that befalls us all.

NOTES

1. Questions of vision preoccupy Chen's work, and this sequence is echoed in the opening moments of his next film, *Double Vision* (2002). Here, the camera zooms in on the eye of a stillborn infant in a symbolic précis of the film proper – a study of perception versus the paranormal, and sight versus truth.

2. Nick Kaldis, 'Monogamorphous Desires, Faltering Forms: Culture, Content, and Style in Chen Kuo-fu's "Zhenghun qishi"', paper given at *Remapping Taiwan*, University of California at Los Angeles, 13–15 October 2000: <www.international.ucla.edu/cira/paper/TW_Kaldis.pdf> (accessed 12 February 2007).

3. Ru-shou Robert Chen, 'Marketing *The Personals*: New Strategies Pay New Dividends', *Cinemaya*, no. 45 (1999): 38–39.

4. Shelly Kraicer, '*The Personals*', chinesecinemas.org, 1999: <www. chinesecinemas.org/personals.html> (accessed 12 February 2007).

5. Norman Denzin, *The Cinematic Society. The Voyeur's Gaze* (London: Sage Publications, 1995), 7–8.

6. Kaldis, 'Monogamorphous Desires', 2.

7. See, for example, 'Privacy in China', *The Economist*, 12 January 2006.

8. Examples include: Bonnie S. McDougall, 'Privacy in Modern China', *History Compass*, 2 (2004): 1–8; and Bonnie S. McDougall and Anders Hansson, eds, *Chinese Concepts of Privacy* (Leiden: Brill, 2002).

9. This lacklustre response may, however, be galvanising into action as various constituencies have begun to mobilise themselves more efficiently in the wake of the promulgation of the 'Measure Governing the Rating Systems of Publications and Pre-recorded Video Programs' ('Chubanpin ji luying jiemudai fenji banfa') in 2004. The degree to which this measure – a clear move towards censorship – has stoked activism is discussed in Ning Yin-bin *et al.*, '"Yuwang, qingnian, wanglu, yundong: cong fanjiafenji yundong tan Taiwan sheyun de xin qingshi". Zuotanhui daoyan' ('Introductory Remarks on a Forum on "Desire, Youth, the Internet, and Social Movements: Discussing Nascent Social Movements in Taiwan from the Perspective of the Anti-Ratings Campaign"', *Taiwan shehui yanhui jikan* (*Taiwan: A Radical Quarterly in Social Sciences*), no. 60 (2005), 179–196.

10. Denzin, *The Cinematic Society*, 7–8.

11. See Laura Mulvey, 'Visual Pleasure and Narrative Cinema', *Screen*, 16, no. 3 (1975): 6–18.

23 *PTU*: Re-mapping the Cosmopolitan Crime Zone

Vivian Lee

This essay looks at Johnnie To's *PTU – Police Tactical Unit* (2003) as a manifestation of 'post-nostalgic imagination' in Hong Kong cinema – an awareness of the here and now as a site of critical re-engagement with time past, and especially the visual imagination of the past.[1] More specifically, I situate *PTU* within the permutations of the action film as a struggle with its own memory, both in the form of an emotional attachment to local cultural tradition and a sharpened awareness of the genre's need to reinvent itself amid changing conditions of the local film industry. Existing writing on To's work gives credit to his ability to balance aesthetic innovation with commercial considerations, especially his effort to reinvigorate the action genre through self-reflexive parody and experimentation.[2] My reading of *PTU* focuses on the displacement and reinterpretation of generic conventions in the construction of an urban space where order and chaos are purely contingent and coincidental, where human agency is less defined by individual (heroic) qualities than by desire and circumstance. I argue that, on the one hand, the urban space in *PTU* reinscribes the familiar local 'crime zone' within a defamiliarised visual composition in which the familiar contours of the urban space look strange and unreal, so that the immediacy of action is dissolved into psychological and visual vignettes that de-emphasise the heroic and the good/evil binary. On the other hand, the surrealistic dreamscape subtly reintroduces a local flavour through intertextual references and inflections. The end product is an existential landscape in which the parameters of action – and lack of action – are redrawn. My discussion suggests that it is a revisiting and reinvention of the action film's legacy, an effort born out of the tensions between cinematic nostalgia and 'contemporaneity', between a sense of identity anchored in the local film-making tradition and the urgency of self-reinvention amid the chaotic flux of the present.

HEROISM, GROUP IDENTITY AND 'CORPORATISM': CHANGING FACETS OF THE ACTION HERO

From the mid-1990s on, many Hong Kong action films have shown a growing interest in probing the limits of 1980s-style heroism popularised by John Woo, who has come to represent the so-called 'hero films' in Hong Kong cinema ever since *A Better Tomorrow I* and *II* (1986, 1987). Woo's 'cinema of crisis'[3] signifies an important landmark in the development of the action genre, and by extension an aesthetic response to the versatile political and social realities of Hong Kong in the 1980s and 1990s closely associated with the nostalgic, *fin-de-siècle* apprehension of the 'end of (colonial) history'. However, since the mid-1990s there have been efforts by other Hong Kong film-makers to downplay the heroic prototype in favour of less idealised, more psychologically and morally conflicted characters struggling to survive the challenge of the moment. The 'countdown' to the change of sovereignty further facilitated this critical reflection as film-makers sought to look beyond the 1997 deadline, in order to resituate and redefine Hong Kong's 'local' identity and its relationship with the 'nation' (China). Meanwhile, the decline of the local film industry beginning in 1993 continued throughout the decade. Market depression deepened as a result of the Asian financial crisis in 1997–1998, and the already pervasive pessimism grew more pronounced during the SARS pandemic in 2003. Thus the mid-1990s to the first half of the 2000s was a time of enduring crisis for both Hong Kong society and its cinema, a time when film-makers struggled to maintain morale and creativity in local productions.[4]

As far as the action film is concerned, there was an obvious effort to reinvent itself through a self-reflexive revisiting of its own legacy. These explorations into new possibilities were also a function of the shortening life cycle of popular trends in the mainstream cinema[5] and the domination of Hollywood productions in the domestic market. The deconstruction of the hero and heroic individualism (e.g. Wai Ka-fai's *Too Many Ways to Be No. 1*, 1998) undermines the *agency* of the central characters in controlling their own fate. A shifting emphasis from the individualistic hero to the group was also an emerging trend that gained momentum in the wake of the new millennium. In Gordon Chan's *First Option* (1996), Johnnie To's *Lifeline* (1997) and *The Mission* (1999), to name a few examples, loyalty to an entrenched patriarchal tradition, usually symbolised by a father figure, is replaced by a more dynamic, forward-looking and flexibly managed collectivity defined by a relational network, or the group.

In this respect, Johnnie To's Milkway films have made some important breakthroughs.[6] For example, *Expect the Unexpected* (1998) subjects a team of police officers to a cruel twist of fate. *Lifeline* is entirely devoted to the creation of a group identity (firemen) as an embodiment of the heroic in everyday life *without* any resort to the good/evil binary. Inspired by Kurosawa's *Seven Samurai* (1954), To experiments with a kind of 'motion in stillness' in *The Mission*.[7] The film privileges the group (five bodyguards) over the authority of the father figure (the triad gang boss), as it evolves from an emotionally detached mechanical operation into an organic community bonded by a deep sense of brotherhood. On the other hand, their professionalism (visible through the immaculate dark suits and extremely efficient, target-oriented teamwork) opts for flexible solutions to defend the status and authority of the boss without obeying his order to execute one of their own. This flexible 'group philosophy' extends further into To's later police stories, *PTU* and *Breaking News* (2004), and gangster films, *Election I* and *II* (2005, 2006). In these films, the group, be it a police unit or a triad society, exhibits a corporate spirit that emphasises the need to survive in an increasingly versatile, crisis-stricken and business-oriented world. Here, heroism is repeatedly sidestepped by professionalism, emphasising self-/group preservation, operational efficiency, and shrewd and unscrupulous decision-making.

If the Woo-style 'hero film' dramatises the heroic *act* as a spectacle in and for itself, in To's films there is a movement away from action-as-spectacle to action as part of, if not subsumed under, an unfolding psychological drama. If *The Mission*, *PTU* and *Breaking News* are the 'unofficial trilogy' of To's 'group movies',[8] *PTU* presents an interesting case study as a midway exercise that builds upon the group theme and formal experimentation in *The Mission* and anticipates the kind of corporatism he further developed in *Breaking News*. More importantly, in *PTU* formal experimentation results in a 'distilled' image of the urban landscape from which a 'post-nostalgic' imagination emerges to capture and re-envision the local, an experiential space within which the nostalgic is reconfigured as part of the film's deconstructive aesthetic.

THE CRIME ZONE REVISITED

The story of *PTU* takes place during one night shift of a Police Tactical Unit (PTU) squad in Tsimshatsui, one of the busiest commercial and shopping areas in Hong Kong. The narrative consists of three main strands: a police investigation into the murder of a gangster leader nicknamed Ponytail; the search for a lost gun by a criminal investigation division officer Lo, and his fellow PTU officers; and the PTU's investigation of a series of vehicle break-ins in the area. As Lo believes that his gun has been stolen by Ponytail's men, he switches his mobile phone with Ponytail's in the hope of tracking down the hoods, inadvertently attracting the suspicion of his superior, Leigh Cheng. The PTU squad, led by Mike and Cat, covers up for Lo and as a result gets involved in the gun search.

Throughout the film, the camera follows the excursions of the three parties – Lo, the PTU squad and the murder investigation team – into obscure corners of the district. As they keep crossing paths

PTU

with one another, the three lines of action converge in a crossfire in which the PTU squad, the criminal investigation team, two gangster heads and four heavily armed mainland Chinese criminals fire at one another during an accidental encounter. My interest here is in how, and to what effect, the camera indulges in the police on the beat – who resemble what Michelle Huang calls 'walkers' in Wong Kar-wai's *Chungking Express* (1994)[9] – and the act of walking, as a means of exploring the city at night by using defamiliarising techniques, so that the familiar urban space of the 'crime zone' becomes strange. *PTU* mediates cinematic nostalgia and an awareness of its own contemporaneity. This inevitably works to circumscribe the nostalgic through a defamiliarising re-imagination of the urban space.

PTU is arguably the most representative example of To's fondness for the city at night so far.[10] The entire action takes place in one night, and the visual composition of the night city is carefully manoeuvred to create an eerie, surrealistic dreamscape with little resemblance to the clichéd nightlife image of Hong Kong. What immediately strikes the viewer is emptiness: the usual crowds have disappeared, and for the better part of the film, the city is devoid of a human background. In fact, the *mise en scène* strictly limits our vision to the activities of the police by doing away with the multitudes, a far cry from many quick-paced action films where high-speed chase and crossfire take place amid busy traffic on crowded streets for maximum thrill and sensation. Deserted by the masses, the city broods in a resounding emptiness as the drama unfolds, while the frequent use of wide-angle shots further extends the perceived space and distance of movement as the cops patrol the streets in a tightly controlled rhythm. The manipulation of spatial perception is further enhanced by the use of sound and lighting. Watching the film, our attention is repeatedly drawn to certain magnified diegetic sounds – footsteps, doors, beacons, telecommunications devices – as either markers of the main action or the potentiality of action, whereas the usual humming background noise is effectively subdued. A good example is the shot where Ponytail's body is being carried away in a casket. The sounds of police communication devices and the medical crew's footsteps are so magnified that other diegetic sounds are virtually submerged. As the crew move slowly across the screen, the background lighting darkens, leaving

the police minivan in spotlight at the centre before a complete blackout. In this and many other scenes, our sense perception is geared toward the silence that envelops the action on screen.

Rather than reinforcing cinematic verisimilitude, this 'sound-image', together with the alternate blue/white lighting, provides the basic rhythm and ambience for the action to take place, and an audio-visual grid for the walkers – and viewers – to navigate the topos of the city. The film's filtering out of the familiar in this visual mapping is also noticeable in the absence of the 'signature' skyline with its ultra-modern architecture, a favourite backdrop of many Hong Kong action (and non-action) films (e.g. John Woo's *A Better Tomorrow*, Andrew Lau and Alan Mak's *Infernal Affairs* [2002–2003] trilogy and To's own *Running Out of Time I* [1999] and *II* [2001]). Instead of tracing the skyline as an image of the city threatened by a crisis of disappearance, and hence a nostalgic yearning for lost times, *PTU* takes the alternative path to study the city at the ground level: the back streets, an old-style café, a local eatery, a videogame arcade and old rundown buildings. As the police-walkers stroll the streets in search of Lo's gun, the camera, following their footsteps, not only sketches the contour of the night-city but also transforms its texture in the process.

As an exercise in formal experimentation, To's reconstructed 'crime zone' borders on the theatrical. In the scene where Lo meets Ponytail's father, Bald Head (Lo Hoi-pang), in the hope of finding his gun, Ponytail's crew, naked and heads shaven, are locked up in tiny iron cages as a punishment for 'being alive' after their master's murder. The whole scene is designed like a stage performance: the minimal props leave a broad empty space in the middle with the lighting-accented cages on two sides. After a brief dialogue with Lo, Bald Head strikes his hammer repeatedly against one of the cages while the naked man inside cries out in pain and terror. As we watch Lo walk out of the unit, the sound of the hammer and Bald Head's ominous voice are still echoing in the background. While graphic depiction of physical torture is a stock-in-trade of local gangster films, this scene presents torture as a carefully choreographed ritual, emphasising the *visuality* of torture as part of the cinematic language with a generic pedigree.

Stylisation, it seems, is central to the film's visual mapping. In a 'stairway' scene, Mike leads his men up an evacuated building to check out Ponytail's accomplices in their hideout. The PTU squad moves slowly upstairs in a highly rhythmic and co-ordinated pattern to the tune of the synthesiser soundtrack, their flashlight signals going on and off in the dark. Visually, the whole scene is choreographed like a stretched-out dance sequence; without dialogue, the viewer's attention is effectively focused on the body language of the police officers. In Hong Kong action films, the staircase is a preferred setting for pursuit and raid scenes, where action stars can display their extraordinary acrobatic acumen. In *PTU*, the staircase is transformed into a space of suspense and circumspection, revealing the psychological tension of the cops caught in the midst of great uncertainty. Conscious posing is also evident in the film's emphasis on the body language of 'cool'.[11] A good example is the long shot of the PTU squad coming out of a back alley. In their accustomed slow and measured steps, they stop and spread out horizontally under the bright yellow neon sign of Tom Lee Music (a local 'signpost' in the area) as if to pose for the camera before they walk into the foreground and out of frame, one by one, their silhouetted figures standing in sharp contrast to the neon sign above. Shaped by their respective spatial settings – i.e. a narrow staircase and a camera-enhanced outdoor location – these stylised performances display an affinity to the adroitness in the utilisation of space for maximum visual expression in Hong Kong films, while giving new inflections to conventional practices.

If the controlled and measured tempo of the police-walkers enables the camera to indulge in a nostalgic revisiting of the night-city, the resulting dreamlike vision suggests a self-imposed circumvention of its own nostalgia. As a distilled image, the city beckons for recognition as tokens of familiar signs are folded into a surrealistic dreamscape that defies accustomed perception. The displacement of the familiar into the unfamiliar also challenges the viewer to look for similarities between the two contrastive perceptual realms. The frequent references to street names and local signposts, both visually and in dialogue, evoke memories of the local by providing a fictionalised topographical index to the cops' itineraries. In its distilled form, the city *becomes* recognisable through the camera's (and our) active decoding of its self-effacement. This déjà vu, or feeling of revisiting a scene from the past in the present, is recovered

from what Ackbar Abbas calls the *déjà disparu* in 1980s–1990s Hong Kong film culture: 'a handful of clichés … a cluster of memories of what has never been … an inability to read what is given to view'.[12] The sense of tension is reinforced by the time factor: the PTU squad has to find the gun before daybreak. Thus, despite the camera's slow-paced visual mapping, beneath the police-walkers' calm composure is a heightening sense of urgency and anxiety. They are literally 'running out of time' (a recurrent motif in To's recent films, e.g. *Running Out of Time* and *Breaking News*). If the surrealistic image of the night-city has the qualities of a dream, there is also a tacit understanding that this dream will end, or disappear, with the night. In between a *flâneur*-like movement over space and relentless temporal flow, the film seeks out the *symbolic* potential of nostalgia by dissolving the components of the past into its own film medium that goes beyond the nostalgic. The productive tension between the *déjà vu* and the *déjà disparu* in *PTU* is where the post-nostalgic imagination emerges as an effort to mediate between a desire for some anchorage in the past, hence an identity derived from a sense of place and its cultural imaginations, and a desire to dislodge itself from the 'handful of clichés' in order to imagine 'what *is*'.

LOSS AND ABSENCE: 'CITING' THE HEROIC

Johnnie To and his Milkyway team are well known for their production and marketing agility that balances commercial viability and aesthetic innovation. These dual objectives are realised in their best films through self-conscious parody and subversion of generic conventions. *PTU* is among To's hybrid creations that defy strict genre definitions by mixing elements of drama, action and the kind of dark humour that characterises Hong Kong's popular cinema. If, in John Woo's cinema, space is a spectacle born out of a spiritual force moving dialectically toward an ultimate transcendence in the form of a hero's sacrifice or redemption,[13] in *PTU* the deserted 'film city' is rendered as a stage where heroism, and the moral package of knight-errantry, is re-examined through a different lens.

If nostalgia is the desire to recover a 'lost sense of moral community',[14] in many Hong Kong films in the 1990s it is also 'traceable in the intertextual relations of the past and the present'.[15] In Hong Kong action films, nostalgic intertextuality is most vividly present in the adaptation of martial arts gallantry in hero films. Film-makers in the mid-1990s usually recast the heroic within an ironic, self-referential narrative. But parallel to this 'rebellious' aesthetic is also an awareness of its connection to the 'older' tradition, a formative influence that gave Hong Kong action film its initial generic hallmark, and to whose visual aesthetic the later films frequently refer.[16] Such intertextuality is discernible in *PTU*'s deconstruction of the conventions of *policiers*. Unlike many of its predecessors, the film's 'break' with the past goes beyond parody and mockery of the hero's machismo. Instead, it relies more on exploiting the *image* of uniformed police to destabilise the boundaries between good and evil, order and disorder, and finally the apparently incongruous *narratives* of heroism and corporatism.

The film begins with Lo's missing gun and ends when he finds it after slipping over the same banana skin for the second time in a back alley. Although sloppy and incompetent, Lo is the centre of gravity of the film's main action. His blunders not only motivate the action but also directly lead to the climactic gun battle, where two teams of police officers open fire with armed criminals, and two gangster bosses kill each other in a cowboy-like duel. If possession of a gun is a symbol of power, Lo's missing gun justifiably removes him from the privileged position of power. The missing gun in *PTU* can be read as a self-reflexive reference to To's earlier film, *A Hero Never Dies* (1998), in which the Leon Lai character says, 'God is he who has the gun', which in turn is a variation on a line by Mark (Chow Yun-fat) in *A Better Tomorrow*: 'A god is someone who can control his own destiny.' Stephen Teo revises this motto into 'A hero is he who has the gun.'[17] This reference to the gun, or more precisely the *possession* of one, is not only central to the identity of the hero but also to the moral universe that the hero strives to uphold against evil enemies.

In *PTU*, the missing gun does not so much signify the urgency to reinstate the hero's power as *distract* the police officers from their presumed missions. Even Lo himself is misled by Bald Head (whom he believes has taken his gun) into facilitating Bald Head's revenge on Eyeball (whom Bald Head believes masterminded Ponytail's murder). From beginning to end, the missing gun functions more as a decoy than a vehicle of power through which justice can be served. It seems in *PTU* that To has self-

consciously revised his (and Woo's) motto: 'Both the hero and the gun are tokens of mischievous Fortune.' By establishing Lo as a loser and 'black sheep' of his group at the outset, To retains a comic dimension typical of the black humour of Hong Kong action films, while at the same time inserting an ironic comment on 'cool' in the film narrative.

As an attribute of the *image* of the hero (individual or group), 'coolness' is undercut by its ambivalence as a signifier of the heroic. Throughout the film, we see the coolest cops inflict physical torture on their targets as a routine practice. On the other hand, the film carefully avoids any direct portrayal of gangsters seriously doing their business. (They eat, play videogames, pour yellow paint onto Lo's car and beat him up without inflicting fatal injuries.) Most of the time they are either ripping each other off or being ripped off by the police – those who have guns.

If there is a trait of heroism remaining, it exists in a highly negotiated form – the PTU leader Mike, who at the very beginning admonishes his subordinates to observe the code of conduct: 'Anyone wearing the uniform is one of our own.' Apparently a straightforward and somewhat clichéd dictum on loyalty and brotherhood, it becomes more problematic than it first seems as the film proceeds. As early as in the opening scene, Mike's remark is undercut by Cat's more pragmatic rejoinder: 'Whatever happens nothing beats returning home safely.' Sitting on facing benches on the police truck, Mike and Cat are already positioned to represent different values, and different *interpretations* of what it means to be 'wearing the uniform'. The second and last time this line is reiterated, Mike's voice is replaced by a much disliked orderly, who turns the hero's logic against itself: the 'uniform' is not about covering up for an individual at the expense of the group, but the other way round. Surprisingly, the most looked-down-upon member of the team manages to change the course of events – Mike finally backs down, and the whole team heads for the shooting ground.

In sharp contrast to Lo's, Mike's image comes closest to the cool-headed, intelligent and unflinching cop-hero ready to violate any procedural guideline to protect 'one of his own'. However, he is *not* a conventional hero, for his action lacks the moral stature typical of the accustomed roles of a 'good cop' (or 'good gangster'). Throughout the film, Mike, as well as his team, is often cast in shadows. In the scene where Mike tortures a young hood in a videogame arcade, a low-angle shot shows Mike in full command, but half of his face remains shaded. Later on, the camera shows Mike addressing his squad in a close-up, but his authority is marred by the front lighting that grossly flattens his features.

These portraits of the hero invite comparison with those of Lo, the anti-hero. On at least two occasions, Lo is given a well-defined close-up that draws attention to his vulnerability: when he tries to bargain with Bald Head in the latter's headquarters, and when he runs away in terror from the violent shootings at the end. The first scene, rendered in alternate close-ups of the two characters, subtly sketches Lo's helplessness and fear at the sight of Bald Head torturing the young hoods in iron cages. In the second close-up, Lo gives the most emotionally intense and 'human' performance: shot in slow motion, the scene emphasises his bandaged, panic-stricken face as he cups his ears, screams in panic and flees for his life.

In the end, Lo's street-smart philosophy saves the day of the police teams when he advises Leigh to cover up her cowardice during the shooting: 'Fire a couple of shots, Madam – it will look good in your report.' If Mike's solemn declaration of brotherhood in the name of 'the uniform' (a visible form of power like the gun) harks back to lost times and lost values that no longer apply, Lo's remarks suggest how these values can be recuperated under a different rubric. Ironically, Lo's rather unheroic flight leads him to the missing gun: a moral failure turned into a victory of a different sort, occasioned by chance and sheer luck.

In *PTU*, Hong Kong is a 'clockwork metropolis'[18] where human agency is a function of contingence and circumstance rather than heroic intent. Marginal characters out of nowhere (e.g. the pre-teenage biking boy who steals coins from parked cars and the harmless-looking mainland criminal who runs into Lo at the phone booth right before the gun battle) can be the ones who pull the strings of a 'heroic' drama – an absurdist 'police story' rewritten into the official account of the night's events. Before the police crews disappear into the depths of the night, Lo, Mike and Leigh respectively dictate their reports orally. Their interwoven lines match perfectly to create yet another *image* of police chivalry – a series of blunders skilfully crafted into a well-orchestrated (co-)operation in which 'good' eliminates 'evil'.

This self-reflexive 'testimony' can be read as the film's ironic comment on the aesthetic of the gun, which is given full expression in the 'Woo style' in the grand finale. The use of slow motion, highly stylised body movement, and the 'miracle' of blood-spurting criminals firing back several times before they fall dead – all these are conscious encodings of the hero film popularised by Woo's cinema. However, the spectacle is out of proportion with the reality of its aftermath. The *absence* of the conventional hero in this spectacle of gunfire and his replacement by Lo as the centre of gravity suggest that the visual codes of the hero film are less required by the plot than a kind of citation, a tribute to an 'origin' and a witty exploitation of its signifying potential. The self-referential happy ending short-circuits the visual logic of the hero film by foregrounding the *fictionality* of heroism (a nostalgic intertext in Rey Chow's sense), for embedded in the co-authored police report are two mutually incompatible *narratives*: heroic action and corporate wisdom. In an ending shot, instead of occupying opposite positions as before, now Mike is seated next to his teammate Cat on the truck as he 'reconstructs' his account of the team's activities of the night. This, I think, is the last stroke of dark humour played upon the cops. If, as To says, Cat is merely a 'housewife' figure whose only concern is to go home safely,[19] it is her 'housewifely logic' that Mike succumbs to, a difficult but necessary choice between two *possible* narratives of loyalty and brotherhood.

If post-modernist culture has a tendency toward ironic, self-reflexive transgression of boundaries to reveal the 'overdetermined' nature of signs and meanings, *PTU* can be regarded as a post-modernist decoding and recoding of pre-existing genre conventions. It can be read against the local film culture since the 1980s in terms of a post-nostalgic re-engagement with earlier texts through stylisation, intertextuality, displacement and citation. What emerges from the film's visual mapping is a defamiliarised 'dream city' where the action cinema's own legacy is reconfigured in the process of self-transformation.

NOTES

1. I am grateful to Stephen Teo for the opportunity to read part of his unpublished manuscript on Johnnie To during my research for this essay. Teo's study, *Director in Action: Johnnie To and the Hong Kong Action Film*, was subsequently published by the Hong Kong

University Press in 2007. All references to Teo's book in this essay refer to the published work.

2. See Andrew Grossman, 'Johnnie To: A Belated Auteur', *Senses of Cinema* (January 2001): <www.sensesofcinema.com/contents/01/12/to.html>; David Bordwell, 'Movies from the Milkyway', in *Milkyway Image, Beyond Imagination – Wai Ka-fai + Johnnie To + Creative Team (1996–2005)*, ed. Lawrence Pun (Hong Kong: Joint Publishing, 2006), 16; and Stephen Teo, *Director in Action*, Chapter 4.

3. Tony Williams, 'Space, Place, and Spectacle: The Crisis Cinema of John Woo', *Cinema Journal*, 36, no. 2 (1997): 67–84.

4. Stephen Teo, 'Sinking into Creative Depths', *Hong Kong Panorama 97–98* (Hong Kong: Provisional Urban Council of Hong Kong, 1998), 11–13.

5. The 'triad kid fad' triggered by the *Young and Dangerous* series ran its course in about eight months, despite the later release of the final instalment in 1998. Li Cheuk-to, 'Young and Dangerous and the 1997 Deadline', *Hong Kong Panorama 96–97* (Hong Kong: Urban Council of Hong Kong, 1997), 10.

6. Beginning as a production assistant at Hong Kong Television Broadcast Ltd (TVB), To worked briefly under Chang Che, a famous martial arts film director, and began making his own films in the late 1970s. To founded Milkyway Image in 1996, and 100 Years of Cinema in 2000 with a group of Hong Kong film-makers with a view to reviving the local industry.

7. Lee Cheuk-to and Bono Lee, 'Beyond *Running Out of Time* and *The Mission*: Johnnie To Ponders 100 Years of Film' (interview), *Hong Kong Panorama 1999–2000* (Hong Kong: Leisure and Cultural Services Department, 2000), 48. This aspect of the film is discussed in Teo, *Director in Action*, Chapter 4.

8. To had in mind a third film after *Mission* and *PTU* with an all-female cast. Thomas Shin (interview with To), 'Johnnie To's *PTU*: Blind Loyalty of a Night Voyager', *Hong Kong Panorama 2002–2003* (Hong Kong: Hong Kong Arts Development Council, 2003), 83. 'Unofficial trilogy' is used by Teo in discussing the group movies, in Teo, *Director in Action*, Chapter 4.

9. In her analysis, 'walkers' are the *flâneur*-like characters in Wong's film. See Tsung-yi Michelle Huang, *Walking between Slums and Skyscrapers: Illusions of Open Space in Hong Kong, Tokyo, and Shanghai* (Hong Kong: Hong Kong University Press, 2004), 31–48.

10. Shin, 'Johnnie To's *PTU*', 3.

11. '… they are much more imposing than the real cops … and should look smart in uniform.' Ibid., 82.

12. Ackbar Abbas, *Hong Kong: Culture and the Politics of Disappearance* (Hong Kong: Hong Kong University Press, 1997), 25–26.

13. See Williams, 'Space, Place, and Spectacle', 77–78.

14. Linda Lai Chiu-han, 'Film and Enigmatization: Nostalgia, Nonsense, and Remembering', in *At Full Speed: Hong Kong Cinema in a Borderless World*, ed. Esther Yau (Minneapolis: University of Minnesota Press, 2005), 235.

15. Rey Chow, 'A Souvenir of Love', in Yau (ed.), *At Full Speed*, 224.

16. E.g. the world of the *jianghu* (lit. rivers and lakes), an alternative social order in the martial arts tradition. Teo calls it an 'inner world' with its own codes of conduct. Teo, *Director in Action*, Chapter 4.

17. Ibid.

18. Jeff Smith, '*PTU*: Johnnie To and the Clockwork Metropolis', in Pun (ed.), *Milkyway Image*, 236.

19. Shin, 'Johnnie To's *PTU*', 83.

24 *The Red Detachment of Women*: Resenting, Regendering, Remembering

Robert Chi

INTRODUCTION

Given the recent resurgence of People's Republic of China (PRC) nationalism, the increased willingness within China to re-examine the Maoist period (roughly 1949–1979) in both academic and non-academic discourses, and the increasingly varied and sophisticated ways in which cultural theory has informed Asian studies, it has become both possible and necessary to fit the Maoist period back into China's long twentieth century. The most promising recent scholarship has proposed two strategies: first, crossing the period's beginning and ending markers (especially 1949);[1] and second, focusing on the psychic, aesthetic, affective and everyday dimensions of experience during the Maoist period.[2] With respect to cinema, we are faced here with two questions. First, how might we reconsider the functioning of culture and the arts under Maoism? Second, how are we to think of cinema as both a public art and a site for mass experience? To these more obvious questions I would like to add a third: what aesthetic and political operations take place in the name of memory? These questions are intimately connected in the many films of the Maoist period that combine revolutionary history with the coming-to-consciousness of a single representative character. One of the best and most influential of these is *The Red Detachment of Women* (Xie Jin, 1960).

Red Detachment is set on Hainan Island, off the south coast of China, and begins in 1930. In the first part of the film, a Communist cadre disguised as a rich merchant encounters the local landlord, Nan Batian. By chance an intractable maidservant has run away only to be recaptured and flogged. When the cadre leaves, Nan Batian gives the maid, Wu Qionghua, to the cadre. As they pass Boundary Ridge, the cadre frees Qionghua and directs her to a Communist women's militia – a red detachment of women – that is forming nearby. Along the way Qionghua

meets another embittered woman, Fu Honglian, and the two of them follow the newly formed militia. Qionghua pleads with the (female) company commander to let them enlist. Now in uniform, the cadre, Hong Changqing, arrives with the local (male) division commander, and the two men allow the two women to enlist.

In the second part of the film, Qionghua and Honglian are sent to spy on Nan Batian. Hungry for personal revenge, Qionghua violates the rules of discipline and fires at him. Nan Batian is wounded in the left shoulder, and the women retreat. Back at the base Hong Changqing confines Qionghua to quarters. A few days later the cadre dons his rich merchant disguise again and takes Qionghua and several others to trap Nan Batian. They capture the landlord and parade him through the village. The landlord, however, escapes; giving chase, Qionghua is shot in the left shoulder. After recuperating at a field hospital, she returns to the red detachment. Along the way, she encounters Hong Changqing; passing by Boundary Ridge again, they have not a love scene but a scene

Qionghua enlists in the red detachment of women

of instruction. For Qionghua proposes to go under-cover to kill Nan Batian, whereupon Hong Changqing takes her back to base to show her a map of China. The point is that Hainan Island is only one tiny part of China, and so only collective struggle, not individual vendettas, can liberate the whole country. Qionghua applies for Party membership, and later Honglian marries a fellow Communist soldier.

In the third part of the film, the Kuomintang (KMT) Nationalist government sends an expeditionary force to Hainan Island to fight the Communists. The KMT army and Nan Batian's militia defeat the red detachment at Boundary Ridge. Qionghua and the other women soldiers retreat, but Hong Changqing is captured and then burned alive in front of the villagers. The KMT commander refuses to pursue the red detachment, which he considers a negligible threat, but Nan Batian – now bent on personal revenge – wants to attack. The red detachment captures the landlord, and the rest of the Communist forces defeat the KMT troops. Qionghua finally kills Nan Batian, ostensibly in self-defence. The film closes with Qionghua taking Hong Changqing's place as Party cadre for a second red detachment of women.

Previous analyses of *Red Detachment* have usually focused on its questionable vision of women's liberation, given the way that Hong Changqing dominates Qionghua's trajectory as saviour, teacher, role model disciplinarian, forbidden lover and symbolic creditor.[3] This is not to discount its affective appeal. But recognition of the latter usually turns on a gendered notion of melodrama as excess. This tends to reduce the film to a Rorschach test: it gives women the illusion of freedom only within an essentially patriarchal system, or it belies a patriarchal panic at the figure of woman as other, or it allows women a spectatorial room of their own. The notion of melodrama as excessive can also combine with a scepticism towards socialist realism, resulting in the dismissal of the film as exaggerated and unrealistic (as well as exoticist, being set on a tropical island) and hence ultimately ineffectual to all. My analysis is based on a re-evaluation of melodrama, namely that the latter is neither strictly gendered nor strictly a genre, which is why the film is able to fold women into a masculinist vision of women's liberation. More importantly, melodrama here shares a common genealogy and articulation with non-cinematic practices under Maoism, all of which place memory-work at the centre of the struggle for liberation.

MEMORY-WORK

Four theoretical contributions to the critical discourse on memory are particularly useful here. First, Maurice Halbwachs argues that memory is always essentially social: specific memories are always associated with, tagged according to and triggered by social contexts.[4] Second, Paul Connerton looks more closely at just 'how societies remember', drawing attention to bodily practices in particular.[5] These include periodic commemorative rituals where the anamnestic function is overt and conscious, as well as pedagogical activities that unconsciously convey and condition subjects as followers in a long tradition such as that of a particular writing system. Third, Pierre Nora suggests that one can speak of memory only when there is an effort to remember.[6] That effort might not appear to be conscious or overt or intentional; it may work out in unexpected ways; and it may fail as well. Nevertheless, Nora's distinction is useful because it implies agency and hence the motivating anxiety of *not* remembering. For memory is often thought of as an effort against negation: 'never forget', 'we will/must always remember', and so on. Fourth, Ian Hacking has proposed the notion of 'memoro-politics' as a science of the soul.[7] It complements Michel Foucault's anatomo-politics of the body and bio-politics of populations. All three are sciences of power/knowledge that construct a normative model of the subject. Memoro-politics in particular has to do with the notion that subjects have interiority, dimensionality and depth, as well as the notion that absence – what is forgotten, not what is remembered – determines us. Thus for Hacking memory operates through a productive repression, just as for Foucault sex does. Moreover, both memory and sex operate specifically on the body, and they may even be interconnected via an erotics of memory. Such an erotics would not just be represented in a film through, for example, character sexuality. More importantly it would be felt through spectatorial engagement grounded in the body, such as through intense emotions and their somatic correlates. It would be a question of desire, love and pleasure – even the pleasure of suffering, violence and death.

Memory is often contrasted with history on the grounds that the latter is a selective and repressive official narrative and hence the former is a site for political resistance. But this is a misleading contrast, since the state itself often openly engages in mnemonics. Obvious examples of this include monuments and memorials, as well as museums, textbooks, holidays, currency, postage stamps, and the naming of public spaces and architecture. During the Maoist period culture played a crucial role in the overall effort to narrate the origins of the People, the Chinese Communist Party (CCP) and the PRC. Privileged topics included the organisational efforts of the leftists and the Communists during the 1920s through the 1940s, as well as the armed conflict against the KMT and the Japanese. Such narratives appeared in a variety of forms and genres. For example, fictional and semi-fictional narratives appeared in literature and drama, while non-fictional narratives included reportage, interviews and memoirs.

To be sure, for cinema historians the Maoist period is quite heterogeneous, mainly because the Cultural Revolution (1966–1976) saw very few new films produced – or old films screened. In contrast what in Chinese is referred to as the Seventeen Years (1949–1966) was a period of abundant production, wholesale expansion and reconfiguration of the film industry, and numerous overlapping sub-periods marked out by the interactions among politics, economics and culture. The Seventeen Years saw over one hundred feature films about the revolutionary wars or revolutionary history in general, as well as many documentary films on similar subjects. In the decade after its release, *Red Detachment* itself was turned into a revolutionary ballet, then a revolutionary model opera and then finally into filmed versions of both of those, in 1970 and 1972, respectively. Even today revolutionary history films continue to be central to what in the post-Cultural Revolution years have been dubbed 'main melody' (*zhu xuan lü*) works – witness the parade of often two- or three-part films since the 1980s recounting major battles, campaigns and CCP leaders.

At the same time, PRC history has seen a whole procession of anniversary observances. Throughout the Seventeen Years there were many anniversaries, holidays and commemorations of revolutionary events. Moreover, they usually involved generically heterogeneous memory-texts, making such memory-work what textual studies calls simply intertextuality, allusion, reference, tradition. For example, the original film version of *Red Detachment* was released on 1 July 1961 as part of a week-long series of new films – the series itself being only one of a range of works

and events – celebrating the fortieth anniversary of the founding of the CCP. The films included feature films, children's films, documentaries and educational films.[8] As one might expect from a commemoration of the CCP at that point, more than half of the films (among the fifteen advertised in the *People's Daily*) – including both fiction and documentary films – are about revolutionary history. Similar events take place today as well, such as the various film series, theatrical performances and museum exhibits in Shanghai during the summer of 2001 that celebrated the eightieth anniversary of the founding of the CCP.

Besides these reproducible and transportable works, live public acts of storytelling have been crucial to the formation of revolutionary subjects. Before 1949 one of the most significant symbolic devices and social practices under the CCP had been the public airing of grievances or *suku*, the recounting of suffering under China's 'feudal' conditions. It is important to note that imagining and expressing interiority in this way – as in, for example, judicial proceedings – long predated the CCP. But during its years of revolutionary struggle the latter turned it into a means of publicity, recruitment, motivation, training and organisation. Even after the establishment of the PRC in 1949, such narrative recollection continued to integrate the recollection of past suffering, the revolutionary struggle for liberation and the imperative not to let the 'feudal' past repeat itself. Such public airings of grievances were institutionalised in the form of mass rallies and public denunciations. They included visual-somatic elements such as the baring of scars and the shedding of tears, both of which figure prominently in *Red Detachment*. This served to focus particular attention on the body as the site of both memory (as suffering, as an effort against negation) and sociality – this latter being in fact the interface between individual and collective, or simply the mass public experience. The public airing of grievances continued to be a crucial technique for the formation of revolutionary subjects, as shown by the far-reaching land reform and anti-counterrevolutionary, anti-corruption and anti-capitalist campaigns of 1950–1952, as well as the all-too-common denunciations of the Cultural Revolution.[9]

Ci Jiwei has analysed the Party's memory-work in terms of a 'calculus of debts'.[10] *Red Detachment* thematises this on screen and diegetically through the

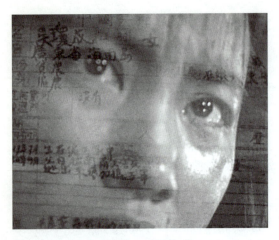

Qionghua and her application to join the Party

circulation of coins, as do other films of the Seventeen Years such as *Daughter of the Party* (Lin Nong, 1958).[11] In *Red Detachment*, when Hong Changqing grants Qionghua her freedom at Boundary Ridge he immediately monetises that debt by giving her four silver coins to buy food on her journey to the red detachment base. Later, as Qionghua and the other women soldiers are preparing to retreat from the battle at Boundary Ridge, Hong Changqing tells her that her Party membership application has been approved. She gives him the four coins as payment of her Party dues. After witnessing Hong Changqing's execution Qionghua recovers the cadre's bag, which contains her now-approved Party application form and the four coins. This last sequence is the emotional climax of the film and provides little plot-related

Body, image, monument: Qionghua enters the Party

action. Instead it is dominated by close-up reaction shots of Qionghua witnessing the execution and then walking home benumbed. This culminates in the prolonged series of close-ups of Hong Changqing's bag, the four coins in Qionghua's hand, and a remarkable montage of dissolves and superimposed images of Qionghua in tight close-up and her Party application, which she is ostensibly reading. Amid this is a barely diegetic monumental close-up of her clenched fist, in which she has just grasped the four coins, held aloft in the Communist salute. The repeated swelling of the Internationale on the soundtrack holds the whole three-minute sequence together.

By working through memory, the calculus of debt ensures the interiorisation, the *making one's own*, of that indebtedness to the Party. The Communist salute clenching the four coins serves to transvalue the latter from money to *memento mori*, and even more important than the Communist oath, the gesture's unspoken verbal component is 'I shall never forget'. As Wang Hui argues in one of the best Chinese-language commentaries on the film's director Xie Jin, what is at stake is not compliance but a willingness to comply, not just control but a belief in the legitimacy of that control.[12] Thus when Qionghua is confined to quarters after breaking the rules of discipline, she has a heart-to-heart talk with Honglian. While fingering the four silver coins, Qionghua marvels: '[Hong Changqing] lectures you, he disciplines you, and even as he is disciplining you, he makes you [want to] comply wholeheartedly [*jiao ni kou fu xin fu*, literally 'makes your mouth and heart submit'].' If *Red Detachment* mobilises memory in the service of the Party, just how does it turn audiovisual images from mechanically reproducible and publicly circulating tokens to iconic talismans with inestimable sentimental value?

THE RED ATTACHMENTS OF WOMEN

The director of *Red Detachment*, Xie Jin, is perhaps the single most important film-maker during the first half-century of the PRC. Born in 1923, Xie Jin began working in the film industry in Shanghai in 1948, on the eve of the establishment of the new China. After several years as assistant director, he made his first film as director in 1951. Among his pre-Cultural Revolution films, *Woman Basketball Player No. 5* (1957), *The Red Detachment of Women* and *Stage Sisters* (1965) are especially notable. Xie Jin's films continued to be popular and critical successes after the Cultural Revolution; examples include *The Legend of Tianyun Mountain* (1980), *The Shepherd* (1981), *Garlands at the Foot of the Mountain* (1984) and *Hibiscus Town* (1986). These later films in particular played a crucial role in the negotiation of the state's 'main melody' in the reform era. Even after 1989 Xie Jin's films continued to be noteworthy if only for the way that they stubbornly hewed to the 'main melody' – witness *The Opium War* (1997) commemorating the return of Hong Kong, as well as *Woman Soccer Player No. 9* (2000), a remake of *Woman Basketball Player No. 5* that doubled as a feature-length advertisement for the PRC women's national soccer team.

Xie Jin's major films both before and after the Cultural Revolution all engage in one way or another with the problem of the individual experience of history, a history that in the PRC is always writ large as a story whose protagonist is a collective one – the People. More specifically, the embodiment of that individual experience is usually a woman, and the mode of experience is melodrama. The vexed notion of 'Asian melodrama' is outside the scope of the present essay, and certainly any notion of a 'Chinese melodrama' can find local or 'traditional' sources and conditions that account for Xie Jin's privileged mode. However, it is useful to note that recent re-evaluations of melodrama see it as neither a genre nor a deviation or excess with respect to the norm of classical or mainstream cinema. For example, both Linda Williams and Christine Gledhill contend that melodrama is a fundamental mode (if not *the* fundamental mode) of mainstream cinema.[13] Melodrama negotiates between morality and feeling, between realism as a mode and modernity as contemporary lived experience, and between fictional and real worlds. This revised notion of melodrama is not in itself gendered as feminine, since it also accounts for masculine genres like Westerns and action films. An apparent hybrid like *Red Detachment*, a women's war film, thus confirms the underlying identity of the two, just as the Maoist practice of the public airing of grievances, itself traceable to pre-Communist antecedents in China, can be seen as a kind of melodramatic theatre.

In both cases that melodrama is figured in terms of memory. Melodrama's aims of stirring spectators to pathos as well as the recognition of moral virtue and innocent victimhood are precisely the aims of the Maoist practice of publicly airing grievances. What the latter specifies is that they are based on historical experience, so the pathos and sympathy of spectators spring from their recognition of common experiences in their own pasts – in other words, identification under the sign of memory. *Red Detachment* foregrounds this by presenting not one but a series of scenes of such grievance airing. In fact, there are three key scenes in which Qionghua announces her bitter personal memories, and these scenes serve to punctuate her trajectory from slavery to liberation, from personal revenge to collective class struggle and from taking orders to giving them. The three scenes consist of the first passage across Boundary Ridge, the enlistment scene and the public parading of the captured Nan Batian. Together the three scenes form a developmental sequence on several levels. In all three Qionghua's speech is interrupted: first by herself, then by the arrival and mere presence of Hong Changqing and finally by Honglian's admonition which results in a redirection of Qionghua's *j'accuse* to praise of the Communist revolution. It takes an increasingly active and external intervention to interrupt Qionghua, which means that she herself is becoming increasingly active in both expression and action. Likewise, the diegetic audiences of the three scenes go from Hong Changqing to the assembled women's detachment to the people of the village. This sequence traces a progression in number as well as an ideological progression from the Party as specular leader to the People themselves.

There are also several supplementary and countering moments that serve to highlight Qionghua's trajectory. First, other characters confess their own personal bitter memories, too. Not surprisingly the two major characters to do so are Honglian and Hong Changqing. They are Qionghua's symbolic partial doubles in that the former remains within the family structure and hence becomes both wife and mother, while the latter is the mentor whose place Qionghua ultimately occupies instead. Hong Changqing in particular teaches Qionghua and the film's audiences about the emotive or 'melodramatic' basis of revolution: when he chastises her for violating discipline and firing at Nan Batian during the scouting mission, the Party secretary asks her rhetorically, 'Do you think that only you feel such resentment [*yuan chou*]? What proletarian's heart is not steeped in tears?' Later, as part of the map-lesson about the priority of collective struggle over personal vendettas, the secretary tells Qionghua of his own background, his own bitter past. Here Hong Changqing is pointedly engaged in a bit of stage business, namely chopping open a very large coconut. Besides adding a bit of exotic local colour or realism, this somatic correlate to the bitter recollection serves to express the secretary's own pent-up resentment as he grips the knife and coconut and delivers the final, violent blow to the latter. But the business ends up being channelled into the productive, positive, nourishing action of pouring and drinking the coconut's milk. Grasping the lesson, Qionghua responds, 'In other words, every proletarian's heart is steeped in tears!' Second, Qionghua has another partial double whose trajectory is the mirror image of hers: Nan Batian. He reflects not alternatives but opposites, his story moving from the pinnacle of power at the beginning of the film to a bullet wound in the left shoulder, escape from his captors and finally a desire for revenge over strategy that proves to be his undoing. Thus the symmetrical contrast between Qionghua and the retrograde Nan Batian further suggests the structural necessity of suffering and the bitter past as the threat of negation that motivates the utopian remembering of Maoism.

The most emblematic of Qionghua's three scenes of grievance-airing is the enlistment scene, when Qionghua and Honglian ask to join the red detachment. When the company commander tells them to submit a formal application explaining why they have come, Qionghua impetuously tears open her blouse to reveal the scars she has suffered under Nan Batian's whip. She shouts that she wants revenge: 'What for? You want to know what for? For this! Revolt! Revenge! Kill the officials! Cannibals! Skin them alive! I … I …' It is at this moment that the film cuts to a counter-shot of Hong Changqing and the division commander entering – and it is this which silences Qionghua's outburst. While the uncovering of scars accompanied by passionate denunciation perfectly combines the public airing of grievances with the iconic low-angle close-up that Stephanie Donald calls the 'socialist-realist gaze',[14] what is most revealing about this scene is its possible alternatives. After making the film Xie Jin wrote his 'Director's Notes on *The Red Detachment of Women*'. There he laments that the scar scene does not express Qionghua's class

identity clearly enough. He writes that upon finally seeing a sympathetic audience of fellow proletarians, Qionghua should have been overflowing with things to say. She should have struggled to find the right words first, before revealing her scars and shouting – instead of doing so right away, without missing a beat.[15] In contrast, the model opera version filmed in 1972 (dir. Cheng Yin) has Hong Changqing and the red-detachment commander welcoming Qionghua immediately and without doubt. They do not ask her what she came for; instead, noticing her scars, Hong Changqing simply invites her to air her grievances before her comrades. This turns into a lengthy (i.e. verbose) aria. The two alternatives bracket the melodramatic aspect of the scene. The former opts for a classical cinematic naturalism of character motivations and behaviour, which moreover should have been indicated precisely by the inability to make oneself understood that is a key trope of melodrama. The latter, coming at the more radically utopian moment of the Cultural Revolution, dispenses with such blockage and deferral, resolving the dilemma through the immediate embrace of the Party.

In his 'Director's Notes' Xie Jin also presents three simple but crucial ideas that summarise how cinema of the Seventeen Years operates as a form of memoro-politics. First, Xie Jin recounts actual responses to a preview screening to show that different viewers indeed interpret the main idea of a film differently: in this case, different audience glosses include 'Chinese women took up arms, the greatest suffering did not deter them, and the Chinese people are invincible'; 'Resistance that springs from the individual is limited, it is necessary to act collectively in order to generate great strength and in order to defeat all enemies'; and 'Dare to struggle, dare to win'. Second, he attributes this difference to the fact that each reader or spectator of a work associates the latter with his or her own experience.[16] Finally, he insists throughout that the measure of a film is to what extent it moves its audience as if in a 'mutual cry' or resonance [*gong ming*] with its characters.[17] Spectatorship as resonance here resides at the intersection among affect, cognition, soma and memory, and is figured specifically as an oral-aural experience. Given the real past experiences of individual spectators – which in turn form their interests, tastes and concerns in the present – a film aims to fore ground characters as sites for identification and hence education. Cognitive self-reflection on that education, here expressible in the form of summaries of the main idea of the film, can vary widely. But what is ultimately at stake for Xie Jin is the affective-somatic aspect of identification. In other words, the revolutionary call to action consists not only of ideological education but of moving the spectatorial body – moving both as somatic gesture and as emotional stimulation.

The abundance of narratives and commemorations of revolutionary history in the PRC reminds us of just how important it was – and still is – to popularise and multiply memory-images of the struggle for liberation. The further fact that relatively little critical attention has been focused on this unmistakeable link between pre-1949 China and post-1949 China confirms that memory is a supplement, without necessarily being a site of resistance, to the master narrative of dramatic leaps and breaks in the course of inexorable forward progress away from the past – the temporality of revolution or historical abjection. Cinema under Mao was part of this attempt to radically restructure subjectivity – a wholesale 'cultural revolution' – and in films such as *The Red Detachment of Women* that revolution takes place 'where the heart is'.

NOTES

1. For example, see Tang Xiaobing, ed., *Rereading: Mass Culture and Ideology* (*Zai jiedu: dazhong wenyi yu yishixingtai*) (Hong Kong: Oxford University Press, 1993); and Peng Hsiao-yen, ed., *Literary and Art Theory and Popular Culture* (*Wenyi lilun yu tongsu wenhua*), 2 vols (Taibei: Zhongyang yanjiu yuan Zhongguo wen zhe yanjiu suo choubei chu, 1999).

2. For example, see Ban Wang, *The Sublime Figure of History: Aesthetics and Politics in Twentieth-century China* (Stanford, CA: Stanford University Press, 1997). In fact, the Cultural Revolution in particular did inspire many attempts at psychological analysis of Mao Zedong and of the Red Guards. These were sometimes combined with historical analysis under the rubric of 'psychohistory'. See, for example, Robert Jay Lifton's remarkable studies *Thought Reform and the Psychology of Totalism: A Study of 'Brainwashing' in China* (New York: Norton, 1961) and *Revolutionary Immortality: Mao Tse-tung and the Chinese Cultural Revolution* (New York: Random House, 1968). Such psycho-historical studies do take the realms of the psychic and the everyday seriously, but they do not offer much specific analysis of cultural forms such as literature, cinema, theatre and the fine arts.

3. *The Red Detachment of Women* has been the subject of much passing commentary in English-language scholarship, but there have been few published attempts to analyse the film in detail. In one of the best of those analyses, Shuqin Cui shows how the film sublimates gender difference into class struggle. See her *Women through the Lens: Gender and Nation in a Century of Chinese Cinema* (Honolulu: University of Hawaii Press, 2003), 79–95.

4. Maurice Halbwachs, *The Collective Memory*, trans. Francis J. Ditter, Jr. and Vida Yazdi Ditter (New York: Harper & Row, 1980).

5. Paul Connerton, *How Societies Remember* (Cambridge: Cambridge University Press, 1989).

6. Pierre Nora, ed., *Realms of Memory*, English edition, ed. Lawrence D. Kritzman, trans. Arthur Goldhammer, 3 vols (New York: Columbia University Press, 1996–1998).

7. Ian Hacking, *Rewriting the Soul* (Princeton: Princeton University Press, 1995) and 'Memory Sciences, Memory Politics', in *Tense Past: Cultural Essays in Trauma and Memory*, ed. Paul Antze and Michael Lambek (New York: Routledge, 1996), 67–87.

8. See advertisements published around this time in the *Renmin ribao* (Beijing) and the *Wen hui bao* (Shanghai).

9. For more on the public airing of grievances and the psychic significance of such narrative practices, see David E. Apter and Tony Saich, *Revolutionary Discourse in Mao's Republic* (Cambridge, MA: Harvard University Press, 1994); and Ann Anagnost, *National Past-Times: Narrative, Representation, and Power in Modern China* (Durham, NC: Duke University Press, 1997), esp. Chapter 1.

10. Jiwei Ci, *Dialectic of the Chinese Revolution: From Utopianism to Hedonism* (Stanford, CA: Stanford University Press, 1994), 82–85.

11. The film *Daughter of the Party* is based on the 1954 short story 'Party Dues' by Wang Yuanjian, and there are also various stage versions of *Daughter of the Party* – all of which confirm the centrality of the premise of indebtedness to the Party.

12. Wang Hui, 'Politics, Morality, and the Secret of their Displacement: An Analysis of Xie Jin's Films' ('Zhengzhi yu daode ji qi zhihuan de mimi – Xie Jin dianying fenxi'), *Film Art* (*Dianying yishu*), no. 2 (1990): 23–45.

13. Linda Williams, 'Melodrama Revised', in *Refiguring American Film Genres*, ed. Nick Browne (Berkeley: University of California Press, 1998), 42–88; and Christine Gledhill, 'Rethinking Genre', in *Reinventing Film Studies*, ed. Christine Gledhill and Linda Williams (London: Arnold, 2000), 221–243.

14. Stephanie Hemelryk Donald, *Public Secrets, Public Spaces: Cinema and Civility in China* (Lanham, MD: Rowman & Littlefield, 2000), 59–64.

15. Xie Jin, 'Director's Notes on *The Red Detachment of Women*' [*Hongse niangzi jun* daoyan zhaji], in *The Red Detachment of Women: From Screenplay to Film* (*Hongse niangzi jun: cong juben dao dianying*) (Beijing: Zhongguo dianying chubanshe, 1962), 278.

16. Ibid., 271–272.

17. Ibid., 291–292.

25 *Riding Alone for Thousands of Miles*: Redeeming the Father by Way of Japan?

Faye Hui Xiao

INTRODUCTION

This essay examines Zhang Yimou's recent film, *Riding Alone for Thousands of Miles* (hereafter *Riding Alone*). Compared to Zhang's previous father–son narratives, *Riding Alone* visualises a more democratic and sensitive father figure, played by Japanese star Takakura Ken. Here 'democratic' is used in the sense of 'interpersonal democracy' practised through the bonding of intimate relationships in people's every-day life, which will be elaborated in the later parts of this essay.[1] While a remorseful Japanese father embodies a new patriarchal ideal in this film, Tokyo is depicted as the site where human relationships are alienated and traumatised. Hence, the father–son bond can only be materialised through the mediation of reinvented 'traditional' Chinese culture. The contradictions, negotiations and competitions between the narratives of 'Japaneseness' and 'Chineseness' in this cross-cultural and inter-ethnic melodrama invite two central questions. First, if Zhang's 'sentimental return' in his late-1990s' films indicates 'a distinctively nationalist quality' associated with historical specifics, then how should we read the national, ethnic and historical ambivalences in *Riding Alone*?[2] Second, how does this democratised father–son narrative articulate its relation to an emerging 'Greater China' discourse while simultaneously maintaining its appeal to a transnational audience? To explore these issues, I will situate my reading of the film within the theoretical framework of transnational Chinese cinema while taking into account the cross-current of a burning 'consumer nationalism'.[3]

In the face of Chinese cinema's increasing integration into a world film market, Sheldon Lu posits 'an essentially transnational nature' of 'Chinese cinemas'.[4] Yingjin Zhang also points out that the film-makers in mainland China, Hong Kong and Taiwan have not only competed against each other but also worked in 'close *cooperation* as an effective transregional strategy since the 1980s'.[5] Pertinent to current developments in the Chinese film industry, the transnational perspective can serve as a fresh and effective approach to studies of Chinese cinema. However, Lu's and Zhang's arguments about transnationalism have overlooked two key issues. First, they focus on the commercial and cultural transactions between Chinese cinema(s) (including mainland China, Hong Kong and Taiwan) and Hollywood. They barely touch upon the influences from and interactions with Japanese and Korean cinema as well as other forms of regional popular culture such as soap opera. Second, theory about the increasing global and regional interconnectedness in film production and consumption does not fully examine the escalating tensions between transnational capital flows and rising 'consumer nationalism'.

For example, recent Sino-Japanese diplomatic conflicts have affected the circulation and consumption of popular cultural products. The former Japanese Prime Minister Junichiro Koizumi's regular visits to the controversial Yasukuni shrine caused large-scale protests in China. A call for boycotting Japanese products ensued at some of the largest Chinese Internet portals, such as sina.com, tianya.net and ebay.com.cn.[6] Under the great pressure of this nationalist campaign online and offline, the release of *Memoirs of a Geisha* (2005) was cancelled in China, despite the usual appeal of Hollywood big-budget films among Chinese audiences.[7] Zhang Ziyi, the icon of a transnational Chinese cinema, has been severely attacked as a 'shameful traitor' (*hanjian*) for 'accepting the role of the beautiful geisha Sayuri without considering Chinese national pride'.[8]

Given the outbursts of 'consumer nationalism' in contemporary urban China, the warm reception of *Riding Alone* is thought-provoking and worth exploring. Setting a box-office record for Chinese arthouse films, this small-budget Sino-Japanese co-production has been praised for its adept build-up of emotional resonance and mutual recognition transcending linguistic barriers and ethnic boundaries between a Japanese father and a Chinese son.[9] It was selected as the Best Foreign Language Film at the 2006 San Diego Film Critics Award, while Takakura Ken won the prize for Best Actor. When *Riding Alone* premiered as the Opening Film of the 2005 Tokyo International Film Festival, audiences responded to this visual narrative of a cross-cultural emotional tie with overflowing tears and enthusiastic applause.[10]

Centring on a border-crossing journey of promise and redemption, *Riding Alone* is Zhang Yimou's second most recent film at the time of writing and was produced in close co-operation with Japanese director Yasuo Furuhata. It opens with a medium shot of the lonely figure of Takata Gouichi (Takakura Ken), a fisherman in a small Japanese village. He is summoned by his daughter-in-law to Tokyo to see his terminally sick son. Returning to Tokyo for the first time after nearly twenty years, Takata feels alienated by the rapid modernisation of the city. His sense of loss is heightened by his son's refusal to see him, due to an unspecified past misunderstanding between them. As he leaves, his daughter-in-law hands him a videotape to help him know his son better. The tape is a visual chronicle of his son's obsession with Lijiang, a tourist spot in south-western China. At the end of the video, his son makes a promise to Li Jiamin, prestigious performer of the local *Nuoxi* opera, that he will come back to watch Li's exciting performance of *Riding Alone*, a time-honoured *Nuoxi* play. To fulfil his son's promise, Takata embarks on the first transnational journey of his life. Arriving in Lijiang, he finds that Li has been jailed for assault. Takata manages to get permission to go to prison and videotape Li's performance. However, when they get there, Li is unable to perform and bursts into tears. He tells Takata that he also longs to see his own son, an illegitimate child who lives in Stone Village. Takata then makes a trip to Stone Village and builds up an inalienable bond with Li's son, Yang Yang.

The father–son relationship has been an enduring leitmotif in the works of the Fifth Generation Chinese film-makers. Dai Jinhua suggests that the most prominent feature of the Fifth Generation's earlier works is a patricidal complex, which is a political allegory for the film-makers' scathing attack on Chinese mainstream culture, and specifically the party-state

ideology and Confucian patriarchy.[11] Zhang Yimou's earlier films engaged in this patricidal tradition, in which a visual narrative evolves around a strong desire to subvert the Law of the Father, or 'a feudal patriarchal system' in Zhang's own words.[12] From his debut film, *Red Sorghum* (1987), an anti-Japanese war epic that also presents a father–son story, to this recent melodramatic narrative of paternal bonds, Zhang's visual representations of the father–son relationship have taken a sharp turn.

A STORY OF A JAPANESE FATHER BECOMING CHINESE?

When China began to open up to the outside world and develop a market economy in the late 1970s and early 1980s, there was a nationwide debate about the 'besieged masculinity' of Chinese men.[13] Among all the cinematic and televisual masculine figures of the time, Takakura was regarded as *the* embodiment of a new vision of masculinity, the subject of modern individualism as a negation of Chinese collectivism. Fully aware of Asian audiences' nostalgic memories of Takakura, Zhang Yimou regarded the performance of this Japanese star as a major selling point of *Riding Alone*.[14] To get Takakura's consent to play the Japanese father, Zhang kept revising the screenplay for six years.[15] The tactic of invoking audience nostalgia has aided the transnational advertising and marketing of the film. Many audiences were in tears at the magnified screen image of Takakura's familiar face, stern, weather-beaten but still endearing.[16] Nonetheless, an international cast has become a common practice of transnational Chinese cinema, and it does not necessarily guarantee the success of a film. Therefore, I propose that *Riding Alone* makes Takakura's star image more intriguing and acceptable through a narrative of reinvented 'Chineseness'.

The film title comes from a well-known chapter of the ancient martial arts classic *The Romance of Three Kingdoms*. In it, the Lord Guan, symbol of traditional Chinese masculinity and Confucian virtues, rides alone on a long journey to carry out his promise for Liu Bei, his sworn brother and sovereign lord.[17] *The Romance of Three Kingdoms* has a time-honoured aura among East Asian audiences, and the term *danji* (pronounced *tanki* in Japanese), conjuring up a romantic masculine image of a solo rider on horseback, has circulated from Chinese literature to Japanese travel writings. This transnational appeal has been translated into the central thread of this film, in which seeking the *Nuoxi* performance of Lord Guan's heroic feat is the vehicle for healing the Japanese father's trauma and rebuilding the father–son relationship. Through his cross-cultural journey, Takata re-duplicates Guan's legendary deed of riding alone on a long journey to reconnect a male bond. This conflation of the images of the Chinese hero and the Japanese star is visualised in the film poster, which advertised its Chinese release from 25 December 2005. Against the backdrop of the picturesque landscape and distinctive architecture of south-western China, Takakura's image is merged with a *Nuoxi* mask of the Lord Guan that he reverently holds close to his heart. Thus, Lord Guan, the regional emblem of Confucian ethics, becomes a central image linking not only a Japanese father and a Chinese son, Han Chinese and Naxi ethnic minority, but also audiences of a contemporary film and readers of traditional Chinese literature.

In addition to drawing on the trans-East Asian popularity of *Romance of the Three Kingdoms*, the narrative of 'Chineseness' also revives some anachronistic Maoist revolutionary values. The residual socialist belief in the 'redemptive power' of labour is demonstrated clearly through the characterisation of the Japanese father.[18] Takata rejects the urban middle-class lifestyle in the cosmopolitan metropolis of Tokyo. Instead, he chooses to make a living through heavy manual labour in a remote fishing village. In sharp contrast with the helpless characters confined within an enclosed walled space in *Ju Dou* (1990) and *Raise the Red Lantern* (1991), *Riding Alone* strikes

Chinese poster for *Riding Alone for Thousands of Miles*: Takata holds a *Nuoxi* mask of Lord Guan

audiences with its visualisation of the Japanese father's repeated border-crossing in the vastness of a transnational open space. All through the film, audiences witness Takata's body in motion, busily fishing, videotaping, walking, and so on. Travelling on a plane, in a minivan, a taxi cab or on a tractor, he sutures not only Japan and China, and the minority frontiers and cosmopolitan metropolises, but also the totally different value systems of the past and present. As idealised socialist labour aesthetics promises, in the end all his sweat, labour, suffering and bitterness are rewarded with redemption. The lost paternal bond and ethical truth are retrieved 'through a dialectic of pathos and action'.[19]

His heavy reliance on the collective help of local Chinese people to achieve his final goal makes this Japanese father more Chinese. For example, Jiang Wen, the woman interpreter from Kunming, helps Takata to communicate with villagers over the phone. Qiu Lin, Takata's aide in Lijiang, volunteers to help him for free. Under the leadership of an elderly patriarch, the Stone Village people help Takata to get Yang Yang and set up the spectacular mile-long *liushui xi* ('running-water' banquet) to celebrate the coming together of the Japanese father and the Chinese son. Rather than an individualistic hero like his earlier characters in Japanese films, this time Takakura is portrayed almost as a socialist hero. In contrast to the image of a solo rider featured by the film title, he treasures the tradition of making communal efforts for a common good and carries on the communist 'mass line' (*qunzhong luxian*). Constantly revealing that he himself can achieve nothing without the help of the people, Takata resorts to mass mobilisation as well as official support to achieve final success. Furthermore, the past utopian values of collective consciousness and communal bonding obliterate any traces of the consumerism that has encroached on even the most 'primitive' frontier areas and commercialised interpersonal relationships in post-Mao China.

DEMOCRATISING THE FATHER

Nonetheless, it would be oversimplified to conclude that *Riding Alone* is merely a story of integrating the cultural Other into a nationalist narrative. While making the Japanese father Chinese, this film also capitalises on the global currency of overflowing sentiments and human connections. With its 'universal' appeal, it is believed that this sentimental narrative can overcome vast differences of gender, class, locality or ethnicity. Whether in Kunming (capital city of Yunnan province), Lijiang (internationally famous tourist spot) or Stone Village (a small Naxi community with an ancient history), Takata's repeated narration of his family story makes Chinese people – Han or non-Han – immediately identify and sympathise with him. His performance of a 'universal' father–son melodrama made possible with the aid of visualising technologies transforms him into a close member of the community. Just as the reason for Takata's rift with his son is never specified, any reference to historical trauma or recent Sino-Japanese antagonism cannot be found in the idyllic picture of harmonious coexistence and interaction of different generations, ethnicities, languages and cultures.

Unlike the almost invisible patriarch in *Raise the Red Lantern*, the oppressive pervert in *Ju Dou* or the literally and metaphorically blood-sucking communist cadres in *To Live* (1993), the local officials in *Riding Alone* (played by real Lijiang government officers) are portrayed as sensitive and compassionate individuals rather than abstract and impersonal symbols of the patriarchal system. On the Japanese father's arrival, they never contemplate any unpleasant associations connected with the exacerbated Sino-Japanese antagonism. Deeply touched by Takata's confession of the past wrong and his desire to find redemption, these communist cadres relate to this failed father and go out of their way to help him to rebuild the broken paternal bond.

Let's take the following sequence as an example. When Takata takes his camcorder to the local prison, the official in charge readily grants his request to videotape Li Jiamin's *Nuoxi* performance in jail on one condition: Takata must not produce a deliberately 'distorted' video of prison life and sell it to some 'ill-intentioned' ('*bieyou yongxin*') Western media to denigrate China's image on the international stage. It cannot be clearer that these exhortations are targeted at numerous Euro-American reports and films about China's human rights violations. Takata gives his consent and gains admission to the jail. Via Zhang Yimou's camera, audiences get to see the austere but personal interior of the prison, the strict but humane management, and a highly organised music band composed of some talented prisoners. This narrative device of re-humanising the state apparatus serves as

a rebuttal not only to Western reports about China's human rights conditions but even more to the earlier charge against Zhang of producing self-Orientalising accounts of China to pander to Western audiences.[20] The place of the isolated and suffocating patriarchal Orient is taken by a harmonious China intimately bonded with the outside world through powerful expressions of inner feelings and emotional empathy.

In tune with this gesture of reconciliation towards the Father's law, the ideal of a democratic father is personified through Takakura's filmic role. This image is consummated in a sequence leading to the emotional climax of the film. After all the hardships and frustrations encountered on his border-crossing journey, Takata finally locates Yang Yang. On their way to the local prison to meet the boy's father, Yang Yang unexpectedly runs away. Takata catches him after a long chase through the hilly karst relief. Unfortunately, they get lost. Spending a night alone with Yang Yang, Takata fosters a close emotional tie with the boy and starts to reflect upon what kind of father he is in his son's eyes. The following morning, the rescue team sent out by the villagers and local police finds them. Takata begs the village chief to ask why Yang Yang refuses to see his father. When he finds out that the boy ran away because he has never met his father since his birth, Takata disagrees with the elderly village patriarch that they, as seniors, are entitled to force Yang Yang to see his father. Takata decides that a child's feelings and decisions should be respected. Before he leaves alone, Takata hugs Yang Yang tightly. His usually stern face breaks into an affectionate smile, while the boy starts laughing heartily. The emotional crescendo of the consolidated paternal bond is visualised in a lingering low-angle close-up shot of the two happy faces against the brilliant backdrop of the vast blue sky.

This rewriting of the father's image in the spirit of love and democracy draws on the aesthetics of regional melodrama. Since the late 1970s, foreign films and television dramas have come to dominate the Chinese cultural market, as well as the popular imagination of a new lifestyle and its accompanying structure of feeling. In the 1980s, Sino-Japanese racial and cultural affinity, as well as friendly diplomatic relations with Japan promoted by the Chinese government, meant that Japanese cultural products were better received by Chinese audiences than Hollywood films. Through the regional distribution of these popular cultural products, a 'media regionalism' was spurred by 'the development of consumerism and electronic communication technology'.[21] The palpable craze for Takakura's earlier films is one example of this Japan-centred 'media regionalism'. Another is Chinese audiences' enthusiastic embrace of Japanese television mini-series and anime including *Oshin*, *Doraemon* and a number of family melodramas starring Yamaguchi Momoe and Miura Tomokazu. Coincidentally or not, Yasuo Furuhata, the Japanese film-maker who helped to make *Riding Alone*, was one of the major producers of 1980s popular melodramas.

Since the late 1990s, the landscape of Chinese popular culture has changed significantly. As a result of an emerging Korean cinema and Chinese consumers' rising nationalist sentiments against Japanese products, the 'Korean Wave' (*hallyu*) has taken Japan's dominant place in the Chinese cultural market. Thanks to the sweeping popularity of his character in the television melodrama *Winter Sonata* (2002), Bae Yong Jun, a Korean star, has become the latest dream lover for Chinese female audiences. In comparison to Hollywood counterparts, Chris Berry states, Chinese film melodramas of the 1950s and 1960s put more 'emphasis on ethical expectations based on hierarchically defined social and kinship position'.[22] This ethical orientation is not limited to Chinese cinema, but also emphasised in 'Asian-style' melodramatic narratives produced in Japan and Korea.

On the other hand, melodramatic narratives targeted at modern Asian audiences have also contributed to a new vision of enacting the fantasy of democracy in people's everyday life and intimate relationships. In a number of Korean melodramas, we can identify a trend of democratising traditional family ethics and gender ideology through everyday resistance and negotiation. For example, Bae's roles are often portrayed as caring and sensitive lovers and primarily hailed by female audiences. *My Sassy Girl* (2001), a best-selling Korean film embraced enthusiastically by Asian audiences, features a rebellious and aggressive Korean girl and her submissive and devoted boyfriend. Through the regional circulation and consumption of these popular melodramatic narratives, the legitimacy of the conventional gendered division of labour and absolute authority of patriarchs is generally undermined, though also reinforced from time to time.

Discussing the transformation of everyday life and interpersonal relationships in modern society, Anthony Giddens contends that '[t]he possibility of intimacy means the promise of democracy'. He continues to argue, in marriage, parent–child relations, as well as other forms of kinship, 'egalitarian communication' serves as a mechanism through which interpersonal democracy can be pursued.[23] Cashing in on the transnational appeal of 'Asian-style' melodramas, *Riding Alone* exemplifies how this mode of 'egalitarian communication' between different generations, genders, localities, languages, cultures and ethnicities can be made possible, not through words but emotional power and ethical truth conveyed in the 'universal' language of transnational visuality. Ironically, in this transnational visual politics of 'egalitarian communication', the one who has lost his language is not Takata, but the local village people who are rendered impenetrable and unable to speak for themselves. Instead, they can only be accessed and understood through the lenses of visualising technologies, which are of course associated with Japan. Once more, Japan's technological superiority is endorsed by the circulation and consumption of transnational visuality.

CONCLUSION

In her essay, Dai Jinhua articulates the deep anxiety that the Fifth Generation film-makers felt in the 1980s: 'Their generation, following a historic act of Patricide, faces the castrating power of the double weight of ancient Eastern civilization and assaults launched from the West.'[24] In the light of Dai's argument, the final scene of a suicide attack launched by Chinese villagers against the intruding Japanese army in *Red Sorghum* can be viewed as a desperate gesture by the 'son-generation' against the invasion of a new order driven by the joint forces of the state and the market.

However, since the 1990s the position of the 'son-generation' of film-makers in a reconstituted power structure has evidently changed. Following Deng Xiaoping's famous inspection trip to the south of China in 1992, the Chinese market economy has expanded. Chinese film-makers, among other urban elite groups, are the major beneficiaries of this historical process of urbanisation and globalisation. Privileged by their ready access to the lion's share of transnational capital, government sponsorship and the domestic film market, 'the son-generation' has formed a formidable alliance with the Father's law, renewed through the logic of the market economy and global consumerism. While gaining membership of the club of the New Rich, they are also confronted with a dilemma caused by the exponential globalisation of the Chinese film market. The opening up of the Chinese film market brings in overseas capital as well as the dual threat posed by imported Hollywood big-budget films (*dapian*) and sweeping 'Asian-style' melodramas produced mainly in Korea since the 1990s. Facing a new invasion of popular cultural products and the government's recent tightening control over the mass media and cultural market, instead of a heroic 'suicide attack', 'the son-generation' has turned to manufacturing their own melodramas with 'Chinese characteristics' to get an edge on the competition for market share as well as to produce a new politics of transnational visuality. Read in this context, a reconstructed father–son narrative in line with 'traditional' Chinese ethics marks a re-orientation of Zhang's 'transregional strategy' that intersects with a new 'Greater China' discourse.

While China's booming economy is moving the country away from its marginal position on the world stage, an emerging 'Greater China' discourse sponsored by the party-state promotes the new image of a 'harmonious' China. This seems to be a belated response to the 'clash of civilizations' theory.[25] One hundred and twenty-three government-sponsored Confucius Institutes 'in 49 countries and regions' extend a nationalist ambition to secure ethical-linguistic cohesion.[26] According to Tu Wei Ming, the centre of this 'Cultural China' lies in the Chinese diaspora living outside the geopolitical boundaries of the nation-state of China.[27] However, 'by making its traditional value systems known to the world', the Chinese government now attempts to allay worries about the 'China threat' and reclaim a central position in the 'imagined community' of a 'Cultural China'.[28] As stark political ideology is losing its appeal nowadays, the 'Greater China' discourse often resorts to cultural means to create the pleasure of consuming a melodramatic 'structure of feeling', in which 'the ideological principles that support a given arrangement of power are translated into regularised patterns of emotion and sentiment'.[29]

Stripped of their historical contexts and socio-political relevance, traditional Confucian ethics and vestiges of socialist labour aesthetics are re-presented as the eternal emotional and ethical truths of human interiority in pursuit of a unifying power transcending geopolitical boundaries as well as ethnic barriers. Along this line of rendering a discursive 'Greater China' as a gripping melodrama, a harmonious picture of Chinese and Japanese, the Han ethnicity and Naxi minority, and the central government and the frontier people is engendered in *Riding Alone*. Commenting on *Riding Alone*, Ni Zhen, one of the mentors of the Fifth Generation film-makers, said that it promotes an 'Oriental' ethics as a therapy to alienated interpersonal relationships caused by the prevalent modern individualism. More productions of films like this will enable Chinese national cinema to play a decisive role in promoting the image of a harmonious China.[30]

Joining hands with global consumerism and the 'Greater China' discourse, melodramatic nationalism based on the reproduction of a 'traditional' structure of feeling is materialised and circulated through the 'universal' language of 'technologized visuality'. The transnational circuit of affective values derived from 'reified spectacles'[31] of Chinese ethnographic detail is presented as a redemptive force to bridge the divide caused by generation gaps, class stratifications, ethnic differences or historical traumas. At the intersections of localisation, regionalisation and globalisation, the 'national' comes back to play a pivotal role in the context of transnational Chinese cinema. However, as a contested 'imagined community', the parameters of the 'national' have already been stretched, reconfigured and transgressed by intersecting and oftentimes conflicting forces of nationalist sentiment, transnational capital and image flows, and regional cultural production and consumption patterns.

ACKNOWLEDGMENTS
I would like to extend my heartfelt thanks to Chris Berry, Lawrence Chang and Matt Hale for their insightful comments and suggestions.

NOTES

1. Anthony Giddens, *The Transformation of Intimacy: Sexuality, Love and Eroticism in Modern Societies* (Stanford, CA: Stanford University Press, 1992), 188.
2. Rey Chow, 'Sentimental Returns: On the Uses of the Everyday in the Recent Films of Zhang Yimou and Wong Kar-wai', *New Literary History*, 33, no. 4 (2002): 652.

3. An increasing amount of scholarship has been devoted to the discussion of the relationship between consumer culture and nationalism. For a few examples, see Laura Nelson, *Measured Excess: Status, Gender and Consumer Nationalism in South Korea* (New York: Columbia University Press, 2000); Jian Wang, 'The Politics of Goods: A Case Study of Consumer Nationalism and Media Discourse in Contemporary China', *Asian Journal of Communication*, 16, no. 12 (2006): 187–206; and Xudong Zhang, 'Postmodernism and Post-Socialist Society: Cultural Politics in China after the "New Era"', *New Left Review*, no. 237 (1999): 77–105.

4. Sheldon Lu, ed., *Transnational Chinese Cinema: Identity, Nationhood, Gender* (Honolulu: University of Hawaii Press, 1997), 2. For a more elaborate argument concerning transnational Chinese cinema(s), see Sheldon Lu, *China, Transnational Visuality, Global Postmodernity* (Stanford, CA: Stanford University Press, 2001).

5. Yingjin Zhang, *Screening China: Critical Interventions, Cinematic Reconfigurations, and the Transnational Imaginary in Contemporary Chinese Cinema* (Ann Arbor, MI: Center for Chinese Studies, 2002), 36 (original emphasis).

6. One boycott petition widely spread at various online forums can be sampled at: <forums.ebay.com.cn/thread.jspa?threadID=1100063221&tstart=0&mod=1172323548163> (10 March 2007). This petition claims that Japan's economy will collapse if Chinese people stop purchasing Japanese goods. Additionally, a group of Chinese nationalists have founded the Patriot Alliance (*aiguozhe tongmeng wang*: <x.1931-9-18.org>) to urge the Chinese government to stop importing Japanese goods and technology.

7. David Barboza, 'Citing Public Sentiment, China Cancels Release of "Geisha"', *New York Times*: <www.nytimes.com/2006/02/01/movies/01geis.html> (1 February 2006).

8. Antoaneta Bezlova, 'Chinese Pride and Geisha Prejudice', *Asia Times*: <www.atimes.com/atimes/China/HB09Ad02.html> (9 February 2006).

9. Tan Zhengji, '"Mou" faxing: xuanxiao hou chushou' ('The Distribution of Zhang Yimou's Films: Launched after All the Marketing Ploys'), *Xinxi ribao* (*Information Times*), 6 December 2005, B6; and Li Jun and Luo Wenjing, '*Danji* quanguo gongying Shanghai tiqian dianying jiucheng guanzhong jiaohao' ('*Riding Alone* Released Nationwide 90 Per Cent Audiences at

its Selected Screening in Shanghai Hailed'), *Shanghai qingnian bao* (*Shanghai Youth Paper*), 23 December 2005, A19.

10. Qiu Haitao, *Ren Gao Cangjian de gushi: Cong Zhuibu dao Qianli zou danji* ('Endurance – Takakura Ken's Story: From *Kimi yo funme no kawa o watare* to *Riding Alone for Thousands of Miles*') (Shanghai: Wenhui chubanshe, 2006), 197–198.

11. Dai Jinhua, 'Severed Bridge: The Art of the Son's Generation', in *Cinema and Desire: Feminist Marxism and Cultural Politics in the Work of Dai Jinhua*, ed. Jing Wang and Tani Barlow (London and New York: Verso, 2002), 13–48.

12. Mayfair Mei-hui Yang, 'Of Gender, State Censorship, and Overseas Capital: An Interview with Chinese Director Zhang Yimou', *Public Culture*, 5, no. 2 (1993): 301.

13. A more detailed description of this movement can be found in Xueping Zhong, *Masculinity Besieged? Issues of Modernity and Male Subjectivity in Chinese Literature of the Late Twentieth Century* (Durham, NC, and London: Duke University Press, 2000). Takakura Ken's masculine image is briefly mentioned in Zhong's book on pages 3, 41 and 46.

14. Zhou Hui, *Shei zhizao le zhongguo dianying de shenhua* (*Who Has Created the Myth of Chinese Cinema*) (Beijing: Zhongguo qingnian chubanshe, 2006), 164.

15. Qiu, *Ren Gao Cangjian de gushi*, 181.

16. Ma Dan , '"Qianli zou danji" cui lei Gaocang Jian budongshengse guanzhong ku zhong yan' ('Tear-jerking *Riding Alone for Thousands of Miles* Takakura Ken Stays Cool Audiences Cried Their Eyes Out'), *Huaxi dushi bao* (*Western China City Daily*), 23 December 2005, 10.

17. Luo Guanzhong, *Sanguo yanyi* (*Three Kingdoms: A Historical Novel*), trans. Moss Roberts (Berkeley: University of California Press, 1999), Chapter 27.

18. Chow, 'Sentimental Returns', 644.

19. Linda Williams, 'Melodrama Revised', in *Refiguring American Film Genres: History and Theory*, ed. Nick Browne (Berkeley: University of California Press, 1998), 42.

20. There have been a large number of articles criticising Zhang Yimou's 'self-Orientalisation' published in China and beyond. The most frequently quoted is Dai Qing's 'Raised Eyebrows for *Raise the Red Lantern*', trans. Jeanne Tai, *Public Culture*, 5, no. 2 (1993): 333–337.

21. Koichi Iwabuchi, 'Uses of Japanese Popular Culture: Trans/nationalism and Postcolonial Desire for "Asia"', *Emergences*, 11, no. 2 (2001): 206.

22. Chris Berry, '*Wedding Banquet*: A Family (Melodrama) Affair', in this volume.

23. Giddens, *Transformation of Intimacy*, 191.

24. Dai, 'Severed Bridge', 14.

25. Samuel P. Huntington, 'The Clash of Civilizations?', *Foreign Affairs*, no. 72 (2003): 22–49.

26. Xinhua, 'More Seeking to Learn Chinese', *China Daily*, 3 January 2007, 2.

27. Tu Wei Ming, ed., 'Cultural China: The Periphery as the Center', in *The Living Tree: The Changing Meaning of Being Chinese Today* (Stanford, CA: Stanford University Press, 1994), 33–34.

28. '"China Threat" Fear Countered by Culture', *China Daily*, 29 May 2006, 2.

29. Christina Klein, *Cold War Orientalism: Asia in the Middlebrow Imagination, 1945–1961* (Berkeley: University of California Press, 2003), 7.

30. Ni Zhen, '*Qianli zou danji* jianshu yaoyuan de ai' ('*Riding Alone for Thousands of Miles* Tells a Story about Remote Love'): <ent.sina.com.cn/r/i/2006-01-04/1641949386.html> (9 February 2007).

31. Chow, 'Sentimental Returns', 651.

26 *Spring in a Small Town*: Gazing at Ruins

Carolyn FitzGerald

After Fei Mu (1906–1951) was denounced by the Chinese Communist Party during the late 1950s, his 1948 classic, *Spring in a Small Town*, was banned for several decades.[1] However, in the wake of Mao's death in 1976, softer-line scholars and critics conceded that the Party had made a mistake and overturned their previous indictment of Fei Mu. As a result, his film became available for viewing by the younger generation of film scholars and directors in mainland China, who embraced it as a newly 'discovered' classic.[2] In 2002, Tian Zhuangzhuang, for example, produced a remake of the film, paying homage in the credits to 'China's pioneering filmmakers'. Also, in the same year it was voted the best modern Chinese film of the past hundred years by the Hong Kong Film Association.[3] In addition, like many other directors, Zhang Yimou praised Fei Mu as a master of modern Chinese film,[4] and Hong Kong film director Stanley Kwan even paid a tribute to him in his 1992 film, *Centre Stage*. A large number of essays were written by scholars in mainland China, Hong Kong and Taiwan praising Fei Mu's deployment of traditional aesthetics, including elements of Chinese opera, poetry and painting.[5] As film critic Liu Chenghan, for example, wrote, '… *Spring in a Small Town* is not only a classic treasure chest of Chinese aesthetics, but even more is one of the great works of international film …'.[6]

In contrast, however, to these interpretations, which view the film as a 'timeless' masterpiece characterised by a quintessentially Chinese national style, this essay will instead seek to better historicise Fei Mu's film within the period when it was produced, in the wake of the War of Resistance against Japan (1937–1945) and in the midst of escalating civil war between the Nationalists and the Communists (1945–1949). Having provided a brief background on the post-war period and on Fei's work directing and editing the film script of *Spring in a Small Town*, I

will analyse the film's modernist formal experimentation from the perspective of traumatic memory. Focusing on its deployment of voice-over narration and long-take cinematography of ruins, I will argue that Fei Mu's use of these two techniques reflects his effort to mimic the traumatised consciousness of people living in the ruins of war. While the film's unreliable narrator Yuwen draws attention to the epistemological and psychological problematics of the representation of trauma, the long-take camera gazes meditatively on the ruins of war.

THE POST-WAR PERIOD: VICTORY AS DEFEAT AND THE WOUNDED MALE BODY

After Japanese forces surrendered unconditionally to the Chinese on 15 August 1945, victory parades and celebrations broke out all across China. However, in the weeks and months following the war's end, excitement over victory quickly began to fade. Grappling not only with immense destruction of lives and property resulting from eight protracted years of full-scale colonial invasion by the Japanese, Chinese people also had to face the escalating civil war. The assassination in 1946 of beloved poet and intellectual Wen Yiduo by Nationalist government secret agents sparked a series of protest rallies and mourning in cities throughout China. Realising that the violence of the long war had in no way ended, intellectuals were plagued with a feeling described by Paul Pickowicz in his essay on post-war film as one of 'victory as defeat'.[7]

A memorable scene at the end of Ba Jin's famous 1947 novel *Cold Nights* captured this sentiment particularly well when it portrayed a tubercular protagonist suffering in bed as he listened to victory celebrations outside, too sick to participate. As in Ba Jin's novel, the feeling of defeat in the face of victory appeared frequently in post-war literature and film.

Spring in a Small Town

Well-known post-war epics, *The Spring River Flows East*, *Eight Thousand Miles of Clouds and Moon* and *Distant Love* (all from 1947), for example, portrayed emasculated male characters who were unable to prevent the disintegration and demise of their families.[8] Like post-World War II film in the United States and Europe that according to Kaja Silverman focused 'obsessively and at times erotically on the physical and psychic mutilation'[9] of male characters, so too did Chinese films dwell on male illness and powerlessness in their depiction of the wounds of war.

Filmed in the ruins of a former Jiangnan mansion, Fei Mu's *Spring in a Small Town* also features a sick male protagonist Dai Liyan, the eldest son of a declining elite family. Suffering from lung and heart disease, Liyan lives in separate rooms from his wife, Zhou Yuwen, in the ruins of their former estate. They also live with the family's one remaining servant, Lao Huang, and Liyan's sixteen-year-old sister, Daixiu. The couple barely talks to one another, and Yuwen spends most of her time walking alone aimlessly along the crumbling city wall. One day their lives in the small town are disrupted when Liyan's friend Zhang Zhichen, a doctor of Western medicine, comes to visit. Unbeknown to Liyan, Yuwen and Zhichen used to be sweethearts during their youth, and upon seeing one another, their feelings are rekindled. Stultified by her life with Liyan in their crumbling estate, Yuwen longs to leave with Zhichen. However, feeling weighed down by a sense of responsibility towards her husband, she decides to stay on to care for him. The film ends with Zhichen leaving for the train station, accompanied by Daixiu and Lao Huang.

Unlike other post-war films, which employed large casts and told epic stories of wartime struggle, *Spring in a Small Town* was shot in only three months with five people, using three interior sets.[10] This approach was adopted in part to save money. In an interview with Hong Kong film critic Huang Ailing, the film's lead actress, Wei Wei, recalled that Wenhua Productions opted to shoot amateur screenwriter Li Tianji's film at a low cost in order to make enough profit to cover the expense of their larger production *A Good Husband and Wife*.[11] According to Li Tianji, the film's minimalist aesthetic also resulted from the fact that Fei Mu asked him to cut out almost two-thirds of the script.[12] As Li recalls in his essay 'Hurrying to Make Films for Food', Fei Mu prompted him to reconsider whether the story in fact was about love, and upon reflection he conceded that it actually had more to do with 'dejection' (*kumen*).[13] Originally entitled *Bitter Love*, the name of the film was first changed to *Lost Love*, and eventually to *Spring in a Small Town*.[14] Rather than portraying a sentimental story about a failed romance, Fei Mu instead employed a minimalist plot and let the ruins of war tell their own story through cinematography. As Li later recalled in an interview, Fei Mu had explained his editing of *Spring in a Small Town* and his decision to film in an old mansion with the comment that, 'Sometimes a cinematic frame can speak volumes'.[15]

Also, Li remembered other changes that Fei Mu made, including telling the story from the perspective of Yuwen, removing Liyan's traditional doctor from the story and transforming Zhichen into a doctor of modern medicine. In addition, Li writes that Fei Mu changed the beginning and ending of the film:

> ... I [Li Tianji] originally began the film with Zhichen walking into the small town, and ended with him walking out of the small town, facing the sunlight. After the film was changed, it opened with Yuwen, and ended on Yuwen and her husbands' bodies.[16]

Reminiscent of male protagonists such as Juehui in Ba Jin's *Family* (1957), or Lu Xun's I-narrator in 'My Old Home' (1921), the protagonist in Li's earlier version thus left behind his feudal hometown in the countryside in pursuit of a brighter future when he walked towards the sunlight at the end of the film. However, unlike Li Tianji, and more importantly unlike Lu Xun, Fei Mu's reworking of the film did not portray the modern intellectual embarking on a hopeful journey. Instead, he portrayed a very different story when, at the end of the film, he positioned the camera behind Yuwen to show her perspective from the ruins of her home, as she stands waving goodbye to her former love, the modernised doctor.

With this ending, Fei Mu not only refused to offer a vision of hope for the future but also to valorise the modern doctor and intellectual. In contrast to Lu Xun, who saw himself as the kind of doctor who could cure the soul of the Chinese people,[17] Fei Mu depicted Zhichen as a much less powerful and central figure. Although Zhichen manages to save Liyan from dying, the image of Liyan walking feebly with a cane at the end of the movie suggests that the Westernised doctor lacks any long-term solutions to the problems of the old society and dying landowning class. Yet, Fei Mu also refused to valorise a traditional-style hero as he had in earlier works such as *Filial Piety* (1935) and *Confucius* (1940), which featured 'modern sages' (*modeng shengren*) who solved the problems of the modern era by applying Confucian virtues and values according to the popular dictum of 'Chinese essence, Western techniques' (*zhongti, xiyong*).[18] In contrast, *Spring in a Small Town* portrayed neither the modern intellectual nor the traditional landowner as a figure possessing solutions to rebuilding the ruins of post-war China. Instead, Fei Mu depicted Liyan as someone more like himself, a victim of heart disease and also the eldest son of a landowning family who had accepted his parents' arranged marriage. As Fei Mu commented in a letter to fellow director Yang Ji about the bleak, hopeless ending of the film, in *Spring in a Small Town* he and Li Tianji were unwilling to force the portrayal of a facile 'way out' (*chulu*) for China.[19]

THE UNSTABLE NARRATOR AND THE REPRESENTATION OF TRAUMATIC MEMORY

Apart from changes made to the script, in his filming of *Spring in a Small Town*, Fei Mu also experimented with elements of modernism and film noir, and added the voice-over narration of the female protagonist Yuwen.[20] This addition is one of the most salient and, in some respects, most disturbing features of the film, partly due to its convoluted depiction of time. Commenting at the beginning of the film on Zhichen's arrival, for example, Yuwen states, 'He came from the train station. He walked through the city wall. I had no idea that he would come.'[21] Although Yuwen, the character in the story, has 'no idea' that Zhichen will come, Yuwen the narrator apparently knows a lot more, and describes Zhichen's arrival as though it were a past event. However, Yuwen's voice-over then reverts to the position of a character in the story who is unsure whether or not the newly arrived visitor is Zhichen, before shifting again from third to second person to hold an imaginary conversation with Zhichen in her mind.

Yuwen's vacillating use of tense and person makes it unclear whether she is talking about an event that occurred in the past or present.[22] In particular, given that Chinese is an uninflected language, the tense of the film remains ambiguous and open to multiple interpretations. One possible reading is that the film describes an event that occurred in the past, but as Yuwen remembers the past, it seems so real, she forgets and slips into present tense. As such, her confusion highlights the presentness of the past, the traces of which are everywhere in the ruins of war. This past-tense reading of the film is also bolstered by Fei Mu's use of flashback. The film's opening shot of Zhang Zhichen, Lao Huang and Daixiu leaving for the train station is repeated at the end of the film, suggesting that the entire film is a memory recollected by Yuwen as she walks repeatedly along the crumbling wall.

However, Yuwen not only has trouble remembering the past but at times also actively attempts to forget it. In one scene, for example, she sits by the window in her sister-in-law's room and talks to herself: 'It seems the sun is especially nice sitting in this room. I've long since forgotten the past. I'll never think about anything again.' Yet, despite her desire to forget, Yuwen is continually drawn back to the past as each day she walks 'with no particular destination in mind' along the crumbling wall that serves as *mise en scène* of the destroyed past. The arrival of Zhichen acts as a catalyst that brings to the surface memories and smouldering passions she has tried to forget. Throughout his visit, she wavers between clinging to these memories and trying to distance herself from Zhichen. In many scenes, the two characters appear to be engaged in a kind of dance, wherein they move close to one another, only to shy away and later return again. While Zhichen, who arrives in the film wearing a suit, represents all that is new and Westernised,

Liyan, with his crumbling house and decrepit body, represents the old society. On an allegorical level, the film thus depicts Yuwen's vacillation between past and present, old and new, oblivion and a compulsive attachment to the past.

Although Yuwen's beautiful memories of past romance suggest nostalgia for the old society, they are also marked by confusion and disorientation. To use more clinical terminology, one might say that Yuwen exhibits signs of post-traumatic stress disorder characterised by 'a symptomological dialectic of hypermnesia and amnesia', wherein 'memories are not mastered, but rather are experienced as involuntary, hallucinatory repetitions, or, alternatively, are blocked'.[23] Her narration of a past that she cannot and does not want to remember, and yet is unable to forget, implicitly raises issues about the representation of traumatic memory, and specifically memories of World War II. How is it possible to represent the traumas of war according to ideological paradigms, such as the victory of democracy over fascism, or the leftist denunciation of the Nationalists and the landlord class, when massive destruction of millions of lives does not fit into neat explanations or make logical sense? How can one realistically portray the memory of something one has tried to block because it is too horrible to remember? Yet, how can one not attempt to narrate or make sense of the past when its traces and impact are felt everywhere? Thus, rather than telling a realist narrative, Fei Mu's film most often expresses its story through gaps that speak volumes about his characters – gaps between characters, in the lapses of their faulty memories of the past, in the deteriorating walls of their home and city, and in the chasm between the present and a past that can never be recovered. Though the War of Resistance and the civil war are never actually discussed, through this repression, their impact is perhaps felt more deeply.

THE LONG TAKE: GAZING AT RUINS

While *Spring in a Small Town* became an emblem of cultural authenticity and Chineseness after its 'rediscovery' during the 1980s, Fei Mu's deployment of the long take has often been singled out as reflecting an inherently Chinese aesthetic. In his book *The Roaming Lens*, for example, Lin Niantong, describes Fei Mu's and other Chinese directors' use of the long take as embodying the aesthetic of *you* or unrestrained

roaming found in traditional literature, and especially in scroll painting.[24] To some extent, these interpretations draw from Fei's own assessment of the film in his letter to Yang Ji as a 'bold and crazy experiment' in which he intended to portray the 'bleak mood of traditional Chinese culture through long-takes, a slow moving camera, and dim light'.[25] In addition, many of Fei Mu's essays stress the need to incorporate components of traditional aesthetics, including elements of Chinese painting, poetry and opera, into modern film. For example, in his 1942 essay, 'The Problem of Making Traditional Chinese Drama into Film', Fei Mu discusses his experience producing film versions of traditional Chinese operas, and argues that 'in the heart of the director there often exists a desire to create national painting'.[26]

In keeping with Fei's theorisations, many of the long takes in *Spring in a Small Town* resemble traditional landscape painting, as a small figure appears against the line of the broken city wall, and the camera pans slowly across the scene like an unfurling scroll. In addition, the film apparently reflects Fei Mu's effort to match emotion and scene according to the Chinese poetic conception of *qingjing jiaorong* (fusion of scene and emotion), and the bleak ruins mirror the broken lives of the characters who inhabit them. At times, in fact, the characters blend so well with the background against which they are framed that they appear to become lost or engulfed by the backdrop. As Liyan, for example, states in one scene about his decrepit body, which mirrors the broken ruins he inhabits: 'I'm afraid my health [*shenti* (lit. body)] is like this house, destroyed beyond repair'. However, with such images Fei Mu succeeds in conveying a dystopian sense of doom and agoraphobia, rather than a harmonious scene from a traditional landscape painting. Moreover, the film's resemblance to an unfurling scroll is undercut when Fei Mu employs modernist techniques such as oblique camera angles and frequent fade-outs in the middle of scenes.

Rather than simply re-creating the experience of a Chinese scroll, long takes in the film often serve the function of drawing attention to ruins. In particular, given the film's minimalist aesthetic, long takes of ruins, rather than an action-packed plot, become a central focus of the film. Recalling Yuwen, who returns each day to meander along the collapsing city wall, the camera also moves slowly and repeatedly through the crumbling estate. In addition, the panning of the camera across ruins re-creates the gaze of the film's characters as they view their hometown. This reading of Fei Mu's long-take cinematography draws from Ban Wang's essay 'Trauma, Visuality, and History in Chinese Literature and Film', in which he argues that 'The long take … functions as a metaphor for the traumatized patient, who when asked to tell a coherent story is repeatedly and helplessly seized by a singular persistent image.'[27] Just as Fei Mu's inclusion of Yuwen's voice-over narration affords the viewer a glimpse of her troubled psyche, so too does his cinematography thus mimic the perspective of a witness 'seized' by the ever-present image of post-war ruins.

In addition, Fei Mu's cinematography also reproduces the barred and vulnerable perspective of the characters by shooting many long takes from low angles, behind windows and curtains, or blocked by pieces of rubble. Such disorienting positioning of Fei Mu's camera stands in contrast to a more omniscient perspective provided in other post-war films. In *Eight Thousand Miles of Clouds and Moon*, for example, characters' travels within the interior during the war are accompanied by maps so that the viewer never loses track of them. However, in *Spring in a Small Town*, the viewer is never clear where the 'small town' is or what exists outside of it, just as the characters often find themselves lost amid the cavernous, rambling ruins of the family estate.

Yet, while Fei Mu's film in some respects differs from other post-war films, his use of the long take parallels a similar trend in both Chinese and European post-war cinema.[28] André Bazin, for example, describes a rise in long-take cinematography in Europe during the late 1940s.[29] Also, in *Cinema 2*, Gilles Deleuze writes about post-war film directors' growing interest in the 'time image' (his term for the long take). Discussing this trend in post-war cinema in his essay in this volume on Jia Zhangke's *Xiao Wu*, Chris Berry links interest in the long take with the destruction and 'falling away of faith in the modern project' brought about by World War II and the Holocaust that made it difficult for directors to readily view time-as-movement or time-as-progress. As such, Berry argues that the long take, with its protracted gaze, often on empty space, served to accurately convey a sense of purposeless and unprogressive passage of time experienced by people living in the wake of the war.

This reading of the long take as expressing a lack of faith in time-as-progress accords with Fei Mu's convoluted portrayal of time in the film and his rejection of the perspective of the 'enlightened' modern intellectual. Also, it concurs with the film's preoccupation with ruins, a focus found as well in European wartime intellectual Walter Benjamin's work, the *Arcades Project*. As Susan Buck-Morss argues in her essay 'Historical Nature: Ruin', Benjamin's allegorical treatment of ruins in this work shows that 'the crumbling of the monuments that were built to signify the immortality of civilization becomes proof, rather, of its transiency'.[30] Reading Fei Mu's cinematography of ruins in dialogue with European wartime film and intellectual thought, it thus becomes possible to draw linkages between wartime disillusionment and modernisms in both Europe and China. Moreover, a historicised approach offers an alternative paradigm for understanding the use of the long take in earlier Chinese films from the 1920s and 1930s. Instead of simply interpreting the prevalence of the long take in modern Chinese cinema as evidence of a national style, it becomes possible also to see it as bespeaking of disillusionment with modernity on the part of intellectuals living in a society wracked by repeated wars and foreign invasions.

However, apart from suggesting a lack of faith in time-as-progress, Fei Mu's cinematography of ruins also conveys a sense of unutterable loss over the destruction of traditional society. This predicament is represented allegorically by the plight of Yuwen, who can neither leave with Zhichen to head towards a bright future, nor return to her home as it was before the war. The film thus portrays an impasse of not only loss of faith in Westernised modernity but also an inability to return to a past that has been reduced to ruins. This unresolved tension likewise mirrors Yuwen's inability either to remember or forget, and the film's uneasy blending of traditional aesthetics stressing harmony with destabilising modernist techniques such as flashback, voice-over narration and mid-scene fade-outs. Clearly, Fei Mu longed to find harmony between 'tradition' and modernity, as is evident in his fascination with the 'modern sage' and his extensive study and theorisations on Chinese art and aesthetics. However, the power and artistry of *Spring in a Small Town* lies not in its unproblematic adherence to a signature national aesthetic grounded in 'tradition'. Rather it stems from the film's vivid psychological portrayal of the traumatic rupture between past and present experienced by people living in the wake of World War II, and from its elegiac expression of yearning for the ruins of what has been destroyed.

Moreover, the impasse portrayed in the film between new and old reflects not only on post-war realities but also on the schizophrenic political situation Fei Mu witnessed as he faced China's growing civil war. Prior to filming *Spring in a Small Town*, Fei Mu spent two years directing *Majestic Mountains and Rivers*, a film that depicted the harmonious resolution of conflict between the Nationalist and Communist Party. However, due to both financial problems and widespread criticism, he was never able to finish his project.[31] Though he longed to help find a peaceful resolution to the battles between warring political factions in Shanghai, he was ultimately rejected by right and left-wing directors, who both held him in contempt and suspicion.[32] Following the release of *Spring in a Small Town*, Fei Mu went to work in Hong Kong. When he attempted to return to China after the end of the civil war in 1949, he was met coldly by many left-wing workers in the film industry. Required to write a self-criticism, he refused and thereafter returned to Hong Kong, where he died in 1951 of heart failure.

NOTES

1. I would like to acknowledge gratitude to individuals who gave me feedback on earlier drafts of this paper. In particular, I would like to thank Paul Pickowicz for his many insightful comments. Also, I am very grateful to Lydia Liu, David Rolston, Song Hwee Lim, Julian Ward, Feng Jin, Benjamin Ridgway, Miranda Brown and Ning Qiang for their helpful suggestions.

2. Chen Mo, 'Timeless *Spring in a Small Town*' ('Buxiu de *Xiaocheng zhi chun*'), in *Retrospective on One Hundred Years of Chinese Film (Bainian dianying shanhui)* (Beijing: Zhongguo jingji, 2000), 175.

3. See the Hong Kong Film Awards website: <www.hkfaa.com> (23 December 2006).

4. See the interview between Zhang Yimou and Zhu Jun online at: <book.qq.com/s/book/0/5/5498/70.shtml> (19 April 2007).

5. See, for example, the essays collected in Wu Zhongli, ed., *The Film Aesthetics of* Spring in a Small Town – *A Tribute to Fei Mu* (Xiaocheng zhi chun de dianying

meixue – xiang Fei Mu zhi jing) (Taiwan: Shenshi yishu, 1996); see also Huang Ailing, ed., *The Poet Director – Fei Mu (Shiren daoyan – Fei Mu)* (Hong Kong: Hong Kong Film Critics' Association, 1998); Chen Mo, *Essays on Fei Mu's Films – Wandering Bird and Spring Dream (Fei Mu dianying lungao – Liuying chunmeng)* (Beijing: Zhongguo dianying, 2000).

6. Liu Chenghan, '*Spring in a Small Town*: A Model of Exposition, Explicit, and Implied Comparison ('*Xiaocheng zhi chun*: fu, bi, xing de dianfan'), in *A Collection of Filmic Exposition, Explicit, and Implied Comparison (Dianying fu, bi, xing ji)*, ed. Liu Chenghan (Hong Kong: Tiandi tushu, 1992), 68.

7. Paul Pickowicz, 'Victory as Defeat: Postwar Visualizations of China's War of Resistance', in *Becoming Chinese: Passages to Modernity and Beyond*, ed. Wen-hsin Yeh (Berkeley: University of California Press, 2000), 342–365.

8. For a discussion of the prevalence of weak male figures in post-war film, see also Brett Sutcliffe, '*A Spring River Flows East*: "Progressive" Ideology and Gender Representation', online at: <www.latrobe.edu.au/screeningthepast/firstrelease/fir1298/bsfr5c.html> (16 November 2006).

9. Kaja Silverman, *Male Subjectivity at the Margins* (New York: Routledge, 1992), 53.

10. Huang Ailing, 'Interview with Wei Wei' ('Fangwen Wei Wei'), in *Poet Director*, 203.

11. Ibid., 201.

12. See Li Tianji's essay on his three meetings with Fei Mu to edit his script, 'Receiving Instruction Three Times: Distant Parting Forever' ('Sanci shou jiao: youran yongjue'), in Huang, ed., *Poet Director*, 189–193.

13. Li Tianji, 'Hurrying to Make Films for Food' ('Wei le fanwan ganshang dianying'), in *Selections of Li Tianji's Film Scripts (Li Tianji dianying juzuo xuan)* (Beijing: Xuelin, 1996), 331. In an essay about her father, Fei Mingyi also recalls that when she mistook *Spring in a Small Town* for a romance, her father told her that she must have been exposed to too many Hollywood films; see 'Mr Fei Mu – My Father' ('Fei Mu xiansheng – wo de fuqin'), in Wu, ed., *Film Aesthetics of* Spring in a Small Town, 8.

14. Li, 'Hurrying to Make Films for Food', 331.

15. Zhu Tianwei, 'Interview with the Screenwriter and Composer of *Spring in a Small Town*' ('Dui *Xiaocheng zhi chun* juzuojia he zuoqujia de fangwen'), presented at the 'Conference on Research of Fei Mu's Films',

held at the Beijing Archives on 3 March 1997. Quoted in Chen, *Essays on Fei Mu's Films*, 361.

16. Li , 'Hurrying to Make Films for Food', 337.

17. See, for example, Lu Xun's 'Preface to *Call to Arms*' ('*Nahan* xuyan'), in which he describes his decision to become a writer rather than a doctor.

18. For a discussion on the figure of the 'modern sage' in Fei Mu's early works, see Chapter 9, 'The Modern Sage', in Chen, *Essays on Fei Mu's Films*, 112–124; for an analysis of Fei Mu's earlier propaganda film *Filial Piety*, see Paul Pickowicz, 'The Theme of Spiritual Pollution in Chinese Films of the 1930s', in *Modern China*, 17, no. 1 (January 1991): 57–61. Although several of Fei Mu's earlier films were produced for the Nationalist government's 'New Life Movement' that promoted traditional morality, the recurrence of the 'modern sage' in his film suggests his genuine admiration for this figure.

19. Fei Mu, 'Director, Script Writer – Written for Yang Ji' ('Daoyan juzuozh – xie gei Yang Ji'), dated 9 September 1948, in Huang, ed., *Poet Director*, 99. Also, in this letter, Fei Mu comments that he portrayed Liyan as a landowner in order to represent the plight of a class of people who could 'no longer collect rent, nor sell their land'.

20. For a discussion on film noir techniques in post-war European film, see Sheri Biesen, *Blackout: World War II and the Origins of Film Noir* (Baltimore, MD: Johns Hopkins University Press, 2005).

21. For the Chinese film script of *Spring in a Small Town*, see Wu, ed., *Film Aesthetics of* Spring in a Small Town, 104–144. For an online English translation by Andrew Jones at MCLC website, see: <mclc.osu.edu/rc/pubs/spring/default.htm> (1 March 2007).

22. Chen Mo also describes the uncertain tense of the film in his *Essays on Fei Mu's Films*, 421–422.

23. Joshua Hirsch, 'Post-Traumatic Cinema and the Holocaust Documentary', in *Trauma and Cinema: Cross-Cultural Explorations*, ed. Ann Kaplan and Ban Wang (Hong Kong: Hong Kong University Press, 2004), 116.

24. See Lin Niantong, *The Roaming Lens* (*Jingyou*) (Hong Kong: Su ye, 1985); also see Lin Niantong, 'Consciousness of Space in Chinese Film' ('Zhongguo dianying de kongjian yishi'), in *E hu* (*Goose River*), 109 (July 1984): 42–50.

25. Fei, 'Director, Script Writer', 99.

26. See Fei Mu 'The Problem of Making Traditional Chinese Drama into Film' ('Zhongguo jiuju de dianyinghua wenti'), in Huang, ed., *Poet Director*, 84–87 (83).

27. Ban Wang, 'Trauma, Visuality, and History in Chinese Literature and Film', in *Trauma and Cinema*, ed. Kaplan and Ban, 238.

28. For a discussion on long-take cinematography in post-war Chinese films, see Lin, *Roaming Lens*, 5–10.

29. André Bazin, 'An Aesthetic of Reality: Neorealism', in *What is Cinema?*, vol. 2, trans. Hugh Gray (Berkeley: University of California Press, 1971), 28.

30. See Susan Buck-Morss, *The Dialectics of Seeing: Walter Benjamin and the Arcades Project* (Massachusetts: MIT Press, 1989), 164.

31. See Huang, 'Interview with Wei Wei', 202–203.

32. Ibid.

27 *A Time to Live, A Time to Die*: A Time to Grow

Corrado Neri

A Time to Live, A Time to Die (1985) is an autobiographical film by Hou Hsiao-hsien, in which the director, who was born in China in 1947 but grew up in Taiwan, recalls his youth and adolescence. The movie is part of a 'biographical trilogy', through which the director reconstructs the memories of his generation. Hou had acquired a solid technical background in the early part of the 1980s, when he directed three successful musical comedies. The turning point was *The Sandwich Man* (1983), a portmanteau feature film that marks the birth of the New Taiwan Cinema movement and for which he directed one part. Then came *Boys from Fenggui* (1983), a partly autobiographical film, in which Hou, still hovering between commercial film-making and personal expression, started investigating the themes that remained the focus of his later work – growing up, the generation gap, sexuality, Taiwan's economical and political problems, and the rural–urban dichotomy. He also started investigating a new language to express these themes, by experimenting with non-professional actors, long takes, still camera shots and elliptic editing. *Boys from Fenggui* is still experimental, but the biographical trilogy demonstrates maturity. The first chapter is *Summer at Grandpa's* (1984), based on the memories of the writer Zhu Tianwen. The second is *A Time to Live, A Time to Die*, which is autobiographical (the screenplay was co-written by Zhu Tianwen, as all other Hou movies have been). The third is entitled *Dust in the Wind* (1986), and is based on the experiences of Wu Nianzhen, the famous Taiwanese screenwriter, actor and director.[1]

The very first film of the Taiwan New Cinema, *In Our Time* (Edward Yang, Ke Yizheng, Zhang Yi and Tao Dechen, 1982), also deals with memory, as the directors were asked to work on an episode taken from their youth. The New Cinema opposed artistic movies to commercial comedies, realism to studio-made films, non-professional actors to the star-system, and reflection on society and human lives to pure escapism. The directors, and in particular Hou, started describing their own experiences, trying to put reality back on the screen by dealing with the familiar landscapes of memory. Hou, with his Taiwan trilogy of *A City of Sadness* (1989), *The Puppetmaster* (1993) and *Good Men, Good Women* (1995), Yang Dechang, Wu Nianzhen and the other Taiwan New Cinema directors undertook a very precise process moving first to deal with autobiography, and then with history *tout-court*. Because of the socio-political commitment of Chinese artists, the investigation of the past cannot stop at personal feelings and nostalgia; it also has to deal with the nation itself, society and cultural identity.[2] *A Time* is consistent with the Chinese tradition of placing the personal story within the greater context of history, and Hou's cinematic style is consistent with the Confucian vision of a committed artist. As I shall note later, it should be emphasised that some stylistic procedures also express the director's deepest feelings, even if in an implicit and poetic manner.

Biography, and particularly autobiography, is traditionally a literary genre that links back to history as its original source. As Nienhauser reminds us, 'The principal aim of autobiography was to celebrate one's name and make known one's parents.'[3] The first autobiography in China is usually identified as the *Lisao*, a famous poetic composition by Qu Yuan, which starts with a description of the poet's genealogy.[4] The autobiographical notes by Sima Qian in the conclusion of his historical *opus magnum*, the *Shiji*, are also noteworthy.[5] Here the presentation of the author's life is justified and takes on significance owing to and through the text itself. The intertextual references form a network from the past to the present, inscribing the writer in a rich and noble tradition that gives order to the world. The identity of the individual man is to be found and understood in this semantic context, thanks to his being part of a larger scheme. The historian finds his place in society and the meaning of his life by defining himself as the one who hands down and keeps the memories of past events alive. He finds a way to be remembered by remembering.[6]

Autobiography (*zizhuan*) is far from the modern Western tradition of autobiography, characterised by romanticism and psychology.[7] It is more a matter of finding a place in society (and nature) that can provide a sense of harmony in existence. It is also a way to pay respect to the memory of parents and family, which is, together with society, the greater context of human existence.

In accordance with Chinese cultural tradition, Hou speaks of himself in an indirect manner. (It is significant that nothing in the film suggests the fact that Hou will become an artist.[8]) He evokes the most personal memories and re-creates images of his youth on screen. These were the strongest images that had marked his imagination and have gone on to become obsessions in later years. However, this procedure is carried out through a de-personalisation of the narration, putting his intimate feelings at a distance and choosing a detached perspective, as if he were merely a spectator of his own story and not the protagonist. The real protagonists are his family and his country. The scholar Ni Zhen writes:

> Hou Hsiao-hsien's systematic and highly stylized cinematic prose expresses very incisively and vividly the ethical spirit of Confucian culture and the emotional attachment to the native land typical of the Orient. The family is a cohesive, highly symbolic unit of Confucian culture, the fundamental space within which to view and examine the psychological world of the Chinese.[9]

The movie also features some cultural traits that emerge indirectly: Hou seems to revitalise the *biji* tradition. The *biji* is a literary genre dating back to the Song Dynasty. It is a diary form in prose, a miscellany made up of annotations, which are often very refined and poetic.[10] The most remarkable example is Shen Fu's eighteenth-century *Fusheng liuji* (*Six Chapters from a Floating Life*). 'This work, now consisting of four chapters … amounts to a systematically arranged autobiographical review of the author's life; within the Chinese tradition it is unusual for its detail and candor.'[11] It is difficult to classify the *Six Chapters*

among the literary genres. It anticipates some features of the modern novel (*xiaoshuo*), because it contains an atypical expression of the self as well as a self-conscious pleasure in pure writing that is neither socially nor politically engaged. The latter is a characteristic that Lu Xun ascribes to the novel.[12] However, we do not find classical narration with a beginning and an end, but a juxtaposition of impressions and strong images, characters and landscapes. Therefore, the *biji* is a mix of a very traditional sensitivity, as well as an innovative and modern way of dealing with memories. It refuses exposition according to the logic of cause and effect, preferring an impressionistic approach and refusing to write a *Bildungsroman* in which the characters are exemplars. We will not find catharsis, redemption or a climax, but the placid rhythm of life floating along. Another important characteristic of the autobiographical *biji* narrative is that it has an episodic structure, and does not follow chronological criteria. Hou's films do follow a chronological line, but like the *biji* form they accumulate their details according to atmospheric affinities and the similarity of various visual impressions. So, like this typical Chinese form and unlike the Western tradition of autobiography, Hou's films are repetitive and apparently not demonstrative, and proceed by accumulation and not by synthesis. Certain scenes repeat like a hypnotic rhythm through the film: the women of the family talking while they sit on the wooden floor in a medium-long shot; the eldest son working at the father's desk in a medium shot with the camera placed outside the room; the grandmother sleeping on the floor in a medium shot, and so on. Hou uses autobiography as a means to express personal feelings and to develop a unique style of his own in an episodic manner that recalls the *biji* tradition, as well as to describe and hand down the experiences of his family and country in the *xiaoshuo* tradition.[13]

As for his visual approach, it is interesting that Hou does not admit any direct inspiration, but cites only the 'panoramic vision' of Shen Congwen (1902–1988).[14] The writer's influence on Hou could only be indirect. Shen's autobiography[15] starts with a wide perspective on the writer's hometown, the houses and the people, and only later is his character introduced. This is exactly what happens in Hou's movies, which also follow this descriptive technique of proceeding by successive reduction. This is how

Hou introduces himself into the narrative of *A Time*. After the description of the house in Hou's own voice-over over a few still shots, the grandmother goes to the village looking for her grandson. There is a wide pan shot of the little town, then a cut to a medium shot that focuses slowly in on a group of children playing. Hou must be among them, but which one is he? This is a very elegant and discreet way of introducing himself into the story. The beginning of the film already introduces the poetics of the contemplative slow rhythm, the aesthetics of the long take and the composition of long shots including blank spaces.[16] Unlike other writers of the period, Shen Congwen had only been negligibly influenced by Western literature (as Hou is not ostensibly influenced by Western cinema). Their approaches to creation are very instinctive and unmediated. Both are strongly attached to the soil of their motherland and celebrate it in their works, and both rejected formal schooling to learn from real life. Their attitude is somehow similar, and quite atypical in the Chinese context. Furthermore, as in Shen Fu's memories, Hou Hsiao-hsien and Shen Congwen's works both display an alternation between an intimate description of the author's inner feelings that is doubly striking given their position as distant observers and a detached description of their backgrounds, often made up of an enumeration of family names, place names and visual details, transferred in Hou's case into cinematic language by the use of the long-take description of village life and geometric compositions that inscribe the characters in their family and social context.

Made up of very long takes, elliptical narrative, an aesthetics of stasis and elaborate geometric compositions, Hou's mature aesthetic reached complete harmony in *A Time*. This aesthetic claims the status of art for film-making, and imposes a distinctive authorial gaze and the patient habit of careful observation. The long shot is used with a full understanding of its possibilities: every frame is divided into multiple frames made up of windows, doors and mirrors. The frame is balanced and in perfect stillness, the movements of the characters providing an internal rhythm. Once again, this is a stylistic strategy, but it also corresponds to the way things were perceived at that time, when all doors and windows were always open, when people were used to talking for hours sitting on the doorsteps of their houses, before skyscrapers, tiles, pollution and the urbanisation of Taiwan. Thanks to

these techniques, the spectator feels as if he were an intimate witness, just like little Hou.[17]

Hou works on reality, flirting with documentary film – almost all his actors are non-professionals. He tries to revive old pictures of his family, re-creating the exact conditions of the past for new people. One sequence shows his sister's class, all in a line in a medium shot, and a photographer taking a picture. The students are still but moving; they comb their hair and arrange their clothes. The image cuts to an old black-and-white picture of a class. With this editing, like a poetic juxtaposition placing the real picture against the fictional shot, Hou signals one sense of the movie; it is a new form of archaeology, an attempt to re-create the past by restoring movement back to a still image and bringing the subjects back to life.

This attitude also confirms a deep interest in memory and historical reconstruction. 'It can be argued that this desire to (re)construct a family or regional history is in itself the result of an obsession with history, which is certainly a dominant Chinese cultural trait', argues Leo Ou-fan Lee.[18] Memory is fragmented, and Hou, free from any demonstrative project or a romantic representation of the self, creates particles that can be inscribed in history.

One of the indirect ways to introduce history in narration is to use the eyes of witnesses as a filter, especially the bewilderment in the eyes of children. Another formal strategy (frequent in *A City of Sadness*) is to utilise news from the radio to let the historical context filter into the private lives of the family. Hou's family, following his father, moved to Taiwan only two years before the separation from the mainland. As suggested in the film, Hou feels the island is his homeland because he lived there all his life; but his parents cannot help feeling they are exiles. They cannot find their place in the new country where they were supposed to live only a few months, but where they find themselves obliged to stay for ever. The strongest symbol of this situation is undoubtedly the character of the grandmother. The old lady disappears from time to time and is found walking lost in the neighbourhood. She is looking for a mythical bridge that can take her back home, because she cannot stand to be far from the graves of her ancestors. With this significant character, Hou creates both a touching figure of a 'time to die' and the unstoppable decay of body and mind, as well as a metaphor of exile. Bai Xianyong argues in some of his best

A Time to Live, A Time to Die

short stories that the Chinese in general are parricidal because they 'killed' the legacy of Confucius in the first decades of the century, denying the importance of tradition while worshipping the idea of an imported modernity.[19] If this is true, the Chinese-Taiwanese must be even guiltier, having severed the ties with their motherland. Another important symbol of the father's generation's sense of exile is provided by the father's chair – the same metaphor as used in *Boys from Fengui*. It is made, as is the rest of the furniture, of bamboo. As the sister discovers by reading her father's journal after his death, this was not an aesthetic choice but a practical need. Bamboo is cheap, flexible and light. The father did not want to settle down in Taiwan and was always ready to return to the continent as soon as the KMT Nationalist army took it back. The Hou family's bamboo furniture becomes both a sign of the premature death of the father and subsequent economic difficulties and a metonymy of Taiwan, an empire born from exile, from retreat, loss and emptiness. There are other elliptical strategies indicating the tense situation of the times. For example, one morning after a sleepless

night for Hou's father, the people of the village find huge tank tracks in the mud outside their poor houses. War is thundering just outside the door, with its fearful rumble. Tension is created, and a sensation of malaise and threat filters into the film in a very subtle way. This visual procedure also corresponds to Hou's real experience, as he was just a child in the early 1950s and only became aware of the situation and drama of his relatives by small clues and brief intuitions in exactly this manner. The spectator never sees the threat waiting off screen, only its shadow drawing over the serenity of daily life. Last but not least, this is also an expressive example of how a low-budget movie can resolve problems without sacrificing strong meaning and deep impact.

It is significant that after the most dramatic sequences, which imply time to be linear, there is a shot focused on clusters of trees and the sky, suggesting a circular idea of time. Historical or private tragedies are to be reconstructed and re-created in front of the camera, but the sky is always the same, the same blue now as when Hou was a child. The episode thus preserves its significance, engraved for ever in memory, but is also seen as inscribed in the serene circularity of nature.

Could this mean that there is no lesson for the young Hou to learn? Perhaps it is useful to return to the idea of the *biji* form and the English title of the film.[20] The structure of the film, though apparently very simple and linear, is punctuated by key images that create an echo, linked together by the artist's retrospective eye. It is possible to classify life experiences according to various inventories. As Shen Fu catalogues his experiences under titles like *Of Small Delights in Idleness* and so on, Hou lists the peaceful moments and the pleasures, and the violence and the mourning, under the categories of 'a time to live' and 'a time to die', respectively. The time to live includes the nostalgic description of his youth, childhood games, first loves, lost sensations of summer smells, long talks around a table and the anticipation typical of every adolescence, as well as the feeling of loss (conveyed by the long, still takes). In these moments, the movie seems free, spontaneous and almost random.

The time to die is the hidden structure of the movie, the trace of signification. Even if these tragic events seem to flow with the natural movements of the seasons, they are actually symbols of crucial moments in Hou's life. They are different stages, each of them bringing a different awareness.

The first death is the father's. In Hou's process of growing up, this signifies lack, an awakening and awareness of emptiness, and rupture. (It is possible to use the same terms for the Taiwan nation, as well.) The father's death occurs during a blackout; his passing away is not shown, but the screen remains black for several seconds. After a few scenes, there is another powerful ellipsis, the most significant temporal ellipsis of the film. After long scenes of mourning, there is a medium shot of young Hou going to the bathroom. Hearing a cry, he turns his head. There is a close-up of the young Hou, his eyes wide open with fear. The next cut to a medium shot shows that it is his mother who cried out. Then there is another close-up on Hou, who is now a teenager. Something like ten years have passed. This is an efficient and surprising stylistic choice, made even more notable because close-ups are so rare in the film. This cut occurs after one hour, almost midway through the movie. Significantly, Hou decides to avoid representation of the mourning period and the difficult years

without his father, so that these dramatic and painful events remain off screen. They are not seen, but their presence casts a shadow on the rest of the movie, implicit, but strong nonetheless. The boy's existence is built on emptiness, on a sense of loss. In this way, it is exactly like the film, for Hou's voice-over at the beginning of the film states, 'this film is about my father'. However, the father passes away very soon, so more precisely, it is a film about the absence of the father. This absence had profound consequences for Hou, the most direct being loss of respect for authority and lack of respect and projects for the future, which his gang of friends shares and expresses in pointless violence and rebellion against authority.[21]

Childhood ends, in Hou's experience, with death and pain; ellipsis itself is a loss, things missing. Furthermore, the cut is on a pair of eyes: the first express the terror of a child who sees his family broken; the second just give the lazy glance of an annoyed teenager. But can the audience not see in that gaze the shadow of a past tragedy? It is an invisible reflex, a faded trace, but by approaching the two dimensions of his character in this manner, Hou suggests a dark continuity. This continuity is the impotence that exists when faced with loss. Hou manages to describe the more imperceptible consequences of drama (and of history), like the trace of infinite sadness in the eyes of his characters, and he entrusts the unspoken, the suggestion and minimal description of small details to mirror ineffable feelings.

The death of the mother is also treated with a particular stylistic strategy that creates the invisible architecture of the film. It underlines the peculiar structure of echoes and repetitions, and establishes a connection between sexuality (the son's puberty and first sexual experience) and death (the mother's illness).

I do not think this reveals a vision of sexuality as sin or implies an oedipal relationship, but rather it underscores the cycle of the seasons, and of life and death. Perhaps, by dealing with such delicate and difficult themes together, there is also an attempt to accept them as complementary and inscribe them in the natural flow of events. Besides that, the sequence of the mother's agony is similar to that of the father's. This gives a sense of the creeping circularity of time, like nature always repeating its own fearful symmetry. These must have been terribly strong images that the young Hou could not elaborate until the making of the film, and they remain identical and obsessive. They filter experiences, while also lending poetic unity to the film as leitmotifs. In this sense, I believe that behind the veil of the interest in history and society, it is possible to glimpse traces of deep reflection, and the author's feelings and obsessions. Hou gives flesh and blood to the ghosts imprinted on his retina, crucial points where everything dropped away and then all resumed. The long takes and the other formal features discussed above allow these images to penetrate into the eyes of the spectator as they penetrated Hou's eyes, like ink absorbed by paper.

The last strong image is the death of the grandmother, an image that gives Hou the possibility to state indirectly what he will be. She dies in her sleep. The nephews find her when some ants are already walking over her body. First we see a close-up of the young Hou writing, then a long shot of the house from outside as the voice-over starts again, followed by a medium shot of the grandmother lying on the floor (possibly sleeping, as usual). Then there is a close-up of her hands, with ants running over her fingers, a medium shot of the woman, in which it is evident that her face is white, and then a long-take long shot as the nephews arrive. This end is lyrical (the quiet silence of the image, the sweet death of the woman) and prosaic (the voice-over speaks with apparent detachment), violent (the clotted blood, the neighbourhood reproaching the three nephews because they did not discover the body earlier) and tender (the three hovering close to each other). The film ends with Hou's voice-over as we see a medium shot of the nephews looking at their grandmother's body. He says, 'I remember', and it is as if he were taking over his mother's role, for she was always remembering family histories and refused to let the doctor operate on her because she would not have been able to speak, and that is what she needed to do. Now she is dead, and the role of the person who speaks and remembers and tells the stories must be filled again.

Tied with love and modesty to his recollections and to his lost adolescence, Hou, who comes together as both character and director only at the end of the film, is a sweet murmur of memory. He is the one who is not going to forget, who is going from one village to another to remember his people, the way it was in the lost time of their youth. This voice cries on a chaotic island, in a city of sadness, in a country rocked by the post-economic boom and by forced Westernisation, and from an alien country repudiated by his own native land, seeking success and modernisation with dangerous enthusiasm. Hou murmurs about time lost and time found, using cinema not as an amazing machine but as art; a potential madeleine both personal and social. The hiatus between a time to live and a time to die must be filled (or, it is full to the brim) with other times, especially a time for reflection and a time for memory, and this movie represents them softly, with a gaze full of affection. Hou, the character, facing his dead grandmother, does not think, but remembers. In this way, he grows.[22]

NOTES

1. See Bérénice Reynaud, 'Taiwanese Cinema: From the Occupation to Today' ('Cinema di Taiwan: dall'occupazione giapponese a oggi'), in *The History of World Cinema* (*Storia del Cinema Mondiale*), vol. 4, ed. Gian Piero Brunetta (Turin: Einaudi, 2001), 857–877; Peggy Chiao (Jiao Xiongping), *New Taiwan Cinema* (*Taiwan xin dianying*) (Taipei: Shibao wenhua chuban qiye youxian gongsi, 1988); Marco Müller, ed., *Taiwan: New Electric Shadows* (*Taiwan: nuove ombre elettriche*) (Venice: Marsilio, 1985); Yingjin Zhang and Zhiwei Xiao, *Encyclopaedia of Chinese Film* (New York: Routledge, 1998).

2. See Robert Hegel, ed., *Expression of Self in Chinese Literature* (New York: Columbia University Press, 1985); Wendy Larson, ed., *Literary Authority and the Modern Chinese Writer; Ambivalence and Autobiography* (Durham, NC: Duke University Press, 1991).

3. William H. Nienhauser cites the Confucian scholar Liu Chih-chi in *The Indiana Companion to Traditional Chinese Literature* (Bloomington: Indiana University Press, 1986), 842.

4. 'Descendant of the ancestor Kao-Yang,/Po-yung was my honoured father's name./When the constellation She-t'i pointed the first month,/on the day keng-yin I was born.' In Burton Watson, trans. and ed., *The Columbia Book of Chinese Poetry* (New York: Columbia University Press, 1984), 54.

5. The Grand Historian [the author's father] grasped my hand and said, weeping, 'Our ancestors were Grand Historians for the house of Zhou … will this tradition end with me? If you in turn become Grand Historian, you must continue the work of our ancestors. … Now, filial piety begins with the serving of our parents; next, you must serve your

sovereign; and, finally, you must make something of
yourself, that your name may go down through the
ages to the glory of your father and mother.
In Theodore de Bary and Irene Bloom, *Sources of
Chinese Tradition*, vol. 1 (New York: Columbia
University Press, 1999), 370.

6. See Stephen Owen, *Remembrances: The Experience of
the Past in Classical Chinese Literature* (London:
Harvard University Press, 1986), 136–137.

7. C. T. Hsia, *The Classical Chinese Novel* (New York:
Columbia University Press, 1968), 312.

8. Hou says: 'I have always been searching for a
particular Chinese style and method of expressing
feeling. The Chinese people have always gone about a
tortuous and roundabout route in expressing
emotions.' Peggy Chiao, 'History's Subtle Shadows',
Cinemaya, no. 21 (1993): 8.

9. Ni Zhen, 'Classical Chinese Painting and
Cinematographic Signification', in *Cinematic
Landscapes: Observations on the Visual Arts and Cinema
of China and Japan*, ed. Linda C. Ehrlich and David
Desser (Austin: University of Texas Press, 1994), 75.

10. Wilt Idema and Lloyd Haft, *A Guide to Chinese
Literature* (Ann Arbor, MI: Center for Chinese
Studies, University of Michigan, 1997), 58–59,
161–162.

11. Ibid., 188.

12. Lu Xun, *A Brief History of Chinese Fiction* (Beijing:
Foreign Languages Press, 1976), 80–81.

13. Lu Xun cites the *Han Dynasty History*: '*Xiaoshuo* were
the talk on the streets … All the talk of the streets and
highways was recorded.' And then, citing the scholar
Chi Yun: '… the *xiaoshuo* writers were successors of
the Zhou dynasty officers who collected information
… the task of these officers was to help the ruler to
understand country ways and morals.' Lu, *A Brief
History*, 4, 6. The word *xiaoshuo* is now used to
indicate the novel.

14. In Michel Frodon, ed., *Hou Hsiao Hsien* (Paris:
Cahiers du Cinéma, 1999), 73.

15. Shen Congwen, *Recollection of West Hunan*, trans.
Gladys Yang (Beijing: Foreign Languages Press, 1982).

16. For discussions on the 'Chineseness' of this style, see
(among others) Lin Niantong, 'A Study of the

Theories of Chinese Cinema in Their Relationship to
Classical Aesthetics', *Modern Chinese Literature*, 1, no.
2 (1985): 185–198; Yeh Yueh-yu, 'Politics and Poetics
of Hou Hsiao-hsien's Films', *Postscript*, 20, nos. 2/3
(2001): 61–76. Note also that there are at least two
versions of the film in circulation, one of which does
not begin with the voice-over.

17. In Stanley Kwan's 1996 documentary, *Yang + Yin:
Gender in Chinese Cinema*, Hou says he feels a strong
sense of nostalgia for a time when life was lived in a
community. Now, he complains, everyone is hidden
behind thick walls of concrete. This sensation is
transmitted in his movies.

18. Leo Ou-fan Lee, 'Afterword: Reflections on Change
and Continuity in Modern Chinese Fiction', in *From
May Fourth to June Fourth*, ed. Ellen Widmer and
David Der-wei Wang (Cambridge, MA: Harvard
University Press, 1993), 378. The author refers to Lao
Shi, Ba Jin, Shen Congwen, Mo Yan and others.

19. See Bai Xianyong, 'Winter Nights', in *Chinese Stories
from Taiwan: 1960–1970*, ed. Joseph Lau (New York:
Columbia University Press, 1976), 337–354.

20. I am aware that the original title conveys a different
meaning (*Tongnian wangshi* means 'the past things of
youth'). Still, as in every Taiwanese production, the
original title is accompanied by an English title,
directly chosen by the director himself.

21. It is possible to make a comparison with the gangs in
Tsai Ming-liang's films, especially *Rebels of the Neon
God* (1992). These latter are much more nihilistic and
desperate; they live in a modern city. If the young Lee
Kang-sheng in *The River* (1997) is a kind of Oedipus,
the strangers in *A Time* are like his daughter,
Antigone, forced into exile. As Lee does not blind
himself, but sees everything and goes on living,
indifferent, here the Antigones, with the natural
indifference of time and the seasons, simply get used
to the new place. If still some contrasts exist with the
generation of Hou's parents, his generation is like a
river that creates its new bed, with time and patience,
and without tragedy.

22. In *Yang + Yin*, Hou says that he wants to teach his
children two values: respect for themselves and the
ability to adapt.

A Touch of Zen: Action in Martial Arts Movies

Mary Farquhar

This essay is about action in *A Touch of Zen* (Parts 1 and 2, King Hu, 1971). Action – or combat – is the essence of the film and of the martial arts genre, known in Chinese as *wuxiapian, wudapian* and *gong-fupian* (*gongfu/kung-fu* movies are the southern subgenre). *A Touch of Zen* is acknowledged as a pioneering martial arts film in the northern swordplay subgenre, containing some of the best-known action sequences in the Chinese cinema.

Released after three years of production, *A Touch of Zen* won prizes in Taiwan and at Cannes in 1975. *A Touch of Zen* is part of a body of work by King Hu in the 1960s and early 1970s that reshaped martial arts action into a mainstay of the Hong Kong and Taiwanese film industries, influencing subsequent action film-makers such as Tsui Hark, John Woo, Jackie Chan, Ang Lee and, now, Zhang Yimou.

In much writing on martial arts film, action is treated in isolation as a purely formal delight. Here, *A Touch of Zen*'s action is analysed as narrative, as spectacle and as morality play under the rubric of a cinema of spectacle-attractions. The approach extends the Western framework to non-Western cinemas, building on my earlier work on Chinese cinematic modes.[1] Overt theatricality is a feature of early cinematic spectacle in the West. In the earliest Chinese cinema, this spectacle is operatic, recasting martial arts movies as contemporary 'shadow opera' and a mode of Chinese film-making developed out of indigenous literary tradition and in operatic performance. King Hu's films best illustrate this point. They are feature films. But their theatricality was so obvious that a contemporary reviewer described them as a 'cinematisation of Beijing opera' (*pingjude dianyinghua*).[2] Another wrote that both story and form emerged from 'the womb' of opera.[3] Stephen Teo later called King Hu's films 'cinema opera' (*xiqu fengwei dianying*).[4]

The concept of cinema opera is a starting point for analysing action in *A Touch of Zen*. Action cannot be considered in isolation. Its meaning is related to its location in the text on two levels. First, action is integrated into narrative, not isolated from it. This is generally the case in the martial arts genre. Second, action is not purely abstract, but culturally over-coded. The essay outlines an interrelated aesthetic *and* ethic of action in *A Touch of Zen* that propelled King Hu's work in 'the martial arts genre into the ninth heaven of cinema abstraction'.[5]

ACTION AS PART OF NARRATIVE

While combat is the core attraction of the martial arts genre, the plot usually triggers action sequences. Otherwise, action would be pure display. Furthermore, action does not suspend so-called realist storytelling. Even the most extraordinary martial arts combat scenes contain drama as counterpoint and continuation of the storyline. Hence action is enmeshed in the narrative as both spectacle and storytelling device.

Nevertheless, everyone knows that martial arts movies are about action as novel display in its own right. Hence twentieth-century martial arts movies – whether swordplay such as *A Touch of Zen* or *gongfu* – provide spectacular action as the novel attraction. Novelty ranges across the surreal in the 'ghost-and-demon' film *fantastique* of the early twentieth century; the highly physical in the *gongfu* subgenre from the 1970s; and the dreamlike ballet atop the bamboo in Ang Lee's *Crouching Tiger, Hidden Dragon* at the turn of a new century. The dance, the physicality and the *fantastique* are all present in the diverse action sequences of *A Touch of Zen*.

The story provides this action with its moral framework. It is adapted from a famous Qing dynasty short-story collection. Yang Huizhen is the warrior-daughter of an upright Ming dynasty minister, who is executed when he offends the Chief Eunuch. Her father's powerful enemies – the Chief Eunuch's palace guard – now hunt her and her father's friends in forbidding landscapes on the edge of empire. There are three cumulative movements to the narrative: the personal, the political and the spiritual.[6] The personal is a romance between Yang and the scholar, Gu Shengzhai. The film's first combat scene ends this movement. The second movement is the political combat between Yang's group and her enemies. It contains the bamboo-forest fight sequence, one of the most famous in the genre. The third movement shifts to the spiritual, ending with a cosmic combat involving this world and beyond. The fight sequences are therefore vital narrative elements in the story's suspense, building towards an extraordinary climax in which a mysterious monk with supernatural martial powers hovers between humanity and Buddhahood – between life and death, earth and sky, real and surreal, matter and void, victory and defeat. The monk gives the film its English title, *A Touch of Zen*. Its Chinese title, *Xianü* or *Lady Knight Errant*, focuses on the warrior heroine rather than on the magical monk who comes to her aid.

Narrative therefore supports action in the martial arts genre. Christian Metz has argued that the merger of cinema and narrativity is 'a great fact, which was by no means predestined'.[7] It follows that the Chinese merger may diverge from Western models. We have already demonstrated that, unlike the West, complex narrative and visual display were concurrent elements in China's earliest films and the merger continues in such contemporary films as *Farewell My Concubine* (Chen Kaige, 1993). King Hu developed the narrative format of martial arts movies, minimising plot to focus pleasure on combat spectaculars.[8] So action or at least the expectation of action dominates the form.

The pleasure of action may be postponed to heighten the effect. The first combat scene in *A Touch of Zen* comes almost an hour into the film. Before this, there is growing tension as Scholar Gu meets strangers in the village, including the beautiful Yang Huizhen with whom he falls in love. But who are these strangers? Like Hitchcock, King Hu builds suspense through point-of-view shots, off-screen looks and restricted knowledge, primarily attached to Scholar Gu. Yang Huizhen refuses his marriage proposal but invites Scholar Gu to her house one night.

Part of the novelty is the film's delicious shift away from Confucian domestic propriety and female subordination to warrior virtues and gender equality. It begins as Gu arrives to find Yang Huizhen playing a lute under the moon, singing a poem by Li Bai as he moves towards her. She is caught in his gaze but the audience knows that she has contrived his gaze and the moonlit setting. Her song ends:

> The moon sways with my song,
> My shadow moves with the dance,
> After we've drunk, we part
> But we cherish our feeling
> Until we meet – if ever we meet – again.

She now looks back at him, he smiles and she beckons him inside. Images and sounds of nature suggest lovemaking and birdsong suggests dawn. Then, to the sound of cymbals, the door is pushed open by unknown hands. Yang awakes and tickles the sleeping Gu with a strand of grass. Commander Ouyang Nian, a spy for the evil palace guard, then enters the room and orders Yang home. The fight begins suddenly. Gu sees his lover change from feline softness to deadly swordswoman, from *wen* arts (poetry, wine, lute and love) to combat (*wu*), from graceful singer to acrobatic swordfighter, and from bedroom seductress to family avenger, fighting through grasses, trees, forest, rocks, battlements and turrets. Ma Guoguang describes the film as 'blood draining into poetry'.[9] David Bordwell analyses Hu's action technique in this and other scenes as 'the aesthetic of the glimpse'.[10] In part, the glimpse aligns with Gu who runs outside to follow the fight, falls, and looks up at the sun in a shot reminiscent of Kurosawa's famous sun-shot in *Rashomon*. He faints. The action ends. The film then cuts to the second movement. Scholar Gu is summoned to the magistrate's to learn of the Yang family's outlaw status. The first combat scene and its surrounding narrative therefore resolve the mystery about the strangers who come to town. The battle is no longer secretive; Yang Huizhen and Generals Lu and Shi are no longer in hiding; and Scholar Gu is now drawn into the political intrigue, the moral dilemma and therefore the physical combat. In the second movement, Gu's point of view remains the storytelling thread that binds the private to the now public domain.

The first hour of *A Touch of Zen* shows the extent to which action is empowered by a classical narrative format. The audience is not directly addressed as in early cinema but absorbed into the story as in so-called 'realist' cinema. Martial arts movies therefore mix cinematic modes – the aesthetic of attractions and the classical – to great effect. In the literature on a cinema of attractions, scholars note that the star system, music and techniques such as extreme close-ups in contemporary Western cinema are all continuations of early film spectacle. These elements support both the action-attraction and the story-telling in *A Touch of Zen*. For example, extreme close-ups of Scholar Gu and Ouyang Nian, as they look off screen, suggest that there is a dark reality beneath the ordinary small-town façade that fills the film's first movement. This façade is peeled back at the first movement's end and in the subsequent narrative. Action provides the first climax. It rips apart the illusion of everyday life to reveal realities behind realities until the final combat ends in a landscape reduced to colour and form. The film's *finale* suggests a central tenet of Buddhist philosophy: the illusion (*maya*) that is the phenomenal world. Thus, the martial arts genre in King Hu's hands operates in merged mode. It is a narrative cinema that foregrounds action-attraction, pushing visual symbolism and bodily action to the limits of credibility. Here, action starts slowly. In other works, martial arts combat explodes on the screen much earlier. Either way, the audience expects it.

AESTHETICS: THE *YIN-YANG* OF ACTION (AND INACTION)

There is therefore an aesthetic of action at work in *A Touch of Zen*. King Hu choreographed combat. His innovation was to conceptualise martial arts action as operatic dance. The dance is a rhythmic interplay around the two poles of *qi* or cosmic energy: a dance of *yang* (movement) and *yin* (stillness).

While martial arts movies are classed as a genre of 'action movies' (*dongzuopian*) in which 'fast, rhythmic action constitutes the film's main interest',[11] the term *dongzuo* does not capture the aesthetic complexity of the dance. Luo Bu writes of the genre:

> Yes, film is a 'moving' (*dong*) art but the word *dong* should not be narrowed to actual 'movement' or 'action' in *dongzuo*; it should involve such alternative meanings as the *dong* in *liudong* (to float), *yuedong* (to leap) and *sheng-dong* (vibrant, alive). Fierce movements (*dongzuo*) are of

course *dong* but a vital rhythm and dance of *qi* (*qiyun*), a coming alive of characters, and the narrative flow are also *dong*.[12]

One term for martial arts movies, *wudapian*, captures this variety in that *wuda* refers to acrobatic fighting in dance/opera/film. Simply stated, *wuda* is rhythmic fighting akin to dance. King Hu is quite explicit on this point. He said that his combat moves do not come from *gongfu* or martial arts techniques (*wushu*); they come from Beijing opera, which he constantly watched as a young boy in Beijing. He said, 'In fact, all the action scenes come from fighting in Beijing opera, that is, they are a kind of dance.'[13]

Action choreography is now considered crucial to the genre. Since King Hu, this is the province of the martial arts choreographer. Indeed, King Hu credited the success of his groundbreaking martial arts style to his own director/choreographer, Han Yingjie. Hu said:

> That [the martial arts in my films are so new] has a direct link with my martial arts director Han Yingjie. The term 'martial arts director' (*wushu zhedao*) actually started with me using Han Yingjie. It has a lot to do with his ideas. During the making of *Come Drink with Me* it was quite difficult for me to handle the action. I had no problems with handling the story because I had read many martial arts stories. I have never had any training in the martial arts and I don't know how to fight, so I called in Han Yingjie, a Beijing opera actor, to help me out. I studied his martial arts moves and selected the best.[14]

How does this work? What is meant by action as dance? How does film technology transform the action into a *yin-yang* rhythm, the music of *qi*? Han Yingjie has partly explained this in relation to the famous bamboo fight scene midway through *A Touch of Zen*. Yang Huizhen, her two generals and Scholar Gu ambush Ouyang Nian and two others on Green Bamboo Mountain to prevent them reporting to the fearsome Commander Men Da, newly arrived at the frontier. Han Yingjie attributes the stunning effects of such combat scenes first to performance – specifically, to revitalised martial arts styles, well-researched costumes and realistic acting – and second to film editing (*jianjie*).[15]

According to Han Yingjie, action movements were designed in line with King Hu's requirements.

Most shots were improvised on the set but climactic action was storyboarded beforehand. One such climax is the bamboo-forest fight scene.[16] The most spectacular move in this sequence (and perhaps in the Chinese movies) is Yang's free-fall from the top of the bamboo to pierce one of the two bodyguards below. This move is a highly physical merger of warrior and sword and it ends the battle, apart from a short coda when General Shi kills the second bodyguard. The acting is realistic in a comparative sense. The bare operatic stage is replaced by real film locations (such as the bamboo forest) and symbolic operatic gestures are replaced by realistic action (such as the enemy meeting in the forest on horseback). The superhuman action – leaps, somersaults and flying – are achieved with wires, trampolines and stunt[wo]men in the film whereas they are suggested by acrobatic movements in opera. The on-screen performance gains further credibility through meticulously researched historical background and period costumes. In the bamboo-forest sequence, the red enemy costumes are glimpsed through the mist in the first long shot, distinguishing them from the plain costumes of the heroes when the action turns to fast, close combat. The real bamboo forest, the stylised acting, the operatic percussive beat and the period costumes all enhance the spectacle. Hence the overall effect of the action choreography is towards realism (*xieshi*) and away from operatic symbolism (*xieyi*).

For example, the *fantastique* effect of Yang Huizhen's dive in the bamboo-forest scene comes from editing but its visual basis is an actual dive. Han Yingjie said:

> The bamboo forest was located in Taiwan in a place that only had sunshine during noontime. The temperature inside the forest was lower by twelve degrees and the trees were so tall that we couldn't use trampolines or wires. In the end we put the camera in the middle of a lake next to a cliff, and took shots of the stuntmen diving into the lake, then cut back to the forest.[17]

The dive is rendered realistic on screen through rapid cutting, shot juxtapositions and discontinuous movement so that the stunt dive is broken up and barely discernible within the frame. King Hu calls this the aesthetic of 'crookedness' (*quzhe*), 'a twisting and

A Touch of Zen: Yang Huizhen, the lady knight-errant

turning that cannot be grasped in a single glance'.[18] But the action also relies on frozen moments for miraculous effect. For example, Yang's frenetic dive is interspersed with still shots of sunlight and bamboo and extended close-ups of the astonished onlookers, including the enemy just before he is pierced from above. Thus, action choreography is a rhythmic flow between movement (*yang*) and stillness (*yin*), without resorting to obvious trickery and special effects. This is *qi* in Chinese aesthetics, an invisible force that animates voids and phenomena so that the still frames become active intervals in action choreography. Movement emerges out of stillness. Indeed, this scene begins with a slow long shot of shadowy enemy shapes in the bamboo forest and ends with the two exhausted victors, Yang Huizhen at rest and General Shi sheathing his sword. Ouyang Nian escapes. The enemy's martial prowess increases in the second and third movements, moving from Ouyang Nian to Commander Men Da and finally to the Commander-in-Chief, Xu Xianchun, played by Han Yingjie.

Han's pioneering action choreography is now a staple of the genre. Jet Li said that he only signs a film contract once he knows the choreographer's name.[19] Similarly, the action in *Crouching Tiger, Hidden Dragon* (Ang Lee, 2000) is the work of Yuen Wo-ping, who helped establish heroes such as Jackie Chan and Jet Li. Ang Lee said, 'in Yuen's choreography, the martial art becomes a performing art'.[20] Elsewhere, he likens the combat to dance or ballet. Zhang Yimou's foray into martial arts film, *Hero,* also features an established Hong Kong choreographer. The film's breathtaking Mongolian fight is again likened to ballet, not to battle.[21] This is the legacy of King Hu and his action director, Han Yingjie.

ACTION ETHICS: THE COMBAT BETWEEN GOOD AND EVIL

The opening shots of *A Touch of Zen* are justly famous. They are a metaphor for evil that ensnares the world. Nine shots of spiders weaving webs at night to trap victims fill the frame in the first sequence. Panoramic shots of misty mountains at dawn follow, almost inviting the viewer into a tranquil Chinese landscape painting. But evil stalks this vista. Like the spider, it exists, it hunts, and it is a force of nature. Evil requires action, which is understood in relation to non-action (*wuwei*) in Chinese philosophy. Action is variously validated in the film's

three worlds: the hierarchical Confucian society of the border town, the brotherhood of the martial arts world (*jianghu*), and finally the Buddhist world of transcendence. We look at each in turn. The common denominator is that evildoers precipitate the violence. Heroes re-act.

The action poetry of *A Touch of Zen* unravels a moral universe that seeks to restore order in disorder through the heroic *wuxia* or lady knight-errant. *Wuxiapian* or martial arts film translates as 'knight-errant movies' so the principle of heroic action against overwhelming evil is fundamental to King Hu's films, which clearly distinguish good and evil. Indeed, good (*Dao* or The Way) and evil (*Mo* or monsters) are in mortal, political and eventually cosmic combat. Confucian rites (*li*), such as filial piety, female submission, marriage and civil service examinations, dominate the first movement until dispatched with wondrous irony in the first fight. Such rites were considered essential to Confucian civilisation, which relies on hierarchies of patriarchal virtue descending from Heaven through the Emperor to clan and family. The social hierarchy is doubly subverted in the film. First, the good Minister Yang is tortured and killed by the evil eunuchs who block his memorandum to the Emperor/Father. Thus imperial order is perverted, not rejected. Second, the father of the Yang family is dead and his lineage threatened in the hunt for his daughter. Yang Huizhen's fight is legitimised by a Confucian system that demands vengeance for the father and declares lack of sons the ultimate unfilial act. She not only fights. She also bears Gu a son and literally leaves him holding the baby in the final act while she retires to a monastery. Hence her martial persona is an extension of the Confucian moral order in times of dire peril. Yang Huizhen acts as a filial daughter in the long tradition of women-warriors.

The Yang family remnants become outlaws with warrants issued for their capture and execution. They escape to a mythic Chinese underworld called *jianghu* (literally 'rivers and lakes') on the frontier, leaving the dangerous spider spaces of city, town and village. Ng Ho has reconstructed *jianghu* as both a real criminal underworld and a mythic realm in Chinese fiction. He writes:

> *Jianghu* was an anarchic, reckless world with no appreciable demarcations between good and evil. It was a martial (*wu*) world unsupported by valour (*xia*).

Chivalrous heroes [*wuxia*] were merely icons conjured by man's desire for an ethical order, answering their need for moral arbitrators in this undisciplined realm. For this reason, chivalrous figures only appear in fiction [and film], seldom in history.[22]

The fictional *jianghu* is not a self-sufficient world. It operates as the mirror image of Confucian society and its virtues are also the opposite of the Confucian order. Warriors (*wu*) displace literati (*wen*) at the top of the hierarchy. Gu Shengzhai personifies this displacement, moving from scholar to military strategist and from law-abiding citizen to outlaw in the second movement.

A Touch of Zen constructs its own version of this world. Yang Huizhen – the chivalrous *xianü* – epitomises military prowess, although her chivalry is discriminating. At one point, she hesitates as an enemy begs for mercy. Gu intervenes, repeating the Confucian dictum that female benevolence always causes trouble. So she plunges the sword into the enemy's belly in full close-up. In *jianghu*, inaction against an enemy is death; chivalry is reserved for the 'brotherhood' of heroes, the righteous and the oppressed. The sword is more than a means of survival. Its supreme mastery by the heroine symbolises a deep desire for moral order that can only come about by the violent overthrow of evil. Hence, combat is more than necessary. It is the central poetry of the martial arts world.

The violence legitimised in these two worlds is rejected in the third world of Buddhist transcendence. This third world shifts *A Touch of Zen* into the 'ghost and Zen' subgenre (*guichanpian*, *chan* being the Chinese term for Zen), which showed King Hu's art at its peak. Huang Ren claims that:

These films [of King Hu] transcend the forms of this world, entering a space where ghostly and human compassion and revenge meet, and where personal grievances are usually abandoned through enlightenment. An example is [the glimpse of] nirvana in *A Touch of Zen*, an elevated conceptualisation of the martial arts film.[23]

The central motif in this third world is compassion (*en*) rather than revenge. *A Touch of Zen* ends with a meditation on action itself in which compassion is concentrated in the Zen master, Hui Yuan, and his acolyte monks. Hui Yuan appears twice in the second movement as the incarnation of stillness and non-violence, despite his (almost) invincible martial powers. This stillness dominates the film's third movement when Hui Yuan confronts the epitome of evil, the weaver of webs, the great exponent of martial arts – Commander-in-Chief Xu Xianchun.

The combat between Hui Yuan and Xu is the clash of good and evil, compassion and revenge, set up in the preceding narrative. The sequence is imbued with mystic symbolism, unearthly power and visual beauty. The third movement reaches its final crescendo as Gu seeks Yang, finds the baby but is then betrayed to Commander-in-Chief Xu. Hui Yuan sends Yang and General Shi to save him but the combat proves Xu to be more powerful. So the monks intervene, defeating Xu but letting him live after unsuccessfully trying to dissuade him from a life of evil. They leave. Ma Guoguang claims that this Xu–Hui Yuan sequence alone is worth the price of the ticket.[24] But Xu is not finished. He waylays Hui Yuan, begs for mercy and then stabs him. This leads to the extraordinary finale as Xu looks up, hallucinates, shakes his head and sees the monk against a cosmic skyscape washed in light. Hui Yuan turns, pulls out the dagger and bleeds gold to the chant of a full male choir. The sky dissolves into greens and reds. Xu leaps, falls to his death, followed by alternating shots of his corpse on the ground and encircling birds of prey in the sky.

The closing minute of this sequence is shot/reverse shots of the three main characters looking at a transfigured Hui Yuan *always* still and *always* at the centre of a panoramic frame.

Medium close-up	A wounded Yang looks up from the desert
Extreme long shot (1)	Hui Yuan is a vague shape suffused with light and centred high in the frame between a shadowy crest of rock and a golden sky
Close-up	Shi falls, looking up in amazement
Extreme long shot	As in (1) but shadowy robes flutter
Long shot	Gu, holding the baby, falls to his knees as he looks up
Extreme long shot	As in (1)

Close-up	Yang rises
Extreme long shot	As in (1) but now a shadowy arm rises, and a sleeve flutters
Close-up	Yang continues to look up
Extreme long shot	As in (1)
Close-up	Yang looks up
Extreme long shot	A silhouette of Hui Yuan's monastery is shown on a dark mountainside against a golden sky
Extreme long shot	The frame then serially dissolves into its negative of red and white, into a silhouette of Hui Yuan (with halo), bathed in light, and into a core of light that irradiates the frame. Then the shadowy figure stands and finally becomes a clear silhouette of Hui Yuan as Buddha with a golden halo. THE END

The final shots alternate between images of the real and of the surreal, between Buddhist redemption and earthly suffering. The soundtrack is now a full female choir. Throughout, Hui Yuan calls the monastic life *kongmen*, the gate to the void. But the image of the void is not empty; it is light, infinite space and changing colour with Hui Yuan – a Buddha – at its centre. It is as if the film-maker is standing in the gateway and showing us two worlds as alternative human options that relate directly to the characters' actions: earthly suffering and the sky of nirvana. Violent action kills enemies so *jianghu* heroes can survive for the next combat. Non-violence cherishes life, kills no one and defeats death itself through karmic transfiguration beyond 'the endless sea of suffering', to use Hui Yuan's own words. Thus, non-action as the choice *not* to kill defeats martial arts action, the art of killing.

The changed ethic is matched by a changed aesthetic that forgoes King Hu's earlier 'twisting and turning' aesthetic of 'crookedness'. Stillness overcomes movement and is presented visually in two ways at the end of the film. Repeated glimpses of Hui Yuan against the sky show a centred, serene, 'enlightened' core of being high in the frame. Hui Yuan's centrality is reinforced by the onlookers' gaze upward and always

at him from different vantage points on the ground. He is encircled by looks of enlightenment, the opposite of earthly desire. King Hu's feat was to visually incorporate this abstract complexity and transcendent world into *A Touch of Zen*.

This discussion on action in *A Touch of Zen* has led us to King Hu's own meditation on (non)action in the martial arts genre.

NOTES

1. Mary Farquhar and Chris Berry, 'Shadow Opera: Towards a New Archaeology of the Chinese Cinema', *Postscript*, 20, nos. 1, 2 and 3 (2001): 25–42.
2. Liu Chenghan, 'Auteur Theory and King Hu' ('Zuozhelun he Hu Jinquan'), 1975, cited without full publishing details in Fu Shizhuan, 'Visual and Auditory Elements in King Hu's Martial Arts World' ('Hu Jinquan wuxia shijielide sheting yuansu'), in *The World of King Hu* (*Hu Jinquan de shijie*), ed. Huang Ren (Taipei: Taipeishi Zhongguo dianyingziliao yanjiuhui, 1999), 235.
3. Luo Bu, 'Hu Jinquan', in Luo Bu, Wu Hao and Zhuo Baitang, *Genre Theory in Hong Kong Cinema* (*Xianggang dianying leixinglun*) (Hong Kong: Oxford University Press, 1997), 41.
4. Stephen Teo, 'Only the Valiant: King Hu and His Cinema Opera', in *Transcending the Times: King Hu and Eileen Chang*, ed. Provisional Urban Council (Hong Kong: Provisional Urban Council, 1998), 19–24.
5. Teo, 'Only the Valiant', 24.
6. Tony Rayns, 'King Hu: Shall We Dance', in *A Study of the Hong Kong Martial Arts Film*, ed. Provisional Urban Council (Hong Kong: Urban Council, 1980), 103.
7. Christian Metz, *Film Language: A Semiotics of the Cinema*, trans. Michael Taylor (New York: Oxford University Press, 1967), 93.
8. Stephen Teo, 'Love and Swords: The Dialectics of the Martial Arts Romance, A Review of *Crouching Tiger, Hidden Dragon*', *Senses of Cinema*, no. 11 (2000): <www.sensesofcinema.com/contents/00/11/crouching.html> (9 January 2001).
9. Ma Guoguang, '*A Touch of Zen*: Blood Draining into Poetry', in Provisional Urban Council, *Transcending the Times*, 65–67.
10. David Bordwell, 'Richness through Imperfection: King Hu and the Glimpse', in Provisional Urban Council, *Transcending the Times*, 33–34.

11. Wang Jie'an, chief ed., *Film Dictionary* (*Dianying cidian*) (Taipei: Dianying ziliaoguan, 1999), 11.

12. Luo Bu, 'The Beginnings of Mandarin Martial Arts Film' ('Wuxia guoyupiande qianlu'), in Luo *et al.*, *Genre Theory*, 21.

13. Huang Ren, 'A Path of Creative Variety' ('Duocai duozide chuangzuo zhi lu'), in Huang, *The World of King Hu*, 115.

14. Hirokazu Yamada and Koyo Udagawa, 'King Hu's Last Interview', in Provisional Urban Council, *Transcending the Times*, 75.

15. Han Yingjie, 'Remembering King Hu', in Provisional Urban Council, *Transcending the Times*, 83.

16. See a shot-by-shot analysis in Cheuk Pak Tong, 'A Pioneer in Film Language: On King Hu's Style of Editing', in Provisional Urban Council, *Transcending the Times*, 60–61. Also see Chris Berry and Mary Farquhar, *China on Screen: Cinema and Nation* (New York and Hong Kong: Columbia and Hong Kong University Presses, 2006).

17. Han, 'Remembering King Hu', 83.

18. Hu Jinquan cited in Fu Shizhuan, 'Visual and Auditory Elements', 245–246.

19. Stephen Short and Susan Jakes, 'Violence Doesn't Solve Anything, *Time* talks exclusively to martial-arts master Jet Li', *Timeasia.com*, 2001: <www.time.com/time/asia/features/hero/int_jet_li.html> (18 January 2002).

20. Ang Lee, 'Working with Fight Choreographer Yuen Wo Ping', in *Crouching Tiger, Hidden Dragon*, ed. Linda Sunshine (New York: New Market Press, 2000), 95.

21. Stephen Short and Susan Jakes, 'Making of a Hero', *Timeasia.com*, 2002: <www.time.com/time/asia/features/hero/story2.html> (18 January 2002).

22. Ng Ho, 'Jianghu Revisited: Towards a Reconstruction of the Martial Arts World', in *A Study of the Hong Kong Swordplay Film (1945–1980)*, ed. Provisional Urban Council (Hong Kong: Urban Council, 1981), 84.

23. Huang, 'A Path of Creative Variety', 118.

24. Ma Guoguang, '*A Touch of Zen*', 67.

29 *Vive L'Amour*: Eloquent Emptiness

Fran Martin

Vive L'Amour (Tsai Ming-liang, 1994), winner of the Golden Lion at the 1994 Venice International Film Festival, is the second part in a film-cycle by Tsai Ming-liang, the Malaysian-born arthouse director working from Taiwan. Following *Rebels of the Neon God* (1992) and preceding *The River* (1997), *Amour* contributes to Tsai's continuing filmic exploration of the conditions of human subsistence in millennial Taipei.[1] His films' settings amid the city's dismal concrete and neon streetscapes, their minimalist stories of the aimless days and nights of drifting, marginal characters and their austere cinematic style have earned Tsai his name as filmic philosopher of existential anxiety in post-'economic miracle'Taiwan.[2]

Tsai's films have been discussed by critics within Taiwan and internationally mainly in relation to their distinctive cinematic style and their thematic explorations of post-modern alienation.[3] But within Taiwan's local lesbian and gay (*tongzhi*) communities Tsai's film-cycle is frequently analysed in relation to its representations of homosexuality, a topic less often foregrounded in existing English-language scholarship at the time of writing.[4] Taiwan's *tongzhi* movement, encompassing activist and social groups as well as *tongzhi*-directed cultural production and consumption (including film-making, filmgoing and film criticism), emerged during the 1990s as part of the series of popular movements proliferating in the wake of the Kuomintang government's lifting of martial law in 1987.[5] In what follows, I assume the context of *Vive L'Amour*'s production in 1990s Taiwan, in the same cultural moment that saw the emergence of the *tongzhi* movement. Bearing in mind Tsai's films' popularity with *tongzhi* audiences, I consider how *Vive L'Amour* indexes current transformations in constructions of sexuality and family. My approach to Tsai's film thus differs from much existing work less in its methodology than in its thematic focus and its emphasis on the film's social context. Rather than reading the film as an expression of a generalised, global post-modern malaise, on the one hand, or of nostalgia for a mythic, lost 'Chinese family', on the other, I will suggest that *Amour* indexes a particular moment in the transformation of available discourses on sexuality in 1990s Taiwan. I will analyse the film's representation of *tongxinglian* (homosexuality) through its organisation of space and through the characterisation of Xiao Kang (Lee Kang-sheng), the central character who has appeared in a lead role in all of Tsai's films to date.

With its principal cast carried over from *Rebels* (Lee Kang-sheng as Xiao Kang, and Chen Zhao-rong, who played A'Ze in *Rebels*, as A'Rong), *Amour*'s plot concerns the ephemerally intertwined lives of three characters, A'Rong, Mei-mei and Xiao Kang, as they cross paths in a vacant luxury apartment awaiting sale. Mei-mei (Yang Kuei-mei) is an estate agent who spends her days driving between apartment and empty apartment, making calls on her mobile phone in the hope that someone will turn up to view the properties. Taking a break for a cigarette and a drink in a crowded coffee shop in the Hsimenting entertainment district, she encounters A'Rong, an itinerant salesman who peddles women's clothing illegally on the street outside a department store. After a protracted exchange of glances, A'Rong follows Mei-mei from the coffee shop to a vacant luxury apartment Mei-mei handles, and the two have sex. Unbeknown to either one, a spare key to the same apartment has been swiped by the third character, Xiao Kang, who makes his living pre-selling funerary niches in a crematorium. At a measured pace, the film explores each character's relationship with the others as they return to the apartment at various times and for various purposes over the days that follow. Mei-mei goes to the apartment in order to show the property to potential buyers (and also to eat her lunch from polystyrene *biandang* lunchboxes, and to take an occasional nap). A'Rong goes there to have sex with Mei-mei (also to masturbate with a porn magazine, sleep, take a bath in the jacuzzi and eat hotpot with Xiao Kang). Xiao Kang goes there initially to attempt suicide (and, later, to stage a one-man bowling game with a watermelon, model a little black dress, feather boa and heels from A'Rong's merchandise bag, and hide under the bed where A'Rong and Mei-mei have sex, then emerge to kiss the sleeping A'Rong's face).

As the Taiwanese critic Jiang Xun notes, each of the character's occupations represents an aspect of the underside of Taiwan's 'economic miracle'. Mei-mei is a middle-person in the property boom, but cannot legitimately share in the luxury lifestyles she sells – her working-class accent makes a stark contrast with her expensive-looking outfits, and her own apartment is decrepit by comparison with the five-star properties she handles.[6] A'Rong possesses heightened mobility in two opposite senses: he earns enough for regular trips to Hong Kong to buy merchandise; yet at the same time, selling his wares in the informal street economy, he is forced into an uneasy state of perpetual motion by regular police raids on the floating market that hovers at the doorstep of the high-end department store. Xiao Kang, meanwhile, letterboxes ads for the tiny funerary niches that are often the only viable option on a small island where skyrocketing land values have put a grave site in a traditional cemetery outside most people's reach.

Along with Taiwan's rapid industrialisation and urbanisation, the structure and practice of the family (or *jia*, a term meaning both 'family' and 'home') has also transformed over the past three to four decades. Post-1960s generations have abandoned the villages for the big cities of Taipei and Kaohsiung, and the agricultural basis of village economies has been rapidly eroded with the expansion of first the manufacturing and more recently the service sectors. As many commentators have observed, Tsai's film-cycle foregrounds the resultant crisis and reconfiguration of the *jia* in turn-of-the-century Taiwan.[7] While *Rebels* and *River* both deal directly with *jia* at the level of the story by foregrounding Xiao Kang's relationship with his father (played in both films by Miao Tien), it is in *Amour* that the idea of *jia* and its apparent absence is most arrestingly present at a symbolic level, in the metaphor of the empty apartment. Taiwanese feminist scholar Chang Hsiao-hung argues convincingly

that what we see in *Amour* is not so much a dramatisation of the tragic breakdown of some mythic 'traditional Chinese family', as has been suggested by some, but rather an 'emptying out' of the *jia* itself that compels a fundamental re-thinking of its significance in relation to current transformations in Taiwan's society and culture.[8] In what follows, I will consider how Chang's notion of the emptied-out *jia* can help us think through other, related interpretations of the film's various figurations of 'emptiness'. In particular, I will suggest a possible correlation between the film's representation of 'emptiness' and its figuration of *tongxinglian*.

Like *Rebels*, *Amour* and *River*, and other Taiwanese films including *The Wedding Banquet* (Ang Lee, 1993), the independent film *The Love of Three Oranges* (Hung Hung, 1998) frames the subject of homosexuality in relation to the *jia*.[9] Also like *Amour*, this quirky first-time feature from Hung Hung examines a complex interplay between three characters: young lesbian lovers Star (also called Pony) and Mimi, and Star's high-school boyfriend who has reappeared after two years away on military service. Near the beginning of the film, Star has a conversation with her ex-boyfriend in which she tells him that she and Mimi plan to have a baby and raise the child together. When he asks how she means to do this, Star implies that she's prepared to have sex with a man in order to get pregnant. Shortly thereafter, she begins to have regular sex with the ex-boyfriend. Mimi grows jealous, and a love triangle is formed that resolves, at the close of the film, with Mimi's marriage to Star's ex-boyfriend/lover.

At one point, the ex-boyfriend secretly reads Mimi's diary. Mimi has written: 'Star's high-school boyfriend showed up. Star says she can't forget him, because she was once pregnant with his child. If what is between [Star and me] cannot produce a real child, then do our kisses count as real?' In this question, the lesbian love between Mimi and Star is constructed by Mimi as 'false' because it does not promise the presumed 'realness' of reproductive heterosexuality. Mimi's question crystallises the tension between homosexual love and the reproductive demands and desires of the *jia* that suffuses and organises the film as a whole. In Ang Lee's *Wedding Banquet*, the reconciliation of the desires of a gay son with the demands of his family that he enable his ageing father to 'hold his grandson' (*bao sunzi*) is achieved by the creation of a situation in which the son becomes able to produce an heir, as it were, *despite* being gay. Indeed, the tension between patrilineal heredity and homosexual desire is a central theme of Tsai's film-cycle as well, and comes to a climax in *River*.[10] All these films suggest that in the context of contemporary Taiwan, where the requirements of the *jia* are socially and psychically entrenched in the lives of individual sons and daughters, the imperative to familial reproduction remains a force to be reckoned with in the elaboration of liveable ways of being for *tongzhi* subjects.

It is for this reason that Mimi asks herself whether lesbian kisses can be considered 'real' if they cannot produce children. In asking this question, Mimi follows the lead of a dominant culture that has tended to construct *tongxinglian* as an unreal, empty or ghostly counterpart to reproductive heterosexuality. As Naifei Ding observes, in the 1990s literary movement of *tongzhi wenxue* (queer literature), *tongxinglian* was frequently aligned with ghostly or cipher-like non-human (*feiren*) forms. Ding interprets this tropology as demonstrative of the fact that *tongxinglian* transgresses the rules of the 'human' when the human is defined by its relationship of interiority to the heterocentric *jia*.[11] For example, the popular *tongzhi* author Hsu Yoshen begins his first novel, *Man Betrother, Man Betrothed* (*Nanhun nanjia*), a semi-autobiographical coming of age story, with the following words, figuring the narrator's gay life as a posthumous state: 'The year I turned thirteen, my queue stood on end – you know what I mean: I died. Because that year, I realised I was an incurable homosexual.'[12] Similarly, Chen Xue's lesbian short story 'Searching for the Lost Wings of the Angel' commences with the protagonist's description of herself and her lover as insubstantial beings suspended between worlds, wingless 'angels': 'We're both angels who have lost our wings. Our eyes are fixed on a height attainable only in flight; our bare feet stand on the searing, obdurate earth, and yet we have lost the direction mankind ought to have.'[13] Qiu Miaojin, author of the now-classic lesbian novel *The Crocodile's Journal* (*Eyu shouji*), parallels her lesbian protagonist's story with that of an anomalous urban crocodile which lives invisibly among the people of Taipei yet at a distance from them, due to its inability to disclose its true identity.[14] Meanwhile, the queer Gothic fiction of Lucifer Hung (Hong Ling) is peopled by vampires, werewolves, demons and other such unquiet spirits.[15] Following Foucault, this figuration of *tongxinglian* by *tongzhi* authors through cipher-like, non-human figures can be interpreted as a reverse-discourse: a form of resistance to the dominant discourse that would place *tongxinglian* beyond the bounds of the human due to its perceived threat to the reproductive, heterosexual *jia*.[16] In the light of this conceptual linkage between *tongxinglian* and the cipher, in what follows I want to read *Amour*'s often noted foregrounding of emptiness alongside its representation of *tongxinglian* in the character of Xiao Kang.

Vive l'Amour reveals an obsession with emptiness on several levels. First, at the level of the graphic space of the screen itself, many shots appear empty by virtue of the harsh composition with simple blocks of flat colour dissected by stark lines produced by architectural frames like balustrades, window frames and doorways. This composition is seen in the first shot, a close-up of a key hanging from a lock in a deserted corridor, ultimately grabbed by an out-of-focus Xiao Kang. The shot is dominated by the vertical lines of the walls and doors in the corridor, and the camera remains fixed on these solid architectural forms before and after the blurry human forms enter and exit the frame, giving an impression of the ephemerality of this human movement against the stolid substantiality of the concrete artifice. Similar shots, with flat screen space dissected by harsh framing devices that seem both to circumscribe and render trivial the movements of the characters, proliferate throughout the film.

The film's soundtrack, too, is characterised by an uncomfortable emptiness. There is a brutal refusal of dialogue and extra-diegetic music; we hear instead the inconsequential sounds of everyday life: traffic, other people's half-heard conversations, footsteps, the characters' breathing, the sounds of Mei-mei and A'Rong having sex, construction racket, Buddhist muzak in the crematorium, the ringing of cash registers in convenience stores and supermarkets, dogs barking in the distance, the calls of street vendors, sirens, Mei-mei's mobile phone's ring-tone.

The film's most concrete representation of emptiness is of course its depiction of the three-dimensional architectural spaces of the apartment. This apartment in which the three characters uneasily cohabit is conspicuously devoid of settlement: it is minimally furnished, but lacks the comforting detritus of everyday

Vive L'Amour: A'Rong and Mei-mei cruise each other

life. The bedroom in which Mei-mei and A'Rong first have sex, for example, has a double bed but no bed-linen, and is otherwise unfurnished except for a lone pot plant and a bedside rug. The other apartments Mei-mei handles are just as cavernous and imper-sonal, if not more so. The second apartment where we see Mei-mei, squatting in the foreground dwarfed by the desolate vacancy of the space, is a huge void made by two units knocked into one. Given the depress-ingly useless expansiveness of this space, in which surely no one could imagine actually living, Mei-mei's cheery greeting to prospective buyers rings with a cer-tain irony: 'Come in, come in – the place is pretty big!' It is these most thematically and diegetically central representations of emptiness that occasion Chang's argument on the key significance of the emptied-out *jia*.

All this emptiness contributes to the sense of an existential vacuum that commentators have fre-quently noted in Tsai's films, a sense that concretises for many in this film's closing scene, in which Mei-mei weeps inconsolably for a full four minutes in the muddy construction-site void of what is to become Da'An Forest Park.[17] And yet, in the light of the film's parallel thematisation of *tongxinglian*, this emptiness may turn out to signify something in excess of the existential ennui so routinely attributed to Tsai's films. When contextualised in relation to the prevalent cultural logic that links *tongxinglian* with notions of emptiness, *Amour*'s parallel thematisation of these two subjects seems quite clearly overdeter-mined. The metaphorics of emptiness, and the emptied-out *jia* in particular, can be interpreted as encoding an implicit reference to *tongxinglian*, asso-ciated as that subject is with cultural anxieties over a *jia* 'emptied out' from within through a failure of het-erosexual reproduction. In this sense, the film's paral-leling of the homosexual theme with its obsessive focus on graphic, architectural, aural and metaphysi-cal emptiness rehearses the familiar cultural logic that makes *tongxinglian* merely the cipher of heterosexual plenitude. To consider what the film does with this idea, having raised it at a connotative level, necessi-tates a closer analysis of the film's denotative repre-sentation of *tongxinglian*.

Underpinning *Amour*'s subtextual reference to *tongxinglian* through its foregrounding of emptiness and the emptied-out *jia* is its explicit representation of *tongxinglian* through the character of Xiao Kang. As Chris Berry observes:

> We are given plenty of material enabling us to interpret Hsiao Kang [Xiao Kang] as a young man gradually coming to terms with his homosexuality: the attempted suicide is followed by a growing interest in Ah Jung [A'Rong]; a scene in which he tries on some of the women's clothes Ah Jung is selling; and finally, the morning after he has hidden under the bed on which Ah Jung and Mei-Mei are having sex, a scene in which he tentatively kisses the sleeping Ah Jung.[18]

In addition, Xiao Kang's character can be read as conforming to the representational convention that links *tongxinglian* with the realm of the ghost and the cipher. Jiang Xun remarks:

> If Yang Kuei-mei is a salesperson of homes for the living, then Lee Kang-sheng is a salesperson of homes for the dead. An atmosphere of death saturates the ghoulish presence of the Lee Kang-sheng character: he seldom speaks; tries again and again to kill himself; and lives a hermit-like existence in the apartment awaiting sale whose key he has stolen.[19]

Drifting about the city on his scooter peddling funerary niches, with his characteristically expressionless demeanour, Xiao Kang indeed appears rather ghostly. His ghoulish air is particularly intense in the scene in which he wears a somewhat formal and old-fashioned black suit and tie, and sits in a dimly lit café solemnly stapling his name-card to his niche ads that urge potential customers: 'Be together with your ancestors.' This written exhortation, on which the camera lingers, explicitly cites the ideology of the continuing family line while also elliptically intimating the 'death' of this model – since the precondition for getting together with your ancestors in a funerary niche is that all of you are dead. This linkage of familial ideology and death in Xiao Kang's advertising material reinforces the triangulation between *jia*, ghosts and *tongxinglian*, according to the central logic in which *tongxinglian*'s perceived threat to terminate the family line and effectively kill off the *jia* is deflected defensively back onto *tongxinglian* itself, which is then, in place of the *jia*, made to appear 'dead' and ghostly. This scene, where a spectral and (it will emerge) probably homosexual Xiao Kang quietly

prepares his ads for final resting places for dead families represents a key point in the film's interrogation of the homophobic syllogism that opposes 'human', '*jia*' and 'life' to 'non-human,' '*tongxinglian*' and 'death'.

Elaborating on the same theme is the scene in which Xiao Kang watches a group of office workers play a corporate bonding-style game similar to musical chairs. In the game, the odd one out calls out a rhyme answered by all the other players, who are organised into three-person make-believe family units: 'I want to move house (*ban jia*)!' 'Who wants to move house?' '[Mothers/fathers/sons/everyone] move house!' Following this, there is a general upheaval as the 'families' rearrange themselves in a new configuration. Throughout the game Xiao Kang, again wearing the black suit, watches silently from the sidelines, utterly separate and apparently unseen by anyone including one man who has to pass directly by him to enter the office where the game takes place. Xiao Kang's invisibility and insignificance to the players in the 'family game' again aligns his character with the extra-familial ghost or cipher.

Further associating Xiao Kang with the ghostly, Xiao Kang's growing interest in A'Rong in *Amour* parallels Xiao Kang's 'haunting' of the Chen Zhaorong character, A'Ze, in *Rebels*. In that film, Xiao Kang's haunting of A'Ze as the incarnation of the rebellious boy-god Nuozha is foreshadowed and paralleled by the 'haunted' lift in A'Ze's government apartment building. The lift always stops unbidden on the fourth floor (*si* meaning 'four' being a homophone for *si* meaning 'death') because, as the girl A'Gui remarks just before A'Ze and Xiao Kang cross paths and Xiao Kang begins obsessively to shadow the other boy, 'There's a ghost on the fourth floor, isn't there?' The fourth-floor ghost in A'Ze's building is soon joined by the spirit of Nuozha in Xiao Kang, who haunts A'Ze throughout the days that follow. In *Amour*, Xiao Kang again haunts the Chen Zhaorong character, A'Rong.

But while Xiao Kang exemplifies the ambivalent metaphor linking *tongxinglian* with the ghost and the cipher, the kiss scene between him and A'Rong reworks the film's paralleling of *tongxinglian* with emptiness in a new way, and to different effect. This scene, in which Xiao Kang emerges from under the bed where A'Rong and Mei-mei have had sex, to lie down with A'Rong then kiss him, represents a key turning point for the film both formally and thematically.

After Xiao Kang appears from under the bed where A'Rong sleeps following Mei-mei's departure, the camera follows Xiao Kang as he creeps around the bed and enters the dark alcove that leads to the door. But after hesitating a while, Xiao Kang – once again, with a certain spectral air – soundlessly re-emerges from the darkness of the alcove into the light of the room and stands immobile for several moments, still framed by the dark rectangle of the door alcove, gazing at the slumbering A'Rong. Finally, he walks out of this dark frame towards the bed. The next shot is a high-angle mid-shot of the two men lying on the bed, with Xiao Kang, like some shy novice vampire, gathering his courage and drawing slowly towards A'Rong's inert form, lips parted. Interestingly, during Xiao Kang's lengthy approach, a series of (perhaps incidental) children's shouts is faintly audible in the background, as though somewhere in another part of the building a child were perhaps waking and getting ready for school. The cries of the invisible child are too faint to make out with certainty, but in the clearest of them, the child seems to call urgently: 'Baba!' ('Daddy!'). At the moment when the film's most direct depiction of homosexual desire is taking place on screen, such a desperate plea to the father from a unseen child fits aptly into the cultural scheme that I've argued this film, like the others in Tsai's film-cycle, addresses: the crisis of the patrilineal *jia* that *tongxinglian* is presumed to occasion.

From the mid-shot of Xiao Kang's approach to A'Rong, the film cuts to its only extreme close-up: of A'Rong's out-of-focus face across the lower foreground of the shot as Xiao Kang approaches from over his shoulder. With this unprecedented filling of the screen by a human face, the alienating distance of the previous scenes, dominated by medium and long shots, is challenged for the first time. This shot is also conspicuous as the only close-up with two faces in frame: the sex scenes have been mainly mid-shots, often with only A'Rong's or only Mei-mei's face in frame at one time. In this sense, too, the kiss scene breaks the formal rules that have governed the film up to now and replaces emptiness, distance and solitude with fullness, proximity and union. Following the shot with A'Rong's face in the foreground is a close-up from above with the two men's heads against the background of the white bed, now facing each other as A'Rong rolls over in his sleep and throws an arm about Xiao Kang. The

shot is graphically arresting in its contrasting of the pale background with the darker tones of men's faces. As Xiao Kang draws slowly nearer to A'Rong, the empty white space separating the two men is bridged and finally overcome by Xiao Kang, when he gently kisses the other man's lips and their heads fill the screen to the all but total exclusion of the white background.

In some ways, the kiss scene looks forward to the conclusion of *The River*. In particular, the soft, blue dawn light that illuminates this scene adumbrates the dawn that greets Xiao Kang and his father in the Taichung hotel at the conclusion of the later film. In *River*'s final scene, Xiao Kang walks out onto the balcony and wanders off screen for a moment, then returns, looking about him in the light of the new day in what Tsai has interpreted as a gesture of hope.[20] Even more specifically, the close-ups of Xiao Kang and A'Rong's faces as they lie in bed foreshadow another scene with two men in bed: Xiao Kang and his father in *River*, after they return from the sauna where they have unwittingly had sex together. In *River*, as in *Amour*, the scenes of Xiao Kang in bed with another man are remarkable for their use of close-ups and the absence of the harsh architectural framing devices that have created the sense of claustrophobia in each film up to that point. In both films, Xiao Kang's sexual connection with another man marks a crucial shift in the film's formal composition, suggesting the defeat of distance by closeness, and the overpowering of emptiness by the plenitude of a different kind of love. In one sense, the queer plenitude of these films seems the opposite of the existential emptiness critics frequently read in Tsai's oeuvre; yet this plenitude is also fixed in a dialectical relationship with emptiness insofar as it is the unravelling of older social systems that at once occasions existential crisis and creates space for new ways of being.[21]

In the ways outlined above, *Vive L'Amour* references the homophobic cultural logic that opposes *jia* to *tongxinglian* and relegates the latter to the realm of ghostliness, emptiness and unreality. But it cites that system only to destabilise it by suggesting, at the last moment, that love between men might, on the contrary, occasion a hitherto unimagined fullness and connection. Additionally, in direct contradiction of the system that opposes *jia* to *tongxinglian*, of the three main characters it is Xiao Kang, ghostly as he may be, who seems most eager to turn the eerie apartment into a kind of alternative *jia*.[22] As Chang observes, it is he who devises a scheme to make a washing machine of the jacuzzi by adding detergent and dirty laundry, and he also goes food shopping and prepares a hotpot meal to share with A'Rong. Appropriated and re-imagined in these ways by Xiao Kang, the space of the apartment becomes a liminal one, somewhere in between the familial *jia* and a new kind of 'post-*jia*' social space that is as yet in the process of being imagined: a space, perhaps, where non-traditional forms of love and intimacy might be more fully elaborated.[23]

Thinking of the empty apartment, in the way Chang suggests, as a liminal space that indexes the need for a new kind of social space makes it possible to rethink the figures of ghost and cipher along similar lines. Ghosts, too, are liminal figures, hovering unquietly between the world of the living and the world of the dead. Equally, the cipher-like beings such as angels, crocodiles and vampires associated with *tongxinglian* in fiction and film could be interpreted as liminal figures caught between humanity as it is currently imagined, and something new, and emerging at a time when, as Taiwan's *tongzhi* groups insist, what is urgently required is a collective imagining of new ways of being human – new ways of thinking and practising culture and sexuality in social contexts so thoroughly transmuted. In this sense, *Vive L'Amour* contributes to the 1990s wave of *tongzhi* cultural production that reworks *tongxinglian*'s association with emptiness and ghostliness to figure a nascent sexual subjectivity, struggling to emerge into the anxious spaces excavated by cultural transformation.

NOTES

1. Tsai's films *The Hole* (1998) and *What Time is it Over There?* (2001) utilise the same pool of actors once again (Lee Kang-sheng, Yang Kuei-mei, Miao Tien, Chen Zhaorong and Lu Yi-ching [formerly known as Lu Hsiao-ling]) and extend the general theme of urban alienation. However, the use of song-and-dance sequences in *Hole* sets this film apart stylistically from the first three, to a certain degree, and it is questionable whether the story traceable in the first three films is continued in *Hole*. Miao Tien plays Xiao Kang's father again in *Time*, but again the transnational setting (Paris and Taipei) sets this film apart to a certain degree from Tsai's first three features.

2. Jiang Xun, 'Body Heat and Salvation' ('Tiwen yu jiuduxin'), *Vive L'Amour* (screenplay) (*Aiqing wansui*), Tsai Ming-liang *et al.* (Taipei: Wanxiang, 1994), 144–151.

3. Chuck Stephens, 'Intersection: Tsai Ming-liang's Yearning Bike Boys and Heartsick Heroines', *Film Comment*, 32 (September–October 1996): 20–23; Tony Rayns, 'Confrontations', *Sight & Sound*, 7 (March 1997): 14–18; Richard Read, 'Alienation, Aesthetic Distance and Absorption in Tsai Ming-liang's *Vive L'Amour*', *New Formations*, 40 (Spring 2000): 102–112.

4. But see Chris Berry, 'Where is the Love? The Paradox of Performing Loneliness in Ts'ai Ming-Liang's *Vive L'Amour*', in *Falling for You: Essays in Cinema and Performance*, ed. Lesley Stern and George Kouvaros (Sydney: Power Publications, 1999), 147–175. For Chinese-language discussion of Tsai Ming-liang's films in relation to *tongzhi*, see Ke Jiazhi, 'A River Flowing toward the Dawn: Tsai Ming-liang's Films and My World' ('Wang liming liutangde he – cai Mingliangde dianying yu wode shijie'), *Isotope Electronic Bulletin* (*Tongweisu dianzibao*), 28 April 1998: <www.south.nsysu.edu.tw/sccid/today/isotope/98/04/isotope980428.html> (15 November 2001); Chang Hsiao-hung, 'An Erotic Map of Taipei' ('Taibei qingyu dijing'), in *Queer Desire: Gender and Sexuality* (*Yuwang xin ditu: xingbie, tongzhixue*) (Taipei: Lianhe Wenxue, 1996), 78–107; and Chang Hsiao-hung, 'A Queer Family Romance: *The River*'s Mise-en-scene of Desire' ('Guaitai jiating luomanshi: *Heliu* zhongde yuwang changjing'), in *Queer Family Romance* (*Guaitai jiating luomanshi*) (Taipei: Shibao, 2000), 111–141.

5. For more detail on this history, see Fran Martin, 'Queer Comrades: The Emergence of Taiwan's Literature of Transgressive Sexuality', *Angelwings: Contemporary Queer Fiction from Taiwan*, trans. and ed. Fran Martin (Honolulu: University of Hawaii Press, forthcoming).

6. Jiang, 'Body Heat and Salvation', 148.

7. See, for example, Berry, 'Where is the Love?'; Chang, 'Erotic Map'; and Chiao Hsiung-ping, 'Lonely Taipei People' ('Gujide Taibeiren'), in Tsai *et al.*, *Vive L'Amour*, 152–156.

8. For an example of a nostalgic reading of the breakdown of the *jia* in Tsai's cinema, see Chiao, 'Lonely Taipei People'; Chang, 'Erotic Map', 96–97.

9. Chris Berry has written at length on the tendency in East Asian film to represent homosexuality in relation

to blood family. See, for example, Chris Berry, 'Asian Values, Family Values: Film, Video and Lesbian and Gay Identities', *The Journal of Homosexuality*, 40, nos. 3/4 (2000): 211–232.

10. For an extended discussion of this question, see Fran Martin, 'Perverse Utopia: Reading *The River*', in *Situating Sexualities: Queer Narratives in 1990s Taiwanese Fiction and Film* (Hong Kong: Hong Kong University Press, 2003).

11. Ding Naifei in discussion in 'Homosexual Politics' ('Tongxingliande zhengzhi'), in *Visionary Essays in Sexuality/Gender Studies* (*Xing/bie yanjiude xin shiye*), vol. 1, ed. He Chunrui (Taipei: Yuanzun, 1997), 189–229.

12. Hsu Yoshen, *Man Betrother, Man Betrothed* (*Nanhun nanjia*) (Taipei: Kaixin yangguang, 1996), 8 (my translation).

13. Chen Xue, 'Searching for the Lost Wings of the Angel' ('Xunzhao tianshi yishide chibang'), trans. Fran Martin, *positions: east asia cultures critique*, 7, no. 1 (1999): 51–69 (51).

14. Qiu Miaojin, *The Crocodile's Journal* (*Eyu shouji*) (Taipei: Shibao, 1994).

15. For a detailed account of the *tongzhi wenxue* movement, see Martin, 'Queer Comrades'.

16. I find the idea of the cipher particularly suggestive due to its double meaning: both 'non-entity' and 'code'.

17. But Chang interprets the construction site as an optimistic metaphor, and actress Yang Kuei-mei understood this scene to represent hope, since as she cries her face is illuminated by a ray of sun. Chang, 'Erotic Map', 102–105; Tsai Ming-liang interviewed by Shelly Kraicer, *positions: east asia cultures critique*, 8, no. 2 (2000): 579–588 (582).

18. Berry, 'Asian Values', 170.

19. Jiang, 'Body Heat and Salvation', 149.

20. Tsai Ming-liang, 'A Life of Desire, Repression, and Fragmentation' ('Yuwang, yapo, bengjiede shengming'), interview with Chen Baoxu, in *The River* (screenplay) (*Heliu*), ed. Chiao Hsiung-ping (Taipei: Huangguan, 1997), 52–76 (59); see also Martin, 'Perverse Utopia'.

21. Cf. Chang, 'Erotic Map', 104–105.

22. On this point, see ibid., 100.

23. Ibid., 103.

30   *Wedding Banquet*: A Family (Melodrama) Affair

Chris Berry

Most existing critical discussion of Ang Lee's *Wedding Banquet* (1993) focuses on issues of identity politics. However, this short analysis considers the film in the context of its genre – the family melodrama. When scholars talk about the family melodrama, in fact they usually mean the American or Hollywood family melodrama. A genre analysis of *Wedding Banquet* challenges this presumption that the Hollywood form is universal or a default category. In many ways, the story of *Wedding Banquet* is similar to those found in typical Hollywood family melodramas. However, I argue here that while audiences used to Hollywood films may see *Wedding Banquet* as a variation on a familiar pattern, that 'variation' is in fact the trace of a different category of family melodrama – the Chinese family melodrama. *Wedding Banquet* returns to and rejuvenates both the Hollywood and the Chinese family melodrama, which focuses less on the individual in conflict with the family and more on the family as a collectivity in crisis. In *Wedding Banquet*, this manifests itself in both the narrative conventions and in the tropes and patterns of filmic discourse, promoting audience empathy and identification not with any one individual but with the Confucian family unit as it negotiates the interface with globally hegemonic American culture. With this understanding, we can not only begin to insist that scholars specify melodrama historically and socially, but also begin to grasp the specificity of the Chinese genre and the ideological terrain it negotiates.

Perhaps it is not surprising that identity has captured the attention of most critics writing about *Wedding Banquet*, because it can claim to be the first mainstream Taiwanese and possibly even the first Chinese-language film to portray homosexuality seriously and sympathetically. In the film, Taiwanese migrant landlord Wai-Tung lives happily in New York with his Anglo boyfriend Simon. Their bliss is interrupted only by the long-distance efforts of his Taiwanese parents to find him a bride. Simon suggests a marriage of convenience to Wei-Wei, a mainland Chinese tenant in need of a green card. However, the comedy really gets under way when Wai-Tung's parents, the Gaos, insist on visiting and throwing a lavish wedding banquet. Simon and Wai-Tung 'de-gay' the house, move Wei-Wei in and have Simon pose as 'landlord and friend'. On the night of the banquet, Wei-Wei 'liberates' Wai-Tung and gets pregnant. The Gaos' departure is delayed by Mr Gao's ill-health, which provokes Wai-Tung to come out to his mother. She makes him swear never to tell his father. However, Mr Gao reveals to Simon that he has already figured the situation out, and swears him to secrecy, too. Asked why he is maintaining the charade Mr Gao explains, 'Otherwise, how would I have got my grandson?'

Most responses to *Wedding Banquet* judge it according to hopes and expectations for the representation of various identities, including not only gay Chinese men, but also Asian-Americans and Chinese women. For example, Gina Marchetti quotes a variety of contrasting audience reactions, from disappointment that 'gay relationships must compromise themselves and bow to traditional, straight values and family structures' to praise for the film's demonstration that 'family relationships actually do mean something to us'.[1] Sheng-mei Ma believes *Wedding Banquet* and other Ang Lee films challenge stereotypes by 'undermining fixed categories in racial, cultural, and sexual identities'.[2] Along similar lines, Cynthia Liu notes that the film challenges the gay stereotypes of the 'rice queen' and 'potato queen' as young effeminate Asian man and older white man, a point also discussed in detail by Marchetti.[3] But Liu's main argument is about gender, and she notes that, 'under the guise of "cultural difference", the narratives of Lee's trilogy exhibit a punitive tendency in his constructions of the feminine'.[4] Given that Mrs Gao is portrayed as little more than a sweet but stupid wife and mother and that Wei-Wei sacrifices her independence and rebellion to take on the most stereotypically conformist of female roles, her claims are persuasive.[5]

Some writers on these questions of identity are confident they can discern a clear message in the film. Cynthia Liu's article is based on her conviction that 'the patriarch [is] the character through which film viewer's [sic] sympathies are so inexorably channeled'.[6] Shu-mei Shih agrees that 'the patriarch always wins', even though she notes the 'flexibility' of Lee's films as they play differently to Taiwanese and American audiences.[7] Gina Marchetti places her main emphasis on this latter aspect, concluding that '[P]roduced, distributed, and marketed within a transnational matrix of economic, political, cultural, ethnic, and linguistic relationships, The Wedding Banquet does not posit a singular position for an abstract, "ideal" viewer'. Although she also notes that the need to play to different audiences limits the degree to which the film can be ideologically challenging, this suggests a more open text.[8]

In her essay on Crouching Tiger, Hidden Dragon in this volume, Felicia Chan argues that ambiguity and ambivalence are hallmarks of Ang Lee's films produced by the mixing of different genres. Taking this lead, I examine the generic genealogy and hybridisation of Wedding Banquet in order to address the question of how the text works on spectators, as well as to delineate the cultural and historical specificity of different kinds of melodrama. Is there a clear message or is it an open text? I argue that playing on different versions of the family drama genre is both part of and enhances the openness that Marchetti notes. But I also argue that although the viewer is not placed to identify with the individual patriarch (Mr Gao), openness is limited by an overall perspective that takes certain values for granted.

Although farce is clearly one of the genres that Wedding Banquet draws on, its main genre is the family melodrama.[9] The film matches the primary characteristics of the Hollywood family melodrama, and in particular the coming-out story subgenre. In this subgenre, an individual discovers a personality trait (homosexuality) in dramatic conflict with the values of his family and strives to express that trait, often leaving the blood family and seeking out a chosen family in the gay, lesbian or transgender community.[10] Wedding Banquet seems to tell the story of a man who has done just that, but has omitted the crucial stage of telling his family, which the film addresses.

Thomas Schatz notes that in Hollywood, the general term '"melodrama" was applied to popular romances that depicted a virtuous individual (usually a woman) or couple (usually lovers) victimised by repressive and inequitable social circumstances, particularly those involving marriage, occupation and the nuclear family.'[11] Wai-Tung appears as a virtuous character according to conventional Chinese or American middle-class virtues. In the opening scenes, he is shown to be concerned about his parents and also so hard-working that his partner Simon is resentful they have been unable to take a planned vacation together. But he is also so caring that, over a romantic dinner for two, he promises to make up for this by taking Simon to Paris. Although he is a slum landlord, he is concerned enough about his tenant Wei-Wei to take one of her paintings in lieu of rent and buy her an air conditioner. The pressure from his parents to marry presents itself as Schatz's 'inequitable social circumstances' concerning marriage. In so far as homophobia and misogyny in both Chinese and American cultures link gay men and women, he is even edged towards the conventional focus of the Hollywood melodrama on women.

Schatz also argues that generic elements of the Hollywood family drama include 'The aging patriarch ... the search for the father/lover/husband ... the male intruder-redeemer who regenerates and stabilizes the family, the household itself as locus of social interaction, and the ambiguous function of the marital embrace as both sexually liberating and socially restricting ...'[12] Mr Gao, who has already had one stroke in Taiwan and is concerned about getting his only son to continue the family line, represents the ageing patriarch perfectly. And by having the Gaos and Wei-Wei move into Simon and Wai-Tung's New York brownstone, Wedding Banquet not only creates the pressure cooker of confinement that helps to generate frantic farce but also fulfils 'the household itself as locus of social interaction' requirement. The gay 'twist' in this version of archetype generates some interesting complications concerning the redeemer/intruder. Is it Simon or Wei-Wei, or maybe both, who fits this part of the model? Certainly, given that Wai-Tung is gay but that Wei-Wei's pregnancy liberates him from his parents' pressures, the marriage and formation of the couple – or is it a *ménage à trois?* – at the end of the film fits the ambiguous formation of the couple.

In Schatz's analysis of the genre, implausibility can prompt questioning on the part of the audience and therefore create an ironic and critical dimension. For example, he cites 1950s melodrama director Douglas Sirk's comment that 'there is no real solution of the predicament the people in the play are in, just the *deus ex machina*, which is now called "the happy end"'.[13] Certainly the miracle of a woman made pregnant by a gay man and agreeing to marriage and motherhood despite her previous commitment to independence strains credulity, not to mention the willingness of his parents to accept the complicated domestic arrangements that appear inevitable. However, it also true that *Wedding Banquet* is shot in a conventionally realist fashion, featuring none of the mannered play with colours, lighting and framing that critics like Schatz associate with a self-reflexive subversion in Sirk.

Given the many Americans involved in making Ang Lee's films and his own many years in the United States, it is not surprising that *Wedding Banquet* follows the pattern of the Hollywood melodrama in many ways. But what about the Chinese family melodrama? The term 'melodrama' is commonly used in the discussion of Asian cinemas in general and Chinese cinema in particular.[14] Yet all the existing accounts of the development of Hollywood melodrama trace complicated genealogies through many different branches of stage productions, literature and popular cultural forms – all of them exclusively European and American.[15] Such considerations lead Nick Browne to ask, 'On what basis can an aesthetic ideology so embedded in the popular entertainment forms of Western culture – Christian and capitalist – be treated as significant, culturally speaking, to the form and meaning of contemporary Chinese film?'[16]

An attempt to trace a genealogy of the Chinese family melodrama in general is beyond the scope of this article. However, two basic factors should be noted. First, Western stage forms were introduced into China in the early part of the twentieth century, meaning that Chinese dramatists and film-makers are familiar with Western melodrama. On the other hand, although popularisation of Western stage forms

like melodrama in China coincides with the advent of modernity, as Peter Brooks has noted is also the case in Europe,[17] this was not part of a transition to secularity, because dominant Confucian ideology was already secular in focus. What, then, do Chinese scholars and critics mean when they use the term 'melodrama'?

Wimal Dissanayake has noted that none of the Asian languages has a synonym for 'melodrama',[18] and this is also true in Chinese. In 1986, the Hong Kong International Film Festival's annual retrospective was on 'Cantonese Melodrama 1950–1969'. The Chinese title of the catalogue and all the essays in it use 'melodrama' as a translation of *'wenyipian'*. This term literally means 'literature and art film'. But as Li Cheuk-to notes, although it is different from the European melodrama because the *wenyipian* is defined more by subject matter than mode, it has many dramaturgical characteristics in common with the European melodrama: 'highly schematic characters, plots punctuated by fortuities and coincidences, extreme emotions and conflicts …'[19] Taiwanese critic Cai Guorong traces the general form and history of the *wenyipian* to the 1920s and defines it by theme, setting and tone as films about family and romance, set in modern times, and with a lyrical focus on emotion.[20]

However, when we turn to the family melodrama, it is notable that the Chinese term translated in this way is not 'family *wenyipian*' but instead 'family ethics film' *(jiating lunlipian)*.[21] This is significant, for *lunli* is a specifically Confucian term for ethics, referring to the Confucian code of reciprocal ethical obligations. These are the five relationships *(wulun)*: emperor–subject, father–son, husband–wife, elder brother–younger brother, friend–friend. As Ma Ning notes, 'although the *wulun* relationships are asymmetical and structured as patron–client relations, they are naturalized in ethical terms'.[22] This emphasis on ethical expectations based on hierarchically defined social and kinship position leads Ma to add that 'the Chinese melodramatic narrative facilitates the construction of a subjectivity that can be best described as intersubjectivity'.[23] This understanding of selfhood has grounded narratives in China for many centuries, as contradictions between different obligations or between obligation and personal desires can motor all manner of stories.[24] In contrast to this relationally defined 'intersubjectivity', a hallmark of the transition to secularity in Europe discussed by Brooks as grounding the emergence of European melodrama is the emphasis on the individual 'personality' understood as a unique and natural individual psychology.[25] The resultant emphasis is not on ethics (behaviour) but on morality (good or bad character).

In these circumstances, the distinction between the European family melodrama and the Chinese family *lunlipian* produces a tension between two different models of secular subjectivity, one based on psychology and its expression and the other based on ethically defined social and kinship roles. In so far as the emergence of the modern Chinese melodrama is coincident with the Chinese experience of modernity as a European import, we may therefore hypothesise that the Chinese family *lunlipian* is itself a modern and hybrid form that stages the tension between 'tradition' and 'modernity' as a tension between different models of subjectivity, with competing value systems for judging behaviour. In the remainder of this essay, I would like to examine how *Wedding Banquet* can be read as a *lunlipian* as well as a Hollywood-style family melodrama, and how this is manifested not only in narrative but also in *mise en scène* and editing to create ambiguity around the message of the film and ambivalent audience engagement.

Homosexuality is ripe for melodramatisation in the Western tradition as a personality trait in conflict with dominant social values. It is also ripe for narrativisation in the tradition of the *lunlipian*. Here, however, the drama is driven by the potential ethical difficulty of being unable to fulfil one of the most fundamental obligations expected of a son: the production of a grandson to continue the family line.[26] Wai-Tung's discussions with Simon early in the film concern homosexuality as personality – he is lying about who he is and should he just come out to his parents? However, when a potential match sent from Taiwan tells Wai-Tung about his father's stroke, she also tells him that his father has said his greatest wish is to see his grandson before he dies – emphasising the Confucian ethical dimension of the situation.

These tensions between what can be seen as ethical practice or oppression and self-expression or selfishness animate the rest of the film. They extend beyond Wai-Tung and are often made explicit in heart-to-heart conversations. Wai-Tung's father is a retired career army officer who everyone refers to as 'the commander'. But soon after arriving in New York, he tells his son he joined up to escape an arranged marriage. Indeed, he only got married at all after learning that his family in the mainland had died, leaving the responsibility of continuing the family line to him. Since Wai-Tung is an only son, the ethical parallels are clear. But it is also clear that Mr Gao's own experiences include the negotiation of parallel tensions.

After the truth has come out about both Wai-Tung's sexuality and Wei-Wei's pregnancy, Wei-Wei feels obliged to return the Gaos' wedding presents to Mrs Gao. Mrs Gao refuses, insisting that she wants her grandson. Wei-Wei responds, 'What about my future?' But after this stand-off between ethical kinship obligation and self-realisation, Mrs Gao tells Wei-Wei she envies younger women and their independence and education, and Wei-Wei responds that she came to regard the Gaos as her own parents because she is so alone in America. Again, both women live the struggle between different ideological systems and corresponding modes of subjectivity.

Even Simon is unconsciously caught up in these tensions. He tries hard to fulfil the ethical obligations of a traditional daughter-in-law, cooking and cleaning diligently for Wai-Tung and his parents. Although his motivation for suggesting marriage to Wei-Wei is selfish – getting Wai-Tung's parents off their backs – this act mimics the ideal behaviour of a barren daughter-in-law in suggesting a second wife to enable her husband to produce an heir. However, when things go wrong, Simon starts going out with friends and tells Wai-Tung he plans to leave, presumably because the complex situation is not satisfying his needs. Towards the end of the film, Wai-Tung and Wei-Wei decide to keep the baby and ask him to co-parent. When he nods, Wai-Tung asks tentatively, 'So you'll stay?' But the ironic clincher is Wei-Wei's invocation of the Western equivalent of kinship obligations: 'You must, for the sake of the child.'

This double thematic focus on mutual obligations and self-expression certainly helps audiences of different backgrounds to engage with *Wedding Banquet*. But the moral ambivalence produced by mixing the two sets of values is a distinctly new feature of the film. Both the Hollywood and Chinese family melodrama had a very clear sense of right and wrong. Indeed, they functioned to rehearse and affirm well-known values. But so much of the drama in *Wedding Banquet* is produced not only by the clash between

Wedding Banquet: Wei-Wei's wedding night

values but also the acknowledgment of both sets of values by the central characters that the result is a new characteristic for the genre – deep-seated moral and ethical ambivalence.

This ambivalence makes it less easy to determine how the film works to position audiences. Is it organised to promote a primary identification with any one particular character? In the opening credits sequence, only Wai-Tung appears, working out at the gym. This might seem to indicate that this is his story. His mother's voice on the audiotape letter pressuring him to marry might be taken to promote further sympathy and identification with him, especially for audiences already favourable to the idea of self-expression and steeped in Hollywood melodrama.

But in the scenes that follow, other characters are introduced. Although Simon and Wei-Wei's relationships to Wai-Tung are quickly established, in each case we are first given a sense of their lives beyond him. In Simon's case, we see him at work as a physiotherapist before the sequence continues into a dinner date with Wai-Tung. The next morning, we see Simon running into a gay friend outside the house he shares with Wai-Tung and they touch upon

HIV-AIDS activism briefly, a theme that will be picked up again later in the film. In Wei-Wei's case, she is first shown alone in her overheated basement studio in Wai-Tung's building, sweating, drinking, listening to loud music and working on her abstract paintings. Only then does Wai-Tung arrive. Although it is unlikely anyone could claim that *Wedding Banquet* is primarily Simon's or Wei-Wei's story, these scenes make it harder to see it as Wai-Tung's alone.

Furthermore, these narrative techniques are complemented by camerawork and editing enabling the audience to perceive how different characters feel, rather than tying them into seeing things from one character's point of view only. Some of the most often cited work on Hollywood film has emphasised the potential for ideological persuasion through the use of point-of-view shots and other techniques that align the audience with the perspective of a particular character.[27] Setting aside for the moment at least thirty years of argument about how true this might be in Hollywood studio-era cinema, it is important to note that this is not the technique deployed in *Wedding Banquet*.

First, *Wedding Banquet* does not align audience perspectives with the literal point of view of any one character. Although point-of-view shots are used, in particular, as a way of heightening dramatic tension in scenes where people argue, I cannot discover any privileging of one character's point of view. Indeed, the film does not privilege the point-of-view shot as an identification device at all. Instead, in many scenes, the dominant device is the arrangement of the characters in the *mise en scène* and the editing so as to give the audience access to the different reactions and ideas of all the main characters. This is mainly produced by keeping everyone in the same frame with their faces visible to the camera, as for example in the scene where Wei-Wei returns the gifts to Mrs Gao. But it may be produced by editing. For example, prior to the wedding banquet Wei-Wei and Wai-Tung kneel before Mr and Mrs Gao. It is not possible to view all of the characters' faces at once. The camera cuts back and forth so that we can see Mr and Mrs Gao getting happier as he makes his long paternal blessings speech, but also Wei-Wei and Wai-Tung getting more uncomfortable.

This example brings up a second important point about audience perspective. This scene depends for its effect on our superior narrative knowledge. At this stage of the film, we know more about each character's background and feelings than any one character does, and we are moved because the clash of emotions is invisible until, much to Mr and Mrs Gao's surprise, Wei-Wei breaks down in tears. I have referred to this device elsewhere as a kind of spectatorial 'third place', but I would further specify that we can call the pleasure of superior knowledge 'epistemophilia'.[28]

Nick Browne notes in his article on *Stagecoach* that superior knowledge can override the identification potential of the point-of-view shot. He analyses a scene where point-of-view shots align the audience physically with disapproving gazes upon the character of Dallas, a prostitute. However, prior knowledge has established audience sympathy with her, which overrides this alignment and makes its use only a way of poignantly underlining prejudice.[29]

Just prior to telling Wai-tung why he joined the army, Mr Gao has a point-of-view shot that is strongly marked, both because such shots are unusual in the film and it is not motivated by a movement or sound drawing his attention. He (and we) look at the two empty chairs in the garden of the house. Does this mean the audience is aligned with the patriarch, Mr Gao? First, the film gives us no idea what he is thinking about these two chairs, although if Simon is the live-in landlord and Wai-Tung and Wei-Wei are his tenants – as he has been told – the arrangement may seem odd. And second, we already know far more than he does, meaning that we certainly do understand the significance of the chairs. Therefore, the use of the shot is deeply ambivalent.

Similarly, at the end of the wedding banquet itself, Wei-Wei and Wai-Tung watch Simon lead Mr and Mrs Gao off. Are we to understand our perspective as anchored in either Wei-Wei or Wai-Tung's vision or both? And what emotions are we to attach to this view? Nothing in the text prompts a definitive answer. We may look at it from either character's perspective, or our own. We cannot be sure if Wai-Tung and Wei-Wei are happy or feel manipulated. This ambivalence is even more heightened in the final scene of the film, where Wei-Wei, Wai-Tung and Simon see off Mr and Mrs Gao at the airport. Prior to the notoriously ambivalent final shot where the film freezes on Mr Gao raising his arms in what could be interpreted as surrender or as triumph, the family looks at the wedding-photograph album. The scene seems like a self-referential retrospect. We cut back and forth between shots of their facial reactions and their point of view of the pictures in the album. Should we identify with one character's point of view? Do we need to identify with any individual perspective? The text seems more open.

However, although these techniques produce considerable flexibility and ambivalence the film is not completely open. Rather, it produces its ideological effect through a different set of devices than point-of-view shots. The combination of narrative knowledge and camerawork offers the audience access to the feelings of all the central characters and enables knowledge that exceeds that of any one character, enabling different audience members to work through the film with different trajectories. However, the text itself forecloses upon certain crucial narrative possibilities. All the characters strive hard to understand and satisfy the needs of the other characters, whether based on individual self-expression or the fulfilment of social and kinship roles. At no point is any serious criticism of either set of values voiced within the film itself. Nobody denounces Mr Gao's obsession with the family line, and nobody denounces Wai-Tung and Simon's sexuality as immoral or selfish. Of course, a real audience member may always bring their own ideas from outside the film to bear upon their interpretation of it. But the film's ambivalence is itself an ideological move appropriate to the sustenance of globalised liberal capitalism, for it enables that system by finding a way to maintain simultaneously two otherwise incompatible value systems that it brings into proximity. In this way, it produces a new melodramatic hybrid appropriate to the negotiation of the 'moral occult' of globalism.

NOTES

1. Gina Marchetti, '*The Wedding Banquet*: Global Chinese Cinema and Asian American Experience', in *Countervisions: Asian-American Film Criticism*, ed. Sandra Liu and Darrell Y. Hamamoto (Philadelphia: Temple University Press, 2000), 281.

2. Sheng-mei Ma, 'Ang Lee's Domestic Tragicomedy: Immigrant Nostalgia, Exotic/Ethnic Tour, Global Market', *Journal of Popular Culture*, 30, no. 1 (1996): 191.

3. Cynthia W. Liu, ' "To Love, Honor and Dismay": Subverting the Feminine in Ang Lee's Trilogy of Resuscitated Patriarchs', *Hitting Critical Mass: A Journal of Asian American Cultural Criticism*, 3, no. 1 (1995): 37–40; Marchetti, '*The Wedding Banquet*', 285–288.

4. Liu, ' "To Love, Honor and Dismay"', 9.

5. However, one largely overlooked identity dimension of the film in all the critical discussion is ethnicity. For further analysis see Chris Berry and Mary Farquhar, 'Where Do You Draw the Line? Ethnicity in Chinese Cinemas', in *China on Screen: Cinema and Nation* (New York and Hong Kong: Columbia and Hong Kong University Presses, 2006).

6. Liu, ' "To Love, Honor and Dismay"', 14.

7. Shu-mei Shih, 'Globalisation and Minoritisation: Ang Lee and the Politics of Flexibility', *New Formations*, no. 40 (2000): 92–93.

8. Marchetti, '*The Wedding Banquet*', 292–293.

9. Scholarship over the last twenty years or so has challenged the idea that melodrama is a generic type, and argued instead that it is a mode of cinematic narration that can be found in all manner of genres including the Western and the gangster film. Crucial though this argument is, it does not undermine the status of the family melodrama as a distinct genre deploying the melodramatic mode. The key essay on this topic is Christine Gledhill's 'The Melodramatic Field: An Investigation', in *Home Is Where the Heart Is: Studies in Melodrama and the Woman's Film*, ed. Christine Gledhill (London: BFI, 1987), 5–39. Gledhill makes it clear she believes the effort to confine the melodramatic mode to the Hollywood genres of the woman's film and the family melodrama are motivated by misogynistic prejudice against emotion and excess. Linda Williams extends the argument to revise our understanding of classical Hollywood cinema as a whole and attack the common division between realist cinema and melodrama in 'Melodrama Revised', in *Refiguring American Film Genres: History and Theory*, ed. Nick Browne (Berkeley: University of California Press, 1998), 42–88.

10. Ken Plummer, *Telling Sexual Stories: Power, Change and Social Worlds* (London: Routledge, 1995), 83.

11. Thomas Schatz, 'The Family Melodrama', in *Hollywood Genres: Formulas, Filmmaking, and the Studio System* (Philadelphia: Temple University Press, 1981), 222.

12. Ibid., 229–230.

13. Ibid., 244.

14. See, for example, the essays collected in Wimal Dissanayake, ed., *Melodrama and Asian Cinema* (New York: Cambridge University Press, 1993).

15. In addition to accounts in Gledhill, Schatz and Williams, see Thomas Elsaesser, 'Tales of Sound and Fury: Observations of the Family Melodrama', in Gledhill, *Home Is Where the Heart Is*, 43–69.

16. Nick Browne, 'Society and Subjectivity: On the Political Economy of Chinese Melodrama', in *New Chinese Cinemas: Forms, Identities, Politics*, ed. Nick Browne, Paul G. Pickowicz, Vivian Sobchak and Esther Yau (New York: Cambridge University Press, 1994), 42.

17. Peter Brooks, *The Melodramatic Imagination: Balzac, Henry James, Melodrama and the Mode of Excess* (New Haven, CT: Yale University Press, 1976), 15–18.

18. Wimal Dissanayake, 'Introduction', in Dissanayake, *Melodrama*, 3.

19. Li Cheuk-to, 'Introduction', in *Cantonese Melodrama 1950–1969 (Aoyu Wenyipian Miangu 1950-1959)*, ed. Li Cheuk-to (Hong Kong: The Urban Council, 1986), 9.

20. Cai Guorong, *A Study of the Modern Chinese Melodrama (Zhongguo jindai wenyi dianying yanjiu)* (Taipei: Taiwan Film Archive, 1985), 3–7. For further

discussion in English, see Law Kar, 'Archetype and Variations', in Li, *Cantonese Melodrama*, 15.

21. This Chinese term appears as the original on page 8 translated into English as 'family melodrama' on page 9 in Li Cheuk-to's introduction, for example. The same translation can be found comparing the Chinese original and the English original of Stephen Teo's 'The Father–Son Cycle' ('Fu yu zi–aoyupian zhuti de yanxu'), in Li, *Cantonese Melodrama*, 42–47 and 37–41 respectively. This essay forms the foundation for Chapter 4 of Teo's own book, Stephen Teo, *Hong Kong Cinema: The Extra Dimensions* (London: BFI, 1997), 61–72. Cai Guorong also uses the term in his book on the general category of the *wenyipian*.

22. Ma Ning, 'Spatiality and Subjectivity in Xie Jin's Film Melodrama of the New Period', in Nick Browne *et al.*, *New Chinese Cinemas*, 18.

23. Ibid., 23. For further discussion of the early origins of these and related concepts, see Donald J. Munro, *The Concept of Man in Early China* (Stanford, CA: Stanford University Press, 1969).

24. Andrew H. Plaks, 'Towards a Critical Theory of Chinese Narrative', in *Chinese Narrative: Critical and Theoretical Essays*, ed. Andrew H. Plaks (Princeton, NJ: Princeton University Press, 1977), 343–345.

25. Brooks, *The Melodramatic Imagination*, 42.

26. These questions of homosexuality and the space and ideology of the family are discussed further by Fran Martin in this volume. I have also considered the question at greater length in various essays, including 'Asian Values, Family Values: Film, Video, and Lesbian and Gay Identities', in *Gay and Lesbian Asia: Culture, Identity, Community*, ed. Gerard Sullivan and Peter A. Jackson (New York: Harrington Park Press, 2001), 211–233.

27. The two most famous examples are probably Daniel Dayan, 'The Tutor-Code of Classical Cinema', in *Movies and Methods*, ed. Bill Nichols (Berkeley: University of California Press, 1976), 438–451; and Laura Mulvey, 'Visual Pleasure and Narrative Cinema', *Screen*, 16, no. 3 (1975): 6–19. The second article works on the gendered quality of these structures.

28. Chris Berry, 'Sexual Difference and the Viewing Subject in *Li Shuangshuang* and *The In-Laws*', in *Perspectives on Chinese Cinema*, ed. Chris Berry (London: BFI, 1991), 30–39.

29. Nick Browne, 'The Spectator-in-the-Text: The Rhetoric of *Stagecoach*', in *Film Theory and Criticism: Introductory Readings*, ed. Leo Braudy and Marshall Cohen, 5th edn. (New York: Oxford University Press, 1999), 148–163.

31 *Woman, Demon, Human*: The Spectral Journey Home

Haiyan Lee

The mainland Chinese woman director Huang Shuqin's opera film *Woman, Demon, Human* (1987) has long been regarded as one of the few truly feminist films in People's Republic of China (PRC) cinematic history. It is based on the life of the Peking opera performer Pei Yanling (b. 1947) who specialises in male roles on stage.[1] Its artful use of theatrical transvestism has provoked, almost by academic reflex, much discussion about gender identity and gender performativity. Shuqin Cui and Dai Jinhua, for example, have both shown how the film problematises gender through protagonist Qiu Yun's choice of on-stage personae – most notably the male demon king Zhong Kui – a choice that attests to her refusal to be a good woman and to the difficulty of female self-representation.[2] But the narrow focus on gender, I believe, often produces a circular argument about gender ambiguity and ultimately fails to arrive at a compelling feminist reading of the film. The problem, paradoxically, begins with the English translation of the Chinese title *Ren gui qing* as *Woman, Demon, Human*, instead of a more literal rendition like *A Human-Ghost Affair*. The addition of 'woman' and the omission of '*qing*' (passion, love or feeling) set the film on a critical course that seldom ventures beyond gender consciousness and identity politics. It is my intention to argue that while the film deploys an explicit gender discourse and parades rich gender imageries, it is more appropriately a celebration of human attachment that transcends binary gender identity. As an opera film, it mobilises the aesthetics of the 'cinema of attractions' that departs significantly from contemporary, more high-profile filmic appropriations of the operatic form. It uses the theatrical metaphor to configure radical identities and to urge men and women to look beyond romance and marriage to forge more inclusive, creative and emancipatory forms of sociality.

OPERA FILM AS CINEMA OF ATTRACTIONS

The prevalence of cross-gender casting in traditional Chinese theatre has proven irresistible to film-makers and cultural theorists alike. But just because a film incorporates theatrical transvestism does not make it subversive of gender norms or dominant gender ideology. Chen Kaige's epic film *Farewell My Concubine* (1993) is a case in point. The first part of the film depicts a delicate-featured boy named Douzi being trained for female *dan* roles and forced to sing 'I am by nature a girl, not a boy'. But Douzi somehow instinctively knows that he is a boy and stoically defends his 'innate' or 'true' gender identity, blurting out 'I am by nature a boy' again and again and inviting repeated whackings from the sadistic headmaster of the opera academy. Douzi grows up to become an acclaimed actor (adopting the stage name of Cheng Dieyi), who harbours unrequited love for his stage partner. His 'homosexuality' is portrayed as the pathetic expression of a distorted gender essence, the product of a human artifice meddling with natural gender difference. It is a nodal point that condenses all his failings, emotional, moral and political. For all its opulent theatricality, *Farewell My Concubine* perpetuates a gender essentialism that undercuts its critique of the politicisation of art in PRC history. Indeed, Dieyi is already a wreck long before the onslaught of the Cultural Revolution and its vulgarisation and butchering of Peking opera as the epitome of traditional high art. Chen Kaige therefore misses the opportunity to exploit the theatrical trope for the space it might *open up* in terms of gender and sexual performativity, or the feminist thesis that gender and sexuality are socially constructed and continually consolidated and revised through iterative performance.[3]

Commenting on the preponderance of opera movies in early twentieth-century mandarin cinemas on the mainland and mid-century dialect cinemas in

Woman, Demon, Human

Hong Kong and Taiwan, Chris Berry and Mary Far-quhar consider opera film the mainstay of a Chinese 'cinema of attractions'.[4] Indeed, opera film's sumptu-ous display – costume, movement, action, music and vocals – is a source of pleasure that is largely inde-pendent of cinematic diegesis, or the 'story'. But above all, opera film's 'attractions' have to do with the prevalent cross-dressing motif and the convention of cross-gender casting in traditional theatre that afford the opportunity for gender performance and gender-bending play. To adapt an insight from Linda Williams in connection with the 'thriller' as an Amer-ican cinema of attractions, we can say that theatrical cross-dressing has the potential of destabilising gender identity by introducing the thrill of imagining other, indeterminate or transgressive forms of iden-tity and belonging.[5]

However, opera film can also be naively literal-minded, construing gender performance as either wilful playacting or an imposed regime of behaviour. Theatrical literalisation can therefore paradoxically reinforce the gender essentialism that structures het-erosexual desire and plot in classical narrative cinema. *Farewell My Concubine*, for example, holds fast to an essentialised psychosomatic conception of gender that is largely absent in traditional theatre and the traditional social world, where gender is defined in relational terms and articulated through sartorial, ges-tural and ritualised tropes.[6] What it fails to grasp is that cross-dressing subverts gender norms not simply because one can don the accoutrements of the oppo-site gender and reinvent oneself, but because it allows one to traverse the boundaries that align the male/female binary with the outside/inside (*wai/nei*)

binary. So it is not cross-dressing per se but the (dis)location of women and men in drag that engen-ders anxiety and fascination and produces disorient-ing and subversive effects.

Moreover, film faces a peculiar dilemma when appropriating opera to fashion a cinema of attrac-tions. This is because film is a medium that no longer tolerates cross-gender casting owing to the entrench-ment of the modern psychosomatic conception of gender. The tension between the traditional perfor-mative conception and the modern psychosomatic conception of gender constitutes a major stumbling block for opera films. But the incommensurability of the medium is also what enables opera film to explore alternative vistas of identity and sociality. *Woman, Demon, Human*, in my view, is a more self-conscious and more creative appropriation of the theatrical that boldly probes the possibilities of non-gender-centred human relationships. These relationships are mod-elled on those between father and daughter and between brother and sister, but only as they are medi-ated through a theatrical trope.

TO BE A GHOST

Woman, Demon, Human begins with a disorienting sequence showing the opera actress Qiu Yun making up her face in the dressing room full of mirrors reflecting either her semi-painted feminine face or her fully dressed theatrical role, Zhong Kui the demon king. In long flashbacks, the film narrates Qiu Yun's childhood and adolescence as she trains assidu-ously and defiantly for the operatic stage. These flashbacks are interrupted by operatic interludes that feature Pei Yanling herself playing the *wuchou* (martial-comic) role of Zhong Kui. The interludes are presented explicitly as fantasy sequences, with a grotesque and clownish Zhong Kui appearing out of nowhere and seemingly prancing in mid-air. As the legend has it, before he became a ghost, Zhong Kui had been an indigent but studious scholar who lived with his younger sister. Impressed by his scholarly promise, his best friend, Du Ping, put up the money for him to travel to the imperial capital to sit for the highest levels of the civil service examination. But on his way there, he was assailed by a pack of goblins, who spitefully disfigured him. He achieved first rank in the palace examination, but the emperor, fright-ened by his hideous appearance, refused to honour his achievement. The heartbroken Zhong Kui killed himself by smashing his head against a pillar; there-upon the remorseful emperor appointed his ghost as the Demon King and put him in charge of vanquish-ing malevolent spirits. But Zhong Kui has an impor-tant matter to take care of first: he must return to his home in the human world in order to give his sister away in marriage to his benefactor Du Ping.

The operatic interludes in the film focus on one segment of a popular play called *Zhong Kui Marries off His Sister* (*Zhong Kui jiamei*), depicting an anxious Zhong Kui on his homeward journey singing a plain-tive aria about his yearning to see his sister and his fear of frightening her. He sports a long bushy black beard, a hunchback and a crooked shoulder – all indi-cators of his other-than-human status. He is mostly accompanied by a band of spirit attendants who per-form ghoulish acrobatics to the rhythmic beat of a quickened operatic soundtrack. With its spectral fig-ures, rhythmic dance, colourful visual collages and melancholic arias, the ghostly journey is an important source of the film's 'attractions' – attractions that are grounded in the operatic form and heightened through cinematic techniques. As the ghosts hop, stamp, frolic and tumble across a murky-edged frame, the screen itself is transformed into a liminal space between life and death. With the knowledge that the telos of the journey is a this-worldly home and that the object of the demon king's poignant but non-erotic longing is a human maiden comes the pleasure of (momentarily) suspending the ontological certainty of the divide between life and death and the episte-mological certainty of the disinterested spectator.

Zhong Kui's homebound journey is also what the little Qiu Yun grows up watching on stage as her par-ents play Zhong Kui and his sister. In one perform-ance, Qiu Yun's father as Zhong Kui mimes reaching the front gate of the house and calls out to the back-stage: 'Sis, open the door'. But his wife has run away with her lover (Qiu Yun's biological father) and thus fails to appear on stage. The father repeats his call and appears increasingly foolish and exasperated. As Qiu Yun watches the audience shower her father with boos and projectiles, the image of a lonely and belea-guered Zhong Kui who cannot return 'home' becomes the master trope that lends meaning and structure to her life. But precisely what is it about Zhong Kui that appeals to Qiu Yun, for whom other operatic heroes seem no substitute? What or where is the home to which he yearns to return but apparently cannot?

I submit that Qiu Yun wants to play and indeed to be Zhong Kui because he is not a 'man' as such. Instead, he is a composite of the noble and transcen-dent qualities of the Chinese moral universe. In the first place, he is an ideal Confucian male, having mas-tered the classics and imbibed all the essential Con-fucian virtues: he is said to be courageous, upright, loyal, trustworthy, dutiful and selfless – as confirmed by his success in the civil service examination. But because he dies before he is rewarded with fame and power (plus the emperor's daughter for a bride as the cliché goes), he has not had the opportunity to be corrupted by the temptations of office-holding or compromised by the claims of family and associates. He is therefore above the corrosive effects of private interests and truly embodies the Confucian ideal of serving the public (*gong*). In his official capacity as the demon king, he resembles a Daoist shaman or Bodhisattva who guards the *yang* social order against the antisocial forces of the *yin* world by descending into that world. He is also a knight-errant who ren-ders chivalric services to the weak and helpless. Not a romantic hero, he has only paternalistic solicitude for his female charge. Indeed, he is decidedly not a pale-faced scholar (*caizi*) destined to meet his beauty (*jiaren*). And for this reason, he is not prone to for-sake his duties in pursuit of sensual gratification. He is god, demon and human all at once, embodying cosmic justice and freedom.

Jo Riley considers the equivalency of theatre and the afterworld to be the most striking aspect of Chi-nese performance, noting that the exorcist Zhong Kui is part of a repertoire of semi-human, semi-beast fig-ures in Chinese mythology that mediate between the living and dead and regenerate the cosmos through acts of cleansing, consuming or destruction. She writes:

> The Chinese performing body is one which is dislocated from its so-called 'own identity', and reformed as 'other'. It has a different body shape and size, it may be ugly or terrifying to behold, or it may be part-beast (hairy). … The other body is reconstructed as a body from another world (of death, the spirit world, the fictive world of theatre).[7]

In *Woman, Demon, Human*, the 'other body' on stage is the ugly, lame and misshapen Zhong Kui. When Qiu Yun plays Zhong Kui, she is not merely mas-querading as a man, but rather enacting a role that points to another world. The ghost becomes the ultimate metaphor for an alternative, indeterminate form of identity and sociality, whereby a woman need not be inexorably inscribed by gender roles. It is significant that Qiu Yun does not follow the familiar pattern of aspiring to religious transcendence in order to escape Confucian gender inscriptions, even though there is no shortage of models. The most famous one is perhaps Guanyin, the Goddess of Mercy. According to Chinese mythology, Guanyin had once been a devout princess named Miaoshan who was driven out of her father's palace when she defied his wish to marry her off. In a dream journey through Hell, she was revealed to be the Bodhisattva Guanyin and delivered all sinners from their suffering. She then saved her father the king from a mysterious disease with a physic made with her two arms and two eyes. Miraculously, her eyes and limbs grew back as her father attained enlightenment. Thereupon father and daughter ascended to Heaven together.[8]

The difference between the stories of Guanyin and Zhong Kui is that the former ends with transcendence while the latter dwells on the journey 'home' – to accomplish something as mundane as giving away one's sister in marriage. In other words, marriage is the obstacle for one and the goal for the other. Popular stories featuring Guanyin usually present her as an all-knowing and all-powerful matronly figure whose narrative function is primarily that of a deus ex machina. Other than in the legend of Miaoshan, she is never on a quest. She transcends womanhood by renouncing human sociality altogether. In Heaven, her father will simply be another immortal being and the father–daughter relationship ceases at the moment of their heavenly ascension. Zhong Kui, by contrast, is forever a restless wayfarer, drawn by an intense yearning to be home, to see his sister and to discharge his brotherly duty. In this sense, he is profoundly and painfully human. In identifying with Zhong Kui, Qiu Yun makes a very modern choice that affirms the inherent value of 'home' and family life (as opposed to the traditional valuation of the contemplative life), but she refuses to be exhaustively defined by the gender roles of wife and mother. Instead, she seeks a form of emancipation and transcendence that is nonetheless deeply rooted in human attachments and that does not entail a denigration of the quotidian. In the film and

its operatic double, it is the unlikely bonds between a (foster) father and daughter and between a brother and sister – bonds that are outside the five cardinal relationships (*wulun*) in Confucian ethics and hence remain unmarked by Confucian sanctification – that lend power and pathos to this aspiration.

Let us consider Qiu Yun's attachment to her foster father, Old Qiu. Qiu Yun's carefree childhood comes to an abrupt end when she accidentally chances upon her mother's secret tryst with her lover amid some gloomy haystacks – the film's most emblematic *mise en scène*. Choking with fright and bewilderment, the seven- or eight-year-old girl runs back to the camp of the itinerant troupe and plunges into Old Qiu's bosom. Old Qiu comforts her and wipes away her tears. After the lovers elope, Qiu Yun and Old Qiu become inseparable. Old Qiu initiates her, at first against his own wishes, into the world of opera and trains her in its manifold skills and singular spirit. Later, When Qiu Yun is recruited by the provincial opera troupe, Old Qiu stoically fights back tears and sends her off before returning to the farm with a stray dog. In the provincial opera troupe, Qiu Yun first tastes the bitter fruit of love: her romantic relationship with the charismatic Teacher Zhang has no future because the latter has a wife and four children in the countryside and because the leaders of the troupe waste little time in sending Zhang away. A dejected Qiu Yun returns to her father's house vowing to give up opera for good. Old Qiu chases her up and down the farmyard brandishing a stick. Unable to evade him further, Qiu Yun takes a bold stride toward him, daring him to beat her. Old Qiu's stick, however, halts in mid-air when Qiu Yun exclaims: 'you are not my dad!' This line irrevocably transforms the father–daughter relationship from an ascriptive and hierarchical relationship to one of mutual attachment, care and respect, cemented by shared devotion to opera. When the camera cuts to the next scene, father and daughter are walking side by side toward the train station. Old Qiu bids farewell to Qiu Yun with these words:

> When you walk out on the stage at the sound of the gong, the audience are a dark mass in front of you and all you see are the lights. Every darned worry is gone! All you think about is being on stage. That's what acting is. You'll never be famous if you can't get that point.

In his down-to-earth fashion, Old Qiu drives home the point that opera is not about being a man or woman; rather, it is about artifice and artistry that transcend the naturally given, about being utterly alone and yet seen and adored, and about the sheer exhilaration of conjuring up a new and fantastic world. Teacher Zhang makes essentially the same point when one day he catches Qiu Yun making herself up in the feminine *dan* fashion in the dressing room. He tells her that she is beautiful enough to play either a man or woman. However, while she can easily play a coquette, she may never be a Mei Lan-fang – the renowned Peking opera actor who specialised in *dan* roles – for beauty or any such natural quality is no sufficient basis for becoming a virtuoso *dan* actor. But if she 'can play a man *well*, that would be truly sensational'. Again, the idea is that the art of opera is not grounded in gender essentialism; rather, it is about transcending or denaturalising one's received gender.[9]

The only significant relationships in Qiu Yun's life are those mediated through opera, and the only significant men in her life – Old Qiu and Teacher Zhang – are her fellow travellers on and off stage. Her mother, in betraying the world of opera, also betrays Qiu Yun. Heterosexual love in this film is marked as unromantic through a hesitant visual language. This is especially true in the scene in which the adult Qiu Yun finally meets her birth father in a restaurant. Throughout, the man who is her birth father never faces the camera – indeed, he is identified in the credits as 'the back of a head' (*hounaoshao*). Without the opportunity to see his face and observe his emotions, the audience is left with the feeling that there is something truly sordid about what he and Qiu Yun's mother have done, and that he is too stricken with shame to look either Qiu Yun or the audience in the eye. The same goes for Qiu Yun's marriage: the husband never enters the frame except in a wedding photo on the wall of their living room. Addicted to gambling and deep in debt, he is a source of shame and trouble for Qiu Yun. Crucially, he has no taste for opera nor any inkling of what acting is all about. Marriage and motherhood are thus shown in a couple of brief scenes and the film quickly returns Qiu Yun to her opera world. After the interruption of the Cultural Revolution, which the film skips over, she has returned to the stage and resumed playing roles from the traditional repertoire.[10] Moreover, she has quickly achieved international fame and her troupe is scheduled to tour abroad. But before that, significantly, her troupe is to return to her home village in an effort to bring opera to the people. The home visit is where the film reaches its emotional climax.

TO BE HOME

In *Farewell My Concubine*, Peking opera is an art form chiefly patronised by urban elites, be they local hereditary nobility or domestic/foreign army officers. The actor protagonists, coming out of indentured apprenticeship in an opera academy, are floating individuals without deep roots or primordial attachments; their art, too, is easily smothered by overzealous but clueless proletarians. *Woman, Demon, Human*, by contrast, begins with an itinerant troupe that puts on open-air performances on makeshift stages. Old Qiu, in Zhong Kui regalia, is even asked to bless a schoolboy and officiate at a New Year's parade. Opera thus blends into the rural landscape and is very much a part of the vibrant social and ritual life of the countryside. It is then no accident that the film ends with an elite state troupe blithely putting up with the shabby conditions of a rural community. In fact, the chief excitement for the villagers is not so much the performance itself as the return of the village daughter, Qiu Yun. Old Qiu struts about the village practically bursting with pride. When someone compliments him for having such an accomplished daughter, however, he replies with humility: 'Oh, she sings well and the folks like it. That's all.' Instead of the performance itself, the film presents a long sequence of the convivial banquet thrown by Old Qiu the evening before to entertain the actors and the villagers, even though it exhausts all his savings. There is no mistaking the suggestion that opera is a living art form sustained by peasant sociability.

At the end of the banquet with all the guests gone, father and daughter sit together for one last drink and to enjoy a quiet moment. For the first time, we see a truly happy, if a bit tipsy, Qiu Yun with her face glowing softly in the candlelight. She proposes to her father that the next day she play the sister and he play Zhong Kui to marry her off. The inebriated father immediately perks up and vows to catch all the demons of the world. Qiu Yun teases him, 'demons can't be seen or heard, how can you catch them?' She then meditates on her lifetime affair with the Zhong

Kui story and comes to the realisation that her Zhong Kui really does only one thing: matchmaking. He may be an ugly ghost, but he cares about women's fate, and he will not yield until he finds a good husband for his sister. The scene ends with two echoing lines:

Qiu Yun: I think women should marry well.
Old Qiu: Men should marry well too.

If heard out of context, the conversation between father and daughter can be disappointingly banal and frustrate any effort to read the film as an example of feminist cinema. But the film's final sequence offers us a clue for an interpretation that is more in keeping with its larger message about gender and theatricality. Here, for the first time, Qiu Yun comes face to face and converses with Zhong Kui, a scene that recalls the opening sequence with its multiple, fractured images of Qiu Yun and Zhong Kui staring into each other silently in a hall of mirrors. As their conversation continues, Zhong Kui walks away from the by now familiar *mise en scène* of haystacks, which then dissolves into a stage. Zhong Kui's face re-emerges to take up the entire backdrop and his disembodied voice continues to address Qiu Yun, now a tiny figure in the centre of an extreme long shot:

Zhong Kui: I've come to marry you off.
Qiu Yun: You've married me to the stage.
Zhong Kui: Any regrets?
Qiu Yun: No.
Zhong Kui: Farewell!

It would be too facile to say that Zhong Kui is Qiu Yun's alter ego and that in Zhong Kui she finds her true self. What I wish to emphasise is that Qiu Yun is on a quest not to find herself or resolve her identity crisis, but to seek out a mode of human sociality that is both free and fulfilling. In the role of Zhong Kui, she believes she has found such a relationship. Hence, she has no regrets. The relationship is marked by attachment and care, but it is crucially mediated through theatre, through a shared striving to transcend the bondage of institutionalised relationships. Theatrical performativity is in turn couched in the idiom of marriage, which must be taken symbolically. In the eternity of theatrical repetitions, Zhong Kui is forever on his way home to

'marry off' his sister and in the end he marries Qiu Yun to the stage. More than anything else, marriage is an allegory of the theatrically mediated mode of human connection that is beyond the constricting regime of gender and (hetero)sexuality and that is partly lived out between Qiu Yun and her foster father. They reach out to each other in their co-performance of a self-scripted father–daughter/brother–sister relationship.[11] Gender-crossing, in the figure of Zhong Kui who traverses the divide between life and death, is the means by which foster father and daughter effect a new community that is woven into the rural social fabric and yet is freed of its institutional and ideological baggage.

The late 1980s was a heady time when questions of gender, sexuality and subjectivity were at the forefront of the so-called 'cultural fever' (*wenhua re*). Huang Shuqin's film offered a feminist antidote to the feverish celebration of gender difference and the power of libido in the hands of male writers and filmmakers who were not shy of gender essentialism. *Woman, Demon, Human* urges women to look beyond the bourgeois binary norms of masculinity and femininity to forge more inclusive, more creative and more emancipatory forms of human bonding. Finally, we are ready to answer our question: where is home in *Woman, Demon, Human*? Home is the alter-space symbolically constructed through the destabilising poetics of opera film as a cinema of attractions. It is the self-chosen and self-fashioned community in which individuals mutually affirm their defection from institutional bondage and their pursuit of personal emancipation and artistic transcendence. It is where individuals, in their human vulnerability and neediness, come together to see each other through – to 'marry' each other off. If Zhong Kui is Qiu Yun's theatrically crafted self, then we might say that her dedication to theatre is not a flight from home, but an attempt to reach it. When Zhong Kui's face stretches to fill the backdrop of the stage, Qiu Yun is finally home.

NOTES

1. Strictly speaking, 'Peking opera' (*jingju* or *jingxi*) is neither native to Peking/Beijing nor operatic in the Western sense. It is a blend of regional theatrical styles, which met in the capital city and blended with each other beginning in the late eighteenth century. Rather than 'opera', it is more appropriately a

performance art comprised of four basic skills: *chang* (singing), *nian* (recitation), *da* (acrobatics), *zuo* (acting). In this essay, I follow the convention of referring to *jingju* as Peking opera.

2. Shuqin Cui, 'Transgender Masquerading in Huang Shuqin's *Human, Woman, Demon*', in *Women through the Lens: Gender and Nation in a Century of Chinese Cinema* (Honolulu: University of Hawaii Press, 2003), 219–238; Dai Jinhua, '"Human, Woman, Demon": A Woman's Predicament', in *Cinema and Desire: Feminist Marxism and Cultural Politics in the Work of Dai Jinhua*, ed. Jing Wang and Tani Barlow (London: Verso, 2002), 151–171.

3. Judith Butler, *Gender Trouble: Feminism and the Subversion of Identity* (New York: Routledge, 1990).

4. Chris Berry and Mary Ann Farquhar, *China on Screen: Cinema and Nation* (New York: Columbia University Press, 2006), 47–74.

5. Linda Williams, 'Discipline and Distraction: *Psycho*, Visual Culture and Postmodern Cinema', in '*Culture*' *and the Problem of the Disciplines*, ed. John Carlos Rowe (New York: Columbia University Press, 1998), 103.

6. For genealogical accounts of the transformation of gender in China, see Joseph R. Allen, 'Dressing and Undressing the Chinese Woman Warrior', *positions: east asia cultures critique*, 4, no. 2 (1996): 343–379; Roland Altenburger, 'Is It Clothes that Make the Man? Cross-Dressing, Gender, and Sex in Pre-Twentieth-Century Zhu Yingtai Lore', *Asian Folklore Studies*, 64 (2005): 165–205; Tani Barlow, *The Question of Women in Chinese Feminism* (Durham, NC: Duke University Press, 2004); Haiyan Lee, 'Tears that Crumbled the Great Wall: The Archaeology of Feeling in the May Fourth Folklore Movement',

Journal of Asian Studies, 64, no. 1 (2005): 35–65; Teri Silvio, 'Chinese Opera, Global Cinema, and the Ontology of the Person: Chen Kaige's *Farewell My Concubine*', in *Between Opera and Cinema*, ed. Jeongwon Joe and Rose Theresa (New York: Routledge, 2002), 177–197. Ayako Kano outlines a similar transformation in early twentieth-century Japanese theatre whereby the *onnagata* (female impersonator on the kabuki stage) was replaced by the new-style actress on the grounds that womanhood was rooted in the natural body rather than in performance ('Visuality and Gender in Modern Japanese Theater: Looking at Salome', *Japan Forum*, 11, no. 1 [1999]: 43–55).

7. Jo Riley, *Chinese Theatre and the Actor in Performance* (Cambridge: Cambridge University Press, 1997), 84.

8. Glen Dudbridge, *The Legend of Miaoshan*, rev. edn. (Oxford: Oxford University Press, 2004), 24–34, 44–46.

9. On this point, see also Silvio, 'Chinese Opera, Global Cinema'.

10. After the Chinese Communist Party came to power in 1949, cross-gender casting was frowned upon and soon phased out (Siu Leung Li, *Cross-Dressing in Chinese Opera* [Hong Kong: Hong Kong University Press, 2003], 192). During the Cultural Revolution, Pei Yanling was given female roles only in such plays as *The Heroic Sisters of the Grassland*, *The Red Detachment of Women* and *Mount Azalea*.

11. Shuqin Cui also recognises the suggestive parallel of the father–daughter and brother–sister dyads, noting that 'the relationship between father and daughter is no longer a conventional one of familial ties but a complementary signification of each other's desire' (*Women through the Lens*, 236).

32   *Xiao Wu*: Watching Time Go By

Chris Berry

> What I like most in a long take is that it preserves real
> time.
>
> Jia Zhangke

Over the last decade, Jia Zhangke has emerged as the cinematic poet of post-socialist China. He himself has stated that *Xiao Wu* was inspired by his determination to record how China was changing today – something he felt few other films were doing.[1] A recent anthology on China's independent cinema opens with an extensive discussion of his work – implying that he is representative of the entire phenomenon – and he is mentioned in every essay.[2] As Valerie Jaffee points out, 'the main characters of Jia's films are … approximations of the Chinese "average": all live in or are from towns of lower rank than provincial capital, none have college educations or the hope of attaining one'.[3] These everyman figures populate the 1980s transition to the market economy in *Platform* (2000), the influx of foreign popular culture in *Unknown Pleasures* (2002), internal migration in *Still Life* (2006) and the encounter with the global in the local in *The World* (2004).[4] As well as stories on small-town life, 'Jia's fundamental approach to *mise en scène* of keeping real time intact (his fondness for the long take)' has captured the attention of critics and commentators.[5]

Jason McGrath notes that because of these themes and stylistic features, 'It is generally agreed that Jia Zhangke's films embody a bold new style of urban realism.'[6] This is apparent in the two shots that punctuate the opening credits of Jia's very first feature film, *Xiao Wu* (aka *Pickpocket*, 1997).[7] These two shots are unrelated to the rest of the film. Just before the first, road noises are heard, mixed with a racy comic dialogue (*xiangsheng*) in a North Chinese dialect. The dialogue sounds like it may be coming over a loudspeaker or a radio, but no source is visible. The first shot is a medium long shot of a young man

standing by the side of the road. The young man adjusts his sleeve, looks around, then squats down and waits. His direct glance at the camera defies feature film conventions, suggesting this may be a documentary shot. After another title, a long shot of the same scene appears. The greater distance reveals three other figures to the left of the young man. A woman stands next to him, another squats next to her, and an older man stands on the left side of the shot.[8] They all look around, but at different times and in different directions, as if distracted. Although both shots build the world in which the film is set, they impart no sense of narrative progression. The characters are still, the camera is unmoving, and much as the characters glance about as though looking for something to hold their interest, nothing in the shot itself seems to demand our attention, either.

It is this distracted quality in Jia Zhangke's first feature film and the resulting narrative distension that interest me here. Jason McGrath locates Jia's distinctive urban realism between two sources: 'the broader indigenous movement of post-socialist realism that arose among both documentary and fiction film-makers in China in the early 1990s' and 'the tradition of international art cinema, and particularly a type of aestheticized long-take realism that became prominent in the global film festival and arthouse circuit by the late 1990s'.[9] Laura Mulvey discusses the latter trend in reference to Iranian film-maker Abbas Kiarostami as a 'cinema of delay'.[10] Although the complex and distinctive soundscapes of Jia's films are also an important component of his particular realism, this essay follows these leads to focus on time.[11] What do we mean by post-socialism as an era? How can we understand and theorise time under Chinese post-socialist conditions? How are realism and time articulated in the cinema under post-socialism? This essay addresses such questions by examining cinematic time in two senses.

First, there is the time constructed by the individual film text. The essay argues that *Xiao Wu* articulates Jia Zhangke's understanding of those who are not the drivers of China's post-socialist project but instead, at best, its passengers, and more often onlookers at the roadside, watching as it passes them by.[12] This post-socialist realist time is quite different from the utopian progress of socialist realism. However, whereas socialist-realist time is monolithic and replicated in more or less the same way in every text, *Xiao Wu* is an unusual film. Other films articulate other modes of post-socialist time, including the retrospective and critical 'modernist' perspective of Fifth Generation cinema and the consumerist progress favoured by the director of romantic urban comedy hits Feng Xiaogang, whose masterpiece of cynicism, *Big Shot's Funeral* (2001), is discussed elsewhere in this volume by Yingjin Zhang. This leads to consideration of cinematic time in a second sense; the kinds of time constructed by the cinema institution, and the corresponding need to understand time as differential or multiple and disaggregated rather than homogenous.

The first scene of the film echoes the two shots in the title sequence by showing the eponymous Xiao Wu standing by the road, lighting a cigarette and waiting, like the earlier young man. Xiao Wu is also distracted and disengaged. He boards a bus, avoids paying his fare and steals a wallet, immediately establishing him as a pickpocket. We never see him get money by any other means. Xiao Wu is returning to his hometown of Fenyang, a backwater of Shanxi Province where Jia Zhangke grew up. As Jia notes, 'my films deal with people who struggle in life and being failures, they have no other option but to return to their original place'.[13]

At the end of the film, we return to the roadside again, when the crackdown on crime we have been hearing about throughout the film has finally caught up with Xiao Wu. He is led out from the police station handcuffed to an officer, and walked down the street in an extended hand-held long take. The officer has something to attend to, so he handcuffs Xiao Wu to an electricity pole and tells him to wait. The film, which began with a young man waiting by the side of the road, followed by another young man waiting then boarding a bus, ends with that same young man chained to the side of the road. Like the young man in the first shot of the credits sequence,

Xiao Wu squats down by the side of the road, and looks about. The camera swings round to take up a position more or less similar to his. It stares for a long time at the gathering crowd, which stares back at Xiao Wu and the camera, and, by extension, us. This invokes an important literary intertext. As Jia himself says of the final scene, 'Naturally, I also thought of Lu Xun's conception of the "crowd".'[14] Lu Xun's Ah Q is also a loser in the early twentieth-century game of modernisation, who ends up arrested and the object of public scrutiny on the way to his own execution. Although we do not know where Xiao Wu is going, the intertext does not bode well.[15]

In an interview, Jia Zhangke has acknowledged his love of long takes like the one at the end of *Xiao Wu* and their connection to narrative distension. 'What I like most in a long take', he explains, 'is that it preserves real time, it keeps time intact. … You see two people smoking and talking aimlessly … In that long and tedious passage of time, nothing significant happens, they are waiting. Only through time can you convey this.'[16] And indeed, although the frequent claim that almost all the film is shot in long takes is an exaggeration, long takes are prominent in *Xiao Wu*. What should we make of this?

Deleuze's distinction between the movement-image and the time-image is useful here. He designates the movement-image as the way time is apprehended in what we call 'classical' Hollywood cinema and other montage-based cinema. Here, time is rendered as movement: camera movement or physical change within the diegesis marks and measures time in a manner that is logical, linear and corresponds to narrative motivation. In contrast, the time-image designates cinematic tendencies that break down that logic in various ways. (As Deleuze is associated with opposition to the disciplines of modernity, this is presumably positive for him.) For example, if there is no possibility of discerning the measured time relation between one shot and the next, as in those Chris Marker films where one shot can logically be followed by any other shot, linear time-as-movement is not present. Similarly, a fixed gaze upon empty space, as in Ozu's famous pillow shots, might be understood as standing outside logical time-as-movement.[17] Lack of focus and narrative distension in *Xiao Wu* can be also seen as a dismantling of the movement-image and a drift towards the time-image.

Jia Zhangke may not have read Deleuze's work on the cinema. But his own argument that the long take 'preserves real time, it keeps time intact' certainly invokes André Bazin, who comments in reference to depth of field and the long take in *Citizen Kane* (1941), 'Orson Welles restored to cinematographic illusion a fundamental quality of reality – its continuity'.[18] Jia trained as a film theory student at the Beijing Film Academy, where there has been a strong interest in Bazinian aesthetics since the early 1980s. The local journal *World Cinema* translated essays by various Japanese, Soviet and especially Western film theorists at that time, including Kracauer, Arnheim, Mitry, Metz and Bazin. But Bazin appears to have been the most frequently translated, and in 1981, Dudley Andrews's introductory essay on Bazin also appeared.[19]

However, following Lydia Liu's 'translingual practice' and the general debate around cultural translation, the interest in the long take in China in the years following the Cultural Revolution must be understood in its particular context of appropriation and deployment.[20] The same principle should be applied to Jia's use twenty years later of the long take and other techniques that can open up a door to the time-image in *Xiao Wu*. Although Deleuze's examples are mostly American and European, they offer a useful clue for understanding the Chinese context. Most of his examples that illustrate the movement-image are from before the end of World War II, while those for the time-image are mostly classic art films of post-World War II Europe. Although this valorisation of European art cinema seems like a conservative throwback,[21] the World War II watershed corresponds to the falling away of faith in the modern project that many European commentators date to the Holocaust.[22] After this event, any pretence to European superiority was doubtful, and the various anti-Soviet uprisings in Eastern Europe also undermined socialist alternative modernity. For Lyotard, this loss of faith in the grand narrative of modernity is the herald of post-modern culture.[23]

Adapting the Lyotardian model to the Chinese context, Maoist socialism would be the particular grand narrative of modernity that has lost credibility after the Cultural Revolution, and yet which continues to condition all that has developed since. Defined in this way, I have traced the emergence of a post-socialist cultural sensibility in the Chinese cinema to the films of the late 1970s.[24] Of course, to call this 'post-socialism' in China itself would be impossible: it would risk invoking the possibility that socialism is over, even though this is not the implication of post-modernity in regard to the modern. In the People's Republic, this period is often referred to as the 'reform era', and Jia has acknowledged that in both *Xiao Wu* and *Platform* his focus is on the experience of reform for individuals caught up in this 'top-down movement'.[25] (This is a perceptive characterisation, countering the usual assumption that the rollback of the state must have been initiated from below.) To use de Certeau's terminology, these are not the strategists who organise the overall environment, but the tacticians who respond on the ground, seeking agency in the space of the other.[26]

Xiao Wu communicates these vicissitudes by setting its anti-hero up with an alter ego. After his return to Fenyang, Xiao Wu reads flyers about a crackdown on crime and then talks to a friend, who reports that their buddy Jin Xiaoyong is a successful businessman now. Local television covers this model entrepreneur and his upcoming marriage. Both Xiao Wu's friend and the local police chief urge him to emulate Jin. Although the film has already shown Xiao Wu picking pockets, he reassures the police chief that he is not a criminal anymore and is indeed a businessman. However, Jin explicitly refuses to invite Xiao Wu to his wedding, for fear that his presence might remind people that Jin was once a pickpocket himself. Xiao Wu's failure and inability to match his alter ego Jin becomes ever clearer. He does not get into business and continues to rely on picking pockets. He attempts to make a bar hostess his girlfriend, but she unceremoniously dumps him for someone with more money and power. Having retreated to his family in the countryside, his father throws him out of this last refuge after a fight. By following Xiao Wu rather than Jin, the film marks its interest in the losers of the reform era rather than the winners.

How is this related to the film's rendering of time? The pacing of the scenes follows Xiao Wu's faltering attempts to insert himself into the new order and yet retain an old system of honour and obligation towards friends and family. When Xiao Wu attempts to take the initiative or assert himself, the pace is relatively fast and dynamic. But when he runs into obstacles, it slows. However, this variation in pace does not correlate exactly to the use of the long take alone. Although Jia Zhangke notes his particular interest in scenes where nothing much goes on, the use of hand-held camera techniques can produce a lot of dynamic movement, even when the take is extended. A repeated example would be the frequent takes where Xiao Wu is depicted striding through the streets of Fenyang. For example, the scene where Xiao Wu visits Jin to confront him about the lack of a wedding invitation begins with Jin and his workers preparing for the festivities. Although this is rendered in a long take lasting 1 minute and 11 seconds, it is fast-paced because the camera follows first one and then another worker as they busy themselves. It also catches Xiao Wu as he comes into the courtyard and follows him inside the building.

After a relatively short 43-second take while Xiao Wu waits for Jin to join him inside, the confrontation takes place in another long take. However, here the pace slows. This is not only because the take lasts 3 minutes and 45 seconds. It is also because the characters sit down, the scene is framed as a long shot, the camera does not move and the lack of narrative progress produces an effect of distension. Jin refuses to yield an inch to Xiao Wu's challenges, either making desultory excuses for not inviting him or simply staying silent. But it also becomes clear that Xiao Wu will not move beyond verbal challenges about the invitation to a more dramatic or even physical confrontation. Time passes as they are deadlocked. In other long-take scenes following setbacks, Xiao Wu is also shown either sitting or standing doing nothing very much for extended periods of time.

Xiao Wu

The long middle section of the film in which Xiao Wu courts Mei Mei, the bar hostess, is an interesting variation on this pattern. Distension, camera distance, static camerawork and long takes do not necessarily signify failure in this situation, because Xiao Wu's attempt at a relationship with Mei Mei represents a refuge from the hustle and bustle of the town. One day, the bar owner tells him Mei Mei is sick. He goes to visit her. When she says she wishes she had a hot water bottle for her aching stomach, Xiao Wu rushes off and buys one in a fast-paced sequence rendered with plenty of camera movement and cuts. This is typical of the dominant pattern, where stepped-up pace signifies Xiao Wu's efforts to assert agency. However, once he returns, the use of a static long-shot long take helps to signify not deadlock or failure but the transformation of the dormitory into an intimate space of retreat, albeit constantly disturbed by the sound of traffic from the street outside. Mei Mei and Xiao Wu sit side by side on the bed and confide in each other about their frustrations and hopeless dreams. After she sings a sad little song, he responds to her efforts to get him to sing by opening a cigarette lighter stolen from Jin that plays a tinny version of *Für Elise*. Finally, she leans over and puts her head on his knee. The extended sequence in the bathhouse, where Xiao Wu finally does sing once he is convinced he is alone, is another scene where interiors signify retreat and security.

However, the overall downward spiral of ever greater distension, longer takes, static camera and long shots plays out until Xiao Wu is completely immobile, literally shackled to a post. The turning of the camera to take up a position mimicking Xiao Wu's own gaze in this scene, noted earlier, is also part of this pattern and has been used before when defeats encourage introspection. For example, soon after his first meeting with Mei Mei, and following a few scenes showing him at a loose end, he stands above a street scene and spots one of the young men in his gang walking with a girlfriend. The camera takes up Xiao Wu's position and follows his gaze in a long-take long shot that pans with the young couple as they walk along the street. In the next scene, he is back at the bar again, enquiring after Mei Mei. Later, when his father throws him out of the house, a similar panning shot shows Xiao Wu's last lingering look back at his home village before he returns to Fenyang.

The distinctive distended rhythm and pace in *Xiao Wu* stands out from the socialist realism of the 1949–1976 Maoist era, when the grand narrative of socialist modernity was strong. That forward-directed project of progress symbolised by the economic and political plans of the Party-state was embodied in socialist realist narratives. These constructed time in a manner similar to Hollywood's own celebrations of modern progress, with cause and effect eliminating anything extraneous to this logic, usually through ellipsis. As Yingjin Zhang discusses in 'My Camera Doesn't Lie?', because films like *Xiao Wu* mark themselves out from the cinema of the past they also engage in a struggle over realism.[27] Socialist realism's claim to truth was grounded in the Marxist analysis of society and history as a dialectical process of class struggle. In contrast, *Xiao Wu*'s realism and claim to truth is not grounded in an analytical schema, but in a cinematic rendering of the experience of the main character. The pace and rhythm of the film correspond to his moods and difficulties. The look of Fenyang corresponds to how it looks to the human eye, unadorned by the optimism of 'revolutionary romanticism'. And empty time often passes – without ellipses produced by cuts – as it does for Xiao Wu himself – especially in shots marked as replicating his own contemplative gaze.

The experiential realism of the loser that characterises *Xiao Wu* is far from dominant in China today. Indeed, *Xiao Wu* is engaged in an ideological struggle about what reality is, not only with socialist realism but also with other cinematic realisms and anti-realist modes with truth claims in the post-socialist era. This suggests that there may be more to post-socialist time than a simple succession from one time mode to another. Not only do we need to understand other modes of post-socialist time but also how it is possible for there to be more than one post-socialist construction of time in circulation. This calls into question the assumption that there can only be one time mode in each era. It also shifts our attention to the cinema as a social institution shaped by power in ways that determine the time modes it can construct and circulate.

To detail all the other realist and non-realist cinematic modes with claims to truth produced in the post-1976 era is impossible in this brief essay. However, they are multiple and almost all of them are posed against socialist realism in one way or another.

There are a number of analytical and expressive modes, including late-1980s cycles of absurdism and expressive psychological realism. Most prominent, however, is the critical modernism associated with 'Fifth Generation' film-makers and films such as Chen Kaige's *Yellow Earth* (1984), Zhang Yimou's *Red Sorghum* (1987), *Ju Dou* (1990) and *Raise the Red Lantern* (1991), Zhang Junzhao's *One and Eight* (1983) and Tian Zhuangzhuang's *Horse Thief* (1986). Whereas socialist realist cinema is forward-looking, linear and progressive, all the Fifth Generation examples listed are retrospective and analytical, working from a vantage point in the present and using a historical story set in the past as a parable or metaphor to answer the question 'How did we get here?'[28]

A mimetic realism or documentary impulse has also manifested itself in many different films since the early 1980s.[29] *Xiao Wu* participates in this tendency through its use of real locations, minimal lighting, non-professional actors, and so forth. However, as Jason McGrath has discussed, the most important realist tendency is the independent documentary cinema itself.[30] These films frequently feature the same kind of distension found in *Xiao Wu* and also the same kind of focus on those struggling in the post-socialist era. To cite two early examples, Wu Wenguang's *Bumming in Beijing* focuses on independent artists trying to figure out how to get by in the wake of the 1989 Democracy Movement, while Li Hong's *Out of Phoenix Bridge* (1997) focuses on maids who have come from Anhui to work in Beijing. Like *Xiao Wu*, a considerable proportion of these films is given over to watching time go by.[31] In contrast, mainstream television documentaries and cinema, such as Feng Xiaogang's urban comedies, are dominated by logic-driven realism, whether socialist or consumerist.

How should we account for this multiplicity of post-socialist time schemes in the Chinese cinema? In *The Politics of Time*, Peter Osborne makes two important points. First, he notes that postmodernism operates within the logic of modernism. Unlike other time schemes, modernity is itself purely temporal. In contrast to time schemes that are tied to nature (days, hours and seasons), to religion (BC and AD) or to dynastic rises and falls (the xth year of the so-and-so emperor), modernity is defined by the purely temporal category of newness.[32] In this sense, post-modernity is another modern category of time, ironically and paradoxically defined as new in contrast to established modernity. In the context of late capitalism, post-modernist consumerism is associated with the succession of atomised sensations symbolised in televisual time in Jameson's analysis.[33] This is just such a paradoxically modern post-modern culture – one that continues the modern logic of capitalist 'development' at the same time as it produces new cultural forms appropriate to the logic of consumption rather than the earlier (but also modern) logic of production. Appropriated and adapted for the People's Republic of China, the continued domination of materialist ideologies of progress on both sides of the post-socialist and socialist historical divide helps to account for the continuation of modern modes of time as progress in mainstream television documentary and feature film work in the People's Republic.

Second, Osborne also emphasises the idea of 'differential time'. This concept questions any assumption of time as singular and unified, such as the mechanical Marxist model that would see 'time' as a cultural construct determined at the level of the base. Within such a monolithic perspective, each era – however defined – would have a corresponding singular type of time. In contrast, 'differential time' insists that diverse understandings of time can exist alongside each other, intersecting but also operating according to their own logics.[34] In this sense, it is not surprising that different experiences of social formations should be manifested in different constructions of time, including the distended sense of watching time go by in *Xiao Wu*.

Logically, we might expect that different experiences of time exist in all periods. However, they are not always manifested in public discourses like cinema, especially if blocked by censorship. Maoist socialism may well have also been experienced by many Chinese as something that happened to them; at best a vehicle on which they were passengers and at worst one that ran them down. However, under socialist conditions, this was excluded from public discourse. To account for this, we must pay attention not only to the cinematic modes of time constructed in the texts but also to the time of the cinematic institution and the determinations upon it that make possible – or impossible – the construction of certain discursive modes of time. In writing about post-modernity, various authors have noted its fragmented nature. While pessimists lament this,

optimists emphasise that this change opens up the possibilities for those previously excluded from access to public discourse.[35] Under post-socialism, this characteristic is even clearer. The monopoly on all public discourse enforced by the Party-state apparatus under socialism has been rolled back, allowing for films like *Xiao Wu*. Until recently, such films have been limited to the world of the 'underground', facilitated by cheap and lightweight digital equipment but blocked from cinema release. With *The World* in 2004, Jia Zhangke and many of his colleagues came 'above ground'.[36] Now, only time will tell the fate of their apprehension of post-socialist time in this new environment.

NOTES

1. Lin Xudong, Zhang Yaxuan and Gu Zheng, eds, *The Films of Jia Zhangke: Xiao Wu* (*Jia Zhangke dianying: Xiao Wu*) (Beijing: Zhongguo mangwen chubanshe, 2003), 106.

2. Paul G. Pickowicz and Yingjin Zhang, eds, *From Underground to Independent: Alternative Film Culture in Contemporary China* (Lanham, MD: Rowman & Littlefield, 2006). My thanks to John Yu Zou for his valuable feedback and suggestions for the first draft of this essay, and to other readers for their comments on the initial unpublished version of the essay.

3. Valerie Jaffee '"Every Man a Star": The Ambivalent Cult of Amateur Art in New Chinese Documentaries', in Pickowicz and Zhang, *From Undergound to Independent*, 79.

4. Shuqin Cui examines Jia's focus on the negotiation of the global and the local in 'Negotiating In-Between: On New-Generation Filmmaking and Jia Zhangke's Films', *Modern Chinese Literature and Culture*, 18, no. 2 (2006): 98–130.

5. Stephen Teo, 'Cinema with an Accent – Interview with Jia Zhangke, Director of *Platform*', *Senses of Cinema*, no. 15 (2001): <www.sensesofcinema.com/> (22 March 2002). Other biographical details are also drawn from this interview.

6. Jason McGrath, 'The Independent Cinema of Jia Zhangke: From Postsocialist Realism to a Transnational Aesthetic', in *China's Urban Generation*, ed. Zhang Zhen (Durham, NC: Duke University Press, 2007), 81–114 (82). McGrath notes that his essay is in conversation with the earlier version of this one, meaning that now the conversation continues here.

7. Michael Berry discusses Jia's short films culminating in *Xiao Shan Going Home* (1997) in his extensive and important interview with the director in *Speaking in Images: Interviews with Contemporary Chinese Filmmakers* (New York: Columbia University Press, 2005), 184–189.

8. Lin Xiaoping identifies this as a family of three, but I am not so certain: 'Jia Zhangke's Cinematic Trilogy: A Journey across the Ruins of Post-Mao China', in *Chinese-Language Film: Historiography, Poetics, Politics*, ed. Sheldon H. Lu and Emilie Yueh-yu Yeh (Honolulu: University of Hawaii Press, 2005), 190.

9. McGrath, forthcoming.

10. Laura Mulvey, 'Abbas Kiarostami: Cinema of Uncertainty, Cinema of Delay', in *Death 24x a Second: Stillness and the Moving Image* (London: Reaktion Books, 2006), 67–85.

11. For example, Jin Liu examines his use of local languages as a mark of realism in 'The Rhetoric of Local Languages as the Marginal: Chinese Underground and Independent Films by Jia Zhangke and Others', *Modern Chinese Literature and Culture*, 18, no. 2 (2006): 163–205.

12. Yingjin Zhang correctly emphasises the subjective dimension of Jia's realism (and realism in general) in 'My Camera Doesn't Lie? Truth, Subjectivity, and Audience in Chinese Independent Film and Video', in Pickowicz and Zhang, *From Underground to Independent*, 28.

13. Teo, 'Cinema with an Accent'.

14. Berry, *Speaking in Images*, 203.

15. Lu Hsun (Lu Xun), 'The True Story of Ah Q', in *Selected Stories of Lu Hsun*, trans. Yang Hsien-yi and Gladys Yang (Beijing: Foreign Languages Press, 1972), 65–112.

16. Teo, 'Cinema with an Accent'.

17. For the movement-image, see *Cinema 1: The Movement Image*, trans. Hugh Tomlinson and Barbara Habberjam (Minneapolis: University of Minnesota Press, 1986); and for the time-image, *Cinema 2: The Time-Image*, trans. Hugh Tomlinson and Robert Galeta (Minneapolis: University of Minnesota Press, 1989). D. N. Rodowick uses Marker's serial montage to illustrate the time-image in *Gilles Deleuze's Time Machine* (Durham, NC: Duke University Press, 1997), 4. Deleuze discusses Ozu in *Cinema 2*, 13–19. For him, what are usually known as Ozu's 'pillow shots' are examples of empty space and any-space-whatever.

18. André Bazin, 'An Aesthetic of Reality: Neorealism', in *What Is Cinema?*, vol. 2, trans. Hugh Gray (Berkeley: University of California Press, 1971), 28.

19. Chris Berry, 'Real to Reel: Long Take Long Shot Aesthetics in Chinese New Wave Cinemas' (paper presented at the annual meeting of the Association for Asian Studies, Washington, DC, April 2002).

20. Lydia H. Liu, 'Translingual Practice: The Discourse of Individualism between China and the West', *Positions*, 1, no. 1 (1993): 160–193.

21. Rodowick, *Gilles Deleuze's Time Machine*, xiii–xiv.

22. Hannah Arendt would be a good example. Of course, the slave trade, the Opium Wars and other much earlier instances of horrific violence puncture European modernity's claims to 'civilisation'. However, it was only when they turned on themselves that Europeans began to perceive this; as long as they were doing it to 'others', no such crisis occurred.

23. Jean-François Lyotard, *The Postmodern Condition: A Report on Knowledge*, trans. Geoff Bennington and Brian Massumi (Minneapolis: University of Minnesota Press, 1984).

24. Chris Berry, *Postsocialist Cinema in Post-Mao China: The Cultural Revolution after the Cultural Revolution* (New York: Routledge, 2004).

25. Teo, 'Cinema with an Accent'.

26. Michel de Certeau, *The Practice of Everyday Life*, trans. Steven Rendall (Berkeley: University of California Press, 1984), xix, 34–38.

27. In Pickowicz and Zhang, *From Underground to Independent*, 23–39.

28. For further discussion, see Chris Berry and Mary Farquhar, *China on Screen: Cinema and Nation* (New York and Hong Kong: Columbia and Hong Kong University Presses, 2006), 32–34.

29. For further discussion on the early 1980s, see Berry, 'Real to Reel'.

30. McGrath, forthcoming.

31. For futher discussion, see Chris Berry, 'Getting Real: Chinese Documentaries, Chinese Postsocialism', forthcoming in *China's Urban Generation*, ed. Zhang Zhen (Durham, NC: Duke University Press, 2007).

32. Reinhart Koselleck, '"Neuzeit": Remarks on the Semantics of the Modern Concepts of Movement', in *Futures Past: On the Semantics of Historical Time*, trans. Keith Tribe (Cambridge, MA: MIT Press, 1985), cited in Peter Osborne, *The Politics of Time: Modernity and Avant-Garde* (London: Verso, 1995), 9–13.

33. Fredric Jameson, 'Postmodernism, or The Cultural Logic of Late Capitalism', *New Left Review*, no. 146 (1984): 53–92.

34. Osborne discusses this problem in Marxism, citing the discussions of Gramsci and Althusser among others, in the second half of his first chapter; *The Politics of Time*, 13–29. In his second chapter, 'One Time, One History', he questions the assumption that it must be possible to unite these different time schemes under one overarching scheme (pp. 30–68).

35. See E. Ann Kaplan's discussion of what she calls 'utopian post-modernism' in 'Introduction', in *Postmodernism and Its Discontents: Theories, Practices*, ed. E. Ann Kaplan (London: Verso, 1988), 1–9.

36. For discussion, see Paul G. Pickowicz, 'Social and Political Dynamics of Underground Filmmaking', in Pickowicz and Zhang, *From Underground to Independent*, 1–3.

33   *Yellow Earth*: Hesitant Apprenticeship and Bitter Agency

Helen Hok-sze Leung

Writers and artists concentrate everyday phenomena, typify the contradictions and struggles within them and produce works which awaken the masses, fire them with enthusiasm and impel them to unite and struggle to transform their own situation … To sum up, the creative labour of revolutionary cultural workers transforms the raw material of everyday life into literature and art that serve the people.

Mao Zedong, 'Talks at the Yan'an Forum on
Art and Literature' (1942)

The sun has gone down behind the clouds,
My mouth says nothing but my heart is grieving.
Green grass and cow stool cannot put out a fire,
So these mountain songs cannot save Cuiqiao.
Me, Cuiqiao! Ah, the lot of a woman!

Folk song in *Yellow Earth*
(Chen Kaige, 1984)

If Mao were to have his cultural workers 'transform' Cuiqiao's song, the bitter assertion that 'these mountain songs cannot save Cuiqiao' would probably be the first line to attract their editorial attention. The suggestion that folk songs may be useless for the improvement of one's material situation is surely not the best way to 'awaken the masses, fire them with enthusiasm and impel them to unite and struggle to transform their own situation'.[1] Yet, the very 'useless-ness' of Cuiqiao's songs, which call attention to the limits of the singer's agency, offers other kinds of transformative possibilities. Chen Kaige's remarkable first film tells the story of an encounter between Gu Qing, a cultural worker from the Eighth Route Army, and the peasants whose songs he is supposed to collect and transform. The film is at once a critique of Mao's dysfunctional political project and an embodiment of the desire such a project inspires but is unable to fulfil.

Since its controversial release in 1984, followed by a critically acclaimed reception at the Hong Kong International Film Festival in 1985, *Yellow Earth* has sparked a number of important debates, not only in the study of Chinese cinema, but more generally in the consideration of Chinese culture, nationalism and the ambivalent legacy of the Communist Revolution. The initial critical reaction to the film in China largely comprises of literal interpretations that focus on questions of historical accuracy and the image of the peasantry.[2] By contrast, critics in the West seem much more interested in the film's figurative aspects, which appear to conceal far more than they reveal. For many critics, the elusive character of the film's symbolism creates a rupture in the text: a dimension of otherness that resists the film's dominant structure and ideology. Esther Yau locates this otherness in the 'non-perspectival presentation of landscapes' which decentres the gaze and instigates a Daoist aesthetic contemplation that undercuts the narrative strands of the text and resists her own 'Western analysis'.[3] Mary Ann Farquhar develops this argument further and argues that the film's 'blank' shots of nature and sounds of silence are figures for the repressed and ignored Daoist principle of yin, the dearth of which results in a cosmic and seasonal disorder.[4] Wary of attributing too hastily a 'Chinese difference' to the film, Rey Chow calls attention to the scene of the film's own dilemma: how to represent China through the arguably non-Chinese technology of the cinema.[5] Chow suggests that the film stages conflicting notions of reform: the filmic image is aligned with a politics of identity while music, which 'empties out' rather than anchors the image's signification, alludes to a politics of difference.[6] In a more recent article, Stephanie Donald also seeks to locate 'points of disruption' in *Yellow Earth* by analysing the film's landscape as a 'demon lover' that devours 'the object of its passion and the agency of its rivals'.[7]

These figures of otherness, whether interpreted as blank spaces, silence, music or the landscape, are pitched against the ideological rigidity of the Maoist project, apparently signified by Gu Qing. Chow characterises the soldier's presence in the village as symbolic of a 'politics of record' that 'signifies the thorough nature of political intervention in civilian life'.[8]

Donald also understands Gu Qing to be an 'agent of the Party' whose agency disappears as he becomes integrated into nature, because he 'cannot move forward as a successful agent of the Party' when he 'occupies a harmonious position in the circulation of the natural world'.[9] The Maoist project is thus perceived to be absolutely incompatible with the film's trope of alterity: an outmoded historical moment that is superseded and displaced by the film's new aesthetic.

While my reading of *Yellow Earth* owes a great deal to these insightful analyses, I wish to address the relative inattention they pay to the proximity between the desire of the Maoist project and that of the film itself. Chen Kaige, like most of the intellectuals, writers and artists of his generation, had spent parts of his early adulthood in the countryside as a sent-down youth. Mao's injunction in this campaign to 'apprentice' urban youths to the peasantry was driven by ideological assumptions very similar to those behind Gu Qing's assignment. Like many of his contemporary film-makers and writers, Chen often returns to the scene of this early 'class apprenticeship' in his works, most explicitly in *King of the Children* (1987). In fact, Chen's description of how he and his cinematographer Zhang Yimou prepared for the filming of *Yellow Earth* is curiously reminiscent of Gu Qing's sojourn in the village: 'We went to the area where we were going to shoot for a month. We stayed with the peasants, lived with them, ate with them. We didn't have a car or a bus. We walked.'[10] The actual practice of making *Yellow Earth*, which involves the film-maker's apprenticeship to his film's subjects, thus *repeats* the soldier's narrative. Like Gu Qing, the film-maker wrestles with the problematic but utopian desire to undo the fixity of one's class origins through a radical cultural practice. Throughout the history of Communist China, such desire has haunted the lives of many intellectuals (who in the Party's eyes are as likely to hold on to their class privilege as they are to 'defect' to the side of the masses) as they struggle to live up

to the demands of the revolution. Yet, the film neither documents nor instantiates the fulfilment of this desire for what Gayatri Spivak has, in another context, provocatively termed 'class deconstruction'.[11] Rather, the film's elusive tropes of otherness, i.e. of what remains *persistently* desired, marks the impossibility of fulfilment. I will show that the failure of both Gu Qing's and the film's enterprise is a necessary corollary – and precisely the radical implication – of the logic of the enterprise itself.

MUTUAL APPRENTICESHIP AND THE MASS LINE

Yellow Earth begins with an encounter between sound and image. We hear a short folk tune, followed by the sound of wind blowing, as a short description of the film's setting scrolls down the screen. The archaic script of the text recalls the immense historical significance of the Shaan-Gan-Ning border region as the cradle of early Chinese civilisation and, subsequently, the heartland of an imperial culture. While this 'four-thousand-year-old culture' provides a powerful ideological symbol for a 'national culture', the resolute iconoclasm in Chinese nationalism also condemns it as a burden of tradition that stands in the way of modernity. The very incongruity of an archaic calligraphy scripting a story about the Communist Revolution ironically recalls the charge Chen Duxiu levied on the ideographic script as a 'home of rotten and poisonous thought' which is 'incapable of communicating modern ideas'.[12] In this opening scene, folk culture (the musical tune) is associated with nature (the sound of wind) and orality. It remains marginal to the image of the written text and functions as a possible resolution to the contradiction exemplified by the image.

Gu Qing's assignment is an example of Mao's attempt to create a national and modern culture that is at the same time revolutionary in character. Mao does not advocate the abandonment of all traditions, but rather an 'assimilation' of the 'democratic' aspect of traditional culture:

A splendid old culture was created during the long period of Chinese feudal society. To study the development of this old culture, to reject its feudal dross and assimilate its democratic essence is a necessary condition for developing our new national culture and increasing our national self-confidence, but we should never swallow anything and everything uncritically. It is imperative to separate the fine old culture of the people which had a more or less democratic and revolutionary character from all the decadence of the old feudal ruling class.[13]

The injunction to separate the 'fine old culture of the people' from the 'decadence of the old feudal ruling class' would privilege Shaanbei folk songs over Tang poetry (which is arguably also 'indigenous' to the region) as the defining ingredient of a national culture. Unlike Tang poetry, which is the fruit of imperial glory, this 'fine old culture of the people' has in fact been nurtured by adversity and oppression. When Gu Qing naively asks the old peasant how it is possible for people to remember so many folk songs, the peasant replies that one remembers 'when life is hard'. The unique character and the most dynamic radicalism of the Communist Revolution was also fostered in dire material conditions, exemplifying Mao's belief that backwardness is an asset, rather than an obstacle, to the building of socialism. Yan'an politics, which deviated from more orthodox Comintern principles, was characterised by an emphasis on the revolutionary potential of the spontaneous consciousness of the masses and a deep suspicion of the rigid organisational structure of the Leninist vanguard party. The notion of the 'mass line' – which provides the motive for the Gu Qing's assignment in the film – was developed at this time. Mark Selden describes the 'mass line' in these terms:

> Mass line conceptions of leadership brought honour and status within the grasp of every youth or adult who was prepared to devote himself wholeheartedly to the revolutionary cause, regardless of his class, formal training, or family background. If peasants could 'rise' to leadership through struggle and self-education, students, bureaucrats, and traditional elite elements could 'descend' by means of 'to the village' and production campaigns to unite with and lead the people within the confines of the village. In either case, leadership implied a break with the elitism of the past and the acceptance of a multiplicity of roles which traditionally had been separate and distinct.[14]

Gu Qing's assignment is thus supposed to serve a double purpose: to create a new national culture by 'assimilating' the 'democratic essence' of the culture of the region, as well as to foster the 'mass line' through cultural workers' efforts to 'unite with and lead' the peasants. The collection of folk songs is important both in and of itself, and as a process through which a community may be built on 'the acceptance of a multiplicity of roles which traditionally had been separate and distinct'.

The insistence on *mutuality* presents some suggestive problems. In a talk delivered to the cultural workers of the Shaan-Gan-Ning region in 1944, Mao refers to a dilemma Gu faces in the film:

> Our culture is a people's culture; our cultural workers … must act in accordance with the needs and wishes of the masses. All work done for the masses must start from their needs and not from the desire of any individual, however well-intentioned. It often happens that objectively the masses need a certain change, but subjectively they are not yet conscious of the need, not yet willing or determined to make the change. In such cases, we should wait patiently. We should not make the change until, through our work, most of the masses have become conscious of the need and are willing and determined to carry it out.[15]

For Mao, consciousness-raising is necessary because class location and class identification do not necessarily – or even usually – coincide. The Party collects and transforms folk songs as a means to instil a 'subjective consciousness' in the peasantry. At the same time, Mao realises that class identification cannot be imposed from without, least of all by members of another class.

In the film, Gu Qing follows this demand faithfully as he constantly engages the peasant on issues of revolution and women's emancipation, but refrains from actively intervening in Cuiqiao's situation. Gu is committed to learning from the peasants at the same time that he tries to educate them. The most provocative lesson arises, however, when what Gu learns actually disproves the fundamental assumptions of his enterprise. What if the peasants are 'subjectively' thoroughly conscious of their 'objective' needs but are still not impelled to follow the 'objective' solutions prescribed by the Party? What if the Party's solutions do not always satisfy the masses' needs, but merely instigate their desire to find other solutions? What if the truly radical implication of a 'mutual apprenticeship' between the Party and the masses demands that the Party relinquish its own authority as a representative of the masses?

BITTERNESS AND AGENCY

These questions are most clearly raised by the following scene, which takes place when Gu eats with the peasant's family after ploughing the fields together:

> Peasant: Young officer, what was it you said last night that you came here to collect?
>
> Gu: I'm collecting folk songs [*min'ge*] from Shaanbei.
>
> Peasant: (laughs) What folk songs, they're just bitter tunes [*suan qu'er*]!
>
> Gu: Do you know how to sing them, Uncle?
>
> Peasant: I'm neither happy nor sad, what's the point of singing?
>
> Gu: There are so many folk songs in the region. Tell me, how do people remember them all?
>
> Peasant: When life is difficult, you'd remember … Why are you collecting bitter tunes?
>
> Gu: To put new words to them, so that soldiers of Cuiqiao's age can sing them. When people hear them, they'll know why they're suffering, why women are beaten, why workers and peasants should rise up. When our army hears them, they'll fight the rich and the Japanese even more bravely. Chairman Mao and Commander Zhu both love listening to folk songs. Chairman Mao doesn't just want us to learn how to sing, but also to learn to read and write. He wants all the people of China to eat properly.

The ordering of Gu's wants implies that consciousness-raising (through singing, reading and writing) is the precondition for material well-being (eating properly). This belief assumes that when people's consciousness is raised, agency follows. It is, however, a 'directed' agency. The songs should spur people's will to participate in a political movement organised by the Party, which would, in turn, ensure the material well-being of the people it represents. The insistence on such 'direction' means that any undirected (i.e. unintended and unforeseen) consequences of the consciousness-raising project must be eradicated at all costs.

The peasant's response to Gu's questions illustrates a different understanding of the relation between consciousness and agency. He does not understand why the soldier is so interested in folk songs, which to him are 'just bitter tunes'. The soldier uses the term *min'ge*, which refers to 'folk songs' or 'songs of the people'. By contrast, the peasant refers to the songs as *suan qu'er*: bitter tunes. This term drops

out any mention of the 'folk', privileges the songs' melody over their lyric, and draws attention to the element of lament (bitterness). To the peasant, these songs are not important as part of a folk tradition or as raw material to be revolutionised by the Party. They are simply to be sung spontaneously, when one is happy or sad, and are remembered when 'life is difficult'. Folk songs are, according to the peasant's understanding, affective responses to one's lived experience. They exist solely within, and not a moment beyond, the immediate context of their spontaneous production. It would thus make no sense to 'collect' them. The film presents many moments of folk singing to illustrate this understanding of 'bitter tunes' and its critical implications for the soldier's project.

Worried that the soldier may be reprimanded by his leaders for not having collected enough folk songs, the peasant sings for him for the first and only time. This compassionate 'performance' on the eve of the soldier's departure suggests, in two distinct ways, that the peasant's understanding of the world far exceeds the assumptions behind the soldier's project. First, the composition of the shot that shows this

Yellow Earth: Cuiqiao

performance draws attention to the peasant's 'bitter' compassion for his daughter. A close-up of the peasant's face is juxtaposed with a blurred image of Cuiqiao in the background, listening while she works. The song is a lament for the suicide of a young widow. Prior to this scene, we have learned that the peasant has arranged a marriage for Cuiqiao to a much older man. Between her mother's funeral and savings for his little brother's future bride-price, there is little money left for a dowry and hence the prospect of a good match. In Gu Qing's eyes, the peasant is an unenlightened patriarch who does not understand his daughter's oppression. Yet, this song, ostensibly a performance for the soldier, also functions as a lament for his daughter, whose future is likely to be similarly tragic. It shows that, contrary to the soldier's belief, the peasant is neither unconscious of nor unsympathetic to his daughter's situation, even though such awareness and empathy do not in themselves lead to any action or change. The 'bitterness' of these songs thus derives not only from the sentimental music or the tragic scenario depicted by the lyric, but more fundamentally from an awareness of a discontinuity between subjective awareness and objective change. Second, the peasant sings for the soldier even though, as the scene discussed above clearly shows, he does not believe in the soldier's project. In fact, it is because the peasant does not believe that the collection of folk songs for revolutionary use is tenable that he stages this performance for the soldier. The peasant understands with insight that the project will fail. Out of empathy and compassion, he sings for the soldier so that he would have something in his 'collection' and not be reprimanded by his superiors. The actual moment of 'collection' thus belies the logic of the project. Yet, it should be valued precisely because it could facilitate the 'mutual apprenticeship' Mao envisions.

Cuiqiao's songs also question the relation between consciousness and agency. Her songs depict the condition of her oppression, yet they fail to articulate any possibility for change. Bitterness in song is not even considered an articulation in and of itself: thus Cuiqiao sings, 'I wish to speak my mind but I don't know how', even when she has just spoken her mind in a song. However, Cuiqiao's desire to sing prompts her to search for something beyond both the songs and the soldier's promise. Gu Qing's political ideals initially appeal to Cuiqiao because they propose equality for women. Gu argues with her father that women shouldn't be forced into arranged marriages and should be given educational opportunities. He 'shows off' his sewing skill to Cuiqiao to demonstrate that men in the Communist Party share responsibilities that are traditionally designated to be women's concerns. However, these apparently feminist principles actually marginalise Cuiqiao in their own ways. The rhetoric of equality is underwritten by a process of masculinisation that inscribes the ideology of masculinity as the norm in which everyone may 'equally' participate. The film illustrates this process by contrasting the cinematic representation of Cuiqiao's singing with that of the waist-drum dance at Yan'an. Cuiqiao's songs – as yet 'unassimilated' by the revolution – are sung to sentimental orchestral accompaniment and linked, by means of parallel editing, to images of nature which are filmed in natural lighting and extreme long shots, minimally edited in slow panning long takes. Combined with the shadowy images of Cuiqiao's solitary figure and markers of her feminised labour (a water-bucket, a spinning-wheel, a bellows), these sequences reinforce the association of 'pre-revolutionary' folk culture with femininity, which is in turn associated with emotions and nature. By contrast, the waist-drum dance is filmed in a well-lit open space, edited at a frenzied pace, and foregrounds the male dancers' expressionless faces and highly co-ordinated movement. The image of disciplined and masculine collectivity bears a resemblance to the rain dance performed by male peasants at the end of the film. The parallel suggests that the 'revolutionary transformation' of folk songs marginalises feminine 'bitterness' in the same way that the rural patriarchal order, in a desperate bid for survival (during a famine), also substitutes 'bitterness' with collective discipline. The particular feminist rhetoric of Gu Qing's assignment is thus unwittingly complicit with a suppression of femininity in the interest of organisational discipline and ideological certainty.

There is, however, one very important and suggestive difference between the two scenes I compared above. In contrast to the high-angled long shots which film the rain dance as a spectacular upsurge of mass energy, the waist-drum dance is filmed in the style of hand-held motion photography. The systematic and co-ordinated movement of the dancers is incongruously represented in erratic and jerky shots. A shot/counter-shot links this agitated perspective to a close-up of the hesitant and anxious expression of Gu Qing watching as an onlooker. When the waist-drum dance becomes the object of Gu Qing's gaze – in short, the gaze of someone who has submitted himself to the Maoist pursuit of the 'mass line' – its status as 'revolutionary culture' becomes extremely unstable. Uncertainty and anxiety lurk beneath revolutionary ardour and discipline. What has the soldier learned from (the failure of) his assignment that produces this moment of anxiety? What is the relation between his lesson and Cuiqiao's? I shall consider this question by discussing the most prominent figure of elusiveness in the film: nature.

RESPECT

Images of nature abound not only in the film, but also in Cuiqiao's folk songs, the aesthetic of which is related to the film's cinematography. Cuiqiao's songs always juxtapose a natural imagery (the frozen yellow river in June) with a social situation (being forced by one's father to get married). There is, however, no semantic link that would compel the listener to make a specific correspondence between the two. It is thus impossible to establish whether the frozen river resembles the situation of forced marriage or the girl's sorrow, or whether it is simply the scenery in front of her eyes when she sings. Similarly, the film's cinematography uses jump-cuts to juxtapose images of Cuiqiao's singing to that of the natural landscape, without diegetically connecting the two. Images of nature are thus not exhaustively assimilated to the narrative movement of both Cuiqiao's songs and the film's plot.

The film thus suggests that nature cannot be assimilated to the soldier's assignment and, by extension, the revolutionary project of the Chinese Communist Party that, like all other great revolutions of its time, is tied to the ideology of modernisation. One of the soldier's biggest blunders during his visit is his failure to understand the peasant's reverence for the natural landscape. In response to Gu's disrespectful laughter when he ritually sprinkles grains onto the ground before eating, the peasant says: 'You young people would not understand. This piece of yellow earth – you tread on it, step after step; you plough it, mile after mile. How can you not respect it?' What appears to the soldier to be merely a superstitious ritual signifies the peasant's particular lived relation to the land. Unlike the soldier's 'revolutionary' attitude

towards rural life, the peasant does not regard nature simply as raw material. The yellow earth enables his livelihood but is not reducible to that function. The 'respect' it demands from him is a marker of this irreducibility.

The film also pays respect to nature precisely by its refusal to assimilate it, visually or diegetically, to an exhaustive signifying function. The dramatic sequence of Cuiqiao's departure illustrates the critical import of this gesture of respect. The camera cuts from a long shot of Cuiqiao rowing her little boat into the Yellow River to extreme long shots of the natural landscape wherein the human figure has disappeared from sight. The significance of the editing remains unclear. Has nature 'swallowed' her boat, thus rendering her desire and agency irrelevant? Or has it carried her to the other side, thus providing a bridge between her desire and concrete changes? There is nothing in the cinematography or the subsequent narrative to supply the link between these images. The fate of Cuiqiao – as well as the role nature plays in it – remains ambiguous. As Cuiqiao sets out into the river, we hear her sing the revolutionary song that the soldier taught her brother. The last line of the song is, however, not completed: 'The salvation of the people/Depends on (the) Communist –.' Curiously overlooked by many critics, it is only the word 'Party' and not the word 'Communist' that has been silenced by the sounds of wind and water. Just as Cuiqiao may have survived, so the salvation of the people may depend, not on the Party – which is shown to have failed to live up to its promise, a failure ironically caused by its own ideological rigidity – but the utopian ideal (communism) it claims to serve. In contrast to the project of the Party, which seeks to suppress feminised figures of uncertainty, the film respectfully gives in to the irreducibility of nature. Images of nature are irreducible to the limits of signification imposed by the act of filming/reading, in the same way that folk songs are not reducible to their function as raw material in the service of the revolution.

This strategy of editing is used again at the very end of the film, in a similarly respectful act of refusal to assimilate the figure of the peasantry. This sequence shows the soldier's return to the village. It is unclear if he has come to continue his unfinished project, to (belatedly) fulfil his promise to Cuiqiao, or to start something new. The film cross-cuts between shots showing the soldier walking away from the horizon, and that of the peasants performing the rain dance. Hanhan stands out among the peasants as he waves to the soldier and desperately tries to run against the crowd to meet him. At the end of the sequence, the soldier has disappeared from view and the final shot simply shows an image of the infertile earth. Does the soldier finally meet up with Hanhan or does the frenzied crowd keep them separate? Echoing the uncertainty of Cuiqiao's fate, the film again refuses to supply the answer. This closing image of the earth is accompanied by Cuiqiao's voice singing the words of the revolutionary song, not to the original melody, but to the melody of her bitter tune. This song does not belong to the scene of that frame because Cuiqiao is either dead or has joined the army and is nowhere near the village during the drought. The song signifies the fulfilment of the soldier's assignment: a harmonious and mutual assimilation between the folk and the revolutionary. It remains an impossible utterance under the circumstances presented to us in the film, and thus exists in this last shot only as a ghostly echo, recalling the truncated song (and the as yet undelivered promise of communism) that circulates over the natural landscape after Cuiqiao has disappeared from the scene.

These ambiguous 'openings' in the film – Cuiqiao's departure and the soldier's questioning gaze and return to the village – are products of the Party's initial project, even though they are not its intended results. They are accidental corollaries of the revolutionary project, unaccounted for by its projections and subversive of its authority. Historically, such openings were consistently and ruthlessly shut down so that the authority and ideological certitude of the Party could be maintained.[16] The film poses the challenging question: What if these openings were pursued rather than suppressed? It critiques the revolutionary history of the People's Republic of China on its own terms, while revealing the unrealised utopian potential of that history. What is impossible to articulate, and remains ambiguous within the diegetic logic of the film, becomes figures for what may be possible elsewhere, outside the medium of film and under different historical conditions.

NOTES

1. Mao Zedong, 'Zai Yan'an wenyi zuotanhui shan de jianghua' ('Talk at the Yan'an Forum on Literature and Art'), in *Mao Zedong Xuanji* (*Selected Works of Mao Zedong*), vol. 3 (Beijing: Renmin chubanshe, 1991), 866. English translation in *Mao Zedong on Art and Literature* (Beijing: Foreign Language Press, 1960), 19.

2. For a summary of the film's critical reception at the time of its release, see Geremie Barmé and John Milford, eds, *Seeds of Fire: Chinese Voices of Conscience* (New York: Hill and Wang, 1988), 251–269.

3. Esther Yau, '*Yellow Earth*: Western Analysis and a Non-western Text', *Wide Angle*, 11, no. 2 (1989): 22–33.

4. Mary Ann Farquhar, 'The "Hidden" Gender in *Yellow Earth*', *Screen*, 33, no. 2 (1992): 154–164.

5. Rey Chow, 'Silent is the Ancient Plain: Music, Filmmaking and the Conception of Reform in China's New Cinema', *Discourse*, 12, no. 2 (1990): 87–89.

6. Ibid., 96–99.

7. Stephanie Donald, 'Landscape and Agency: *Yellow Earth* and Demon Lover', *Theory, Culture and Society*, 14, no. 1 (1997): 97–112.

8. Chow, 'Silent is the Ancient Plain', 94.

9. Donald, 'Landscape and Agency', 110–111.

10. Chen Kaige, 'Breaking the Circle: The Cinema and Cultural Change in China', *Cineaste*, 17, no. 3 (1990): 29.

11. Gayatri Spivak, *In Other Worlds* (New York: Routledge, 1988), 182.

12. Cited in Lin Yu-sheng, *Crisis of Chinese Consciousness* (Madison: University of Wisconsin Press, 1979), 77.

13. Mao, 'Xin minzu zhuyi de wenhua' ('The Culture of New Democracy'), *Xuanji*, 2 (January 1940): 707–708; Mao, *On Art and Literature*, 75.

14. Mark Selden, *The Yenan Way in Revolutionary China* (Cambridge, MA: Harvard University Press, 1971), 276.

15. Mao, 'Yan'an zuotanhui ' ('Yan'an forum'), *Xuanji*, 1012; Mao, *On Art and Literature*, 117.

16. See Merle Goldman, *Literary Dissent in Communist China* (Cambridge, MA: Harvard University Press, 1967) for an account of the consequence of dissent within the Chinese Communist Party (especially from cultural workers) during the revolutionary period; and her *China's Intellectuals: Advise and Dissent* (Cambridge, MA: Harvard University Press, 1981) for the post-revolutionary period under Mao's regime.

34   *Yi Yi*: Reflections on Reflexive Modernity in Taiwan

David Leiwei Li

If Fredric Jameson's well-known treatise in *The Geopolitical Aesthetic* put Edward Yang (Yang Dechang) on the map of Anglo-American academic criticism, the director's cinematic mapping of Taipei over the decades has culminated most masterfully in *Yi Yi* (2000). The film won the Best Director prize at Cannes, garnering long overdue popular renown for a serious artist, whose oeuvre articulates the local condition of transnational capitalism in manners 'more deeply symptomatic and meaningful than anything the enfeebled centre still finds itself able to say'.[1] While Yang's thematic elaboration of originality and copy in *Yi Yi* is, following Jameson's suggestive judgment on *Terrorizer*, 'archaically modern', the film's treatment of men mired in money and mobility is exemplary of a 'post-modern' 'proliferation of the urban fabric that one finds in the First and Third Worlds alike'.[2] Jameson's brilliant take on Yang dismantles the conceptual binary of East and West as tradition versus modernity, enabling readings that recognise both the border-transcending flow of global commerce and the reflexive capacity of residual local cultures.

It is in this interpretive promise, ironically, that Jameson's generous inclusion of Yang within the post-modern sentiment of the deceased subject and displaced morality seems to come short. For him, Yang's Taipei becomes synonymous with any 'international urban society of late capitalism' where 'moral judgements are irrelevant'.[3] While the disintegration of extended and nuclear family forms and the decentring of the self are everywhere evident in *Yi Yi*, Yang does not seem to subscribe to the inevitability of a post-modern planetary amorality or the demise of artistic agency. It may be helpful if we break the stranglehold of the modern and post-modern debate to situate Yang's work – and by extension, artistic productions from all societies whose historical experience of capitalism is both relatively recent and

radically condensed – in the framework of 'reflexive modernity'.

Developed by Ulrich Beck, Anthony Giddens and Scott Lash, 'reflexive modernity' shares with 'post-modernity' the recognition that the organised capitalism of earlier industrialisation is over. However, contrary to post-modern dystopic resignation to the impossibility of truth claims, proponents of reflexive modernity seize the tumultuous global transition to disorganised capitalism as a moment of reflection and reorganisation. Since this phase of modernity has set free individuals from such collective structures as 'class, nation, [and] the nuclear family', they argue, it must be viewed 'with the decline of influence on agents of class structures', 'with the crisis of the nuclear family and the concomitant self-organization of life narratives'. Reflexivity is thus at once structural and subjective, in which agents are called upon to reflect on the 'rules' and 'resources' of dysfunctional structures and to institute self-regulation against the 'heteronomous monitoring' or externally imposed governance of the previous era.[4] *Yi Yi*'s representation of the Taiwanese family in *weiji* or 'crisis' stands as Yang's most illuminating reflection to date on the 'jeopardy' and 'opportunity' of reflexive modernity. (The Chinese word *weiji* or 'crisis' is made of two characters that, read independently, mean 'jeopardy' and 'opportunity'.) The film reveals that Taiwan's transition to satellite state in the late capitalist universe and 'silicon island' in the information age has heralded a fundamentally new experience of time and space, which in turn demands an appropriate ethical imperative.[5]

1.

The film opens with a wedding, sandwiches a birth in the middle and ends with a funeral. Beyond its focus on the multi-generational family, it also includes its members' interactions with neighbours, friends, schools, businesses, the local city space, and the global sphere of media and commerce. If the cradle-to-grave story suggests a traditional narrative linearity, the imaging of radiating global city space reminds one of the 'concentric circles' that inform both Tu Weiming's neo-Confucian revival and Martha Nussbaum's working of the Stoics.[6] Both posit an ideal of social affinity that extends from the individual self, to the immediate family, to the local community, and onwards to national and global societies. The problem, however, is that the sense of beginning and ending requisite for any narrative and the solidity of a centre, necessary for the sustenance of the ever-extending circles, are not at all self evident. For in reflexive, late or post-modernity, individuals are no longer significantly or singularly interpellated into the biological family, or for that matter, into the biological destiny.

Yang frames this difficulty earlier on with the wedding pictures. First is the ideal composition of the big family photo: families and friends saunter over and gather under the lush canopy for a group picture that symbolises the vitality of 'the living tree' and its ever-expanding roots and branches.[7] The serenity of nature's green, however, is followed by the crimson red of the banquet hall that suggests less festivity than the intense heat of contention. The groom's old flame, Yunyun, literally bursts into the wedding party, vociferously accusing the bride of hijacking her man while frantically apologising to the groom's mother for failing to become her daughter-in-law. Amid the commotion and confusion, the gigantic photo blow-up of the newlyweds, Adi and Xiaoyan, is misplaced. Heads down towards the floor, smiles turned into grimaces, it reverses optical logic just as the obvious pregnancy of the bride disrupts the old social sequence of marriage and child bearing. No wonder Popo, the grandmother of the family, withdraws from the ceremony and suffers shortly afterwards a stroke that puts her into a coma.

The doctor prescribes that the family 'talk with' grandma to stimulate her brain and enhance her chances of revival. What is meant as therapy for the ancestor on life support, however, turns out to be torture for the progeny. Son and groom Adi, the self-proclaimed champion talker, assures his mom that he is out of his money trouble but soon runs out of

words to say. Daughter Minmin gets so depressed by the poverty of her daily routine and the perfunctory minutes by Popo's side she cannot help but weep. A sagacious matriarch of a bygone age and a retired teacher who cannot talk, let alone instruct, Popo is Edward Yang's object-correlative for the newly built-in obsolescence of the old filial authority while the breakdown of generational interlocution is his overall figure of familial disintegration.

What Yang cinematically exposes in terms of 'the great transformation' in Taiwan, or historically mixed and compressed modernity in East Asia, coincides with what Alisdair MacIntyre engages in his philosophical critique of the Enlightenment Project.[8] Both seem preoccupied with the consequences of the disappearance of both the density of social fibre and the teleological understanding of individual destiny. Though unquestionably liberating, the kind of instrumental rationality underlying the formation of the sovereign modern individual is for MacIntyre ultimately unsatisfactory, because it is devoid of significant societal dimensions and detached from a 'narrative' and thus a social conception of the good:

> The key question for men is not about their own authorship; I can only answer the question 'What am I to do?' if I can answer the prior question 'Of what story or stories do I find myself a part?' We enter human society, that is, with one or more imputed characters – roles into which we have been drafted – and we have to learn what we are in order to be able to understand how others respond to us and how our responses to them are apt to be construed.[9]

While sharing MacIntyre's insistence on the ascriptive or given condition of the self and its necessary imbrication with the discursive and the historical, Yang is hardly as prepared as MacIntyre to evoke the construction of traditions and 'local forms of community' that are pre-modern in historical origin and relatively enclosed socially.[10] The director of *Yi Yi* is not 'after virtue' in the abstract; he is more interested in revealing how the 'imputed characters' or given roles of individuals have necessarily become more complex after modernity and how under conditions of globality the 'local forms of community' are no longer bounded by its own centripetal energy.

2.

The attenuation of filial linearity as the central motif of self-actualisation coincides with the everyday dispersion of activities: individuals in reflexive modernity are living on multiple planes with ever-expanding social horizons. Yang figures this world of layered complexity and blurring boundaries with his ingenious use of abundant glass in metropolitan architecture, which, whether in Tokyo or in Taipei, is the transnational space his characters traverse. Unlike masonry walls, glass panes mark space without total delimitation, suggesting permeability, liquidity and flexibility, typical of the age of transnational capitalism or reflexive modernity. Yang foregrounds the visual prominence of the glass immediately before the presentation of Ota (the Japanese computer legend) when NJ and his colleagues ride in Dada's car, debating rescue plans and exit strategies for their struggling company. One suggests searching for a copycat Ota in Taipei while another banters about Dada's retirement to San Francisco. The characters appear one moment through the windscreen and disappear the next in the curve of the auto-glass, as the reflection of office buildings in the uniform international box style rolls over, engulfing their visage. Yang conveys through the medium of glass the intertwined connectivity and intricate fluidity between global capital flow and the motion of business and people. But this double play of transparency and reflexivity also becomes a larger metaphor for the collapse of the older binaries that Jameson describes as the 'depth model', such as 'essence and appearance', 'latent and the manifest', and 'authenticity and inauthenticity'.[11]

Although implicitly privileging the depth and composure of character more favoured in the earlier modernity and capital of 'inner direction', Yang shows that the 'other direction' of reflexive subjectivity is more symptomatic of the material abundance of a consumer society. Yang shares David Riesman's analysis that yesterday's telos-driven self-discipline of 'inner direction' is yielding to a peer-prompted and mass communication-mediated 'other direction' of today.[12] And he is especially sensitive to the sway of that 'other direction' on his characters when Taiwanese society swings far more suddenly than American society did towards a post-industrial information economy. Minmin's anguish about life's monotony is a case in point. After an extraordinarily long take, the camera steers away from the sobbing Minmin, the mirror image of her back and the semi-open venetian blinds filtering the intermittent light of car traffic below. Her husband NJ pauses, looking at his wife pensively, and turns his back to close their bedroom door and shield the children from the sorrow. The camera cuts to a long shot outside the apartment, with street lamps in the distance, headlights rushing towards us and the reflection of the house lights mixed together on the same plane of vision. The apartment next door is then illuminated at the upper-left corner of the screen, showing the silhouettes of lovers in a bitter squabble against the indifference of nocturnal city motion. The camera pans in towards the domestic sphere of Minmin as NJ paces towards the window, and slowly closes the venetian blinds as though to contain the troubles. We can no longer see the inside but we are overwhelmed by the outside: the windowpane-reflected urban panorama of pitch darkness is broken by dotted white lights, the neighbours' bickering now commingling with Minmin's whimpering.

Glass as a visual trope of dimensions that one can see through or dimensions that are overlaid with reflection and refraction thereby comes to denote horizontal 'other direction' in reflexive modernity, a dialogical formation of subjectivity that displaces the centrality of the linear 'inner direction' of old. Glass also figures the growing indistinguishability of the inside and outside that Michael Hardt and Antonio Negri describe as characterising the generation of 'imperial subjectivity'. 'The enclosures that used to define the limited space of the institutions have broken down,' they argue in *Empire*, 'so that the logic that once functioned primarily within the institutional walls now spreads across the entire social terrain.'[13] The sequence on Minmin we have followed amply illustrates the invasion of the outside, or the internalisation of the external, that engenders much psychological and social instability. Husband and wife are not the principal agents of their own ennui but subjects in conversation with other social forces in a much larger nexus of economic and emotional exchange. The transparency and reflexivity of the glass enables the camera's panning to establish visual simultaneity and spatial complementarity not only between the two apartments but also their relation to the city as an engine of social as well as individual change. Although the residents may entertain the illusion of their sovereign existence in separate units, Yang convinces us that they actually inhabit the same condominium of 'the lonely crowd' and without optimal escape routes.[14]

To drive this point home, the director frames Minmin before a mammoth window again, this time at her office. We see her at the beginning of the shot almost completely immersed in the gloom, standing motionless and staring blankly at the void, which as we recognise all too quickly is the reflection of the city below. In the distance is the reflection of the steady flash of a stop signal positioned precisely where Minmin's heart would be if we had X-ray vision. The audience is absorbed in the rhythmic beat of the red light at the intersection of a far-away surface street, the perpetual swishing of the tyres on the nearby freeway the only sound audible. The heart is where the light is, their separate pulses regulated by a parallel surge of synergy and a parallel arrest of stagnation. The human–machine interface is figured in this over-layering, a breathtaking image of the total interpenetration and interpellation of society and subjectivity, and of exteriority and interiority. 'Haven't you gone back yet?' enquires Nancy after she steps into the office. After a long-drawn-out moment, Minmin replies, 'I have nowhere to go.'

3.

The sense everywhere of having nowhere to go is surely symptomatic of reflexive modernity, a global risk society whose predicament is defined by Ulrich Beck as 'unintentional self-dissolution or self-endangerment'.[15] As NJ puts it to the comatose Popo after Minmin has left home, 'I am not sure about anything these days. Every morning, I wake up feeling uncertain.' 'If you were me,' he asks Popo, 'would you like to wake up?' The vanishing certainty about old social structures and systems of knowledge entails the use of a new decentralised expert system, according to Anthony Giddens, wherein the reflexivity and circularity of social know-how can help the subject change her condition of action.[16] Minmin's retreat to the Buddhist temple, a Chinese equivalent of the therapist's couch in the West, certainly indicates how the traditional folk or new age spirituality can reclaim authority alongside other burgeoning expert systems in late modernity. But this does not hide director Edward Yang's distrust of the expert: the master monk is later shown to be a travelling priest, coming down the mountains apparently to recruit NJ but returning happily with his fat cheque. For Yang finally, self-reflexivity will have to involve self-reflection, not reflection as the bouncing back and forth of images or the superficial suturing of subjectivity but as the possession of knowledge and the apprehension of totality.

This reflective search for knowledge is also couched in the film as a cinematic dialectic of vision. As the boy protagonist Yangyang puts it to his father NJ, 'I can only see what it is in front of me and not what's behind. Does it mean that we can only see half of the world?' Yangyang is evidently a junior alter ego of Director Yang. With all his intellectual precocity, Yangyang is concerned about vision and cognition in at least two different senses. One is the urge to transcend partial and peripheral for holistic vision, an attempt at grasping social and spatial interdependency and integrity. The other is the desire to recognise a temporality of sight, to couple the forward-looking eye/I with the history of its own immanence and the origin of its imminent becoming. If Yangyang pictures the rear of people's heads to enable their self-perception, the director of Yi Yi wants to locate the failure of constructing totality in the post-modern fracturing of time and space and at the same time recuperate its possibility.

Ironically, the loss of holistic vision results from a contemporary saturation of vision – a vision of life burdened with sensorial overload and its absolute satisfaction. 'Fatty' tells Tingting after their trip to the movies that the invention of cinema has extended human life: 'the experience we get through the movies at least doubles what we experience in real life'. To illustrate, he cites the movie as a manual for murder. Only when Fatty is arrested for that crime does the audience realise the importance of cinematic foreshadowing. The boundary between fantasy and reality has been abolished while the pursuit of intensified virtual experience in actuality becomes Yang's apt allegory of moral collapse. Not rejecting modern technologies and the enrichment of life movies and video games can bring, Yang encourages his audience to keep sight of the life narrative.

If the audience has so far been frustrated by the random dispersal of families and friends, they are illuminated by the sequence of frames that intercut NJ and 'Sherry' with Tingting and Fatty. On learning of NJ's business visit to Ota, his now married first love

Sherry flies from Chicago to Tokyo to meet him. The camera captures both waiting at a Japanese commuter train station, catching up on old times and new stories. 'I get jealous as my daughter is growing into a woman,' NJ says, 'knowing that she'll eventually be with someone else.' Before his voice tails off, a passing train obscures NJ and Sherry, and the film cuts to Tingting standing at the corner of a Taipei theatre. As Fatty slowly walks into view the clucking of the train fades into the din of city traffic. Tingting asks, 'What's the time?' 'Nine,' replies Fatty. 'It's almost ten now. Eight a.m. Chicago time,' Sherry's voice jumps in, just before the film cuts back to her. 'Nine p.m. in Taipei,' murmurs NJ as they saunter towards a railroad crossing. Time and space of transnational proportions are radically compressed into living immediacy to exemplify the arrival for some of the condition of a global village. Sherry remarks on the crossing's resemblance to the one near their school, harking back in late modern Japan to a modernising Taiwan three decades ago. 'That's long gone,' NJ updates her, 'but I remember the first time I held your hand there, before our going to the movies.' We hear this as the camera cuts from the quiet night of the Japanese town to the hustle and bustle of the Taipei street crossing, where Tingting and Fatty are waiting for the pedestrian light, silently holding hands. 'I'm holding your hand once again,' continues NJ's voice, speaking to Sherry off screen, 'only at a different place, at a different time, at a different age.' The lens closes in on Tingting and Fatty, hands clasped together, crossing the street, as Sherry's voice finishes NJ's sentence, 'but the same sweaty palm'.

In his cinematic correlation of romance across separate international time zones, different generations and varied speeds of motion, Yang signifies both generational distinctions and identity. The remarkable simultaneity of overlapping concentric circles that exemplifies reflexive modernity is set against the unchanging cycle of the generations, of human procreation, of economic production and of the origination of subjectivity that defies the immediacy of time. The contemporary dispersion of subjectivity in the multiple spheres of work and leisure should not distract us either from an awareness of our origins or an anticipation of our demise. While global capital's perpetual manufacturing of difference and engineering of sensation threatens to compact our sense of time into ephemeral pleasures, we ought not to lose sight

The same sweaty palm across generations and geopolitical time zones

of such simple beauty as the generational repetition and duration of locked hands and hearts. *Yi Yi* is not content with merely stating the finitude of human life; it wants the recognition of this finitude to effectively counter a normative conception of time in late modernity as instantaneously self-fulfilling.

Fatty's formula of experiential expansionism in the episodic mode thus provides the backdrop against which NJ's deliberation resolutely rails. Indeed, NJ's interlude with Sherry in Japan is not fundamentally different from the flights of fancy that plague Fatty or his in-laws, neighbours and friends, who all wish for the thrill of novel experience. There are no impeccable characters on Yang's late modern landscape immune to the passage from industrialising society to a consumer one with their respective cultural logics, the 'delay of gratification' for one and the 'delay of payment' for the other.[17] However, some are less vulnerable and more capable than others to recall Yangyang's dialectical tale of hindsight and foresight, to weigh the excitement of the moment with the progression of a chosen trajectory.

After considerable reflection – in postures evocative of Auguste Rodin's 'The Thinker', one in a silhouette behind a Japanese screen and another on an embankment stretching out to the ocean – NJ turns down Sherry's proposal to start their life anew, and goes back to his Taipei family and company. With Popo's death and Minmin's return, Yang has finally brought the couple together in the same frame for the first time in the film, reminiscing about their absence from each other:

> NJ: How was it up in the mountains?
> Minmin: It was OK. In fact, it was not that different. It was as if they [the monks] were talking to Mom, except our roles were reversed. They were like me and I was like my mother. They took turns talking to me about the same things, repeating them several times a day. I've come to realise that so much is in fact not complicated. But why did they ever appear so?
> NJ: Right. Can I say this? While you were away I had a chance to relive part of my youth. I thought that if I had had the opportunity to do it again, things would have turned out differently. They turned out pretty much the same. I suddenly realised that even given a second chance, I would not really need it. It is quite unnecessary.

If Minmin has emerged from the confusing complexity of reflexive modernity by grasping the kernel of simplicity underneath, NJ has refrained from the tantalising prospect of a fresh start and an apparent alternative to his perceived rut. Having wandered lonely as a cloud in the lonely crowd, husband and wife have literally landed on their bed, an image of re-embedding after their disembedding ventures into the exhilarating unknown.[18]

The reconciliation of the couple hinges on a shared refusal of endless experiential experiments, and a restoration of binaries, boundaries and brakes (traffic lights and slow or stop signs abound in the film as cautions against reckless movements and unbridled mobility). For Minmin, the recognition that appearance can be deceiving leads to her conviction of an inarticulate essence. For NJ, that essence is defined by his reconceived needs and obligations as opposed to his equally reticent and ultimately repressed wants. Both have embraced, through their individual routes of discovery, a generational cycle of perpetuity that entails a limitation of individual gratification. The centrifugal forces of reflexive modernity that engender much confusion for Yang's characters have finally occasioned the reflection necessary for self-regulation and reorganisation to occur.

Although the site of the biological family appears the cinematic centre of this recuperation from and within radiating reflexive modernity, the film is not endorsing a model of traditional patrilineal governance. An earlier coupling of Popo and Tingting's hands, the symbolic gesture of affection and affinity between maternal grandma and granddaughter, for instance, receives its visual encore in Tingting and NJ towards the movie's closing, suggesting a disruption of paternal heritage as well as the preservation of kindred sentiments.[19] A similar logic of the visual duet is at work in the film's successive frontal framing of Tingting and NJ, Yangyang and NJ, and Ota and NJ together behind the windshield, intimating a transgender, transgenerational and transnational solidarity of spirit, at once locally embedded and embodied yet befitting contemporary globality. By contrast, Adi's ride with NJ is shot from behind just as NJ is put in the passenger seat when Dada drives: neither seems NJ's true fellow traveller nor shares with him his ideal universe. If Adi's crass materialism is condemned in the rapid boom and bust of his fortune, Dada's chase of Ato, the copycat of Ota that cannot deliver, is a lesson against instant profits. The kind of instrumental reason or rational choice that matches means to ends economically turns out neither ethical nor efficient. Whether it is in the arena of emotional or economic transaction, those who seek short-term interests fare much worse through Yang's lens than those who are committed to the durability of reciprocal benefits.

Such mild melodramatic Manichaeism is reminiscent of Henry James and Balzac's unveiling of the 'moral occult', a 'domain of spiritual forces and imperatives that is not clearly visible' but 'believe[d] to be operative' in a 'desacralised' post-Enlightenment world.[20] An exemplary film at the turn of a new millennium, Yi Yi provides a similar yet more radical dramatisation of Taiwan's passage into another world of risk-ridden modernity. There, the providential is no longer viable, the filial and the local no longer stable, yet rediscovery of the ethical imperatives that used to depend on them remains vital. Edward Yang seems to have possessed an identical urge as the masters of early modernity to register into consciousness the power of the residual, to recover a weakened sense of historicity, a narrative conception of the self and a teleology of the human species. Cultural capital properly belonging to a previous era yet not entirely eradicated in the mixed and compressed modernity of Taiwan seems to hold promise: Tingting, Yangyang, NJ and Ota are emblems not of the past but of the potential of our planet where 'the end of history' is yet the indeterminate future.[21]

'I'm sorry, Popo. It wasn't that I didn't want to talk to you. I thought whatever I told you, you would have already known,' Yangyang says in tribute to Popo at her funeral. 'I know so little, Popo. But you know what I'll do when I grow up? I will tell people what they do not know and show them what they cannot see.' Reflexive modernity finally requires that social 'knowledge spiral in and out of the universe of social life, reconstructing both itself and that universe as an integral part of that process'.[22] The film has shown us a world of jet travel, bullet trains and instant electronic transfer of money, image and information. But it has also illuminated the incontrovertible limits of nature on human life, Popo's death being the most striking sign, despite the scientific overcoming of space and time. Yangyang's remark thus implies that the ever-expanding circles of social knowledge, enabled by the liberating technologies of global modernity, must be appropriated with full recognition of nature's limits and the cycle of the species.

'Throughout human history,' argues Zygmunt Bauman, 'the work of culture consisted in sifting and sedimenting hard kernels of perpetuity out of transient human lives [and] actions, in conjuring up duration out of transience', and in 'transcending thereby the limits imposed by human mortality by deploying mortal men and women in the service of the immortal human species'. It is not incidental that Bauman deploys the past tense in his summary of that history, for 'demand for this kind of work is', as he puts it, 'shrinking'.[23] Bauman's concern with the waning of such demand and the devaluation of immortality is Edward Yang's as well, for both are preoccupied with the decisive turning point in human history when the sovereign individual – the figure of 'Yi', 'the One' – is

becoming the figure of hegemony in global modernity. No one can fully anticipate the consequences of globalisation as a radical individualisation of culture, but it may not be premature to recall a cultural outlook that has sustained the divergent groups of humanity thus far. 'I miss you, Popo, especially when I see my still nameless newborn cousin. I remember that you always say that you feel old. I'd like to tell my cousin,' the boy Yangyang declares, 'I feel old too.' Childhood and age, and innocence and experience finally converge in this articulation of a continuous life narrative, and with it, a reiteration of an ethical imperative so often submerged in the fragments of late modernity. Unlike the pre-modern resignation to fate and or a post-modern deferral of death in instant consumption, Yangyang's signification on Popo's silence suggests a collective triumph over atomic mortality, a cultural transcendence of the individual earthly sojourn. The film Yi Yi has come to affirm a sense of purposeful time in order to embody a notion of spatial and social relatedness, a version of neo-Confucianism perhaps, or the tenets of a planetary communitarianism regardless of civilisational origins.[24]

NOTES

1. Fredric Jameson, *The Geopolitical Aesthetic: Cinema and Space in the World System* (Bloomington: Indiana University Press, 1995), 155.
2. Ibid., 121, 117. For an informative Chinese-language study of Yang's film career up to *A Confucian Confusion*, see Huang Jianye, *A Study of Yang Dechang's Films* (*Yang Dechang dianying yanjiu*: Taipei: Yuanliu, 1995).
3. Ibid., 128.
4. Ulrich Beck, Anthony Giddens and Scott Lash, *Reflexive Modernization: Politics, Tradition and Aesthetics in the Modern Social Order* (Stanford, CA: Stanford University Press, 1994), 115–116.
5. 'Silicon island' is Yang's reference to Taiwan in his comments on the DVD version of *Yi Yi* (New York: Windstar TV and Video, 2001). All English dialogue in the text is based on this edition's subtitles and my own translation.
6. See Tu Weiming, 'Human Rights as a Confucian Moral Discourse', in *Confucianism and Human Rights*, ed. Wm. Theodore de Bary and Tu Weiming (New York: Columbia University Press, 1998), 297–307; and Martha C. Nussbaum, 'Patriotism and Cosmopolitanism', in *For the Love of Country*, ed. Joshua Cohen (Boston: Beacon, 1996), 2–17.

7. See Tu Weiming, *Dædalus*, 120, no. 2 (1991): *The Living Tree: The Changing Meaning of Being Chinese Today*.

8. See Robert M. Marsh, *The Great Transformation: Social Change in Taipei. Taiwan since the 1960s* (Armonk, NY: M. E. Sharpe, 1996); and Alisdair MacIntyre, *After Virtue: A Study in Moral Theory* (Notre Dame, IN: University of Notre Dame Press, 1984).

9. Ibid., 216.

10. Ibid., 263. See also John Haldane, 'MacIntyre's Thomist Revival: What Next?', in *After MacIntyre: Critical Perspectives on the Work of Alisdair MacIntyre*, ed. John Horton and Susan Mendus (Notre Dame, IN: University of Notre Dame Press, 1994), 91–107.

11. Fredric Jameson, *Postmodernism, or, The Cultural Logic of Late Capitalism* (Durham, NC: Duke University Press, 1992), 12.

12. David Riesman, *The Lonely Crowd: A Study of the Changing American Character* (New Haven, CT: Yale University Press, 1961), 14–25.

13. Michael Hardt and Antonio Negri, *Empire* (Cambridge, MA: Harvard University Press, 2000), 196.

14. Riesman, *The Lonely Crowd*.

15. Beck *et al.*, *Reflexive Modernization*, 176.

16. Ibid., 187.

17. Zygmunt Bauman, *Life in Fragments: Essays in Postmodern Morality* (Oxford: Polity Press, 1995), 5.

18. This resembles the denouement of Zhou Xiaowen's *Ermo*, as I analyse in my essay, 'What Will Become of Us if We Don't Stop? *Ermo*'s China and the End of Globalization', *Comparative Literature*, 53, no. 4 (2001): 442–461.

19. NJ is practically married into Minmin's family since Popo is his mother-in-law. The scenario of Tingting and Nainai, or her paternal grandma, holding hands would suggest some sort of straight patrilineal descent.

20. See Peter Brooks, *The Melodramatic Imagination: Balzac, Henry James, Melodrama, and the Mode of Excess* (New Haven, CT: Yale University Press, 1976; 1995), 15, 20–21.

21. Francis Fukuyama, 'The End of History?', in *Globalization and the Challenges of a New Century*, ed. Patrick O'Meara, Howard A. Mehlinger and Matthew Klein (Bloomington: Indiana University Press, 2000), 161–180.

22. Anthony Giddens, *The Consequences of Modernity* (Stanford, CA: Stanford University Press, 1990), 15–16.

23. Zygmunt Bauman, *Liquid Modernity* (Cambridge: Polity Press, 2000), 126.

24. See Tu, 'Human Rights', 299, and also Daniel Bell, *Communitarianism and its Critics* (New York: Clarendon Press, 1993).

Chinese Names

Compiled by Wang Dun and Chris Berry

This list consists of characters for Chinese names that appear in the essays in this volume. The names included are personal names for film-makers, actors and characters, as well as those of authors of Chinese-language publications. The list is organised alphabetically according to family name. However, the names are given as they appear in the essays. For example, 'Maggie Cheung' is listed under 'C' for 'Cheung'. Because there are no standard translations or transcriptions for Chinese names, different translations of the same name may appear in different essays. In these cases, each translation receives a separate entry.

A Cheng	阿城	Chang Chung-hsiung	张俊雄	Duncan Chow	周坤达
A Gui	阿贵	Eileen Chang	张爱玲	Chow Mo-wan	周慕云
A Ying	阿英	Chang Hsiao-hung	张小虹	Stephen Chow	周星驰
A'Gui	阿桂	Terence Chang	张家振	Chow Yun Fat	周润发
A'Rong	阿荣	Chang Tso-chi	张作骥	Chow Yun-fat	周润发
A'Ze	阿泽	William Chang	张叔平	Cui Zi'en	崔子恩
Adi	阿弟	William Chang Suk-ping	张叔平	Cuiqiao	翠巧
Ah Cheng	阿城	Chen Baoxu	陈宝旭		
Ah Mei	阿梅	Chen Baozhu	陈宝珠	Dada	大大
Lawrence Ah Mon	刘国昌	Chen Chuhui	陈楚惠	Dai Jinhua	戴锦华
Ah Q	阿Q	Chen Duxiu	陈独秀	Dai Liyan	戴礼言
Ah Wah	阿花	Chen Gongbo	陈公博	Daixiu	戴秀
Ann Hui	许鞍华	Chen Kaige	陈凯歌	Daji	妲己
Aunt Yee	珊三仪	Chen Kengran	陈铿然	Dame Huang	黄二姐
		Chen Kuan-hsing	陈光兴	Deng Guangrong	邓光荣
Ba Jin	巴金	Chen Kuo-fu	陈国富	Deng Xiaoping	邓小平
Bai	白铁男	Leste Chen	陈正道	Ding Naifei	丁乃非
Bai Xianyong	白先勇	Chen Mo	陈墨	Director Gu	谷燕山
Baosi	褒姒	Chen Shui-bian	陈水扁	Dou Jiangming	斗江明
Bei Cun	北村	Chen Wu	尘无	Douzi	豆子
Bi Yan Hu Li	碧眼狐狸	Chen Xue	陈雪	Du Jiazhen	杜家珍
Mr Biao	彪哥	Chen Yanyan	陈燕燕	Du Ping	杜平
Black Monster	黑山老魔	Chen Yin-jung	陈映蓉	Duan Xiaolou	段小楼
Broken Sword	残剑	Chen Yu-chieh	郑有杰		
Bu Wancang	卜万苍	Chen Zhaorong	陈昭荣	Ermo	二嫫
		Cheng Dieyi	程蝶衣		
Cai Chusheng	蔡楚生	Leigh Cheng	张丽君	Fan	芬
Cai Guorong	蔡国荣	Cheng Pei Pei	郑佩佩	Fei Mu	费穆
Chai Xiaofeng	柴效锋	Alfred Cheung	张坚庭	Feng Xiaogang	冯小刚
Anthony Chan Yau	陈友	Jacky Cheung	张学友	Fleur	如花
Fruit Chan	陈果	Leslie Cheung	张国荣	Flying Snow	飞雪
Gordon Chan	陈嘉上	Maggie Cheung Man-yuk	张曼玉	Fu Biao	傅彪
Jackie Chan	成龙	Cheung Po-tsai	张保仔	Fu Honglian	符红莲
Chang Che	张彻	Chiao Hsiung-ping	焦雄屏	Fu Shizhuan	符诗专
Chang Chen	张震	Ching Siu-tung	程小东		
Chang Cheng	张珍	Zero Chou	周美玲	Mr Gao	高先生
				Mrs Gao	高太太

Yuen Wo-ping	袁和平	Zhang Yimou	张艺谋	King Zhou	(商)纣王
Yunyun	云云	Zhang Yiwu	张颐武	Zhou Shuangyu	周双玉
		Zhang Yuan	张元	Zhou Shuangzhu	周双珠
Zhang Che	张彻	Zhang Zhen	张震	Zhou Xiaowen	周晓文
Zhang Damin	张大民	Zhang Zhichen	章志忱	Zhou Xuan	周璇
Zhang Fengyi	张丰毅	Zhang Ziyi	章子怡	Zhou Yuwen	周玉文
Zhang Huike	张慧科	Zhao Dan	赵丹	Zhu Jian	朱剑
Zhang Huizhen	张惠贞	Zhao Shuxin	赵韦信	Zhu Shilin	朱石麟
Zhang Junzhao	张军钊	Zhenbao	振保	Zhu Shuren	朱淑人
Zhang Liang	张良	Zheng Junli	郑君里	Zhu Tianwen	朱天文
Zhang Nuanxin	张暖炘	Zheng Xiaoqiu	郑小秋	Zhu Wen	朱文
Zhang Shichuan	张石川	Zheng Yunbo	郑云波	Zhu Wenshun	朱文顺
Teacher Zhang	张老师	Zheng Zhengqiu	郑正秋	Zhu Xijuan	祝希娟
Zhang Xuan	张煊	Zhong Kui	钟馗	Zhu Yingtai	祝英台
Zhang Yi	张毅	Zhou Changmin	周昌民	Zhuangzi	庄子

Chinese Film Titles

Compiled by Wang Dun and Chris Berry

This list includes all the characters for the titles of Chinese films as they appear in the essays in this volume. The list is organised alphabetically according to the English translations of the titles. Because there are no absolutely standard translations of film titles, different versions of the same Chinese title are used in some essays. In these cases, each English translation receives a separate entry.

12 Storeys	12楼
The Actress	阮玲玉
After Separation	大撒把
Army Daze...The Movie	新新兵小传
As Tears Go By	旺角卡门
Ashes of Time	东邪西毒
Au Revoir Shanghai	再会吧，上海
Autumn Moon	秋月
Be with Me	伴我行
A Better Tomorrow	英雄本色
Between Life and Death	阴阳界
The Big Mill	大磨坊
Big Shot's Funeral	大腕
Bitter Love	苦恋
Black Cannon Incident	黑炮事件
Blind Mountain	盲山
Blind Shaft	盲井
Blue Gate Crossing	蓝色大门
Beat People	投奔怒海
The Bay from Vietnam	来客
Boys from Fenggui	风柜来的人
The Boys from Fenggui	风柜来的人
Breaking News	大事件
Bullet in the Hand	喋血街头
Bumming in Beijing	流浪北京
Camel Xiangzi	骆驼祥子
Catch	国士无双
Cell Phone	手机
Centre Stage	阮玲玉
Children of the Storm	风云儿女
Children of Troubled Times	风云儿女
A Chinese Ghost Story	倩女幽魂
Chocolate Rap	巧克力重唱
Chungking Express	重庆森林
A City of Sadness	悲情城市
Classic for Girls	女儿经
Come Drink with Me	大醉侠
Coming Back	归来
A Confucian Confusion	独立时代
Confucius	孔夫子
Conned Once	上一当
Crazy Stone	疯狂的石头
Crouching Tiger, Hidden Dragon	卧虎藏龙
Crows and Sparrows	乌鸦与麻雀
Cut	剪
Dawn over the Metropolis	都会的早晨
Days of Being Wild	阿飞正传
Declawing the Devils	斩断魔爪
Devils on the Doorstep	鬼子来了
Ding Jun Shan	定军山
Distant Love	遥远的爱
Do Over	一年之初
Double Vision	双瞳
The Dove Tree	鸽子树
Durian Durian	榴梿飘飘
Dust in the Wind	恋恋风尘
Eating Air	吃风
Eight Thousand Miles of Clouds and Moon	八千里路云和月
Election I	黑社会
Election II	黑社会2: 以和为贵
The Emperor and the Assassin	荆柯刺秦王
The Emperor's Shadow	秦颂
The Enchanting Shadow	倩女幽魂
Enemy of Women	女性的仇敌
Ermo	二嫫
Eternal Summer	盛夏光年
Evening Bell	晚钟
Expect the Unexpected	非常突然
Fallen Angels	堕落天使
Farewell China	爱在别乡的季节
Farewell My Concubine	霸王别姬
Fate in Tears and Laughter	啼笑姻缘
Filial Piety	天伦
First Option	飞虎
A Fishy Story	不脱袜的人
Floating Life	浮生
Flowers of Shanghai	海上花
Flowers Reborn	再生录
Flying Drogon, Leaping Tiger	龍腾虎躍
Forever Fever	狂热迪斯科
Formula 17	十七岁的天空
Garlands at the Foot of the Moutain	高山下的花环
Gen Y Cops	特警新人類2
Girls of a Special Economic Zone	特区打工妹
God or Dog	大巴窑杀童案
The Goddess	神女
Gogo Boys	当我们同在一起
A Good Hushand and Wife	好夫妻
Good Men Good Women	好男好女
A Good Woman	良家妇女
Goodbye Dragon Inn	不散
Happy Time	幸福时光
Happy Together	春光乍泄
The Harbour	海港
The Heirloom	宅变
Her Fatal Ways	表姐，你好嘢！
Hero	英雄
A Hero Never Dies	真心英雄
Hibiscus Town	芙蓉镇
Hold You Tight	愈快乐愈堕落
The Hold	洞
Hollywood Hong Kong	香港有个好莱坞
Home, Secret Home	我想有个家
Homerun	跑吧！孩子
Horse Thief	盗马贼
Huayang Nianhua	花样年华
I Not Stupid	小孩不笨
In Our Time	光阴的故事
In the Mood for Love	花样年华
Infernal Affairs	无间道
Island Tales	有时跳舞
Joyous Heroes	欢乐英雄
Ju Dou	菊豆
Keep Cool	有话好好说
Kekexili: Mountain Patrol	可可西里
The Killer	喋血双雄
King of Children	孩子王
King of the Children	孩子王
La Méladie d'Heléne	心恋
Labourer's Love	劳工爱情
A Lady of Shanghai	上海一夫人
Lan Yu	蓝宇
The Legend of Tianyun Mountain	天云山传奇
Li Shuangshuang	李双双
Liang Po Po: The Movie	梁婆婆重出江湖
Liang Zhu	梁祝
Life	人生
Lifeline	十万火急
Lin Family Shop	林家铺子
Little Cheung	细路祥
Little Toys	小玩意
Long Arm of the Law	省港旗兵
The Longest Summer	去年烟花特别多
Lost Love	迷失的爱情
Love Eternal	七彩胡不归
The Love Eterne	梁山伯与祝英台
Love of May	五月之恋

Index

Page numbers in **bold** indicate extended analysis; those in *italic* denote illustrations; *n* = endnote.

LIST OF ILLUSTRATIONS

While considerable effort has been made to correctly identify the copyright holders, this has not been possible in all cases. We apologise for any apparent negligence and any omissions or corrections brought to our attention will be remedied in any future editions.

15 (*Shiwu*), 2003, © 27 Productions/© Singapore Film Commission; *Big Shot's Funeral* (*Da wan*), 2002, © Columbia Pictures Film Production Asia; *Black Cannon Incident* (*Hei pao shi jian*), 1986, Xi'an Film Studio/Manfred Durniok Film- und Fernsehpr; *Blind Shaft* (*Mang jing*), 2003, © Li Yang/© Tang Splendour Films Ltd; *Boat People* (*Tou bun no hoi*), 1982, Bluebird Movie Enterprises; *Centre Stage* (*Ruan Ling-yu*), 1992, Canal + /Golden Way/Paragon Films/Golden Harvest; *A Chinese Ghost Story* (*Sinnui yauman*), 1987, Cinema City Co./Film Workshop Co. Ltd; *Chungking Express* (*Chong qing sen lin*), 1994, Jet Tone Production; *Crouching Tiger, Hidden Dragon* (*Wo hu zang long*), 2000, United China Vision Incorporated/UCV LLC/Edko Films/Zoom Hunt International/Columbia Pictures/Sony Pictures/Golden Harvest; *Crows and Sparrows* (*Wuya yu maque*), 1949, Kunlun Film Company; *Durian Durian* (*Liu lian piao piao*), 2000, Golden Network Asia/Nice Top Entertainment/Studio Canal +; *Ermo*, 1994, Shanghai Film Studio/Ocean Film Company; *Farewell My Concubine* (*Ba wang bie ji*), 1993, Tomson Films/China Film Co-production Corp./Beijing Film Studio; *Flowers of Shanghai* (*Hai shang hua*), 1998, Shochiku Co. Ltd/3H Films; *Formula 17*, 2004, Three Dots Entertainment; *The Goddess* (*Shennu*), 1934, Lianhua Film Company; *Hero* (*Ying xiong*), 2002, © Elite Group Enterprises; *In the Mood for Love* (*Fa yeung nin wa*), 2000, Jet Tone Production/Block 2 Pictures/Paradis Films/Orly Films; *Kekexili: Mountain Patrol* (*Hoh xil*), 2004, © Columbia Pictures Film Production Asia; *The Love Eterne* (*Liang Shan Ba yu Zhu Ying Tai*), 1963, Run Run Shaw; *Not One Less* (*Yi ge dou bu neng shao*), 1999, Guangxi Film Studio/Beijing New Picture Distribution Co.; *The Personals* (*Zhenghun qishi*), 1999, Zoom Hunt International Production; *PTU*, 2003, © Mei Ah; *The Red Detachment of Women* (*Hong se niang zijun*), 1961, Tianma Film Studio; *Riding Alone for Thousands of Miles* (*Qian li zou dan ji*), 2005, Edko Films/Zhang Yimou Studio; *Spring in a Small Town* (*Xiao cheng zhi chun*), 1948, Wen-Hua-Film; *A Time to Live, A Time to Die* (*Tong nien wang shi*), 1985, Central Motion Picture Corporation; *A Touch of Zen* (*Xai Nu*), 1969, International/Union Film Company; *Vive L'Amour* (*Aiqing wansui*), 1994, Central Motion Picture Corp./Sunny Overseas Corp./Shiung Fa Corporation; *Wedding Banquet* (*Hsi yen*), 1993, Central Motion Picture Corp./Good Machine; *Woman, Demon, Human* (*Ren, gui, qing*), 1988, Shanghai Film Studio; *Xiao Wu*, 1998, © Radiant Advertising Company; *Yellow Earth* (*Huang tu di*), 1984, Guangxi Film Studio; *Yi Yi*, 2000, Atom Films/1+2 Seisaku Iinkai/Pony Canyon/Omega Project/Hakuhodo.